ArtScroll History Series®

Rabbi Nosson Scherman / Rabbi Meir Zlotowitz
General Editors

Rescuing

Published by

Mesorah Publications, ltd

הרה"ק רבי אהרן
מבעלזא זצוק"ל

the Rebbe of Belz

Belzer Chassidus —
History, Rescue and Rebirth

YOSEF ISRAEL

FIRST EDITION
First Impression … April 2005
Second Impression … May 2005

Published and Distributed by
MESORAH PUBLICATIONS, LTD.
4401 Second Avenue / Brooklyn, N.Y 11232

Distributed in Europe by
LEHMANNS
Unit E, Viking Business Park
Rolling Mill Road
Jarow, Tyne & Wear, NE32 3DP
England

Distributed in Australia and New Zealand by
GOLDS WORLDS OF JUDAICA
3-13 William Street
Balaclava, Melbourne 3183
Victoria, Australia

Distributed in Israel by
SIFRIATI / A. GITLER — BOOKS
6 Hayarkon Street
Bnei Brak 51127

Distributed in South Africa by
KOLLEL BOOKSHOP
Shop 8A Norwood Hypermarket
Norwood 2196, Johannesburg, South Africa

ARTSCROLL HISTORY SERIES®
RESCUING THE REBBE OF BELZ
© *Copyright 2005, by* MESORAH PUBLICATIONS, Ltd.
4401 Second Avenue / Brooklyn, N.Y. 11232 / (718) 921-9000 / www.artscroll.com

---

ISBN:
1-57819-059-2 (hard cover)

Typography by CompuScribe at ArtScroll Studios, Ltd.

Printed in the United States of America by Noble Book Press Corp.
Bound by Sefercraft, Quality Bookbinders, Ltd., Brooklyn N.Y. 11232

This volume is dedicated
to the memory of

Eliezer Landau ז״ל

רבי אליעזר נתן בן ר׳ משה דוד הלוי זצ״ל
נפטר ט״ו ניסן תשמ״ט, בירושלים תובב״א

This book could not have existed without Reb Eliezer Landau because he was the great man who was instrumental in saving the Belzer Rav and hundreds of fellow Jews. His courage, dedication and selflessness were awesome. With the help of his wife Sarah, he devised plans to outwit the Gestapo and daringly carried them out with faith in Hashem Yisbarach and the conviction that he was put on this earth to serve Him by helping others.

Reb Eliezer was known as a talmid chacham and an exceptional baal tzedakah, both in pre-War Galicia and post-war Eretz Yisrael. He and his family reached the Holy Land in 1944 and joined in the successful and fruitful effort to rebuild Klal Yisrael in the image of its forebears.

His great desire was that he should be blessed with children and grandchildren following his example, and that fervent prayer was granted him.

We are proud to be the children of such a great man.

Miriam & Issy (David) Tannen
London, England

Rabbi J. D. BABAD

26 Rookwood Road
London N16 6SS
Tel. 0181-802 0310

יוסף דוב באב"ד
———————
דומ"ץ דקהל חסידי בעלזא
לונדון יצ"ו

בס"ד

חודש שבט תשס"ה לפ"ק, פה ק"ק לונדון יצ"ו

הנני בזה להמליץ על ידידי מאז הרה"ח המופלג בתוי"ש ר' יוסף   הי"ו
שהביא לפני חיבור חשוב כתוב בשפת האנגלית בו הוא מתאר השתלשלות
הצלת האחים הק' כ"ק מרן מהר"א מבעלזא זי"ע ועכ"י ואתו עמו אחיו הגה"ק
מהר"ם מבילגורייא זצ"ל מתחת צפורני הנאצים ימ"ש מגיא ההריגה באירופה
לארה"ק תובב"א, ומצאתיו כתוב בטוב טעם ובנוי על מקורות נאמנים כדרכו
מאז כסופר נאמן, וכנצר למשפחת חסידי בעלזא השקיע המחבר עבודה רבה
ועצומה ללקט ולהשוות את החומר עד מקום שידו מגעת כדי להוציא מתחת
ידו דבר נאה ומתוקן.

אמרתי שכדאי ונכון הוא לספר סיפורי נפלא אלו לצעירי הצאן כדי שידעו דור
אחרון את הנסים הגלויים והחסדים שעשה הקב"ה עם כלל ישראל בהצילו את
רבינו הק' רשכבה"ג זי"ע בבחינת אוד מוצל מאש לטובת ולתועלת כל שארית
הפליטה, וכדי שישמעו על התנהגותם של צדיקי הדור בימי הזעם, ועל מסירת
נפשם של חסידים ואנשי מעשה בכל מקומות משבותם בגופם ובממונם לטובת
אחב"י הנתונים בצרה ובשבי', ובפרט שזכה אאמו"ר הרה"ג ר' אברהם משה
באב"ד זצ"ל אבדק"ק סונדרלאנד יצ"ו להיות מהנטפלים למצווה רבה זו, ועדיין
שמור אצלי מכתב קודש שכתב הגה"ק מבילגורייא זצ"ל להודות לאבי זצ"ל
בשם אחיו הק' זי"ע על חלקו בהצלתם.

הנני בזה לברך את ידידי המחבר החשוב שיחי' ומערכת ארטסקרול המו"ל
שיתקבל הספר בנש"ח אצל הקוראים כראי לספר חשוב מלא תוכן ואמונת
צדיקים.

וע"ז באתי עה"ח ברוב הוקרה והערכה על פעולתם הברוכה,

יוסף דוב באב"ד

PREFACE

I N OUR ERA WORDS LIKE "HOLY" OR "SAINTLY" CAN become somewhat devalued by being too widely applied. But Rebbe Aharon Rokach, the previous Belzer Rav, was genuinely holy, a true saint in the intrinsic meaning of the word, a man who was viewed by awestruck contemporaries in the pre-War generation as akin to a *malach*! So it is with some trepidation that one picks up a pen to write anything about a saintly personality such as the holy Belzer Rav. Yet he was so forgiving by nature, I pray that any inadvertent mistake or slip of the pen will be pardoned likewise.

Like my previous book, *Colorful Ceremonies in the Beis Hamikdash*, this work grew out of my daytime vocation at London's Orthodox newspaper — the *Jewish Tribune* — where I produced a 10-part series entitled "Saving the Belzer Rav" for the *Junior* pages. Naively, I had thought the story familiar to most adults from Moshe Yechezkeli's classic book, and thus suitable only for a youthful readership. But that series occasioned two surprises: the immense interest it stirred among mature readers and the wealth of other material that was available.

Since the *Hatzalas HaRebbe MiBelz* was available only in Hebrew and never reprinted since first published in 1962, members of the Belzer fraternity also took an avid and excited interest in the series. I was of course aware that "Moshe Yechezkeli" was none other than the prolific journalist, columnist, and supreme biographer of religious resistance under Nazi oppression — Moshe Prager (whose real name incidentally was Moshe Mark). But I was unaware how his thrilling account of the Rebbe's escape from occupied Poland had been substantially supplemented — and contradicted in some instances — by subsequent books published either by those personally involved in the rescue or authorized by the Belzer establishment.

Foremost among these journals were the personal recollections of Mr. Chaim Shloma Friedman (still available solely in stencil) and the *Devar Chein* by Mr. Berish Ortner. Although the author of *Beis Tzaddikim Yaamod* was too young to have been involved, nor apparently a chassid of Belz, he does add further material and background, while general biographies of the Rebbe by, respectively, R' Yisrael Klapholtz (a close Belzer chassid) and Rav Nosson Ortner (grandson of Reb Berish), together with that of R' Betzalel Landau (the late, noted Israeli author), likewise incorporate many valuable details and anecdotes — as do countless Belz internal publications and annual *yahrzeit* memorials.

The vast bulk of this material, however, has been available only in Hebrew, while the English-reading public was deprived of a thrilling read and of contemplating the modern miracle that is Belz's survival and phenomenal renaissance. Although we have a moral obligation to recognize and recount miracles — *sichu bechal nifle'osav* — the Belzer Rebbe's attitude to his own miraculous escape was noteworthy. On one occasion he refused permission for Mr. Friedman to print his Hebrew account, yet he wholeheartedly granted unofficial permission for the counter-espionage officer who rescued him from Poland to publish an account in Hungarian, shortly after the War.

Furthermore, in his later years, he would personally recount a few supernatural anecdotes on the anniversary of his safe arrival in Eretz Yisrael and encourage his close chassidim to elaborate. Also, he once spent half the night telling the whole story to R' Berish Ortner. Since the Belzer Rebbe rarely confided his actual reasons for most of his actions or views, it is difficult to determine his real motive or guiding principle here. However, several Hebrew volumes have already been published and even Mr. Friedman himself included parts of the Rebbe's unpublished account in his memoirs, later published in English.

When producing the *Junior* series, I had no intention of expanding it into a full-fledged book — which would necessarily entail a large amount of fresh research and rewriting — if not for the warm encouragement and generosity of one man: David (Issy) Tannen. He was anxious to perpetuate the memory of his late father-in-law, Mr. Eliezer Landau, who played a major role in ensuring the Rebbe's relatively lengthy survival in the Bochnia ghetto near Krakow, and who eventually made it possible for the Rebbe to undertake his daring 250-mile flight across occupied Poland to the Hungarian border. In countless ways — both natural and supernatural! — the Rebbe had subsequently signaled his undying gratitude for that kindness.

Mr. Tannen's suggestion fell on fertile ground since my family has cherished connections with Belz. My saintly grandfather was renowned as a prominent *talmid chacham* and a leading chassid in Narol, which was geographically situated within the Belz sphere of influence. As a consequence, my father *zt"l* even walked there on pilgrimage — sleeping overnight in the forest! — since his hometown was within 50 kilometers of Belz. When the Rebbe's brother, the Bilgoraj Rav (father of the present Rebbe), visited London as part of his tour of Europe in 1949 on behalf of the Belzer Rebbe, he foretold my safe birth — anxiously awaited after three sisters!

I must also thank several Belz chassidim in London who have selflessly given of their time and knowledge and treated all my queries with patience, including Dayan J. Babad, whose late father played a positive role in the Rebbe's rescue. In particular I would single out R' Mordechai Mann, who lent me various books and photos while greatly encouraging me; and R' Akiva Osher Padwa, who kindly read through the manuscript, making useful suggestions while providing new information and documents. Finally, I deem it a great privilege that Mesorah Publications, who have displayed exemplary expertise and flair in publishing the trailblazing ArtScroll Series, have included this miraculous tale among their Torah literature.

If, as the Belzer Rav regularly declared, "every War survivor must have been accompanied by *malachim* on either side" — then how many heavenly guardians oversaw his own amazing escape? Beyond the actual circumstances of his rescue, it is noteworthy how Jewish inmates of the ghetto, on the brink of deportation or death, risked life and limb to ensure the holy Rebbe's safe escape from Nazi hands. Since Belz's survival also depended on the unvarnished *mesiras nefesh* of these countless unsung heroes, may this book likewise serve as their tribute.

Yosef Israel
Erev Shabbos Toldos
28 Marcheshvan 5765 / 12 November '04
London, England

לזכר נשמת זקני
הרה"ג ר' משה יהודה לייב ב"ר ישראל האמער זצ"ל
מבני עליה ומגדולי ת"ח בק"ק נארול הי"ד

נפטר לעולמו זמן קצר לפני פלישת הרוצחים
י"ט תמוז תרצ"ט

TABLE OF CONTENTS

CHAPTER I

DER SHTET'ELE BELZ

NOWADAYS, *"MEIN SHTET'ELE BELZ"* OF FOLKSONG fame and legend no longer exists; instead, a sad little village situated just over the border in Ukraine is but a pale shadow of the town's former glory. Little remains of its resplendent Jewish past: a few houses and shops previously owned by Jews; the *hekdesh* (poorhouse) and *mikveh* (bathhouse); the area where the famous synagogue and *beis hamedrash* once stood; two mounds of the ancient, destroyed cemetery; the desecrated "new" cemetery with but four standing gravestones — three Belzer Rebbes and the firstborn of the first Rebbe. In common with much of Poland, the original Belz is now no more than a site of poignant memories on the heritage trail to rediscover family roots — and a pilgrimage to the holy *kevarim* of the Rebbes of Belz.

Few are aware that beyond its connections with the famous Chassidus, Belz actually had a respectable history of its own that predated the advent of chassidic thought and practice. It is hard to believe when contemplating the present size of the small township that Belz was once a fortified city, the administrative center of an entire district, privileged to elect delegates to the semi-autonomous Jewish parliament of *Vaad Arba Aratzos* (Council of Four Lands). By the 1500's, it was still part of "Reissen" (or "Red Russia," comprised of Western Ukraine and Galicia, in contrast to Byelorussia or "White Russia") together with the Lublin and Chelm districts, in the area known as the "Nine *Kehillos*," and under one chief rabbi; in January 1542, King Sigismund I appointed the legendary Rav Shalom Shachna of Lublin to that position.

The arrival of Jews in Belz is lost in the mists of time, but first documentary evidence of Jewish inhabitation dates back to 1439: Apparently, they were confined to a single *Judengasse* and had to pay an extra royal tax toward the upkeep of the fortified walls and cannon. In 1517, native Polish merchants tried to prevent Jewish competition in the local marketplace but Sigismund I came to their defense, granting them equal status and permitting them to display their wares. By 1550 their official number had reached 204 souls owning thirty-two properties, and they were among the prominent twenty-five Polish *kehillos* represented in the *Vaad Arba Aratzos*

Although its population slowly grew through the centuries, Belz steadily lost importance and eventually became subsidiary to Sokal, initially one of its smaller satellites. (Sokal was permitted only two Jewish families in two designated houses in 1578; by 1609 there were eighteen houses, a synagogue and cemetery.) Tradition has it that this unnatural decline was due to a ringing curse pronounced by the renowned R' Yoel Surkis, author of *Bayis Chadash* — popularly known as the "Bach." Rav Yoel was Chief Rabbi of the Belz district between 1615 and 1617, but its irascible communal leaders caused him a great deal of grief while rebuffing any peace overtures.

Matters came to a head when the *rosh hakahal* drew up a letter of dismissal to be delivered on Erev Shabbos! However, the *shammas* bravely delayed handing over the letter until after Shabbos to spare the Rav extra anguish on the sacred day of rest. In response, the Bach blessed him that he merit a great and holy son; as for the community, the Bach said that it should continually decrease in prestige and numbers, the water supply should be nearly undrinkable, the dead should merit no respite, and the president's male descendants should not survive beyond half their allotted life span. His fateful words were fulfilled in total. The *shammas'* son Rav Yitzchak eventually became Rabbi of Belz,

The two large mounds known as "Die alte heilige ort"

and a century later the first Belzer Rebbe, the "Sar Shalom," inherited the position and married into that family (his daughter married Rebbe Henoch of Alesko, who was also a descendant of the *shammas*).

Beyond its steady decline, some of Belz's early inhabitants suffered the ultimate indignity in 1846 when the town mayor insisted — despite Rebbe Shalom's best efforts — on uprooting the ancient cemetery during construction of a new highway. The only grave left in peace was Rav Yitzchak's, the recipient of the Bach's blessing! Meanwhile, the skeletons and consecrated earth were temporarily stored in the ladies' section of the *beis hamedrash*, and those studying there heard unearthly cries that night! Panic stricken, they ran for Rebbe Shalom and suggested he declare a public fast. "You needn't be alarmed," he replied. "These are the remains of those who caused the Bach much pain and were damned to enjoy no rest either in this world or the next!"

After the highway was completed, those remains were reburied near their original site in two large communal mounds known locally as *"Die alte heilige ort."* The "new" cemetery enjoyed no respite either since the ground vibrated from the trains passing nearby; today that railroad has been abandoned but the dead still cannot rest after their cemetery was almost entirely destroyed. (Popular folklore claims this railroad meandered strangely around the town because unscrupulous local farmers seeking lucrative compensation bribed the railway surveyor to draw the proposed route across their land;

naturally, the Jewish residents remained convinced it was Rav Yoel's lingering curse that lay behind their troubles.) Although the Bach left such a strong impact on Belz — even today Belz adherents hesitate to question his rulings or contradict his permitting *chadash* — Belz was graced by other prominent rabbis: Rav Moshe of Przemysl (Premisla), a disciple of the Maharshal and author of *Mateh Moshe*; Rav Yonah Teumim, author of *Kikayon D'Yonah*; Rav Moshe Makh, brother-in-law of the Pnei Yehoshua; and Rav Zechariah Mendel, author of the *Ba'er Heitev* on *Yoreh Deah*, are only a few of several renowned rabbanim who oversaw Belz and the surrounding district. Yet it was Rabbi Yoel Surkis and his blunt condemnation that echoed down the generations.

When the Cossack hordes revolted in 1648-9 just thirty years after the Bach had left town, Belz on the Ukrainian frontier was directly in their line of advance and a prime target. The two hundred local Jewish householders sheltering in the Belz citadel were joined by another thousand families fleeing from other communities. Fortunately, the fortifications were massive enough to withstand the long siege, but many succumbed to hunger and deprivation. Shortly afterwards, the town and fortress were totally destroyed during the Swedish invasion from the north in 1655-6, and they never recovered their former position. When fighting ceased, the Belz town council finally agreed to allow its Jews to settle throughout the town (and not be confined to a ghetto as previously), and ruled that their taxes or disputes should not go directly to the monarch any longer.

In the following decades, Turkey attacked Poland from the south and annexed Podolia, though they had to concede it in subsequent fighting. With the Swedes attacking from the north, the Turks from the south, the Russians from the east, and later Prussia and Austria from the west, Poland repeatedly became a battleground, and each time the Jewish population were scapegoated for attacks and reprisals. After the Russo-Swedish wars of 1700-10, fought on Polish soil and accompanied by a brutal civil conflict, Poland was torn in two. In the 1770's, following an internal religious schism between Catholics and Greek-Orthodox (supported by Russia), Poland was invaded by Austria, Prussia, and Russia, which each annexed large swaths of territory. Austria captured Galicia, Russia took the area around Minsk

A map of the district of Belz in the 1800's

Chapter 1: *Der Shtet'ele Belz* / 15

known as "White Russia" (now Belarus), while Prussia seized the "Polish Corridor." After an abortive uprising twenty years later, yet more territory and independence were lost in the Third Partition.

At that period, the approximate 250,000 Jews constituted nearly 9 percent of the general population in Eastern Galicia, but six townships — including Belz, Sokal, and Brody — were almost entirely Jewish. Yet their number in Belz and surroundings had officially increased to only 716 Jewish souls by 1765 while Sokal, already contained 1,390. Even in 1921, when the Jews were over half the population, only 2,004 of them officially resided in Belz after the town had been badly damaged during First World War hostilities — as it was again in the Second. In population maps of 1931, only nearby Sokal and Rawa-Ruska rate a mention; Belz, with less than 5,000 permanent Jewish residents, is totally ignored. According to local tradition, these two rival communities bickered continually over their relative importance, with the matter settled finally in 1891 by the second Belzer Rebbe, Rav Yeshie'le, who commented when he was in Sokal on a short visit for a *bris*, "Count how many *shas'en* there are in Sokal and how many *siddurim* in Belz." Belz decisively lost the argument when many more *gemaras* turned up in Sokal than prayer books in Belz!

Most of Eastern Galicia was severely affected before and during the world slump and was popularly described by the rest of Poland as the "estates of the *Melech Evyon*" due to its rampant poverty! With the breakdown of Russia during the Revolution of 1917-20, Ukraine on Galicia's eastern borders became a hotbed of anti-Semitic nationalism and bloody pogroms under the leadership of the notorious Semyon Petlyura. By the outbreak of the Second World War and the community's final destruction, many Belz householders had been reduced to catering for the seasonal pilgrimages of chassidim as their main source of income, and half of the

A painting of Belz, 1847

A medallion minted by the Dutch government in honor of Rav Elazar Rokach of Amsterdam

town was given over to pasturage. If not for its association with the world famous Belzer dynasty, the *kehillah* would probably have been long forgotten by mainstream Judaism.

If Belz's town history stretched back further than its size might indicate, the chronology of its chassidic court was far shorter than might be judged by its fame or the spread of its appeal. Indeed Rebbe Aharon, popularly known as "Reb Ahare'le," was only the fourth in line. Although Medzibozh in Podolia, the birthplace of Chassidus, sometimes shared a common administration with Belz (Rav Shalom Shachna, for instance, was in charge of both), and was relatively close geographically — as are the Carpathian Mountains where the Baal ShemTov honed his ideas during a self-imposed seclusion — the ideals and practices of chassidim came late to Belz. They were introduced by the legendary miracle worker and brilliant *gaon*, Rav Shalom Rokach, following his induction as rabbi in 1817.

Rav Shalom was a scion of the distinguished family of Rav Elazar Rokach, the *Maaseh Rokeach*, and renowned Chief Rabbi of Brody and later Amsterdam,[1] and eventual leader of the Ashkenazi settlement in Eretz Yisrael. His great-grandson and namesake, Rav Elazar Rokach

---

1. His appointment in 1735 was honored by a commemorative medallion minted by the Dutch government with an image of his head and shoulders!

of Brody, joined the famous Brody *Kloiz* of *mekubalim* and *talmidei cha-chamim*, where he was a disciple of the Kabbalist Rav Chaim Sanzer. In Shevat 1783 as Rav Chaim lay dying, he consoled his disconsolate *talmid* by declaring that he would return within the week! His cryptic words became a little clearer a week after his passing, when a baby was born to the Rokachs — the young Shalom. This infant inherited a glorious lineage. On his father's side the line stretched back to the me-dieval Kabbalist and Baal Tosafos, disciple of Rav Yehudah HeChassid and among the last of the *Chassidei Ashkenaz*, Rav Elazar Rokach, who was himself a scion of the illustrious Kalonymus clan. On his mother's side, Rav Shalom was a descendant of the noble Abulafia family from pre-expulsion Spain.

Orphaned at a young age, the budding genius was edu-cated by his maternal uncle, Rav Yissacher Ber Ramraz, Rabbi of Sokal. From a tender age it was obvious that the boy had a sublime soul, and when he matured, his uncle chose him as son-in-law, husband to his distinguished daughter Rebbetzin Malkah. Although Sokal was then still a bastion of *misnagdim*, one disciple of the Mezeritcher Maggid, Rav Shloma of Lutsk, author of *Dibros Shlomoh*, had braved the harassment to function as *maggid* in Sokal. Despite hostility even among his own fam-ily, Rav Shalom felt attracted to chassidic teachings and drew close to Rabbi Shloma. Chassidic legend has it that his faithful wife, Rebbetzin Malkah, would let him down by rope at night from their bedroom window so he could secretly study with Rav Shloma without his father-in-law's knowledge. This led to Rebbe Meir'l Premishlaner's apocryphal remark: "*U'Malki-Zedek Melech Shalem* — had his Malkah not been a *tzadekes*, Shalom would never have become a *melech*!"

By this time Rav Shalom had already become known as a legendary miracle worker, and the noted *posek*, Rabbi Shalom Mordechai HaKohen Schwadron of Berezhany (Berzhan), re-called in his responsa (*Maharsham* 3:225) that when someone fell deathly ill one Shabbos in Zlotchow, a local *dayan* — in the guise of *pikuach nefesh* — permitted a non-Jew to dispatch the patient's and mother's names to Rav Shalom in Brody. Rav Shlomo Kluger, Chief Rabbi of Brody, was furious at the desecration, as was Rav

Shalom personally, since the fear of needless *chillul Shabbos* put an undue onus on him to effect a cure; he was successful though, and the man recovered! Indeed, he constantly prayed that the healthy should remain healthy and be spared from all worries.

Although he had drunk deeply from the wells of Chassidus, he still yearned for more and contemplated visiting the miracle worker Rav Yaakov Yitzchak Horowitz of Lublin, famous as the "Chozeh" or Seer. Although his Rebbe, Rav Shloma, was unhappy about losing his prize pupil — "My mind is like a fountain spring and as long as there is a willing receptacle, fresh insights bubble forth" — Rav Shalom eventually went. On his arrival he met Rebbe Naftali Horowitz of Ropszyce (Ropshitz), who peremptorily demanded, "Young man! Bless me!" Rav Shalom looked at him in surprise. "How can I? I'm only a young man, while your honor is famed as a *tzaddik*." But although Rebbe Naftali enjoyed a reputation as a bit of a jokester, he was now deadly serious. Since it was in the midst of an icy East European winter he demanded again, "Why don't you have mercy on me? I'm freezing here from cold!" Reluctantly Rav Shalom blessed him. Later Rebbe Naftali revealed that he had foreseen how tens of thousands would eventually flock to this young man for his blessing — and he wanted be the first! (From then on it became a tradition in Belz for every new Rebbe to accept his first *kvittel* from a Ropshitzer descendant.)

During one *tisch*, Rav Shalom was discovered under the table at the Chozeh's feet and the Lubliner Rebbe predicted, "One day, chassidim will be pushing under your *tisch*, too." Rav Shalom was chosen by the Chozeh to teach a generous but simple donor who had defrayed the marriage cost of two orphans for the celestial reward of gaining admittance to the Chozeh's vicinity in the World to Come. To educate this ignorant man, Rav Shalom was presented with a special copy of the profoundly difficult *Bris Menuchah* (a legendary Kabbalistic work rumored to be capable of reviving the dead) annotated in the Chozeh's own hand. While in Lublin, he also became close to Rebbe Yaakov Yitzchak Rabinowitz, known as the "Yehudi HaKadosh." After the Chozeh's passing on Tishah B'Av 1815, Rav Shalom studied under the fiery Rebbe Uri, the "Saraf" of Strelisk; the saintly Rebbe Yisrael, the Maggid of Kozniece (Kozhnitz); and the venerable Rebbe Avraham Yehoshua of Apta-Opatow. [2]

When the position in Belz fell vacant shortly before the Chozeh's demise, communal leaders approached the Chozeh for a suitable candidate and he unhesitatingly recommended the relatively young Rav Rokach from the neighboring *kehillah* of Sokal. However, Rav Shalom was reluctant to earn a livelihood from his Torah knowledge. Instead, he proposed pooling his dowry with another chassid in order to engage in minimal commerce, for which he received his Rebbe's blessing. Surprisingly, when his prospective partner separately approached the Rebbe for approval, he was advised against the enterprise! Nonplussed, they turned to the Yehudi HaKadosh who encouraged them to go ahead. When they finally began doing business, they encountered one setback after another until Rav Shalom lost all his money. Realizing this must be due to his Rebbe's censure (thus forcing him to become a Rav), he conferred with the Yehudi HaKadosh who revealed that the Chozeh had indeed advised his partner not to go ahead because of impending disaster; he, however, had felt it worthwhile that both lose their money since only thus would Rav Shalom be encouraged to seek a Rabbinical position for the greater benefit of *Klal Yisrael*!

Finally, in 1817, he became Rav of Belz, and after holding this position for almost forty years, town and dynasty were to remain inextricably linked. As tales spread of his legendary ability to heal the sick and paralytic, banish evil spirits or perform wonders transcending the natural order, streams of simple people beat a path to his door. They were followed by hundreds of chassidim eager to

---

2. He once overheard the Chozeh declare, "Whoever lives in the vicinity of the Kozhnitzer Maggid but doesn't meet him will not receive *Shalom* from Mashiach!" and resolved to travel to Kozniece. Yet when Reb Shalom took his leave, the Chozeh remarked, "But you'll be back in Lublin for Shabbos." So after journeying to Kozniece and briefly greeting the Maggid, he immediately took his leave so as to return to Lublin on time. Surprised, Rebbe Yisrael tried to delay him and announced, "*Yungerman!* Stay here for Shabbos and you'll merit to see Eliyahu HaNavi!" But Rav Shalom again gave his hand to make his farewell. The Maggid tried again: "Stay and you'll be shown the *Avos*!" Undeterred, Rav Shalom insisted on taking his leave and returning to Lublin forthwith. When he arrived back in Lublin on Friday, the Chozeh remarked admiringly and publicly, "Neither Eliyahu nor the *heilige Avos,* but to return to his Rebbe — that denotes a true chassid!"

tap this new source of spirituality, and Galicia gained thousands of new recruits. In turn, many prominent Torah scholars visited regularly since the Sar Shalom was above all an outstanding *gaon* who stressed the importance of study combined with chassidic practice. His fame and adherents spread throughout the Austro-Hungarian Empire: Slovakia, Bohemia, Moravia, Carpatho-Russ, and Hungary. Among his illustrious disciples were Rav Shalom of Kaminka, Rav Shimon of Jaroslaw, Rav Yehoshua of Lezsno, Rav Chaim Halberstam (known as the Divrei Chaim) of Nowy Sanz, Rav Moshe Teitelbaum of Uhelji (author of the *Yismach Moshe* and founder of the Sighetu-Satumare dynasty). Regular visits were also paid by Rav Shlomo Kluger of Brody, Rebbe Tzadok HaKohen from Lublin, Rebbe Asher of Stolin, and Rebbe Shmuel of Lubavitch.

The simple lifestyle adopted by Rav Shalom and his Rebbetzin was noteworthy. To remain indistinguishable from his chassidim, he was the first chassidic Rebbe not to don a white *bekeshe* on Shabbos. As Rebbe Yitzchak Issak of Zidichow admiringly recalled, "In Belz we learned how it's possible to be a Rebbe without the white *zjupiecze!*"

By 1820, most opposition to the "new sect" of Chassidus had ceased in Galicia but a more insidious opponent arose — the Haskalah movement of Germany, which struck deep roots in the capital Lvov (Lemberg); even the Orthodox community was officially led by "moderate assimilationists." The Reform leader, Hertz Homberg, originated from Lemberg and had opened four modern boys schools, three girls schools, and a teachers seminary there, but these were all closed down in 1806. Radical assimilationist circles in Lemberg openly identified with German culture, and their ugly battle with Orthodoxy and chassidim was accompanied by groveling informants, governmental pressure, and the appointment of an apostate chief censor who was sympathetic to the Reform movement. Before his baptism he had been virulently opposed to chassidim and their "Wonder Rabbis" — particularly the Sar Shalom of Belz and the Bnei Yissaschar of Dinow — and under his imprimatur no chassidic writings were ever published; they had to be smuggled into Galicia clandestinely.

These assimilationists advocated modernization of traditional Jewish dress in the 1830's. Restrictions against Jewish students attending high schools and university were lifted, resulting in an increasing number of Jewish lawyers, chemists, doctors — and apostates. The Lemberg assimilationists established a Temple and German-Jewish school in 1844, and imported a Reform clergyman from Austria as preacher and school director. When he was confirmed as official rabbi of the entire province, above the heads of the overwhelmingly Orthodox community, opposition boiled over. When this "rabbi" and his family mysteriously died shortly afterwards, attempts were made to direct suspicion against "religious fanatics."

The only effective counterweights to this trend were proactive chassidic adherents who fought a bitter, unrelenting battle against leading *maskilim* while seeking to draw their unwitting followers closer to Orthodoxy. The magnetic personality of Rav Shalom attracted many to the flag of Belz, whether by stories of his legendary wonders and cures, his patent saintliness, or his profound scholarship. Hundreds abandoned their dissolute lifestyle and thousands returned to spirituality. At the same time that the Reform Temple opened in Lvov, Rav Shalom engaged in constructing his famous shul — and this was a legend in itself:

Rav Shalom had made a pact with two colleagues to learn Torah throughout 1,000 nights and thus merit seeing Eliyahu HaNavi. After 300 nights of Talmudic toil, one of the threesome dropped out; after another 500 nights the second partner capitulated, and Rav Shalom persevered alone for the next 200 nights. On the last night, a fierce storm erupted in the area of the synagogue — windows were smashed and candelabra extinguished. His repeated attempts to rekindle the candles failed in the wake of this unnatural storm. In trepidation and anguish, Rav Shalom retreated to the *Aron HaKodesh* to pray fervently with a broken heart. His heartfelt prayers were accepted: the storm abruptly ceased, the candles were relit, and an old, tall man with a shining countenance appeared. Together they sat and studied until daybreak; the last subject he studied together with Eliyahu HaNavi was the halachos of *beis haknesess*. To commemorate this miraculous episode, Rav Shalom built his celebrated shul, overseeing every detail

The famous shul in Belz

— even laboring daily as a common worker — while infusing the sacred building with mystical meditations.

It was designed like an ancient citadel, four stories high, with walls over three feet thick. The castellated roof was supported internally by four massive pillars; the ceiling was made up of nine sky-colored domes, studded with stars (later these were plated in gold), and the exterior battlements were adorned with gilded copper balls.[3] Along the east wall (actually southeast) the *Aron HaKodesh* was elaborately carved and decorated with *esrog* trees with golden *esrogim*. It had room for 5,000 congregants at any one time — the *bimah* alone could accommodate 100 men! — but superb acoustics ensured that prayers were distinctly heard throughout. Until the end, building projects were always ongoing, combined with

---

3. These balls were confiscated by the Russian army during the First World War and melted down for ammunition. In the modern replica that dominates Jerusalem's northern skyline, these balls are made of striking white stone.

sustained fundraising, yet exclusive donations were refused since "all of *Klal Yisrael* should have a share!" Solely used during the summer months, it was not lit by electricity, since the municipal supply likewise served non-Jewish houses of worship. Instead, several massive chandeliers (for candles), beautifully fashioned by a master coppersmith, hung from the ceiling: one donated by the Krakow yeshivah *bachurim* weighed a ton, while another from American chassidim weighed 600 kilos. Inaugurated in 1843, the distinctive shul stood in the main street, alongside the *beis hamedrash* and the Rebbe's *hoif* (mansion) — likewise built by Rav Shalom.

Although in his final years he was afflicted by blindness, the Sar Shalom's holy duties continued unabated and his almost forty-year reign slowly came to an end on 27th Elul 1855. The mantle of leadership immediately passed to his fifth and youngest son, Rav Yehoshua, who loyally consolidated Belz's dominion over Eastern Galicia with an impressive organizational flair all his own. Above all, "Rebbe Yeshie'le," as he was popularly known, was a worthy son of a worthy father. Like his saintly father he was widely respected for his Torah scholarship; prominent rabbanim and illustrious *geonim* from near and far were to be found among the masses of chassidim flocking to his court. Customarily, he roared out the prayers with great fervor and would lift his hands in supplication after each section. *"Der Mitteler Rebbe"* (or "Intermediate Rebbe" as he was later known) inherited his father's gift of leadership, and with his worldly-wise perception proved a forceful counterweight to the wily stratagems of the Galician assimilationists.

Under his capable command, Belz greatly widened Orthodox influence throughout the Austro-Hungarian Empire. Although priding themselves for their strict adherence to tradition coupled with a firm rejection of new and possibly dangerous ideas and trends, Belz took the radical step of establishing a religious-political party and publishing their own newspaper — decades before Agudas Israel took its first tentative steps. In 1848, after popular uprisings in Berlin and Vienna, the promise of emancipation and equal rights had tempted "progressive" Jews to campaign for accelerated assimilation in the hope of achieving comparable status with their non-Jewish neighbors. Their efforts were encouraged by officials of the Austro-Hungarian Empire as a useful vehicle to indoctrinate "superior Germanic cultural values among their backward Slav subjects."

Inspired by these *maskilim*, various anti-religious decrees periodically surfaced under the guise of being enacted for the public good, including agricultural training for unemployed Jews, a modern Theological (or Rabbinical) seminary, and the renewal of the infamous kosher-meat tax to fund Reform institutions. In 1861, the government demanded the establishment of a Rabbinical Seminary and the assimilationists set up the innocent sounding *Chevras Shocherei Toshiah, Hayashar V'hatov* (Society Aspiring for Wisdom, Honesty, and Good). Distorted *kehillah* elections in 1865 allowed reformist Jews to sweep the board throughout the Lvov and Belz

Speech delivered by Rebbe Shalom on the occasion of Emperor Franz Josef's deliverance from assassination

districts. Emboldened by their success, they launched the German cultural *Shomer Yisrael* organization in 1869 accompanied by the weekly *Der Israelit* (or *Izraelita*) in Galician-German (Germanic Yiddish) to overtly spread "education among the Jewish masses and alert them to their civic and social obligations ..." With the propagandizing backing of *Der Israelit*, they formed a joint Jewish-Ruthenian bloc for the 1873 elections and won three seats in the Viennese *reichsrat* (parliament). Nor were they the only assimilationist group. A rival *Doreshei Shalom* group armed with the *Ugoda* newspaper campaigned for Polish nationalism while the radical *Agudat Achim* preached a third brand of assimilation in Galicia.

Orthodox Judaism sought to counter this malign influence both on a local and governmental level, but the turning point in their struggle came in 1878 when *Shomer Yisrael* summoned delegates from twenty-five leading communities to a conference. On the

The newspaper of Machzikei Hadas   A letter of support for Machzikei Hadas

agenda were: (a) modernizing the religious communal structure in their own image; (b) organizing an inter-communal body to represent Galician Jewry to the Austrian goverment; (c) establishing a Rabbinical Seminary to produce modern young rabbis who will spread "enlightenment" among the masses; and (d) renewing the Emperor Franz Josef's fund for modern Jewish day schools.

Fearing that this would allow the Reform minority complete dominance over religion and individual *kehillos*, Rav Yehoshua called a rival conference in Lvov and issued a joint statement with Rav Zvi Hirsch Orenstein, Rabbi of Lvov, denouncing their evil plans as more dangerous than the Spanish Inquisition. In the resulting turmoil, Rebbe Yeshie'le and Rav Shimon Sofer-Schreiber of Krakow (son of the Chasam Sofer) officially established the umbrella organization, *Machzikei Hadas*, covering Galicia and Bukovina. In the previous decade, this organization had functioned almost underground, without permission, since *Shomer Yisrael* leaders with close connections to officialdom delayed its authorization. With that radical step, the Belzer Rav became not merely the spiritual mentor of Galician chassidim but also a leader of *Klal Yisrael* on the world stage; the memorable slogan coined by the Chasam Sofer — "*Chadash assur min haTorah*, Innovations

Rav Shimon Sofer of Krakow

Rebbe Yeshie'le —
"Der Mitteler Rebbe" of Belz

are forbidden by the Torah" — also became the unofficial motto of Belz and the *Machzikei Hadas*. Its statutes were laid down at the founding convention (March 13, 1879) and their own Yiddish publication *Dos Wert Judentum* (The Authentic Judaism) was launched, but it was soon replaced by the Hebrew fortnightly *Kol Machzikei Hadas*. Its 4 Nissan 1879 edition carried a forthright declaration jointly signed by Rebbe Yehoshua and Rav Shimon Sofer, among other prominent person- alities: *We turn to you informing you how the holy federation of Machzikei Hadas has been established by the geonim and tzaddikim of our country ... Please join us in founding branches in every town ... nor be discouraged by the empty proclamations that are inevitably issued by Shomer Yisrael, etc. Our central offices are based in Lvov because that is where the center of Maskilim and Assimilationists, members of Shomer Yisrael, are situated; they call them- selves the "party of progress," but most desecrate the Sabbath, eat nonkosher food, and scheme to introduce new customs into Jewish affairs ... They claim to be concerned for the Jewish community ... Is it not a farce to accept the words of such people who seek to entrap innocent souls within their net and take control of the kehillos?*

As a counterweight to *Shomer Yisrael*, they had a two-pronged agenda: on an official level, to designate their own independent representatives to deal with governments; and on a spiritual level, to inspire Galician youth back to their traditional lifestyle. In the Austrian *reichsrat* elections of that year, they put forward four candidates, but only Rav Sofer was elected, and he joined the "Polish club" in direct opposition to assimilationist members of parliament. In 1882 the Rebbe's enthusiastic aide, R' Mordechai Peltz, organized an impressive conference attended by 800 *kehillah* representatives and 200 rabbanim to shore up religious communities and rebuff reformist or progressive tendencies; only Jews observing *Shulchan Aruch* would henceforth enjoy full communal voting rights.[4] The successful meeting ended on 23 Shevat and Rebbe Yeshie'le exclaimed excitedly, "Let's hope this date will be remembered always — until the coming of Mashiach!" but the full and ominous significance of these fateful words did not become apparent for another twelve years.

The assimilationists continued to target the *cheder* system and sought to ban Talmud study altogether as "no longer relevant to modern society in the 19th century and an obstacle to better inter-ethnic relations." Under their influence, Austrian officials summoned a meeting in Vienna where only three religious Rabbinical delegates were invited, opposed to twelve assimilationists. But after these outnumbered rabbanim, led by Rav Sofer, successfully argued that these radical proposals would split Austro-Hungarian Jewry in half and irretrievably destroy the underpinnings of the Jewish people, the status quo was allowed to continue. Despite the untimely death of Rav Shimon Sofer in 1883 at age 63, this vital endeavor continued, since by then the first Zionist organizations in Galicia (whose influence was to grow as Reform waned) began taking root. During 1887 in the *reichsrat*, the assimilationists proposed closing down every *Talmud Torah* in Galicia. Branches of *Machzikei Hadas* throughout the Galician towns and villages were galvanized into drafting fierce protests and Vienna quietly shelved the proposal.

For Torah study, Rav Yehoshua preferred the system of *pilpul* which had the added advantage — as he once remarked — "that sometimes you need a complicated *pilpul* to exonerate a fellow Jew

---

4. Surprisingly, Mr. Peltz of Lemberg personally grew up in an assimilationist home until his bar mitzvah; his father and brother were early *maskilim* and members of *Shomer Yisrael*, but he was later entrusted to the religious care of his maternal uncle, a disciple of Belz. He was a formidable activist: rich, kind, charming, bubbling with energy, and possessing exceptional organizational and diplomatic skills.

from his *aveiros!*" Although he was fastidious by nature, in his final years he would drink vile tasting castor oil to the last drop to maintain a pure body for prayers. Eventually, in his 69th year, he elected to undergo life-threatening surgery in Vienna against his family's wishes. "I'm prepared to risk my life if there's a chance I can *daven* with a pure body!"[5] He had few illusions about the likely outcome of the surgery, and just before he left home, whispered ominously to *Dayan* Mordche Weinberger of Belz, "Your wife will very shortly give birth to a boy — and you can name him Yehoshua!" Rav Mordche promptly fainted on the spot and by the time he recovered and was finally persuaded to divulge the portentous secret, vital time had passed.

Rebbe Yissachar Ber, known as "Der Fri'erdiger" Rebbe of Belz

Although the Rebbe's family desperately raced to the station in a frantic effort to cancel the journey, the train had already steamed out with the Rebbe on board and could not be recalled.

One of the Viennese specialists was an irreligious Jew, but the Rebbe promised him *Olam Haba* if he would repent and believe totally in the Messiah. The doctor accepted Rebbe Yeshie'le's rebuke and accompanied him back on the train to Galicia where he was part of the *minyan* at the *petirah*; a genuine *baal teshuvah*, he passed away just a few weeks after the Belzer Rav. Although the operation had been a technical success, Rav Yehoshua lost his battle for life on Tuesday, the 23rd of Shevat 1894, early on the homeward journey, but the sad tidings were not released until his train reached Belz without mishap. Despite the news blackout and the icy cold, the *levayah* on Wednesday was accompanied by an estimated 20,000 mourners; the date — as he predicted — would be remembered for posterity.

---

5. The Arugos HaBosem writes in his *hesped* that he was *moser nefesh* to be able to pray for *Klal Yisrael.*

His second son and successor, Rebbe Yissachar Dov (Ber), retained a strict control on Belz chassidim and institutions, though following his marriage to a grandchild of Rebbe Aharon Chernobyl, Rebbetzin Basha Ruchamah Twersky, in 1868, he adopted some ideas and influence of Chernobyl Chassidus at variance with Belz tradition. Although only 3 years old at the passing of his *zeide*, the Sar Shalom, he clearly remembered sitting on his grandfather's lap while the Sar Shalom whispered confidentially in his ear, "Know that Hashem chose Moshe Rabbeinu as a leader because of his ability to find *zechusim* for *Klal Yisrael* even when they had no obvious merits. You will one day be a leader, so you ought to know this and become a good defender of your people!" Notwithstanding the hubbub and excitement of a chassidic center, his *hasmadah* was legendary and he became renowned from a young age for his erudite mastery of Torah and *p'sak* — even beyond his fame as an *oveid Hashem* and *tzaddik*. Prominent rabbanim visiting Rebbe Yeshie'le were most impressed by Rav Yissachar Ber's wide knowledge and sharp Torah insights, and he frequently corresponded with the leading Galician authors of *teshuvos*. In the Responsa of *Beis Yitzchak* (Rav Yitzchak Smelkish), *Ohel Yehoshua*, or *Chavazeles HaSharon* (Rav Menachem Munish Babad), he is cited as the final arbiter of halachah.

Despite his position, Rebbe Yissachar Ber remained sincerely humble. Composing the text of a wedding announcement for one of his children, he suggested he might be entitled *hatzaddik hamefursam* ("the famous saint ...") and the in-laws as merely *hatzaddik*. Noting the astonishment of his chassidim he explained: "I am known widely as a *tzaddik* only by repute, whereas he is genuinely saintly!" True to Rebbe Yissachar Ber's nature, "simple" chassidim who harbored no pretensions beyond their station were made more welcome in Belz than those who felt they had somehow earned a certain degree of prestige or honor. Likewise, he did not believe it below his dignity to address the womenfolk exclusively before *Kol Nidrei* in the *graiser-stieb* with penetrating words of *mussar*; the sobs and wails of his audience could be heard in the distance and were powerful enough to melt the hardest of hearts.

The Belzer Rav's appearance, pithy sayings, and wise advice gained him countless adherents, while his fervent and fiery *tefillos* ignited the spirit of all who merited to hear them. On the way to shul he never sheltered under an umbrella even during the strongest downpour, since "we are soldiers marching to the front! Have you ever seen soldiers using umbrellas?" On the High Holy Days he roared out prayers alternating from desperate pleading to joyful dancing, depending on the context, his differing emotions faithfully mirroring the prayers' meanings (he would shed copious tears whenever reciting verses describing *galus*). After *Tashlich*, the chassidim would dance for hours while the Rebbe periodically blessed them with, "Life, abundance, *berachah*, and *parnassah* for all of *Klal Yisrael!*" His charity too was legendary. While his personal needs were simple, his concern for the destitute and downtrodden was almost beyond limit.

During his tenure, what otherwise could have been described as a disaster was treated as a welcome opportunity. The *beis hamedrash*, which had been built by the Sar Shalom, was constructed entirely of timber — now old and dry — and late on the night of Shemini Atzeres 1924 the *schach*-covering of a neighbor's *succah* accidentally caught fire from an unattended candle. With nobody in R' Moshe Itzikel's *succah* at the time, the blaze spread to the nearby *beis hamedrash* cellar where sacks of *sheimos* were stored, and the conflagration rapidly reduced the ancient house of learning to smoking cinders. Fortunately, no one was hurt and the *Sifrei Torah* were saved.

To everyone's great surprise, the Rebbe showed little sadness at the news; on the contrary, he seemed assuaged. Until now he had felt unable to demolish the old wooden building which had grown too small for its purpose; now they could build a larger and more substantial edifice with bricks and mortar. As with the synagogue and Rebbe's rooms, the new *beis hamedrash* was illuminated solely by candles and never connected to the municipal electricity grid that supplied non-Jewish houses of worship. When it was completed, it housed up to 1,000 scholars at any one time and was extensively utilized by the *yoshvim*.

Under his guidance, the existing system of Belz *yoshvim* — whereby chassidim left their families for months or years to study Torah and remain close to the Rebbe — was considerably expanded and developed. *Yoshvim* during Rebbe Yeshie'le's reign had been older, married, and knowledgable in Torah, whereas now many *bachurim* just commencing intense Torah study were welcomed — a reflection of changed circumstances and competing influences in Galicia. Since Belz always stressed pure Torah learning, these essentially constituted an unofficial *yeshivah gedolah* with R' Mechel'e of Zolkove delivering up to six different *shiurim* to hundreds of teenagers during a 16-hour day. Wherever they went, *yoshvim* were recognized as an elite who steadfastly upheld tradition and custom without the slightest deviation and were always available as a praetorian guard to do the Rebbe's bidding. Even prominent rabbanim would occasionally join the massed ranks of *yoshvim*, where they could shed all communal concerns and abandon the trappings and protocols of office. Unadulterated *chinuch* remained at the heart of Rav Yissachar Ber's concerns, as he once remarked: "Teaching children is mentioned in *Krias Shema* alongside the duties of *mezuzah* and *tefillin* to demonstrate how even the tiniest deviation renders education *pasul* as it would *mezuzos* or *tefillin!*"

Surprisingly, he unhesitatingly gave a warm blessing of support and encouragement to Sarah Schenirer's[6] radically new religious girls day school that blossomed into the renowned Bais Yaakov movement, despite Belz's well-rooted opposition to any innovation — even when introduced with the best of intentions. Although Belz's *Machzikei Hadas* movement had predated Agudas Israel's founding by decades and ostensibly both political parties shared similar aims and platforms, the Belzer Rav remained officially neutral and steadfastly distant from that new organization. About the Religious Zionists he was more disparaging, and once remarked half-jokingly they had taken the title of "Mizrachi" since they are opposed to the holy *Shechinah* that according to the Talmud (*Zevachim* 54b) resides on the *maarav* side!

Rebbe Yissachar Ber's fierce and lifelong battles against alien movements and ideologies or the slightest deviation from tradition made him famous beyond the confines of Galicia. His saintly father had introduced him early to public affairs — remark-

---

6. She was the daughter of a prominent Belz family.

ing, "Without my Berele, I can't move!"— but whereas Rebbe Yeshie'le had to campaign against Reform and creeping German acculturation, now it was necessary to combat the Zionism and Socialism that made deep inroads among *kehillos* and the youth.[7] Although he zealously fought each skirmish against enemies who harbored few scruples and stopped at nothing, he was never rash and considered every step carefully. Likewise, he vehemently opposed the well-intentioned but misguided attempt to establish Galician schools that included a vocational training curriculum. At the successful conclusion of that bitter campaign he commented sadly, "My father had to battle those entirely outside Judaism and at least knew their place; I am forced to fight genuine rabbanim!"

During the inevitable hiatus after Rebbe Yeshie'le's passing, assimilationists in the Austrian *reichsrat* had legislated German as the official language of instruction in Galician *Talmud Torahs*, and instituted that all rabbis in the Hapsburg Empire must be fluent in German and also proficient in secular subjects. A sea change in official attitudes occurred when Rebbe Yissachar Ber met the Austrian Minister of Culture in Lemberg to persuade him to drop the proposed stipulation that only rabbis with secular grades would receive government accreditation. The Rebbe was accompanied by his faithful aide, Mr. Dovid Schreiber — "for the merits of your grandfather, the Chasam Sofer!" — and Mr. Schreiber asked him what they would tell the minister. "I have here the Rebbe Reb Elimelech's personal copy of *Tehillim*, first let us recite a *kapitel*!" On the way up to the minister's office, they met Baron Shmelke Von Horowitz — a die-hard reformer. "And where is the Rebbe going?" he asked scornfully. "Up to the minister? You're wasting your time ..." But the Belzer Rav replied sharply, "We're ascending while your decline begins now and continues!"

At first the minister was nonplussed by the Rebbe's opposition — "Rabbis ought to have some secular education; it's for their

---

7. Rebbe Yissachar Ber also foresaw how the Palestinian *Yishuv* under Zionist influence would never enjoy peace with its Arab neighbors.

own good." However, Rebbe Yissachar Ber argued that if the minister wanted to construct a new house or a state carriage, he would surely consult the experts. So too with the rabbinate: He should value the professional opinion of the rabbis themselves, not take advice from amateurs like Baron Horowitz who have never officiated as rabbis! The minister accepted the point and was genuinely impressed by the chassidic leader's sharp insight and worldly-wise perspective. After their hour-long audience, he canceled the new decree and subsequently upbraided Baron Horowitz for dismissing the Belzer Rav as an obscurantist simpleton; indeed, the reformist Baron's influence waned from that day onwards.

However, the political and religious map was radically redrawn by the First World War, and by its end in 1918, the Austrian-Hungarian Empire ceased to exist. On the "Eastern Front," fierce fighting in Poland and Galicia had ravaged many *kehillos* while most of their religious leadership fled (on hearing how the tzar's secret police planned holding them hostage in Siberian prison camps). After initial setbacks, Germany captured Western Poland and Galicia during the winter of 1914-15, taking almost the total remaining land area of Poland and Galicia, plus Lithuania and parts of Russia during the 1915 offensive. Tzarist Russia counterattacked across German lines in 1916 with a massive army but made only limited headway before being beaten back with huge losses. To the demoralized Russian people, this was the final blow; revolution and counterrevolution broke out before the Communists seized power and signed a humiliating peace treaty with Germany in 1918. Anarchy, socialism, and nationalism were unleashed by the upheaval, while Poland — and eastern Galicia in particular — was a bitter battleground before being put under a strict German military occupation.

As the war front reached Belz on Tuesday, August 11, 1914, Rebbe Yissachar Ber led his family across the border to Hungary and settled temporarily in Racsfehert (Ujfeherto, north of Debrecen) for the next five years. They headed for Racsfehert at the express invitation of the town rabbi who recalled how the previous Belzer Rav, Rebbe Yeshie'le, had hinted to him years earlier that Racsfehert would constitute a welcome sanctuary during wartime! While taking a walk in the Hungarian forests they came across notices supporting the army, causing Rebbe Yissachar Ber to exclaim angrily, "The Germans believe they control the land, the English claim to rule the waves, but I declare in truth, 'To Hashem is the sea which He created while His hands formed the dry land'!"

Continuing hostilities nearby, as well as pogroms and hazardous highroads, reduced the flow of chassidim, allowing him the respite to compose two volumes of *chiddushim* on *Kodshim*. When the battlefront moved further away, masses of chassidim — including numerous fresh Hungarian recruits to Chassidus charmed by the Belzer Rav's personality and wisdom — arrived. Four and a half years later, on Russia's entry into Racsfehert, he left shortly after Purim 1919 and over the next three weeks migrated over 90 miles northeast to the acclaimed border community of Munkacs (Mukacevo) closer to Ukraine and, despite

During their WW I occupation, Russian soldiers requisitioned the historic shul as a field hospital!

local difficulties, only returned to nearby Eastern Galicia after Purim 1922.[8]

The traumatic war years had taken their toll. Belz had been consecutively afflicted by many problems: the invading Russian army burned down half the town while soldiers robbed all remaining valuables and locals vandalized the rest; smallpox, typhus, and cholera epidemics; slave labor to the retreating Russians; conscription into battle by the returning Austrians; and pogroms by demobilized Ukrainians — the notorious *"Hallerchiks"* — whose short-lived regime cut the city off from the surrounding area. Many of its children were orphans reciting *Kaddish* and subsisting on a free bread and cocoa kitchen run by the Joint. As the Rebbe later remarked, *"Es iz mir shwartz gevaren far die oigen zehen'dik die fermachte penim'er* — Seeing their compressed faces (from deprivation and despair) was a black day for me!" The famous shul and the Rebbe's residence had both been damaged in the fighting — the Russian army had even expropriated all ironwork, copper, and gold decorations for the war effort and utilized the priceless shul as a field hospital and the *beis hamedrash* as a stables for their cavalry! So Rebbe Yissachar Ber stayed in Holeszyce near Jaroslaw until repairs were completed in 1924. Although the universal suffering had a profoundly detrimental effect on his health, he selflessly continued his duties without deviation. By 1926 he was mostly bedridden, yet he insisted on blowing the *shofar* and leading the prayers on Rosh Hashanah and Yom Kippur. Though he had to be carried to shul seated on his chair, his vigorous and heartfelt rendering of the *tefillos* remained unchanged. Less than a month after Succos, on Friday night of *Chayei Sarah*, 22 Cheshvan (October 30, 1926), as his health deteriorated further, he ordered four chairs be set out in mystical welcome for *"tzaddikim* of previous generations." Concentrating on reciting *Krias Shema* for the

---

8. Later, during Shavuos of his first year as Rebbe, Reb Ahare'le instructed his chassidim in Munkacs to desist from all dispute with the community — "which only gives succor to the Zionists!" — even if that implied substantial monetary losses from building separate communal institutions.

last time, he slipped away at the age of 73 after thirty-three years of leadership.[9]

The *levayah* took place on Sunday accompanied by many thousands, led by hundreds of rabbanim and Rebbes who had flocked to the scene from great distances. After emotional *hespedim* by his sons, the funeral was interrupted by the local community ceremoniously proclaiming his eldest son Rebbe Aharon as the new Rav of Belz, at which bystanders pressed forward to the grave site to wish the late departed Rebbe, "Mazel Tov"! Later it was revealed how Rebbe Yissachar Ber had earlier predicted the day of his passing and had broadly hinted at his last wish that Reb Ahare'le should succeed him.

Leaving the Rebbe's house for the shul during Rebbe Yissachar Ber's levayah

9. Throughout, his eldest son Rebbe Ahare'le stood to the side of the sickbed, staring at his pocket-watch; suddenly he cried out, *"Nu, shoin"* — at the very moment his father's soul departed! A similar mystical instance occurred earlier, in Holeszyce during his father's *succah* preparations: Rebbe Yissachar Ber traditionally began laying small amounts of *schach* on the day following Yom Kippur, before Minchah prayers, surrounded by his sons and sons-in-law. One year after ascending the ladder, Rebbe Yissachar Dov fell into a deep reverie while all his family stood around in silence; Rebbe Ahare'le waited at the side, staring at the floor as usual. But suddenly, he ran forward to tug at his father's sleeve, crying *"Tatte, shoin, shoin"* — Rebbe Yissachar Ber immediately roused himself and laid the *schach*. Nobody else present seemed to have any inkling of what was going on.

The levayah of Rebbe Yissachar Ber

The matzeivos of the Belzer Rebbes

CHAPTER 2

REBBE AHARON ROKACH OF BELZ

EVEN IN THE PRE-WAR GENERATION OF SPIRITUAL giants, Reb Ahare'le, as he was popularly known, was a phenomenon for his ascetic, almost angelic existence. Stories proliferated in Poland and Hungary of his determined detachment from the coarse and vulgar, his pure innate holiness, lengthy fasts, and minuscule meals (save on Shabbos), routine denial of sleep or any other of the common creature comforts. The needs and appetites of ordinary mortals apparently had no meaning for him when he might spend hours sitting almost motionless with eyes closed as he meditated on heavenly affairs and *dveikus*. So he was the natural choice as successor — and not merely because he was the eldest son.

The circumstances surrounding his birth were yet another link in the chain of miracles that enveloped his illustrious personality. Although his saintly father had married in 1868, his marriage was not blessed with children at first. Rebbetzin Basha Ruchamah Twersky, from the Chernobyl dynasty, was a worthy helpmate, and as her son Rebbe Aharon was later to recall, "Great Jews testified how she attained lofty

Rebbe Aharon of Chernobyl

madreigos in charity, and was an embodiment of *yiras shamayim, tzedakah* and *chessed!*" When Rebbetzin Basha Ruchamah presented her father-in-law with a *kvittel* for children, she exclaimed in distress, "Anyone in the whole world who needs salvation approaches *der shver* and is helped by his prayers — please *daven* for us too!" But Rebbe Yehoshua retorted, "What can I do when your husband seeks the kind of soul that has not been down here on this earth for the last 500 years?"

For the first decade of marriage they lived in her parents' *kehillah*, where Rebbe Yissachar Ber became extremely close to her grandfather, Rebbe Aharon of Chernobyl, while he began to record his personal Torah *chiddushim* in deference to his father's wishes. Before one Yom Tov, his own father asked him to return to Belz with his collection of *chiddushim*, but all of them were stolen en route — to Rebbe Yissachar Ber's immense distress. "My son, don't fret yourself," Rebbe Yehoshua comforted him. "In exchange for your stolen *chiddushim*, Hashem should bless you with a son who will light up the world!" Rebbe Yissachar Ber discovered the missing manuscripts on his return to Chernobyl; apparently a prank had been played on him. Rebbe Yissachar Ber declared he was prepared to be *moichel* and might even forego his precious *kesavim* — but on no account his father's promise.

Reb Ahare'le was born on 17 Teves 1880, twelve years after his parents' wedding. Rebbe Yehoshua was overjoyed at the glad tidings and expressed the wish that his son's firstborn forge another illustrious link in the chassidic dynasty. Ostensibly the young boy was named after his maternal great-grandfather, Rebbe Aharon of Chernobyl, but Rebbe Yissachar Ber revealed eventually, "*Der velt* assumes I called him after the Chernobyler Rebbe, but they're mistaken! He is actually the namesake of the great Reb Aharon of Karlin: Just as the great Reb Aharon accepted upon himself those *tzoros* threatening *Klal Yisrael*, ultimately my son will likewise absorb Jewish suffering!" A portentous prediction that was to prove only too true during the years before, during, and after the World War.[1]

Even as a young child, his purity of soul and purpose were already noticeable. When the prominent Sieniawa (Shiniva) Rebbe visited Belz, Rebbe Yeshie'le proudly led him into his grandson's bedroom. "See him sleeping in his crib?" he whispered. While they stood there a fly buzzed above the toddler's head and the boy pulled his sleeve down before scratching his hair — to avoid touching his head with his bare hands — even while deeply asleep! "Just see that *kedushah*," whispered the visiting Rebbe wonderingly, but Rebbe Yehoshua waved that aside. "And on his holy, *ugehitene* eyes you have nothing to say?" Indeed, his *zeide* would say that the young baby had the face of a *tzaddik* and prophesied, "He is going to become great, and great, and great, until no one will be able to comprehend him!"

His parents were no less admiring. "I don't know how such a great *neshamah* came down for me," admitted Rebbe Yissachar Ber humbly. Sadly, on the Noam Elimelech's *yahrzeit*, 21 Adar 1884, when Reb Ahare'le was only 4 years old, his mother passed away leaving two orphans: Ahare'le and his younger sister Chanah Rachel (who later married the renowned Rebbe and *tzaddik*, Reb Pinchas Twersky of Ostilla). Before her *petirah*, she entrusted the orphans to her mother-in-law while commenting, "The *Borei Olam* alone knows how these two came down to this world!" In later years, Rebbe Aharon would credit his mother for his extraordinary punctiliousness with *netilas yadayim*.

Although he had other grandchildren, the Belzer Rav soon took this young prodigy under his wing for singular guidance, and they naturally grew very close. While sitting on his grandfather's couch during the Pesach Seder, the boy turned to Rebbe Yehoshua at *Shefoch Chamascha* and exclaimed, "Look at that strange Jew who just walked in!" But his grandfather quickly silenced him with a sharp, "You don't

---

1. Surprisingly, despite all he personally underwent before and during the War, Reb Ahare'le would always insist with perfect faith and in all honesty that he had never experienced *tzoros*!

have to reveal everything you see."[2] Before *Mah Nishtanah*, Rebbe Yissachar Ber had made a number of odd changes and irregularities but the young boy accepted everything passively without question until other family members intervened in exasperation. "Can't you see how your father wants you to ask what's going on?" Yet he replied simply, "I have no *kashes* on my father's actions; everything he does must be worthy of study and emulation."

During *Aseres Yemei Teshuvah*, the young Ahare'le was discovered sitting on the steps of the Rebbe's house, sobbing his eyes out. No, nobody had hurt him or pushed him around — "But everybody's crying, something terrible must have happened!" The chassid hastened to reassure him: "There's no cause for you to cry; everybody cries before Yom Kippur over their *aveiros*. But young boys without sin don't have to cry ..." The young boy simply looked up at him in disbelief. "Yet *Zeide's* crying too — and he has no sins either!"

In a revealing episode, when several grandchildren converged in Rebbe Yeshie'le's room with their fathers, he bestowed his rabbinic fur *kolpik* on the young Ahare'le's head. Ahare'le ran excitedly to his father to show off his joyful acquisition. Rebbe Yeshie'le remarked knowingly, "The *kolpik* suits you! Keep it on your head and go with it!" (Earlier, Reb Yeshie'le had placed the *kolpik* upon the older Nachum Aharon — son of Rebbe Leibush of Magrov — but the child had thrown it off and fled the room in panic. The Rebbe of Magrov instantly understood the significance of these actions and was sorely disappointed that his boy had missed a singular opportunity. His brother Rebbe Yissachar Ber left the room rather than intensify his despondency.)

As a tender young child watching his grandfather accept *kvittlech*, he dozed off until Rebbe Yehoshua remarked, "You'll have to stay up many nights listening to people's *tzoros* and sympathizing with their suffering — it's only right you get used to it already now!" Once his grandfather handed him a substantial slice of *sherayim* and his father tried to signal him not to eat it all by himself, but Rebbe Yeshie'le intervened: "What do you want from the child? He already knows how a

---

2. Years later, at his own Seder, Reb Ahare'le once sent one of his grandsons to open the door and subsequently asked the boy whether he had seen Eliyahu HaNavi. When his grandson admitted he had not, the Rebbe admonished him, "When a Jew perfects himself, he can see Eliyahu!"

Jew ought to behave." Indeed, by then the young boy hardly touched his food or slept more than a few hours; all that interested him was a life of spirituality. His father was moved to comment, "His eyes are diamonds, his mouth a pearl, and all his thoughts are bound up 24 hours a day with *Kidshah Berich Hu!*" To bolster his strength, Ahare'le's lunch usually included chicken liver. When a chicken's *kashrus* was called into question after he had already left for *cheder*, Rebbe Yissachar Ber was asked to send an urgent warning to his son who ate only *glatt*. "No need!" replied Rebbe Yeshie'le confidently, waving their fears aside. When the boy returned that evening they discovered the piece of liver still safely packed in his satchel, untouched.

On a visit to Belz, Rebbe Yechezkel Shraga Halberstam (famed Rav of Sieniawa and son of the *Divrei Chaim*, whose son was a son-in-law of Rebbe Yeshie'le) noted the young Ahare'le's relentless spiritual ascent and remarked in wonder, "It seems that the *yetzer hara* has forgotten this 12-year-old child completely!" Likewise, his uncle Rebbe Yechezkel Shraga of Cieszanow noticed that when Rebbe Yissachar Ber rebuked each of his children individually, he appeared to ignore his oldest son completely. "He's totally devoid of sin," explained Rebbe Yissachar Ber, "and doesn't require *mussar!*"

Although the young boy regularly deprived himself of all superfluous comfort, he delighted in attending to the needs of others; he eagerly served visitors to his father's house and their satisfaction was his greatest reward. Usually his conversations were limited and his words carefully chosen, but not when assisting another individual. Typically scrupulous was his reply to a passerby's request for the time: "Twelve-and-a-half minutes past 2 ..." And when chassidim jested, "Are you trying to show how well you can tell the time?" he immediately explained, "*Chessed* performed for a fellow Jew must be carried out thoroughly."

Because of his unremitting spartan lifestyle, he was the despair of the personal *shammas* appointed to safeguard his health and well-being. He took absolutely no interest in food, never complaining at whatever was set before him, and always eating sparingly — if at all. But one early morning on returning from immersion in the *mikveh*, he asked the *shammas* to prepare a cup of coffee and some tasty slices of *lekach* cake, adding for good measure, "Make sure it's excellent coffee and piping hot!" Eagerly, the *shammas* hastened to do his bidding, vainly hoping this marked a radical change in behavior. When he returned, flourishing the tray overflowing with tempting food and drink, the saintly boy asked him to quickly deliver the tray to an impoverished local tailor!

When the piqued *shammas* hesitated, he urged him to hurry, "while the coffee was still good and hot!" The tailor was no less astonished than the *shammas* — what connection did he have with the Rav's son? However, he eagerly devoured the food, for it had been years since he could afford coffee or such a spread of cake and delicacies. Suddenly he let out a whoop of realization. "I remember now! A half-hour ago I was relaxing at the *mikveh* changing room just as the Rav's son was passing through, and I happened to remark, 'After this hot *mikveh*, how pleasant it would be to have some cake and good hot coffee — *mamesh* a *mechayeh nefesh!*' A typical comment of us simple people, I never imagined he'd hear me, never mind take me seriously." Obviously Reb Ahare'le had surpassed himself hoping to perform a kindness and "revive" a fellow Jew he hardly knew.

Later, he once quoted his father as saying that one may take pride in a good character trait where it is a natural instinct inherent to one's innate make-up, since one cannot grow haughty over *middos* not acquired by effort. "For instance, I was born with the *middah* of *rachmanus*," he added. "When I see a Jew eating, that sight gives me *a shtik gezunt!*" This from a man who personally ate and slept the barest minimum.

His saintliness cloaked his scholarship, for his prowess in Torah was likewise extraordinary. Only those closest to him were aware of his deep and wide knowledge of *gemara, midrash, poskim, rishonim,* and *acharonim.* All hours of his day were spent entirely engrossed in learning; he was oblivious to the tumult around him. His father encouraged him in this as Rebbe Ahare'le recalled over a half century later: "As a child I once arrived 5 minutes early for Minchah and stood at the *sefarim shrank* idly watching the busy Belz *beis hamedrash* until my holy father came in and remarked, 'Don't you know that one can also become a *masmid* from 5 minutes?' "[3]

---

3. Many years later in Tel Aviv, during critical eye tests by an optician, Mr. Elkana Seidner, the Belzer Rav was asked to concentrate his failing vision at the sky and follow a bird's flight. He revealed, "What can I do? In my whole life, I've never looked up or watched a bird fly! Even as a child I didn't because I never had the time! I always had so much to learn; when I finished my quota I felt obligated to review and review again. I never had time to gaze at the Heavens!"

When Reb Ahare'le reached the age of 12, Rebbe Yehoshua suggested he develop original *chiddushim* in the Galician style of *pilpul* challenging the *Ketzos HaChoshen*.[4] Accordingly, he recorded numerous wide-ranging and profound *chiddushim* on the margin of his private copy. Such was his innate modesty and reticence that he prefaced them with the words, "On the instructions of my grandfather ... ," and even his closest confidants were denied sight of Reb Ahare'le's *Ketzos*. Only during the annual pre-Pesach book cleaning could they catch a glimpse at his *Toros*, which then rapidly spread by word of mouth or clandestine copies throughout the local network of Talmudic scholars.[5] His *melamed* was likewise impressed and encouraged him to develop this talent by expounding his *chiddushim* openly. However, when word reached the Rebbe how the boy was already lecturing in public while his tutor freely admitted he had nothing more to teach him, Rebbe Yehoshua advised his grandson to stop. Immediately, Reb Ahare'le ceased publicizing his Torah knowledge — just as he painstakingly concealed all his accomplishments — throughout his lifetime!

At his bar mitzvah, on Tuesday, 17 Teves 1893, he added his personal postscript at the end of the customary *derashah*. Basing himself on the words of *Shir HaMaalos*, he described how a father "walks along weeping as he carries the burden" of his son's sins when he is still a juvenile. But when he reaches the age of 13 (*yavo* is the numerical equivalent of 13), the father "rejoices" at his release from responsibility since his son now "bears his own bundle" of sins. When Rebbe Yehoshua heard this *vort* he removed his festive *shtreimel* from over his eyes and leaned forward to stare at his young grandson with evident wonder and admiration.

Throughout his early years, the boy was often to be found in the room of Rebbe Yehoshua, who nurtured him for his role as a Torah leader. Sadly, the close relationship between grandfather and grandson lasted only just over another year. When Rebbe Yeshie'le succumbed to illness and surgery on 23 Shevat 1894, the young

---

4. Apparently, this had mystical overtones: As a descendant of the *Oheiv Yisrael*, Rebbe of Apta (Opatow), he had to redress insulting behavior perpetuated against his ancestor in Stryj, community of the *Ketzos*.

5 .The renowned Trzebinia (Tchebiner) Rav, R' Dov Berish Wiedenfeld, initially a leading chassid of Rebbe Yissachar Ber, still recalled several examples over fifty years later.

A letter from the Trzebinia Rav in support of the yeshivah of Belz teenager who had been orphaned from his mother at 4 felt as if he had become a *yasom* all over again. Rebbe Yehoshua had accurately predicted on his sickbed, "Two will miss me the most: my little daughter — and my grandson!"

Yet Reb Ahare'le's relentless climb to spiritual perfection continued unabated. Any commendable custom or stringency mentioned in *mussar sefarim* or adopted by earlier luminaries was eagerly embraced by the "Rav's son." Yet every adopted *chumrah* had to have a halachic basis, as he once declared, *"Baruch Hashem ich bin nisht kein frummer; az men vet lernen vet men zehn az alles shteht* — Thank G-d I'm not sanctimonious, but if one studies hard enough they will see that everything is soundly based!" Although his father's tradition — as indeed the practice of Belz — was to utilize food and drink for *avodas Hashem,* he extended his abstinence from food or sleep. He ate sparingly and infrequently, while he slept no more than three hours in every 24-hour period, so disparaging slumber to his contemporaries that they all felt it a disgrace to sleep! (One *shammas,* R' Shloma Kahane, later recalled how during the three weeks that he attended to his needs, the young Reb Ahare'le was careful never to have more than one hour of unbroken sleep. For decades he never used a proper bed and during Elul he would instruct his *shammas* to wake him up every 18 minutes!) Concerned for his physical welfare, relatives persuaded Rebbe Yissachar Ber to reprimand his son for espousing an ascetic lifestyle inimical to the Belz heritage.

"From where did you choose this new course of behavior?" he asked sharply. Although Reb Ahare'le's respect for his father was boundless, he staunchly replied, *"Der heiliger Zeide* taught me that when a man chooses a new path in *avodas Hashem,* he need not change his mind even when hearing to the contrary from real *malachim!"* Rebbe Yissachar Ber accepted this rebuttal and never reproached him again; rather he was upset at the relatives for their interference. He openly described his eldest son as *"a Himmel-mentsh"* and once remarked, "I envy those who will merit to be with him under one roof!" (The Trzebinia Rav once recalled noticing how Rebbe Yissachar Ber secretly wanted to show respect when Reb Ahare'le entered his room: He pretended to drop a piece of paper so that he could stand up to retrieve it!)

Rav Shmuel of Sokal,
the father in-law of Rebbe Ahare'le

Yet Rebbe Aharon's humility was breathtaking; he would regularly berate himself with, "What will be my *sof*; what's the *tachlis*?" or "The clock races onward and I have accomplished nothing with my life ..." This, despite a constant immersion in *avodas Hashem* coupled with utter indifference to mundane distractions! From his teens, he would not begin Shacharis before reviewing several *masechtos* by heart, and when his *shammas* once informed him that there remained 14 minutes till the time for prayers, he replied, "In that period one could review a whole *masechta*!" *Hasmadah* in learning was to become one of his constant themes in his annual pre-*Kol Nidrei* sermons, reiterating in the name of his father that this achieved a greater *kapparah* than the scapegoat in the Temple service.

Although Rebbe Yissachar Ber once spoke of his son's looks as reminding him of Rebbe Yaakov Yitzchak Horowitz, the renowned Chozeh of Lublin, he more usually described Reb Ahare'le's features — "besides one wart" — as being identical to his maternal great-grandfather, Rebbe Aharon of Chernobyl.[6]

When he came of age, his marriage was arranged with his cousin, Rebbetzin Malkah, a daughter of Rav Shmuel — elder brother of Rebbe Yissachar Ber and Rabbi of nearby Sokal. The wedding that took place in Sokal two years later was graced by many leading rabbanim and luminaries — not only because of his father's prestige but also out of admiration and wonder at the young bridegroom whose fame extended throughout Galicia and Poland. On the day before the local *poritz* paid his customary courtesy visit to convey his personal

---

6. Indeed, when the Belzer Rav later visited Vienna for medical treatment, Rebbe Yisrael Friedman of Chortkow advised his sons, "If you want to see how our grandfather, Rebbe Aharon of Chernobyl, looked — go and observe the Belzer Rebbe."

An invitation letter to the wedding of Rebbe Ahare'le

congratulations, Rebbe Yissachar Ber instructed his *chassan*, "I'm sure you'll want to stare at the ground as usual because his wife will probably accompany him. Well, there's no need. The Torah tells us not to be led astray by our hearts and eyes — what the heart disallows, the eyes won't see." Nonetheless Reb Aharon stared fixedly earthward in the *poritz's* presence, even shading his eyes with his hands.

Rebbetzin Malkah was a worthy helpmate, forsaking every luxury or creature comfort to ensure that her husband continued his upward ascent to ever greater spiritual heights. Her warmhearted generosity toward the destitute and downcast was legendary — a trail of poor women led to her door, to be greeted with a warm welcome, abundant food, and a listening ear; she affected no airs and graces, simply treating and talking to these unfortunate ladies as if they were her equal.

Following their marriage, Reb Ahare'le was maintained at his father-in-law's household for several years, as was customary. Yet he continued his strict regime of seclusion, deprivation, and asceticism until he became seriously weakened. His doctors advised

Rav Munish Babad

a complete change of locale for a time at a spa. Accordingly, he traveled to the health resort of Kreniec to recuperate, but even there he ate very little, returning almost all the food untouched. After their marriage they had several children who died within hours of birth, although they appeared perfectly healthy and of full weight. Distraught, the Rebbetzin exhorted Rebbe Yissachar Ber, "Thousands come to you for *berachos* and are helped by your *tefillos* — and *davka* your own son you can't help?" The Rebbe replied gravely, "What can I do if he tries to bring down such lofty and holy souls that cannot abide this world?" Those children that did survive were sickly — two daughters were both hearing- and speech-impaired and the others were weak and ailing, but Reb Ahare'le accepted the Heavenly decree lovingly and without complaint.

Eventually, he returned to the family fold in Belz where he grew further in Torah and piety under his father's close tutelage. Even while quoting a well-known *Rashi*, Rebbe Aharon would say, "My father said that *Rashi* says ..." and at the *tisch* he would sit opposite his father, absorbing every word or gesture. Since he could repeat his father's discourses verbatim — these were transcribed in his rooms where he would correct or add to them — he was the final arbiter whenever the leading *yoshvim* harbored doubts as to exactly what was said or meant.

This rapt attention was not limited to the *tisch*. Rav Munish Babad, Rabbi of Tarnopol, once noticed him modestly standing at the back, listening earnestly and fearfully to a discussion taking place in his father's rooms. Yet, judging by the laughter of all the other chassidim present, Rebbe Yissachar Ber's conversation appeared entirely lighthearted. Since Rav Munish was embarking on an important series of meetings in Warsaw and had been instructed by the Rebbe to discuss them with Reb Ahare'le before leaving Belz, he approached him there and then. But Rebbe Aharon took him by the hand and silently led him outside. "Tarnopoler Rav!" he exclaimed. "My father is currently talking of subjects situated *b'rumo shel olam*! How can one forego hearing such holy speech?" And without another word he returned to his father's rooms — obviously discerning far more than most.[7]

His father remained his guiding light and Reb Ahare'le once remarked, "Should all the kings of east and west try to change my ways I wouldn't modify anything learnt from my father — and I wouldn't change anything from my grandfather even when commanded by angels and *Seraphim*!" Rebbe Yissachar Ber once advised him to rest during the day for health reasons, so Rebbe Aharon would retire to bed (still dressed in his *kolpik*!) for a few minutes to be *"mekayem kibbud av"* — each day for the rest of his life! After his parents' passing, Rebbe Aharon would briskly dismiss any comparison with his father; *"Der heilige Tahte is gevehn a Malach!"* The regard was mutual. Rebbe Yissachar Ber respected his eldest son enormously and arranged for attendants to ensure that he ate and slept enough to at least keep body and soul together. Occasionally he would declare that "a Jew like Reb Ahare'le had already lived in this world — the Kozhnitzer Maggid! So frail he had to be helped in and out of bed, yet when it came to *avodas Hashem*, he became energized like a lion."

Because of his chronic sleep deprivation, Reb Aharon could only walk slowly and found it difficult to stand. Although his daily meal consisted of a slice of cake dunked in a cup of milk after midday, he was simply unable to eat any more. But when it came to Shabbos he appeared a different man: taller, stouter, robust, walking easily and forcing himself to eat from all the Shabbos food with obvious relish and encouraging others to do likewise. Instead of shielding his eyes and directing them earthward as usual, he

---

7. Rav Dovid Menachem Munish Babad was eventually to remark, "In my lifetime, I've traveled to three Belzer Rebbes, yet whenever I enter Rebbe Aharon's presence, I feel exactly like I first did at his grandfather's! In fact you can openly and tangibly sense Rebbe Aharon's holiness far more than you could with his father or grandfather! He's unique in his *kedushah* and *taharah*!"

would now gaze around the Shabbos delicacies with joy and satisfaction. In contrast to his weakened constitution, his stamina in *avodas hakodesh* was phenomenal.[8]

In his modesty, Reb Ahare'le before he became Rebbe would *daven* at the entrance rather than disturb a large congregation or cause them to stand up for him. Despite his seclusion and preoccupation with Torah study, his fame spread and many visitors tried to get closer to him, but he only discussed his views on spiritual matters with the leading *yoshvim*. According to his young *shammas*, R' Yisrael Dovid, one could tell who was about to enter Reb Aharon's room by his behavior: If he suddenly closed his eyes it meant he sensed a female petitioner was waiting outside. His *shemiras einayim* was already legendary and he would customarily walk in the street with head bowed and eyes closed while led by a loyal *shammas*.

His saintliness was matched by his erudition. While learning with a *nigun* his face would light up and he appeared revitalized, much as he did during *tefillah*. For a short period he studied *Yoreh Deah* together with Rav Yisrael Raver (of Rawa-Ruska) who rose from the ranks of *yoshvim* to become a leading *dayan* in Galicia. However, when Reb Ahare'le began learning at speed — a practice he henceforth maintained throughout his life — Rav Yisrael could no longer keep up with him although *Yoreh Deah* was Rav Yisrael's speciality and he had every *Pri Megadim* at his fingertips. Later, during the First World War exile in Racsfehert, Reb Aharon learned *Yoreh Deah* with R' Isumer Domb from Lubitch-Lubaczow — a top *yosheiv* with exemplary *middos*. Although a renowned *talmid chacham* deemed worthy to be a Rebbe in his own right, he too was unable to keep up with Rebbe Ahare'le's relentless pace. (Eventually he returned to a tiny apartment in Krakow where he became a respected Rosh Yeshivah; in the ghetto he was to play a significant role in the Rebbe's rescue.) Rebbe Yissachar Ber once asked all his sons and sons-in-law to explain a difficult *Tosafos* in *Pesachim* commenting on the complex *sugya* of Rav Chanina S'gan HaKohanim

---

8. Even in old age, visitors who spent a Shabbos with him were shattered by the late nights or little respite and needed a week to recover, but he carried on his demanding schedule regardless. On arrival in Eretz Yisrael he instructed his *shammasim* to prepare the traditional Belzer Shabbos and Yom Tov delicacies, even teaching them the recipes where necessary, though — as he often declared — he had never set foot inside a kitchen.

(dealing with the esoteric subject of ritual impurity). Reb Ahare'le returned after a short interval with a solution to which his father exclaimed in wonder, "So quickly!"

Eventually Rebbe Yissachar Ber graded all their replies: "This answer shows sharpness; this explanation reveals a wide-ranging knowledge...," but when he came to his eldest son he merely commented "... Who can possibly compare to someone who learns *Torah lishmah* undistracted by petty personal motives? It has a *geshmak* of its own."

Later, Reb Aharon attended a meeting of leading rabbanim, together with the renowned Galician luminary Rav Meir Arik, at which an intense Torah discussion took place. As though he could not follow and had nothing to add, Reb Ahare'le sat silently while they painstakingly constructed a dazzling intellectual thesis, but when taking his leave privately from Rav Meir Arik, Rabbi of Tarnow, Reb Ahare'le let slip one small comment that brought their whole scholarly edifice crashing down. Rav Meir exclaimed, "How could you have just sat there without saying a word?" Rav Meir returned to the meeting to inform them of the devastating critique while remarking, "Only the son of Rebbe Yissachar Ber can sit back with no concern for his own *kavod*; someone with such self-control and reserve surely learns *Torah lishmah*!"

Rebbe Aharon's eldest son, the saintly Reb Moshe'le, once revealed, "Before my father performs any mitzvah — whether Biblical or *mi'd'Rabbanan* — he mentally reviews in his mind all halachic opinions from the earliest *rishonim* to the latest *acharonim* and endeavors to fulfill them all! It is this mental strain that lies at the root of his frailty, not his asceticism!"

During the First World War, when Rebbe Yissachar Ber temporarily settled in Racsfehert (Ujfeherto in Hungary, north of Debrecen) with his extended family, Reb Ahare'le was arrested upon crossing the Hungarian border and was beaten by the police. Although his weakened and emaciated body was covered with welts and bruises, he did not complain, merely retreating to a quiet prison corner to spend his days in Torah and prayer. At his eventual release, his father referred to the episode while reciting Torah during the *tisch* "... Was it just a coincidence that he — alone from the whole family — was maltreated?

Rebbe Ahare'le as a young man

Thrown into prison and thrashed with birch? I called him with the name of the great Rav Aharon of Karlin — a sublime soul that descended to this world to bear *Klal Yisrael's* suffering and lighten their lives. My son too, Reb Aharon, has been designated by *Hashem Yisbarach* to lovingly accept *yissurim* on behalf of *Klal Yisrael."*

Reb Aharon once asked Racsfehert's town Rav, Rav Shaul Rosenberg, whether he had to fast when his *tefillin* straps twisted and revealed the unpainted side. The *p'sak* was fairly unique: "Strictly speaking, one only has to fast if they twisted during *Krias Shema* — yet the son of the Belzer Rav should really adopt extra stringencies. But with your regular abstinence a fast will have little effect so I suggest you instead eat double what you're accustomed to as an affliction!"

According to Reb Aharon's *shammas* in Munkacs (Mukacevo, where the Belz entourage took refuge from Nissan 1919 to Adar 1922), he would take up to two hours to return to his lodgings after his father's *tisch*! To avoid crowds, he routinely detoured down quiet alleyways or hastily slipped into nearby back streets whenever he saw families congregated at front doors. Throughout these digressions he would be totally engrossed in heavenly thoughts — never even noticing when his slip-on shoes fell off! For a time, his lodgings were adjacent to his father's and since Rebbe Yissachar Ber usually began his Shabbos meal after his sons had completed theirs, he often stood by his window to watch Rebbe Ahare'le reciting *Kiddush*. Once a chassid even caught him secretly listening to his son's *Kiddush* — and shaking! (At the end of his life, when Rebbe Yissachar Ber grew too frail to recite *Kiddush* aloud, he advised his rebbetzin to hear Rebbe Aharon instead — adding: "Indeed, I too ought to listen to his *Kiddush*!")

Traditionally, ever since the Sar Shalom, the Belzer dynasty had held the twin positions of town Rav and chassidic Rebbe. But by the time the

A family of Belzer chassidim in Munkacs

war damage was repaired and the Belzer entourage finally returned home from Holeszyce before Purim 1924, Rebbe Yissachar Ber was already 70 and delegated the duties of local Rav to Rebbe Ahare'le. Characteristically, though he was now forced to display some of his scholarship, Reb Aharon still sought to conceal the breadth of his knowledge. Where he could avoid an in-depth Torah discussion, he would often content himself with listening to the *dayanim's* views and analysis in total silence, rapidly scanning through halachic volumes and responsa before issuing a terse ruling. Occasionally, however, he did reveal some of his genius.

The two colleagues, Rav Dovid Menachem Munish Babad of Tarnopol and Rav Avraham Yaakov Horowitz of Prubynznia, were once aligned against each other on behalf of a complicated lawsuit involving substantial amounts of money. When Rebbe Ahare'le was chosen as their final arbiter, he agreed to rule only if both these leading rabbanim set down their arguments in writing. Rav Babad wrote a lengthy sixteen-page responsa, painstakingly divided into sections and clauses. When this was handed to Rebbe Ahare'le, he skimmed through it so fleetingly that Rav Babad assumed he was merely counting the pages before studying it in depth — until

Rebbe Ahare'le in middle age

Reb Aharon looked up and remonstrated, "Tarnopoler Rav, with the greatest respect! There are contradictions between several of the sections ...," and proceeded to lucidly explain his objections. No mean scholar himself, Rav Babad was so astounded at Rebbe Aharon's rapid insight coupled with deep comprehension that he frequently recounted this episode.

In the last decade of his life, Rebbe Yissachar Ber also sought to involve Reb Ahare'le in public affairs. Rebbes, rabbanim, and communal activists were dispatched to confer with "the Rav's son," and though he did not hesitate to voice his opinion on even the most crucial decisions, he always modestly prefaced his views with *"B'gezeras Kibbud Av ..."*! Likewise, petitioners were occasionally sent to consult with him about their business and private affairs. Such was his boundless love for a fellow Jew that he interrupted his diligence in Torah and *avodas Hashem* to solve someone else's problems, displaying uncanny insight despite his almost total removal from worldly matters. Yet when his father repeatedly pressed him to take a more active role he adamantly refused with customary humility to accept *kvittlech* or affect the mannerisms of a chassidic leader. He simply saw himself as personally unsuitable to lead a mass movement of chassidim with their everyday problems; nor was he capable of filling his father's position since his sole interest was Torah study — nothing else. Reb Aharon was the obvious choice to everyone but himself!

Nonetheless, when the travails of war, old age, and ill health claimed Rebbe Yissachar Ber on 22 Marcheshvan 1927, Rebbe Aharon, 47 years old at the time, reluctantly accepted the mantle of leadership. His succession was announced during the large *levayah* held after Shabbos at which mourners wished the late Rebbe, "Mazel Tov"! (Although supported by the *gabbaim*, Reb Aharon Yehoshua Landau and Reb Mendele Landman, Rebbe Ahare'le stumbled and fainted at the funeral and had to be revived; by contrast he was the only one not to display emotion at the actual *petirah* on Friday night: amid the cries of the rebbetzin and the daughters, he calmly interjected, "Today is Shabbos, it is forbidden to cry" — before *davening* Maariv and conducting the Shabbos meal as usual.)

The first three *kvittels* were received from Ropshitzer descendants — in keeping with Belz tradition. Then, a venerable Rav, Reb Yissachar Dov of Bisk, who had previously petitioned the Sar Shalom (at least seventy-two years earlier!), Rebbe Yeshie'le, and had presented an inaugural *kvittel* to Rebbe Yissachar Ber, now again showed his allegiance to Belz by presenting the inaugural *kvittel* to Rebbe Aharon. Thus continued the reign of the noble House of Belz without pause or hesitation.

CHAPTER 3

HIS EARLY YEARS

RELUCTANTLY ACCEPTING THE YOKE OF CHASSIDIC leadership at the age of 47, Rebbe Aharon was to guide his flock for the next thirty years through the most calamitous era Belz had ever encountered. The 23rd of Cheshvan 5687 was less than ten years after the close of the First World War — and thirteen years before the outbreak of the Second World War. The economic slump that overshadowed the 1930's world-wide hit Eastern Galicia and Ukraine particularly hard — an area popularly described by the rest of Poland as the "estates of the *Melech Evyon*" due to its rampant poverty. Following the defeat of the Austrian-Hungarian Empire, Galicia was once again under Polish administration and the Jewish plight was exacerbated by the newly independent Poland implementing a nationalistic and viciously anti-Semitic program — replete with officially inspired boycotts, workers' and shoppers' strikes, confiscations, discrimina-tory regulations, and restrictive practices — to exclude "non-Polish" shopkeepers and businessmen from the national economy. Coming so soon after the Russian army had laid the area waste and the German army had looted factory machinery and merchandise, the

Polish government's xenophobic measures effectively bankrupted many Jews' small businesses and shops — especially after the Poles succeeded in establishing an alternative manufacturing and distribution network — and laid the groundwork for physical persecution in the Nazi paradigm.

On regaining its independence in 1919 after 130 years of partition, Poland had solemnly promised the Allied Powers to guarantee the civil and political equality of its minorities, to grant them the prerogative to establish their own educational, religious, charitable, and social institutions, and to safeguard their citizens' rights. Never were these promises fully honored, and by the mid-30's they were revoked and reversed. Recurring pogroms plagued independent Poland (often perpetuated by *"Hallerchiks"* — demobilized Polish-Ukranian soldiers under the Austrian-Polish General Haller); Jews were abused and beaten on trains and buses; vocational schools and universities restricted Jewish applications; the increasingly fascist government circumscribed *shechitah* — and almost banned it altogether — while legislating a torrent of anti-Jewish decrees. The three and a third million Polish Jews, a tenth of the overall population and a sizeable cultural and economic factor, were everywhere met with jealousy and downright hostility. Despite having been a welcome Jewish haven for over a thousand years, anti-Semitism struck deep roots in Poland — even before the Nazi invasion — and found a particularly fertile soil in Ukraine, where the mainstay of Belz Chassidus resided. Chassidim abroad fared little better, since Jew-baiting flourished around the world and religious Jews were an obvious and visible target. One of their few comforts remained a loving and compassionate Rebbe.

In the new Belzer Rav they could sense a deep love for every Jewish soul and saw how — despite personal disinterest in physical comfort and concerns — he was supremely solicitous for the personal welfare of his chassidim, scrutinizing their *kvittlech*[1] and praying for their salvation and success. Once a name was submitted for attention he could recollect the connection for decades afterwards, and

---

1. In his latter years he would have them read to him, since in a *kvittel* "*zeht men der gantse mensch* — I can see the entire person," and he did not want to observe anyone's shortcomings!

Rebbe Ahare'le with his gabbai,
Reb Aharon Yehoshua Landau

he proffered practical advice to his many supplicants despite his personal aloofness from worldly affairs. He had not deliberately set out to deprive himself of food or sleep; they simply did not interest him. Personal pain and illness he likewise bore with fortitude. Yet when it came to others, he was greatly concerned about any discomfort, infirmity, or the slightest lack of sustenance or rest. His concern for every Jew, coupled with an amazing ability to see the best — and only the best — in both the religious and non-religious, was legendary.

One revealing episode in particular exemplified his attitude to fellow human beings: Late one afternoon there were screams on the streets of Belz — apparently an unidentified small Jewish boy had tumbled into a well. When the tumult reached his house, Reb Ahare'le groaned loudly. "*Oy*! Perhaps it is my son who has fallen in?" Seconds later he burst out, "Woe is to me! What did I say? Why did I groan? Is not every soul — whether my child or otherwise — a creation of *HaKadosh Baruch Hu*?" Immediately he launched into an intense *teshuvah* and for the next half-hour he wandered about his room berating himself bitterly, "Woe is to me for my remark!" Someone who witnessed this remarkable scene commented later, "*Halevai* we should conduct as earnest a repentance on *Kol Nidrei* night as the Belzer Rav did for a momentary aberration in putting his own family before others!"

Rebbe Aharon also began a strange activity — consulting with doctors! Every few days he would summon a doctor but would not submit to a physical examination; instead he would describe his aches and pains verbally for the doctor to prescribe some medicine. Usually these medicines were left in his cupboard, never to be taken; sometimes he would not even bother to buy them from the pharmacy. Yet a few days later he would repeat the process with another doctor or specialist! Those closest to him were extremely puzzled at this strange behavior until they noticed that the Rebbe was careful to bless each doctor before leaving that *der Eibeshter* should send a *refuah sheleimah* to all of their patients. Only then did they realize how their Rebbe's sole concern lay with the welfare of the sick and ailing. Later his miraculous powers to effect cures when top specialists had already despaired was to become legendary.

Such was the adulation and undying respect for their saintly leader that the chassidim unquestioningly accepted obvious inconvenience and modifications to the regular schedule. The regular passing of day or night hardly seemed to matter any more. *Tefillos* were mostly completed when daylight was almost over; the *tisch* conducted in the early hours of the morning; and sleep or food counted for little. For despite his new role, Rebbe Ahare'le maintained his spartan, ascetic lifestyle, developing the ability to remain heavenly and reclusive while simultaneously being intimately involved with crowds of adherents, both the elite and the common folk. His days were still totally engaged in nonstop learning and prayer. Only the hours after nightfall were now devoted to the needs of his flock who queued all night long for a private word with the Rebbe. This entailed radical changes to the traditional timetable in Belz: Henceforth it would function beyond the constraints of either time or nature — as did the Rebbe himself.

At first, he tried to limit the queues to five petitioners a night; not from lack of interest but rather from his overwhelming concern and empathy — "I simply can't take these *tzoros* of *Klal Yisrael!*" — since he felt each person's problem as deeply as if it were his own, literally. Hours after chassidim had left him, their loads lightened and their spirits revived by blessings and encouragement, the Rebbe would still be sitting, staring sadly at the mound of *kvittlech* with his heart torn asunder by the depth of other people's burden. Yet he soon gave way to pressure and allowed in a growing flood of supplicants, although he sometimes complained, "Their problems they spread out before me but they forget to tell me when they have gained relief!"

When accepting *kvittlech* he remained mindful of his followers' financial burden — to a greater degree than they personally recognized. On one of his annual trips to Marienbad he detoured via Humene where he stayed over *Shabbos Pinchas*. Thousands turned up for Shabbos but when they took their leave, the Rebbe refused to accept them individually; instead they had to deposit their *kvittlech* in a large sack! Naturally, his chassidim were extremely upset and sent a delegation of three elderly disciples to remonstrate — until the Rebbe explained. "When the fundraiser Reb Yeshiye Rawer (R' Yehoshua Pach of Rawa-Ruska) returned from Hungary, he reported that the poverty-stricken chassidim were bitter at being unable to afford the journey to Belz. So I came this way — nine extra hours rail journey which critically weakened me — for your sakes, just to be with you. And I thought to myself: individual *kvittlech* would be too expensive for you, paying the *gabbaim* plus a *pidyon*; better to put them all together in a sack and I'll read them separately at home!"

Officially the position of "Belzer Rav" included being Rabbi of the local township, as all preceding members of the dynasty had been, but Rebbe Ahare'le insisted he simply could not spare due time or attention to rule on *shailos;* instead two *dayanim* were appointed to deal with daily queries and only consulted him on difficult and complicated questions of halachah.[2]

From the first, the Rebbe trod his own individual path. When he began leading the prayers during his year of mourning for his father, chassidim were surprised by how substantially his *nusach* differed from the late Rebbe Yissachar Ber. Sensing their disappointment, he eventually explained a little of his motives to Rebbe Yissachar Ber's widow: "What do they want? That I should *daven* exactly like *der heilige Tahte*? Then they will hardly feel they've lost anything!" Likewise his behavior in composing the inscription on his father's *matzeivah* may superficially have appeared disrespectful but was en-

---

2. Interestingly, at the *petirah* of Rebbe Yissachar Ber, his rebbetzin had pressed for splitting these traditionally linked positions: Reb Ahare'le as Rebbe and one of her offspring as Rav. But both the chassidim and the *kehillah* rejected her radical proposal.

tirely based on devout dedication to his father's memory — "For *der heilige Zeide's* headstone my father didn't inscribe the words *'yachid bedoro'* since he said there remained another person who served Hashem with equal perception. So I followed my father's example and didn't write *'yachid bedoro'* on his *matzeivah* either, although I know that in his case, he was truly unique!"

In the early months of his ascendancy, Rebbe Ahare'le locked himself up in his room and refused all the trappings of leadership, until prominent chassidim threatened to break his door down! During the first Shavuos, Rebbe Feivush Rubin of Jabrow was in a nearby room and overheard the Rebbe's preparations for Shacharis: after lengthy contemplation Rebbe Aharon removed his folded *tallis* from his shoulder while quietly asserting to himself, *"Nu memeile,* they flocked to my father and grandfather because they were truly angels — but why are they coming to me?" After musing on this for several long minutes, he added, "But since *baruch Hashem* I never made any efforts to cause them to come here, *Hashem Yisbarach* must have sent them all — the *Eibeshter* should also help them!"

The trend whereby throngs of young adherents of rival chassidic dynasties in Galicia and Hungary switched their allegiances to Belz accelerated under Rebbe Ahare'le. Thousands of chassidim bursting with enthusiasm made the three-hour rail journey from Lemberg (seasonally subsidized by the government) and many budding young recruits joined its ranks as Belz's influence continued to grow apace under the Rebbe's guidance: "A Belzer chassid must be a shining example of how chassidim ought to behave — in every action, behavior, and even thought! Physical needs like eating, drinking and other necessary requirements should be sanctified." The uncompromising stance of Belz had considerable impact in Galicia when its chassidim entered all spheres of communal life and were unafraid of strife. The assimilationists, nationalists, modernists, socialists, Yiddishists, and Zionists all faced a formidable enemy in Belz, and the old-time communal leaders from the ranks of the wealthy landowners and industrialists had to trim their sails in the turbulent decades following World War I. Belz further strengthened its hand when the *Machzikei Hadas* organization, first established by Rebbe Yeshie'le in 1879, was revitalized under Rebbe Aharon.

Hardly had the year of mourning for his father been completed when a series of meetings were held across Galicia — both east and west — to unite religious Jewry in the newly galvanized organization. The first preliminary conclave was arranged in Tarnow on Monday, 11 Kislev (December 5, 1927), where they decided to set up a committee to represent rabbanim of Western Galicia and agreed to their participation in a central meeting in Lemberg. A second meeting ten days later in the Galician capital, Krakow, agreed on an agenda for the central meeting, amendments to the proposed communal constitution, committee rules, and electing committee officials. The Central Meeting itself was preceded by a rousing declaration signed by leading rabbanim: Rav Dovid Menachem Munish Babad (of Tarnopol and the Rebbe's right-hand man), Rav Dovid Halevi Horowitz (of Stanislawow), Rav Yosef Nechemiah Kornitzer (of Krakow), and Rav Avraham Menachem Mendel Steinberg (of Brody) signed in addition to tens of Galician Rebbes and Rabbis.

> To the great Rabbanim, Geonim and Tzaddikim, Rebbes, Leaders of Israel, Respectable Householders, Those who fear Hashem, and Chareidim everywhere.
>
> In the Name of Hashem and in the name of all the great rabbanim and tzaddikim we approach our colleagues, alerting them that the time has come to awaken from slumber and join together in common defense and protect the walls around the Holy Torah that are sadly breached so often for our great sins! Anyone who holds Hashem's Torah dear weeps in private at the depressed state of Judaism and lack of due reverence to the Torah; its statutes and warnings are publicly desecrated chas veshalom with no one standing guard or holding the breach. How long shall we stand with our arms folded, watching the lost flocks straying into foreign vineyards while the vineyard of Hashem is abandoned to trespass? Are we not afraid that an account for these lost sheep will eventually be demanded?
>
> Therefore we have agreed to summon an assembly, gather all shepherds in charge of the holy flocks, rabbanim and teachers, tzaddikim and Rebbes, precious religious householders, this coming Tuesday Parashas Vayigash 5688 in Lvov, to take counsel how to strengthen the flame of Torah and repair the damage. There we will also weigh up the proposed innovations in our communal constitution which

— in the eyes of most religious communities — may be dangerous: threatening destruction of communities and the Torah's foundations chas veshalom. We trust in Hashem that if we act as one, with one heart and mind, and frame a suitable reply to the honorable government, she will favor our request and repeal those troublesome rules or change them for the better.

Thus we strongly implore every Rav in each town and their respectable baale battim, yereim and chareidim who seek the best for their community in the light of the Torah to attend this meeting from the outset and take part in its sessions. May Hashem Yisbarach in His great mercy take pity upon us and illuminate our way to find the wisest direction to observe its statutes and commandments in every particular with love and fear and truth without any obstacles. And He should oversee our efforts for the best result.

On Tuesday, 3 Teves (December 27, 1927), the central meeting duly opened in Lemberg and made an unforgettable impression. Some 300 leading rabbanim attended, as well as the Rebbes of Bobov, Boyan, and Atunia among others. Rebbe Aharon was welcomed with great respect by government representatives and was followed everywhere by crowds numbered in the tens of thousands! They had set themselves a six-point agenda strengthening religion and faith: Shabbos observance, family purity, and kashrus; improving Rabbinical stature; communal affairs; and establishing groups for religious education. Rav Kornitzer was chosen as chairman and was joined on the presidium by the Rabbis of Tarnopol, Prubynznia and Dembrowa, and R' Dovid Schreiber from Drohovitch (mostly Belz devotees). Rabbi Mester became honorary secretary.

The inaugural session was opened by the Belzer Rav and deliberations continued for three days. It was decided to establish an *Agudas Rabbanim* uniting all religious rabbis throughout Galicia (this was in addition to the general *Agudas HaRabbanim* linked to Agudas Israel, which covered all of Poland and Lithuania with branches in Europe and America). Some delegates proposed to set up separate organizations for Western Galicia (surrounding Krakow) and Eastern Galicia (around Lemberg), but the Belzer Rav was determined on uniting all of Galicia in the sacred battle for hearts and minds. On his behalf, the Tarnopol Rav mounted the podium and declared passionately,

A contemporary drawing of the historic meeting in Warsaw

"We cannot allow any split within Galicia; it is tantamount to Shlomo HaMelech's classic threat to cut the disputed baby in half!" Although the new group officially represented all of Galicia's *chareidim* and was a tremendous source of encouragement, most of its activities were essentially carried out by Belzer chassidim, since many of their renowned *yoshvim* had considerable political acumen.

Within only a few years of becoming Rebbe, Reb Aharele's leadership received an even higher profile throughout Poland and the Jewish world when secular groups associated with the Bund persuaded the Polish government in 1929 to issue a four-point program for modernizing their community: henceforth all rabbis will have to obtain degrees in general education; school and *cheder* teachers must likewise pass secular exams; and secular studies and Polish would be added to school curricula. In addition, an umbrella religious council would represent "all strands" and its decisions would be binding throughout Poland! Naturally, these ominous decrees threw the religious establishment into turmoil and the aged *gadol*, the Chafetz Chaim (Rav Yisrael Meir Kagan — already over 90), made the arduous journey to Warsaw from Radin in the Vilna district to reverse this rash decision. He arrived on Monday, the 25th of Teves, and decided to summon a gathering of all the leading *gedolim.* When the Tarnopol Rav, who always represented the Belzer Rav, arrived, the Chafetz Chaim insisted that the Rebbe attend in person by the coming Sunday.

After he was cabled that his presence was vital, the Belzer Rav agreed to travel the over 200 miles to Warsaw, breaking his journey overnight in Lublin. Since there were few Belz devotees in Warsaw — a bastion of Polish, not Galician, Chassidus — some were concerned he would not receive due respect, but the Tarnopol Rav retorted, "We don't have to worry about the prestige of such a *tzaddik* whose *kavod* comes directly from Heaven!" Indeed he was met by tens of thousands of well-wishers — including several rabbanim and Rebbes — immediately on his arrival in Warsaw and the enthusiastic reception he received was a veritable *kiddush Hashem*![3] The street outside 9 Noviniarski, residence of the Zlatapoli Rebbe (Reb Velvel Twersky, uncle and host of the Belzer Rav) continually hummed with visitors and dignitaries coming and going.

The meeting duly opened on Monday, 5 Shevat (February 3, 1930), where the venerable Chafetz Chaim sat at the head with the Rebbe of Gur on his right — and the relatively young Belzer Rav on his left! At the meeting it was suggested that they send a top-level delegation to Professor Bartel, the Minister of Culture, but the Belzer Rav strongly rebutted the suggestion that a prominent Rav, fluent in Polish, lead this delegation. "No! No, we cannot allow this! It runs contrary to everything we're claiming! Here we're arguing that a rabbi must be learned in Torah alone — and not secular knowledge or languages — and then we ourselves choose just such a one as our representative."

Although they privately agreed with him, the Lithuanian rabbanim present, such as Rav Elchanan Wasserman and Rav Aharon Kotler, were amazed and impressed at how this ostensibly inexperienced Rebbe had the temerity to state his radical opinion so forcefully in the presence of older and more experienced *gedolim*. The aged Chafetz Chaim immediately concurred with the Rebbe — "We do not believe differently than the *tzaddik* from Belz!"

Finally, it was decided that the delegation would include the Rebbes of Gur (Gora Kalwaria), Aleksandrow, and Belz, and be led by the Chafetz Chaim personally; they were accompanied by Polish-speaking senators R' Asher Mendlesohn and R' Dovid Schreiber. The Polish Agudah had proposed including their senior *Sejm* representative — a respected Rav, leader of *Agudas HaRabbanim*, and an experienced *shtadlan* in this and countless other religious issues — but the Belzer Rav overrode Zeirei Agudah objections and insisted the delegation be comprised solely of recognized *gedolei Yisrael*.

---

3. When vacationing at Bad Homburg during 1929, he briefly visited Berlin, where Eastern European Jews or *Ost-Juden* were in a minority, and received a royal welcome — being described in German newspapers as the "uncrowned king of the Jews" — as he did when visiting Vienna later to consult with eye specialists.

The official reception for this delegation was an emotional affair since the Chafetz Chaim spoke directly to Professor Bartel — in Yiddish! "According to our tradition, Cyrus the Great merited to order the rebuilding of the Holy Temple because he had wept at the destruction of the First Temple. Sixty-four years ago I watched Polish prisoners in chains being tormented by the tzar's policemen and Cossacks on their way to exile in Siberia. This tragic scene saddened me and I retreated into my private room and with tears in my eyes I cried out, 'Ribono Shel Olam! These Poles are in the right! All they want is to live freely and independently. Why do they deserve such torment?' Since I wept at the collapse of the Polish Revolt, I merited to see Poland win independence! Do you want me to suffer anguish again because of Poland?... G-d looks after the persecuted! Do not forget, Honored Minister, that the time will come when the Jewish nation will also be liberated and the Almighty will free us from the yoke of our oppressors. The Poles, recently liberated from tyranny, ought to know how to treat us — they shouldn't prevent us from living our lives unfettered."

While delivering this speech, Rebbe Yisrael Meir burst into tears; there was not a dry eye among the minister and his aides either. When the senators offered to translate the elderly rabbi's words, Professor Bartel waved them aside — "Enough! There's no need to translate it. I understand the language of the heart!" — and promised to rescind the controversial proposal (though the government subsequently tried to retract that promise). The unusual delegation made an enormous impression on both Jews and non-Jews, religious and non-religious; undoubtedly the Belzer Rav's insistence that it be made up solely of authentic rabbis unversed in secular studies or foreign languages played a vital part in this.

Beyond the impact on the general public, Rebbe Aharon also cemented close relations with contemporary *gedolim*. When he first met the Chafetz Chaim in Warsaw before the meeting, an unusual rapport sprang up between them. The Belzer Rav asked the doyen of the Lithuanian "yeshivah-world" leaders to bless him, and though he was generally reluctant to bestow blessings, the Chafetz Chaim (who was a Kohen) immediately responded by reciting *Bircas Kohanim*. Later the Belzer Rav often spoke admiringly of Rebbe Yisrael Meir and his scrupulousness in speech — "He has a pair of gold scales in his mouth ... all his words are measured and carefully weighed" — while Rebbe Aharon's own strictness in rebutting any slanderous comments about others was legendary. Sensing a kindred spirit, the Rebbe remarked revealingly on his return from Warsaw, "They send him Heavenly messages just as they do in Belz!" Interestingly, he always referred to Rebbe Yisrael Meir as "the Radiner" rather than the "Chafetz Chaim" because of his personal strictness never to quote half-*pesukim*. (The verse *Mi ha'ish hechafetz chaim* ... recited during Shabbos morning prayers derives from *Tehillim* 34.) Likewise, the Chafetz Chaim often referred respectfully to the young Belzer Rebbe since their meeting.

Some measure of that respect can be gauged from the Chafetz Chaim's behavior at the preliminary meeting: As author of the *Mishnah Berurah* and leading proponent of the Vilna Gaon's views, Rebbe Yisrael Meir habitually was meticulous to complete the afternoon Minchah prayer before sundown, but at that meeting he twice ignored the whispered urging of his son-in-law, Rav Mendel Zaks, to *daven* Minchah. Only shortly before nightfall, when the Belzer Rav announced, *"Men vet gein davenen Minchah"* did he stand up to secretly pray Maariv with two *Shemoneh Esrei's* (to compensate for his missed Minchah)! When his son-in-law remonstrated that one can do this only after an *oness* when compelled by force of exceptional circumstances, the Chafetz Chaim replied forcefully, "The Belzer Rebbe's honor is also considered an *oness*!"

The unusual closeness between them extended to their leading disciples. An eyewitness at the Warsaw meeting recorded how Rav Elchanan Wasserman and Rav Aharon Kotler met regularly with the Belzer rabbanim of Tarnopol and Prubynznia at the chassidic hotel in 13 Twarda Street to plan strategy and reflect upon their respective mentors' views in an atmosphere of seriousness and responsibility. Rav Wasserman described the Belzer Rav to his yeshivah *bachurim* in Baranowitz as, "I saw an *emeser Yid* in Warsaw," and whenever relaxing in Marienbad, spent most of his time at the Czechoslovakian spa in the Rebbe's company! When asked why a Lithuanian Rosh Yeshivah and apparent *misnaged* should seek the society of a chassidic leader, he confided his reverence for someone who does not

Walking on a bridge; to the far right of the Rebbe is Reb Yosel Gold of Yarotschev

make a move or action without pure intentions! (Indeed, only his perceptive *gabbaim* recognized how the Rebbe never even changed his clothes without silently whispering some *kavannah* or *yichud*.) This respect was mutual. On the return journey from Warsaw, the Rebbe characterized Rav Elchanan as "a *kedosh elyon*" and, when Rebbe Pinchas of Dobrumil questioned this, added: "Had you watched him as carefully as I did, you also would have seen!"[4]

Also, since that meeting mutual admiration existed between Belz and the Rebbe of Gur, who described the Belzer Rav as "someone who seethes 24 hours a day in *avodas Hashem*!" When he paid a courtesy visit to the Belzer Rav after the latter underwent intensive eye

---

4. Likewise Reb Yosel Gold of Yarotschev, the Rebbe's close attendant and popularly known as "Minister of Interior" of Belz, with his charm, good humor, quick wits, and fervor, successfully parleyed with prominent *misnagdim* and Agudah leaders to convey the Rebbe's viewpoint. Unfortunately, some friction still remained and when one Agudah speaker began his address to the meeting by removing his hat and covering his head with a *cappel* alone — whereas the Belzer Rav never appeared without his *gartel*, hat and topcoat even at the risk of physical discomfort, Reb Yosel strode up to him to confide: "*Yungerman, a bissel derech eretz*! There are *gedolei Yisrael* in the hall!" The speaker took this amiss and retorted angrily, "Who is this *ketzel*?" until Rav Munish Babad interjected, "This cat has already expelled many mice!"

treatment in Krakow, he specifically asked the Rav not to trouble himself in repaying that visit (they only met again officially after World War II in Jerusalem, where he publicly showed unique respect and remarked, "Even if he had lived in the era of the Apta Rav, he would have been a *chiddush*!").

Meanwhile, the Belzer Rav continued to nurture Belz's independent status via his grandfather's *Machzikei Hadas*. Taking advantage of the new reality in Poland (as Agudas Israel had earlier), the organization was restructured as an internal political party. At a convention in Gorodok on Tuesday 12 Teves (December 22, 1931), delegates from one hundred communities relaunched the mass movement, inviting lay membership from every city, township, and village. In time the party was seen in Galicia as a serious rival to the Agudah, as was its cross-community Galician *Agudas Rabbanim* established in 1927.

Nonetheless, Belz subsequently made its stance widely known during the parliamentary elections by a surprising decision to field no candidates of its own! Adamantly opposed to separate Jewish lists that could likely lead to anti-Semitism, the Rebbe circulated his call for everyone to support the Polish government list: "To our Jewish brothers everywhere ... Since the *Sejm* and Senate elections are approaching and *Chazal* have warned us to support the honored government we must therefore vote for government candidates on the List number 1 ... *B'ezras Hashem*, through this great favors can be achieved for the Holy Torah and our Jewish brethren in all their physical and spiritual needs ... May Hashem grant that we always find grace and favor in the eyes of government ministers ... so they seek our welfare in everything ..."

During that election, a bombastic and provocative campaign against government policies mounted by the Zionist leader Itschak Greenbaum only heightened anti-Semitism in official circles; Polish and Ukrainian spokesmen publicly claimed indigent Jews were not true patriots since their heart lay in Palestine and they only remained in Poland to exploit the native workers and peasants![5] At

---

5. The Belzer Rav openly opposed Greenbaum's misguided electioneering; later, Greenbaum was to become notorious for his anti-religious platform under the inflammatory slogan, "*A todt klapp fur die religose Judenthum*; a death blow to religious Jewry!" and there was grievous disappointment when he was officially put in charge of wartime rescue by the *Sochnut*.

The Rebbe's proclamation urging everyone to vote for the official government list

a period when fierce propagandist polemic prevailed between the religious and non-religious political groupings or "clubs" in Poland, plus the open suspicion that the nationalist government of the dictatorial Marshal Pilsudski supported much of the anti-Semitic abuse, the Belzer Rav's decision aroused much controversy. Yet he was motivated not by the spurious allure of popularity but by a deep concern for the welfare of Jewish communities and villagers.

Moreover, the religious youth were currently tempted by the twin threats of socialism, represented by the Bund, and Jewish nationalism, epitomized by Zionism; burgeoning xenophobia also drove many into the ranks of those offering a secular panacea. Despite intense pressure by non-religious circles to establish a common front against government policies, and in full knowledge of the inevitable backlash, the Belzer Rav continued the traditional — and tested — method of old-fashioned *shtadlanus*: maintaining good relations with the prevailing administration in order to obtain concessions for those in need.

The Rebbe's approach was misunderstood by some local townspeople and young Zionist sympathizers too, who claimed he had been initially inclined to back the Zionist candidate, Dr. Shimon Federbusch, a Mizrachi leader in Lemberg. The Rebbe's final decision to endorse a Pilsudski protégé with alleged anti-Semitic links infuriated them. Some of their hotheads shouted down the Shabbos announcement of the Belzer Rav's voting instructions, smashed windows during his *shalosh seudos tisch*, heckled or threw things when his entourage went to vote, and periodically sang an irreverent ditty describing the welcome the government candidate received on his personal visit to the Belz establishment.

Secularist writers sought to stereotype this Belzer policy as yet another example of the archetypal *"Mah Yofis"* Jew fawning over the local *poritz* and stifled by a *galus* mentality. Quite the contrary. Belz were proud of their tradition and custom, risking embarrassment, major inconvenience, or loss of income rather than compromise their deeply held religious principles. It was precisely because they were closer to the people — whose aspirations and needs were at risk from government malevolence — than many remote "leaders" and "spokesmen" who drew their inspiration from alien sources.

Rarely did the common populace or *"amcha"* confide their problems in those self-proclaimed representatives, and certainly never presented them with a *kvittel* or poured out their heart in private — as they did to the Rebbe. Indeed, the Belzer Rav had become so distraught and ill at the mounting tide of heartbreak that he had to temporarily discontinue the practice of perusing each *kvittel* personally and had his *gabbaim* read their contents to him instead.

In the dangerous early years of Polish nationalism, the Belzer Rav was ever mindful of the opinions of national and local government officials and their likely adverse reactions to their Jewish subjects. On one of Poland's national holidays, the Rebbe mounted the podium to deliver a speech on the occasion — in his capacity as town Rav — on brotherly behavior. In the presence of and to the great satisfaction of high-ranking government representatives, he declared that all humans, Jews and gentiles alike, are brothers. Likewise, at the *Agudas Rabbanim* founding conference in Lemberg during 1927, the Belzer Rav personally intervened to have the customary courtesy cable to the government and the despotic Marshal Josef Pilsudski rewritten — to the surprise of other rabbanim present who saw it as little more than a formality. Only later did they hear from a non-religious activist, Dr. Wasser, how the reframing of that telegram had averted a decree that threatened many Jewish families!

His concern for his fellow Jews naturally also encompassed those beyond the borders of Galicia and Poland. In 1937, Prince Peter of Greece expressed a wish to visit Belz during Rosh Hashanah 5697 and meet the Rebbe personally. Since the Prince was a cousin of King George VI of England, which then administered the Mandate over Palestine, the Belzer Rav made time for the royal visitor. In their conversation, conducted by R' Sinai Singer (a former officer in the Austrian army and now one of Belz's *yoshvim*), the Rebbe discussed the unhappy predicament of Jews around the world then and particularly dwelt on the precarious security situation in Palestine. Although the prince tried to reassure the Rebbe that the British army was doing its level best to contain Arab terrorism, the Belzer Rav was not assuaged by verbal assurances and pressed the prince to take an active interest in Palestine's affairs and use his undoubted influence to ensure peace.

Internally, Belz continued to flourish under the Rebbe's guidance. The *yoshvim*, first instituted during Rebbe Yehoshua's tenure and expanded under Rebbe Yissachar Ber, now grew to include, besides the married men, over 500 *bachurim* from Germany, Austria, Switzerland, Romania, Hungary, and Czechoslovakia, as well as Poland and Galicia. Their humility, dedication, and idealism was extraordinary, abandoning home and comforts for intensive Torah study and spiritual refinement — and instant fidelity to their Rebbe's every wish. Rarely did even married *yoshvim* venture home to inquire after family or livelihood (except during the Rebbe's annual break) and were instead totally involved with the almost continuous learning sessions. Since the overnight *mishmar* and early morning *mishmar* overlapped, the *beis hamedrash* was always open, and leading *yoshvim* grew into formidable scholars.

Unlike ordinary chassidim on their annual pilgrimages who customarily met the Rav only fleetingly during their week's stay, the *yoshvim* enjoyed a closer familiarity with Rebbe Ahare'le. Yet, despite this, their awe of the Rebbe was if anything all the greater, although Rebbe Aharon made an enormous effort to appear 'approachable to his followers. In a rare moment, the Belzer Rav once confided that his chassidim do not know how to truly fear him — "If I were a chassid I would flee through the window from overwhelming trepidation!" Seeing through his veneer of simplicity, the *yoshvim* discerned the exalted personality concealed behind layers of modesty.

Since childhood he had always been reticent in displaying his scholarly prowess, and once he became Rebbe, he rarely spoke in learning even with close acquaintances. The prominent Rabbi, Rav Menachem Munish Margulies of Krasnobrad, originally from Hibniv (Uhnow near Belz), was a childhood friend and colleague who had spent countless happy hours studying and debating together with the Rebbe. Although they remained close, every time Rav Menachem Munish attempted to clarify uncertainties in his learning or simply discuss Torah subjects with the Rebbe, he would swiftly switch the discussion to *aggadata* or Chassidus. Despite his closeness, Rav Margulies remained a devoted chassid who regarded the Belzer Rav with as deep a respect and veneration as any of the *yoshvim*.

A rare picture of the beis medrash before World War I

The *yoshvim* were greatly respected in their own right and wherever they appeared, knots of young, aspiring acolytes would gather round, eager for instruction and guidance. This Belz institution received much moral and financial support; furthermore, around Chanukah, Purim, and a week before Rosh Hashanah, the ranks of the *yoshvim* were boosted by prominent rabbanim, adherents of Belz, temporarily shedding their communal responsibilities to refresh the Torah and chassidic allegiance of their youth. Although the most venerable of these distinguished rabbis had risen to prominence in the days of Rebbe Yeshie'le, they willingly — and indeed fearfully — accepted the mastery of Rebbe Ahare'le. Since they had to lead their own respective communities over the *Yamim Noraim*, they customarily visited Belz on the Shabbos before *Selichos*.

The first day of *Selichos* was a day of intense spiritual arousal and introspection in Belz. After Shacharis the Rebbe personally led the large congregation in the complete recital of *Tehillim* before they flocked to the *beis hamedrash* to devote their day to intensive learning. Meanwhile, masses of chassidim continued flocking to Belz for the Yamim Tovim. On the days before Rosh Hashanah and Yom Kippur, thousands more began arriving from Poland and abroad by train, bus, cart and even on foot! These so-called *"Zeckel-Yudelach"* were too poor to afford even horse and cart. Instead they cadged rides or tramped for days and even weeks; their shoulder packs contained little more than challos, jars of homemade pickled fish, and paper-wrapped meat portions for their prospective Yom Tov *seudah*! (Food and rooms for all visitors were available in Belz at a premium since many Belz householders relied on the annual pilgrimages for their year's income and these penurious chassidim could ill afford the prices.)

The *Selichos* of *"Zechor Bris Avraham"* on Erev Rosh Hashanah again heralded a day of intense spiritual arousal and introspection; the sublime appearance of the Belzer Rav, his face aflame with an ethereal light, moved many to aspire to ever higher ideals. Although the famous shul had a seating capacity for a few thousand — and the two *polishen* (side halls) on the left and right with party windows, built by Rebbe Yehoshua and Rebbe Yissachar Ber respectively, could each accommodate another five hundred — it was still very cramped for the growing congregation by the time Rosh Hashanah arrived. The Belzer Rav led the prayers for Maariv, Mussaf and *tekias shofar*, alternately trembling like an abject slave appearing in front of his all-powerful master on the day of justice or roaring as a lion when proclaiming Hashem's majesty. On the first night of Rosh Hashanah, as the Rebbe completed *Adon Olam*, everybody jostled for a closer position in breathless silence as he slowly intoned three times, *"Leshanah tovah tikaseivu v'seichaseimu l'alter l'chaim tovim ul'shalom."* The atmosphere was intensely joyful: They had personally merited to hear the Rebbe wish them a Good Year! Everyone cheerfully wished their neighbors, *"A gut Yom Tov! A gut yohr!"* before lining up in a long straggling queue, organized by the redoubtable *yoshvim*, to file past and take *shalom* individually from the Rebbe — which took some considerable time.

Then the Rebbe retired to his private quarters while the chassidim began their Yom Tov *seudah*. Those who could afford it went to their hostels and private hosts while others ate with the *yoshvim* who had their own dining hall and provided challos, fish, and meat. However, the *Zeckel-Yudelach* repaired to a quiet corner to recite *Kiddush* over their dried challos. They also lacked sleeping quarters and slept on benches in the *beis hamedrash* or in the *graiser-stieb* after the *tisch* had finished. The evening *tisch* lasted almost until daybreak, the morning prayers till late afternoon. Despite this and their meager meal, they were well satisfied and content. For a week or so they could forget their daily grind and difficult life while basking in the holy glow of the saintly Rebbe.

By the time Shacharis, Mussaf, and the *seudah* were completed in Belz it was quite late, yet *Tashlich* — led by the Rebbe — was recited with great fervor and customarily followed by a lengthy *rekidah*. Afterwards the Belzer Rav blessed all those present with a *gut yohr*, Hashem should fulfill all their needs for the best. Then he would instruct them to quickly return to the *beis hamedrash* and continue their learning program. Indeed, many *chassidim* stayed over in Belz to spend the week before Yom Kippur learning with the *yoshvim*. As a consequence, the *beis hamedrash* was packed solid all day during the *aseres yemei teshuvah* — far beyond its 1,000 seat capacity. Some sat on the stairs of the *aron hakodesh* or *bimah*, others even sat on the floor while holding their *gemaras*! Meals too had to be taken in shifts. The *beis hamedrash* reverberated to the loud sound of Talmudic debate and *pilpul* since the gathering included renowned rabbis from abroad, learned householders, and budding young geniuses with a wide knowledge of many tractates. Rich and poor, workers and magnates, shopkeepers and unemployed, all were equally committed to increasing their learning quota by day or night, by natural light or flickering candle. In the crucial days of judgment, nobody had time for idle conversation or gossip, and their only interruption came when slipping out to present a personal *kvittel* to the Rebbe. The mounting pressure of *kvittlech* arriving by hand and mail grew so massive that sacks of supplications were brought into the Rebbe's room on Erev Yom Kippur.

On Yom Kippur too, the Belzer Rav led the prayers for *Kol Nidrei*, Mussaf, and Neilah and, like his father before him, prior to the prayers delivered an exclusive rebuke to the ladies assembled at his house. Before *Kol Nidrei*, the Rebbe ascended the steps in front of the *aron hakodesh* to deliver a *mussar* lecture. He called for increased Torah study and *teshuvah,* and everybody burst into tears. Usually he would reiterate his late father's words about how Torah study delivered forgiveness as effectively — or even more effectively — than that achieved by the Yom Kippur scapegoat in the *Mikdash*! Then he slowly recited the *Vidui* of the *Ramban*, which everyone weepingly repeated. The packed shul with its hundreds of glowing candles made an indelible impression, and even non-Jews from the surrounding area would come in groups for a glimpse.

As a general rule, Rebbe Ahare'le shied away from giving *mussar*, judging himself unworthy! Rarely did he upbraid the townspeople — only two such *derashos* are recorded before the War — and even then he would first justify himself by quoting the Chasam Sofer that this formed part of every publicly funded Rav's duties. Furthermore Jews were not really sinners, merely sometimes unaware of the seriousness of the offense. (Yet on one memorable occasion he summoned all the townspeople, both male and female, to a fiery sermon on various breaches and instituted some *tznius takanos* while warning that those who ignored them would lose their credibility. This was no idle threat since without a solid reputation for reliability, most locals would forfeit their main livelihood of hosting and catering to the chassidim.) However, throughout Elul, he began adding words of *mussar* during *shalosh seudos*, though he excused himself by mentioning that his father had done the same and besides, "Once anyone hears my words they are moved to repentance by themselves."

The morning *tefillos* on Yom Kippur were preceded by the recital of the entire *Tehillim*, which naturally added to the already hallowed atmosphere. After Yom Kippur, the Belzer Rav, consumed by an inner fire, would wander around the empty shul, pausing at certain corners and areas as if he were elevating individual prayers that had not yet ascended to Heaven! The abiding impact of the *Yamim Noraim* ensured that the majority of chassidim did not depart immediately after Yom Kippur. Many returned to the *beis hamedrash* and their trusty *gemaras* — staying on until Succos, Hoshana Rabbah or Simchas Torah. "Tishrei is a month with many mitzvos," the Belzer Rav was wont to say. "And according to the *Reishis Chochmah* one ought to do *teshuvah* before every mitzvah."

Every year when the *Yamim Noraim* and particularly Hoshana Rabbah arrived, the Rebbe began to hurry himself as soon as day broke while instructing the *gabbaim* that everything must be ready so they might not *chas veshalom* forfeit *z'man tefillah.*[6] All day long he

---

6. Hoshana Rabbah in Belz was an unforgettable occasion: Guileless villagers streamed in from the surrounding countryside and the fervent *tefillos* lasted till 3 p.m.

would protest that *"es geessed blut fun zech"* (blood is flowing from me) for fear his prayers may be too late. Yet despite this he was never able to start the *tefillos* until such time as he felt personally qualified, and placed as much stress on the mental preparations, or *"hachanos,"* as on the actual deed of prayer. Whenever the Rebbe had to pray for *Klal Yisrael*, his preparations and exertions were extraordinary — taking up to half an hour even when time was pressing. He would donate substantial *tzedakah* with phenomenal concentration, personally handling the money even though he never usually touched cash directly. Since he was totally preoccupied with his sacred preparations, every Shacharis, Minchah, or Maariv had no set time. "In Belz they *daven* not with the clock but with the heart!"

Yet the crowds waited patiently and despite the long delay, his chassidim could listen to him for hours without tiring. To their mind, "All the expense and effort traveling to Belz is worth it just to hear the Rebbe recite the morning *berachos* — all the rest is sheer profit!" Another leading chassid added, "Anyone who hears him intone '... *v'al tevi'eini l'yedei cheit v'lo l'yedei aveirah v'avoin ...*' with such a broken spirit can see how he honestly believes himself to be the biggest *baal aveirah* in existence!" His prayers were not accompanied with loud cries or clamor but were clearly enunciated with fear, awe, and usually — in common with the Belz tradition — speed. Occasionally he was so consumed by a fiery passion that he would roar out whole sentences and paragraphs in one breath. But on other, rarer occasions his fervent prayers would stretch for protracted periods. As the minutes raced past he would utter little more than intermittent groans and sighs, but his coloring would change rapidly: Sometimes small clouds of worry would cross his face, later his countenance would glow with an ethereal light. With the onset of prayers, all his many physical frailties — the despair of his personal physicians — fell away as if they had never existed. He was a man reinvigorated in Hashem's service, his face aflame with an inner fire, his *tefillos* animated with warmth and spirit.

Frequently, the Belzer Rav invoked the early example of Rebbe Yechiel Mechel of Zlotchow: "He was one of the first among the disciples of the Baal Shem Tov to pray late. I have a tradition from my fathers in the name of the Lubliner Rebbe that had Rebbe Mechel'e prayed promptly, he would have hastened the Redemption and Mashiach would have come! The reason for Rebbe Mechel'e's delay was because he was so weak he was unable to *daven* on time ..." Since he would repeat this sentiment so often, it seemed fairly obvious he was hinting at his own predicament. Certainly he kept trying to complete his preparations early and pray punctually; once he expressed his wonderment and admiration of Gur, whose original tradition was to *daven* late yet had recently switched to praying early — the exact opposite of his own experience.

The Rebbe with bandaged eyes recuperating from an operation

When recuperating from an eye operation in Krakow during the winter of 1938, he was visited by the famed *Chachmei Lublin* Rosh Yeshivah and *mekubal*, Rebbe Shimon of Zolkove, who blessed him: "*Hashem Yisbarach* should send Rabbeinu a *refuah sheleimah* and his eyes should be healed." But the Belzer Rav replied, "Reb Shim'ele! Bless me that I should be able to *daven* on time! You know that the Lubliner Rebbe *davened* early in the morning and many other great *tzadikkim* prayed on time. But the Rebbe Reb Mechel of Zlotchow *davened* late and people say that had the Rebbe Reb Mechel'e *davened* earlier he would have brought Mashiach! Therefore I beg you, bless me to be able to pray *bizmanah*."

Rebbe Aharon also laid significant stress on tradition, whether in education or lifestyle; indeed, Belz and its conservative dynasty remained a sturdy bulwark against the inroads of modernism, and proudly carried the flag for full-blooded Orthodoxy — unrepentant and unembarrassed. While discussing chassidic clothing with another *gadol*, he recalled the example of a Belzer businessman who had to conclude an important deal with a non-Jewish manu-

Rebbe Shimon of Zolkove

facturer during Chol HaMoed Pesach. Embarrassed to wear his fur *shtreimel* in alien surroundings, he concealed it about his person. At the conclusion of the negotiations, they shook hands and the factory director offered him a glass of beer to seal the bargain. Since this businessman was so engrossed in the deal at hand, he accepted the beer and totally forgot it was Pesach! Fortunately, he first wanted to make a *berachah* with his head covered properly, as is customary among chassidim, and groped for his hat — and turned up his *shtreimel*. He stared at it in complete surprise. What was that doing here? Why had he brought it? Then realization finally hit home — "*Ribbono Shel Olam*! I almost had *chametz* on Pesach!"

"We see from this how due to his traditional *chassidishe levush* and *shtreimel*, he was saved from an *issur kares*!" concluded the Belzer Rav triumphantly. "They are a great protection against all kinds of *aveiros*." On another occasion he declared wearing a *shtreimel* a *segulah* (amulet) for nurturing good children, just as having *payos* longer than necessary is a *segulah* for piety. He also spoke out strongly against the modern practice of sporting a quiff of hair at the forehead. "Not only is that a *chatzitzah* for *tefillin* but I heard from my father how someone who is *megadel bluris* might become disqualified as a kosher witness! And you can publicize that in my name!" Likewise, he vehemently disapproved of *chassanim* meeting their fiancées during the engagement. When he heard of one groom who intended doing just that, he sent his *gabbai*, Reb Gershon, with an urgent message. "Tell him: he shouldn't think this is just a chassidus; it's a *Shulchan Aruch*!"

Under his guidance, existing *chadorim* (traditional institutions) were encouraged, new establishments were founded, and Galician activists were encouraged to preserve and protect tradition. In his drive to safeguard time-honored education or *chinuch*, children were favorably treated by the Rebbe. A charming custom was instituted for Shemini Atzeres. Following Mussaf and when the shul had been cleared of all menfolk, the *Aron HaKodesh* was reopened and all the ladies entered with their infants to kiss the *Sifrei Torah*. At the Shabbos day *tisch* (that more usually took place in late afternoon) the Rebbe exclusively distributed *sherayim* from the *lekach*-cake after *Kiddush* to the *cheder* children. A long line of eager boys aged 4 to 10 would queue up, their faces alight with anticipation and assurance: Now they were at least temporarily recognized in their own right, with privileges denied to adults! While giving out *sherayim* the Rebbe would frequently comment, "*Na-dir*, take it as a *segulah* for *yiras Shamayim*!"

As the fish *sherayim* were being distributed, the youngsters continued to be favored and when fathers came forward with their sons, the Rebbe would add a portion for each young budding chassid while gently warning him, "*Gebt achtung*! Be careful of the bones!" (Generally, the Belzer Rebbes preferred salmon at the Shabbos and Yom Tov table, even though these were a rarity in the locality.) On exchanging *Shalom* with the younger generation, he would check how they were progressing in learning and which establishment they attended, since he fought an unremitting battle throughout his incumbency against modern or non-religious schools, and publicly berated fathers who enrolled their offspring in institutes where radicalism or heresy flourished. Probably because of his lifelong avoidance of any possible impediment in his pursuit of purity and holiness, whenever Rebbe Ahare'le shook hands with children he did so through a towel!

His self-isolation from the profane and polluted had to be seen to be believed. To give some minor examples: he would not study Torah nor utter words of holiness in any room containing dirty washing until it was stored within two containers, one inside the other. Nor could he countenance anyone in close proximity with impure ideas, and he would sometimes announce at the *tisch*: "Keep your thinking clean so you don't confuse my thoughts!" (So as not to shame anybody in public, *chalilah*, he was careful never to direct these remarks at anyone in particular.) For the same reason, the *gabbaim* would periodically proclaim at the Simchas Torah celebrations, "*Bliebt mit yishuv hadaas*!" Besides his legendary exertions to attain purity, such as frequent hand-washing, ritual *mikveh* immersions, or

The mikveh in Belz

shielding his eyes, he had an uncanny ability to read people's minds. Countless stories exist of his swiftly solving petitioners' dilemmas — and even rabbanim's complicated *shailos* — before they had even voiced them. Even in his early years as Rebbe, contemporary *gedolim* compared this aptitude with that of the Baal Shem Tov.

One modest manifestation of his second sight or *ruach hakodesh* was revealed during January 1928, on attending the wedding of his youngest brother, Rav Shalom of Apta (Opatow) to the daughter of Rebbe Yisrael Perlow in Stolin. (Remarkably, this match had been predicted by the *chassan's* namesake, the Sar Shalom, when the bride's grandfather Rebbe Asher Stoliner had visited Belz eighty years earlier!) At this wedding, the Stoliner Rebbe mentioned to the Belzer Rav how the family also had an heirloom from the Sar Shalom: One of the twelve small challas traditionally set out at the *tisch* was bestowed as *sherayim* to Rebbe Asher during that visit. However, at the same period Rebbe Asher had received a similar challah from Rebbe Meir'el Premishlaner, and now the family could not tell the two apart. When Rebbe Ahare'le was shown these near identical challas he unhesitatingly reached for one and clasped it with both hands while murmuring excitedly, "This is from *der heilige elter Zeide*, the Maharash!"

The Belzer Rav had an inherent longing for Mashiach that often revealed itself during the Yamim Tovim. On *Shabbos Chazon* (before Tishah B'Av) the *Krias HaTorah* was interrupted to allow the Rebbe to speak on the subject of Mashiach and the approaching *geulah*. For Tishah B'Av he was meticulous to purchase a simple *Kinnos* without commentaries; nor was his copy put aside for next year — did they not fervently believe that Mashiach would surely have arrived by then? Yet his innate yearning for the Messiah never swayed him to consider forcing the issue. The Erloi Rav, Rabbi Shimon Sofer, floated the idea of sacrificing the *korban Pesach* even though the *Beis HaMikdash* has not been rebuilt. He asked his nephew and president of Kollel Galicia, R' Dovid Schreiber, to approach the British Mandate authorities in Palestine for their permission, while his son R' Moshe Schreiber, who was close to the Belzer Rebbe, should ascertain his views.

When R' Moshe asked the Rebbe if it was permissible to sacrifice the *korban Pesach* without the *Beis HaMikdash* or Mashiach, the Rebbe did not reply definitively but instead urged him to learn through the responsa of *Yad Dovid* by Rav Dovid Friedman of Karlin and report his conclusion. After R' Moshe Schreiber studied this responsa in Belz's *beis hamedrash* and came back with his negative decision, Rebbe Ahare'le concurred that the *korban Pesach* should not be sacrificed in our generation. This was despite the harsh reality that by 1934, when this debate took place, *Klal Yisrael* faced major, possibly insurmountable, calamity, and it must have been tempting to push for Mashiach.

CHAPTER 4

THE
GATHERING STORM

PRIVATELY, BELZ HAD VIEWED THE RISE OF Hitlerism with grave foreboding from the start. This was in sharp contrast to the native German Jews, passionately patriotic, who defiantly reacted to Nazi electoral success by futilely asserting *"Daseinrecht"*: the right to maintain a Jewish presence in Germany as a legal entitlement, moral imperative — and a religious mitzvah! They penned eloquent yet ineffectual editorials and coined empty slogans like, "Wear the Yellow Badge with pride!" or "No one dare violate our constitutional rights nor rob us of our homeland and fatherland." Later, far too much later, deep remorse beset those misguided writers and leaders for not advising their followers to flee at once and at all costs.

Belz, however, had harbored few illusions from the beginning. There was a tradition that a *mechutan* of Rebbe Yeshie'le, Rebbe Yechezkel Shraga Halberstam (the famed Rav of Sieniawa and son of the *Divrei Chaim*), was profoundly perturbed during the night of 19th Iyar (April 20) 1889, and came down to ask the chassidim to pray fervently: "An evil soul has come down to this world who could turn out to be an enormous *rasha*! We must pray and plead that his dreadful schemes never come about." (Likewise, the Karliner Rebbe openly predicted how Polish Judaism would be destroyed in a hurricane of looting and slaughter — based on a surviving letter from the Baal Shem Tov which he corroborated with the aged Rebbe of Gur at the outbreak of World War II.) The Belzer Rav himself later disclosed, "My grandfather divulged to my father that the First World War will eventually break out! And my father likewise revealed to me this next World War, many years before it occurred!" When Reb Yehoshua Pach of Rawa-Ruska heard the Rebbe's comment on the Nazi rise to power — "We are approaching a second world war which brings the *geulah* and Mashiach closer!" — he wept openly, crying out, "If the Rebbe already sees the Light of the Messiah, who knows how much darkness now exists in the world? Light is more clearly visible from among the darkness!" Certainly the Belzer Rav was aware of more than just the likelihood of war and regularly repeated his view, "*Fun dem rasha darft men antloifen!*" — in marked contrast to the "worldly advice" of the progressive German-Jewish leadership. Remarkably, the Rebbe never referred to Adolf Hitler *yemach shemo* by name, instead talking of "*Der Deitsch*," "*Der rasha*," or more usually, "*Der meshugene hint!*" which most effectively summed up his opinion.

The growing East-European Jewish community in Germany, derided as "*Ost-Juden*" by native Jews and non-Jews alike, watched the Jew-baiting — painfully familiar from Eastern Europe — with increased trepidation, unlike the half-million established Jews who assumed the hateful phenomenon must soon pass. Native Jews had enjoyed at least partial emancipation since 1812 and had experienced accelerating acculturation, assimilation, and intermarriage ever since. They could not fathom how an uncouth guttersnipe, shiftless, ill-spoken, failure, of questionable lineage (his father was Alois Schicklgruber-Hiedler, an illegitimate child whose parentage was unknown) could aspire to lead the most cultured and intellectual nation in Europe. Who would dare force Germany's top professors, scientists, doctors, lawyers, civil servants, writers, musicians, entertainers, bankers or businessmen back into the ghetto? This nightmarish vision could be nothing more than a passing phase, and the Nazis' premature attempts at grabbing power in 1923 had been dismissed with raucous laughter — scorn and ridicule which the Nazi leaders determined to avenge at the first opportunity.

Founded in the aftermath of the First World War debacle, the National-Socialist (Nazi) Party capitalized on general unrest — hyper-inflation, colossal unemployment, vindictive and punitive war reparations — while exploiting decades of anti-Semitism to grow rapidly in strength and influence. By sordid backstairs political intrigue and massive electoral support, the self-styled Fuehrer was appointed in early 1933 as chancellor, presiding over a coalition cabinet of right-wing nationalists and Nazis, but he controlled only 42 percent of *Reichstag* members. Early elections during February were accompanied by unbridled violence, the burning down of the *Reichstag*, arbitrary arrests and bloodcurdling propaganda; and secured him 43 percent plus another 8 percent of his nationalist partners that brought him to the paper-thin majority of 51 percent. Yet he needed over two-thirds to suspend the democratic process by constitutional means — which he proceeded to accomplish by banning the Communist vote under an emergency decree and buying off the Catholics by promising a Concordat with the Pope (eventually ratified on September 10).

Swiftly, Hitler outlawed or dissolved all opposition parties, suppressed the unions, radio, newspapers, media and publishing houses, while thousands vanished overnight either abroad or into newly established concentration camps. In a reign of terror, totalitarian rule was imposed by the ruthless Gestapo secret state police, the SA brown-shirted storm troopers and the widely feared black-uniformed SS "protective squads." Every German citizen was subject to a pyramid of strict controls stretching down from the Fuehrer via Gauleiters, ward-leaders, cell-leaders, to 480,000 block-wardens who spied on each tenement. The millions unemployed were enrolled in the Reich Labor Service for compulsory work and indoctrination, the youth were enrolled in the militaristic *Hitlerjugend* on which often depended their admission to high school and university, millions more joined the Nazi party or the subordinate Farmers' League, German Labor Front, the SA or the SS.

All this applied to pure-blooded German citizens; the hated *Jude* were rapidly thrust beyond the pale. Nazis had excelled in Jew-baiting and violence from their inception and proposed anti-Semitic legislation wherever and whenever they had attained even temporary authority; now the Party had effectively become the State. Governing unfettered throughout Germany, they could set every evil scheme into execution. On achieving totalitarian rule in March 1933, their first action was to organize a large-scale boycott of Jewish business and stores "to combat the falsehoods spread abroad"! A series of unofficial boycotts against businesses and Jewish professionals plus the looting of department stores (all large department stores were by their warped definition a "Jewish target"!) had drawn worldwide criticism, while America threatened to boycott German goods. In retaliation, the Nazis organized an official three-day violent mass boycott (scheduled to start on Shabbos, 5 Nissan or April 1) of all Jewish businesses, published lists of businesses and individuals to be ostracized, and forced Jewish leaders to inform their foreign brethren that "all the atrocity stories were groundless."

Simultaneously, hundreds of judges, lawyers, journalists, musicians and professors were forced to resign; retroactive legislation (accompanied by mob violence) then extended this discrimination throughout the civil service, schools, universities, media, honorary officialdom and medical and dental professions, rapidly reducing the status of Germany's Jews to that of the preceding Dark Ages. This was not the only reversal of the 1812 Emancipation for which German Jewry had fought so energetically and in whose cause many had abandoned religion, culture, and self-respect. Even assimilated Jews down to the third generation were reclassified as non-Aryan (later all males had to add the name "Israel," and all females, "Sarah") and everyone was debarred from inheriting farmland. *Ost-Juden* additionally had their naturalization cancelled, and *shechitah* was outlawed as inhumane.

Most Protestant and Catholic clergy welcomed these measures in common with most Germans, as long as their own rights were guaranteed. Native German Jews, by contrast, were traumatized and often suicidal — suicide rates rose by 50 percent — and the vulnerable small village *kehillos*, where tradition and religion had remained most steadfast, entered a process of decline and disintegration. Additionally, thousands fled Germany in despair, particularly *Ost-Juden*, yet the majority thought they could tough it out. Although the Belzer Rav desperately wanted to comfort his flock, his instincts and insight told him otherwise; the rise of Nazism had made him extremely fearful since 1933. Six months after the Nazis swept to power, when a visiting journalist asked what he thought of Hitler, the Rebbe began to weep bitterly. Between his sobs, he cried, "He is the *Sitra Achra*; the *avi-avos* of *tumah*! The exact opposite of holiness; the veritable pinnacle of impurity! More than Amalek or Haman *harashah*! But sooner or later we must prevail and overcome him ... You can tell Jews in my name that with Hashem's help he will eventually be completely humbled!" Despite his grim forebodings, his impetus bestowed solace and reassurance rather than generating panic.

According to his eldest son, the saintly Rebbe Moshe'le, much of the delays and disorder in the Belz timetable were exacerbated in 1933, and this was solely due to the Rebbe being disturbed by those fiends — "*Der rasha hot dah fardreyt die sedarim!*" Sensing the evil abyss to which those Nazi leaders aspired, he felt driven to extraordinary exertion in *tefillah* — beyond time and physical constraints. From that period, he began fervently reciting *Tehillim* 46 each morning after *Birchas HaTorah*. Since that psalm graphically describes the ravages of a final war to "the ends of the earth" — nations roaring, kingdoms tottering, countries devastated, weapons destroyed, vehicles burnt (and global battles that pit city against city, nation against nation, according to *Radak's* commentary) — his closest chassidim gained some premonition of the approaching upheaval, though no hostilities were currently in the offing.

Those not party to Divine inspiration, however, consoled themselves that the worst must surely be over. As very little new legislation or spectacular "street action" took place during 1934, hopes surfaced that perhaps the Nazi bloodlust had been sated. This wishful and illusory optimism received an apparent boost when the Nazis turned on each other with brutal internecine slaughter. Sadly this was a fatal misreading of the situation. The notorious "Night of the Long Knives" on June 30 did not signal an end to arbitrary terror by the uncontrollable brown-shirts but was an ugly massacre unleashed by rival criminal gangs with few scruples in butchering their own comrades if they threatened authority, or when it suited their lust for further power.

Ernst Roehm, leader of the brown-shirted storm troopers, had become frustrated at being overlooked for the coveted post of defense minister while his rank and file had grown restive with the conviction that all anti-Jewish measures thus far were "too moderate." Despite Roehm being an intimate and trusted conspirator since 1919, Hitler ruthlessly agreed to double-cross him for army promises to back him as their preferred successor to the ailing President Hindenberg. He persuaded his old friend to send his storm troopers on temporary leave pending a top-level conference in Bavaria.

Before dawn of the scheduled "conference," when Roehm and other top leaders were still in bed, Hitler arrived with hand-picked SS assassins to summarily gun them down for "treason." SS Chief Himmler organized a simultaneous bloodbath in Berlin, while SS operatives throughout Germany went down a 200-name blacklist, methodically liquidating them. Although all were roundly accused of treason, many had nothing to do with the brown-shirts but had previously incurred Hitler's hostility. Most Germans heaved a collective sigh of relief, hoping they had been spared a bloody civil war, and did not even demand an explanation. Their government had rapidly descended from psuedo-legality into naked aggression and terror, yet few seemed to mind. Even German Jews who had fled to neighboring countries ventured to return, mistakenly believing that the bloody purge signaled a change for the better.

In actuality, the brutal butchery marked the tightening noose of tyranny. The Fuehrer was recognized as commander-in-chief of the armed forces, his party sidelined their coalition partners in government, and the sinister SS rose to supreme power and dominated the growing web of concentration camps where anti-Nazis and Jews were subjected to fiendish tortures, debilitating slave-labor — and a terrifying example to those who did not toe the official line. 1935 saw not only the Saar district on the French border reoccupied; the Versailles Peace Treaty disarming Germany defiantly repudiated; conscription, rearming, and remilitarization reintroduced, but more anti-Jewish edicts. They were barred from swimming baths, holiday resorts and places of entertainment; small businesses and newspapers were paralyzed by violent boycotts; and the *Reichstag* ratified the infamous Nuremberg Laws. This racist legislation designated as a *Jude* anyone with a Jewish grandparent; these *Juden* were henceforth forbidden to intermarry with "pure German blood," employ young female domestics or fly the German flag. Furthermore, they could only be considered subjects and never citizens, effectively disenfranchised and legally outside state protection.

It could hardly escape anyone with even minimal religious knowledge that the age-old Biblical admonitions of retribution when sinners do not mend their ways "unto the third generation" were hitting home with a vengeance, just as the public boycotts of Jewish businesses began on Shabbos — previously widely desecrated in pursuit of profit and convenience. Indeed, the early years of Nazi persecution in Germany saw a reawakening of religion and practice as Jews were forced to fall back on their native resources: synagogues filled to overflowing, day schools flourished, hitherto aloof professional classes were driven back to their roots. In the face of the universal threat, most felt more comfortable and certainly safer in the company of their coreligionists. Meanwhile the Gestapo and SS continued to tighten their control over communal affairs.

Ostensibly, the next few years of Nazi rule were committed to economic regeneration, but their Four Year Plan contained a vitriolic preface ranting on the necessity to battle against "Bolshevik-Judaism" and ominously providing for the expropriation of all Jews when Germany went to war. Jewish nationals of Russia, mostly escapees from the 1917 Bolshevik Revolution, were expelled as 1938 dawned. On January 25, the wholesale arrests of able-bodied Jews and "other anti-socials" began; they were dispatched to Buchenwald and Dachau for forced labor. In preparation for a mass influx of Jewish prisoners, Dachau inmates were ordered to sew Magen Davids onto prison uniforms. Ever since *Mein Kampf* had first seen the light of day, war with ideological and race enemies had loomed large in the warped Nazi doctrines entwined with dogmas like *Lebensraum*: enlarging Germany's already substantial territory and eliminating Jews from European society. These perverted policies advanced hand in hand: War provided the opportunity for unrestricted oppression and terror; those running the Four Year Plan legalized the compulsory confiscation and "voluntary Aryanization" of Jewish businesses and property.

Earlier, at a secret meeting during November 1937, the timetable for unprovoked attacks the next year on Austria and Czechoslovakia "with lightening speed" was discussed with military chiefs and foreign ministers — "Where can Germany achieve the greatest gain in living space at the lowest cost? Austria and Czechoslovakia are the first obvious targets!" For years Nazi rallies had reverberated to the psuedo-monotheistic, *"Ein Volk, ein Reich, ein Fuehrer,"* and German-speaking Austria, with a similar racial background and language, was a natural candidate for "voluntary" union. Already in July 1934, Austrian Nazis attempting a *putsch* (a sudden attempt to overthrow a government) invaded the Viennese Chancellery and tried to assassinate Chancellor Dollfuss while conspirators seized the main radio station to announce the takeover by a Nazi government. Fortunately, the conspirators fled to Munich when the surviving ministers, led by Dr. Schuschnigg, and the Austrian army remained loyal — bolstered by Italian troops rushing to defend the Austrian-Italian border. But the growing friendship between Mussolini and Hitler unnerved Schuschnigg, who concluded a face-to-face "Gentlemen's Agreement" in July 1936, which granted amnesty to all Austrian Nazis imprisoned for arson or terrorism and allowed their sympathizers into the government. (Surprisingly, when Viennese Jews presented *kvittels* on behalf of German and Austrian Jewry and repeatedly pleaded for the Jews of Vienna, the Rebbe would only offer a general, *"Der Eibeshter zoll helfen alle Juden* — The Almightly should help all Jews," a cryptic statement that only became clearer with the passage of time.)

Despite this agreement, Viennese police uncovered a fresh Nazi plot for a *putsch* in January 1938 and an overstrained Schuschnigg desperately embarked on another face-to-face conference — only to be harangued, blackmailed, and bamboozled into abject terms: Legalize Nazis, place police and the ministry of interior under Nazi leader Seyss-Inquart's control, and integrate Austria's economy with the Reich! While Austrian Nazis celebrated with riots and wild demonstrations, the *Wehrmacht* suspended its invasion preparations along the border in the obvious expectation that Schuschnigg's far-reaching capitulation would automatically lead to his overthrow. In a last desperate bid to save his small country's integrity, Schuschnigg called a national referendum for Sunday, March 13, where Austrians should freely vote whether they desired continued independence or union with Germany.

Two days before that proposed vote, Friday, March 11, events rapidly plunged downhill — catching even the Austrians by surprise. Early Friday morning, border traffic was halted when *Wehrmacht* units took up offensive positions all along the frontier. Germany first demanded the referendum be immediately cancelled; Schuschnigg abjectly agreed. Next they urged that he hand over all government power to Seyss-Inquart! Although some of his cabinet ministers advocated defiance, Schuschnigg acquiesced to even this to avoid a civil war, and then broadcast his resignation over the radio. The public takeover by a Nazi cabinet was followed minutes later by Schuschnigg's arrest and a formal request for German troops to assist in "protecting Austria from (non-existent) internal threats."

Throughout Friday night *Wehrmacht* columns rolled unchallenged across Upper Austria en route to Vienna. Shabbos saw the arrival of Gestapo officers led by Himmler and Heydrich to organize their terror machinery throughout the length and breadth of Austria. 80,000 prominent Jews, Social Democrats and others vanished within days into concentration camps; provincial Jews were summarily expelled from the *Siebenbergen* border districts; ordinary Jews were subject to public humiliation, beatings and torture. Less than 24 hours after seizing the Chancellorship, Seyss-Inquart resigned in favor of the Fuehrer and proclaimed Austria's *Anschluss* (accession) to the Reich. Rarely had tyranny gained such an easy victory as when *Grossdeutschland* became the bitter reality. Almost all native Austrians rapturously cheered their involuntary takeover and in the subsequent referendum voted in favor of incorporation into the Greater Reich by a factor of 99.75 percent!

The repercussions were felt immediately, even in faraway Belz. Those who arrived for *Shabbos Zachor* were surprised when the Rebbe delayed his regular entrance for Friday night prayers for an inordinate length of time. When the *gabbaim* went to discover what was detaining him they found him restlessly pacing his room, deeply absorbed in profound thought and Divine devotions. They quickly realized that something, somewhere was seriously amiss but had no idea what it might possibly be. It was only on Motza'ei Shabbos when the first radio reports filtered through with the dire news — Nazi troops have taken over Austria and entered Vienna! — that they finally understood the significance of last night's disruption. Since *shalosh seudos* lingered on after nightfall, chassidim awaited a strong reaction, but surprisingly the Rebbe said only *"Der Eibeshter zoll helfen az die Deutsche alein zollen em arop'nemen tief indr'erd* — Hashem should help that the Germans themselves drag him down, deep into the earth!"

At *Shefoch Chamascha* during the Pesach Seder he added, *"Ich bet Dem Bashefer az die Amolekim fun heint zoll Er oich traben b'af un tashmidem mitachas She'mei Hashem* — I beg the Creator that today's Amalek too should be pursued with anger and wiped out from beneath the heavens!" Even then, few realized how these unexpected and distressing events would shortly intrude upon Eastern Europe directly; naïvely they thought such threats were confined to "Greater Germany" like Austria and perhaps adjacent German-speaking areas. But the Rebbe obviously perceived far more than they did. From then on his severe delays in routine, particularly *tefillos*, became ever more acute as he sensed the looming danger to their thousand-year-old history and heritage.

Shortly after Shavuos, the Belzer Rav was beset by personal tragedy: his daughter Rebbetzin Mirele, married to her cousin Rebbe Moshe Eliyakim Beriah of Hibniv, suddenly became mortally ill and was hospitalized in Lemberg for several months. Her father came to visit her but she passed away, leaving behind her grieving husband and two young orphans, Yeshie'le and Raizel. Everybody was shocked and heartbroken, particularly her close family; the only one to display no visible signs of grief was the Rebbe himself. At her *levayah* he made an extraordinary statement: Addressing his daughter directly, he declared, "You valued only what ought to be appreciated and disliked what ought to be deplored; you did not read unsuitable books; you had faith in *tzaddikim*. Go! Go! You have nothing to fear! You had grandfathers who strolled around the *Kisei HaKavod* like children under their mother's apron!"

Meanwhile the situation on the European mainland continued its downward spiral toward bloodshed and devastation. Czechoslovakia had earlier been earmarked as next in line for Nazi dismemberment, and following Austria's rapid integration, the Reich now threatened the Czech state from three sides. Created after World War I as a new democratic republic enjoying high living standards, Czechoslovakia housed substantial foreign minorities including over 350,000 Jews who wholeheartedly supported the nascent state that granted them religious freedom and full citizen rights. However, they were heavily outnumbered by Slovakian separatists, Polish and Hungarian nationalists — and three million Sudeten Germans under Nazi patronage, the most troublesome of all. Czech democratic traditions were shamelessly exploited by "Gauleiter" Henlein, immediately following up each concession by the Prague government with fresh outrageous demands, demonstrations, and riots.

After the British government dispatched a peace envoy to investigate the "trouble spots" during August 1938, the Germans encouraged Poland and Hungary to lay claim to Czech frontier districts while the *Wehrmacht* were ordered to prepare Operation Green for an armed invasion by October 1st at the latest. Czechoslovakia, however, with an efficient and well-equipped army and Skoda munitions (the largest armaments plant in Central Europe), would be no pushover. German army generals were shocked and tried to refute the decision but their warnings were brushed aside; their chief of staff, General von Beck, courageously resigned, yet it made not the slightest difference. Instead, a vitriolic anti-Czech harangue at the notorious Nuremberg Party Rally brought national tensions to a boiling point. In a last ditch effort to avoid war at all costs, Britain's aged Prime Minister Neville Chamberlain boarded an airplane for the first time and flew to Germany for urgent discussions.

Intense diplomatic maneuvers ensued, during which Britain and France guaranteed Czechoslovakia's safety while forcing the country to accept a gradual transfer of disputed areas to the Reich. The Czechs were horrified at losing the mountainous border region that constituted their defensive front line, but this painful concession did not mollify the Fuehrer, who was secretly furious at being deprived of the need — and excuse — for war. Twisting in the knife, he demanded that his army occupy the surrendered Sudetenland immediately, by October 1! The result of this latest ultimatum was the infamous Munich Conference between France, England, Italy and Germany — Czech delegates (and their likely allies, the Soviet Union) being rigorously excluded from a conference deciding their own fate! In an ultimately futile gesture of appeasement, the "Big Four" abjectly agreed that the *Wehrmacht* could march in the next day, October 1. Czech leaders were gravely warned against any action that might precipitate war, while Russian half-hearted promises of assistance were effectively blocked by Poland. Betrayed and abandoned by their guarantors, the Czechs had little choice but to acquiesce in the dismemberment of their land-locked country.

Such was the relief in England at not having to fight for a "quarrel in a faraway country between people of whom we know nothing." Cheering crowds met Chamberlain's plane in Croydon returning with "Peace in our time"! In Germany, the wild nationalistic celebrations were based on more solid foundations. Not only had their flimsy claims, bluster and brinkmanship gained them large areas in western Czechoslovakia with hardly a casualty or risk on their side, but they had also imposed their will on those prominent European powers who had so recently enforced their *diktat* on a severely defeated Germany after World War I. For the Czech Jews the rapid turn of events was a catastrophe, but German and Austrian communities already suffering an intolerable situation were now inflicted with a nationwide pogrom.

As war fever gave way to xenophobic rejoicing, the Gestapo began rounding up Polish *Ost-Juden* in Germany, where about 50,000 resided, and expelling them. To forestall their repatriation, Poland annulled the citizenship of all nationals living abroad for over five years and lacking a new consular stamp to be entered in their passport before October 1st. Then Polish officials refused the *Ost-Juden* this requisite stamp, effectively denaturalizing them and rendering them stateless overnight. In retaliation, the Germans loaded them onto trains and deported them to the border. Since the Poles had closed the border and the Germans refused re-entry, whole families were stranded in an inhospitable no-man's-land at Zbaszyn under appalling winter conditions, without shelter, warmth, or basic amenities. Among the first batch of these unfortunate Jews were the Grynszpans who had lived in Hanover since 1914. Their son, Hershel, was a student in Paris and the suffering of his innocent parents embittered him so deeply that he determined on vengeance: He went to the German Embassy, there shooting and seriously wounding Ernst vom Rath, the Third Secretary.

Anti-Jewish incitement moved into high gear as the first news reports were aired in Germany; and on November 9th, when early Nazi leaders usually met in Munich to commemorate the anniversary of their premature *putsch* of 1923, news broke that vom Rath had died of his wounds. After conferring at length with Goebbels and agreeing that "the SA should be allowed to have their fling," Hitler left early without addressing the meeting, presumably to distance himself from the subsequent outrages. Goebbels then spewed out an inflammatory peroration demanding "spontaneous demonstrations" to avenge the death; in response, a nationwide pogrom was quickly organized by the brown-shirted storm troopers, ever eager for violence. Led by the SA, sadistic mobs across Germany and Austria set fire to synagogues and Jewish institutions, smashed and ransacked shops and homes and threw their contents out of the windows. The streets were littered with shattered glass — up to half of Belgium's annual production of plate glass! — which the Germans mockingly dismissed as *Kristallnacht*.

According to conservative official estimates, 101 synagogues or temples were burned down and another 76 were demolished, 7,500 stores were ransacked, 35 (actually nearer 100) were killed, and 30,000 men were thrown into Dachau, Buchenwald and Sachsenhausen concentration camps, while thousands more terrified Jews were beaten, manhandled, and publicly humiliated. Acting on official orders, the police and fire services stood idly by, only interfering to prevent fires from spreading to non-Jewish property, to stop private looters, and to protect foreigners. They were also available to arrest "as many able-bodied male Jews — especially rich ones — as local police cells can hold," men who would then have to buy their freedom by abandoning their possessions and emigrating immediately. As if this officially inspired physical violence was not awful enough, German Jewry was hit hard in the pocket by a torrent of fresh decrees rapidly banning them from crafts, export mail-order and stores. Insurance payments for the enormous damage inflicted during *Kristallnacht* was diverted to the government instead, while the victims were forced to pay for these repairs out of their own pocket. Also, existing Jewish businesses and factories were forcibly "Aryanized" and replaced with non-Jewish management. Profits from these state-sponsored seizures, augmented by an enormous and arbitrary billion-marks fine, bolstered near bankrupt government coffers while effectively depleting Jewish financial resources.

Kristallnacht marked a turning point in German society. Jew-baiting had become so respectable and commonplace that small objection was raised by the general populace at the unbridled looting, firebombing, vandalism, public humiliations, beatings, murder, unjustified arrests and incarcerations. Five years of Nazi rule and propaganda had successfully set the stage for unrestrained persecution and genocide. Consummating their goal of "solving the Jewish Question, once and for all, one way or the other ..." the Nazis hastily met to discuss curfews, ghettos and particularly emigration along the lines of their Austrian experience, where rampant SS terror, concentration camps and systematic public humiliation coupled with a centralized "Office for Jewish Emigration" had dramatically reduced the Jewish population. A Central Reich Office *fur die Judische Auswanderung* was duly set up in Germany to accelerate emigration while expropriating any remaining Jewish wealth (later this office was to organize the wartime death trains deporting victims across Europe into the mass killing industrial complexes).

Naturally, the Belzer Rav grew increasingly alarmed at the mounting crisis. As usual, many chassidim arrived for Purim and the previous Shabbos, *Shabbos Zachor* (4 March '39). When R' Yechezkel Reich, the *shochet* of Dembitz, took his leave together with R' Zundel Glantz, instead of contenting himself with the customary blessings the Rebbe turned to them and declared somberly: "Since we Jews became a people, *Klal Yisrael* has never suffered such trials as they are now! Truly I ought to travel myself to Lizhensk (Lezajsk) to the holy Rebbe, Reb Elimelech, *zechuso yagen aleinu*. But Heaven knows that I cannot ... therefore I wish to appoint you two as my emissaries!" This was a little surprising since the Glantz family was descended from a respectable line of Kohanim, yet the Belzer Rav instructed them to visit the shrine the following week, on the *yahrzeit*, 21 Adar. The Rav said that they should approach close to the *kever* on his behalf and recite all of *Tehillim* while concentrating "that the *rasha* should receive a *mapalah* — downfall." On no account should they mention that evil man's name, "since that empowers the *Sitra Achra*"! (As already mentioned, the Rebbe was always careful to never use the Fuehrer's personal name.)

Foreign affairs meanwhile continued to deteriorate and again the setting was Czechoslovakia. The Munich Conference had also ordered the Czech government to grant autonomy to the Slovak nationalists led by the anti-Semitic Catholic priest, Monsignor Jozef Tiso. But the Slovakians, stimulated by Germany, were dissatisfied with mere autonomy and demanded full independence and secession from Czechoslovakia. President Hacha, the new Czech leader, tried to prevent the breakup of his country by dismissing the regional Slovak government but Tiso appealed directly to Hitler. Threatening war once again, Hitler summoned the aged Hacha to Berlin and under threats of aerial bombardment proposed brutal terms: total Slovakian independence plus German occupation throughout the remainder of the dismembered state! Hacha fainted on the spot but medical treatment revived him sufficiently to sign a communiqué "placing the fate of the Czech people in the hands of the Fuehrer"! Barely two hours later, as the 15th of March 1939 dawned, the *Wehrmacht* rolled unchallenged across the Czech border and into Prague.

This latest naked aggression, unjustified and inexcusable, stiffened even arch-appeasers like Chamberlain and shocked the world at large. Most fearful of all were Europe's Jewish communities. Now even those who enjoyed the tolerance and hospitality of the Czech democracy became subject to the vicious Jew-baiting that ruled in "Greater Germany." Where would it all end? Polish Jews, just across Czechoslovakia's northern borders, were particularly apprehensive since the Nazi army now directly menaced them from both the west and south while Communist Russia to the east was a capricious ally at best. The Polish communities had overwhelming problems of their own following the destruction of their religious infrastructure in the

German and Russian invasions of World War I, and from which they had still not fully recovered. Relations with the Polish government and populace, furthermore, were on a downward slide.

Following newly won independence after World War I, an increasingly vociferous Polish nationalism manifested itself by harsh economic and educational discrimination culminating with widespread personal attacks and even pogroms. The poisonous influence of Nazi legislation and oppression seeped across the border, encouraging the neo-fascist government of 1935 to propose the "evacuation" of numerous Jews from Poland, disenfranchising Jewish citizens abroad, and almost succeeding in outlawing *shechitah*. Naturally the ocean of torment and suffering resulted in a flood of requests and supplications pouring into Belz for the Rebbe's *berachah* and prayers, as one of his *gabbaim* described in a letter to an American chassid:

> ... As to your asking, "Vos zogt Der Rebbe zum matzav — What does the Rebbe say to the present situation?" I must tell you that generally we hear nothing. But when we read him telegrams or messages from abroad such as from Germany, Vienna, Czechoslovakia, Hungary and also Poland — it is evidently visible how intensely he identifies with their plight. His face is like a flaming beacon! Also, whenever he prays at the Amud as at a yahrzeit, when he utters the tefillah of Lamalshinim and enunciates the words se'aker, u'seshaber, u'semager very clearly and at great length — everyone present hearing those words from his holy mouth shakes with fear and trembling! May Hashem Yisbarach take mercy and hearken to the prayers of the tzadikei hador and rapidly rescue us from this bitter galus, for our brethren are presently in a terrible crisis and have no one to turn to but our Father in Heaven ...

Shortly after Shavuos (May 24-25, 1939), the Belzer Rav distractedly paced his room, groaning loudly while quietly repeating to himself: "What should the Jews do now? Where can they run to? During the last war they fled to Hungary where they found sanctuary. Now the borders are closed — and what will happen there?" When his *gabbai* R' Nachman Hirsch revealed this ominous scene to intimate chassidim, they received some small inkling of the approaching catastrophe.

The Rebbe at the train station in Marienbad (in previous years)

Obviously, the enormous mental and emotional effort placed a great strain on the Belzer Rav's weakened physique, but his favorite place of convalescence, the spa-town of Marienbad, was now under Nazi occupation and off-limits. Indeed, following the German invasion, some Marienbad hoteliers had in the first instance fled to Belz, with which they had developed an affinity over the years. "If they would ask me to visit Lowicz," the Rebbe once mused aloud, "I wouldn't refuse." Lowicz was a quaint historical town on the Bzura River west of Warsaw (on the Sochaczew highway), rather undeveloped and noted for its clear, refreshing air. When the community heard of his statement, a delegation traveled to Belz to invite him. Surprisingly, although he went there for the clean air, he asked that the windows of his room be left tightly shut. When his host suggested that he perhaps enjoy a short walk outside in the fresh air, the Rebbe replied enigmatically, "I've heard that the *Divrei Chaim* said that where the air is good, it goes through the walls!"

Unusual though this attitude was and hardly the general idea of rest and vacation, he had consistently acted this way. In the pre-War years, following medical treatment from Berlin specialists during 1928, he spent time recuperating in the nearby spa-town of Bad Homburg. His rooms had been booked in advance by his

Rebbe Yissachar Ber in Marienbad; to the right is Reb Yosel of Yarotschev, to the left is the gabbai, Reb Aharon Yehoshua

close chassid R' Chaim Nota Katz (later of England), but when the Rebbe arrived he remarked, "You hired a *guteh dirah* ... yet you forgot one thing — it does not have double-windows." Although he was racked with pain and mostly bedridden, those windows remained tightly shut throughout his six-week stay! (Indeed, he agreed only reluctantly to make a small meal of buttered bread just once a day after persistent pleading by his Rebbetzin — who promised to personally prepare his food exactly as her namesake and great-grandmother Rebbetzin Malkah had for the Sar Shalom — combined with the gentle persuasion of his "loyal chassid and good friend" R' Chaim Nota.)

Earlier still, after his father specifically instructed him to benefit from the pure air when taking his annual breaks, he would open his window once a day while reciting, "I hereby wish to fulfill the Biblical commandment of *kibud av*," take just one gulp of fresh air and shut it again until the morrow! Likewise, when Rebbe Avraham Mordche Alter of Gur, the *Imrei Emes*, visited Rav Yissachar Ber at Marienbad before World War I, he found that while the entire Belzer entourage had gone out to take the energizing waters and breathe the enticing air, Reb Ahare'le remained steadfastly in his rooms. "To travel these great distances to be with his father yet not venture out-side at all?" he pondered in admiration. "What an amazing young man the Belzer Rav's son is!" (as recalled by his own son, Rebbe Yisrael, the *Beis Yisrael*, over forty years later). Similarly, when Rav Yissachar Ber ordered a nourishing meal for his ethereal son in Marienbad during 1915, Reb Ahare'le feasted his eyes on the heaped tray, gratefully described its contents in detail — before designat-ing his *shammas* R' Shmuel Stroitzer as his personal *shaliach* to eat it all for the mitzvah of *kibud av*! But now, of course, the only visitors enjoying the delights and spa waters of Marienbad were the hateful Nazi occupiers and their sympathizers.

On the international scene, the invasion of Czechoslovakia moved England and France to offer cast-iron guarantees to Poland, Germany's next presumable victim. (Italy's unprovoked attack on Albania also prompted guarantees to Greece and Romania plus an agreement with Turkey.) In reaction, Germany canceled their German-Polish Pact of 1934 as well as their Anglo-German Naval Agreement of '35. Tension mounted when Lithuania yielded the border port of Memel after ultimatums from Nazi Foreign Minister von Ribbentrop; this in turn put pressure on the Polish port of Danzig — officially an international Free City under the post-War Versailles Treaty — where local Nazi sympathizers rallied to the emotive cry, *Heims ins Reich* (Back to the Reich).

One key to the Polish situation was held by their contentious neighbor to the east — Soviet Russia — through whose terri-tory any Western aid would have to be funneled. Yet Russia's tentative overtures to the West were tainted by mutual distrust. Public and political opinion in the West was split over the is-sue: many preferred the Nazis as a European bulwark against the "Red Menace"; others hoped these two powerful enemies would destroy each other, leaving the West the ultimate victors; it was mainly left-wingers who welcomed Communist Russia to a common front against fascism. The campaign at the League of Nations in Geneva by Maxim Litvinov, Soviet foreign minister, to surround and disable Germany with "Collective Security" had gained ground but it was severely undermined by Stalinist purges and show-trials back in Russia, and in May 1939 Litvinov was suddenly dismissed by Stalin. Over the years Litvinov had been persistently vilified by Goebbels for being a Jew, a leading Communist, supporter of the League of Nations, a peace advocate and an effective campaigner against fascism; with characteristic opportunism, expediency and deceit, Nazi foreign diplomacy rapidly swung into action.

Russia had signed the Rapallo Treaty of friendship with Germany in 1922 but that had lapsed with the Nazi rise to power and their virulent anti-Bolshevism: the "rotten Bolshevik Empire ripe for dissolution" had long been their target of enmity and eventual invasion ever since the publication of *Mein Kampf*. Now, however, the Germans quickly prepared to "make a pact with Satan"! What began as Russian weapon supply problems from the munitions factories of Skoda in Czechoslovakia, now occupied by Germany, swiftly developed into a full blown Russo-German treaty to the amazement of all concerned. Germany was in an extraordinary hurry because they had already drawn up military plans for Poland's invasion, their army was ready and waiting at the border, and political pretexts had already been cynically manufactured. Moreover, they had already fixed the date for Operation White since they wanted their *blitzkrieg* campaign against Poland completed before the autumn rains arrived.

Rapprochement between the two archenemies proceeded at a bewildering pace in comparison with the normal diplomatic calendar: On April 17, the Russian ambassador to Berlin paid a rare visit to the German Foreign Office to discuss Skoda's arms supplies and offered the bait of "normal or even better relations." On May 3, Litvinov was summarily replaced by Vyascheslav Molotov, a ruthless and tough non-Jew close to Stalin who was willing to adopt a pro-German line. On May 30, the German Foreign Office advised their Moscow ambassador, Count von Schulenberg, "In a reversal of previous policy, we have now decided to undertake definite negotiations with the Soviet Union." Schulenberg duly established contacts with Molotov and undercover trade talks continued throughout June against the backdrop of continuing tension and violence against Poland in Danzig and the Polish Corridor. On August 19, Stalin informed his astonished Politburo of their new trade pact with Germany.

Meanwhile Schulenberg asked if von Ribbentrop — ex-champagne salesman and now Germany's top diplomat — might make a personal visit. Acutely embarrassed, Russia hesitated to permit the Nazi foreign minister to set foot in the Soviet capital, but Hitler intervened with an urgent and personal request to Stalin and on August 23 (just three days before the scheduled date for the Polish invasion) Ribbentrop flew in for high-level and fast-paced talks — leaving the rest of the world aghast and apprehensive. All afternoon he conferred with Stalin about a proposed Non-Aggression Pact; the text was agreed upon by evening and signed after midnight! Ostensibly obligating both parties to merely "desist from violence, attack or aggression individually or jointly with other powers," secret protocols of the Nazi-Soviet Pact demarcated their future spheres of influence in a carved up Eastern Europe — giving Germany a free hand in western Poland and Lithuania. Germany, with its overwhelming superiority in manpower and equipment, was now free to crush Poland while Stalin held the ring to the east. The fate of Europe and its vast reservoir of Jews was now cynically sealed.

Yet there was a slight delay. The proposed secret date for the unprovoked invasion was Saturday, August 26, but a day earlier Britain finally formalized its written guarantee to Poland. As a result, Germany temporarily suspended Operation White while attempting to detach the British government from its solemn commitment. Ribbentrop suggested to the British ambassador that Germany be allowed a free hand in Europe in return for the Nazis guaranteeing "the integrity of the British Empire" — an offer even Chamberlain rejected out of hand. Operation White was rescheduled for September 1, 1939 (17 Elul 5699, *Erev Shabbos Ki Savo*) and 1½ million German troops lined up all along the border. German Radio broadcast a 16-point "Peace Plan" they falsely claimed Poland had rejected while manufacturing another pretext for aggression: a faked attack on their own radio transmitter at Gleiwicz, Silesia with the aid of SS commandos and a murdered concentration camp inmate camouflaged in a Polish army uniform.

Until then Germany had gained territory by bluff and stealth; for the first time it was to be open and remorseless warfare. Although they had initiated a treaty of friendship with Poland just five years earlier, now they were to wage ruthless, relentless combat with little justification — even according to their own propaganda — yet few Germans or army leaders raised objections. Instead they willingly executed the orders of the lowly corporal now termed "Supreme Commander" and shared an intense national pride in the *Wehrmacht's* stunning success. At 6:30 a.m. four massive Panzer columns breached Poland's international borders and advanced rapidly from the north (East Prussia), northwest (Pomerania), southwest (Silesia), and south (newly occupied Slovakia), while the *Luftwaffe* quickly achieved complete air superiority after knocking out most Polish planes on the ground and shattering Polish communications. Fast moving German motorcyclists and their armed sidecar comrades easily defeated the Polish cavalry, which was still using horses! Behind them rumbled heavy tanks and the latest weaponry, all working in close tandem with their air cover overhead (standard tactics now but an innovation then). The main campaign was largely decided in a week.

Meanwhile, the invasion was met by a deafening silence emanating from Western capitals. Apparently Chamberlain still hoped against hope that Mussolini, the Italian dictator, might yet be able to persuade his fascist allies to withdraw their invasion troops. Urgent contacts with France and Britain continued for the next few days until the British ambassador to Berlin finally delivered an ultimatum: unless all German troops withdrew from Poland and all aggressive action ceased by 11 a.m. Sunday, September 3, a state of war would exist between Britain and Germany. A few hours later France sent a similarly blunt message. But tough words were not followed by tough action.

The only hope for Poland and its substantial Jewish population — now that Soviet Russia had tacitly acquiesced in Poland's dismemberment — would be a powerful attack on Germany's western borders while the bulk of its army was still entangled in Poland since, in a high-risk strategy, only twenty-three German divisions had remained behind to defend the Fatherland. Yet

France, with 110 well-trained and armed divisions (augmented by British Expeditionary Forces) under its command, contented itself with ineffectually patrolling their huge line of fortifications along the Maginot Line — a defensive tactic, although no German attack could have been in the offing. Aggressive Nazi *blitzkrieg* was met by passive French *"zitzkrieg"* since France's High Command were already fearful of Germany's rapid conquests in Poland and their likely counterattack if France honored their treaty with Poland too literally. By their hesitation, they betrayed Poland and allowed the Allies to be picked off individually nine months later. Had they attacked when the *Wehrmacht* was unsure of itself and the Nazi leadership still insecure, millions of innocents might yet have been spared, and years of untold slavery and suffering avoided. Sadly, the very last chance to halt the aggressors in their tracks was badly bungled; appeasement at Munich was now compounded by military vacillation: "phony war" versus "total war."

By contrast, German tactics were ruthless, remorseless and brutal. With total air superiority in Poland, they rained death and destruction down on military and civilian targets without distinction, repeatedly dive-bombing town centers or gleefully swooping down to strafe and machine-gun swarms of panic-stricken refugees fleeing along the highways in all directions. Warsaw alone was consecutively bombed from the air for twenty-three days, and that peaked on Thursday, September 13 (Erev Rosh Hashanah) when they singled out the Jewish Quarter, collapsing blocks of housing and setting whole streets on fire. Yet despite their hopeless military position, the Poles fought on in the vain hope that the West might finally come to their aid.

Within two weeks most of their large country was overrun and Warsaw was under siege, yet with the Mayor's stubborn leadership the capital refused to surrender. On Sunday, September 17, the day the Polish government fled to the Romanian border (and eventually to Britain), Russia announced, "The Republic of Poland has ceased to exist!" and dispatched its army to easily overrun the eastern half in accordance with its secret agreement with Germany. Finally, on September 27 (Erev Succos), Warsaw capitulated and German troops swaggered in; their Polish campaign was successfully complete. The next day von Ribbentrop and Molotov met again to agree to a new Boundary Treaty adjusting their respective "spheres of influence," with Germany conceding even more ground in eastern Poland and the Baltic states.

Back in Warsaw, there had been no let-up in the fighting for three weeks. Thousands lay dead or dying, and it was barely a few hours to Yom Tov. Yet Jews frantically scavenged among the bombed ruins to rebuild hundreds of *succos* and later queued for hours to recite the blessings over the few complete sets of *arba minim* that had evaded the bitter siege. With the German soldiers intoxicated with conquest and power it was dreadfully dangerous to be out on the street. Every Jew — particularly religious Jews — was a prime target for attack and persecution. Everything that had been inflicted upon German Jewry incrementally during the last six years was rapidly visited upon the Jews of Poland in swift succession.

In countless speeches, articles and films, Nazi propaganda had spewed out hatred and venom; now in conquered Poland they had ample opportunity under war conditions to carry out their warped racist policies. Everything that had been perpetrated against the hapless Jews until now was as nothing compared to the horrors that were to come. In the lies and double-talk that characterized Nazi statements, the Fuehrer had publicly warned in the *Reichstag* at the end of January 1939: "... If international finance Jewry within Europe and abroad should succeed once more in plunging the peoples into a world war, then the consequences will not be the Bolshevization of the world and therefore a Jewish victory, but on the contrary, the destruction of the Jewish race in Europe!" Blunt words, but few took them literally, just as they had earlier ignored his equally candid threats in *Mein Kampf*. (In the last chapter he had even written that at least 12,000 or 15,000 of "these Hebrew corrupters" should have been held under poison gas during the First World War.) In his declaration of war against Poland in the *Reichstag* on September 1st 1939 he further threatened: "Whoever fights with poison will be fought back with poison gas. Whoever deviates from the rules for the humane conduct of war can expect nothing else but that we will take the same steps!" As usual he projected onto his enemies — real or imagined — his own monstrous intentions.

The persecution began immediately upon the invasion since special squads — the notorious SS *Einsatzgruppen* — were attached to the army, and their sadistic atrocities and wholesale murders shocked even *Wehrmacht* generals despite their thorough indoctrination to look on innocent Jews as "parasites and vermin to be completely cleaned out." Pogroms and duplicate *Kristallnacht* were repeated in every new district captured by the Nazis; amid a welter of looting and burning, most synagogues were destroyed or turned into stables, *peyos* and beards brutally shorn, religious Jews forced to clean streets with their *talleisim* or burn holy *sefarim* and dance around the flames. After conferring with military headquarters to ensure they did not interfere with the SS' "essential tasks," a major conference was held in Berlin on September 21, while the fighting was still going on, to organize an *Einsatzgruppe* master-plan for isolating and decimating the Jewish population.

Schemes agreed upon included forcing Jews out of rural areas into the cities, concentrating them in ghettos confined with curfews and adjacent to rail junctions (for further secret measures), and establishing *Judenrat* "fully responsible to German orders under severest penalties" to list all inhabitants by age, gender and useful occupation. As soon as economically feasible, all Jewish businesses and factories would be Aryanized and transferred to non-Jewish ownership. Jews in the Reich, meanwhile, were to be transported in freight wagons to join their Polish brethren. Detailed copies of these plans were circulated to the army, government departments and the civil administration of the occupied territories — the entire German bureaucracy — but ominously they stressed that the unspecified "final aim" of these measures must remain strictly secret.

In early October, Poland itself was divided between the northwestern territories now annexed by Germany and strictly off-limits to Jews (the industrial town of Lodz a notable exception) and the newly designated *General-government* which became a general dumping ground for all undesirables in Nazi eyes. At the same time, Nazi leaders created a vast "Jewish Reservation" in the

Lublin district (in Eastern Poland) and at first deported tens of thousands there from the Reich and the newly annexed territories. Later they spoke of a "Madagascar Plan" to forcibly transport all Jews to the French island colony off Eastern Africa, but both schemes were abruptly dropped. Also in early October, the evil supremo of the Gestapo and SS, Heinrich Himmler, was appointed Reich Commissar for German reclamation and racial purity, thus effectively placing his terror apparatus in overall command in Poland, above the civil governors and even the army. In the first six months of occupation Jews were required to wear identifying arm bands, liable to forced labor in camps and German installations, forbidden access to city centers, and allotted smaller food rations, while thousands were killed at random and all were subject to arbitrary terror and violence. The stage for the most horrendous crime in human history had been set.

CHAPTER 5

THE OUTBREAK
OF WAR

CONTRARY TO NAZI PROPAGANDA, THE SECOND World War was not a "Jewish War" — and certainly not the Polish Jews' war. They had all too painful memories of the previous German invasion during the "Great War" — the First World War that, it was falsely claimed, would end all wars. At first the Germans had suffered setbacks in their early battles with Russia on the Eastern Front and had been rebuffed in Poland. But the appointments of Field Marshal Paul von Hindengburg and General Frich von Ludendorf turned the tide. In the winter of 1914-15, they captured Western Poland and Galicia; then went on in 1915 to take most of Poland, Lithuania, the rest of Galicia and parts of Russia, which they held until the end of the war. While the behavior of the German military and administration in World War I was in no way comparable to their unspeakable conduct during World War II, it was way short of being beneficial.

Even when the fighting was over, their civil administrators had treated Poland as a backward and primitive colony to be forcibly "civilized" by a flood of autocratic directives, while they looted Poland's wealth and shipped whole factories and their contents back to Germany

Residents of Belz digging trenches before the advance of the German army

— this, when Polish industrialization was in its infancy. They beggared a rising class of Jewish magnates; poverty and disease were rampant, especially near the various battlegrounds. Rebbe Yissachar Ber and his large family were not alone in being forced to flee to Hungary. Many rabbis and *kehillah* members fled likewise while the general communal structure in Poland and Lithuania collapsed; it was fully recovering only at the onset of World War II. Now it was to be destroyed forever.

Belz's geographic position in the east of Galician Poland and nearer to Russia meant it had little strategic significance during the early phase of the invasion. As a consequence, it was spared the fierce and bloody land battles when German tank divisions destroyed the outdated Polish cavalry. Nonetheless, Belz's local railroad depot and outer suburbs were among those ruthlessly bombed from the air in the first days of hostilities. In reaction, the Polish army moved anti-aircraft batteries into Belz. Since the famous shul had been so solidly constructed — almost as a castle — the army stationed their anti-aircraft guns on the synagogue roof and began fashioning camouflage cover. Fearing the precious shul would become a target for vicious German bombing, Rebbe Aharon managed to persuade the area's supreme army commander to relinquish the position. In any event, the Polish army retreated peacefully from Belz, hardly firing a shot.

The shul before the War

As a relative oasis of calm among an inferno of remorseless warfare, Belz was soon flooded by panic-stricken civilians desperately seeking sanctuary under the protective wing of the holy Belzer Rav. To cope with the emergency, several of the *yoshvim* — more usually geared to catering to the regular influx of chassidim arriving for the Yamim Tovim — swung into action. Under the Rebbe's instructions, they ensured that nobody went without the basic necessities of food or shelter. Local householders were persuaded to relinquish even their own beds in favor of the penniless refugees and their families. With the halachic sanction of the town *dayanim*, some fugitives were permitted to board in the various shuls. On the eve of Rosh Hashanah, the Belzer Rav ordered that food be prepared for all the many "guests" and also decreed that food shops remain open over Yom Tov so that any refugees could freely help themselves on his account! This bold move guaranteed that all the fugitives had more than enough to eat over Yom Tov.

However, many of the Rebbe's closest advisers were not happy about his remaining in Belz over Yom Tov and wanted the Belzer Rav to evacuate much further eastward "until the *Wehrmacht* had finally been repulsed." Had not his saintly father Rebbe Yissachar Ber left Belz for Hungary during the previous war? It was no secret that the Nazis would persecute all Polish Jews in short order, and there were the most alarming reports from areas already captured. Wherever the German army marched, they had repeated the outrages of *Kristallnacht:* singling out shuls for burning while robbing, torturing and murdering members of the *kehillos.* Shocked eyewitnesses related how they had particularly selected religious Jews and their leaders for humiliation and slaughter.

Most worrying of all, Nazi propaganda before the War had repeatedly publicized photographs of the Belzer Rebbe visiting Marienbad among pictures of other *Wunder Rabbiner,* so he was likely to be one of their prime targets. Nor was there any hope the War would pass them by, as those three large bombs earlier dropped on Belz had rudely reminded them.

Keeping ahead of the rapidly advancing German army was a formidable challenge. Above all, there was a grave shortage of adequate vehicles or transport since most had already been requisitioned by the Polish army during their confused retreat. Some trains were still operating but only in an erratic fashion due to the shifting battlefront. With unpredictable alterations to the schedule, route and destinations, there was no guarantee any train might not instead deliver the fleeing refugees straight into the hands of their hated pursuers.

While well aware of the dangers, the Rebbe resolved to remain in Belz until the last moment rather than abandon his post. As a compromise, he agreed to station a wagon and horses at the ready, prepared for all emergencies. Now the Belzer Rebbe felt responsible for the welfare of the horses bought on his orders and was concerned that in the confusion and panic, his household would forget to care for the animals now under their charge. He refused to eat his meager — and only — meal late at night after his usual day-long *tefillos* until he was assured that those horses had been fed first. "And what is with the horses?" he would cross-question his faithful *gabbai.* "Did anybody remember to feed them? Were they not bought for my needs, for any emergencies? *Al pi din* I cannot eat anything until I check this out!"

His consideration for animals was not a recently acquired character trait. In peacetime, the Rebbe had bought horses and assigned them to the care of a local wagon driver, just to share in this particular mitzvah of granting priority to feeding one's animals each morning before eating oneself. It had also given him the opportunity to obey the Biblical injunction against working one's animals over Shabbos. Reportedly, the Belzer Rebbe would personally refrain from traveling in a wagon drawn by a single horse so as not to overburden a lone cart horse.

Other than ordering the horses and cart for emergencies, Rebbe Aharon Rokach calmly continued his saintly *avodas hakodesh* almost as if nothing had happened. The normal *tisch* continued as usual, chassidim still arrived for *berachos* and advice, groups of young men known as *yoshvim* remained engrossed in learning and *tefillah*. One major change, however, was in his approachability. Until then, chassidim often had to queue for hours until they were admitted to the inner sanctum. Now, in response to the troubled times, he was available at set times to offer reassurance and comfort, "healing broken hearts and bandaging their sorrows."

Naturally, the bloodcurdling reports of early Nazi oppression gave the Belzer Rebbe no respite. As he told one close chassid, "*Yidden* are wandering the streets and I should rest here? They are being persecuted and exiled from one place to another. *Ich ken nisht zitzen! Es stecht mir yedem eiver!* I can't stay here any longer! The suffering pierces my every limb."

In addition to the innumerable refugees who had thronged to Belz, hundreds of chassidim arrived for the hallowed days of *Yamim Noraim*, encompassing Rosh Hashanah and Yom Kippur. From the Shabbos announcing the onset of Elul, an intense atmosphere of seriousness and introspection would descend on Belz. Crowds of ardent chassidim would push forward each Rosh Hashanah Shacharis to hear the unforgettable roar of "*HaMelech!*" uttered by their quivering and trembling Rebbe. Usually, the number of chassidim attending the holy days in Belz could be numbered in the many thousands, but not this year. All the roads were blocked with advancing and retreating armies and crowded with thousands of confused families fleeing in all directions. Only the bravest of souls with the closest empathy with

The Rebbe in an open, horse-drawn carriage

the Rebbe and the necessary self-sacrifice for Chassidus still struggled through to Belz against all obstacles.

Those fortunate to have arrived earlier vividly remembered how the Belzer Rav fervently intoned the first *Selichos*, particularly the chant *B'Motza'ei Menuchah*, as he sobbingly entreated, "*P'nei na el ha'teloyos v'al lachata'os* (Be swayed by the sufferings and not by transgressions) ... *Tar'em nisecha Oseh gedolos* (Show them Your miracles, O Performer of outstanding deeds) ..." His listeners could palpably sense the major battle being waged in Heaven between the forces of good and evil. Several times his closest chassidim heard him implore repeatedly, "*Nor nisht in die hent fun dem folk* — At least not in the hands of this nation." By "this nation," most understood him to be referring to the bloodthirsty Germans whom his father Rebbe Yissachar Ber had frequently castigated since the outbreak of the First World War.

Because of the exceptional situation, Rebbe Aharon instituted some changes for Rosh Hashanah. Generally, all the townspeople of Belz would gather with the chassidim in the large shul for prayers and *tekias shofar*. This year, the Belzer Rav ordered that a separate *minyan* be arranged for his closest chassidim in the *graiser-stieb* — the large hall adjacent to the Rebbe's residence, with a capacity for between 2,000 and 3,000 men, where the *tisch* was usually held. This allowed the chassidim to sing the traditional *nigunim* and *daven* all the *Yotzros* as usual, until late in the afternoon, while sparing the many hungry refugees the long Belzer *tefillos*. Because the Rebbe had dispatched his *baal tefillah, baal kriah* and *baal toke'ah* to conduct the official town *minyan*, which began earlier, the Belzer Rav personally prayed this year with the chassidim.

On the second evening of Rosh Hashanah (September 15), as they were seated at their *seudah* in the *beis hamedrash*, panic-stricken messengers arrived with terrifying news. In response to the general breakdown of law and order following the German invasion, a local militia had been established in the Belz area, mainly with Jewish volunteers, but this was apparently an insufficient deterrent. Taking advantage of the uncertain war situation, a large group of Ukrainian villagers had now gathered to attack and loot the Jews of Belz. Immediately, the men sprang up from their festive meal and raced outside, uttering bloodcurdling screams. When the Ukrainian gangs saw hundreds of men running toward them ready to do battle, they dropped their weapons and fled back into the forests in panic. Not a single marauder remained in the vicinity of Belz. For the moment, the Belz *kehillah* was safe, but this respite was not to last as the area passed from hand to hand.

On Monday, September 19, the first German combatants arrived. It was a small, lightly armed, forward patrol of thirty soldiers, but the terror they caused the civilians of Belz was worthy of a large armored brigade. First, they swooped on the local police station to confiscate their weapons before pushing on. But they informed the police to expect the arrival of regular *Wehrmacht* troops that same evening. The alarming news spread through the town like wildfire, precipitating panic and pandemonium. Obviously, the Jewish population was the most agitated, and communal leaders hastened to the Rebbe, urging him to flee.

However, the Belzer Rav was still engaged in prayer and he signaled that he had no intention of leaving until he completed his *tefillos*! Given the extreme danger, his reply made little sense unless he had no wish nor intention of leaving town just yet. Nonetheless, none of his closest chassidim dared question why he was not thinking of escaping at the last moment, since they were fully convinced of the Rebbe's prescience. It was obvious to them that he did not accept the general consensus either that the German arrival was imminent or that the situation had now become *pikuach nefesh* (life threatening).

By the time the Rebbe's prayers were completed, night had already fallen. In that precarious situation, nobody dared venture out after dark or suggest traveling anywhere. Anxiously, everybody waited for the approaching heavy tread of German tanks and motorized troop carriers, but nothing untoward ensued. After a night of fearful apprehension, the residents of Belz awoke to the glad tidings that there had been a "change of plan" and the Germans would not be coming after all.

While the *Wehrmacht* had indeed been stationed in nearby Hibniv (Uhnow) as the patrol had claimed, they had not driven straight down the short distance to Belz but had instead advanced on other strategic positions in the surrounding countryside. The next few days passed relatively peacefully until Friday, Erev Yom Kippur (September 22), when the Polish army suddenly returned to Belz in strength to prepare for a major clash with German battalions in the vicinity.

All through the night of Yom Kippur and the next day, Polish army convoys rumbled constantly through the small town. Many of the Jewish soldiers and officers desperately wanted a *berachah* from the Holy Miracle Rebbe. Before Shacharis, they queued up to importune the Belzer Rav that they be shielded from any religious predicament and return safely home from the battlefield. As a consequence the Rebbe delayed joining the Yom Kippur *tefillos* until 2 in the afternoon. As before, the Rebbe *davened* with his chassidim in the *graiser-stieb* while the famous shul was given over to the countless refugees.

The Polish army marched out to battle that morning in an orderly fashion, but they were no match for the better equipped German forces. By *Neilah*, at the completion of the Yom Kippur prayers, their confused retreat had begun back toward Belz. The army

The Rebbe's house in Belz before the War

commanders rapidly realized they had no hope of defeating the invading Germans; they would only achieve record numbers of dead and wounded for no visible benefit. During their short clash, the Poles had taken heavy casualties indeed. Consequently, they advised all their men to make their own way home as best they could. Since most of Belz's non-Jewish residents had already fled, those injured in battle were abandoned to their fate.

Stepping into the breach, the Rebbe instructed the *kehillah* that all the wounded Polish soldiers be billeted at Jewish homes and institutions where they were to be treated with indescribable care and kindness. In addition, on the day following Yom Kippur, long tables laden with food were set up in the courtyards of the famous shul and *beis hamedrash,* and needy Poles and Jews were served alike without distinction. The food was prepared in the Rebbe's own kitchens — although severe shortages were already evident — and clothes were likewise distributed to all who needed them.

A day later (September 25), at 11 p.m. Monday night, Russian army trucks suddenly arrived to park on the large square in front of the Rebbe's house (where previously, local wagon drivers gathered to ferry chassidim home after Yom Tov and Shabbos). Most of the townspeople were already asleep; only the *yoshvim* were still engaged in learning at the *beis hamedrash*. Investigating the source of the unusual noise, they were confronted by the serried ranks of unfamiliar army vehicles. Fortunately, one of the *yoshvim* knew some Russian and was able to communicate with the soldiers. Apparently, many of their high ranking officers were Jewish and some even claimed kinship with the Belzer Rav since they too were descendants of the Chernobyl-Twersky dynasty!

They insisted on entering the Rebbe's residence to assure him that he had nothing to fear since he was now under their protection. They would keep a close eye on him and ensure that he would come to no harm. Accordingly, the trepidation in Belz lessened somewhat, but worrying rumors soon surfaced that the area might yet be surrendered to the Nazis.

Following the infamous "non-aggression" Ribbentrop-Molotov Pact signed on August 23, 1939 dividing "spheres of influence" between Nazi-Germany and Communist Russia, the Soviet army had first waited on the sidelines for two and a half weeks while Poland was largely overwhelmed. By September 17, Poland's defeat was only a matter of time and the Polish government retreated to a safe haven on the Romanian border. Claiming Poland had ceased to exist as a separate sovereign entity, Russia invaded from the east to take their share of the spoils. Two days later, they met up with German army units outside Brisk before fanning out to establish a presence in as much territory as possible. During this unofficial partition of Poland, only Warsaw, the capital, still held out against vicious aerial bombardment and shelling.

Once Warsaw capitulated, von Ribbentrop and Molotov were due to sign a new treaty adjusting the extent of their respective spheres of influence. Although Russia's army had taken just a small share in the fighting and he was being freely handed dismembered parts of Poland on a plate, Stalin drove a hard bargain. In the cynical horse-trading which passed for diplomacy in Russo-German relations, the Soviet totalitarian leader pressed for more ground than had originally been agreed upon. In addition to southeastern Poland, he demanded that the three Baltic states of Latvia, Estonia and Lithuania should also be included in his sphere of influence. The Germans countered by trying to reduce the amount of territory in Poland proper that would be awarded to Russia as their prize for "non-aggression." While the Russians had wanted the new boundary drawn down the large River San (that would have included Belz as part of their new territory), the Nazis now suggested that the border run along the equally large River Bug — which would have meant their controlling Belz.

So even if the Russian army had taken up residence in Belz, it was by no means clear that they would retain it indefinitely. Although Communist Russia was strictly anti-religious, Russian rule was eminently more preferable to German, judging by the first reports from the zones under Nazi occupation. The Belzer Rav took great interest in these negotiations and remarked, "At least the Russians don't burn down shuls and yeshivos!"

Unfortunately, even the friendly army commanders in Belz were not privy to the latest, accurate information. Warsaw eventually capitulated to the *Wehrmacht* on Wednesday, 14 Tishrei, Erev Succos, thus successfully concluding the German campaign. On the morrow, the first day of Succos (September 28), Ribbentrop and Molotov finally signed their German-Soviet Boundary and Friendship Treaty with several secret protocols that adjusted the borders agreed upon in their previous pact a month earlier. Even then, the Russian commanders in Belz professed not to know of any impending withdrawal and as a result, rumor and counter-rumor flourished, based on speculation and half truths.

On Yom Tov the community had other, more immediate concerns too. Because of the brutal fighting and occupation that isolated Eastern Poland, there were few sets of *arba minim* available. To obtain an *esrog* with the beauty that the Rebbe was accustomed to was asking for the impossible. Yet precisely the impossible transpired due to what superficially appeared to be a fortuitous oversight. Imperfect *esrog* samples for Belz's *succah* decorations were customarily shipped out by *Mendel Friedman & Sons Esrogim* in Meah Shearim every year since the days of Rebbe Yeshie'le. (When these *esrogim* and apples that hung in the *succah* were ritually given out to excited chassidim after Yom Tov, the privileged recipients celebrated that almost as a festival of its own!) In addition, Reb Mendel Friedman would also select a few choice *esrogim* for the Rebbe's own use and dispatch these in a separate box.

Naturally, these perfect samples were not entrusted to the ordinary mail but were hand-carried by overseas visitors for Succos. As talk of war escalated, few travelers set out that year and even fewer arrived, and none with the special *esrogim*. However, shortly before Rosh Hashanah, the Belzer Rav uncharacteristically asked if the mail had arrived yet. "Only the usual flood of Rosh Hashanah wishes and *kvittlech,* plus a note from the post office about some parcel," replied the *gabbai,* suppressing his surprise. "*Git! Zehr git! Zeits moichel* and send someone please to fetch that parcel." Curiouser and curiouser, the *gabbai* could hardly wait to see what was in this mysterious package, so he was quite disappointed at the label. "*Ach!* It's from Palestine, from Friedman, the usual — it's only *pusele esrogim* for *noi succah!*"

"*Git! Zeits moichel,* bring it in and open it up please." The *gabbai* did so and his eyes almost popped out of their sockets. Instead of imperfect samples, the box was full of choice *esrogim,* each more beautiful than the next, and hardly damaged from the indifferent handling of ordinary parcel post. Thanks to the unusual surprise, the entire district had excellent *esrogim* for Yom Tov. Characteristically, the Rebbe instructed his *gabbaim* to pen a warm letter of gratitude.[1]

During Chol HaMoed Succos, rumors began circulating in Belz that the Russians had conceded all areas east of Lublin (over 100 kilometers west of Belz). This sparked enormous panic, and community leaders once again pressed the Belzer Rav to escape before the accursed Germans arrived. In response, the military authorities issued a stern proclamation that "... the Socialist forces take a grave view of malicious rumors spread by capitalist anti-Soviet agents ...

---

1. Because of the war situation, that letter never arrived, but the Belzer Rav thanked R' Mendel personally on his arrival in Eretz Yisrael. Mr. Friedman was taken aback. "Glad to have helped out so many Jews ... but there must have been some mix-up ... *Och!* I remember now! A whole box of my most expensive esrogim — designated for my best customers — went missing ... we even accused a new worker of stealing them! Although he always denied it, we took the loss off his wages and never employed him again! We will have to make it up to him — a *malach* must have sent Belz my best merchandise!"

We wish to make it perfectly clear that this district will remain under our military rule until peace and sovereignty return to Poland ... Anyone found guilty of spreading unsubstantiated rumors will be severely punished."

Threatening to shoot all rumor-mongers did little to reassure the public or calm the febrile atmosphere. But it did make the Belzer household curb any preparations to flee — or even discuss their plans — for fear of being arrested. Most residents, whether Jewish or non-Jewish, were uncertain what to believe or what action to take. Recognizing how the Belzer Rav had good connections with high-ranking army officers and would probably be the first to know of any change in their situation, most contented themselves with keeping a close watch on the Rebbe's household. All the local *poritzim* (squires) and municipal officials stationed personal representatives outside the Rebbe's house to check for any unusual developments.

Meanwhile the festival of Succos continued amid dread and apprehension: dread that the hated Germans might suddenly turn up, and apprehension of summary military justice meted out by the distrustful Russians. Late on Hoshana Rabbah they received warning that the last train would be leaving Belz that night. No more trains were scheduled to run from Belz and all the local squires and officials were boarding that train with their families. This time, the Belzer Rav finally agreed to leave town on condition that the *dayanim* ruled that he was allowed to travel on the Yom Tov of Shemini Atzeres. Since it was considered a life-threatening emergency if the Nazis caught up with the Belzer Rav, a *hetter* was immediately forthcoming and they frantically began to load the waiting wagons.

Despite the panic outside, the Rebbe calmly entered the great shul to *daven Maariv* as usual — and begin the *Hakafos*. These held special significance in Belz, and their founding Rebbe, the Sar Shalom, is reported to have remarked, "What these dances actually are I cannot tell you, but this much I can reveal: Every prayer that was unable to soar heavenwards during the year ascends tonight through the *rekidos*!" Traditionally, in Belz there are different tunes and songs for each of the seven *Hakafos*; and the Rebbe ordered that they conduct these *Hakafos* with the special

Belzer *nigunim* and *zemiros*; none should be left out or cut short. Regularly, he raised his hand as a signal to his chassidim, encouraging them to ever greater fervor in singing and dancing to the limits of their endurance. The Rebbe's saintly appearance took on the heavenly glow of a *malach*. Nobody who merited to take part in the final *Hakafos* in Belz could ever forget the indelible impression these imprinted on their soul.[2]

Eventually, these lively *Hakafos* came to an end. On the instructions of the Belzer Rav, the approximately 150 *Sifrei Torah* were collected together to be taken somewhere safe. (Later, they were spirited across the border to Rawa-Ruska under Russian control.) Meanwhile, everyone filed past the Rebbe's place while he wished them all individually a *"Gut Yom Tov!"*

Then he made his way to the *graiser-stieb* next to his residence, where the *tisch* was usually held. Here he asked if there were any new developments on the military and political situation. The information that several of the nearby towns had already fallen to the Germans only strengthened his resolve to leave that night on the train, despite it being Yom Tov. Instead of directing the usual *tisch*, for which there was no time, the Belzer Rav merely made *Kiddush* on a double quantity of wine to circumvent the need for an accompanying meal. When he instructed his large household to make for the railroad depot, his *shammasim* advised all the men to exchange their *shtreimels* for their weekday hats so as not to attract unnecessary attention, but no one dared recommend the same drastic course of action for the Rebbe himself. However, as the Rebbe stood by the *mezuzah* prior to leaving his beloved Belz, he suddenly called out, *"Gibt mir iber der golus klieder* — Hand over my *galus* clothes!"

His whole entourage made for the waiting horse-drawn wagons. Actually, several leading citizens of Belz had offered to ferry the Rebbe across the border in their private cars but on hearing that there would be insufficient room for his entire extended family, the Belzer Rav refused the kind offer since he was not prepared to split

---

2. At a poignant ceremony, these selfsame tunes were sung sixty years later by the present Rebbe at the dedication of the massive new Belzer Shul dominating the Jerusalem skyline.

up the Belzer household. Their procession to the railroad depot was a sorrowful occasion. Usually, the Rebbe's departures and arrivals had been spirited affairs attended by large crowds of excited, jostling chassidim, but now he was leaving — perhaps forever — quietly, almost as a fugitive. What future lay in store for them? Where would this *galus* lead them? Would they ever see their cherished Belz again? Yet it was Shemini Atzeres and Simchas Torah! What had always been one of the most colorful and joyful dates on the Belzer calendar had been cruelly transformed into an occasion for sorrow and anxiety. *"The joy of our hearts has ceased; our dancing has turned to mourning"* (*Eichah* 5:15).

As the townspeople watched the exodus of coach and horses silently driving out of town on the night of October 4, 1939, most sadly realized that this was probably the end of Belz as they had known it. Much of the town rapidly emptied as remaining Jews and non-Jews alike followed suit, hurriedly throwing a few possessions together prior to rushing off for that last train before the Germans' arrival. However, no change of demeanor was at all visible on the Rebbe's countenance. Whatever the circumstances, he remained composed and in total control of his emotions.

CHAPTER 6

SOKAL,
THE FIRST GALUS

AT BELZ'S RAILROAD DEPOT, STILL HALF DESTROYED from the initial bombing raids, they were informed that the train would travel only as far as the nearby town of Sokal, popularly known as "Sukal." Fortunately, this was just on the other side of the proposed border between Russian and German control. As the last scheduled train, it was heavily crowded with fleeing refugees, both Jewish and non-Jewish. Despite this and the sound of distant explosions, the Rebbe calmly began his Yom Tov meal (because of their hasty departure from Belz he had only made *Kiddush* so far) and handed out *sherayim* — the "leftovers" from his personal plate — to the accompanying *yoshvim* as if he were conducting his customary *tisch* among conventional surroundings.

The military and political situation was still confused, with pockets of German-controlled enclaves scattered amidst Russian-held territory. So the train took a circuitous route and it was 1 a.m. before they finally arrived in Sokal. This *kehillah* had long been within the Belz sphere of influence: the first Belzer Rebbe was the son-in-law of Reb Yissachar Dov Ramraz, Rav of Sokal; likewise

On the train to Sokal before the invasion

Rebbe Aharon was the son-in-law of a later Rav of Sokal, his uncle Reb Shmuel Rokach; while the current Rav of Sokal was his cousin and brother-in-law. Obviously, Sokal never suspected that the Belzer Rav might suddenly arrive in the middle of the night or during Shemini Atzeres, and no preparations had been made to meet or welcome him.

While the refugees waited at the Sokal rail depot, a few intrepid souls braved the curfew to alert his closest chassidim to the Rebbe's predicament. Immediately, they began looking for suitable accommodations. The rav, Rabbi Shalom Rokach, had already emigrated to America, and his son — Rebbe Aharon's nephew — generously set aside most of his large house for the Rebbe and his extended family. As news spread of the Rebbe's sudden arrival, hundreds gathered outside to welcome him. Unfortunately, when the Russian authorities saw this large crowd they arbitrarily began grabbing men at random, dragging them away for compulsory labor.

The shul (left) and the Rebbe's house (right)

Meanwhile the Belzer Rav settled in as best he could. The Yom Tov *tefillos* were conducted in the large town *beis hamedrash*, as was the *tisch*. Only the bravest of chassidim attended, since the *tisch* took place after the regular curfew of 9 p.m. Following Simchas Torah, news from Belz filtered across the border.

In the aftermath of the *kehillah's* hurried evacuation, Ukrainian gangs had returned to torch the Jewish Quarter and destroy their homes and assets. Such was these Ukrainians' abiding anti-Semitism that this unprovoked attack had been unleashed entirely voluntarily, in the hiatus between the Russian withdrawal and the Germans taking control. When the Nazis finally arrived, they had immediately begun searching for the famous *Wunder Rabbiner* with the help of their Ukrainian collaborators.

On discovering that the Wonder Rabbi had escaped at the last minute, they turned their attention to the renowned synagogue. Although this historic building was famous throughout Poland, they tried to set it alight — yet it would not catch fire. Twice they

Rare picture of the shul and beis medrash (taken in 1923)

exploded dynamite underneath it but the edifice, built one hundred years earlier with tremendous thought and application by the Sar Shalom, did not collapse! By now this unnatural phenomenon was the talk of the town and the superstitious Ukrainian helpers were too terrified to take any further part in the shul's destruction.

Still, the Nazis persevered. First, they avenged their wounded pride by expelling all the remaining Jews of Belz. Eventually, they established a ghetto on the outskirts of Belz where they incarcerated Jews from other localities. Then the synagogue was auctioned off as building material to their Ukrainian cronies who in turn forced Jewish slave labor gangs to slowly take the shul apart, brick by brick.

Even so, the baneful project continued to terrify the non-Jews. In the *Protocol* report (officially written for the Polish Government in Exile), the Belz Judenrat President Dr. Tauber of Krakow personally related how non-Jewish neighbors of the shul described a ghostly bearded figure of an elderly *Yid* appearing among the dark ruins, night after night, frightening all passersby off the street. This was confirmed by another Judenrat member, originally from Lodz. A local *poritz* (squire) added that he saw that legendary old man crying out in a loud voice and this figure appeared so lifelike, he had

The buildings surrounding the shul before the destruction

wanted to dive in to rescue him. Earlier one local looter was struck totally blind as soon as he crossed the shul's threshold.[1]

Since the Bolshevik Revolution, Jewish traditional, religious and communal organizations had been suppressed (as were the Zionist, Socialist-Bundists, and other modern national movements). At first, only the official Jewish section of the Communist Party — the infamous *Yevseksia* who actively collaborated by denouncing religious activity and promoting a Yiddish version of Bolshevik sacrilegious culture — had been permitted. But during the Great Purge of the

---

1. Despite their tenacity, the Nazis did not succeed in totally erasing all memory of the shrine. A Belz survivor who revisited the town in 1949 recounts how even from the war-damaged railroad depot, the skyline was dominated by three tall walls around a large ruin. On closer investigation, he found these three bare walls were all that remained of the historic landmark, while the *beis hamedrash* next door had been razed to the ground with only a pile of rubble to mark the site. The northern Jewish district beyond the *"rijnek,"* or central marketplace, torched by the Ukrainians on their own initiative before the Germans took control, had remained uninhabited, overgrown with weeds or cultivated with vegetable patches. Eventually the Russian authorities cleared the area in 1955 (the same year the Rebbe laid the Jerusalem yeshivah foundation stone) and erected a large school and play area. More recently, religious heirlooms, sacred writings and manuscripts — priceless to the Belzer dynasty — were finally recovered from the site while several surviving bricks were extracted and incorporated in the present grand Jerusalem shul.

The "rijnek," or central marketplace, in Belz

mid-1930's, even their institutions were liquidated while their misguided leaders were executed, imprisoned or exiled. Officially, under the Bolsheviks Jews enjoyed civic status equal to all other nationalities of the Soviet Union, but they were hardest hit when Communist officialdom nationalized all factories or private property and confiscated most money and jewelry. Wealthy Russian Jews were transformed into paupers — some even falsely accused of "sabotage against the Soviet State" — and never seen again.

However, the Polish refugees were generally treated fairly well by their new masters who, gullibly swallowing their own propaganda, saw the influx as "escapees from capitalism" to be given preferential treatment during distribution of food, clothing or housing. In parallel, a wave of confiscations and harassment was promptly directed against men of property and assets. Religious Jews were a particular target of the anti-religious communists, so once they became aware of his whereabouts, crowds of chassidim made the perilous journey to the Belzer Rav in Sokal to complain of their appalling problems under Communism. Yet the Belzer Rav had to be extremely careful when giving *berachos* or advice not to say anything which could be used by the numerous NKVD spies and *agent provocateurs* to make trouble. It was no secret that the Party *apparatchiks* were not happy about the Belzer Rav's presence, and their officers were constantly watching for any "anti-Russian or counter-revolutionary activity." Shleuma, the Soviet mayor, visited the Rebbe to interview him and concluded his visit by remarking, "You, Rabbi, will obtain no employment from us!" but stopped short of actual harassment. Some claimed that Sokal's communists were charmed by the Rebbe's personality while others insisted Shombura, the local Party leader, was behind their policy of non-interference. This Ukrainian owned a large horse-drawn carriage before the War and had conveyed the Rebbe from the railroad depot on several occasions. He had been generously rewarded as usual and apparently was now repaying in kind.

Thus the usual *tefillos* and *tisch* continued in Sokal much as they would have in Belz. Ever since the Baal Shem Tov, the eating of fish at their Shabbos table formed an integral part of chassidic Rebbes' *avodah,* and the Belzer Rav was no exception; he customarily insisted that live freshwater fish be bought, and preferred if several breeds were cooked. However, this proved difficult in Sokal since their local river, the important Bug, now formed the border between German and Russian forces; every so often when tension rose there were incidents of sniping — scaring off the local fishermen. One Shabbos when there was absolutely no fish to be had the Rebbe was so upset that his chassidim promised one fisherman a handsome reward if he brought some fresh fish. To the Rebbe's great delight, he successfully caught a large fish in the Bug which was duly served at the Friday night *tisch*. During the *tisch* the Belzer Rav remarked, "This fish is not from here! This type doesn't live in the Bug. It comes from the Solokija River that flows past Belz and into the Bug — it comes from Belz!"

In general, their stay in Sokal was free from "alarms and excursions," but one day a top Russian general barged into the Rebbe's house. All the chassidim fled in panic as the general shouted in a drunken rage, "We know very well that you're all involved in speculation!" ("*Speculatsia,*" as the communists preferred to label ordinary business enterprise, was also considered a crime.) Fortunately, Yitzchak'l, one of the Rebbe's *gabbaim* who was nicknamed "the Commissar" for his fluency in Russian, managed to calm the drunken officer and persuade him to leave peacefully.

At the time, the authorities were distracted by tightening their grip on the nominally independent Baltic States, designated in the final draft of the Ribbentrop-Molotov Treaty as within the Soviet sphere of influence. Under concerted pressure, Estonia, Latvia and Lithuania reluctantly agreed to transfer some of their territories to the Russians and grant them military bases (though in return Lithuania received their ancient capital, Vilna, back from Poland — a temporary expedient which nevertheless was to prove a welcome escape conduit for thousands of Jews).

Finland, however, having declared its neutrality at the outbreak of war, refused outright its consent to any "frontier-rectifications" and was eventually invaded by Russian forces on October 30, 1939. Initially, the Soviet army made little headway despite their overwhelming superiority or convenient bases in neighboring Leningrad, but by March 1940 Finland conceded all Russian demands, thus allowing the Soviet authorities to turn their full attention to the Polish refugees. Not to be outdone, Germany ruthlessly attacked two other neutral countries by invading neighboring Denmark and Norway by sea, air and land. Denmark surrendered immediately but Norway struggled on in a valiant but ultimately hopeless contest until after Pesach.

In Russian-held Poland, the Pesach festival began peaceably enough on April 23, 1940, but on the morrow and during Chol HaMoed all refugees were presented with a difficult dilemma when the military authorities offered everybody in their new territories the option of becoming full-fledged Russian citizens. At the time, most realized that accepting Russian citizenship would almost definitely entail abandoning all hope of returning to their hometowns in the near future. Certainly, that decision was critical enough but few comprehended the appalling implications of refusing the apparently innocuous but duplicitous offer — ramifications which became brutally clear within only a few short months. Although the refugees ostensibly had the free option to make their choice either way, they and their families would have to live or die by the dire consequences directly resulting from their decision.

According to official statistics, approximately 85 percent of Polish Jews availed themselves of this citizenship offer but religious Jews, fearing further discriminatory decrees, hesitated since they stood to enjoy greater protection by remaining foreign citizens. Belzer chassidim who conferred with the Rebbe were mostly advised to refuse. Surprisingly, the Belzer Rav did counsel a few solitary individuals to accept Russian citizenship. Even more surprising, it was eventually revealed that the Rebbe had secretly decided to become an official Russian citizen personally, together with his extended family. It was only with the benefit of hindsight, after years of confusion, that the Rebbe's advice and conflicting personal policy were better understood.

Events in the wider world did not stand still. Shortly after Pesach, three more neutral countries — and one official belligerent — were sucked into the ever widening war. On Friday, May 10, the day Winston Churchill finally assumed the leadership of Britain, huge Panzer columns swept into Holland, Belgium, Luxembourg and France. Facing unprovoked *blitzkrieg*, Holland collapsed after five days and Belgium surrendered after nineteen when the *Wehrmacht* reached the Channel coast and cut off the British Expeditionary Forces. Inexplicably, the rapidly advancing troops slowed down, allowing 350,000 British soldiers to escape from Dunkirk without their armaments while the Germans drove on to Paris. The French capital fell on June 14, the weekend after Shavuos, and surrender terms were dictated a week later.

By the stupendous success of their fast moving, highly maneuverable campaign, the Nazis had effectively wiped out the shame of their humiliating First World War defeat. In five short weeks they had smashed three powerful nations and captured one million French soldiers. In all of Europe, only England stood defiant — and alone. Its isolation was soon brought brutally home by a strategy of merciless aerial bombing against military and civilian targets, the infamous air-*blitz*, as a "softening-up process" in preparation for outright invasion. All these catastrophic setbacks

A communal memorial stone for Belz

on the world stage cannot but have had a sharply demoralizing effect on Jews worldwide.

Meanwhile, in the Soviet Union, the unlikely ally of fascist Germany, the situation of the refugees had taken a sharp turn for the worse. Before Shavuos, thousands of chassidim made their way to Sokal. The first day Shavuos *tisch* had always been among the highlights of the Belz calendar, as the Rebbe would personally sing three verses from Shabbos morning *zemiros* (*Yom Shabbason*) beginning with "*Uva'u kulam bivris yachad; na'aseh venishmah, amru k'echad* — They all enrolled in the Covenant; 'We shall obey and harken,' they proclaimed as one." In a play on words, this *tisch* was colloquially known as the "*Uva'u kulam tisch*" or "Everybody arriving *tisch*."

When observing their Rebbe's ecstasy they could imagine themselves assembled at the foot of Mount Sinai to hear the fateful roar of "*Anochi ...*" Emotions ran particularly high when the Rebbe sang the verse "... *ha'am asher na'ah* — the nation that wanders, straying like sheep, may Hashem remember them favorably according to His *bris* and promise, so no harm befalls them, just as promised after Noach's flood." The Rebbe fervently repeated these sentiments three times, an obvious supplication that the thousands on the move should come to no harm.

Unfortunately, when the Russian authorities noticed hundreds of strangers — many without permits — traveling from all directions to Sokal near the border, they became doubly suspicious. Sokal was a sensitive area in Russian memory. During the First World War, it was first held by the Austrian-German Alliance along their sector of the Eastern Front; its daring recapture by Russian cavalry in June 1916 heralded the Austrian rout in Galicia. Moreover, nobody was allowed to travel within the Soviet Union without an internal passport and official permission; and some of these strangers had arrived even from the German zone![2] Perhaps a secret Jewish gathering was being organized without authorization! Thousands were summarily arrested and held in prison pending investigation.

Naturally, most chassidim protested their innocence and explained that they had merely been on a pilgrimage to their religious leader. Although the Rebbe willingly corroborated their account, the NKVD remained adamant that serious crimes may have been in the offing since Sokal was a sensitive military zone, situated on the border. It began to look as if thousands of chassidim, after undergoing considerable hardship on the journey, would spend Shavuos in prison cells. However, after a great deal of perseverance and the help of local Jewish residents of Sokal, who had their own lines of communications or *protexia* to top Communist officials, all the chassidim were freed before Shavuos.

Their relief was short-lived. Not only had the unpleasant episode aroused the mistrust and ire of Party *apparatchiks* but it had also encouraged spiteful non-Jews of Sokal to make their own representations — applying for the removal of the *Wunder Rabbiner* from Sokal entirely! The trouble began early Wednesday afternoon, the first day of Shavuos, in the midst of the *tisch*. Although the Sokal *beis hamedrash*, where the *tisch* was held, was being carefully monitored by plainclothes detectives stationed outside, they did not interfere with or molest the thousands of chassidim crowding the building.

The Belzer Rav completed singing the three verses from *"Uva'u kulam bivris yachad"* and had just begun delivering Torah on the topic of *Kabbalas HaTorah* when armed soldiers suddenly burst into the crowded *beis hamedrash*, sowing alarm and confusion. "A top NKVD official has arrived!" they barked. "Everybody outside to hear his urgent announcement!" Naturally there was enormous panic but the Rebbe calmly completed his words of Torah and the customary *nigunim* before urging his chassidim outside to hear what the Russian official had to say. The official proclamation was brutally short and to the point:

---

2. When Rebbe Chunah Halberstam of Kolaczyce was told Belzer chassidim were endangering their lives to visit their Rebbe, he remarked, "If they're going to the Belzer Rav, they've nothing to fear!"

SOKAL IS ON THE BORDER. IT IS STRICTLY FORBIDDEN UNDER SOVIET LAW FOR NON-RESIDENTS TO LINGER HERE. NONE OF THE REFUGEES HAVE ANY PERMIT TO BE HERE AND NONE MAY REMAIN IN SOKAL AFTER 12 P.M. TOMORROW, THURSDAY, JUNE 13, 1940. ANYONE REMAINING AFTER THAT DATE WILL BE DEEMED AN ESPIONAGE AGENT UNDER SOVIET MILITARY REGULATIONS AND LIABLE TO THE DEATH PENALTY.

Everybody was deeply shocked and fearful. This decree would have meant everyone dispersing on the second day of Shavuos, with all the *chillul* Yom Tov that would obviously entail. Moreover, was this arbitrary expulsion a harbinger of worse to come? After further representations by local residents, the authorities agreed to allow the refugees to stay until the day after Yom Tov. Naturally, the next day's *tisch* and festivities were decidedly low key. Despite the relief, many were acutely disappointed since Belzer chassidim traditionally remained for *"Shabbos-nach-Shavuos"* — the *Shabbos Naso* immediately following Yom Tov. Under the circumstances, the Rebbe urged everyone to leave as soon as possible that Friday.

On Sunday, all remaining non-residents were arrested. Most were exiled to Siberia but some were dispatched to the battlefront. Suddenly, distinctive NKVD wagons descended on the Rebbe's residence with orders to transfer the Belzer Rav with his extended family to "an unknown destination." The trepidation and consternation this baleful plot caused can hardly be imagined. Until then they had fondly believed they could establish an amicable working relationship with Communist officials. Now they could see a giant chasm yawning in front of them. Once again considerable representation was successfully exercised to have this latest threat rescinded.

This temporary respite notwithstanding, the ominous episode signaled the end of the first tolerable phase in the Belz dynasty existence under the atheist, anti-religious Communist regime. No longer could it function almost as it might have done back home in Belz; in the future it would have to maintain a lower profile just to be tolerated. Although the local authorities issued an official permit and assured the Rebbe he would now be free from further harassment, he was no longer prepared to trust them.

Even though his chassidim were not protected by a similar permit, they displayed extraordinary heroism in fulfilling his wishes. He asked if two of his followers would not mind relaying a message on his behalf at the grave sites of his father-in-law, Reb Shmuel Rokach; and his great-grandfather, Reb Yissachar Dov Ramraz, Rav of Sokal; and Rebbe Shloma Lutsker, the Maggid of Sokal. He wanted his saintly ancestors to know that he was in great difficulties and forced to wander from place to place. Despite people being shot the previous day on the road to that cemetery, two brave chassidim hastened to obey the Rebbe's wishes. They went and returned safely, without mishap.

Immediately after Shabbos, the Belzer Rav sent emissaries to chassidim in surrounding *kehillos*, in an effort to locate a suitable and quiet neighborhood where he might establish a residence undisturbed. The Rebbe insisted on leaving Sokal on his own volition and relocated to Radichow on Thursday, the 14th of Sivan (June 20, 1940), even before his couriers returned. Although Radichow was only a temporary stopover, Rebbe Aharon conducted prayers and *tisch* (*Shabbos Beha'aloscha*) at the central synagogue and *kloiz*, and also accepted private petitions (*kvittlech*).

On Tuesday, the Belzer entourage was on the move again. At first the Rebbe attempted to settle in Boisk, reportedly a suitable venue, but the regional NKVD Commissar — who was incidentally Jewish — raised such an outcry that they quickly moved on to nearby Galina, where they were hosted by the local Rav. The Belzer Rav recognized that each place he stopped must be part of his preordained *galus* and endeavored to discover the Divine purpose. At one location he even asked those around him, "Does anyone know why I had to come here?" without explaining what he meant.

Eventually, after a fortnight by dint of further representations and "expenses," they received official permission to transfer to Przemyslany, a *kehillah* with famous chassidic antecedents and popularly known as "Premishlan," which already enjoyed a substantial Belzer presence. Przemyslany was over 100 kilometers south of the border and so officially "safe" for refugees. While the Rebbe settled in during the week of *Chukas* as best he could, his chassidim were not so fortunate. Russian retribution for refusing their devious offer of Soviet citizenship earlier, during Pesach, had finally arrived on *Shabbos Korach,* 30 Sivan (July 5, 1940). Just over three weeks after the Shavuos expulsion from Sokal, the Russian security forces struck. Late Friday night (specifically chosen to catch Jews totally unprepared, at home), they swooped down on all the Polish refugees who had expressed a wish to eventually return home, designating them as unsafe elements and a security risk.

Thus, 200,000 Polish Jews — men, women and children — were unceremoniously dragged from their beds, bundled into waiting boxcars and dispatched on a painfully slow railroad journey into the cruel *galus* of Siberia! Included with the hapless victims were many prominent rabbanim — but the Belzer Rav was not among their number, due to his accepting Soviet citizenship. For the Rebbe, badly weakened from years of self-mortification and with a natural susceptibility to cold, expulsion to Siberia would have constituted a death sentence. So it was understandable that, with his premonition, Rebbe Aharon personally applied to become a Russian citizen. Yet why had he advised most chassidim not to apply?

Naturally, the exiles were bitter at their sudden calamity and felt badly let down by misconceived decisions. Most thought this was the worst disaster to befall them and it was much later before the exile was revealed as a miraculous blessing in disguise. Throughout their years of isolation — and even during their postwar homeward journey — they could hardly wait to recount the full extent of their travail to their relatives back home. It was only when they returned to Polish territory that they finally comprehended how their own suffering was as nothing compared to the unimaginable horror that had befallen their birthplace, and their brethren left behind, in their absence.

Only then was the Rebbe's advice revealed as totally valid for each individual situation. Approximately eight out of every ten refugees survived the cold, hunger and slave labor of the icy Russian wilderness — by contrast, at least nine out of every ten Polish Jews who had remained behind were sadistically murdered by the Nazis. Those few petitioners recommended to accept Soviet citizenship had used the opportunity to migrate further into Russia and from there to eventual freedom. Had the mass of chassidim remained in the Russian controlled zone of Poland as they had desired, they would have been among the first victims of the looming bloodbath.

CHAPTER 7

SURVIVING PRZEMYSLANY

E VEN IN PRZEMYSLANY AND ARMED WITH SOVIET
citizenship, the Belzer Rav was not safe from the expulsion decree. Although Przemyslany was not situated on
the border as was Sokal, it was still considered off-limits
for erstwhile refugees. Yet the Rebbe was anxious to remain in
Przemyslany because of its substantial presence of religious Jews
and a high proportion of Belzer chassidim. Repeated representations and a large dose of old-fashioned bribery finally secured the
acquiescence of the atheist *apparatchiks.*

While his large extended family thought they would now be safe in
Przemyslany until the War ended, the Belzer Rav was more cautious.
Due to the continuing danger from Communist agent provocateurs,
he ordered the family to split up and settle in the surrounding villages to attract less attention. Here the Belzer Rebbe was reunited
with his brother, Rebbe Mordechai Rokach of Bilgoraj (father of the
present Belzer Rebbe), who had earlier escaped to nearby Brijshani.

"Reb Mottele," as he was popularly known, was born in 1902 to
Rebbetzin Chayah Devorah (Pecsenik) when Rebbe Yissachar Dov
was already middle-aged, yet his father's close interest in his educa-

*Rebbe Mordechai of Bilgoraj,
brother of the Rebbe
and father of the present Rebbe*

tion trained him in outstanding Torah scholarship and diligence. Reb Mottele's popularity owed much to his humble manner and his ability to mingle easily with people without assuming any airs or graces; he closely resembled his father in nature and sentiment and was unexcelled in his ability to recollect and interpret his father's every intimation.

Despite growing up in the shadow of World War I, with the family seeking refuge abroad, he ignored all distracting rumors from the battlefront to mature into a renowned *baki*, knowledgeable in *Shas* and *Poskim*, and was often delegated to resolve difficult halachic issues.

In 1927 he accepted the *Rabbanus* of Bilgoraj where he founded a dynamic school and encouraged the establishment of yeshivos. Rebbe Mordechai rapidly earned respect in wider circles and was even offered the prestigious rabbinical position of Lemberg; yet, in deference to his saintly brother's advice, he remained in Bilgoraj until the outbreak of war.

Rebbe Mordechai in Bilgoraj, where he established a yeshivah

The large shul in Berezhany destroyed by the Germans

At the beginning of hostilities, Bilgoraj was bombed from the air and most of its residents fled. Reb Mottele planned to return to Belz, fearing it would likely be abandoned as it had been during the previous war. Knowing how his saintly elder brother was habitually engrossed with heavenly matters at the approach of Rosh Hashanah, he intended to assist him in any evacuation (as he later recalled in the *Protocol*). But as the flood of refugees from the Lublin area streamed toward the nearby Volhynia district of Ukraine, Rebbe Mordechai and his family migrated with the flow to Poritsc (only several kilometers north of Sokal) from where he had maintained a constant correspondence with the Belzer Rav. More recently, he had moved to Berezhany (Berzhan), barely three kilometers southeast of Przemyslany — and was destined never to leave his brother's side throughout their miraculous escape.

By virtue of their extreme caution in Przemyslany, the Belzer Rav and his entourage survived, despite the strong suspicions of the Communist authorities for almost a year. Consequently, the Belzer Rav limited his *tefillos* and *tisch* in public and instituted strict controls on visits by the chassidim. Henceforth, they could not just turn up in Przemyslany for Shabbos and Yom Tov whenever they saw fit, but were only allowed in on a tightly regulated rotational basis. Any chassid with an urgent request was generally encouraged to visit quietly during the week. Despite the restrictions, many chassidim still found a way to smuggle themselves into Przemyslany. Claiming they were only visiting their "*Zeide Meir'l*" — the holy grave of Rebbe Meir of Premishlan, the famous miracle worker who was highly respected by Jews and non-Jews alike — wagonloads of bearded Jews would creep down quiet village roads in an effort to avoid the ever watchful eye of the hostile NKVD. Even when halted by security patrols, the magic words "*Da Stari Meir'l*" usually permitted their free passage.

Before Rosh Hashanah, Reb Yosel Gold of Yarotschev, a close attendant and "Belz Minister for External Affairs" circulated to all chassidic centers throughout Galicia a confidential communiqué with an urgent request from the Rebbe. Belzer chassidim were instructed not to make the traditional pilgrimage to the *tisch* unless they had an important message (*shelichus*) to deliver. Reluctantly, the chassidim accepted the edict and remained in their places of refuge — though each naturally sought some important commission to justify their attendance at the Rosh Hashanah *tefillos* and *tisch*. Even so, more chassidim turned up than originally envisioned. Yet they still numbered in the hundreds rather than the customary thousands.

In any event, the Belzer Rebbe's *tisch* was run totally as normal, with no modifications. Even though far fewer chassidim attended in comparison with previous years and there remained ample room for everybody, the Rebbe still begged his sadly diminished audience "not to push (*shtip*)" as if he were surrounded by many thousands as usual![1] Those fortunate to attend this *tisch* forgot, if only temporarily, their personal predicament and felt that they were almost on a different planet, experiencing a higher plane of spiritual existence.

Although the Rebbe traditionally read the *Megillah* personally, few chassidim dared to make the perilous journey to Przemyslany. However, one famous devotee, Torah scholar and renowned *badchan* R' Yisrael Hubniver (of Uhnow, who had personally taught many

---

1. Interestingly, whenever the Rebbe had vacationed at the spa in prewar years with only a few close devotees, he would also utter these admonitions at regular intervals — undoubtedly, these had a paranormal rationale. Likewise, he would sometimes instruct his *gabbai* at night to tell "those outside to go" — although there were no living souls outside to be seen!

of the Rebbe's family), was present. As the Belzer Rav later recalled, "Do you know who Reb Yisrael was? Under the Germans when there was only a small *olam*, he still sang *grammen* to cheer up the Jews — and he was successful! I saw them laughing with my own eyes. That was my Reb Yisrael!"

Generally, the chassidim were not overtly molested by the Soviet regime; however, at first they did obstruct the baking of traditional matzos for Pesach. Fortunately, Reb Mottele in his wisdom managed to persuade the hostile *Natchalnik* that since matzos were *"lechem oni"* — the historical bread of affliction, representing their liberation from slavery — they epitomized the true bread of socialism! Despite the close watch maintained by the NKVD and particularly its Jewish-born agents, Jewish soldiers and even high-ranking Soviet officers still approached the Rebbe covertly to unburden their regrets about their present lifestyle or to confide their fears for the future.

Outside Russia, meanwhile, chassidim and well-wishers concerned for the Rebbe's well-being began making tentative inquiries to rescue him from his plight. Because of difficulty in communications and tight censorship during wartime, with little precise information as to the Rebbe's whereabouts or welfare, wild rumors and scare stories proliferated. Witness this inaccurate report in the newspaper *Ha'aretz* on August 10, 1940, under the screaming headline —

BELZER REBBE DEPORTED TO SIBERIA! EXILED FROM SOKAL TOGETHER WITH HIS CHASSIDIM:
Istanbul*: We have received reports that the Belzer Rebbe, Rabbi Aharon Rokach, who had earlier fled the German invasion and resettled in Sokal in the Soviet zone, has been recently arrested and transported together with groups of his followers and admirers to hard labor in Siberia. As we have already reported in the Ha'aretz, the Germans have burnt down the large synagogue of Belz. In the early days of the Belzer Rebbe's sojourn in Sokal, he was persecuted by Jewish communists and imprisoned. However, he was freed after a fortnight and resided in relative peace. Many of his closest followers visited Sokal and attended to the Rebbe's upkeep and that of his family.*

It is relevant to note that the Rebbe of Belz is frail in body and suffers from ill health. His exile to Siberia, therefore, constitutes a threat to his life.

Usually, *Ha'aretz* was reliable, but the only truth in the report was that the Belzer Rav had indeed been forced to leave his residence in Sokal when many of his chassidim had been deported to Siberia. But these false reports spurred chassidim to become more actively involved in rescue efforts. Leading Belzer chassidim — including R' Elimelech Ashkenazi, R' Dovid Perkovitz, R' Avraham Prester, R' Hillel Vind and R' Mordechai Sprung — met in Jerusalem before Pesach and decided to write to prominent Rebbes in America, asking for their assistance.[2] Apparently, religious leaders in America whom they approached were privy to more accurate information and were aware that the Rebbe remained detained in Galicia. (One source of information was Rabbi Aaron Pecsenik, a cousin of the Bilgoraj Rav. Although an American citizen, he had been trapped in Lemberg and lodged for a few months with his uncle Rebbe Avraham Yaakov Friedman of Boyan. One day a messenger somehow got through from Przemyslany, with an urgent message from the Belzer Rebbetzin Chayah Devoire'le: "The Belzer Rav wants to leave for Eretz Yisrael! Please see to it when you get back to America ..." Rabbi Pecsenik eventually made it back to the United States during January 1941 and passed this message on.)

In reply, the Modzhitzer Rebbe, Rav Shaul Yedidiah Eliezer Taub, related how he had immediately conferred with Rav Avraham Yehoshua Heschel (the Kopicznitzer Rebbe), Rav Levi Yitzchak Grunwald of Tzelem and Rav Chaim Halberstam of Czchov (Chechov). They all agreed that their best rescue plan would be to obtain entry visas to the American continent with the aid of a Latin American passport, which would necessarily entail a great deal of effort both in the United States and in Poland. However, the other rabbanim were hesitant since they had previously heard that the Belzer Rav was unwilling to leave his place of refuge, primarily because his large extended family depended on him.

To clarify their doubts, these rabbanim dispatched a telegram to one of the Belzer Rav's close supporters who was in direct contact

---

2 Interestingly, when they petitioned the miracle-working Rebbe Shloma Goldman of Z'vil, he cryptically replied, "About him you don't have to worry — they won't have any power over him!"

by regular mail and currency transfers, but the reply that eventually came back solely requested urgent funds with no intimation whether the Belzer Rebbe had any intention or wish to emigrate.[3] In view of this response, the Modzhitzer Rebbe decided to halt any further moves until he received more definite information of the Rebbe's wishes from his chassidim; and he advised the Lubavitcher Rebbe likewise.

By then, however, the Lubavitcher Rebbe, Rav Yosef Yitzchak Schneersohn, who was related to the Belzer Rav through the Twersky dynasty, had already sent a sharply worded letter on 24 Nissan (May 1, 1941) addressed to the Agudah leader, Rabbi Moshe Blau, demanding that he obtain a Palestine Mandate entry certificate. He was confident that Agudas Yisrael was taken seriously by the British authorities then in charge of Eretz Yisrael; surely the influential Agudist leaders Dr. Pinchas Cohn and Rabbi Dr. Isaac Breuer have contacts capable of assisting the saintly Belzer Rav. Although neither he nor the Belzer Rav were Agudah members or supporters, narrow party interests should not apply since what was at issue was literally a matter of life or death! Rebbe Yosef Yitzchak concluded by begging them wholeheartedly to leave no stone unturned, no avenue unexplored, until they rescue the Belzer Rebbe — their efforts were sure to meet with success.

In fact, obtaining an entry certificate was far more difficult than the Lubavitcher Rebbe's letter implied. Due to Arab agitation in the years leading up to the War, the British Government had been severely restricting Jewish immigration under their notorious

---

3. Lack of funds remained a severe problem in Przemyslany, but one source of support was the Feder family in Lubaczow, who had owned a textile shop before the War. When the Russians exiled the parents to Siberia they left the daughter in charge of their merchandise, but the Communists conducted periodic searches for "capitalist wealth," confiscating valuables and arresting their owners. Her host feared an imminent raid but she reassured him that the Russians would not touch anything since she had already pledged half of it to the Belzer Rebbe! Indeed when the Communists swooped down on neighboring houses and seized anything they saw, they visited her temporary home but left everything untouched. She religiously divided all sale proceeds in half, sending them to the Rebbe's family in Sokal and Przemyslany where they were sorely needed. The Rebbe never forgot her kindness and treated her considerately after her arrival in Israel.

Rabbi Akiva Sofer of Pressburg

"White Paper" policy, which set tight, inflexible limits on the quota of foreign Jews allowed in annually. Thus the Balfour Declaration promising to "favor a Jewish Home in Palestine" — upon which Great Britain received their mandate from the League of Nations — was exposed as a sham. Furthermore, Agudas Yisrael was restricted yet further. Even within the limited amount of lifesaving entry certificates available, the Agudah's allocation was reduced to a paltry 6 percent because of their alleged anti-Zionist stance. Thus were the overwhelming majority of religious Jews in Eastern Europe denied a safe haven from Soviet tyranny or Nazi oppression.

Nonetheless, the Agudah leadership took the Lubavitcher Rebbe's request most seriously. Rav Akiva Sofer of Pressburg read his missive with great interest before summoning Rabbi Blau and Dr. Cohn to make representations. However, after several days they had to regretfully report that their mission was impossible as "the British Consulate in Russia had no interest in issuing visas at present, since they did not want to encourage any influx of refugees into Palestine."

Later, spurred by the Lubavitcher Rebbe's insistence to explore every avenue, Rabbi Moshe Blau embarked on a bold, though somewhat unorthodox, stratagem. Meeting directly with the British High Commissioner for Palestine, Sir Harold MacMichael, Rabbi Blau proposed that an important personage like the world-famous Belzer Rebbe should be awarded an entry visa outside the annual quota. Had this venture been successful, it might have likewise proved a lifesaver to other important Rabbinical personalities in a similar predicament. Unfortunately, the result was ultimately counterproductive.

Although he usually enforced the White Paper restrictions rigidly, the High Commissioner was initially receptive to the unusual request and began urgently processing the necessary paperwork, but suddenly the whole procedure came to an abrupt halt. As it subsequently transpired, British army intelligence was adamant that their principle of not granting entry permits to anyone leaving Nazi jurisdiction — on the suspicion they might be German spies — must be strictly complied with. Although their rationale was ludicrous when applied to the Belzer Rav (as it was indeed with all Jews fleeing German persecution), the application was summarily turned down. As far as the official circles were concerned, the Belzer Rav's place of residence would likely count against him in any future applications on his behalf.

This was not the only attempt originated by the Lubavitcher Rebbe. Concurrent with his conferring with the Modzhitzer Rebbe and writing a letter to Rabbi Blau, he also involved his relative and emissary, the *gaon*, Rav Shlomo Yehuda Leib Eliezerov of Jerusalem (previously Hebron). Rav Eliezerov's first step was to invite the leading Belzer chassidim to a meeting. The ten chassidim who attended showed him the response that the Modzhitzer Rebbe had received, yet most still believed that the Rebbe's unusual silence did not prove he was unwilling to leave Poland. Quite the reverse, they speculated, he might be under such close scrutiny that it was too dangerous for him to give a positive reply. Rav Eliezerov concurred with their view and after meeting with Rabbi Blau, whom he acknowledged had better placed connections, he approached his *mechutan*, the Supreme Court Judge Gad Frumkin, for assistance in obtaining exit visas from Russia and entry visas into Palestine.

After a short correspondence, Justice Frumkin discovered that there was no possibility of obtaining entrée for the Belzer Rav and his family since the British were not issuing any certificates at all; the British Consulate in Russia was not issuing visas to anyone without a passport; and the Soviet authorities were not providing passports. Unbeknown to Rav Eliezerov or anyone else outside Russia, the Belzer Rav had already obtained a Russian passport, but whether the British Mandate authorities would have been more accommodating in these circumstances is a moot point.

Perhaps the only way out of this impasse, Rav Eliezerov concluded, would be if the Modzhitzer Rebbe revived his original

Wehrmacht troops lead the invasion of Sokal across the Bug River in 1941

plan to obtain a South American entry visa instead. Meanwhile, the Modzhitzer Rebbe made extensive inquiries trying to ascertain the personal wishes of the Belzer Rav. On 25 Elul (August 17) he was able to confirm to R' Dovid Perkovitz the latest information received: the Belzer Rebbe was still in Przemyslany and felt unable to leave since at least sixty members of his large, extended family depended on him. As long as the Rebbe's life was in no immediate danger, though existence under Soviet rule was fraught with danger, he was reluctant to abandon his post.

Even as this correspondence was continuing, the situation of the Jews in the Soviet zone deteriorated drastically when scarcely a fortnight after Shavuos, on June 22, 1941, the German army had invaded the territory of their erstwhile ally. Frustrated by their inability to make any headway in the "Battle of Britain" air war (though it reduced Britain's ability to influence Europe's fate), Germany had switched attention back to Russia. Soviet power was a natural ideological enemy for fascists, and *Mein Kampf* had described "the colossal Bolshevik Empire as ripe for dissolution."

Notwithstanding the non-aggression pact signed between their two states less than two years earlier, the Nazis made plans for an unprovoked attack — code named Operation Barbarossa — plus organized administrative authority to resettle millions of Slavs while "eliminating" hundreds of thousands of Jews and other "undesirable elements" in their future control. Although Churchill had sent repeated intelligence warnings, Stalin refused to take them seriously and instead embarked on a series of political purges that left his army officer corps leaderless and demoralized.

Yet Operation Barbarossa was delayed because of the Balkan War, which erupted when Germany reinforced its military presence in Hungary, Romania, Bulgaria and Yugoslavia in preparation for their successful invasion of Greece. In response, patriotic Serbian army officers staged a coup in Yugoslavia on behalf of Britain. This surprising turn of events threw Hitler into a paroxysm of fury and he abruptly postponed Operation Barbarossa to wreak unbridled vengeance on Yugoslavia in general and Belgrade in particular, which was flattened by repeated, vicious dive bombing raids. By the time Yugoslavia had been dismembered into separate, intractable zones, the Russian invasion had been put back by over a month — a critical delay as the campaign unfolded.

Ultimately, the massive German invasion along a 2,000 mile front suddenly materialized on *Motza'ei Shabbos Shelach*, 27 Sivan — June 22nd, which by an unbelievable coincidence was the very date Napoleon had chosen 129 years earlier for his ill-starred thrust on Moscow. This was not to be the only similarity between the two offensives. Until then, the Belzer Rebbe had taken little close interest in the wider strategic implications of each campaign, but now he uncustomarily paid avid attention to the route taken by the *Wehrmacht*. When he discovered the Germans were advancing on a straight line toward Moscow, he thoughtfully remarked, "Now the *rasha* will experience a halt to constant victories! But then there remains the fear that the oppression of Jews will increase as a result of his setbacks!"

Only much later did the Rebbe confide in his brother the background for his cryptic remarks. "When I was a little boy, *der heilige Zeide* (Rebbe Yeshie'le) *zechuso yagen aleinu*, took me into his room, drew a rudimentary map and showed me the route taken by Napoleon after crossing the River Neiman into the depths of Russia toward Moscow. Then our *Zeide* commented, 'If Napoleon would have chosen a more circuitous route, he would have succeeded in subduing Moscow and Russia. But Napoleon's route invited retribution and caused his downfall.'

"At the time, I did not comprehend the *Zeide's* meaning. It was only with this German invasion that I finally understand the deep significance of *der heilige Zeide's* remarks!"

His brother, Rebbe Mottele Bilgoraj'er, asked curiously, "And what is the other, more roundabout route?"

"That, I'm afraid, I am not at liberty to reveal," replied the Belzer Rebbe gravely.

At first, the *Wehrmacht* successes were stunning, even by the Nazis' previous record of *blitzkrieg*. Stalin's political purges had irretrievably weakened the army while Soviet industrial might and distribution had been all but destroyed by the wholesale dismissal of top managers, engineers and technicians. Harsh policies in the Communist satellite states and frontier districts coupled with mass deportations had led to popular anti-Russian hostility, and the German army was initially welcomed as liberators. The chaos along the border rapidly spread to the interior as huge areas were overrun with lightning speed and staggering losses. Within months, Germany's incredibly ambitious targets of Leningrad in the north, Moscow in the center, and the food rich Ukraine in the south all looked within its evil grasp.

Whereas most of the Ukraine fell to the invaders, by the time the Panzer divisions reached the outskirts of Leningrad and Moscow they were running out of momentum and the Russian winter soon set in with Arctic severity. Furthermore, despite their immense losses — amounting to millions of dead, wounded and captured troops — the Russian army remained resilient and even mounted successful counterattacks. Not only was the Russian army more suited to winter warfare, but early Nazi bloodletting transformed their initial favorable reception by the local populations into burgeoning resentment.

Just as the earlier invasion of Poland had also been closely followed by *Einsatzgruppen*, this time the extermination squads' remorseless tactics were strikingly similar and their blood toll along the Eastern Front was staggering. Across Eastern Poland, Ukraine and Russia, Jews who had escaped deportation to Siberia were now rounded up in the thousands, ordered to surrender their valuables and dig large pits before being machine-gunned to death. In the first few months of the invasion, hundreds of thousands were brutally massacred. Sokal, on the front line, fell to the German invaders on the first day of the attack while Przemyslany was subjected to heavy shelling.

In Przemyslany, there was total panic. The Russian army had been caught completely unawares with no inkling of an attack, and most fled without even a token show of resistance. By then, no Jew harbored any illusions about Nazi cruelty and violence, and dreaded the imminent prospect of falling prey to the butchers. The Belzer chassidim were particularly concerned for the safety of their Rebbe, since according to frequent reports, Nazi agents had made extensive inquiries as to the Belzer Rav's whereabouts. *"Wo ist der Wunder Rabbiner aus Belz?"* they demanded, flashing a photograph of the "Wonder Rabbi" on a prewar visit to Marienbad, previously published in the infamous *Der Stürmer*. Leading chassidim considered arranging for the Rebbe to flee with the retreating Russian army despite the obvious dangers that might entail, but all motorized vehicles had already been requisitioned by the army. Since the Russians were totally panic stricken there was literally no one whom the chassidim could approach for assistance.

As a preliminary precaution, the Rebbe moved into hiding at the house of a non-Jewish landlord, with only a select few chassidim privy to his secret location. Even his family was kept in the dark and had to communicate by infrequent messages — as did all other chassidim with urgent requests — relayed by the five close chassidim still in contact. His long standing *gabbai*, R' Aharon Shea (Yehoshua) Landau, was replaced by two young boys, Sholom'l Kohl (from Sokal) and Yisrael Mendel (from Przeworsk), chosen for their "Aryan" appearance; they played their part by disguising themselves as Polish *"shkotzim."*

German troops reached Przemyslany on Tuesday night, the 24th of June, moving quickly through in pursuit of the retreating Soviet army. They only consolidated their hold there a week later, on Tuesday, July 1. Their first action was to "clear out nests of resistance," which amounted to house-by-house searches accompanied by their Ukrainian auxiliaries who promptly dynamited any dwelling that aroused their suspicions. When the house two doors away from the Belzer Rav's residence collapsed, all their own windows shattered. As the net closed in, the Belzer Rav intoned two *pesukim*, *Lishu'ascha kivisi Hashem* and *Nafshi Lashem mishomrim laboker*, in the somber *nigun* of *Kol Nidrei*, and the patrol turned away.

Shortly afterwards, on Friday, July 4 (9 Tammuz *Erev Shabbos Chukas*) they were awakened by the sounds of screams and turmoil. With the full encouragement of the Nazis, the Ukrainians had torched the main shul in Przemyslany where the Rebbe had previously *davened* and had once hid. The fire spread rapidly through the entire quarter, comprising the *beis hamedrash* and other institutions, and also the residences of prominent *kehillah* members and its Rabbinate. As the residents ran into the street to escape the flames, all males were grabbed by the Germans searching for Jews to humiliate or force into demeaning slave labor. They were surrounded by a raging sea of terror and confusion while the unchecked blaze roared and raged as it relentlessly consumed the district. Outside, large trucks waited ominously for victims destined for an unknown fate.

The Rebbe's secret location was a little distant from the conflagration, so his two closest chassidim, R' Yeshayah Prager of Rawa-Ruska and R' Yosel (Yosef) Gold of Yarotschev, decided to remain there to avoid the German snatch squads out on the streets — particularly since the Rebbe was confined to bed, weakened from nights of fasting and praying. However, the Nazis again went from house to house, seizing men and cramming them onto their waiting vehicles, amid blows and curses. They were closely followed by Ukrainian looters who stole everything of value. When the Germans reached the Rebbe's residence, the two chassidim begged to be allowed to continue ministering to the "elderly patient" in their care. At first they were successful but the next patrol that arrived a few minutes later paid no attention to their entreaties — apparently they mistakenly suspected that the venerable Rav Yeshayah Prager, who had a refined and distinguished demeanor, might be none other than the missing *"Wunder Rabbiner"* and that R' Yosel Gold was his *gabbai*.

Screaming abuse, they beat him up without mercy before throwing R' Yosel down a steep flight of stairs. After tormenting him mercilessly and pulling out his beard, they press-ganged him into back-breaking slave labor all Shabbos. Fortunately, they did not discover the authentic Belzer Rebbe who was resting in an inner room. Shortly afterwards, the Ukrainian looters burst in and stole whatever they could, even the Rebbe's shoes placed at his bedside. Abandoned

The Rebbe's son, Rebbe Moshe'le (right), and his son in-law, Rebbe Shmuel Frankel (left)

and alone in bed, the Belzer Rav was obviously in grave danger, especially in his weakened state.

By the time his two young *shammasim* who had stolen away to seek assistance returned, the flames were already licking at the exterior of the house. Instantly, both decided to risk their lives, come what may, to rescue the Belzer Rav from his perilous plight. Throwing all caution aside, they raced into the Rebbe's room and quickly helped him dress. Then all three ventured into the pandemonium outside, the Rebbe still bereft of shoes. Luckily the patrols and looters took small notice of them and contented themselves by jeering and throwing stones at them. Fortunately, these missed their target and the three men made it safely to a Jewish house on the outskirts of Przemyslany before Shabbos.

His close chassidim were released from their ordeal only after Shabbos, shattered and crushed. Others were less favored. It was during Shabbos that the disquieting absence of prominent members of the Rebbe's family and chassidim was noted, and they did not return with the eventual release of the slave laborers. Only from the subsequent report of women survivors were they able to piece together the awful truth. Rebbe Moshe'le Rokach, the Belzer Rav's

A letter from Rebbe Moshe'le to the Shotzer Rebbe of London eldest son and a *tzaddik* in his own right, had been residing near the main shul and was unsure of the Rebbe's actual hiding place. When his house caught fire, he had run out into the street together with the venerable R' Rafael Rawa, R' Arye Diss and R' Yosef Artziger. Suddenly, Rebbe Moshe'le noticed the main synagogue in flames and, believing the rumors that the Belzer Rav was still hiding in the attic above the shul, cried out in a panic, *"Vie iz der Tahte* — where is my father?" This alerted the German murderers, who grabbed all four and threw them into the burning shul!

Later, the women were forced to bury forty-two charred bodies in a common grave. As soon as the chassidim discovered the bitter truth, they reburied them individually. Naturally, they were hesitant to inform the Rebbe of the terrible tragedy but the Rebbe had already sensed that something was gravely amiss. All night long, he was heard groaning loudly and crying out in pain, *"Vie iz mein Reb Moshe'le? Vos haben zei nebbech gevolt fun mein R' Moshe'le? Vos hot mein R' Moshe'le zei geshtert?* Where is my Reb Moshe'le? What did they want from my unfortunate R' Moshe'le? What has my R' Moshe'le ever done them?"[4]

Rebbe Moshe'le was the Rebbe's firstborn and extremely close to his father. Saintly and well-learned, he was blessed with a phenomenally sharp brain and extraordinary diligence in Torah study, yet he found the time and energy to exercise charity and kindness. Renowned for his piety and virtue, he was one of his father's most fervent chassidim and his obvious successor. It was hardly surprising that the Belzer Rav respected him so highly. Yet when he was finally told the bitter truth, confirming his worst fears, Rebbe Aharon scarcely reacted and calmly accepted his fate as a Heavenly Decree. He rarely spoke of the tragedy and never kept his *yahrzeit* — although the date of Reb Moshe'le's brutal

---

4. Thirty years later one survivor, Sheva Mautner, graphically recalled in the *Belz Yizkor Buch* how she had emerged from her hiding place to see an unknown Jew with a scorched face, bloodied and wounded, frantically fleeing for his life. As he was closely pursued by the Ukrainian rabble intent on resuming his beating, he screamed, *"Yidden! Ratavert!"* She vainly tried to pull him toward their house but the wild mob continued to chase him. Alerted by the tumult, her mother sprang out and immediately identified the fugitive — *"It's Reb Moshe'le, dem Rebbe's!"* But it was too late and he was forced back to the burning synagogue.

murder, 9 Tammuz, was well known — perhaps so as not to commemorate a personal loss amidst universal suffering. When somebody brought up the subject in the presence of the Briger Rebbe, then a refugee in Przemyslany, the Belzer Rav remarked, *"A chessed fun Der Bashefer* (A kindness from the Creator)! Now I too have paid my dues and presented my *korban!"* — a remarkable statement which spoke volumes of his characteristic fortitude, moral stamina and utter acquiescence to Divine Will.

Rebbe Moshe'le's uncle, the Bilgoraj Rav, later recalled that in the very first days of the German invasion, Rebbe Moshe'le had sensed the grim future and repeatedly implored his father to avert the impending catastrophe. *"Tahte! Daven* that the evil decree be torn up! Pray that the *rasha yemach shemo* should have his downfall very soon — now, immediately!" But the Belzer Rav would only sigh deeply and reply, "It's all in the Hands of Heaven; we can do nothing against the Will of Hashem. It's His Decree ... Yet the bitter end of that *rasha* has surely been decided; he will definitely perish." Even so, with his abiding love for *Klal Yisrael*, Rebbe Moshe'le would not desist *"Tahte, Tahte.* I know that it is in your hands to hasten his downfall ..."

CHAPTER 8

A CHANUKAH MIRACLE

FOLLOWING THEIR SURPRISE ATTACK OF JUNE 1941, Germany now controlled both zones of Poland — plus the Baltic states and huge swathes of Russia — yet although the two halves were incorporated into their *"General-government,"* they were not treated equally. Jews in the northwestern half of Poland, captured in the previous unprovoked attack of September 1939, were subjected to arbitrary humiliation, intermittent slave labor, sporadic murder and random sniping; those in the newly captured territories to the southeast, where Przemyslany was situated, were exposed to prolonged terror and systematic mayhem. In the 1939 invasion, the *Einsatzgruppen* had contented themselves with an orgy of burning and looting before deporting age-old communities and forcibly cramming them into the main cities. With Operation Barbarossa, Nazi oppression had entered an advanced stage in the mass murder of thousands upon thousands. Life in both areas under Nazi domination was awful beyond description, but for the majority of ghettoes in the western half it was survivable, at least at first.

After the brutal slaying of his beloved son, the Belzer Rav went into hiding at the home of one of his chassidim by the name of Pfeffer.

Rebbe Mottele

Besides the two young "Aryan" boys, no family member or follower now knew of his whereabouts — not even R' Aharon Yehoshua Landau, his seasoned and trusted *gabbai* — because of the immediate danger. However, his younger brother, Rebbe Mordechai of Bilgoraj, twenty-two years his junior, was summoned from nearby Berezhany. Although Berezhany was hardly three kilometres distant from Przemyslany, it was inordinately hazardous for any Jew to venture out and Reb Mottele was reluctant to leave his place of refuge, where he had succeeded in establishing an intricate network of charitable and social support services for the starving refugees. Yet when a secret messenger arrived with a personal note in the Rebbe's own handwriting, he complied immediately.

On his arrival, he learned of the Rebbe's total isolation and how no one else of the family had been permitted to call on the Rebbe. So Reb Mottele bravely resolved to visit regularly. To Reb Mottele's great surprise, the Belzer Rav refrained from mentioning his own tragedy. Instead, he related the grim tidings of late July: the *Petlyura Aktion*, with its "Black Friday" culminating in the bloody slaughter of 12,000 Jews in Lemberg (Lvov), among them leading rabbanim and Rebbes — including Rav Benzion Halberstam, the renowned Bobover Rebbe, and Rav Aharon Lewin, the Rabbi of Reischa (Rzeszow) and *Sejm* senator. They had been arrested on July 25 and imprisoned in Gestapo headquarters at 4 Palcinski St. After torture on the following Monday, 4 Av, the Ukranian mob murdered them in a forest off the Yanov highway; surprisingly, their surviving relatives remained unsure of their fate and expended superhuman efforts to release them. (The action was named for the notorious anti-Semite Semyon Petlyura, the virulently anti-Communist, nationalist leader and army commander of Ukraine, where bloodcurdling pogroms were rampant since the winter of 1919. After his escape to Paris he was assassinated by the Jewish poet and Communist fighter, Shalom Samuel Schwartzbard, on May 26, 1926.) The Belzer Rav

The Bobover Rebbe, Rav Benzion Halberstam (seated, second from left), in Lemberg just before the German invasion. To his right is his son and successor, Rebbe Shlomo; to his left are Rebbe Aharon Levine of Reischa, and his son-in-law, Rebbe Moshe Stempel; standing on the left is the Rebbe's son, Moshe Aharon

bitterly bewailed Lemberg's harrowing fate, yet he did not utter a word about Reb Moshe'le's murder, though it had occurred within days of the Lemberg massacre.

Przemyslany's dire situation under German military control continued to deteriorate. Rosh Hashanah and Yom Kippur, normally commemorated in Belz with such fervor amid an excited multitude, now passed off dismally in exile. None of the chassidim were allowed to visit and the Rebbe *davened* alone and forlorn in his private room. The day after Yom Kippur was "celebrated" by German snatch squads grabbing Jews for the slave labor camps of Kyrbitze and Jacturov, followed a fortnight later by the first officially recorded Nazi massacre in Przemyslany, when Ukrainian auxiliaries aided by the military authorities butchered approximately 500 Jewish victims in the nearby forest.

Chassidim in Przemyslany, trapped within the eye of the storm, were helpless to protect their venerable leader. Outside the area, few Belzer chassidim realized the perilous situation of their revered Rebbe, since communications between the two halves of Poland remained almost totally severed. The old borders were still hermetically shut to civilian traffic, and vehicles were strictly searched. All Jews trying to enter the civilian controlled *General-government* from areas previously controlled by Communist Russia were automatically assumed to be "Bolshevik agents" and immediately condemned to death by hanging.

Nonetheless, nebulous yet wild rumors of their Rebbe's fate began to circulate in the clandestine *shtiebels* of Western Galicia. "Have you heard anything lately?" chassidim anxiously questioned each other. "I've heard terrible things, the worst of stories have happened to the holy Rav! Can they possibly be true?" Despite frantic inquiries, they could discover very little beyond appalling reports of early Ukrainian brutality, with the open connivance of the German tyrants. Long known for their unbridled anti-Semitism, the Ukrainians had immediately embarked on a campaign of unfettered pogroms. With mounting trepidation, the Belzer chassidim realized that no atrocity was improbable under the inhuman military regime controlling Eastern Galicia.

After a few weeks, they were relieved to learn that their Rebbe had survived the first pogrom in Przemyslany, but they were shocked to the core to hear how Reb Moshe'le had been slain together with leading chassidim. Reb Moshe'le had been enormously popular for his noble character and selfless charity, and they could scarcely imagine how his father, with whom he had been so close, had accepted the dreadful tidings. Immediately, they resolved to smuggle the Belzer Rav out of the Russian areas to the western half of Poland where it was relatively safer. But would the Rebbe agree to leave his large, extended family? Indeed, he had earlier refused to do so.

Unfortunately, the Krakow area, where the most active cell of Belzer admirers in Western Poland dwelt, was just then undergoing a traumatic upheaval of its own: it had been officially proclaimed that the ancient *kehillah* was to be arbitrarily rendered *Judenrein* but for a small ghetto of 10,000 essential workers. Most chassidim were served with *ausweis karten* (deportation notices), which effectively meant they would have to abandon their homes, businesses and precious possessions. Obviously, now was not the right time to organize a hazardous rescue bid, nor did anyone possess the peace of mind to resolve the complicated details.

Yet concrete steps to extricate the Belzer Rav were soon taken and discreet inquiries initiated as to the best possible refuge in the Krakow area for the Rebbe's comfort and safety. Eventually they located Wisnicz (popularly known as Vishnitza or Vichniowitz), a tiny village which did not appear on most maps. Due to its inaccessibility, without railroad or adequate road system, it could only be approached indirectly by horse and buggy on a five-mile journey from Bochnia. Its sole claim to national fame was that it housed one of the largest prisons in Poland. As a consequence, Wisnicz had never been visited by the German authorities.

This small *kehillah* (not to be confused with its Romanian namesake, home to a famous Chassidus) dated back over 700 years but had often suffered persecution at the hands of its Ukrainian and Polish neighbors. During the Cossack upheavals of the 1640's (infamously known as "*Gezeiros Tach V'Tat*") they were decimated by the Tartar invasion and only slowly recovered. The city became briefly famous as the *kehillah* of Rav Leibush Charif (better known as author of *Arieh Debai Iloye*), a leading chassid of the Chozeh of Lublin, son-in-law of Rav Moshe Teitelbaum of Uhelji (author of the *Yismach Moshe* and founder of the Sighetu-Satumare dynasty) and father-in-law of Rav Yechezkel Shraga Halberstam, the famed Rav of Sieniawa.

Beyond the official requirement to wear a yellow armband identifying the wearers as Jewish, Wisnicz inhabitants might hardly have sensed they were under occupation. Its main synagogue and three yeshivos continued to function as usual and chassidim still wore their complete traditional attire — both on Shabbos and during the week — without harassment. No ghetto had been established there, allowing its Jews to work normally, generally in food manufacture, and several had succeeded in amassing substantial profit. In short, Wisnicz represented an island of tranquility in a sea of oppression and an ideal haven for the Belzer Rav.

A devoted young Belzer chassid from Krakow, R' Chaim Shloma Friedman (who aspired to a prominent role in rescuing the Rebbe), sought to somehow contact the Belzer leadership in Przemyslany and convey this information to the Rebbe. Assuming that Yechezkel Halberstam, the youthful grandson of Bochnia's rabbi, had left Belz and Sokal together with the Rebbe and was probably still in close proximity, he wrote privately to the Belzer Rav, care of Halberstam, informing him that the Krakow chassidim had heard of the terrible calamity and believed Przemyslany to be an unstable area where further trouble could break out at any moment. Instead, they thought Wisnicz would be preferable as an alternative sanctuary until the end of the war.

Young Yechezkel showed the letter to the leading Belzer chassidim, R' Yeshayah Rawa (Prager) and R' Yosel Gold (of Yarotschev), who found the whole plan faintly ridiculous. Surely the Rebbe would never abandon his family to travel alone to Western Galicia. Furthermore, traveling across Poland was dangerous, crossing the old border was perilous, and living in the western half precarious for any Jew known to have come from the Russian zone — and particularly so for a *"Wunder Rabbiner"* who already figured high on the Gestapo wanted list. How on earth would they keep the Rebbe's arrival secret? Gestapo informants had infiltrated the Jewish community of Krakow as thoroughly as they had elsewhere.

Although they determined to dismiss the whole scheme as unworkable and unsafe, they nonetheless showed the letter to the Rebbe to corroborate their decision. To their great surprise, the Belzer Rav immediately agreed to the plan. Obviously, much had changed since he discouraged all escape strategies and had flatly refused to abandon his family. The only condition stipulated was that his brother accompany him. Rebbe Mordechai was obviously tempted since, as he later wrote,"... crossing over to the western half was seen then as akin to passing from *Gei-Hinnom* to *Gan Eden* ..." Yet how could he leave his own family and his vital charity network behind in Berezhany? In deference to his saintly brother's wishes, he reluctantly agreed to accompany him to Krakow if he so desired.

Within a few days they replied, citing the Rebbe's agreement in principle but demanding to know more details of the escape plan. Now the Krakow chassidim had to seriously consider their options and several ideas were floated. An ingenious scheme to smuggle the disguised and heavily bandaged Rebbe in a Red Cross ambulance was turned down as too risky. An alternative plan to transport their Rebbe in a military vehicle driven by German policemen was likewise dismissed as even more dangerous. True, the border guards were unlikely to inspect one of their own vehicles, but who could trust the German police escort not to double-cross them? Who knows what Germans might do were the Belzer Rav entrusted to their sole care? Besides, the Jewish contact who set up this plan was demanding the large sum of 6,000 *zlotys* for their dubious services.

Was there no other more reliable courier? How about Salo (Solomon) Greiber, the assimilated Jewish overseer of the Bochnia labor camp? The large Greiber family was well established in Bochnia, south of Krakow, but Salo had lived in Germany as an *Ost-Jude* for many years before the War and was no longer personally religious. Even after his deportation back to Poland, he had kept up his business contacts with large, influential concerns in Germany. Due to his useful contacts he had managed to establish efficient and relatively humane "workshops" (i.e., small factories) employing approximately 2,000 Jews in Bochnia under *Wehrmacht* auspices, which was infinitely more bearable than SS control. As the expert buyer of the *Bau-Dienst*, Greiber was often allowed to scout round the newly captured territories to expropriate raw materials jettisoned by the fleeing Russian army. Perhaps he could be persuaded to bring an extra passenger back from Przemyslany? Yet who was to persuade him? Salo Greiber was a secular, non-religious Jew who had but a vague inkling what a leading chassidic Rebbe embodied.

R' Chaim Shlomo Friedman had only recently moved to Bochnia following deportation from nearby Krakow and had no close contact with the Greiber family. Under the influence of Rav Benzion — son-in-law of the Vielipoli Rebbe and *dayan* in Bochnia — Salo's religious father, Hershel, finally badgered his son to safely ferry the Belzer Rav from Przemyslany to Bochnia in his own car. At the last minute, however, Salo Greiber backed out of the agreement and set the chassidim back to zero.

Desperately, they discovered one of the *Volk-Deutsche*, native Germans who migrated to Poland in previous centuries. These ethnic Germans were mostly Nazi collaborators and the racial tensions they had warranted had been utilized by the Nazis as a pretext for their unprovoked attack on Poland. This particular *Volk-Deutsche* offered to smuggle the Rebbe out in his private car for a huge ransom. Yet after taking the money and visiting Przemyslany, he likewise let them down.

Finally they found a Polish prince from a distinguished aristocratic family who was employed as a "Commercial Inspector" for the German civilian authorities and was equipped with a military vehicle. As part of his official duties he was empowered to visit farming villages and agricultural enterprises to check on their produce. For a down payment of 10,000 *zlotys*, he agreed to convey the Belzer Rav in his official car from Przemyslany to Wisnicz. From all reports, the man was believed to be reliable but he refused to budge until he had all the money in hand.

Raising those large sums was an arduous task, especially when the whole plan had to be kept a closely guarded secret. Most of the Krakow chassidim had been widely dispersed by the deportations and only a minority had entered the Ghetto set up in the Podgorze district. Surrounded by high walls, over 20,000 Jews (from a previous population of almost 70,000) had been crammed into a few small streets and condemned either to starving or laboring with the Nazis for a pittance — none could afford much money for the Belzer Rav's rescue attempt. Instead, R' Moshe Stern of Bochnia, who customarily collected funds to support the Rebbe's household in Przemyslany, exclusively approached the leading chassidim of each district; because of German travel restrictions he had to resort to sending begging letters that inevitably evoked a less generous response. By mid-December '41, they still had a shortfall of nearly 4,000 *zlotys*.

Meanwhile, R' Chaim Shloma Friedman was temporarily relieved from slave labor when his whole family went down with typhoid, and he took this opportunity to personally collect for the great cause. Although he soon became infected with typhoid and had to fight off a raging fever, he heroically embarked on his self-appointed emergency mission, instead of being hospitalized with his family. Armed only with forged travel documents and with nowhere to eat or sleep, he braved the ever-present Gestapo scrutiny to smuggle himself on and off trains to collect the missing funds, face to face. In a *blitz* campaign, he visited Tarnow, Mielic and Reischa within three days and raised 3,100 *zlotys*. He had intended to continue his successful campaign after Shabbos but the strain and lingering typhoid got the better of him and he could not step out of bed for the next week — by which time his forged travel pass had run out. Nonetheless, his intervention almost closed the financial gap and their emissary, the Polish prince, soon set off.

Early one winter's morning the Polish prince finally arrived in Przemyslany — shortly after America joined the War (following the treacherous attack on Pearl Harbor). But there was an immediate delay. Although the Belzer Rav was willing to entrust himself to his care, he refused to drop his original stipulation — namely that he be accompanied by his younger brother, the Bilgoraj Rav. Accordingly, the prince waited for another day while a Polish police officer was despatched to nearby Berezhany to fetch Rebbe Mordechai Rokach. Rebbe Mottele was most apprehensive when a police car suddenly pulled up outside his home and the officer jumped out. Entering the house, the police officer announced, "I have orders to bring you to Przemyslany, straight away!"

When he saw the panic his words had caused, he added soothingly, "Don't be scared. I have come from the *tzaddik* and I can give you proof; you are about to go on a journey with the *tzaddik*!"

There was no time to hesitate. Hurriedly, Rebbe Mordechai took his leave from his family — who knew not when they would ever meet again, if at all — and entered the police officer's car. (The Bilgoraj Rav's family moved on to Kobrin, where his father-in-law lived, while the Belzer Rav's family stayed on in Przemyslany under the care of R' Yosel Gold of Yarotschev.) But when he reached the Belzer Rav's hideout in Przemyslany, the prince strenuously objected to taking him or any other extra passengers. Only when he was promised more money with the Rebbe's authorization did the prince give way. Even so, he insisted they adopt a less Jewish appearance — by removing their distinctive chassidic garments and also their beards and *peyos* — to reduce the danger of their being stopped en route. The Rebbe agreed even to this repugnant stipulation and both brothers were shorn of all visible signs of their Jewishness.

Neither of them had any official documents or travel permits, and the prince planned to leave after dark — after *lecht-bentching* on the seventh night of Chanukah 5702 (Rosh Chodesh Teves, December 21, 1941). At the last minute two young chassidim close to the Rebbe, R' Nachman Hirsch Singer and R' Dovid Getzel's Erdman,

The Przemsyl Bridge over the River San before the War

joined them as *"gabbaim,"* likewise disguising themselves as non-Jews. As planned, they drove right through the center of Lemberg (Lvov), the scene of dreadful massacres. Lemberg was brightly lit up with armed German patrols accompanying reinforcements rushing to the Eastern Front, where the *Wehrmacht* was reeling from Russian counterattacks at Rostov-on-Don and Moscow. Miraculously, none of these patrols took any notice of the strange car, nor stopped to question its terrified passengers.

After safely exiting Lemberg, they cautiously made their way toward Przemysl on the other side of the old border, still heavily guarded. Because of the everpresent danger, the prince took side roads and followed an indirect, twisted route. "Who knows if we will be able to escape the many patrols in the border zone?" the prince remarked nervously as he peered through the windshield. Suddenly he called out, "Pray to your G-d! We are in great danger!" At that moment, they drove across a bridge over the River San. Everyone held their breath until they reached the other side. By a miracle, the two guards on duty had fallen asleep in their sentry box and did not see the car racing past them. The prince signaled that they had made it to safety by gulping down some strong spirits in celebration.

Yet a couple of hours later he anxiously begged them to pray again. "We are approaching Tarnow, site of the Gestapo headquarters for the whole of West Galicia," the prince explained tensely. "They are notorious! Pray to your G-d that He should help us!" Once again they passed through the center of a dangerous town without a problem.

But as they sped through the dark, quiet streets away from Tarnow, disaster struck. Overcome with exhaustion and fear, the passengers had fallen asleep and apparently their aristocratic driver's attention had also began to wander — perhaps he had treated himself to another celebratory drink ... Suddenly there was a terrific crash. The driver had lost control and the car ran off the road into a ditch. The heavy car rolled over onto its roof, throwing the passengers together into a confused heap, each person sprawled on the one below, with the crushing weight of the wreckage bearing down on them all. The car doors had jammed shut, trapping them among the broken shards of metal and shattered glass.

They truly thought their end had come. As the Bilgoraj Rav began to suffocate, he could clearly hear his brother the Belzer Rav quietly reciting *Vidui*. After a few dazed moments, the Bilgoraj Rav managed to catch a breath of fresh air "in the merit of our holy fathers." With a superhuman effort he pushed his way out of the wrecked car and then successfully pulled the Rebbe free. Finally they freed the Polish prince and the two *gabbaim*, R' Nachman Hirsch Singer and R' Dovid Getzel's Erdman. Hardly had they dragged themselves away from the car when the engine caught fire and exploded. Burning debris flew in all directions, but fortunately none hit any of the escaping passengers.

All were badly shaken and bruised by their ordeal, and some were seriously injured. When Rebbe Mordechai tended to the Belzer Rav, he was shocked to discover that though the Rebbe did not utter the smallest groan or complaint he had a deep wound in one leg, while blood was running down his face.

Their situation was extremely dangerous. It was long after the curfew — 3 in the morning — and they were stranded out on the open road, strangers to the area, without permits or official papers. Meanwhile their main protection against German scrutiny, the official car with military markings, lay wrecked and abandoned in a roadside ditch. Despite the late hour, German army patrol cars rushed back and forth along the main road to nearby Tarnow with its bloodthirsty Gestapo henchmen. Amazingly, no one seemed to notice them. Eventually, the Polish prince decided to limp back into Tarnow for assistance while his forlorn Jewish passengers waited nervously at the side of the highway, abandoned to their fate.

Suddenly a horse-drawn cart rode past them, out of the darkness. Bravely, the Bilgoraj Rav stepped forward and hailed the driver in Polish. The driver pulled up, stared sharply at the strange figures and then called out in a loud Yiddish, *"Yidden! Vos tit ihr doh? Veist ihr nisht az der Gestapo zennen doh dernebben? Eire leben iz nisht vert a prutah!* — Jews! What are you doing here? Don't you know the Gestapo headquarters are close nearby? Your lives are not worth a penny!"

In desperation, Rebbe Mordechai begged the driver to take them somewhere safe although, in accordance with the Belzer Rebbe's instructions, he did not reveal their identity. The cart driver hesitated. "It's far too dangerous to take you lot into Tarnow," he muttered. "The furthest I can take you is to a nearby inn along this road, outside Tarnow."

This inn was the only one remaining in the entire area still managed by a Jewish innkeeper, a Slovakian refugee. At first, when the cart driver hammered loudly on the front door, they were greeted by a deafening silence. Only after prolonged knocking did they finally hear a desperate whisper, "Please. Go away. Leave us alone. I am not allowed to let anyone in."

Even when the cart driver insisted he take pity on Jews wounded in some traffic accident, the innkeeper was too terrified to open the door in the middle of the night. Only after the Bilgoraj Rav solemnly promised the innkeeper that he would not regret saving them did the innkeeper finally agree to risk his life and allow them to stay in the woodshed, round the back. But he carefully locked them in and hung a padlock on the outside, to protect himself from any Gestapo investigation.

The fugitives made themselves comfortable on the floor as best they could. While gratitude and relief for their deliverance from immediate danger predominated, their suppressed pain from the accident now engulfed them. One of the *gabbaim*, Reb Nachman Hirsch Singer, was convulsed with agony, and his screams throughout the latter hours of the night disturbed the sister of the innkeeper whose bedroom abutted the woodshed. As soon as dawn broke she opened the woodshed and asked them how she could help. Yet the Bilgoraj Rav merely requested some water to wash their hands for *netillas yadayim*, and a hot drink.

The Rebbe in Marienbad; on his left is Moshe David Leitner

But when she looked round the small group and saw the wounded Belzer Rav, with a red towel wrapped around his bloodstained face, she cried out, "*Vei iz tzu mir*! That's the *Belzer tzaddik*! For sure, it's definitely him and none other!" Tolsha, the innkeeper's sister, was not originally from Tarnow but had escaped in 1938 from Slovakia, where her father, Mr. Moshe David Leitner, had owned a kosher guesthouse in Marienbad. So she easily recognized the Rebbe from his regular visits to Marienbad before the War. Although the Rebbe was almost unrecognizable without his distinctive beard, now that his face was framed by a towel he was easier to identify. Rebbe Mordechai saw as nothing short of miraculous the remarkable fact that her lodging was right next to the woodshed.[1] She urgently summoned her brother to treat the injuries of the group adequately.

The innkeeper hurried in apologetically with hot coffee and milk, and also bandages, iodine and warm water to clean their wounds. Meanwhile, despite the Belzer Rav's strict instructions, the secret about the presence of the Rebbe in the near vicinity of Tarnow

---

1. However, since neither the Bilgoraj Rav nor the Rebbe discussed this episode with them after the War, surviving members of the Leitner family now doubt whether it was actually their relative.

quickly got out and survivors in the ghetto did everything to help him. Early that morning, a rich chassid, Mr. Goldfarb, urgently shook Dr. Joshua (Isaiah) Hendler awake. "Terrible news!" he whispered despondently. "I have only just heard that the Rebbe of Belz was trying to escape from the Nazi murderers. On the way he's had a bad accident and now his life is in danger! Will you accompany me to his hideout to treat him? We will need to slip out of the ghetto with some medical supplies."

Although he was not religious, Dr. Hendler agreed to risk his life by removing his yellow patch and smuggling himself out of the ghetto without a permit. Outside, a cart and horses were waiting and they hastily drove to the inn. The doctor found it difficult to recognize the Belzer Rav, since his face was still covered with dried blood. As the doctor cleaned and dressed the wounds, he discovered a deep gash in the Rebbe's leg. Dr. Hendler carefully treated this injury and bandaged the wound. While he worked he found it impossible to take his eyes off the Rebbe. Despite his strong pain, despite the anxious situation, the Rebbe's holy gaze stared calmly into the far distance, as if he were totally removed from the present mundane world with all its pressing problems.[2] [However, R' Nachman Hirsch's injuries were more serious and he was taken back into Tarnow for further treatment.]

After the doctor cleaned everyone's wounds, the Rebbe offered him payment for his services. Although he had risked his life, Dr. Hendler proudly refused. "Not even a broken *kopek* — I have only done my duty as a doctor and as a Jew!" At that, the Belzer Rav stood up to bless him that Hashem should protect him together with his close family from all danger and mishap. In addition, he presented him with a 20-*zloty* coin which he blessed as a *segulah* while warning him to guard it carefully so that its merit always protect him.[3] As they left, Mr. Goldfarb begged him to sell him that coin for 2,000 *zloty*. "Anyhow, you don't believe in Wonder Rabbis or their charms! Wouldn't it be

2. Even after many years had passed with numerous traumatic experiences, Dr. Hendler could never forget the indelible impression the Rebbe's calm gaze had made on him.

3. The Belzer Rav had a precise procedure when consecrating coins; they had to be placed a certain way and only the coinage of certain countries was eligible.

better to let me have that coin rather, as a *segulah*?" he argued. Once again, the doctor refused. "I received this coin as a keepsake and I won't sell it at any price!" he replied firmly. Even after he was offered 20,000 *zloty*, he rejected all notion of selling it at any price he might name — "To me this coin is priceless; it is worth *mein gantze leben!*"

Much later, Dr. Hendler recalled, "I must confess that I subsequently experienced miracles and wonders! When the Tarnow ghetto was liquidated, tens of thousands were massacred. Only a few Jews were transferred to Plaszow ghetto, near Krakow — and I was among them! There the great majority of Jewish slave workers fell like flies from exhaustion, torment and mass murder. Yet I survived all their tortures and left that terrible hell alive, with my health intact. That respectable chassid, Mr. Goldfarb, fell among their innumerable victims while I was saved. Later I and my sister survived deportation to Germany. Who knows? Perhaps the Rebbe's emotional *berachah* helped me and I survived in its merit. Although I had to bury the coin with my unpublished medical manuscript for safekeeping in Plaszow, I found them both intact after the War, even though our slave labor barracks had been destroyed."

Meanwhile at the inn near Tarnow several more chassidim smuggled themselves out of the ghetto to visit the Rebbe, see to his welfare and ask for his *berachah*. But the prince who had left his passengers alongside his wrecked car did not reappear. Instead, R' Shmuel Gelbwachs, a renowned Belzer chassid from Bilitz who had been deported to Tarnow, managed to rent an alternative vehicle for their onward journey to Wisnicz. After a day of recovering at the inn, they left after dark. Before they took their leave, the Belzer Rav warmly blessed all who had assisted in their deliverance. The innkeeper surely had no reason to regret letting them in, just as the Bilgoraj Rav had assured him.

At Wisnicz, an anxious group of chassidim braved the curfew and waited at the outskirts to guide the driver safely in without arousing any suspicion. They still hoped to keep the Belzer Rav's presence in Wisnicz a secret, particularly because he had come from the Russian zone. If Gestapo agents or informers ever discovered the truth, there would be dire consequences. According to the driver's estimates, the car should have been here already. Where were they? Had another mishap occurred? Or had they been caught, *chas veshalom*? Fortunately, the chassidim did not lose hope or abandon their vigil. Finally the substitute car turned up, very late but safe and sound.

As arranged, the Rebbe moved in with the notable chassid R' Zelig Shechter, who had a comfortable home. R' Zelig allocated two of his rooms for the Belzer Rav while he and his family contented themselves with the remainder of the apartment. Although the accident had been a frightening experience, it could have been a great deal worse, and everybody was grateful the Rebbe had been safely spirited out of the inferno raging in Przemyslany.

As his chassidim contemplated the miracles that the Belz dynasty had merited on *Zos Chanukah* 5702, they were inevitably reminded of past Chanukahs in Belz. Traditionally, Belz celebrated Chanukah almost akin to a Yom Tov. Throughout Chanukah, chassidim would arrive in the hundreds to watch the Rebbe kindling his menorah in the *graiser-stieb*, accompanied by traditional *zemiros*. Later the Rebbe would deliver a Torah discourse before all returned to the *beis hamedrash* to study late into the night.

The celebrations reached their peak on *"Zos Chanukah"* (the eighth day of Chanukah) with an unusual ceremony. All the new *sefarim* purchased during the past year were carried by *cheder* boys in a charming procession from the house of Reb Itzig Warsawer (Sternberg). Led by their *melamdim*, the sweet children, holding flickering, plaited wax candles and slices of *lekach*, filed past the Rebbe's window as he sat watching the parade with great pleasure, blessing the children that they merit to learn from these *sefarim* with bliss. As the procession marched past the *graiser-stieb*, the Belzer band played music.

Afterwards everyone would return to the *beis hamedrash* to conduct lively *Hakafos* around the *bimah*. Finally the new *sefarim* were placed on their correct shelves. This was closely followed by the *"Zos Chanukah Seudah"* which took many hours, at the Rebbe distributing *sherayim* and delivering Torah — just as at a normal *tisch*. Finally, the chassidim conducted lengthy *rekidos* performed with great intensity until Maariv. Such was the elevated and joyful occasion in Belz of old, but now their present situation under Nazi oppression was anything but joyful.

CHAPTER 9

FOREIGN CONTACTS

W ISNICZ'S FAIRLY INACCESSIBLE LOCATION had spared its *kehillah* most of the indignities and persecutions of their brethren. While the Nazi extermination squads wrought havoc in the Russian zone or the newly captured territories, and Krakow had suffered several Nazi *aktionen* reducing its Jewish population to a quarter of its former self, nearby Wisnicz was scarcely affected by the German occupation. Indeed, it was the general hope that Wisnicz might provide a safe haven for the Belzer Rav until the end of the War — as long as the Gestapo did not discover his whereabouts nor his flight from the Russian zone.

Other chassidim were less sanguine and their plans to convey the Rebbe to a neutral country continued apace, though the urgency of their quest varied with the prevailing situation. The correspondence with foreign contacts was initiated by R' Moshe Stern of Krakow (a renowned prewar Belz fundraiser who underwrote the escape to Wisnicz) when the Belzer Rav was still hiding out in Przemyslany. Wartime correspondence had to be written in German and pass the Gestapo's scrutiny, so their task was complicated by the need

Reb Moshe Gross

for cryptic and confusing hints that would slip past the official censor. Writing via Rav Isumer Domb, the Belzer Rosh Yeshivah in Krakow, he informed the youthful Moshe Gross of Geneva how he had received word from Przemyslany that the Rebbe "very much wanted to convalesce in your area for his health, so please let us know what papers are needed in the meantime." The charismatic Czech *bachur* Moshe Gross had been one of Belz's prominent *yoshvim* until he accompanied a sick fellow *bachur* (for whom he had earlier taken responsibility) to recuperate in Switzerland shortly before the War. Armed with the Rebbe's instructions, he had sailed through visa and border restrictions designed to keep out unwanted Jewish refugees and was subsequently advised by the Rebbe to stay "until the troubles were over," with the personal promise that he would remain forever true to his chassidic upbringing. Because of his close and recent connections with Belz, chassidim placed great conviction in his devotion to their cause and their confidence was not misplaced. Moshe Gross tirelessly threw all his energy, skills and time into the cause; but to those trapped under German occupation, every week felt like a year and matters proceeded far too slowly.

Twelve days after the Rebbe's safe arrival in Wisnicz (January 5), R' Moshe Stern wrote again via the *Judenrat* to confirm, "I received both your reply and the express letter. Grandfather arrived with his brother, Nachman Hirsch and Dovid Getzel's. We are doing our best for the family (i.e. those left behind in Przemyslany). As for his convalescence, please send a doctor here to arrange everything. All the paperwork and exit permits (i.e. for the Rebbe) must also be arranged by yourselves. When Grandfather travels, he will need two assistants (i.e. *gabbaim*)." His next letter informed them, "Grandfather was feeling well and his details are as follows: Aaron Singer, born Nemirov Kraus, Rawa-Ruska, 1876. Nachman Hirsch (Singer) born there 1880. Dovid Getzel's (Erdman), 1879. Please send everything necessary for the journey; because of his weakness he can't do anything. I have written to Reb Yosef Yarotschev (Gold) to send the papers. I hope it will be all right. Also a good bed so Grandfather can have a good rest. Please favor me with a swift reply."

To fool the Gestapo, those dates were as inaccurate as the names. Officially, the Belzer Rav registered under the assumed name of "Aaron Singer" but he was at pains to point out to his chassidim that *chalilah* this was not an entirely false identity since his true family name "Rokach" signifies a chemist, an occupation described in colloquial German as "Singer." To disguise their kinship, his half-brother Rebbe Mordechai registered as "Markus Pecsenik," using his maternal family name (the second wife of the previous Belzer Rebbe, Rebbetzin Chayah Devorah, was the daughter of Rebbe Avraham Shmuel Pecsenik of Brzeziny).

This was closely followed by a letter from R' Isumer Domb who wrote, "We received your letter. Grandfather is willing to travel to convalescence only when accompanied by Nachman Hirsch. R' Shemayah should clarify the details, what preparations are needed, the best mode of travel — car or train. Everything must be prepared. Please reply urgently with all news." "R' Shemayah" referred to R' Shemayahu Binder, a wealthy Belzer chassid from Zurich who had habitually visited Belz during Tishrei, almost every year.

R' Stern's letter coincided with an urgent secret missive from Rav Michoel Ber Weissmandl, the Slovakian hero of rescue in Pressburg, who wrote among other items, "... Included here is a letter to Mr. Gross of Geneva regarding saving the holy Belzer Rebbe. Please see that this letter is answered <u>immediately</u> via this messenger; and I mean a <u>proper</u> answer, which should be sufficient for the wise ..." Both "immediately" and "proper" (i.e. money) are underlined in the original.

R' Moshe Stern's next letter to R' Shemayah Binder of Zurich is also more insistent: "My dear friends, R' Shemayah and R' Moshe, I would like to tell you that I visited the Rebbe this Shabbos. He began speaking of you and remarked that he always found you trustwor-

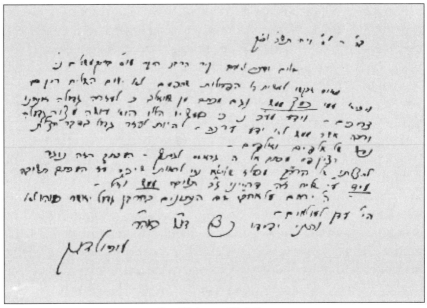

Rav Weissmandl's letter

thy in the past and he is still convinced you will sort everything out for his convalescence as quickly as possible ..." Distressingly, that letter of April 29th was his last before being deported; the correspondence was continued by R' Nachman Hirsch and R' Dovid Getzel's (and occasionally, R' Chaim Shloma Friedman) who used the same conduit to tell R' Shemayah Binder that "I want to relate our *good news* that our mutual friends Moshe Stern and Mr. Yeile have journeyed from here. Uncle has to visit you for treatment before going on to Hirsch (in America). Our friend Leibush Rubinfeld will see it all goes well (i.e. will fund the enterprise) ..." R' Leibush Rubinfeld was a wealthy Belzer businessman from Lugano, with a distinguished reputation throughout Switzerland.

Meanwhile, the Belzer entourage remained in Wisnicz where, prior to the War, Jews formed the overwhelming majority in the townlet and the chassidim more or less ran the *kehillah*. Despite the German occupation, Jews remained free to conduct business or work at whatever they fancied, and they were freely able to buy food on the open market instead of being strictly restricted to meager rations. All the local *chadarim* and shuls functioned normally, as did the three chassidic yeshivos of Radomsk, Bobov and Belz. Although the Rebbe tried to play down the near fatal accident and did not even refer to it on his arrival in Wisnicz, he was bedridden for several weeks. Even so, every Friday night the Belzer Rav arose for *davening* and conducted the prayers and *tisch* as usual. Besides his visible injuries which necessitated constant medical care, the Rebbe was badly bruised all over. Later they discovered that a small shard of rusty metal had lodged in his leg — the cause of

The Bilgoraj Rav after the War

repeated infections and much pain. The Belzer Rav only gradually recovered from his ordeal and suffered the aftereffects of the accident for a long time.

One of the organizers of his escape, R' Chaim Shloma Friedman, was also confined to bed — overwhelmed by typhoid doubtless induced by his superhuman exertions — and only able to visit his Rebbe four weeks later. In Wisnicz, he found the Belzer Rav still recovering in bed; his *gabbai*, R' Dovid Getzel's, introduced him, "*Ot iz doh, Chaim Shloma. Ehr hot gebrengt dem Rabben doh ahehr* — Here is Chaim Shloma, who brought the Rebbe here." The Belzer Rav nodded and replied, "I know, I know." Turning to R' Chaim Shloma Friedman with a warm *Shalom Aleichem*, he thanked him for helping to rescue him from the Valley of Death and expressed his fervent hope that they would all survive to see the *yeshuah*.

Much as they tried, it was almost impossible to keep the Rebbe's arrival secret, since the excitement among chassidim could scarcely be contained. Hundreds exerted themselves to visit Wisnicz and they all had but one central request: "protection from any mishap," as the Bilgoraj Rav later recalled. On Shabbos or Yom Tov, the prayers and *tisch* were mainly attended by residents of Wisnicz — not necessarily Belzer chassidim — but few outsiders would show up. Although Bochnia was within walking distance, they still needed a travel permit, which was most expensive. Ever the generous host, both R' Zelig Shechter and his family, put themselves out for the Rebbe and indeed for any of his chassidim who came to visit.

Generally, the Belzer Rav was able to act openly as a Rebbe with the usual, if reduced, *tisch* surrounded by chassidim in *shtreimels*, while in most other areas, religious Jews cut off their beard and *peyos* to avoid Nazi molestation.

However, they did suffer from occasional scares. One day as R' Zelig Shechter was standing outside his residence — which likewise sheltered the Belzer Rebbe — the Prison Governor, who was an old acquaintance of his, remarked suddenly, "Have you heard that some important *Wunder Rabbiner* has arrived in the area?" R' Zelig hastily gave some noncommittal reply and broke off the conversation, but he was deeply perturbed. Since the prison in Wisnicz was one of the largest in the whole country, perhaps the Governor had heard this information from official circles. Was this a precursor to a Gestapo raid to unearth the Rebbe's whereabouts? If they swooped on Wisnicz and discovered that the Rebbe, already high on their wanted list, had escaped from the Russian zone, then the consequences would be too dire to contemplate! R' Zelig was racked with indecision: if he informed the Belzer Rav of his suspicions, he would cause him untold anxiety and pain. But if he kept it all to himself, might that not abet the Rebbe's capture?

After frantic consultations with leading chassidim and the Bilgoraj Rav, they finally decided to inform the Rebbe of the unpalatable news. Accordingly, they waited until evening, after the Rebbe completed his intensive schedule of prayers; then R' Zelig reported the unnerving conversation and put forward his recommendation that the Belzer Rav temporarily relocate to a safe house while they discovered if anything lay behind the governor's words. Immediately after dark, the Rebbe left R' Zelig's apartment and moved in with Elimelech Miller, a young chassid from Bochnia who lived nearby. Surrounded by his leading chassidim, the Belzer Rav spent a troubled night and day apprehensively awaiting the Germans' next move.

When they saw that the next day passed peacefully with no one making any inquiries after the Rebbe, they finally calmed down and concluded that the Prison Governor had merely been satisfying his own idle curiosity and was not acting under official instructions.

Since his lodgings at the Millers were not suitable, the Belzer Rav returned to his former apartment with R' Zelig Shechter.

While life within Wisnicz itself remained relatively tranquil, macabre rumors swept the district over the probable fate of the deportees. Since early 1942, thousands upon thousands of "non-essential Jews" (i.e. penniless refugees, women, children, the sick and elderly who were incapable of working for the German war machine) were being brutally "evacuated for work in the East" in railroad boxcars, over eighty persons crammed like so much freight into each sealed boxcar. Naturally, their unknown destinations raised morbid fear and few trusted vague German assurances. Besides, what "work" were most of the deportees capable of? Were the massacres of Ukraine and Russia being replicated here? Terrible stories seeped out from the Auschwitz concentration camp erected on marshland not far from Krakow, but nothing yet of systematic mass slaughter. Little concrete evidence of the widescale Nazi atrocities was then available in Poland, so to where were all those hundreds of thousands of Jews vanishing?

Repeatedly, the Belzer Rav was heard to utter heartrending groans behind closed doors: "*Ribbono Shel Olam*! For how long shall those *reshaim* rejoice? What more does that *rasha* want from the Jewish people; downtrodden, broken, orphaned, exiled? Oh, *Ribbono Shel Olam, Imo anochi betzarah* — I identify with their agony." Despite the Rebbe's oft expressed wish to leave Poland, he fully empathized with the plight of the Jews living there. Although still recovering from the motor accident, the Rebbe *leined* the *Megillah* that Purim as usual, and his rendition of Queen Esther's phrase, "How can I bear to witness the disaster approaching my people?" was recited with unusual concentration and emotion. Likewise at the *tisch*, the line from *Shoshanas Yaakov*, "*Arur Haman asher bikesh l'abdi* — Accursed be Haman who sought to destroy me" was repeated three times for extra emphasis.

The day after Purim, they received the first firm indication of what had happened to the deportees. A Belzer chassid, R' Naftali Rubinstein, originally from Krakow and now living in Oshpitzin (the townlet whose name was transposed to the infamous death-camp on its periphery) smuggled a secret letter back to the Rebbe. Its contents were horrific, beyond belief:

> *It was a total lie that the deportees were taken for any work. Throughout a long journey, dragged out for many days, they received not a crumb of food or water — neither the adults nor the children or babies. Whenever they passed near large towns, the Gestapo mercilessly forced back Jewish communities providing food and drink and callously denied their prisoners even a drop of water. Anybody attempting to throw them food from a safe distance was forewarned they would be shot on the spot! Naturally, some of the deportees died before they reached their destination. The boxcars traveled past Rawa-Ruska through a nearby forest on specified tracks to a small town called Belzec, where large crematoriums have been erected. Every day tens of trains arrive with fifty or sixty boxcars full of men, women and children. About an hour after their arrival, terrible screams and shrieks could be heard by the Jews of Rawa-Ruska.*
>
> *According to a few individuals who managed to escape the bloodbath, when the boxcars were unlocked most of the captives were already more dead than alive. They were assembled in a large clearing and addressed by a Gestapo officer who told them that this was not a labor camp, merely an aufenthaltslager (transit camp or sammellager) to sort out workers according to their skills. After this short speech, they were surrounded by many guards (including Jews under duress) and marched to a large shower hall where they were ordered to undress. But instead of water emerging from the showerheads they were all suffocated by some gas! After the first group was killed, the next unsuspecting groups were led in without knowing what had just happened. Meanwhile piles of bodies were dragged further into the forest and burned but since they were incompletely burnt, the stench of decomposing flesh could be smelled throughout the forest and lent credence to the survivor's horror stories.*

When this staggering letter arrived with its gruesome message, even most pessimists found it simply inconceivable. That the sadistic Germans were prepared to murder or torture at will — they all knew this only too well after two-and-a-half years of terror and trauma. But the systematic, cold-blooded slaughter of thousands of men, women and children day after day after day? It beggared the imagination; how could it possibly be true? Were human beings — even Germans — capable of sustaining such calculated wickedness? Yet when they discussed it with the Belzer Rav, who had always excelled at seeing the best in everyone, he groaned deeply and painfully.

At the same time, other more soothing rumors circulated about a wholesale German retreat from the Russian Front, but the Belzer Rav dismissed these as unsubstantiated and premature. "Don't rely on mere rumors," he warned. "Even if they were true, the battlefront is too far away to affect Polish Jews! From here the Nazis will not leave so quickly. Quite the contrary, any setback raises the possibility that the *rasha* may take revenge by stepping up his persecution of the Jews."

Copies of that letter were circulated and the macabre tidings spread by word of mouth to warn Jews of the ghettoes and German "workshops" to take every precaution to avoid "Evacuation." Belzer chassidim, meanwhile, frantically redoubled their efforts to transfer their Rebbe out of Poland by any means available, and the tone of their letters to Switzerland grew increasingly urgent and demanding.

By Pesach, the Rebbe had fully recovered from his injuries and was invigorated enough to conduct his Seder and *tisch* as in former years. However, Chol HaMoed was met with more bad news. After absorbing tremendous losses in men and equipment because of the bitterly cold Russian winter, the *Wehrmacht* had regrouped. With the approach of spring they prepared for their major second offensive toward Stalingrad (coupled with lightning attacks across Northern Africa and through Egypt) and, to protect themselves against the inclement Russian weather, they imposed the seizure of all fur clothing in Poland. The confiscation was carried out with utmost brutality. Women innocently dressed in fur cuffs and collars or men wearing *shtreimels* — with little knowledge of the latest decree — were arbitrarily shot. Despite his habitual sensitivity to cold (probably due to his continual fasting) the Rebbe also had to relinquish his heavy, distinctive *peltz*.

Wisnicz's population was deeply disquieted that German overseers had visited their townlet to confiscate furs, dashing the fragile illusion that Wisnicz might continue to escape Nazi attention. Hitherto, no deportation *"Aktions"* had been perpetrated in Wisnicz, while the bribing of local commanders had ensured that they contented themselves with grabbing men for temporary slave labor. The likelihood that Wisnicz would eventually be sucked into the seething maelstrom around them was acutely unnerving. Their dark mood of pessimism was somewhat lightened by widespread confirmation of enormous German losses and setbacks at the Russian Front, which sparked many anti-Nazi jokes and jingles. Tens of chassidim gathered to share the good news with the Rebbe, and when he heard the tidings after a long day of prayer and mortification, he announced publicly, "Until now it was impossible to do anything! Now we can already ask *Hashem Yisbarach* for the Germans' complete downfall ..." However, the Belzer Rebbe was deeply troubled and remarked sadly (as the Bilgoraj Rav later recalled), "By rights, that *rasha* ought to have his downfall at one stroke! Otherwise an accumulation of smaller setbacks might escalate our calamity. It may goad him into revenging his disgrace on his hapless victims!" The Rebbe's fears were not misplaced.

CHAPTER 10

A PILLAR
OF TENACITY

MEANWHILE, THE FRANTIC PLEAS OF THE BELZER chassidim finally began to bear fruit and the external effort to rescue the Rebbe gathered pace. On Sunday, May 25, 1942 (two days after Shavuos), R' Berish Ortner of Tel Aviv received an official summons from the English censor at the main Allenby St. Post Office. On arrival, one of the officials informed him that a telegram had arrived from Switzerland addressed to him. Yet instead of handing over the telegram, the official proceeded to interrogate him. "Do you know Rabbi Rokach? Do you know a Shemayahu Binder?"

"Yes, I do know Mr. Binder from Switzerland," he answered carefully. "And if by Rabbi Rokach you are referring to the Grand Rabbi of Belz, then of course I know him too, as do many others."

Despite his satisfactory answer, the officials refused to hand over the telegram or even tell him what message it contained. "You will receive the telegram at your home address," observed the English official laconically, waving him to the door. When three days passed without the delivery of the intriguing cable, R' Berish began to get seriously concerned. There was a good chance the cable would be

Reb Berish Ortner

impounded or destroyed altogether and he would never see it. Under the British Mandate during wartime, Palestine was subject to strict military discipline, so every communication from abroad was viewed with grave suspicion; this telegram was apparently more suspect than most. But R' Ortner was never one to be stumped by mere obstacles. In this whole Belzer saga, if ever there was the right man at the right place at the right time, that man was R' Berish Ortner.

He was born at the end of 1882 in Hibniv (Uhnow, in the Rawa-Ruska district) where his paternal and maternal families were traditional communal leaders. Hibniv was subservient to Belz both in influence and geography, at a distance of only 22 kilometers. The young Dov Berish had visited Belz regularly from the age of 8, where Rebbe Yeshie'le had made an indelible impression. He had met and respected old chassidim of the first Belzer Rav, the Sar Shalom. After his marriage, R' Berish set up as a printer and received the all-important license after a prophetic blessing from Rebbe Yissachar Ber. He was also Hibniv's assistant official registrar. In the upheaval of the First World War, he migrated to Berlin where he soon became firmly established — involving himself in countless charitable activities with selfless tenacity. In addition, he took a leading part in overseeing *mikvaos* and religious education, and acted as deputy president and treasurer of the *Ost-Juden Verband* representing Eastern European refugees. Despite his intimate connections with German Orthodoxy, he retained his chassidic heritage, returning each year to Belz for Tishrei, and favored with Pesach matzos from the Rebbe's inner circle. Above all, he combined the inner warmth of a chassid with the punctiliousness and attention to detail typical of German Jewry.

As an outsider at the advent of the Nazis' rise to power, he foresaw the future more perceptively than most native German Jews and obtained the Belzer Rav's blessing to emigrate to Eretz Yisrael — though his "defection" sent shockwaves through Orthodox German Jewry. On Lag B'Omer 1933, Rebbe Aharon agreed and advised him to reside in a large town. In an unusual step, the Belzer Rav accompanied him to the street at his departure, remarking, "If a Jew is traveling to Eretz Yisrael, one must escort him!" As a result he was escorted by large crowds of Belzer chassidim on his departure, arriving in Tel Aviv in Tammuz 1933, at the age of 51. Now with this elusive telegram R' Berish Ortner felt it his life's mission to prepare the way for the Rebbe's arrival, since he was privy to the previous Rebbe's private but intense longing for Eretz Yisrael. For the next two years, he put all private considerations aside in his single-minded goal to extricate the Belzer Rav despite all obstacles. Rather than delegate, he would undertake even the most mundane tasks; instead of employing a secretary for the numerous letters to officialdom, he tapped them all out himself on his personal typewriter. But first, he had to find out what that mysterious cable contained.

As a preliminary step, he met with Dr. Rosmarine, the Polish Consul. By way of introduction, Mr. Ortner reminded the Consul that as Deputy President of the German *Ost-Juden Verband* he had returned to Poland in April 1933 on behalf of East European Jewry and in preparation had secretly met in Berlin with Dr. Pniger and Dr. Wisoski, the Polish Consul and Ambassador respectively. Later he had conferred with the Belzer Rav who had given him several letters of recommendation, including one to Dr. Rosmarine himself (who was then a *Sejm* parliamentarian), and as a result he had joined an urgent meeting in Lvov (Lemberg) which sent telegrams to government ministers and *Sejm* representatives in Warsaw. In response, instructions were sent to the Polish Ambassador, Dr. Wisoski, to convey a protest to the German government — and the German Foreign Office had replied by issuing a directive "not to treat foreign citizens adversely."

"Now," continued Mr. Ortner gravely, "a telegram has apparently arrived from a Belzer devotee, Mr. Shemayahu Binder of Switzerland, referring to the Belzer Grand Rabbi. I am sure he is alive and certainly needs some help. But the censor refuses to hand it over to me; so I would be most grateful if the Consul would assist my receiving it." Dr. Rosmarine replied that he well remembered the campaign on behalf of Polish Jewish citizens in Germany and promised to personally meet with the chief censor, who had a Polish background. "Come back tomorrow, and I will have some news for you."

By then Dr. Rosmarine had arranged an appointment for Mr. Ortner at the chief censor's office on Yafo St. at 11 a.m. "Tell him that I've sent you and if you have any documents about yourself or the Belzer Rabbi, please bring them along. No doubt you will have further cables and he can instruct the officials to hand them over without reservation." Accordingly, on Friday, May 29th (13 Sivan) 1942, R' Berish Ortner finally met Mr. Waituski in his private office, together with three other high ranking officials, where he showed them three newspaper cuttings: a German report from an evening paper on July 5, 1929, described the personality of the Belzer Rav during his visit to Professor Rosen in Berlin for medical treatment. The *Neuer Morgan Lemberger Togblatt* of September 22, 1936 described the courtesy visit of Prince Peter of Greece, a cousin to King George VI of England, to the Belzer Rav during Rosh Hashanah. The Warsaw *Moment* of April 30, 1939 contained the Belzer Rebbe's patriotic proclamation urging Polish Jews to support their government's efforts to raise a National Loan.

After showing them some of his personal documents from Poland and Germany, Mr. Ortner announced, "As soon as I receive the telegram, I will travel to Jerusalem and pass the contents on to the Chief Rabbi of Palestine, Rav Herzog, to the Jewish *Sochnut* and to any other personalities and institutions capable of dealing with this important cause." The British officials studied the documents and newspaper reports carefully before Mr. Waituski concluded, "This all seems satisfactory. You can go now and the telegram will be delivered to your shop at 111 Nachalat Binyamin St. within a few minutes. Any further cables relating to this issue will be forwarded to that address without delay." When Mr. Ortner finally saw the telegram dated May 23, 1942, in the French language, he was not much the wiser:

Obviously, "medical certificates" was a veiled allusion to Palestine
Entry Certificates. But who was Ernest Gelley? Or Dr. Ashur?
Hastily, R' Ortner traveled to Haifa that Friday to consult with
leading Belzer chassidim. However, most of them told him what
he had already discovered — that it was almost impossible to acquire a certificate for those previously under enemy occupation. On
that *Shabbos Beha'aloscha*, R' Berish was awarded an *aliyah* and was
called up for *revii*; his portion ended early on the verse (*Bamidbar*
9:23), "At Hashem's word they camped, at Hashem's word they
moved on, the charge of Hashem they would safeguard, according
to Hashem's word to Moshe." R' Berish instantly saw this as deeply
symbolic. "You see," he exclaimed excitedly to those around him.
"The Rebbe's emissary is called up and his *aliyah* concluded on such
an optimistic note! This is proof that with *Hashem Yisbarach's* help,
the Rebbe will come to Eretz Yisrael!"

On Sunday, R' Berish journeyed to nearby Nahariah to speak to
Ernest Gelley — but to no avail. Mr. Gelley insisted he had no idea
why he was mentioned in the telegram and knew nothing of the
Belzer Rav. On Monday R' Berish went to Bnei Brak to question Dr.
Ashur but he was similarly mystified at the connection and could
not enlighten him. In fact, cryptic references to Gelley and occasionally Ashur continued to appear in subsequent cables but the key to
the enigma surfaced only after several months.

That Monday, R' Berish traveled to Jerusalem to consult the
leading Belzer chassidim at R' Shaul Frankel's apartment, and they
advised him to meet with Rav Akiva Sofer of Pressburg. Because of
his close interest last year (when the Lubavitcher Rebbe had pressed
for entry certificates for the Belzer Rav) he might advise him on
his next move. The meeting with the chassidim broke up late that
evening, yet he went on to Mr. Steinberg (brother of the Jaroslaw
Rav and noted activist); but Mr. Steinberg only arrived home at 3
a.m. from another urgent meeting. As soon as he saw the telegram,

The Bilgoraj Rav (second from left) sitting with Rav Herzog (far right); between them is Dayan Hillman, Rav Herzog's father-in-law; far left is Rav Charlap

Mr. Steinberg straightaway set up an appointment with the Chief Rabbi, Rav Yitzchak Isaac Halevi Herzog, for 9 a.m. On Tuesday morning, R' Berish met the Pressburger Rav at 8 a.m. for nearly an hour, but no practical suggestions resulted.

When his taxi drew up outside Rav Herzog's two-story residence on Ibn Ezra St., Rechavia, he found Rav Herzog delivering a *gemara shiur* to an audience of about twenty men. Rav Herzog interrupted the *shiur* to read the cable before asking, "Where is the Rebbe?"

"In Switzerland!" R' Berish replied in surprise.

"How do you know that?"

"Because the telegram comes from Switzerland!"

Rav Herzog shook his head sorrowfully as he pointed out, "I am *baruch Hashem* capable of reading a telegram — even in French![1] But I repeat, where is the Rebbe now?"

This question hit R' Berish Ortner like a hammer blow: there was no indication to the Rebbe's current location. Since there had been so little information available in Eretz Yisrael as to the Rebbe's whereabouts, he had fondly imagined his Rebbe was safely waiting for his

---

1. Rav Yitzchak Herzog actually grew up in Paris.

entry certificate in Switzerland when he was probably still trapped in Poland under German occupation. As realization dawned as to the gravity of his beloved Rebbe's predicament, he suddenly burst into a flood of tears accompanied with large cries — "*Mamesh* like Yom Kippur before *Kol Nidrei* in Belz!" The participants at the *shiur* were shocked to see a grown, white-bearded man of 60 cry uncontrollably, but Rav Herzog was even more affected and he fell off his chair in a dead faint!

Through his sobs, R' Berish asserted that he was not crying for the lack of certificates but for the joy of hearing that his Rebbe was still alive. "*Der Eibeshter* Who has spared him till now can certainly save him without certificates. Yet since one cannot rely on miracles we must do all we can." Rav Herzog was still shaken and, turning to his *shiur* participants, he remarked in amazement, "Here you can see the strength of a chassid!" Without delay, he took his official stationery and composed a letter to Mr. Moshe Shapira, head of the *Sochnut's* Aliya Department. Because of Mr. Ortner's intense emotion he only managed to read the opening sentence: "Some earn their *Olam Haba* in an hour; now the hour has arrived to earn your World to Come ..."

After Rav Herzog sealed the letter, he handed it over to R' Berish while instructing him, "Go to R' Moshe with *hatzlachah,* and *Hashem Yisbarach* should assist you! Meanwhile, I will contact him by phone." Shortly after leaving, R' Berish met Rebbetzin Henele Perlow, the sister of the Belzer Rav, who asked him to accompany her back to Rav Herzog. But at the door, they were met by the *shammas* who barred their way. "Because of that man," he said, pointing angrily at Mr. Ortner, "Rav Herzog has had to put himself to bed with a high temperature!" Rebbetzin Perlow tried to pacify him. "I am a sister of the Belzer Rav and I would like to meet the Rabbanit Herzog, if I may." The *shammas* reluctantly agreed on the proviso that "this man does not come with you. Do you want the Rabbanit to become as sick as the Rav?" Indeed, R' Berish's visit left an indelible impression on Rav Herzog for years to come, as the Chief Rabbi frequently recalled.

R' Berish then proceeded directly to Mr. Shapira and handed over Rav Herzog's letter with a copy of the telegram and a list of names of the Belzer Rav's family. "I'll give you certificates from all my heart and with everything within my power," Mr. Shapira promised. "But first you'll have to telegraph to find out exactly how many certificates are urgent, plus their names, ages and place of birth."

Despite this favorable response, R' Berish still explored every avenue and approached R' Yitzchak Meir Lewin, the erstwhile leader of Polish Agudah now heading Central Agudas Israel in Eretz Yisrael. "Reb Itche Meir" was naturally reluctant to part with the precious certificates since beyond the tight restrictions imposed by the British, religious Jews were further limited to only 6 percent of the general quota. How could he afford over sixty certificates for all the Belzer relatives? Everybody in Poland, Europe and much of Russia was clamoring for these certificates in the hope that they might save their lives. "The most I could possibly offer are three certificates," he said at last. R' Berish was not content with this and presented a *kvittel* to the Gerrer Rebbe (who had escaped from Poland to Eretz Yisrael in Nissan 1940 together with his son-in-law, Reb Itche Meir):

> *Yerushalayim Ir Hakodesh. Aharon ben Basha Ruchamah, the Rebbe of Belz, shlita, is in great danger according to a telegram I received from Switzerland. The son-in-law of the Rebbe, Rav Yitzchak Meir, shlita, told me today that he will give three certificates from Agudas Yisrael to send to Switzerland. Hashem Yisbarach should help that there be no opposition or obstacle chas veshalom and they will send the certificates immediately so that his holiness the Belzer Rebbe, shlita, can shortly come here to the Holy Land without any problems. Amen.*

In reply, the Gerrer Rebbe gave his blessing while instructing his son-in-law not to delay *chas veshalom* even for a moment. Meanwhile, news of the Belzer Rav's survival and his entreaty for certificates received banner headlines in most national newspapers. After R' Berish Ortner reported back to Switzerland by cable, he discovered that he had been laboring under a misconception. In fact, the certificates were not directly intended to be used for entry into Palestine, rather as a stratagem to acquire transit permits through Switzerland. The Swiss activists had successfully acquired entry visas to Cuba for the same reason, partly with the help of R' Yakir Beigal-Eissen of America, as another letter from the Modzhitzer Rebbe on May 20, 1942 revealed. The Modzhitzer Rebbe also informed them that the Belzer Rav was living in Wisnicz and was not incarcerated by the Nazis, and that his family was being adequately supported by donations from abroad.

Over the next six days, R' Berish explored every avenue to pressure his previous contacts to achieve results. He persuaded the Supreme Court Judge Gad Frumkin (who had earlier made inquiries at the urging of the Lubavitcher Rebbe) to motivate Rav Yitzchak Herzog and also Mr. Eliyahu Dubkin, who chaired the *Sochnut's* Immigration Department together with Mr. Shapira. He presented a second *kvittel* to the Gerrer Rebbe who again instructed Reb Itche Meir to send certificates with all haste and to the best of his ability. Not content with this, he further convinced the rebbes of Husyaten, Boyan, Chortkov, Sadigura, Przemsyl and Zlatapoli (all members of the Rizhin dynasty) to press R' Yitchak Meir Lewin for the certificates.

Rav Zvi Eisenstadt was persuaded to approach both Dr. Rosmarine, the Polish Consul, and Rav Herzog, who later met over tea to discuss tactics. However, none of these stratagems bore fruit and the certificates remained frustratingly absent; scarcely any certificates — destined for "Veteran Zionists" — were available even to the *Sochnut* and certainly none to spare. On Monday the 23rd of Sivan, R' Berish sent a strongly worded express letter to the Chief Rabbi, exhorting him to move more quickly, suggesting that any delay would be queried both by Jews abroad and by posterity, and elaborating on the Belzer Rav's prominent communal role — "Who fits the description 'veteran' more than he?" While the mills of bureaucracy continued to grind exceedingly slowly, Rav Herzog personally invited affluent donors to his residence and persuaded them to contribute financially to the Belz rescue effort; hard-pressed faculty members at Jerusalem's *Chaye Olam* yeshivah skimped on wages and meals to associate themselves with the cause. Meanwhile, Zurich cabled the Belzer Rebbe's details on May 15, 1942:

PRESENT DATES OF REBBE AND COMPANIONS ARE RAV
AARON SINGER BORN 1876 IN MAGROV NACHMAN HIRSCH
SINGER BORN 1880 MAGROV DAVID ERDMAN BORN 1879
MAGROV SEND CERTIFICATES VIA TELEGRAPH TELEGRAPH
IF PAPERS HAVE BEEN GIVEN TO ERNST GELLEY NAHARIAH
SHEMAYAHU BINDER

These changes in their names and places of birth were most fortunate since it effectively side-stepped official British opposition
to anyone residing under German jurisdiction. Objections raised
earlier by British security services — after R' Moshe Blau had directly approached the Palestine High Commissioner on the Belzer
Rav's behalf — could easily have scuppered the whole rescue effort,
but there was less likelihood they would connect "Rabbi Singer of
Magrov" with Grand Rabbi Rokach of Belz. Hardly had R' Berish
passed this cable on to Chief Rabbi Herzog and Mr. Shapira when a
further worrying cable arrived from Zurich on May 17, 1942:

HEALTH OF RAV BAD SEND THREE CERTIFICATES HAVE
YOU GIVEN CHAIM NOTA'S PAPERS TO GELLEY NAHARIAH
FOR DANNENBAUM CABLE SHEMAYAHU BINDER

At that time, early June 1942, Krakow suffered its first *aktion*, as
the Nazis euphemistically termed the deportations. On May 30th
(14 Sivan) the Gestapo suddenly ordered all Krakow Jews to present
themselves to the military authorities to have their papers checked.
Out of 17,000 Jews still remaining in Krakow ghetto, some 5,000 had
their documents invalidated and were herded into Zaguda Square
together with the sick and elderly, and were deported to Sobibor
death camp. A few days later, searches were launched for "illegal"
Jews hiding out without papers, and approximately five hundred
were deported to the Belzec death camp.

Back in Wisnicz, a young man had arrived from Lublin with
harrowing tales of the persecution. After the mass deportations, survivors had at first hoped the deportees had been located in Ukraine
not far from the front. But then a short letter was smuggled in from
a townlet near Lublin with a stark message: *"Please implore the Rebbe*

to pray for our souls. Jews! All are led to death camps without exception! Since the Jews don't know this, they march there without resistance. Better to warn them to flee before they are taken by force."

As the Bilgoraj Rav later recalled, this shocking note confirmed the unbelievable letter received earlier from Belzec and threw the Rebbe's entourage into consternation. Copies were promptly sent to sixteen towns to publicize the warning. Naturally, this spurred the chassidim to redouble their rescue efforts and presumably lay behind Zurich's urgent cable. When he received the latest telegram, Mr. Shapira promised to send three certificates forthwith to their contact Dr. Shefes in Switzerland.

Meanwhile, R' Berish journeyed back to Nahariah to confront Mr. Gelley. Already on June 5, 1942, Mrs. Gelley had let slip that her husband had indeed received amounts of money from England for a "Mr. Dannenbaum," but now Mr. Gelley continued to flatly deny any knowledge or involvement. Consequently, R' Berish urgently cabled R' Chaim Nota Katz in London on June 18, 1942:

TELEGRAPH IF YOU SENT ANY PAPERS FOR THE RAV ORTNER

R' Chaim Nota was a leading Belzer *chassid* and fundraiser in England who had apparently been sending money destined for the Rebbe to private addresses in Palestine to circumvent wartime currency restrictions. Unfortunately, this cable received no immediate reply since it was sent to an old address and it was months before a written letter got through.

Obtaining the vital certificates was also problematic. While Agudas Yisrael had to regretfully inform Belz chassidim that they had none to offer, the *Sochnut* agreed in principle to allocate three certificates from those destined for "Veteran Zionists, Rabbis etc." But they were not prepared to release these until they had firm evidence they actually would be used to extricate the Belzer Rav. Since certificates were in critically short supply during the dire emergency, priority had to be given to urgent supplications from those trying to escape certain death. Under pressure, the most they were prepared to do was have the certificates prepared at their Eretz Israel Office, Geneva, immediately available for all eventualities.

Among several prominent personalities who approached the *Sochnut* on behalf of Belz chassidim was the saintly Rabbi Yaakov Moshe Charlap, who wrote to Mr. Shapira:

> *I cannot contain my deep anguish after hearing the terrible, shocking news. How can we wait and remain silent without saving this Leader in Klal Yisrael? From my heart I beg you to exert yourself to try again, find an avenue by your own inquiries. It will undoubtedly be a great zechus for you. Yesterday I visited Rabbi Fishman (Maimon) and he is prepared to help.*
>
> *I write in tears and distress, your strong friend,*
> *Yaakov Moshe Charlap*

Fortunately, on the basis of Palestine certificates available in Geneva, the Swiss government agreed to issue transit visas on July

Reb Hillel Vind (left) at the Rebbe's side in Yerushalayim

8, 1942 — just over one month after Mr. Ortner was first contacted — though it took some time before the news filtered back to Eretz Yisrael. After Rosh Hashanah (September 12, 1942) Mr. Ortner wrote privately to a leading Belz chassid in Jerusalem:

> To my friend, Reb Hillel Vind, shlita
>
> I would like to tell you that this week Dr. Ashur in Bnei Brak received a letter from his sons in Switzerland who report that the Tzaddik of Belz has been given an entry visa there; but only for himself and they are now trying for at least one gabbai. They are hopeful and believe he will soon be in Switzerland.
>
> I think you should better not publicize this — only to R' Avraham Prester and R' Avraham Mader, but instruct them not to spread it further! I think you can also trust R' Itche Meir Lewin and he should see how they could have helped sooner! But I have not lost hope that Hashem Yisbarach will guard our Rebbe, shlita, until he escapes those sadists.
>
> Of course we should have sent proper certificates and they would already have been there — but everything is in Heaven's Hands ... Wishing you all a Gemar Chasimah Tovah and all Jews should rapidly be helped completely with total help.
>
> With respect,
> Berish Ortner

Unfortunately, extricating the Rebbe from Poland to Switzerland proved futile. At that juncture, obtaining an exit visa — officially or unofficially — was hopeless, despite their best efforts or expenditure of immense sums.

CHAPTER II

SURROUNDED BY DANGER

THE CONTINUING DEPORTATIONS INDUCED ACUTE unease among the Belzer Rav and his chassidim, even in the relative security of Wisnicz. Their first step was to protect the Rebbe with foreign credentials, since foreign Jews or *Auslander* were officially exempt from most onerous Nazi regulations and *Judengezetzen*. Foreign citizens did not have to wear an identifying *Magen David* armband, could live outside the ghetto, and were free of travel restrictions (thus allowing them to engage in many types of business now off limits to their fellow Jews). Even those who preferred to live and work within the ghetto desired foreign citizenship since these travel freedoms enabled them to escape the area whenever an "evacuation *aktion*" was threatened.

As a result, hundreds of Jews petitioned relatives and friends in the neighboring countries of Hungary or Slovakia for foreign papers (usually genuine papers of strangers), and a select few even obtained passports from Uruguay, Argentina, Turkey and Switzerland. Leibish Pflaster, a Bobover *yeshivah bachur*, drew upon his artistic talents to carve a fake Hungarian seal and fabricate Hungarian certification, forging these lifesaving papers even at the expense of

An idyllic painting of Wisnicz and the surrounding countryside

his own escape from Bochnia. However, all these bogus documents had to be authenticated by the Gestapo — a procedure fraught with danger, usually smoothed over by bribery and ingenuity. Fortunately, Bochnia's new chief of gestapo, Schoemburg, took an extremely lax attitude to documentation and would affix his signature and SS seal without question, even to blatantly dubious or counterfeit papers.

Surprisingly for a Gestapo officer, Schoemburg, a 60-year-old German, was not an overt anti-Semite — though he could murder with the worst of them during *aktions* — and he frequently showed visitors around the Sanzer *kloiz* or *beis hamedrash* in Bochnia. As news spread of his benign attitude, a growing stream of documents from further afield arrived for his endorsement, but eventually the Gestapo Headquarters in Krakow vetoed Schoemburg's authentication. In desperation, a Tarnow chassid, R' Avraham Mehr, began issuing counterfeit stamps and signatures which could not be distinguished from Schoemburg's valid endorsements. Even Schoemburg could not tell the difference between the counterfeit and genuine article and, under pressure from Gestapo border controls, he eventually limited their validity outside the Krakow district. (Unfortunately, the Gestapo later "placed all foreign Jews under their protection" and shipped them all off to Bergen-Belsen, where they were closely questioned as to how they had acquired their citizenship. Most did not satisfy the SS and were shot; only the few who had gone to the exorbitant expense of obtaining genuine passports survived.)

The Belzer chassidim did not want to rely on the thriving black market in counterfeit documents since their easy availability debased their value. After prodigious exertion, they managed to obtain a genuine passport from Turkey in the name of a Jewish resident there. In the event of an *aktion*, which generally lasted no longer than two or three days, the Rebbe could be spirited away to another area since the *Einsatzgruppen* extermination squads usually operated in only one area at a time. However, when rumors circulated about a forthcoming raid by the extermination squads, the Belzer Rav remained apprehensive about the actual protection a false passport would afford.

Urgently, he sent a special messenger to summon R' Chaim Shloma Friedman from nearby Bochnia. "The situation is most unpredictable! *Zeit mochel* and try and obtain a separate travel permit for me — just in case. Please keep this top secret!" R' Chaim Shloma often traveled on business to Tarnow with a false travel permit and was greatly experienced in dealing with the black market. A travel permit in the name of "Aaron Singer" was duly acquired and lodged with a reliable chassid, available for whenever the need arose. (Naturally, the Turkish passport could not be used in conjunction with the travel permit since they ostensibly related to two different people.)

R' Chaim Shloma Friedman himself was not totally satisfied with either tactic so they also dug a small "bunker" or underground hideout beneath the Rebbe's residence in Wisnicz. In the event of being caught in an evacuation *aktion* when official papers were of doubtful value, the Rebbe might be concealed from the murderers' scrutiny for a vital few days while the extermination raid ran its bloody course. Then he could be moved to a safer area.

The feared blow fell in early Elul (mid-August 1942). As usual, the first sign of an impending raid in Wisnicz was the unwelcome appearance of Simon Spitz, a hateful Gestapo collaborator from Krakow who had often informed on fellow Jews. Earlier, soon after the Belzer Rav's arrival in Wisnicz, a group of young chassidim had consulted the Rebbe, asking whether Spitz's betrayals might come within the halachic definition of *"rodef"* and thus permit his elimination in self-defense. The Belzer Rav held his head between his hands for a few minutes while he thought deeply. Eventually he replied, "No! One cannot murder a Jewish soul! Perhaps his grandchildren will be *ehrliche* Yidden." Then the Rebbe stared into the distance while he murmured to himself, "Grandchildren? ... Grandchildren? ... Perhaps he himself will yet repent with a complete *teshuvah!*" Those fateful words were later to prove prescient.

Spitz, who originated from Dhibetz, a townlet in Eastern Galicia, had the looks and behavior of a sinister gangster: tall, middle-aged, with a dark complexion and sharp eyes that missed nothing. Like his German masters, he wore knee-high, gleaming leather boots and habitually carried a large whip, so that people instinctively kept their distance. Those who met his displeasure were noted in his reports to the Gestapo and usually arrested within twenty-four hours. The Germans treated him with deference, freeing him from all the onerous regulations and restrictions that applied to other Jews. Officially, he worked as an undercover agent for the political department (targeted primarily at Polish resistance groups whom he frequently betrayed) where he had his own office, but he was often a harbinger of imminent *aktions*. Routinely, he would demand a large ransom to thwart any planned "evacuation" but his payoff usually proved as worthless as his glib assurances of safety — *Einsatzgruppen* raids would inevitably follow. Whenever Spitz appeared in an area, its Jewish inhabitants sensed they were doomed.

Inexorably, in late Av (the second week in August 1942), Spitz duly arrived in the Bochnia ghetto with a group of Gestapo officers and plunged the whole district into turmoil. They summoned a meeting of the Bochnia *Judenrat* and unreasonably demanded 250,000 *zloty* within two weeks; otherwise, they threatened deportations. The *Judenrat* dutifully called a public meeting in the presence of Salo Greiber (the industrial boss of Bochnia slave workers) where several speeches were made appealing for enormous funds to avert the evil decree. Although most suspected that this was nothing more than a German ploy to squeeze every last *zloty* out of the trapped Jews before destroying them, the money still poured in and the immense fortune was raised within only a few days. Despite this, few trusted

German assurances; those who were able to dug bunkers or sought refuge outside the ghetto.

Their trepidation was heightened when they heard how Spitz and his entourage had visited Wisnicz on the same day. *Chalilah*, had he discovered the whereabouts of the Belzer Rav? Would he ferret out the closely guarded secret? Once the Gestapo's star informant unearthed who was hiding behind "Aaron Singer" or "Markus Pecsenik" and how they had escaped from the Russian zone, their cover would be totally blown and they would be in mortal danger. The chassidim's grim foreboding was not misplaced. Spitz quickly sniffed out how one of their prize quarry, for whom the SS had hunted unsuccessfully throughout Galicia for almost three years, was in fact concealed in the hamlet of Wisnicz.

The chassidim persuaded R' Eliezer Landau, a prominent Bochnia businessman who had "connections" with the Krakow's Chief of Gestapo Jewish Section, to visit his contacts to sound out any recent developments behind the scenes. Their worst fears were rapidly confirmed on his arrival when he was immediately interrogated by the section chief, *Obersturmfuhrer* Wilhelm Kunde. "Were you aware that the *Wunder Rabbiner* Rokach is living in Wisnicz? Is it certain he recently arrived from areas under Bolshevik occupation?"

Mr. Landau paled, especially at the last question. Generally, any Jews who had lived under Soviet jurisdiction were automatically suspect of being "Communist agents" — liable to be tortured and killed. Yet how to deny it when the Gestapo appeared fully confident of their latest intelligence; they freely admitted it had come from their loyal informant, Simon Spitz. Mr. Landau realized he had no option but to bargain openly with the killers. After promising them "something special," they agreed not to molest the Belzer Rebbe. As a token of their "sincerity and goodwill" they whispered the secret information that Wisnicz was shortly due for an *aktion* and the *Wunder Rabbiner* would be safer elsewhere ...

Before R' Eliezer Landau could organize extricating the Belzer Rav from Wisnicz, the *Einsatzgruppen* struck. On Sunday, 10 Elul (August 23, 1942), placards were hung up in Bochnia and all the surrounding towns of the district. Signed by the *Judenrat* on behalf of the Gestapo, it ordered all Jews to vacate their homes and relocate to Bochnia by Saturday, August 29, at the latest. Anybody who disobeyed the order would be shot. They were to be eventually housed in the overcrowded ghetto, but "on a temporary basis" they could reside in the disused army barracks, near the railroad depot.

Many Jews did not comprehend the full seriousness of this decree, nor the ominous proximity to the only railroad in the vicinity, and innocently assumed the SS merely wanted to concentrate all Jews in one enclosed precinct. Those around the Belzer Rav were less sanguine and realized that the Rebbe's peaceful sojourn in Wisnicz had come to an end. Initially they planned to ferry the Rebbe to nearby Krakow, away from the immediate area under threat, but rumors surfaced of an impending *aktion* there too. Reluctantly, they decided to convey the Belzer Rav to Bochnia as a preliminary move, but separately from and earlier than the other Wisnicz inhabitants.

Under the influence of R' Eliezer Landau, Salo Greiber dispatched a car to Wisnicz on Thursday, 14 Elul, for the use of the Rebbe, his brother and the two *gabbaim*, R' Dovid Getzel's and R' Nachman Hirsch. Before they could board the car, they were surrounded by all the Jewish residents of Wisnicz — men, women and children — to take leave after the Rebbe's eight-month stay in their *kehillah* and ask for his blessing. As the car pulled away, all of them spontaneously broke down and sobbed. Who knew what the future held ... Who knew whether they would ever meet again in this life ...

The journey to Bochnia passed without incident, but the Rebbe remained apprehensive. Although a loyal chassid, R' Chaim Langer from Bilitz, had vacated his apartment for the Belzer Rav while he and his family found alternative accommodation with relatives (no mean feat in the cramped, vastly overcrowded ghetto), the Rebbe was unsure whether Bochnia itself was safe. Salo Greiber repeated his assurance that as long as the ghetto factories functioned on behalf of the German army, *aktions* would only involve Jews residing in outlying areas. Yet the Rebbe was far from convinced. When his brother the Bilgoraj Rav suggested that they immediately journey on to Krakow — contrary to public sentiment — the Belzer Rav replied, "*A pele* (a wonder)! My heart tells me the same thing!"

Their first night in Bochnia passed peacefully and no official came to inquire how they had suddenly appeared in the ghetto or to examine their papers; nonetheless, the Rebbe was adamant that they must continue on to Krakow. Even when R' Chaim Langer notified them that his apartment contained an excellent and secure bunker which would surely protect them in the event of an *aktion*, the Belzer Rav could not be dissuaded. Indeed, many other Jews desperately sought refuge outside Bochnia rather than rely on official reassurances. In the name of their Rebbe, the chassidim begged R' Leizer Landau to utilize his exceptional contacts in Krakow to organize a hasty escape to Krakow.

Early in the morning, Mr. Landau arrived with a truck of the *Baudienst* (German slave labor detail) camouflaged with piles of clothes. The truck was already crammed full of men, women and children standing, sitting or clinging to the sides. Mostly these were "illegals" escaping from Wisnicz and Bochnia whom Mr. Landau felt bound to save. Many were communal leaders, such as Rebbe Yeshayeh Halberstam of Czchow (Chechov), youngest son of the Divrei Chaim, the Sanzer Rav. The chassidim were appalled and openly argued with Mr. Landau. "How can you endanger the Rebbe like this? You promised a private taxi! Such a large group of people, all without permits, multiplies the risk tenfold and threatens everyone! Nor have any of these passengers an entry permit into Krakow."

R' Leizer admitted that his plan entailed enormous peril and actually asked one of the chassidim, R' Yosef Friedman, who had a forged entry permit to accompany the truck in case of any "unforseen inspection" — but he insisted they had no choice. "Officer Kunde, my Gestapo contact, has flatly refused to help or provide a secure car. It's far too dangerous for me to go back and forth between here and Krakow; I can only make the one trip. Besides, I have a Gestapo permit to ferry workers around in this truck to wherever work is available."

Although some chassidim suspected that Mr. Landau's true motive was to mobilize the Belzer Rav's *zechusim* (heavenly credit) to rescue the other fugitives, they grudgingly agreed to his hazardous scheme. It was difficult to find a suitable place for the Rebbe on the crowded truck, and in his weakened state the journey was a nightmare. Besides the constant fear, the standing passengers swayed and staggered from side to side, as the heavy truck bumped and ground its way to nearby Krakow. Nevertheless, the Belzer Rav displayed his satisfaction that so many Jews had escaped alongside him.

That they were not stopped on the main highway between Bochnia and Krakow was little short of a miracle. Generally, whenever an *aktion* was imminent the Gestapo canceled all travel permits and increased their regular patrols throughout the area to prevent escape. Moreover, this *Bau-dienst* truck was so overloaded with refugees they had to jettison the piles of clothing that should have been screening the escapees. Despite the obvious presence of fugitives, the truck was not detained. Their entry into the ghetto also passed without incident despite the chassidim's well-founded qualms. The truck should have been searched at the gate but the ghetto guards were headed by a German officer, Buskuh, who was a secret anti-Nazi and he personally allowed the suspicious truck in without any checks.

They had escaped deportation by a hair's breadth. The remaining Wisnicz residents arrived early Friday morning in a long convoy of horse drawn wagons and made their way with great difficulty through Bochnia's narrow streets. Instead of being allowed to disembark at the ghetto, the Polish policemen directed them all to the barracks near the railroad depot under heavy guard. Realizing they were being led into a trap, some disobeyed their guards' orders and — abandoning their possessions — jumped off the wagons and mingled with the surrounding crowds where they were soon indistinguishable. Others followed their example when signaled to do so by acquaintances from Bochnia, but the majority were enclosed in the old army barracks. Even those who hid in the Bochnia ghetto were not safe since, despite all the official assurances, Bochnian inmates were also slated for the deportation *aktion*.

Within Nazi echelons there had always existed arguments over whether their chosen role to murder Jews took precedence over harnessing their vital slave labor for the war effort. Now, either by accident or design, the Germans released mixed and confusing signals. Only the day before the scheduled *aktion*, the chief director of *German Textiles Farband* in the *"General-government"* (as the Germans described occupied Poland) visited Bochnia to place fresh orders and reassure them that although all other Polish ghettos were "emptying out," Bochnia was safe for the long term. Their official Nazi newspaper, *Krakower*

The central marketplace and square in Bochnia

Zeitung, published a lengthy and favorable article about the Bochnia enterprises, describing them as a *gross betreib* (substantial industry). None of this helped in the slightest.

The seeds of destruction had actually been sown earlier, in the spring. During April 1942, about a week after the *Krakower Zeitung* published an official notice closing down the large Lublin ghetto (initial deportations had already begun there without warning in mid-March), two top Gestapo officers from Krakow, Kunde and Becher, were invited to Lublin to watch Globocnik in action and learn how it was done. *Brigade-fuhrer* Odilo Globocnik was then officially only head of SS and police in Lublin, but he was to become one of the prime engineers of the extermination program known as Operation Reinhard; his name alone was enough to strike fear into the heart of any Jew.

The *Einsatzgruppen* raid on Bochnia, Shabbos 16 Elul (August 29, 1942), was ruthless and brutal. Of the 8,000 Bochnian residents who assembled in the central square to "have their papers checked," approximately 1,200 were summarily machine-gunned at a mass grave in the nearby village of Baczkow, including rabbanim, chassidic Rebbes, activists, and the elderly and sick. All the rabbis in the Bochnia ghetto were first gathered into one courtyard where the Germans forced them to lie on the ground for hours while they humiliated and tortured them. The shocked remnant (plus the thousands from surrounding villages) were forced onto the freight boxcars waiting at the railroad depot; only about 1,500 were "selected" for work. Many of those hiding in the bunkers were tricked into abandoning shelter when the Jewish police force announced, "Anyone who goes to the trains voluntarily will be sent to a slave-labor camp. But those who are caught will be executed!"

After three days, the *aktion* had rendered Bochnia into a pale, shattered effigy of the former *kehillah*. The 1,500 survivors wandered aimlessly about the blood splattered walls of the ghetto, in a daze after having witnessed parents and relatives murdered before their eyes. Every place bore signs of the unrestrained bloodbath and looting. Even "the all-powerful Ghetto boss," Salo Greiber, had been tortured and murdered after he was caught on the phone complaining to a *Wehrmacht* officer about Gestapo interference with his factories, essential to the war effort. He made the fatal mistake of relying solely on the authority of the army whom he had faithfully supplied with vital goods while ignoring the Gestapo of Krakow and Bochnia. During the *aktion* when the SS had sole charge, they had unleashed their gruesome revenge.

Fortunately, the rumors of an impending deportation raid in Krakow itself timed to coincide with the attack on the Bochnia district were false. Since it had undergone a brutal *aktion* almost three months earlier, in early June, Krakow's inhabitants were safe for the time being. At first, the Rebbe was safely accommodated in the apartment of R' Yidel Diss (son of the saintly R' Chaim Diss from Korzcin). Approximately 20,000 Jews subsisted in the Krakow ghetto officially designated for 10,000, so general accommodation was extremely cramped — several families in one room. The apartment the Rebbe shared with the Diss family barely provided him with a tiny room two meters square.

Now that they were in Krakow, directly under the control of Gestapo headquarters, the chassidim were anxious to keep the Rebbe's identity and arrival a secret. It was a forlorn hope. On the very day they arrived, Simon Spitz wormed the secret out and dutifully hastened to inform his Gestapo overseer. The next day, the Jewish Police Chief Simchah Schapiro arrived with his crony, Prester. Officially, the Germans had established the *Ordnungdienst* (as the Jewish police were known) to keep order in the factories once "Aryan" policemen were withdrawn from the ghettos, but when the pace of deportations quickened, they were forced into the corrupt role of collaborators.

Simchah Schapiro was a case in point. An unassuming and obliging man before the War, he had earned a moderate wage as a Krakow house painter; after the invasion he became a *shammas* to the *Judenrat*. Because of his strong physique he was promoted to the ghetto police force where he rose rapidly through the ranks until he was appointed Police Commissioner of the entire Krakow district. By then he had become a compliant tool in the hands of the Nazis and was roundly feared for his sycophantic enforcement of their cruel decrees. Whereas in his previous incarnation he had even sported a small beard and acted as a *baal tefillah* during the High Holy Days, now he was a egoistic mercenary replete with gleaming uniform, loaded revolver and a large dog always at his side. He took a special dislike to lawyers, doctors and those of the former elite.

On the morrow of the Rebbe's arrival in Krakow, Schapiro swaggered into the Diss apartment with the other police officers. All of them had earned their spurs in the Gestapo's employ by their betrayal of fellow Jews, and their unannounced appearance aroused enormous fear and consternation. Yet the Belzer Rav treated them as honored guests, offering them a chair and refreshments and sitting with them for a short time discussing everyday affairs. Their whole demeanor changed and they were enraptured by the Rebbe's personality, speaking respectfully and gently. As they took their leave, Schapiro declared, "Rebbe! For my part I will do everything within my power for your sake. Not a hair of the Rebbe's head will be harmed as long as he resides under my protection! Only one viper is likely to cause the Rebbe trouble — Shimon Spitz! He is the one who informed the Gestapo of your illegal arrival here and he is the one capable of passing on this intelligence to the higher authorities!"

After the group left, the chassidim contemplated their next step. How were they to legalize the Rebbe's position? How could they neutralize Shimon Spitz? How could they protect the Rebbe from the Gestapo's baleful eye? To their great surprise, the Belzer Rav then suggested they summon Spitz for a meeting! At first they were horrified at the very suggestion. Spitz was infamous for his callous behavior and heartless treachery. At best, he would see the summons as a bad joke. Anybody who approached him risked being a prime candidate for Gestapo attention. But if the Rebbe seriously suggested it ...

The Bilgoraj Rav asked a young man, R' Mottel Ehrlich (son of the late R' Chaim Ehrlich, a renowned Belzer *lamdan* in Krakow), if he would be brave enough to invite Spitz round. Trembling in fear of his life, Mr. Ehrlich went in search of Spitz and found him playing cards. "What do you want?" Spitz snarled in Polish. Ehrlich replied fearfully that the Belzer entourage would like to see him — Schapiro, Prester and a few other Gestapo favorites had already been there and now they would like to meet him. "*Pah!* Can't you see I'm busy? Don't worry, there'll come a time when I'll enter his room!"

This ominous answer threw them all into deep foreboding. The next day Spitz suddenly arrived, but he showed a total lack of respect — he did not even bother to cover his head. Disguising his fear, the Bilgoraj Rav received him courteously and tried to soften his attitude. "Have you ever heard of the Belzer Rav? Do you know anything about him?"

"Of course I've heard of Belz, I was born in East Galicia," Spitz replied scornfully. Patiently, the Bilgoraj Rav explained their quandary, residing in Krakow with no official papers or permit. But Spitz opened his eyes in wonder. "I'm surprised at you rabbis! I used to think you were clever; now I can see you've got no *sechel*! What do you expect from me? Officially, I am not in the Gestapo section dealing with Jewish affairs. Besides, has anybody heard of me — Spitz — having ever done a fellow Jew a favor?"

Even so, the Bilgoraj Rav did not desist; when would he ever have a better chance? Besides, the very fact that Spitz had actually come to visit the Belzer Rebbe must mean something. "Look here," he continued. "This could also be to your own advantage! Thousands of chassidim will respect and trust you; they may even help you where necessary. We need some assistance and you are in the unique position to assist us." This argument made a profound impression on Shimon Spitz who was roundly hated and despised by everyone and desperately craved some devotees of his own. "I'll think about it," he muttered gruffly as he left.

The next day, he reappeared with two work permits signed and stamped by the Gestapo, one in the name of Aaron Singer and the other in the name of Markus Pecsenik. These work permits were then seen almost as a lifesaving passport. However, Spitz was not content. Apparently, he was so taken by the Belzer Rav's personality that he advised his Gestapo bosses to visit the *"Wunder Rabbiner"* for themselves!

Without warning, Spitz reappeared the next day accompanied by Kunde, Heinrich and Hase. Usually, these three angels of death struck morbid fear into any Jew they met, and for good reason: They were under direct orders from Berlin and organized every *aktion* in that region of Galicia. Hase was their chief while Kunde and Heinrich were his deputies; all were present at every *aktion* where they often shot and killed indiscriminately, leaving a trail of corpses littering the street. Now these murderous beasts marched right into the Rebbe's room. The fright they caused can scarcely be imagined; Spitz's presence was the only reassurance that perhaps they meant no harm. Fortunately, the Gestapo leadership sat at the Rebbe's table for only a few minutes before they politely took their leave.

Actually, Kunde and Heinrich had told Mr. Landau of their wish to meet the *Wunder Rabbiner* earlier — when they had first discovered his whereabouts in Wisnicz — and requested that he be properly dressed for the occasion in his "official Grand Rabbi's clothes" including a silk *bekeshe* and a fur *kolpik*! R' Eliezer Landau had attempted to prepare the Belzer Rav for the visit, assuring him that if the Gestapo really intended to maltreat him they already had ample opportunities to do so. At that time, the chassidim had managed to put that unwelcome meeting off; now in Krakow under direct control of the Gestapo they had no such leeway. Doubtlessly, R' Leizer's many "presents" had help soften their attitude to the *Wunder Rabbiner*, officially still high on the Gestapo's Wanted List.

Spitz's next call was hardly less hair-raising. He suddenly burst into the Belzer Rav's room bellowing on top of his voice. "Belzer Rebbe, you may not stay here any longer!" Everybody was shocked into silence at this frightening statement as Spitz continued in a slightly calmer voice, "A different apartment must be found ... something more suitable for the Belzer Rebbe!" Though everyone breathed a sigh of relief, the Belzer Rav was most perturbed: Who knew how Spitz might obtain larger premises in the overcrowded ghetto? He was quite capable of evicting any number of families — or deporting them altogether — in order to requisition their apartment. "Please, *zeits moichel*," the Rebbe begged, "I'm very happy with this room, it suits me just fine! I don't need anything else."

Yet Spitz was not deterred by this; most likely he was acting under Kunde's instructions to provide a larger residence for the Belzer Rebbe. Spitz marched into the Judenrat and demanded they find a better apartment, somewhere nearer his own place, so he could keep a close eye on the Rebbe and ensure he came to no harm. Fearful of Shimon Spitz's authority and willfulness, the Judenrat set to the task in a hurry and soon found a large apartment at 7 Josepynska Street, which shared a courtyard with Spitz's own flat. It was already occupied but the Judenrat persuaded the owner, Mr. Freilich, to vacate two rooms and the large balcony on behalf of the Belzer Rav and his brother. In the densely crammed ghetto this was luxury indeed and the saintly brothers were duly grateful.

CHAPTER 12

UNDER GESTAPO SCRUTINY

I N THE GERMAN SCHEME OF OCCUPATION, CENTRAL
and Southern Poland had been renamed *General-Government*,
and Krakow designated its capital, with Hans Frank reigning as
Governor General at the historic seat of Poland's kings. Before
the War, the ancient Krakow *kehillah* had a population of over 56,000
— equal to many a small country — and their numbers had swelled
to at least 68,000 when the Germans decimated provincial *kehillos*.
Frank was anxious to reduce Krakow's Jewish population to the
minimum so Jews should be neither seen nor heard; expulsions (euphemistically described as "voluntary departures"), deportations
and ghettoization proceeded apace. Most of Krakow's Jews were
served expulsion notices and less than one-quarter were permitted
to remain in the ghetto at the Podgorze precinct. After the June 1942
aktion, only 11,500 Krakow Jews officially remained in the ghetto
situated in the meanest, most crowded neighborhood.

Krakow also housed Gestapo headquarters, which masterminded
the accelerating mass "Evacuation" program. That they had so far
kept their offensive hands off the Belzer Rav, still on their "wanted
list" from the 1939 invasion, was nothing short of a miracle. The

two brothers settled into the cramped ghetto as best they could. Their living quarters were better than most: a small room and kitchen of their own; but this was a far cry from the substantial Belzer *kloiz* back home. Shimon Spitz, erstwhile Gestapo agent, did indeed train a careful eye on the Belzer establishment, in keeping with his commitment.

Hardly a day passed without him dropping in to see the Rebbe, usually late at night. Although he customarily left the Gestapo for home only af-

The Jewish Quarter in Krakow

ter 2 a.m., he would first check on the Belzer residence to ensure there were no problems. Unlike at his initial visit, Spitz now behaved with greater decorum and respect. Before entering the Belzer Rav's room, he would wash his hands in the outer chamber. Once inside, he would sit at the table talking as quietly and as respectfully as any ordinary chassid.

The chassidim soon noted that the Gestapo did not molest the Belzer Rebbe and that many of their agents showed their esteem by their regular visits, joining the *tefillos* or presenting *kvittlech*. Relieved, chassidim came flocking to the Rebbe's address seeking solace and sanctuary. Many were "illegals" who had no official work permits or permission to reside in the Krakow ghetto, having smuggled themselves in — as had the Rebbe himself. Paradoxically, the Belzer Rav's influence grew in the teeth of these awful circumstances and the constant need for concealment; even those far removed from Chassidus or the "superstitious belief in wonder-working rabbis" came for blessings and advice. As the pace of deportations quickened, the Belzer Rav sought to save what could yet be saved or advised petitioners how to escape. Krakow Jews from all circles saw him as one of Poland's remaining treasures, shielding him from harassment and warning his entourage of every possible danger.

On one occasion, a Jewish policeman took it into his head to inspect everybody's papers at the Belzer residence. Sure enough, he quickly discovered a number of Belz chassidim who had smuggled themselves into the Krakow ghetto without any German passes in order to be close to their Rebbe. This policeman stirred up enormous trouble — until Shimon Spitz heard about it. He flew into a rage and swore to take revenge on that Jewish policeman. However, the Belzer Rav intervened and begged Spitz to forgive him and let the matter rest; that hapless policeman never caused trouble again.

Undoubtedly, Spitz's close proximity to the Belzer Rav wrought a fundamental change in Spitz's behavior and motivation. As he later admitted to the *gabbai*, R' Dovid Getzel's, "As soon as I set eyes on the Wonder Rabbi, something stirred within me! His glowing eyes haunted my innermost soul, probing my whole being, seeking out merit and transforming me into another person, a new entity!" Outwardly, little had changed. Spitz still worked for the Gestapo — by then he was in too deep to have much choice — and he continued to be present at *aktions*.

Certainly he openly provided hundreds of resident or work permits for "illegal Jews" not officially allowed into the ghetto. After the Rebbe and his brother had their position legalized (as the Bilgoraj Rav later recalled in his official report), Spitz supplied similar certification for the two *gabbaim*. R' Dovid Getzel's in particular became most friendly with Spitz and when chassidim seeking sanctuary with the Belzer Rav recognized the Gestapo agent's amazing behavioral change, they persuaded the *gabbai* to ask for permits on their behalf.

Spitz listened carefully to the request before promising that he was prepared to *"Kosher"* all documents entrusted to his care. At first, they were unsure whether to trust him. After all, he had been one of the most feared men in the ghetto until very recently, liable to betray any Jew or Pole who crossed his path. Only a few of those in desperate straits with little to lose dared hand over his papers. To their amazement and relief, Spitz returned that evening with their permits properly signed and stamped by the Gestapo.

This quickly became a standard procedure. Every day he would authorize documents from more of the refugees previously seen congregating around the Belzer Rav. Shimon Spitz became so accustomed to the practice that whenever he entered the Rebbe's apartment he would first ask if there were any more permits to be processed before attending to any other business. Interestingly, he would not undertake this anywhere else but at the Belzer residence. This became so well known among religious Jews that many would ask the Belz establishment to legalize their papers.

In a short time, he had voluntarily helped hundreds of Jewish fugitives without being asked, and all for no money or recompense. Undoubtedly, Shimon Spitz was attempting to perform some *teshuvah* for his earlier behavior. Even his bitterest enemies and rivals among the Gestapo network of informers had to admit that ever since Spitz had come under the influence of the Belzer Rav, he had entirely stopped denouncing his fellow Jews to the Gestapo. Previously, thousands of Jews and Poles had been betrayed by him.

The abrupt change was traced back to a fateful meeting soon after the Belzer Rav's arrival in Krakow. Spitz had appeared at the Rebbe's residence in the grip of some deep emotion and insisted in speaking with the Rebbe alone — "between four eyes." Everybody left the room, including the Bilgoraj Rav, while Spitz remained closeted with the Rebbe for some time. Later, people claimed that Spitz had unburdened his soul, wept at the invidious situation in which he had entangled himself, and begged to repent for his enormous misdeeds. Apparently, based on Spitz's future behavior, when he asked the Rebbe to recommend a strict regime of improvement to somehow redress the harm he had inflicted, the Belzer Rav had demanded that at the very least, he refrain from informing on his fellow Jews.

After Spitz joined the *tefillos* or presented a *kvittel*, some of the embittered ghetto inmates began half jokingly referring to him as "*Hechasid Reb Shimon* ..."! Others scoffed at his close connection with the Belzer Rav and openly questioned how a renowned *tzaddik* like the Belzer Rebbe could associate with such a notorious *rasha* and lackey of the accursed Gestapo. Only those with insight and perception recognized the fundamental transformation the Rebbe had achieved even with such unpromising material. Ever since his fateful change of heart, Spitz was frequently closeted with the Belzer Rebbe and would reveal to him secret information of the Gestapo's plans — or so chassidim surmised. Regularly he burst into tears as he sobbed about the terrible predicament in which he had entrapped himself. Although he had served the hated Gestapo loyally, he realized full well that they were planning to get rid of him.

Rosh Hashanah 5703 (Shabbos, September 12, 1942) was Poland's fourth Rosh Hashanah under the heel of the Nazi jackboot, yet in Krakow it passed relatively quietly without any major incidents, and Spitz arranged for suitable protection around the Rebbe's rooms. The Rebbe personally led the *davening* of Minchah and Maariv — the final *tefillah* of the outgoing year and the first of the new year. The *tisch*, conducted late at night, as was customary in Belz, was attended by approximately 100 chassidim, despite it being long past the curfew. Many chassidim from Bochnia and even Tarnow had arrived on forged travel documents and were joined by other brave souls who had risked their lives to smuggle themselves out of the notorious labor camps and into the Krakow ghetto in order to pray in close proximity to the Belzer Rav. Fortunately, they all behaved with such circumspection and caution that none of the German officers or their underlings suspected anything untoward.

Despite their enormous *mesiras nefesh*, their numbers were pitiful when compared with Belz in its heyday. Yet because of the limited space — particularly for *tekias shofar* (on the second day of Yom Tov) — many of the chassidim were forced to arrange separate *minyanim*. Even Simchah Schapiro, the infamous commander of the Jewish Police, presented a *kvittel* on Erev Rosh Hashanah and returned on the second day of Yom Tov to hear the sounding of the *shofar* at the Rebbe's *minyan*. All were amazed to observe how the Belzer Rav continued the customary Belzer *nigunim* and *minhagim* without deviation, even under the oppressive Nazi regime.

Slave laborers sealing off the Krakow ghetto

Shortly after Rosh Hashanah, disquieting rumors swept the Krakow ghetto: Yet another evacuation *aktion* was being planned for Krakow's inhabitants! Would this *chalilah* be their last? Why hadn't Spitz, or any of the other Gestapo collaborators, warned the Rebbe? In fact, Shimon Spitz flatly rejected the scare stories and insisted that there was no truth in them. After several days it was revealed that a major *aktion* had actually been planned but was unaccountably postponed to a later, unspecified date. Despite the general apprehension, Yom Kippur also passed peacefully, and on Erev Succos, Spitz arranged for a ghetto engineer to build a *succah* in the Rebbe's courtyard. On Shemini Atzeres and Simchas Torah (October 3 and 4, 1942), the Belzer Rav *davened* with a relatively larger congregation; doubtless many recalled that emotional final Shemini Atzeres in Belz, three years earlier.

Shortly before the War, in 1938, the Belzer Rebbe had been hospitalized in Krakow for eye treatment, but the operation had been only partially successful. One of the Jewish doctors who had exerted himself for the Rebbe's care then, now renewed his acquaintance in the ghetto and continued to treat him as far he was able without adequate facilities or medical supplies. As the liquidation of the ghettos and their Jewish population accelerated remorselessly, this doctor ventured to ask for the Belzer Rav's blessing. "I bless you that you remain alive," replied the Rebbe.

"But what will happen to my family? Please bless them too!" the doctor persisted. The Rebbe replied, "Your family will also survive." Even then, the doctor was not entirely satisfied. "And what will happen in general?" he continued. This time the Rebbe replied with finality, "Both of us will live and don't ask me any more questions!"

The Belzer Rav was not always so explicit. When one of his close chassidim asked his advice about where to escape, he merely paraphrased the daily *tefillah* of *Hashivah shofteinu*, translating the words *"v'yoatzeinu kevatchilah"* as "we should be able to receive guidance as previously."

Because of his close watch on the Rebbe's household, Shimon Spitz soon realized how they suffered from a chronic lack of food and cash. Numerous chassidim had been deported and others were incarcerated in the horrendous labor camps. Even those still in the ghettos were severely impoverished and overworked, while normal fundraising was rendered impossible by the restrictions on travel and mail or the ever present curfew.

Without further ado, Spitz organized a weekly collection among the various ghetto industrialists and financiers and regularly brought in 1,800 *zloty*, a substantial sum, which the Rebbe mostly forwarded to Przemyslany, where his extended family of over sixty souls was facing serious deprivation and starvation. Even from his hiding place he tried to help fellow refugees as much as he was able and dispatched food parcels to starving *gedolei haTorah*. Spitz also provided chickens for Shabbos and occasionally fish, but the Belzer Rav would not consume these himself; rather he would distribute them among the needy. When Shimon Spitz pleaded in protest, the Rebbe opened a *Tehillim* with *Yiddish teitch* to Psalm 91 and pointed to the words *"imo Anochi b'tzarah ..."* We must identify with universal suffering and not gorge ourselves on fish and chicken while our brethren are starving.

Indeed the Belzer Rav, who customarily ate very little, now frequently went without any food altogether. As the Bilgoraj Rav later wrote to a leading Belzer chassid (R' Chaim Nota Katz):

> His tefillos intoned with sad tunes pierced bystanders' hearts and kidneys. Many times he refused to eat ... because he so closely identified

with the suffering of Klal Yisrael. Praise be to Hashem that several times I managed by persuasion and other means to assuage his grief and encourage him to eat a little ...

Probably due to his abstention from food, the Belzer Rav was habitually susceptible to cold, so at the onset of winter, Spitz arranged for a wood-burning stove with an ample supply of logs — no mean feat when the German occupying forces had requisitioned everything of value for their own use. However, the Rebbe once again refused to take advantage of special treatment while the majority were subject to deprivation.

Immediately after the Yamim Tovim, the situation began to deteriorate markedly. Gestapo officers made repeated visits to the ghetto on various pretexts, usually to check whether any nonworkers (and thus "non-essential" to the German masterplan) might still be hiding out there. Occasionally they conducted house-to-house inspections personally (instead of relying on their usual collaborators), and this caused the Belzer establishment no end of anxiety whenever search teams were in the vicinity. In one incident, it was felt advisable for the Rebbe to temporarily move to the neighboring building that housed the *mikveh* and was less likely to arouse suspicion.

As rumors resurfaced that the postponed *aktion*, scheduled after Rosh Hashanah, was imminent — rumors now confirmed by Spitz and associates — the authorities proclaimed that the "Ukraine" precinct would become off limits for Jews as of October 30, 1942, thus signaling further "thinning out" of the ghetto area and population. In response, leading Belzer chassidim planned to move the Rebbe back to Bochnia, at least temporarily. Since Krakow had been spared since the beginning of June, they reasoned, while Bochnia had more recently undergone a brutal *aktion* at the end of August, it was less likely Bochnia would be targeted again so soon. Indeed the rumors seemed to indicate that only Krakow was to be singled out for "evacuation." Obviously the chassidim kept their plans a closely guarded secret, but they thought it expedient to inform Simon Spitz. With his connections throughout the whole district, he might be able to smooth the Belzer Rav's passage, and he was equally capable of causing trouble if he were to feel slighted or double-crossed.

To the Rebbe's great chagrin, Spitz was adamant that the Belzer Rav remain under his protection in Krakow throughout the *aktion*, and insisted that he would guarantee his safety. The chassidim were astounded. How could any Jew's life be guaranteed during the bloody deportations? Even Spitz himself, for all his slavish service to the Germans in the past, could not be sure they would not turn on him at a whim. True, the SS officer Wilhelm Kunde owed the "Wonder Rabbi" a favor, but woe betide anyone who places his trust in a German's debt of honor. Kunde's young son had recently taken ill and all the specialists had despaired of his life. At the urging of Spitz and Schapiro, he frantically petitioned the Belzer Rav — and his son had made a remarkable recovery! But what Nazi would bother to repay a Jew a favor?

Earlier in the War, during Nissan 1940, *Obersturmfuhrer* Kunde had been seconded as the paid escort from Krakow Gestapo's Jewish Section for the aged Gerrer Rebbe, Rav Avraham Mordche Alter (later known as the *Imrei Emes*) escaping from Warsaw via Krakow, Vienna and Trieste to Eretz Yisrael. Kunde had executed his task on the express train faithfully, obstructing suspicious officials and warding off border controls, and accompanied the party safely to the Italian port of Trieste. But he only discovered who the privileged train passengers or the "old patient" were when *Wunder Rabbiner* Alter — prominent on the Warsaw Gestapo wanted list — had already slipped beyond his grasp, as he frequently grumbled to Krakow's *Judenrat*. He was unlikely to repeat that oversight again.

Spitz insisted he knew from his "sources" that the impending *aktion* would encompass Bochnia too (an assurance later revealed as untrue). The chassidim realized they had small chance of smuggling the Rebbe to Bochnia if Spitz was so adamantly opposed, particularly since surrounding areas were always closely patroled when *aktions* were looming. Reluctantly, they finally concluded that they had little choice but to entrust the Rebbe's safety to the tender mercies of the Gestapo underlings, with all that might entail. Heaven alone could save them now. In any event, it turned out to be sheer terror and horror interspersed with surreal farce.

In case an *aktion* broke out without any warning, a group of volunteers were organized to remain in close contact and be readily available to spirit the Belzer Rav out of danger with Spitz's connivance. One of these lookouts took the opportunity to present a *kvittel* on behalf of his family. But whenever one child's name was read out, the Rebbe repeatedly interrupted and asked him to read the *kvittel* again from the beginning. Eventually, the Rebbe shrugged in puzzlement and motioned him to continue reading. Only later did the father discover that this son had died suddenly, but the rest of his family miraculously survived the war.

On Monday, October 24, 1942, Spitz confided in the Rebbe that the *aktion* would begin early tomorrow and last for two days (16-17 Cheshvan, just three weeks after Simchas Torah). He had earlier suggested that the Belzer Rav sit out the "evacuation" at Simchah Schapiro's apartment — situated in the headquarters of the Jewish Police which Schapiro led, and less likely to be searched — and Spitz now urged him to escape there while there was still time. But the Belzer Rebbe insisted that he would go only if his brother Rebbe Mottele could accompany him. The Gestapo collaborators deliberated and hesitated for some time before they accepted this stipulation. However, when the Rebbe requested that his two loyal *gabbaim*, R' Dovid Getzel's Erdman and R' Nachman Hirsch Singer, also join them, they bluntly refused in case this attracted too much attention.

At 4 a.m., before the mayhem began, Spitz arrived with a waiting vehicle and ferried the two brothers safely across to the Police Headquarters while R' Dovid Getzel's and R' Nachman Hirsch hastily hid with Prester, a collaborator living outside the ghetto and relatively safe from German molestation. At 6 a.m., the ghetto was surrounded by lines of Polish, Latvian and Ukrainian auxiliaries backed up by Jewish policemen and commanded by leading Gestapo officers Kunde and Hase — a sure sign of a deportation *aktion*. Officially, they were only inspecting everyone's papers while checking for "illegal residents," but dozens of orphans were gunned down in the street and all who did not pass their devilish

The Rebbe wearing a fur kolpik

"selections" were loaded onto waiting trucks and dragged off to the *Umschlagplatz* — the freight railroad depot. For two days, Nazi snatch squads searched all ghetto apartments, cellars and attics; anybody who tried to escape was shot on sight.

All this time, the Rebbe and his brother were ensconced in the Police Headquarters near the Gestapo premises, but they were not spared from intense fear and trepidation. Apparently the Gestapo commanders had been apprised of the *Wunder Rabbiner's* secret hideout, amidst the murder and mayhem, and demanded to see the Grand Rabbi directly — instructing that he be appropriately dressed in silk *bekeshe* and fur *kolpik*! The alarm they caused when the arch-killers barged into Schapiro's apartment, accompanied by Spitz, can scarcely be imagined.

Hase wanted to know, "How did you come from Bochnia to Krakow?" Fortunately, when nobody replied, he did not pursue that line of inquiry. Eventually he declared, "As long as Jews remain in the ghetto, you will not be affected in any way. We won't touch a hair!" Unbelievably, they even demanded that the Rebbe pray for German success, "since German victories will be very beneficial for the Jews!" Finally they took their leave without inflicting any violence. But they returned several times during those two terrible days of the *aktion,* stopping just long enough to assure themselves that the *Wunder Rabbiner* was still within their cruel grasp before continuing with the "evacuation." Each time they arrived, Spitz accompanied them, since there was no telling how their murderous moods might abruptly take them.

Although Schapiro's apartment was thought to be secure from the Nazi snatch squads, it was not entirely safe. Suddenly the door

Belongings left behind after the infamous Krakow "evacuation"

swung open and two SS officers stood balefully on the threshold with murderous intent. Mindful of Spitz's strict instructions to guard the Rebbe's safety with his life, Schapiro rushed forward and frantically pressed a large envelope stuffed with money into their hands, while the others begged the SS not to cause any problems. Fortunately, the officers took the bribe and left as quickly as they had appeared.

Finally the dreaded *aktion* was over and it was safe to return home. On the way, the Belzer Rav heard how bad it had been. Out of the 12,000 left from the previous deportation in June, yet another 7,000 unfortunate souls were seized and nothing could be done to save them. Closer to home, they discovered that Prester's lodging had also been raided and all those sheltering there had been dragged away — including the Rebbe's two *gabbaim,* who had been denied the safety of Schapiro's refuge. Perhaps they, at least, could be saved …

Forthwith, the Belzer Rav sent an urgent message to Shimon Spitz asking if he could help. Spitz turned on his heel and raced back to the railroad depot. He had grown to respect R' Dovid Getzel's in particular and had willingly provided numerous official permits on his recommendation. Now he ran up and down the freight wagons like a man possessed, repeatedly shouting out their names, desperately trying to make contact, but to no avail.

Probably neither R' Dovid Getzel's nor R' Nachman Hirsch could hear him above the coarse yelling, screams and tumult that consistently accompanied the brutal deportations. When Spitz reported back on his failure, the Rebbe's entourage was distraught, since all recognized the extreme loyalty of both *gabbaim*. For years, R' Dovid Getzel's Erdman had served Belz well with wise counsel and had successfully accomplished confidential missions; both he and R' Nachman Hirsch Singer were universally respected for their piety and kind deeds. Now they were obscure casualties lost among the countless masses vanishing without a trace.

CHAPTER 13

IN GRAVE DANGER

W HILE THESE DREADFUL EVENTS WERE TAKING
place, Belzer chassidim abroad had not been sitting
idle. Although their information was not always
entirely accurate or up to date due to communication
difficulties, they heroically persevered in trying to rescue their
Rebbe despite all obstacles and expenses. Extricating anyone from
the Nazi murder machine in Poland proved dreadfully difficult.
Shortly after the Krakow deportation, on October 29, 1942, the
youthful Moshe Gross of Geneva wrote directly to R' Berish Ortner
in Tel Aviv, reporting all he knew:

> The renowned Reb Shemayah Binder passed on your letter, asking
> for more details of the Rebbe and his family ... Until several weeks
> ago the Rebbe, together with his brother Rav Mottele and his gab-
> baim R' Nachman Hirsch and R' Dovid Getzel's, were staying in
> Wisnicz. After Yom Kippur they were forced to leave there. Now
> their situation is surrounded with great danger. Last week I received
> a letter from R' Dovid Getzel's begging us to utilize every avenue to
> arrange their removal from there since it is literally pikuach nefesh,
> may Heaven help us! We are trying everything and look for Hashem

Reb Shemayah Binder

Yisbarach's assistance since we are involved in a mighty enterprise.

But my friend, I must write of our main obstacle — our lack of ready finance. To date we have spent large sums sending food parcels to the Rebbe, and also to his family in Premishlan. Now we need further large sums: First for the entry visa into here and, more importantly, for an exit permit from there. So we are at a loss where to go from here.

We get regular letters from the family about their severe deprivation — literally starving from hunger Rachmana litzlan! A few weeks ago I got a letter from Rebbetzin Yente, wife of Rav Yochanan, where she reveals that the elderly Rebbetzin, the wife of the previous Rebbe, has passed away. She also asks that we try and send them food parcels so they can exist ...

If you can help with any breakthrough (a hint for money), please let us know ... and Hashem should help that we soon meet the Rebbe in good health and satisfaction. I repeat that we still need the certificates so we can complete our task ...

A month later, on the 16th of Kislev (November 25, 1942), R' Moshe Gross wrote again with more dire news:

By now you must have received my previous letter. We are still trying everything within our power to rescue the Rebbe. We are still being held up by obstacles and expenses (for the entry visa and exit permits and most importantly traveling out of there). Hashem Yisbarach should grant us that we welcome the Rebbe and his brother Rav Mottele very shortly since the danger there is enormous — mamesh life-threatening. I must ask you for your full support so we can hurry our plans along.

As matters stand, every day there is like a year since more bad news comes from there with every passing day. May Heaven help us, for they have reached breaking point. I enclose a copy of a card I received from my friend Reb Isumer Domb (famous as the chassid Isumer Lubitcher) who was Rosh Yeshivah in Krakow and is now with the Rebbe since the gabbaim Nachman Hirsch and Dovid Getzel's were

A money order sent by Reb Shemayah Binder via the Polish consulate on behalf of the Rebbe

sent some weeks ago to an unknown destination — the explanation of that, *Rachmana litzlan,* you can well guess for yourself! The Rebbe is now left with his brother Rav Mottele presently known as Pecsenik. Again the Rebbe urgently requests his visit here since it is most important to get away speedily. Note also the distressing news about his holy brothers-in-law who went to visit the late Rebbe with all their families!

My hair literally stands on end! May Heaven have mercy on us, have mercy on us soon. Woe to us that such has occurred in our lifetime. What can we possibly add? I am heartbroken over the terrible situation, the likes of which has never happened before; may Hashem protect us very soon. It is important we gird ourselves for the unique task at hand: saving the holy Rebbe which will benefit so many.

I have also received letters from the renowned chassidim *R' Chaim Nota Katz and R' Elimelech Rumpler (both of London) that our fraternity there likewise want to support our effort. I informed them by telegram to send the necessary papers (i.e. money) to Mr. Ernest Gelley of Nahariah and he should in turn telegraph his friend Mr. Dannenbaum, which will be of enormous help to us. Please talk to the above and ask if he received anything from R' Chaim Nota or any other Belzer and inform me immediately exactly what he received.*

While writing these lines I have just been handed another card from Przemyslany in which they write that all the Rebbe's family there are well. May we hear only good news of the Rebbe and his family and may we see him soon in happiness and ease. Looking forward to your positive reply as soon as possible.

The enclosed postcard in cryptic German, mailed via the Krakow Judenrat and smuggled past the German censor by R' Isumer Domb, read as follows:

My dear friends. I write of our health; thanks to G-d we should only hear good news from you. Please take an interest in the medical visit of your dear uncle Aaron Singer and his companion Markus Pecsenik. From the brothers-in-law Twersky and family we have received letters. It is very good for them, they are visiting their father-in-law Sucher Beer. I write in the name of our beloved friend and he awaits your speedy reply. He wishes you everything good. Heartfelt regards ...

Actually, many of these and subsequent communications purportedly written by R' Domb were really composed by the Bilgoraj Rav himself. As he recalled after the War in a private letter to R' Chaim Nota Katz:

... the physical difficulties and enormous expense involved in maintaining a clandestine correspondence with our supporters in Hungary and Switzerland had to be experienced to be believed. R' Isumer Lubitcher scoffed at me when he watched me writing those letters and investing so much money into them. He would say that it was all a waste of time and money, an effort without end or benefit. But I persevered at my post until I succeeded with Hashem's help to find a miraculous way to dispatch messages to Hungary and also used the normal channels to contact Switzerland. With warm words and saddling them with responsibility (with your help) they finally set to the task ...

The cryptic post-card mailed via the Krakow Judenrat by Reb Isumer Domb to Reb Moshe Gross

Meanwhile, in one reaction to the bitter news, R' Berish Ortner publicized the following news item in the Palestine press under banner headlines:

CHASSIDIC REBBES OF OSTILLA AND RAWA-RUSKA MURDERED:

From the Polish Valley of Death has come terrible news of the martyrdom of the Rebbes of Ostilla-Przemysl and Rawa-Ruska with their families. Both were sons-in-law of the late Belzer Rav, Rebbe Yissachar Dov.

Rabbi Pinchas Twersky, Rebbe of Ostilla, was famous throughout Poland. His whole life was dedicated to Torah and piety and he would sit all day in his tallis and tefillin learning, praying and fasting. He was famed for his Torah knowledge and his ability in Rabbinical responsa. A scion of the Chernobyl dynasty and a son of Rebbe Mottele Rachmistrivka who passed away in Jerusalem, he visited Eretz Yisrael several years ago and was sixty-two years old when he was murdered.

Rebbe Yitzchak Nachum Twersky was also Rav and Chief Dayan in Rawa-Ruska and was respected for his greatness in Torah and saintliness. Among the leaders of Poland's Agudas Rabbanim, he was renowned for his exemplary conduct. His father, Rebbe Mordechai of Skver, was likewise murdered. He was fifty-three years old at the time of his martyrdom.

Later it transpired that they had misunderstood the cryptic post-card and in fact Rebbe Pinchas of Ostilla was still alive at the time. R' Isumer Domb was actually referring to Rebbe Yochanan Twersky, Rav of Rubichow. Publicity in the media, of course, was a double-edged weapon and an item published in *Haboker* on Wednesday, 23 Kislev (December 2, 1942) seemed totally irresponsible. On that day, Palestine newspapers appeared with black borders in reaction to Nazi war atrocity stories, and *Haboker* carried reports from the Polish Immigrant Federation which claimed "... the Belzer Rebbe is being hunted by the accursed Nazis ... he is living anonymously in a small Polish town and continues to encourage and comfort his many followers ... his chassidim abroad have provided him with a passport, visa, a large sum of money and entry into a neutral country but he refuses to abandon his tortured brethren ... Before Yom Kippur he declared a forty-day fast to invoke Heavenly mercy ..."

This drew an immediate riposte from Mr. Ortner. Writing in his capacity as a previous representative of the *Ost-Juden Verband* in Berlin, he upbraided the writer for lacking discretion and en-dangering the Rebbe. If he was hiding in a small town under an assumed name, surely that was to throw off all pursuit. Publishing clues of his whereabouts will only alert the Nazis that he is still in Poland. Gestapo agents doubtless scour the Jewish press for useful information, Mr. Ortner warned, and begged the Polish Immigrant Federation to be more careful in the future.

Meanwhile, the situation in the Krakow ghetto continued to deteriorate following the mass deportations. In a unnerving devel-opment, several satellite slave labor camps were rapidly established around the outskirts of Krakow. Most macabre of all was the erection of the dreadfully familiar, elongated wooden dormitory blocks on the site of the Jewish cemetery at 25 Jerozolimska Street and walled in with thousands of uprooted tombstones! Disquieting rumors swept through the 5,000 survivors of the previous deportation: As soon as this new camp was completed, all Krakow's remaining Jews would be forcibly relocated there. When Shimon Spitz next came to visit the Belzer Rav a few days later, Spitz was asked directly to confirm or deny the alarming reports.

To their bitter dismay, Spitz confirmed that this small "Yerusalemka" labor camp was indeed destined to accommodate all of Krakow's Jewish population, starting from March, and was to be run by the infamous hangman SS *Obersturmfuhrer* Goett whose sadistic death toll

The notorious wall around the Krakow ghetto built from looted matzeivos

was notorious. Since Spitz had spoken openly, his information spread like wildfire but people were divided on whether to accept it when other members of the Gestapo hierarchy continued to deny the rumors. The Belzer fraternity, however, were inclined to believe the worst, as Shimon Spitz was usually well informed and had rarely misled the Rebbe. Lending more weight to Spitz's report was the Gestapo's recent insistence on a strict segregation between able-bodied workers still capable of slaving for the Third Reich and "useless parasites" whose physical strength had already been expended. Obviously a fresh *aktion* and exile was in the offing. They could not trust the safety of the Belzer Rebbe to the malevolent mercies of the notorious Goett.

They decided that the Belzer Rav best move back to Bochnia, and this time Shimon Spitz agreed with them. Bochnia had also suffered an *aktion* of its own — during November 1942, a month after Krakow — but it had been less severe than feared. The Gestapo officers *Obersturmfuhrer* Kunde and Heinrich had previously intimated to Eliezer Landau how they looked forward to appropriate refreshments during the deportations! Feverish preparations immediately began to provide a first-rate meal for their unwelcome guests and after these killers had downed an inordinate amount of intoxicating drink, both Mr. and Mrs. Landau began pleading fervently with the two Germans to curtail the *aktion* and spare the "vital workers for the war effort."

Not only was this an extremely brave step to undertake — the Nazis did not take kindly to the slightest interference in their plans

— by this stage in the war, the German occupiers were under direct orders from Berlin to speed up the "Final Solution" and had little leeway to spare favored Jews. Yet after Mrs. Sarah Landau's persistent pleading, and several more glasses of liquor, Wilhelm Kunde miraculously agreed to cut the *aktion* short. Out of the thousands of Jews slated to be deported *"nach austen,* to an unknown destination" (actually the death camp at Belzec, less than 36 miles from Belz), only about 1,000 victims were liquidated. The Bochnia ghetto had survived to endure another nine months.

Now that Spitz was no longer obstructing their plans, the Rebbe's closest chassidim contacted Mr. Eliezer Landau with the urgent request that he utilize his well-placed connections to safely ferry the Rebbe out of Krakow. Leaving the Krakow ghetto or entering the Bochnia ghetto without official permission was hard enough, but for Jews traveling anywhere without documents — particularly while German patrols were greatly increased before *aktions* — was near impossible. R' Leizer Landau's plan was ingenious in its simplicity, though it needed careful planning and groundwork.

In his birthplace, the nearby town of Brigel (Brzesko past Bochnia, further along the road to Tarnow), lived a renowned Polish specialist who presumably was beyond Gestapo suspicion. Induced by Mr. Landau's substantial bribe, he agreed to register the Belzer Rebbe as a former patient requiring further medical care and also consented to ferry the Rebbe out of Krakow in his private car "for urgent treatment" in Brigel. Furnished with forged exit permits and travel documents, the doctor arrived in Krakow in the late afternoon of December 9, 1942, shortly before the onset of the eighth day of Chanukah 5703 — popularly known among chassidim as "*Zos Chanukah*" — a year to the day since the Rebbe Ahare'le and Rebbe Mottele had escaped from Przemyslany. Once again the two brothers had to undergo the indignity of disguising themselves in typical Polish clothing and removing their beards.

Accompanied by Mr. Landau to insure nothing untoward occurred, the hour-long journey passed entirely without mishap. Despite the heightened tension prior to an *aktion*, no patrols stopped them; nobody asked to see their papers or created any difficulties. When the motorcar arrived at the Bochnia ghetto it was already dark and after the curfew, yet R' Leizer Landau ordered the sentries to open the gates and they unquestioningly obeyed!

Hoping to avoid suspicion, the refugees quickly made their way to the apartment of Shimshon Kempler, a reliable Belzer chassid. Without resident permits or official permission to enter Bochnia, their situation was precarious. Although they aimed to keep their arrival a closely guarded secret, such was the inevitable excitement at the Rebbe's safe arrival that the task was almost impossible. When they entered Kempler's apartment, he had just begun lighting his menorah and he nearly fainted from astonishment. However, the Belzer Rav gestured to him not to interrupt the blessings or ceremony and merely asked if he might also light there. R' Shimshon was glad to inform the Rebbe that he even had olive oil because of some good connections with Polish neighbors. The Rebbe was pleased to use simple glasses as a menorah — a far cry from his priceless heirloom. Back in Belz, he had customarily lit on a massive, pure silver menorah, one meter high and weighing eight kilos, beautifully hand-crafted by a top Krakow silversmith. Now they were forced to make do with ordinary glasses.[1]

Despite his unnerving escape, the Rebbe recited the blessings with his customary concentration. Although his arrival was ostensibly a secret, a *minyan* of intrepid chassidim was soon present in the cramped lodgings. Nonetheless, the Rebbe was not overly dismayed and merely asked half-jokingly, "*Vie azoi bistu schoin gevoir gevoren* — How did you already find out?" After lighting, the Rebbe suggested they chant the traditional Belzer *nigunim* but requested that they sing softly so as not to disturb or alert the neighbors. After reciting chassidic Torah, the Rebbe blessed each chassid individually with, "*A guten Chanukah!*" and they all slipped quietly away into the darkness of the Bochnia ghetto.

Settling down in Kempler's tiny apartment was difficult. It comprised barely one room and a kitchen and already housed two families: R' Shimshon Kempler's and his brother-in-law R' David Shapira's, numbering altogether eighteen souls. Both families va-

---

1. Interestingly, the Belzer Rav never replaced his menorah afterwards, using only glasses even in peacetime.

cated the room and crammed into the kitchen in favor of the Rebbe and his brother. As Mr. Shapira later recalled, the kitchen was crowded with his "brothers and sisters, children and grandchildren ... all the children slept together at night above the *fiekalik* (the large kitchen stove) ..." More than once, one of the children would wake up crying and this would greatly distress the Belzer Rav, who was acutely sensitive to any suffering. *"Ober a Yiddishe kind veint!"* he would remark sadly.

Since he was up half the night over the next few weeks trying to quiet the children, Mr. Shapira's feet swelled up from stress. R' David Shapira was himself a refugee from Krakow, where his father had inherited the renowned business of "Shapira's Mead" — with a cellarful of vintage honey-mead famous throughout Poland and patronized by the Polish nobility and presidents. For trying to rescue some of their valuable heritage from the plundering Germans, he had been forced to flee to Bochnia. As a leading Belzer chassid, he was pleased to minister to the Rebbe's needs in place of the Rebbe's deported *gabbaim*. Since he was a Kohen, however, the Belzer Rav would not allow him to serve in a personal capacity.

A 10-year-old child who had been a tenant in that crammed apartment recalls how until then the disgruntled ghetto inmates had grumbled and argued incessantly over the most trivial details. The position of a mattress, the queue for the tiny kitchen stove, or a glass of water assumes major importance when one is deprived, overworked and constantly hungry. With the arrival of the Rebbe, the atmosphere changed dramatically. People became polite and accommodating, gladly yielding a few inches of treasured space to make room for their honored guest. They greeted each other with a faint smile and spoke in hushed whispers while the Rebbe pored over his holy books with the aid of precious candles. (By then, candles were a rare commodity in the ghetto.)

Despite tight security, Bochnian Jews flocked to the Rebbe for blessings and advice. A tiny, overcrowded cubicle was hurriedly constructed in one corner and dark paper was pasted over the windows to provide a modicum of privacy. Shortly after the Rebbe's arrival, Mr. Landau's elderly father, Reb Moshe Dovid Landau, burst into the Belzer Rav's tiny room and threw himself on the floor, sobbing and shrieking. "Where are our *tzaddikim?*" he screamed uncontrollably as he refused to get up. "Such terrible decrees are raining down on us Jews! Jews are being killed in all manner of *misos meshunos* (unnatural deaths) and the *tzaddik* sees what's happening here — and remains quiet?"

The Belzer Rav trembled with all his being yet he would only repeat several times, sighing again and again, "*Es iz a gezeirah fin Himmel* — it is a decree from Heaven!"

On another occasion, while trying to encourage a depressed ghetto inmate, the Rebbe remarked "*Oy!* The *Bnei Yisrael* in Egypt did not slave as hard as this! *Ribbono Shel Olam!* Surely the severity of the hardship ought to cut short the torment." Yet the man retorted bitterly, "During the Spanish Expulsion the Torah leaders gathered together to beg for mercy on *Klal Yisrael* — here the suffering intensifies from day to day, why don't they do something?" The Belzer Rav affectionately clasped the man's hand in his and replied with great emotion, "This is the everlasting battle of Amalek. The disciples of the holy Baal Shem Tov strove mightily to soften the judgment in the generation before Mashiach. In that first battle against Amalek, Aharon and Chur had to support Moshe's hands; now Jews are being destroyed for our great sins and that support has been cut. So the hands of the Torah leader symbolized by Moshe Rabbeinu are heavy. And even back then, Yehoshua succeeded only in weakening Amalek, not uprooting them completely. So it remains a battle for every generation. You should know that every *Yiddishe krechtz* breaks my heart, through and through — I accept all these tribulations with love!"

Mr. Leizer Landau became extremely close to the Belzer Rav, even remaining in the Rebbe's room while he accepted *kvittlech*. At first he was perplexed by the Rebbe's behavior: He kept picking up large *gemaras*, rapidly flicking through their pages as if he were counting them, then picking up another *gemara* and repeating the exercise until he finally began reading the *kvittlech*. Was he looking for something? Every day? When Mr. Landau confided his puzzlement to leading chassidim, they explained that the Belzer Rav had a long-standing custom to study Talmud in depth before accepting *kvittlech* — "He's not counting pages, he's actually reviewing hundreds of *dafim*, quickly and thoroughly!" Mr. Landau was astounded by this explanation and began discussing various Talmudic topics dealt with in these *masechtos* — only to quickly recognize how the Rebbe was intimately familiar with both the text and the explanations of all the commentaries. Even in the pit of distress and oppression the Belzer Rav habitually reviewed numerous *gemara* pages daily. Nor did he modify any of his other customs: in prayer, in Torah, in mitzvos, in *minhag*, in *chumros*, in offering advice, sympathy and blessings to every individual Jew, and in involving himself in their plight. Understandably, this resulted in long queues of frightened and dejected petitioners.

Obviously, there was a limit to how long the two brothers could continue in these cramped premises. For the next six weeks, Belzer chassidim still in Krakow pressured their Bochnian counterparts to find alternative accommodation for the Belzer Rav. Finally, Shimon Spitz lost patience and dispatched R' Mottel Ehrlich to the Bochnia Judenrat with a blunt message: "Either provide a suitable apartment for the Belzer Rebbe within twenty-four hours or else Spitz will personally turn their whole place over!"

The Judenrat were terrified at the explicit threat and Simchah Weiss, who headed the Judenrat, immediately came round with leaders of the police and labor departments to check out the Rebbe's living conditions. After they saw his tiny room, they promised to supply excellent alternative lodgings before the day was out. Nearby at 4 Kublaska Street dwelt an extremely important gentleman in two large, airy rooms, and the Judenrat "persuaded" him to move out of his apartment. But the Rebbe was reluctant to take advantage of anyone's discomfiture. Instead he insisted on speaking personally with the previous occupant, who assured him he was happy with the arrangement. Even so, the Belzer Rav requested that the man's replacement flat be measured to check it was of similar dimensions to the one he had been forced to vacate. Only then was the Belzer Rav prepared to move in. The next day, Spitz arrived to inspect the apartment, and that was the last time he met the Belzer Rav.

It was extremely unusual for individuals to be allotted such a relatively large apartment in the increasingly restricted ghetto. Under the regime of the new *Lagerfuhrer* (camp commandant) Muller, the Bochnia ghetto was divided into two. Ghetto One held able-bodied adults who were all forced to work, men and women alike, and a fence patroled by guards separated them from the non-workers in Ghetto Two, which held children and the elderly and infirm — evidently all "useless eaters" in German eyes and instantly expendable.

Muller further separated the workforce into three divisions: forced laborers (or *zwangsarbeit*) marked with a white "Z" patch on their left side (besides the yellow *Jude*-patch on their right arm); slave workers for the weapons industry (or *rustung*) marked with a white "R" patch; and those forced to work for the *Wehrmacht* wore a "W" patch. Since Ghetto One was now a "workers' camp," husbands and wives were forbidden to live in the same apartment and were only allowed to see each other for two hours in the evening. Also, all workers had to eat together in the communal dining canteen, and private cooking was banned under pain of fines or prison. Anybody caught by the *Lagerfuhrer* breaking these restrictions was brutally beaten — men and women alike!

All the workers had to rise before dawn and rush off to a roll call on Kowalska Street before marching off to work, five abreast, under a police escort. Living conditions in Ghetto Two were relatively easier; people arose at a normal time, did not have to hurry hither and thither, and even had time to attend *shiurim*. But since Ghetto Two seemed obviously slated for elimination — Germans won't "waste" food on useless non-workers — everyone fought to move back into Ghetto One, which was now fenced off and guarded. Officially, accommodation in Ghetto One was solely designated for productive workers: without the distractions of family or private cooking facilities, all rooms were meant to house no furniture beyond beds, neither tables nor chairs — not even a cupboard or suitcase to store their clothes!

To fool the Nazis, Eliezer Landau had registered many old men, the most likely to be murdered, as much younger workers, while young children were registered as teenagers. Since the old men and rabbanim were incapable of much work, the young children exerted themselves to keep the German factories going. Obviously, the Belzer Rav would have been far more comfortable in Ghetto Two where life was as normal as possible under German occupation, but his chassidim believed the Rebbe would be safer in Ghetto One masquerading as a worker.

Accordingly, Mr. Landau arranged for the Belzer Rav to be registered with the *Bau-Dienst* as a master tailor, and his brother, the Bilgoraj Rav, as an expert shoemaker. The tailoring division that produced beautiful uniforms for the Gestapo officers was a central reason why the Gestapo had allowed the relatively unimportant Bochnia labor camp to survive for so long; three hundred and fifty expert tailors were employed by R' Berel Frankel — from the noted factory-owning family in the industrial town of Bilitz-Bielsko — who provided eighty-five sewing machines. Actually, the Rebbe spent all his time as usual, praying and learning under the watchful protection of his chassidim, but tools and trimmings with parts of trousers and shoes were scattered strategically about the room so the brothers could immediately take their places at their workbench the instant suspicion fell upon them.

Meanwhile, the American authorities published their assessment that approximately two million Jews had already died under Nazi persecution and another five million were in acute danger of extinction. Naturally, this spurred on all rescue efforts; and the Belz covert correspondence — containing enigmatic hints and allusions — with outside supporters continued. On January 11, 1943, a cryptic card to Moshe Gross in Geneva was posted in Bochnia:

> *Dear Uncle,*
>> *We received your letter and were very pleased. The photographs requested by the "Master,"[2] we are sending to you. Please write what you are doing.*
>> *Your grandfather Arik and your uncle Mark.[3]*

Eleven days later, on January 22, 1943, another card from Bochnia was dispatched to Geneva, ostensibly from R' Isumer Domb:

> *Dear Moshe,*
>> *Received your letter. What you write, that grandfather should meet your brother-in-law Weinstock, is impossible. Please ask Shemayah*

---

2. Presumably passport officials.

3. I.e., the Belzer Rav and Bilgoraj Rav, respectively.

Binder if he received the letter and photos. I hear you are finally do-
ing something for Uncle A. Singer and his brother Markus Pecsenik.
Grandfather does not feel well, may G-d send him a complete and
speedy recovery.
    Best regards,
    Isumer

After another seventeen days, on February 8, "Domb" wrote again to R' Moshe Gross:

Our Dear Friend,
    We received your letter and you should know how much you have
gladdened grandfather's heart. His great joy at Moses Gross' greet-
ings made a very good impression. Please write precisely if Moses has
arranged everything for uncle and brother.
    In conclusion, with regard to what you wrote, that grandfather
should visit your brother-in-law, is impossible. There it is the same as
here. Regards to our friends Binder and Rubinfeld.
    Best wishes,
    Isumer

Next week, two more cards were sent — on the 15th and 16th of February. The first read:

Dear Cousin,
    I write to tell you that I am very well thanks be to G-d and hope
to hear the same from you. After receiving your letter I am fulfilling
your request. Your grandfather was born in 1893, your father Mottele
in 1900, your uncle Shachna Schapira in 1908. Please pass on regards
to Mr. Weingort from Shalom Arjinieski. He looks forward to good
news. Regards in grandfather's name to Domb. You will receive his
letter any day now since he was ill.
    Yours.

The second, to R' Moshe Gross at Hotel Meyerhof, read:

My Dear Friend,
    Just to let you know our good health. Hope to G-d to hear only
good from you. Received your two letters. Our dear grandfather asks
you do everything possible that our dear uncle Aaron Singer and his
dear brother Markus Pecsenik visit you. If that is impossible, at least

*Rav Michoel Ber
Weissmandl*

show your friendship by sending regards from Mr. Weingort. Our dear grandfather goes without a beard. He and his brother had their photographs taken and sent to our friend Moses Brezner. How is your health? We hear from Yeshie'le that he is well. The grandfather is being served by Asher.

Our dear grandfather heartily sends regards to you and blesses Mr. Weingort, your father-in-law R' Botchko and yourself.

Best wishes,

Isumer

These enigmatic references to R' Gross' brother-in-law, R' Shlomo Weinstock, refer to an escape plan to nearby Slovakia, hatched up by the veteran rescue activist Rav Michoel Ber Weissmandl. Although Slovakia was controlled by a fascist government closely linked to Germany and had already deported many Jews to the concentration camps, Rav Weissmandl's Hatzalah Committee managed to bribe top SS officials to halt the deportations. In addition, he funded an extensive smugglers' network to assist Jewish escapees from Poland; in exchange for their "right" to steal refugees' valuables, the Slovak police smuggled them further into Hungary where they were relatively safe. However, the Bilgoraj Rav believed Slovakia to be as precarious as Poland and pressed for their entry to neutral Switzerland. The "regards" to Rabbi Dr. Saul Weingort of Montreaux probably refers to his supply of South American citizenship papers and passports which offered some protection against *aktions*.[4] Holders of these passports were generally deported to Vittel Camp in France or Bergen-Belsen in Germany where they received preferential treatment as "foreign Jews," but ultimately, most were murdered.

As mentioned, most of Domb's messages were really composed by the Bilgoraj Rav. A parallel though less intelligible correspondence was maintained by R' David Shapira, replete

4. Both he and Rav Eliyahu Botchko, Rosh Yeshivah of Etz Chayim in Montreaux, were close relatives of the Sternbuchs, the pioneers in rescue efforts, but none of them were related to Moshe Gross.

Deportations from Slovakia

with esoteric hints. On January 9, 1943, he wrote to Moshe Gross in Geneva:

> *My Dear Friend,*
>
> *Your letter of December 4 we received and also that of your brother-in-law. But our dear grandfather is too weak to meet your brother-in-law. The only option is that you personally visit Uncle Aaron and likewise his brothers Markus and David. When you have an opportunity, send raisins and also meet our friend Binder and decide together how to greet the dear uncle and his two men. I bless you with alles gut! During my life you have done so much for me. You will see Rabbiner Aharon.*

On February 17th he sent another card:

> *My Dear Friend,*
>
> *Received your letters of February 4 and 5. I am so grateful you remember me. Give my best wishes to your dear uncle, also my cousins Marcus and Shachna Spin as "Mr. Teminas" writes. But if Mr. Teminas does not want to write, you don't have to depend on him. You can write without him and to Aaron Singer or Markus Pecsenik. Be well! Awaiting your reply.*
>
> *Your good friend, Shapira*
>
> ❧
>
> *March 8, Bochnia. My dear cousin Moses!*
>
> *Our situation is well, thank G-d, and we are in good health. G-d should grant that we hear only good from you. I am so surprised not to have heard*

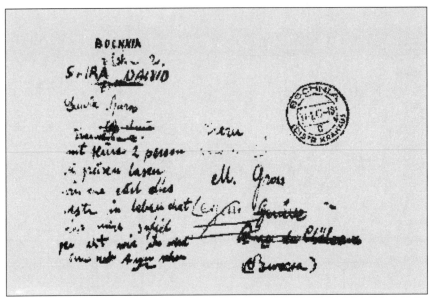

A card from Reb David Shapira in Bochnia to Reb Moshe Gross in Geneva

from you for such a long time. Grandfather especially awaits impatiently to hear from you good news. He asks you write more. Please write if you had regards from Mr. Teminas. Remember that grandfather and his brother await impatiently to receive from you good letters. I hope that very soon we will get a reply from you; don't put it off. I write that we are all working and earning. How are things with you? Heartfelt greetings.

David

Outside Poland the urgent correspondence relating to the Rebbe's rescue gathered pace with increased pressure for Palestine entry certificates. Twenty days after his fleeing to Bochnia, Mr. Gross received the following cable:

> TELEGRAPH WHAT HELP IS NEEDED FOR THE REBBE RABBI LEWENSTEIN SHOULD TELEGRAPH CHIEF RABBI HERZOG JERUSALEM ORTNER

In response, Rabbi Dr. Tuviah Lewenstein, Agudist and Rescue activist of Zurich, sent an urgent telegram on February 24. Meanwhile, Chaim Barlas, who represented the Jewish Agency at the Vaad

Hatzalah, Istanbul, Turkey, also telegraphed Chief Rabbi Herzog on January 12, 1943:

> PLEASE HELP RABBI ROKACH IS WELL AND HOUSEBOUND BARLAS

This coincided with another telegraph to a leading Belzer chassid in Yerushalayim:

> ASHKENAZI MEAH SHEARIM JERUSALEM GRAND-FATHER FEELS BAD AND IS IN EISENSTADT'S PLACE HOPING FOR IMPROVEMENT PERHAPS IN SHMELKE'S HOSPITAL ALL WELL AND WAITING FOR REPLY LUGANO

This last telegram spurred R' Berish Ortner into further meetings with Rabbi Herzog, Mr. Moshe Shapira (Head of the Jewish Agency's Aliya Department), and Chief Justice Gad Frumkin. Sharing the taxi to Jerusalem with R' Moshe Blau, the legendary Agudah leader, R' Berish Ortner showed him the documents and discussed tactics. They remained baffled by the money allegedly sent from London and still missing.

> CHAIM NOTA KATZ LONDON PAPERS FOR REBBE URGENTLY NEEDED FOR CERTIFICATES TELEGRAPH IF SENT ORTNER

Two weeks later, on February 4, 1942, the London *Keren Hatzalah for Yishuv Hayashon* replied:

> BERISH ORTNER NACHALAS BINYAMIN TEL AVIV OVER FOUR MONTHS 1,500 LIRA TOTAL MAAMODOS COLLECTION FOR REBBE TELEGRAPH GELLEY NAHARIAH PLEASE HELP HIM AS MUCH AS POSSIBLE REGARDS FROM MOSHE YITZCHAK'S SON AND ALL CHASSIDIM FOR SHEMAYAH

Obviously, R' Chaim Nota, son of R' Moshe Yitzchak (Eizak) Katz, was the real instigator of that telegram. Another cable demanding the immediate handover of £2,000 for the rescue effort arrived from George Mantello, the honorary consul of El Salvador, on February 2, 1943, via Istanbul. Mr. Mantello was actually a Romanian Jew from Bistritzia with religious parents who — protected by his diplomatic pass — had personally witnessed the Viennese *Anschluss* in 1938, the Prague takeover in 1939 and the Yugoslavian annexation of 1941. He was himself arrested by the Gestapo in Zagreb, Croatia during 1942, but made a daring escape two months later to Switzerland via Italy. Joining El Salvador's consulate in Geneva as general secretary, under the influence of the French Agudah leader Maître Muller, he began mass manufacturing his own Salvadorian "passport" which he dispatched free to Eastern Europe.[5]

Less than a week later, on February 8, 1943, Mr. Ortner received an appalling cable:

SITUATION VERY GRAVE PRAY FOR REBBE'S HEALTH SONS SHMUEL MOSHE YISRAEL ZUNDEL HAVE DIED SUDDENLY WE WAIT FOR YOUR IMPORTANT REPLY AND SPEEDY HELP M GROSS

Mr. Ortner first reacted by publicizing the news in Eretz Yisrael's press, but the information was mostly premature. While Rebbe Moshe'le, the Belzer Rav's eldest son, had already been brutally murdered back in 1941 during the Przemyslany pogrom of 9 Tammuz (July 5), the other sons, R' Yisrael aged 37, R' Zundel aged 35 and the Rebbe's son-in-law Rav Shmuel Frankel aged 41, survived there till the killings of the summer of 1943.

Afterwards R' Berish appealed to Mr. Israel Rokach, Tel Aviv mayor, who was related to the Rebbe, to put him in touch with the influential Greek Prince Peter, cousin to King George VI of Great Britain and now serving in the British army; the prince had paid a

---

5. Later, with a series of strident telegrams to the print media, he ripped the veil of secrecy from the Nazi mass-murder program and thus helped halt the Hungarian deportations.

royal visit to the Rebbe in Belz on the first day of Rosh Hashanah 1937. Eventually the Jewish Agency confirmed that Palestine certificates had been prepared in Istanbul awaiting the earliest prospect of the Rebbe's entry, and on February 16, 1943, Mr. Ortner cabled Geneva:

JEWISH AGENCY SENT ENTRY PERMITS FOR SINGER PECSENIK TO ISTANBUL HOPE JOURNEY HAPPENS SOON WAITING NEWS OF THEIR HEALTH ORTNER

Unfortunately, this rescue bid was overshadowed by a bitter argument between the Orthodox establishment and the *Sochnut* that pitted Chief Rabbi Herzog against the Zionist leadership, including the religious-Zionists — the *"Yaldei Teheran"* scandal. The controversy was rooted in the chaotic population migrations engendered by war when many Polish Jews had fled to the Soviet zone, together with the Belzer Rav, at the 1939 Nazi invasion. Most had been ruthlessly exiled to the inhospitable wastes of Siberia where substantial numbers had succumbed to the icy cold, disease and deprivation. In countless cases, those refugees had been survived by their traumatized children who had witnessed their parents' demise and had personally assisted in their burial. Bands of these orphans — starving, friendless, penniless, assailed by enmity or common criminals — wandered the vast Russian interior for the next three years, heading southwards toward warmer climes. Under force of circumstance they had matured before their time, unnaturally distrustful of strangers and accustomed to sustaining themselves and deciding their own fate. Many believed they had survived those ghastly years by an open miracle; they claimed to have regularly gone to sleep hungry and awakened content.

Eventually some 733 children and teenagers arrived in Teheran where various children's camps had been established and funded by the Polish Government in Exile. From August 1942 this camp was placed under the jurisdiction of Youth Aliya, the *Sochnut's* junior wing, in recognition of the children's racial origin. Although most orphans were from religious homes — some from the most prominent families in Orthodox Poland — and applied to enter

Eretz Yisrael in honor of their parents' last wishes, non-religious counselors were appointed and a corrupt cronyism flourished. The resultant physical and mental maltreatment of these young charges plus a blatant campaign of antireligious coercion, in Teheran or during their sea voyage via India, provoked a storm of protest in Israel. The Orthodox establishment argued that as a matter of halachah all orphans should be placed under the care of a competent *beis din* and receive a religious education — at least under the Rabbanut; besides, these children were overwhelmingly Orthodox. But all that the Orthodox were offered was a shabby compromise whereby the orphans would be placed in homes based on a rough estimation reflecting political parties' electoral support!

All efforts to form a united religious front failed and the Orthodox establishment was repeatedly double-crossed. Religious representatives — even Chief Rabbi Herzog on occasion — were barred entry to *Sochnut* youth camps while visitors were insulted and abused. Many children deliberately had their morals corrupted and were taught to disparage Judaism and hate the pious; only thirty were permitted to enlist in yeshivos (and another forty absconded later). During April and May 1943, in sympathy with despairing cables from Chief Rabbi Herzog, Britain's United Synagogue Beth Din and provincial rabbis together with the USA's Agudas Rabbanim issued a worldwide boycott of Keren Hayesod (Palestine Foundation Fund). To counter a flood of angry telegrams even from ostensible supporters such as the English Board of Deputies or leading American Zionists including Dr. Stephen Wise, the *Sochnut* called a press conference chaired by Rabbi Fishman-Maimon who poured scorn and ridicule on Rav Herzog. Other Mizrachi leaders joined in the virulent campaign; only Mr. Moshe Shapira remained ambivalent. Eventually, under tremendous pressure, Rav Herzog cabled rabbinical personalities abroad asking them to call off their boycott. Obviously, this sad chain of events clouded his relations and influence over the *Sochnut* and cast a long shadow over rescue attempts.

Back in Bochnia, the ghetto itself was beset with high drama: Reb Shloime'le Halberstam, the young Bobover Rav and eldest son of the Rebbe murdered in Lemberg, had been arrested. Surviving relatives of the Bobover dynasty had already been sheltering in Bochnia for the past year and Reb Shloime'le had used his contacts to set himself up as a Hungarian citizen. He was permitted to live outside the ghetto, from where he smuggled countless Jewish children into "safe" Polish homes. When Polish detectives raided his small, rented house on the trail of these missing children during *Erev Shabbos Tetzaveh* (mid-February 1943), they also discovered white flour challos and fresh kosher chicken — forbidden to mere Jews! — and turned him over to the notorious Beck of the Gestapo. Naturally Rebbe Shaye'le Halberstam of Chechov, his venerable great-uncle and youngest son of the Divrei Chaim, began urgent prayers for his safety. Likewise the Belzer Rav asked for his mother's name and chanted *Tehillim* for many hours, only pausing to ask if there were any fresh developments.

After an initial brutal beating, Reb Shloime'le despaired of his fate and began composing his last will and testament, prefacing it as customary with a verse from the weekly *Sidrah: ... And the sound of the golden bells will be heard as the Kohen Gadol approaches the Mikdash* — until he recollected that this *pasuk* actually ends with the comforting words ... *and he will not die* — and determinedly tore up the half-completed will! After he was speedily and painlessly released, he regained his vigor and related this incident to the Belzer Rav who declared, "That omen was a heavenly manifestation of *chizuk* and encouragement! — just so you should not despair!"

CHAPTER 14

STRATEGIES FOR SURVIVAL

W
HILE THE INTENSE EFFORT TO OBTAIN SWISS
entry visas with the aid of Palestinian certificates
continued apace, an exciting new window of opportunity opened up in occupied Poland — direct escape to
the freedom of America! It began with a brief announcement from
the Gestapo during March 1943 asking all Jews with American citizenship to register on a Judenrat list. Naturally this "American List"
engendered great interest and speculation. From past experience
they knew how hidden motives lurked behind every bland pro-
nouncement. Perhaps the Germans hoped to negotiate — and may
have even concluded an agreement — to exchange those eligible
with German citizens arrested in America. Possibly they intended
to use the so-called *Austauschjuden* (exchange Jews) as human barter
for German agents arrested abroad.

Actually, very few true American citizens remained in the
Krakow area who could produce birth certificates or other documents. Instead many took advantage of this opportunity to buy
false documents and letters from Polish master forgers in Krakow
at an exorbitant price. Some even used up their entire life savings

and sold all their belongings in their desperate bid to try this escape route to America. As a consequence, eighty-three Jews in the Bochnia ghetto registered as American citizens. A day before they were due to start their fateful journey, one of them came to the Belzer Rav for his blessing.

The Rebbe took the opportunity to ask him to convey an urgent message to Belzer supporters in America who had concentrated until then on obtaining visas for use in escaping to Switzerland. "We are in a terrible situation here, constantly faced by mortal danger! They must explore every avenue in their power ..." Those eighty-three were duly taken to Krakow's Mantilupi Fortress where all the other "Americans" were concentrated. While their papers were being processed during the next few days, news apparently leaked out to Gestapo agents how most — if not all — their documentation was fictitious. All were dragged to the Podgorze Jewish cemetery where they were summarily shot. Only two of the group miraculously escaped their fate — one was the man blessed by the Belzer Rav.

Meanwhile, the Belzer Rav began surreptitiously conducting a *tisch* and delivering *Toros* for the select few in the know, now that he had relocated to larger premises. Potentially this might easily provoke deep trouble. Indeed, just under three months after their arrival in Bochnia, word of a suspicious gathering at the Rebbe's residence on Friday night, *Parashas Shekalim* (March 6, 1943), leaked out to the Gestapo by early next morning and they apparently deduced from their informants that the Belzer Rav's worker status was nothing more than a sham. As a result, the *Lagerfuhrer* (Camp Commandant) Muller decided to meet the *"Wunder Rabbiner"* personally and investigate the circumstances for himself. Fortunately he mentioned his plan to Mr. Landau, who hurriedly dispatched a Jewish policeman to tip off Belzer chassidim.

Even so, there was hardly time to rearrange the room and clean up from last night's *tisch*. Nor was there sufficient time to prepare the Rebbe for the crucial visit. After a long night of study and *avodas hakodesh*, he had only recently gone to bed when Muller arrived, accompanied by Mr. Landau. The comforting presence of R' Eliezer gave some small reassurance but they were extremely nervous about how to behave. Should they remove their head covering or not? Should they offer the *Lagerfuhrer* a seat or would he be insulted? A wrong move could be fatal. In the end they did pull out a chair but Muller haughtily disdained the offer and instead seated himself on a windowsill near the Belzer Rav's bed.

"So this is the famous *Wunder Rabbiner*," sneered the Camp Commandant scornfully. "And where's his brother, the Rabbi?" The Belzer Rav remained sitting on his bed already deeply engrossed in *davening*, ignoring the officer almost entirely. Instead, the Bilgoraj Rav, who was suitably furnished with a broken shoe to "repair" with a spare shoe sole, offered to answer all his questions in German. The Nazi stared at him before he spat out, "When there are no more Jews in Poland and the Jewish religion vanishes completely — who then will need rabbis?" The Bilgoraj Rav broke out in a cold sweat and was struck almost speechless in fear.

"If your brother's so weak," the Nazi continued, gesturing at the Belzer Rebbe sitting on his bed, "why isn't he in Ghetto Two where all the rest stay? Ghetto One is only for the best workers!" An ominous line of questioning since those confined to Ghetto Two were most likely to be dragged away first. In reply, the Bilgoraj Rav pointed round the room equipped with bits of cloth, finished trousers, scissors, irons, measuring tapes, cottons and needles. "My brother is a master tailor," he declared bravely. "Here is a receipt from the ghetto warehouse showing that Aaron Singer has just delivered a large amount of finished trousers!"

The *Lagerfuhrer* grimaced and asked suddenly, "How can the Wonder Rabbi pray here? Shouldn't there be windows along the eastern wall?" The Bilgoraj Rav explained patiently that in the difficult circumstances of the ghetto it was enough to pray quietly and direct your heart toward Jerusalem. After asking all sorts of questions, Muller finally came to the point. "Explain to me! Why were all those strangers gathered in the Rabbi's rooms last night?" This dangerous question showed that the Gestapo knew of the Friday night *tefillos* with the Rebbe, and possibly the *tisch*. Thinking quickly, the Bilgoraj Rav replied that the Rebbe had given the ghetto workers a rousing speech, demanding that they work harder for the German masters or otherwise there will be no future for the ghetto. Everybody who receives bread from the Germans must deserve it!

Satisfied, Muller nodded and restated the usual Nazi propaganda, declaring all Jews are parasites and swindlers who need to be taught a lesson ... Then he began repeating crude *Der Sturmer* misquotes from the Bible and Talmud to display his "knowledge" of Judaism. Rather than contradict him, they merely nodded quietly.

Behaving more politely, the Commandant announced that from now on the Belzer Rebbe's food would be supplied directly

The building that housed the Rebbe in the Bochnia ghetto

from the kitchens so that he won't have to queue up for it with other workers. He also offered to double his meat ration — of horse meat! As another generous gesture, he appointed him *Lager Rabbiner* (Camp Rabbi) and released him from forced labor. Realizing how dangerous such a position could be, the Bilgoraj Rav thanked him for the kind offer but insisted that the Belzer Rebbe was eager to continue working for the war effort as a master tailor.

After about an hour of "conversation," Muller took his leave. On the way out he met Rav Halberstam of Wisnicz who had been innocently approaching the Rebbe's residence for Shabbos Shacharis, unaware of the ominous visitor. Instead of upbraiding or cross-questioning him, Muller merely remarked, "*A rabbiner geht tsum rabbiner!*" and motioned for him to enter. Indeed the *Lagerfuhrer* was in an exceptionally good mood and workers in his office later remarked how he remained unusually good humored and good natured throughout the day. Of course that did not last, and at the final liquidation of Bochnia ghetto, Muller murdered with the worst of them.

A week after that fateful meeting, the blow finally fell in Krakow. As Shimon Spitz had warned the Rebbe when he contemplated fleeing Krakow, the ghetto would inevitably be eliminated when satellite labor camps around the city were completed. On 6 Adar,

Shabbos Pekudei (March 13, 1943) began the infamous "March *aktion*" which — following the previous deportations of June and October 1942 — effectively destroyed the ancient and glorious Krakow community. Doctors and patients were shot in cold blood at the hospital, 2,000 others were murdered at home, and 6,000 were assembled at the ghetto gate before being transported to the newly erected barracks on the Jerozolimska Jewish cemetery. They had to leave behind almost all their belongings — including their young children and babies whom the Nazi murderers forced them to heartbreakingly abandon at the waste ground near the gate. Those who refused to part with their children were brutally killed together with them.

News of the Krakow *aktion* reached Bochnia on Sunday but they only heard the hair-raising details on *Taanis Esther* (brought forward to Thursday, that year) completely cowing the Purim spirit. Throughout *Shabbos Zachor*, the Rebbe remained in his room and only emerged to *lein Megillas Esther* on Motza'ei Shabbos. On this occasion, his voice was excessively weak and several times he had to pause for breath. Despite this, his grip on tradition and *minhag* remained as steadfast as ever and he asked R' Chaim Shloma Friedman before Purim if he could organize the traditional pair of fish for Purim: one boiled *heimishe* as for Shabbos, the other prepared with raisins as a Purim treat.[1]

Destruction of the Krakow ghetto also brought about the downfall of Shimon Spitz, who vanished two weeks later under mysterious circumstances. There were various rumors as to his death. From the first, Spitz had confided to the Rebbe his fears of how rival German agents were planning his eradication and some now claimed that Berlin had issued orders to eliminate him. The fact that he was murdered by the Nazis was seen by many chassidim as a sign that his *teshuvah* was accepted and that he had received a *kapparah* for his horrendous crimes as a Gestapo collaborator. Others, however, surmised that he had been assassinated by revengeful Poles or even Jewish partisans shortly before Pesach while conducting his usual "negotiations" in the prelude to further *aktions*.

---

1. On finally reaching safety he commented how he had never relinquished any of his many *chumras* or customs during the war years despite all the difficulties!

One Belzer disciple who did escape the Krakow inferno was R' David Singer from Jaroslaw, who managed to bribe a Polish cart driver delivering hay to smuggle his family overnight to Bochnia. However, when the cart driver saw the guards around the ghetto he took fright and, ignoring his agreement or their desperate entreaties, refused to go any further and forced them off his cart. Stranded in the middle of the night on the public highway, they sought to hide behind minimal vegetation until daybreak. As dawn broke a Jew noticed them and directed them to a hidden break in the ghetto fence. After they safely crept in, he went to see the Belzer Rav. As soon as he arrived, the *gabbaim* exclaimed, "Did you give us a night! Several times the Rebbe sensed your predicament and cried out, '*David Yaroslaver darft a yeshuah* — David of Jaroslaw needs salvation!' "

With Pesach approaching in the deprived and famished ghettos, it became commonplace to temporarily permit *kitnios* (certain non-*chametz* foods such as rice and legumes; there was a centuries-old Ashkenazic stringency to refrain from eating them during Pesach). When the Belzer Rav was invited to join an emergency rabbinical conclave to consider allowing Bochnia's inmates to consume *kitnios*, he sent the Bilgoraj Rav in his stead and urged that they invite R' Berel Frankel. This raised some eyebrows — why on earth should they invite Reb Berel? He was neither a rav nor a particularly renowned scholar. Yet in deference to the Rebbe, they agreed to call him.

But Reb Berel, who ran the sewing section for the *Bau-Dienst*, was tied up that evening in a lengthy session with his German overseer and by the time he could safely get away, the meeting was almost over. He burst in just as it was breaking up and after apologizing for his unavoidable delay, asked what it was all about. When he heard how they had reluctantly decided to permit *kitnios* by force of circumstances, he vehemently disagreed: "*Chalilah v'chas*! Don't even think about it! There's no need! On my responsibility, I'll get you a fresh supply of potatoes — I've got good contacts. On my *achraiyes*!" The rabbanim agreed to delay their decision and give him a chance; true to his word, he procured a sufficient supply of potatoes for the ghetto during Pesach. When the Bilgoraj Rav reported back on this remarkable turn of events — almost a *mofes* — the Belzer Rebbe merely remarked, "I knew Reb Berel was a *varmer* Tzanzer chassid who would try to help!"[2]

Meanwhile the owner of their apartment offered to supply the Pesach needs of the Belzer Rav and his brother and to host their Seder. With the heroic efforts of Chaim Shloma Konigsberg and a group of Bobover *bachurim*, a clandestine matzo-oven had been prepared in the ghetto bakery, wheat had been hand-ground in a smuggled coffee grinder, and the oven was fueled with exclusive wooden furniture retrieved from Nazi confiscations. By an oversight, their host prepared roasted meat for the Seder, contrary to accepted custom. Rather than embarrass him, the Rebbe quietly waited until the guests had eaten their share before he gently asked if he perhaps had any boiled meat left over. Defying the fear dominant late at night in the ghetto, they sang and danced the traditional *nigunim* at the conclusion of the Seder, on the Rebbe's instructions. However, he halted the *rekidah* after a few minutes to minimize additional danger. Throughout Yom Tov, the Pesach needs of the Belzer adherents around the Rebbe were supplied by Mr. Chaim Shloma Friedman, and after the festival, the Belzer Rav admitted "The *chevrah* revived me!"

Despite the severe conditions prevailing in the Bochnia ghetto, the Rebbe would not forego a single custom or tradition. In general, he kept to his earlier regime of long fasts broken by a sparse meal.[3] Unfortunately, very little food was available that met the Belzer Rav's high kashrus standards. Desperate efforts were made to obtain potatoes and flour with unquestionable kashrus. As the Bilgoraj Rav later related "... often there was nothing for the Rebbe to drink besides water. Once we had a bottle of milk and I managed to mislead him to think I had already drunk from this milk. (*Chalilah*, I didn't touch a drop — not to deprive my holy brother.) Several times I persuaded him to rest before daybreak and eat something ..."

---

2. Mr. Frankel survived the War and emigrated to Tel Aviv; although he was clean-shaven and hardly the typical Belzer chassid, the Rebbe greeted him warmly and regularly honored him with distinguished *aliyos* for his past dedication to religious customs and for sheltering him in his slave labor division.

3. Indeed, till the end of his life he weighed just 36 kilos — less than many concentration camp victims!

The Rebbe's regular repast after a day-long fast was a half-slice of cake, a cup of coffee and a few spoonfuls of vegetable soup. His attendants would serve him a full plate of soup but he would return most as *sherayim*. Occasionally, after a two-day fast, he would ask the *gabbaim* if they were *"moichel der sherayim."* When he first arrived in Bochnia, he would forego the soup entirely and subsisted on coffee with milk; later they discovered that the soup plates had been used for meat dishes many years earlier — and the Rebbe had sensed this.

The milk for the Rebbe was procured by the superhuman exertions of R' Shimon Kempler, who had first accommodated the Belzer Rav on his arrival in Bochnia. He was employed as an electrical engineer outside the ghetto and when he discovered how essential kosher milk was to the Rebbe's survival, began looking for likely sources. Luckily, next to the fields where they were digging foundations for electric pylons lived a poor Polish farmer who owned one cow. During the half-hour lunch break, R' Shimon would sneak into the cowshed and personally witness the milking. By dint of various stratagems and not a little risk, he managed to smuggle a bottle of this milk past the guards each night. The Rebbe trusted Mr. Kempler implicitly and never questioned whether he had overseen the milking.

As he was once creeping toward the cowshed, Mr. Kempler was caught by Nazi thugs who fell upon their victim with a vengeance. "Where's a filthy Jew running to?" they bellowed as they beat him mercilessly. They would not stop tormenting him until they received some satisfactory answer, but he could not reply without endangering the whole scheme. Only by a miracle did he finally escape their clutches, and it was evening before he deemed it safe to visit the cowshed. By then, the Pole had already milked his single cow. Mr. Kempler took his filled bottle nonetheless and smuggled it back to the ghetto. All the way he debated with himself. This was the first time he had not supervised the milking, and the peasant had personally decanted the milk into Kempler's bottle. On the other hand, he persuaded himself, these were special circumstances and the Belzer Rav's life literally depended on a steady supply of milk. The peasant was familiar with supervision, was aware that his milk was destined for a "famous holy man" and would not likely compromise his standing. In the end Mr. Kempler decided to reveal nothing of the altered status of the milk although total trust had been vested in him.

So he was greatly surprised when the Rebbe sent for him urgently as soon as he was served his milky coffee at the end of a long day of fasting and prayer. "Please tell me, Shimon," he asked gently, "do you stand and watch while the milking is going on?"

R' Shimon was overcome with emotion. "I have to confess," he began brokenly, "that until now I have always been present at the milking. It's never happened that I missed it. But today — for the first time — there was a mishap. Those *reshaim* attacked me and I was unable to carry out my assignment properly. I am so sorry." After Mr. Kempler revealed the truth, the Rebbe pushed his cup aside, remarking, "Thousands of Jewish infants desperately need milk and have to go without! I too can manage without ..."

CHAPTER 15

AVENUES OF ESCAPE

WITHIN MONTHS OF THEIR ARRIVAL IN Bochnia, the Belzer entourage finally had some good news: two, possibly three, escape plans presented themselves before Purim. Their desperate pleas to Switzerland and Hungary had ultimately borne fruit. The first initiative came, indirectly, from the Swiss activists. Despairing that the Rebbe would ever be allowed to travel directly from occupied Poland to neutral Switzerland, R' Moshe Gross advised his Slovakian brother-in-law, R' Shlomo Weinstock, to explore opportunities to smuggle them across the Slovak border. In his postcard of February 16, the Bilgoraj Rav had dismissed Slovakia outright as equally dangerous to Poland, yet Mr. Weinstock, a *shochet* from Bardejov, persevered with the encouragement of Rav Michoel Ber Weismandl, the legendary Slovakian *hatzalah* leader from Nitra.

On his advice, Mr. Weinstock met with R' Yosche Mendelovitch, of the border town of Michalovce, who was friendly with a top Hungarian officer who had apparently carried out similar commissions. After several weeks of waiting for the right time and circumstances to confide in this officer, they finally set up a secret meeting and asked him if he would be prepared to spirit their "uncle" out of Poland for a few thousand dollars. The officer confidently promised to bring their uncle out in his own car. The journey as well as crossing the border would be absolutely no obstacle, he declared; he had a solution for every problem! But he insisted on receiving all the money upfront. Both Mr. Weinstock and Mr. Mendelovitch were naturally suspicious that he was interested mostly in money and had little intention of rescuing their "uncle." Instead, they suggested that the well-known and respected Rabbi Weissmandl in Nitra should hold any outstanding amount in escrow, but the officer would not hear of it.

They left the meeting in trepidation. While dubious about the officer's motives, they were wary of abruptly breaking off negotiations lest he spitefully notify the authorities. So they promised to think the matter over. Mr. Weinstock returned home to consult with Rav Weissmandl. He agreed that the officer was probably planning to double-cross them but it would not be sensible to make an enemy of him. On his suggestion, they informed the officer after a few weeks that their "uncle" had just sent a message refusing to leave Poland. However, they generously agreed to pay his expenses — amounting to a few hundred dollars — to buy his silence.

Meanwhile a fresh avenue of escape presented itself — the Hungarian option. Despite the deceptive calm that pervaded the country until March 1944, Belz activists in Hungary took the Bilgoraj Rav's desperate messages relatively seriously. About a week after the first letter arrived, they held a top level meeting in Budapest to discuss alternate plans. Most were highly imaginative but impractical: spiriting the Rebbe through Slovakia, Austria and Italy to the Mediterranean; or bribing the top Nazi hierarchy to release him. Money was frittered away on schemes that invariably led nowhere. With experience, they slowly learned the severe limits on any rescue mounted from Hungary. Hundreds of kilometers plus rough, hilly terrain separated them from the Krakow area. Any rescue bid would require huge sums, more than they could raise among Belz supporters in Hungary.

After Rosh Hashanah, as spirits sank and rescue efforts faltered, an unmarried Belz *yoshev* from Munkacs by the name of Simchah

Teichman forged a letter, purportedly from the Rebbe's inner circle in Poland. This searing letter demanded to know how Hungarian chassidim could callously abandon their leader to his fate. The Rebbe had personally expressed his amazement that they so nonchalantly ignored the numerous urgent messages. When this missive arrived in Szombathely, where many of the youngest and most fervent Belz devotees resided, it burst upon them like a bombshell.

R' Moshe Dovid Hollander

On Erev Succos they held an urgent meeting and chose two energetic activists, R' Shloma Zalman Kut and R' Moshe Dovid Hollander, to raise large sums and spur the Budapest Committee into greater activity. They found it an uphill task — most chassidim had fully emptied their pockets during previous campaigns. The two were reduced to pawning their possessions just to scrape together travel expenses. In Pupa, they fared no better and Mr. Kut returned home while Mr. Hollander continued on to Budapest. Throughout the winter of 1942, R' Moshe Dovid displayed uncommon single-mindedness to his sacred mission. When occasion demanded, he traveled even on Shabbos, as befitting the rules of *pikuach nefesh*. For months on end, he rarely spent another day at home — arriving shortly before his own son's *bris* and leaving immediately afterwards. Among the hundreds of selfless individuals involved in the glorious saga of saving the Belzer Rebbe, his personality shines out as a beacon of heroism.

By haunting the border area and forging close contacts with seasoned smugglers, he managed to establish irregular links with Belz confidants trapped in Poland, but Mr. Hollander soon exhausted the limited funds at his disposal without getting any nearer to rescuing the Rebbe. Those hundreds of kilometers of hostile territory still separated him from their goal. Yet he learned one fundamental lesson: There was no realistic hope of rescuing their beloved Rebbe without investing substantial sums of money. Undeterred by the formidable task ahead, he returned to Budapest with the insistence that they devote more resources to the cause. Unbeknown to them, their long months desperately casting around for any means to save the Belzer Rav were about to bear fruit. Those who believe in Divine Providence accept that "*refuah kodemess lamakkah,* Heaven often prepares the solution before the misfortune" — in this case Dr. Leon Makh, Polish Consulate General.

One hundred twenty-three painful years of partition between neighboring Russia, Prussia and Austria had preceded Poland's finally regaining independence after World War I. Since many Polish citizens had fled that war to neighboring Hungary, the new state established a consulate in Budapest where Dr. Makh was designated to persuade them to return. Among these refugees were many Jews who found a friendly ear in Dr. Makh's office. He was polite, charming — and spoke a passable *Yiddish*! Meticulous in showing respect to rabbanim, he instructed his clerk to prioritize any Jew with a beard and sidelocks who carried a silver-topped cane. Makh soon became famous among Polish émigrés in Hungary. Although he failed to persuade many to return, he proved immensely helpful opening up import/export opportunities between Poland and Hungary, particularly in agricultural produce and textile manufacture.

In early 1939, just when Dr. Makh's official position finally became crucial with many Polish Jews considering returning to Poland in the wake of Austria's annexation and Hungary's pro-German stance, he was suddenly pensioned off. Yet he remained in Hungary, an active member of the Polish émigré community, and at the outbreak of war he joined the committee of the Hungarian-Polish Refugee Council. Over the years he had become a patron of the internationally famous Stern Restaurant on the street of Rumbach-Sandor utca, popular with Polish émigrés. Members of Hungarian royalty and government also enjoyed a tasty meal on Stern's premises and it became a must with tourists. This kosher restaurant in the center of Budapest was owned by a Belzer chassid, R' Chaim Mordechai Stern, who attributed his phenomenal success to his Rebbe's blessing. Thanks to his acumen and wide clientele, he was entrusted with many secrets and — naturally, a leading member of Budapest's Rescue Committee — was among the first to be told of the Rebbe's whereabouts.

At the restaurant, Dr. Makh made the acquaintance of a resourceful Polish captain who had joined Hungarian counterintelligence and made weekly expeditions into occupied Poland to gather intelligence. Leon Makh had an inspiration: perhaps Captain Shtaier could rescue Jews from the ghettos. Dr. Makh visited a close Jewish contact, Mr. M. Kraus, to make this proposal. Better still, he suggested, perhaps a prominent rabbi whose Hungarian devotees would pay handsomely for the rescue. Mr. Kraus thought the whole idea rather wild but his wife had a Polish background and was aware of the Belzer chassidim's desperate quest to save their Rebbe at whatever cost.

As a consequence, a meeting was set up between Dr. Makh, Captain Shtaier and Mr. Siegmund Berger (chairman, Carpatho-Russ Zionist Federation), with R' Chaim Mordechai Stern and R' Yosef Salgo on behalf of Belz. Leon Makh vouched for Shtaier's reliability and ability while Siegmund Berger guaranteed any shortfall in funding. Since Hungarian counterintelligence was in on the venture and promised their support, the cost was prohibitively high — approximately half a million Hungarian *pengoes* (even then, about $20,000 on the black market), to be split 15/85 between Shtaier and his spy-masters.

Politically, it was an opportune moment for the highly connected rescue bid. Since 1938, Hungary had joined Germany in dismembering parts of Czechoslovakia, Romania and Yugoslavia, and later invaded Russia as German allies. But before Pesach 1942, the pro-German Prime Minister, Laszlo Bardossy, had been replaced by the moderate Miklos Kallay, who sought to disentangle Hungary from Germany and war. He withdrew most Hungarian troops from Russia and rejected German demands to introduce the yellow star and "resettle" Hungarian Jews in Poland. Hungary's ruler, Regent Miklos Horthy, was summoned to Saltzburg shortly after Pesach 1943 for an embittered harangue by Hitler, but Kallay held steadfast to his course. Rescuing a prominent rabbinical personality would serve his political purposes nicely and provide a useful "alibi" should the Western Allies win the war.

Although the chassidim had promised to "save their Rebbe at any cost," they were taken aback at the steep price. Where were they to covertly raise these huge amounts during wartime? One of the few not to be discouraged was the indefatigable R' Moshe Dovid Hollander. As soon as he heard of the scheme with its high price tag, he offered to provide 30,000 *pengoes* within days. In truth he borrowed the entire sum from his rich brother's bank account — his brother had become religious and later escaped from Vienna due to the Rebbe's warm *berachah*. The Rescue Committee was so inspired by the rapid delivery of this substantial injection of *pengoes* that they set to the formidable task of raising the rest with renewed vigor.

Belz chassidim worldwide — in America, Switzerland, Palestine and England — began a clandestine campaign to defray the shortfall. Dispatching funds from America to Switzerland and on to Hungary was not a major problem but sending money out of England or British-administered Palestine was fraught with difficulties. Its life and death struggle with fascism would have bankrupted Britain irrevocably if not for America's generous Lend-Lease scheme, so the authorities took a dim view of any outflow of capital — particularly when they had a shrewd suspicion that its final destination was a country allied with their mortal enemies.

As we have seen, English chassidim had no option but to transfer their money via Palestine (originally through Mr. Gelley in Nahariah). Transmitting the funds from there on to Switzerland, however, was problematic. It needed the personal guarantee of Chief Rabbi Herzog to assure the Palestine authorities that this money originated from a bone fide source and was not destined for a German Axis country (which Hungary in fact was). At a meeting with Rabbis Charlap and Kipnis, Rav Herzog agreed to take the risk and accept full responsibility although he knew British officials would take an extremely dim view if they discovered the truth. Other prominent personalities declined for fear of British retribution, and one remarked admiringly, "I haven't the *mesiras nefesh* for another Jew comparable to Rav Herzog!" In addition, Chief Rabbi Herzog summoned rich acquaintances to select meetings at his residence where he campaigned for the Belzer cause.

A week after receiving Hollander's 30,000 *pengoes* and long before much funding could be solicited, Shtaier was despatched on a fact-finding mission. His "cover" was a training course at the Krakow embassy for Hungarian army officers serving with the *Wehrmacht* on the Russian front. Captain Shtaier arrived in Krakow with a flourish, in an official army car with a Hungarian pennant fluttering on the hood, and booked into a luxury hotel. He was also equipped with an introductory let-

Rebbe Yeshaye'le of Chechov, the youngest son of the Divrei Chaim

ter to the Belzer Rav proposing the new plan, signed by R' Shlomo Weinstock of Slovakia! Although Mr. Weinstock was primarily concerned with Slovakian escape plans, since he had been in regular contact with the Belz entourage and his handwriting was familiar, he was asked to write the secret letter in his own hand and affix his signature. But how was Shtaier to make contact with the Bochnia ghetto without arousing suspicion?

Somehow he discovered that the official interpreter at the course was actually a Jew, Mr. Mijis from Lemberg, feigning pure Aryan ancestry. The interpreter directed him to Mr. Eliezer Landau who was registered as a foreign citizen, thanks to highly placed contacts, and allowed to live outside the Bochnia ghetto with his family. However, Weinstock's cryptic letter did not identify the Belzer Rebbe by name so as not to incriminate him, being merely addressed to "The Rav." Who, puzzled R' Eliezer, could this anonymous Rav be? All the unknown Hungarian officer could tell him was that he was a *Csoda-Rabi* (a wonder-working *tzaddik*) with rich supporters in Budapest. Was it perhaps his Rebbe, Rav Yeshaye'le of Chechov — the last son of the Sanzer Rav, famous as the Divrei Chaim — who was also being sheltered in the Bochnia ghetto?

Accordingly, Mr. Landau called on the Rav of Chechov next morning. "Does the Rebbe have any plans to escape to Hungary?

Does he perhaps have a chassid by the name of Weinstock or has he ever heard of the name?" Reb Shaye'le promptly replied that he had no idea what R' Eliezer was talking about and he was certainly not involved. Mr. Landau then approached the Bilgoraj Rav who quickly confirmed that they had been in regular contact with a Weinstock, though not about Hungary. Obviously, they wanted to know more details, but the letter of introduction was guarded and circumspect in case it fell into the hands of the Gestapo. The Belzer Rav summoned R' Eliezer and asked him for more particulars. "What is the plan? How will it work?" Mr. Landau shrugged. "I don't really know," he admitted "*B'ezras Hashem* everything will work out for the best; the main thing is to get the right contact. Does the Rebbe agree in principle to escape with this Hungarian *hauptman*? He will be staying in Krakow for the next three days."

The Belzer entourage decided to sound out the mysterious captain and discover more details. Besides, if this plan was to succeed, there were surely various technical points to sort out. But how to renew contact? Krakow was now totally Aryan and *Judenrein*, off-limits and extremely dangerous to Jews. Once again Mr. Landau came to the rescue. Thanks to his German "connections," his official status as a foreign citizen and his unruffled penchant to bravely wander where no other Jew dare tread, Mr. Landau went to meet Captain Shtaier at his luxury hotel in Krakow. The captain told him that he had used his preliminary trip to make notes of dangerous crossing points, Gestapo checkpoints and patrols. He intended to smuggle the Rebbe and his companions all the way in an official Hungarian army vehicle. The Budapest Committee had paid for three "passengers" — the Rebbe, his brother and his loyal attendant (*shammas*) Mr. Josef Gold — and he urgently needed photographs (showing them clean shaven and in modern clothing) so he could make up the requisite documents.

This was followed up by another secret missive: "We have decided to rescue the Rav at any price. The emissary is reliable. From you is required *mesiras nefesh* and without your help nothing can be organized. He is capable of finding the way and

The Rebbe with Reb Yosel Gold of Yarotschev at his right

crossing borders. But you must organize everything until the departure. Stern. Salgo."

Producing the necessary photos quickly was a problem but not insurmountable. However, the Budapest Committee was laboring under a delusion when they assumed that the famous Belzer, R' Yosef (Yosel) Yarotschev (Gold) must be at the right hand of the Rebbe. In fact they had been separated for over a year. At his precipitate flight from Przemyslany, the Rebbe had expressly instructed R' Yosef to take charge of the Rebbe's extended family remaining behind in Przemyslany. Since he was renowned for his wise counsel and quick intelligence — and unofficially acclaimed as the "Belzer Foreign Minister" — he was an excellent choice to guide them through German Occupation in the absence of the Belzer Rav. So who should now take his place; who would be the third man? It was not merely whose photo should be handed over, it was rightly seen as a question of *pikuach nefesh*. Mr. Landau pressed for his mentor, the Chechover Rav, to be included in the escape mission. By then, the elderly *tzadaik* — who, like the Belzer Rav, spent his time in the ghetto learning and praying — was debilitated and ailing; this might be the last chance to save his life.

However, when the suggestion was put to Reb Shaye'le, he refused to leave by himself — "How can I abandon Rebbe Yankele, my beloved son and Rav of Sucja, with all his children?" — and there was absolutely no more room for anybody else. As it was, the military vehicle would be fairly cramped with a driver, the captain and three "passengers" in the rear compartment. Since the third place had originally been set aside for the Rebbe's *gabbai*, it was finally decided to substitute R' David Shapira, his loyal *shammas* in Bochnia. Moreover, he worked outside the ghetto, in Baczkow, which would be an ideal secluded area to board the foreign vehicle without attracting too much attention.

When the three photographs were duly handed over, the Hungarian officer reassured Mr. Landau, "It's all going well — I've found out everything I need to know. There'll be no problem getting across the border." He announced cheerfully, "I'll be back very soon!"

Yet when they did not hear another word for the next two months, the Belzer entourage began to doubt that the ambitious Hungarian option would ever become a reality. No doubt, they thought privately, it had run into formidable difficulties and had fallen through like all the others. Actually, the delay was due to the Budapest Committee's superhuman efforts to collect the enormous sums necessary for this rescue bid. But those trapped in Bochnia were not to know that. With most Polish ghettos on the brink of extinction, their situation had become so precarious that they were prepared to consider desperate measures — including perilous escape plans such as the Slovakian smugglers' network.

Among the teams of professional smugglers in Slovakia was one led by a partisan called "Paul" — in reality, David Milgroim of Lodz who had escaped from the Treblinka death camp — who was in direct contact with Rav Weissmandl's *Vaad Hatzalah* in Pressburg (Bratislava). Operating in the area of the "Black Dunajec" (the Dunajec River, near its source below the Carpathian Mountains on the Slovakian-Galician border), these smugglers helped hundreds of Bochnia's Jews escape to Slovakia. Now a Belzer chassid from Bochnia, R' Binyamin Landau, got in touch with "Paul" and asked him to arrange for the Belzer Rav's escape.

Obviously, smuggling a weak, venerable gentleman of over 60 who had spent a lifetime fasting and depriving himself of sleep complicated matters enormously. Crossing the border in that area involved a strenuous climb across the 7,000-foot high Carpathian or Tatra Mountain barrier, fording icy rivers and streams, trekking tens of kilometers through rough country and dense forests, and nights of forced marches up rugged country lanes while trying to keep ahead of the border patrols. (This undeveloped mountainous area is now a national center for winter sports and skiing.) Special care would have to be taken when choosing the most suitable route for the Belzer Rebbe whose *avodas hakodesh* had even intensified during the War in sympathy with the widespread suffering. How could he possibly walk through such a difficult, dangerous terrain? That they could even consider it shows how hazardous the situation in Bochnia had become.

R' Binyamin Landau's nephew, the youthful R' Moshe Schonfeld (later of Jerusalem), presented the plan to the Bilgoraj Rav and subsequently to the Belzer Rav personally. Since the Rebbe felt particularly infirm, it entailed two smugglers conveying him in an armchair over the most difficult terrain; safe-houses for any eventuality were designated along the projected path, with this specific route and stratagem exclusive to the Rebbe's use. Later the Belzer Rav would have to be smuggled further south-eastward across the Slovakian border into Hungarian occupied territory, annexed from Czechoslovakia in late 1938 and early 1939. Although nominally allied with Germany, Hungary was almost neutral and less anti-Semitic. Fortunately, crossing the Hungarian border was relatively trouble free. They estimated it would cost approximately 100,000 *Reichsmarks* and would involve several Slovakian peasants living near the border. The Bilgoraj Rav considered every intricate detail of the scheme before he reluctantly gave his go-ahead.

Fortunately, before they could act upon it, a safer plan — likewise from Slovakia — was put forward. Undeterred by his initial setback, Mr. Weinstock had traveled to Kezmarok on the Polish border, where a number of Jewish activists had already organized several smuggling forays. He contacted one of the leaders, Mr. Schwarz, and informed him of their wish to rescue the Belzer Rebbe "at whatever cost." But special care would have to be taken when choosing the most suitable route and mode of transport for somebody as venerable and weak as the Belzer Rav. First they had to find the right person to carry out the contract.

After some effort, Mr. Schwarz produced a Slovakian peasant who appeared to be honest and reliable. He asked to be shown a photo of the man he was to smuggle out of Bochnia and exclaimed excitedly, "Why — he's the exact image of my father!"(To be safe, their passport photo showed the Belzer Rav without a beard.) The peasant offered to smuggle him out as his "ill father" and provide the necessary documentation. So far so good, but they did not at all like his idea of transporting the Rebbe all the way from Bochnia to Kezmarok and on to Nitra in his horse and cart. Instead they proposed an alternative plan. Using his false Turkish papers, the Rebbe would travel by train from Bochnia — accompanied by the peasant — to the nearest border village, Bialy-Dunajec. From there he would board the cart for the last few kilometers across the Slovak border. For added security, the relevant border guards on that day would be suitably rewarded to look the other way.

While the peasant went down to his local registry office to process his "father's" paperwork with the Rebbe's photo, a message had to be urgently conveyed to Bochnia seeking their approval and introducing this unknown peasant. Fortunately, there were two Jewish youths in Kezmarok who made regular business "trips" into Poland and they agreed to deliver the lengthy letter personally. Meanwhile, R' Shlomo Weinstock returned home to await developments. He had to wait several weeks. On Erev Pesach, he was called to the telephone for a long distance call. On the other end were the two youths — the Bilgoraj Rav had replied that the Rebbe was pleased to see an effort was being made but they needed more details. Since they were returning to Poland on Chol HaMoed, they advised him to give them another letter straight after *Havdalah*. Accordingly, on Motza'ei Yom Tov (of the First Days), Mr. Weinstock raced to Kezmarok in a hired taxi with a detailed letter. Although this was quite some distance and took a fair bit of time, the youths delayed their departure until he arrived.

On receipt of this second letter, the Belzer entourage decided to accept the plan with a few changes: the Rebbe should also be accompanied by these two youths who were experienced hands at crossing the border. As a backup strategy in case the Rebbe's identity was discovered on the train, a car would be waiting to secretly ferry them back to Bochnia.[1] Since their scheme entailed bribing the Slovakian border guards and not all guards were approachable, it was considered expedient to flee Bochnia on Shabbos, 10 Iyar (25th *Sefirah* — May 15, 1943), and the two youths returned for the third time to confirm the arrangements.

Prior to the Rebbe's planned escape, R' David Singer from Jaroslaw, who had miraculously fled Krakow at the last minute, came to the Belzer Rav, clutching his two children — a girl of 6 and a boy of 2. Breaking down in tears he begged the Rebbe to bless him that he and his children survive. The Belzer Rav sighed deeply and bitterly. "What can I do?" he asked plaintively. After a few moments thought he added, "My father *zichrono livrachah* said that a lender and a borrower are a *segulah* for *arichas yamim* for both of them! And I say that giving something over for safekeeping has the same status and likewise is a token of long life! Here is my *kittel*, look after it, and when we meet again with all Jews, you can give it back ..." Then he gave him two coins for the children.[2]

Shortly before Shabbos, the Rebbe requested one of his close chassidim, R' Chaim Shloma Freidman (later of Antwerp), to cut off his beard! Naturally, Mr. Friedman trembled at the execution of the unfamiliar, delicate task — particularly with the imminent approach

---

1. It transpired that these precautions too were probably insufficient: Even *"Auslander"* now required special permits to travel near the border area and the entire Halberstam family attempting this escape route in mid-June was quickly apprehended by police checks in Kalawaria and Neimark. Car passengers were subject to similar stringent scrutiny.

2. Although Mr. Singer later suffered the full horrors of Nazi oppression in the camps, he and his children were finally liberated by British troops in Bergen-Belsen where he was "protected" as an Argentinean citizen. When he made his way to Eretz Yisrael and met the Belzer Rav, the Rebbe remarked animatedly, "Every Jew who was saved was accompanied by two angels! As for saving children — these had to be real *malachim!*"

R' Chaim Shloma Friedman's Aryan papers,
clean-shaven for an Aryan appearance

of Shabbos — but the Rebbe calmed him down. "Don't be scared," he said in a soft voice. "Take your time and do it normally." To everyone's considerable surprise, the Belzer Rav displayed no pain or emotion while this painful exercise took place. Since they were confident of the Rebbe's imminent departure, no Shabbos morning meal was prepared. Unfortunately there was a mishap.

Their escape depended on there being no trouble from guards at the ghetto gate. Afterwards the Rebbe could hide with any "foreign" Jew officially permitted to reside outside the ghetto, while waiting for a signal. Frustratingly, the friendly Jewish guard upon whom they could usually rely had taken ill. However, an influential Jewish policeman intimate with the head of the police, Dr. Rosen, and the Judenrat was a religious bachelor who risked his life for countless favors and mitzvos — seeing to the proper burial of the murdered and personally raising large bribes to release the young Bobover Rav, Reb Shloime'le, from prison — and was considered fairly close to Belz. (Although the Jewish ghetto police everywhere were ultimately Nazi lackeys, the Bochnia *Ordnungdienst* were relatively more benign than their counterparts elsewhere.) After Minchah, the Rebbe summoned this policeman and confided to him their secret plans. "We intend leaving for Slovakia tomorrow morning! Could you just arrange with the guard at the ghetto gate to let us through, no questions asked?"

To their astonishment, the policeman refused. "It's not a good idea; I don't agree with the timing! Now's not a good time. Wait a few days and I'll tip you off when's the best opportunity ..."

he blustered. While he did this with the best of motives out of a genuine concern for the Rebbe's welfare,[3] both the Belzer Rav and his brother stared at him in shock. What *chutzpah*! Finally the Bilgoraj Rav snapped angrily, "We didn't call you here for *eitzos*, for advice! We'll make our own decisions when or whether to go — all we're asking you is merely to assist our leaving the ghetto. Now, if you want to help, well and good. Otherwise — *gei gezunter heit*!"

In reply, the policemen turned on his heel and left. But within minutes the Judenrat and their Jewish police force knew of the Rebbe's intentions — and they were determined to prevent him from leaving Bochnia. As long as he was still among them, it helped foster a (false) sense of calm. Besides, who knew what revenge the Gestapo might unleash upon them when a prime bargaining chip slipped from their grasp? Almost certainly the Judenrat would be suspected of collusion. At an urgent meeting they seriously considered whether to surround the Rebbe's residence with a police cordon; eventually, they dismissed the idea that would inevitably tip off the German guards and Krakow's Gestapo that something was amiss.

Nonetheless, the Belzer entourage had no choice but to postpone the breakout, now that their secret had leaked out. The Slovakian peasant still waited for his "sick father" to appear outside the ghetto; yet how long could he and the two smugglers from Kezmarok loiter in the Bochnia vicinity without arousing suspicion? Their persistence was to be in vain when the situation became even more complicated. Captain Shtaier, the mysterious Hungarian/Polish *hauptman*, had suddenly reappeared after two months of unnerving silence!

On Monday, two days after the failed Slovakian escape bid, the army car finally arrived from Hungary. Apparently, part of the delay (beyond the difficulties of defraying the enormous costs) was due to Shtaier's usual vehicle not being up to the task and the Budapest Committee's having to acquire and equip a substitute. Leaving the army car at a safe spot, he sent an urgent message informing them,

---

3. In his later years he joined a Belz *minyan* in Europe.

"Everything's organized, we're ready to go!" But on examining his plans more closely, they were most hesitant.

His official cover story, in case they were ever stopped, struck them as strange and difficult to sustain. Apparently, the Belzer Rav was to be portrayed as a top Russian general captured on the Eastern front who had finally agreed to cooperate with his interrogators and reveal secrets of Russian defenses and strategy. The Bilgoraj Rav and R' David Shapira were other top ranking Russian prisoners taken in "for questioning." Yet all had no military bearing or knowledge and — most importantly — none of them could speak Russian. If they were ever stopped and questioned, the whole charade must inevitably collapse like a pack of cards and their cover be totally blown.

Captain Shtaier's personal official story was closer to the truth: He was a "special agent" sent by Hungarian Army Staff counterintelligence to escort them to Budapest for further questioning. He seemed unsure of the route and inexperienced in smuggling while at least the Slovakian smugglers had succeeded countless times. Their route, undertaken mainly at night, was relatively short and direct though strenuous; Shtaier had plotted a course which took in hundreds of kilometers across occupied Poland, crossed several checkpoints in broad daylight and could take up to three days. On the other hand, they would be ferried all the way in a comfortable car, officially under the protection of the Hungarian Army. Which option should they choose?

The Bilgoraj Rav preferred the Slovakian plan but a matter of such crucial importance was left to the Belzer Rav's judgment alone. "We need an immediate decision," the chassidim advised their Rebbe. "Both the Slovakian and the Hungarian want an answer straight away."

"Let me think about it," the Rebbe replied, "and I'll tell you after Maariv." But Maariv by the Belzer Rav took hours while everybody waited anxiously. "Despite all the problems," the Rebbe finally told them, "we are going with the Hungarian officer!"

CHAPTER 16

A DARING MASQUERADE

SINCE IT WOULD BE FAR TOO DANGEROUS FOR
Shtɛier's official army car to appear anywhere near the
Bochnia ghetto, it was arranged that they would board
his vehicle tomorrow evening (Tuesday, May 18, 13 Iyar)
at the nearby village of Baczkow, where many "foreign Jews" resided. To veil their departure in utmost secrecy it was thought best
to abscond from the ghetto that very night, but first they took their
leave of the elderly *tzaddik*, Rebbe Shaye'le of Czchow (Chechov),
amid mutual respect and warm blessings.[1]

From past experience, they obviously did not want to confide
in the Judenrat and its minions, nor involve any of them in the
breakout. Indeed, heads of Judenrat had strictly warned the Jewish
guards at the ghetto gate to be extra vigilant and not allow anyone
in or out without carefully checking them over first. Should the

---

1. The Czchower Rebbe's admiration for the Belzer Rav went back a long way. Before
the War, in Krakow, he told one grandson, Rebbe Zusia'le of Chernobyl, "Travel to
Belz, I remember him still as a child — he's holy from birth and has never tasted sin!"
His daughter too once told her grandson, R' Nachum Twersky, "You ask if they ever
discussed the Belzer Rav? Why, they never stopped talking about him!"

Belzer Rebbe somehow manage to escape through the ghetto gate, the guards would be answerable with their life.

What other weakness could they exploit? Unlike the larger Polish ghettos that were surrounded by high brick walls, Bochnia was enclosed by a wooden fence topped by the usual razor wire. Several weeks earlier, tens of Jews had successfully breached the ghetto walls and absconded to Slovakia. Surprisingly, Gestapo agents had not yet discovered the actual site of that breach and those wooden boards remained loose and easy to remove. However, this point was quite some distance from the Rebbe's residence and it was not considered expedient to convey him across the ghetto in his weakened condition without attracting attention.

Actually, the Belzer Rav's apartment at 4 Kublaska Street was on the edge of the ghetto, and its wooden barrier ran along the perimeter of his backyard. Just across the road running alongside the ghetto were houses belonging to "foreign Jews" and a useful haven on their flight to Baczkow and freedom. So near and yet so far. Perhaps they could just break through this fence — right here. When the suggestion was put to the Bilgoraj Rav, he immediately authorized the proposal, by paraphrasing the Talmudic dictum: *"Melech poretz geder laasos lo derech, ve'ein mochin beyado* — A king's royal prerogative to smash boundaries to facilitate his route is beyond dispute!"

Even if they succeeded in passing through the ghetto wall, their problems were not yet over. Though this part of the ghetto wall was out of sight of the German guards at the gate, with the regular disappearance of Bochnia's Jews in the direction of the Slovakian border, security around the ghetto had been substantially increased. Jewish police, answerable to the Judenrat, were stationed inside the walls while Polish policemen with German officers patroled outside the ghetto. With rumors still circulating that the Belzer Rav was attempting to escape, just getting past the Jewish police was difficult enough. How were these "Russian Generals" to depart the ghetto, never mind reach Hungary?

Fortunately, there were still Jewish policemen they could trust and they had to hope there was time enough between a Polish patrol passing and its return (especially when they were lured to the furthest point by distracting noises) to allow the Belzer group to disappear into the darkness without scrutiny. As the last minute plans were hastily laid, the two holy brothers again shaved off their beards and *peyos* and donned modern suits with smart, colorful neckties (supplied by Shtaier) in keeping with the image of generals dressed in the latest civilian fashion. They took no personal possessions with them. Meanwhile, two of the Rebbe's young loyal *shammasim* crept out and — at a signal from the policeman, Mr. Yechezkel Blumenfrucht from Krakow, who was on duty after midnight — began carefully and noiselessly prying away the heavy wooden boards from the fence. Although this was incredibly risky for both R' Yechezkel and the two brave *bachurim*, Yechiel Mendel Green of Krakow and Simchah of Wisnicz, they laid down their lives to save the Belzer Rav. By 1 a.m. their task was complete.

The two brothers cautiously emerged from their apartment and waited for a further signal from Mr. Blumenfrucht indicating that the coast was clear. The first to go quickly through was the Bilgoraj Rav, then the Belzer Rav — assisted by one of the *shammasim*. R' David Shapira did not take part in this escapade since he officially worked at the Baczkow factory and could safely get there under his own steam. Although they had safely slipped out of the ghetto, they immediately ran into their first mishap.

The plan called for them to take sanctuary at an apartment of one of the "foreign Jews" — Mr. Baruch Mordechai Tartner (a nephew of R' Zelig Shechter of Wisnicz). Yet when the *shammasim* knocked at his door, there was no reply. Frantically, they tugged at his bell, but again, no response. The house was as dark and quiet as the grave. Unbeknown to them, there had been a misunderstanding and Mr. Tartner was expecting them only shortly before dawn. To prepare for his early awakening, he had gone to bed hours ago and was sound asleep. How long could they stand there without getting caught? Any second now, the Polish patrol would be on its way back!

In desperation, Yechiel Mendel Green hastily shinned up the outside wall to either force open a window or otherwise attract Mr. Tartner's attention. Fortunately, R' Baruch Mordechai was sleeping in that downstairs room; he shot off the bed and opened the front door — and not a moment too soon. Hardly had the group safely entered his apartment when Yechiel Mendel noticed vague shapes approaching out of the darkness: The Polish patrol was returning! They had escaped disaster by seconds.

Before daybreak, Mr. Yehoshua Schaten — another "foreign Jew" with a permit to own a horse and carriage to transport workers — arrived to drive the Bilgoraj Rav and Belzer Rebbe into Baczkow as arranged. Unfortunately, they were slightly delayed. So though they arrived safely in Baczkow village, they were recognized en route by Jewish workers already marching to German workshops in the area. This second mishap was to have major repercussions and jeopardize the whole escape plan.

Yet another mischance occurred on reaching their destination. Although Baczkow village was outside the ghetto it was not spared the horrors of German warfare. In one *aktion*, hundreds of Bochnia's Jews had been marched into Baczkow forest and brutally gunned down at an open pit. Periodically, German raids and reprisals followed partisan activity from the nearby forests. Because of the increased tension in the area, their host R' Yehoshua Hoffnung (a "foreign citizen" who owned the Baczkow carpentry factory where nearly seventy Bochnia Jews labored for the Germans) thought it would be safer if both rabbanim temporarily hid in a secluded upstairs apartment. Due to a misunderstanding, the Belzer Rav accidentally walked into the neighboring apartment owned by a Ukrainian peasant before being redirected.

Although the Belzer Rav was already disguised in modern clothes and had removed his distinctive beard and *peyos*, the Ukrainian immediately exclaimed, "*Oh, Rabbin!*" R' Yehoshua was terrified that their cover had been blown and they were all in mortal danger. He engaged the peasant in long conversation in which he "casually" revealed how the *Rabbin* needed to be registered at the factory and to make any fuss would not be worth the Ukrainian's while ...

This was to be the least of their troubles. Most of the Jews sheltering in Baczkow and other areas outside the ghettos did so by virtue of their official status as foreign citizens, which likewise allowed them to ignore the curfew or dispense with the yellow armband. Some of these documents were genuine foreign papers of Slovakian, Hungarian and occasionally Swiss or Turkish citizens but reused on false names. Others were blatant forgeries. Yet all had been authenticated by Bochnia's new Chief of Gestapo, Schoemburg, until he was forbidden to do so by Gestapo Headquarters in Krakow. Even then, false papers were produced with the forged signature and seal of Schoemburg and now the Krakow Gestapo had decided — on the very day the Belzer Rav was at his most vulnerable — to check up on all these "foreign Jews."

Thanks to the Gestapo's informants they had an up-to-date list of all holders of foreign citizenship, with their names and addresses — and "Aaron Singer," the official name of the Belzer Rebbe who was registered as a Turkish subject, was on that list! Also on that list was his temporary host, Mr. Hoffnung. Should they discover the Belzer Rav or the Bilgoraj Rav hiding in disguise outside the ghetto without permission, it would be catastrophic, *chalilah*.

When the large number of Gestapo vehicles pulled up at the gates of the Bochnia ghetto unannounced, Mr. Eliezer Landau paled. Obviously, they had come on "important special duties" which could only foreshadow yet more evil for the ghetto and its Jewish captives. He had invested so much guile and effort into establishing the German workshops and prolonging the ghetto's survival; was there another *aktion* in the offing? Gingerly, he approached one of the Gestapo officers with whom he had previously done "business" to discover what was going on. "It's nothing," the Nazi assured him. "We're just checking on the papers of foreign citizens." Mr. Landau's heart froze in shock. His own foreign papers were in order but what would happen when they reached Baczkow? Only desperate measures might work now and he characteristically employed bluff to cloud the issue.

Urgently, he phoned *Lagerfuehrer* Muller in charge of the ghetto. "The Krakow Gestapo has arrived to close down the ghetto! They have long been jealous of our success! Now they want to take revenge. All my best workers will be shipped off — and the German personnel will be diverted to other, less well-paid duties; perhaps even the Eastern front! The *Lagerfuehrer* has to do something to save us. The only idea I can think of is to invite these honored guests round to your house for a first-class meal. If you serve up a royal feast — don't worry, I will provide the best food and drink — you will have an excellent opportunity to explain to them how this ghetto is essential to the German war effort and should be left undisturbed. If the *Lagerfuehrer* is successful, I'm sure we will all show our gratitude ..."

Although the Gestapo had not come to destroy the ghetto, of course, they were nevertheless most impressed by Muller's sudden show of friendship and the excellent repast. They were in no hurry to forego his hospitality and their mouth-watering party dragged on throughout the day. Meanwhile, Mr. Landau secretly sent his wife to Baczkow to deliver an urgent warning to the Belzer Rav. It was fortuitous he did so, since Captain Shtaier had become so alarmed by the sudden appearance of Gestapo patrol cars in the area that he wanted to postpone the escape bid for another day. Had they done so, undoubtedly they would have been apprehended quickly by the Germans.

Until then, the Belzer Rebbe had continued his regular routine of *tefillah* and Torah study as if he were in his customary surroundings and normal circumstances. Most agitated by the dire warning, the Rebbe urged that they leave without any further delay, but Shtaier still felt it would be most unsafe before nightfall. It would be a close call if they could get away before the Gestapo arrived.

As darkness descended, R' David Shapira anxiously waited at the window. "Where's that Hungarian captain already?" he fretted nervously. "He should have been here half-an-hour ago — any minute and the *reshaim* will turn up! Has something gone wrong again?" Suddenly, a large army car pulled into Baczkow, making several unusual maneuvers and signaling with its lights, but its signals were not exactly as agreed. Hesitantly, R' David stepped outside onto the sidewalk where he met a tall army officer, dressed in a foreign uniform, scrutinizing him with a sharp glance.

"*Sind sie der Rabbiner* — Are you the Rabbi?" Shtaier asked in German. "I'm sorry for the delay but like I said, these German patrols are everywhere and I've just been stopped!"

Shapira explained he was only the Rebbe's attendant. "If so, may I ask you to bring the Rabbi — *ober shnell!*" ordered the Captain briskly.

R' David rushed back into the house to announce Shtaier's arrival. "*Nu ...*" replied the Rebbe immediately and hurried outside, accompanied by the Bilgoraj Rav. As arranged, both were

R' David Shapira arriving in Eretz Yisrael

clean-shaven and hastily dressed in military uniforms. Shtaier began to give them last-minute instructions, reminding them to divest themselves of all money or valuables and any personal possessions,[2] when the captain noticed that the Belzer Rav was shivering. The Rebbe was habitually susceptible to cold — his unfamiliar clothes probably added to his present discomfort — but Captain Shtaier wrongly assumed he was scared.

"Do not fear, you are now under the protection of the Hungarian army!" he announced grandly in German, pulling out armbands emblazoned in Hungary's national colors. He motioned R' David Shapira toward the back seat and he was closely followed by the Bilgoraj Rav and the Rebbe. Shtaier and his army driver sat in the front and it was fairly cramped in the back, yet they settled in as best they could while the military vehicle sped away as fast as possible without attracting attention.

Meanwhile, the *Lagerfuehrer's* party finally broke up and the commanders immediately resumed their search for foreign passport holders. They fanned out throughout the district, concentrating on

---

2. To the Rebbe's abiding regret, he had to leave his *tefillin* and all other religious objects and writings behind forever.

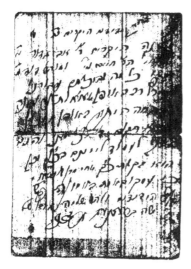

A hurried letter of recommendation written by the Bilgoraj Rav moments before departure, to volunteers on the Slovakia escape route [because of the acute danger he signed himself merely as "Mordechai" and identified the recipients only by broad hints]

the outlying villages where most "foreign Jews" lived. They soon reached Mr. Hoffnung's house.

"Who did you have staying here during the last twenty-four hours?" they demanded suspiciously. Apparently, some of their informants had been keeping them up to date. Fortunately his honored guests had escaped capture by just half an hour and Mr. Hoffnung was able to deny all knowledge and feign complete innocence! Unfortunately, the Gestapo did manage to catch many other Jews whose papers failed to pass scrutiny and these unfortunate people met a bitter end, *Hashem yinkom damam.*

Evading the Gestapo passport checks at the last minute was not the final hurdle the Belzer group had to overcome on leaving Bochnia. For prominent personalities — not to mention a world famous chassidic Rebbe — it was essential that their absence was not noted until it was too late. Otherwise it would be easy enough for the Gestapo to chase them across Poland, set up roadblocks or alert the border guards. Following their thwarted bid to escape last Friday night, the Judenrat were already on the lookout for any further attempts.

Now, however, their plight was yet more complicated and fraught with danger. Due to the delay in ferrying them to Baczkow early Tuesday morning, they had been spotted and recognized by slave workers being escorted from Bochnia. Obviously it did not take long for the news that the Belzer Rav had absconded to Baczkow to filter back to Bochnia. All Tuesday, rumors and counter-rumors swirled around the ghetto — and the Rebbe had not yet left Baczkow. Their situation was dangerous in the extreme.

How could they put the Judenrat — and their German masters — off the scent until the Rebbe was safely beyond their reach?

With a flash of inspiration, some of his closest chassidim embarked on a daring campaign of deception. Against all the evidence to the contrary, they would pretend the Rebbe was still on the premises and nothing had changed. At the urging of R' Chaim Shloma Friedman, Reuven Walkin (a mature *bachur* from Oshpitzin) reluctantly disguised himself as the Belzer Rav despite his legitimate fear that Judenrat or Gestapo informants would discover the ploy. Bravely, he donned the Belzer Rav's distinctive silk *kapota*, white socks and "half-shoes," plus his *tefillin* and Turkish-wool *tallis*, while imitating his voice to perfection. This was a *Purim Spiel* played for high stakes.

The ruse was not as difficult to carry off as it might seem. The Rebbe generally spent most of his day in the inner chamber — even during *davening* — while most chassidim and petitioners waited outside. Only his *shammasim* and closest chassidim usually entered his room. By sitting in the Belzer Rav's chair in his customary place facing the wall and effectively cloaking his head in the Rebbe's heavy *tallis*, Reuven Walkin was almost indistinguishable from the genuine article. The door to the inner room was deliberately left open so all could see the "Rebbe" praying and studying as usual at his *shtender*. Even regular chassidim, whose daily routine included a few hours of learning Talmud and other holy books at the Rebbe's residence while sustaining themselves with steaming glasses of Russian tea, were unaware that it was not their Rebbe sitting inside.

The two young *shammasim* energetically fostered the deception. At intervals, they would come running into the Rebbe's room as if they had been summoned, alternatively fetching a pitcher of water or something to drink and removing the empty containers with conventional bustle after a decent interval. Every so often, Yechiel Mendel Green would appear at the door to shout out, "Simchah! Simchah! *Der Rebbe ruft!*" and his colleague would hurry to his bidding, "*Yoh, Yoh — Doh bin ich. Ich kum shoin!*" At other times Simchah would play the same trick with Yechiel Mendel. Throughout Tuesday, they prolonged this farce.

Yet the rumors persisted. Several workers from Hoffnung's carpentry workshop insisted they had definitely seen the Rebbe traveling in a horse-drawn coach in the vicinity of Baczkow. At midday Salo Greiber, a policeman who had often visited the Belzer Rav in the past, walked into the apartment. "Where's Reb Mottele, the Bilgoraj Rav?" he asked with suspicion, since the Belzer Rav's brother was obviously missing with no "understudy" taking his place. R' Chaim Shloma Friedman replied casually, "Oh. He's just gone out to visit someone ..."

"And when will he be back?" Greiber persisted. Mr. Friedman shrugged, "He should be back in about an hour or so ..." But Greiber was unsatisfied and paced back and forth as if he were looking for something. Those in the know held their breath; evidently somebody in the Judenrat had heard the vague rumor and had sent one of their policemen to check it out. As Greiber's footsteps took him close to the Rebbe's door, purposefully left slightly ajar by the *shammasim*, he snatched a quick glance through the crack and saw the "Rebbe" at his usual place. Abruptly, he turned on his heel and hurried out of the house.

But an hour later he was back. "Where's Reb Mottele? Isn't he back yet?" he asked. Now his suspicions were confirmed. As before, he began wandering about the outer chamber toward the Rebbe's room, and once again he peered in through the open door: The "Rebbe" was still sitting at his *shtender* apparently praying and learning as he usually did most of the day. Salo Greiber finally left and never returned, evidently convinced that the rumors were unfounded.

Meanwhile back in Baczkow, R' David Shapira labored at his official work at Hoffnung's carpentry factory, though he was due to escape that night with the Belzer Rav. To cover his tracks, he had taken his usual place at the huge powersaw and did more than his regular share of slave labor. However, he had smuggled in a small pack of personal possessions and already had taken his leave from his closest family. Since he was known to be familiar with the Rebbe's movements, he was closely cross-questioned by Judenrat officials asking if there was any truth to these rumors — "If something happens and the Rebbe makes a run for it, you'll pay for this with your life!"

Mr. Shapira assured them that the rumors must be baseless. "What reason does he have to leave Bochnia? The Judenrat are on his side. Even the *Lagerfuehrer* helps every way he can. Why should he go? Where else will he find anything as safe as here?" These arguments helped to mollify the Judenrat somewhat though they remained skeptical.

When the Baczkow workers returned to Bochnia at the end of their working day, the rumors resurfaced with a vengeance. "I'm telling you, with my own eyes I saw the Belzer Rebbe traveling in a coach! I saw it myself, early this morning!" several workers insisted. These assertions sparked off heated discussions as Jews in the ghetto argued about the probability of the stories.

Suddenly one official intimate with the *Arbiets-leiter* strode into the Rebbe's apartment, which was unusual. The workers' administration had never shown the slightest interest in Belz before; obviously, he had been sent by somebody higher up in authority. He too peered in through the open door and left immediately. Pushing into the crowd arguing outside, he swore up and down — in fact, he was prepared to bet 500 *zloty* — that the Rebbe was still here! Just this minute, he had been upstairs and had personally seen the Rebbe sitting in his chair!

Inevitably, rumors spread as the arguments continued; those who had no previous inkling of the Belzer Rav's escape soon heard some version or other. Many felt that even if the stories were not accurate, they were at most premature and the Rebbe was probably planning some escape bid. Accordingly, a larger crowd than usual — men and women — visited the apartment to take their leave from the *tzaddik* before it was too late.

Leading chassidim in attendance explained that "the Rebbe" was not accepting visitors in his room at present. This was not entirely unusual — the Belzer Rav had undergone periods of semi-seclusion before — however, they did agree to convey short *kvittlech*. As they watched the *gabbaim* through the open door reading out their petitions, "the Rebbe's" muffled blessings were clearly audible from his alcove. Reuven Walkin's masterly duplication of his mentor's voice and mode of blessings was indistinguishable from the original and most outsiders left well pleased that they had managed to receive the Rebbe's warm blessing at that pivotal juncture in Jewish survival. Who knows when, or indeed whether, they would yet merit to see the Belzer Rebbe again?

That evening, a much larger crowd arrived for Minchah-Maariv; all were curious to see for themselves if the Belzer *tzaddik* was still there or not. The outer room was totally full, more packed than it had ever been when the Belzer Rav had been in residence. Fortunately, the Rebbe regularly *davened* Shacharis and Minchah by himself in his room, leaving his door ajar to join in the communal prayers. As the time for Minchah arrived, one of the *shammasim* emerged from the inner room, went up to R' Chaim Shloma Friedman and announced, *"Der Rebbe beht ihr zol tzu-gehn tzum omud!"*

On cue, Mr. Friedman hurried to the *shtender* and waited anxiously for the next command. The *shammas* emerged again and called out urgently, *"Nu!"* and Mr. Friedman began — urged on by the *shammas* standing in the doorway, and calling out, *"Nu! Nu!"* as he watched the "Rebbe" as usual to check where he was up to. *Korbanos, Ashrei, Kaddish, Shemoneh Esrei* and *Kedushah* flew by at breakneck speed in the Belz tradition, until *Aleinu.* Throughout the *tefillah,* all the outsiders crowded at the open doorway to catch a glimpse of the elusive Rebbe; many were gratified to see him for themselves, seated at his *shtender!*

After Minchah, the door was firmly closed since Maariv would be an insurmountable problem. No way could they conceal the Rebbe's absence. All year round, the chassidim were allowed into the Rebbe's room for Maariv and particularly now when traditionally the Belzer Rav personally chanted the *Sefiras HaOmer* with much emotion and accompanied by loud cries. Furthermore, if Reuven Walkin attempted to imitate the Rebbe's counting of the 29th *Omer,* the foolhardy deception would surely be recognized by veteran chassidim. It was one thing to copy his voice when muffled in a *tallis* and heard at a distance, quite another in public and at close quarters. What if some suspicious soul pushed forward and caught a view of his face? The whole elaborate charade would collapse like a bad dream.

Instead, the *shammas* emerged from the Rebbe's room, shaking his head regretfully: They would have to disappoint the large congregation waiting to hear the *tzaddik* recite *Sefiras HaOmer,* but he was not yet ready for *davening.* In fact, he would not be ready before 9 p.m. — the time of the German curfew. In order not to endanger so many people, he had instructed them to pray outside without him. This had occurred in the past, but infrequently, and it naturally raised suspicions, particularly among those who had been waiting until Maariv to conclusively verify the truth of those rumors, one way or the other.

Some Judenrat officials recognized the deception but decided to keep their doubts strictly to themselves. Others, however, passed on their suspicions to the Gestapo with a few ominous nuggets of information: the strange disappearance of the Bilgoraj Rav, the unusual absence of the Belzer Rav during evening prayers, and repeated sightings of him near Baczkow, outside the ghetto. Miraculously, the Gestapo did not react directly but merely forwarded the report to the Judenrat without comment.

Since Belz chassidim assumed their ploy had been successful, they decided to continue the tactic the next morning. But they were suddenly tipped off by another chassid. "Take care!" he whispered urgently, "Muller, Rosen and Weiss (respectively, the *Lagerfuehrer*, Jewish police chief and Judenrat head) are coming! They're already in the building, officially checking if everyone's at work!" Obviously, their real reason for this unexpected visit was the rumors about the Belzer *Wunder Rabbiner*; the chassidim knew their game was up, literally. As the fearsome trio painstakingly checked from room to room, Walkin hastily tore off the Rebbe's vestments and all made their escape — heading for an abandoned ruin in Ghetto Two — except for the loyal *shammas*, Yechiel Mendel Green. Despite the peril, he refused to abandon the Rebbe's precious possessions to the sadistic fancies of the Germans and their underlings. Perhaps, because of his young age, he might not be held responsible for the Belzer Rav's disappearance.

Imposing in his tight fitting uniform, Muller strode directly into the Rebbe's room, sharply scrutinizing everything and everywhere. Grabbing the frightened youth, he barked menacingly, "*Wo ist der Rabbiner?*" Green shook his head in puzzlement, "I don't know," he admitted.

"How is that possible? You are always together with the *Rabbiner*!" Green nodded slowly in agreement, "That's true ... He must have gone missing overnight. When I got up this morning, I saw he wasn't here!"

By now, Muller's fury was almost uncontrollable. Angrily, he ordered the *shammas* to follow him and they all marched off to the

Judenrat. On arrival, Green was taken to one of the offices where he was forced to strip naked. Then his interrogation began, accompanied by a savage beating. At first, Muller gave the rod to a Jewish policeman but when he perceived he was not flogging him sufficiently ruthlessly, he grabbed the club and exercised his violent temper by meting out a merciless beating. Yechiel Mendel was even thrown to the floor from a height of seven feet (over two meters) and the poor *shammas'* cries could be heard across the ghetto. Nonethelesss, he bravely stonewalled to save the others.

First, the *Lagerfuehrer* asked him, "Tell us, where has the *Rabbiner's* traveled to?"

"I don't know."

"Who were those involved in planning his trip?"

"I don't know any of them."

"But these people came regularly to the *Rabbiner*; what did they discuss with him?"

"I still don't know. Whenever anything of importance was discussed, I had to leave the room."

"Who played the part of the *Rabbiner* yesterday?"

"I did!"

"How is that possible? You were always outside as an attendant."

"That is true. I with my colleague, the other attendant, played the parts. Sometimes I was the *Rabbiner* and he was the attendant and sometimes we switched roles."

"Why did you carry out this act?"

"The *Rabbiner* told us to — if he ever went missing!"

"Where is your colleague?"

"I don't know."

It was obvious from these questions that the *Lagerfuehrer* had received a full report of the goings-on at the Rebbe's residence. After he completed his interrogation, he ordered the Judenrat to bring in the other attendant to check if their stories tallied. Naturally, Simchah's family was reluctant to see their son undergo a similar beating; besides, no one knew where the chassidim were all holed up. Well aware that they were prime suspects in the Judenrat's eyes, they all stayed hidden for two days — only one of them ventured out at night to find out what was going on.

Fortunately, R' Eliezer Landau stepped into the picture. He had actually considered escaping from Bochnia at about the same time as the Belzer Rav, but he had solemnly promised Dr. Rosen, head of the Judenrat's police, that he would stay to smooth things over. In preparation for the inevitable repercussions, Mr. Landau acquired a rare diamond of three carats weight. Hurrying to Muller's office, he quickly placed it on his desk. *"Herr Lagerfuehrer*, this would make an excellent present for your wife's birthday!"

"First tell me, where's your *Wunder Rabbiner* gone?" demanded the Ghetto Commandant, eyeing the glittering stone distractedly. Mr. Landau shrugged. "He's a Wonder Rabbi, capable of miracles! He's left me behind as well. What am I to do?" After receiving some more "presents" and bribes, the Nazi calmed down and freed Yechiel Mendel Green. Yet he still demanded to see the other attendant.

Before Simchah came forward the Judenrat had to promise he would not get beaten up, yet Muller still slapped him roughly about the face. By then Simchah had already met up with Yechiel Mendel to compare notes, so his interrogation satisfied the *Lagerfuehrer* who freed him immediately. Next he consulted with the Judenrat and their O.D. (*Ordnungdienst* — police officers). Muller asked them plaintively, "Why did the *Lager Rabbiner* flee without my permission? He only had to tell me he would like to leave for Hungary and I would have sent him with great honor!" — a comment that is reminiscent of the fake protestations uttered by Lavan the Aramean, as recorded in the Bible!

As the furor miraculously died down, leading Belz chassidim hesitatingly reappeared in public. Despite their immense fright and trepidation, they felt the charade had been well worthwhile, keeping the Gestapo off the Belzer Rav's trail for a crucial few hours. They did not yet know how the Gestapo was to expend enormous efforts to trace the Rebbe's route and whereabouts in order to officially demand his immediate extradition back to Poland.

CHAPTER 17

THE MIRACULOUS JOURNEY

F
OR JEWS TO TRAVEL ACROSS OCCUPIED POLAND under the noses of the Nazis was no easy matter, and Rebbe Aharon himself later remarked, "The *nissim* and *nisei nissim* that occurred en route to Budapest are impossible to describe!" Even leaving the Bochnia area was a major miracle, and when the Gestapo patrols checking on the status of "foreign Jews" finally arrived in Baczkow, it missed seizing the Belzer Rav and his companions by minutes. Furthermore, since they would shortly have to pass through numerous *streife* or police checkpoints and cross sensitive military areas, it would be relatively easy for the Gestapo to issue a nationwide alert and apprehend the fleeing car before it got too far.

Thankfully, Reuven Walkin's brave masquerade confused the Germans and their informants long enough; they entirely failed to pick up the Rebbe's trail until it was too late. Had the Gestapo realized the direction the vehicle took, they might easily have caught it. But at first the Germans assumed the fugitives would use the usual short route southwards, direct to Slovakia. Instead, they went on a long drive eastward across occupied Poland, retracing their earlier flight back toward Lvov and the Ukraine. Captain Shtaier insisted on this circuitous route since the direct route to Slovakia was closely guarded by hundreds of German troops searching for partisans. Unaccountably, Shtaier lost his way out of the Bochnia district although he had personally rehearsed the route to Przemysl three or four times.

The only explanation he could offer was the strangest weather phenomenon he had ever encountered. Although the night — as indeed the previous day — had been clear without a hint of rain, now their army staff car was enveloped in a weird mist. Ahead of them the road was clearly visible under a bright moon, but both sides and the rear of the car were cloaked in an unworldly damp fog that clouded their vision. Amazingly, the road surface remained dry and unaffected by the moisture surrounding their car; the vehicle glided along effortlessly as if in a dream, as R' David Shapira later recalled. Even when they traveled on roads monitored by SS patrols, none approached their car to check on its suspicious passengers; it was as if the strange mist that blanketed the vehicle served to shield it from hostile scrutiny. German controls they had to pass through were found to be unmanned because of another strange weather phenomenon — as Captain Shtaier later recollected — sudden violent downpours of driving rain. This occurred each time they approached German checkpoints and also happened outside the Bochnia ghetto, covering their escape.

On the first leg of the journey, on the main road between Bochnia and Przemysl, the army staff car suddenly broke down. It looked like a major mechanical failure. Even if they found a garage mechanic willing to repair it, no questions asked, it would still take at least half a day. Where would they conceal their "Russian generals" in the meantime? Desperately, both Captain Shtaier and his army driver tried to make some repairs but they were unable to get the car going. The situation was dire. Despite the lateness of the hour, convoys of German army vehicles hurried toward Przemysl and every so often Gestapo, SS and police cars drove past. It could only be a question of time before one of these would pull over to investigate — it was scarcely believable that none had done so yet — and then no slick cover story would help them. Recognizing the enormous danger, R' David Shapira began to recite *Vidui* with great emotion. Even Shtaier was close to despair. The only thing that gave him the courage to continue was the sight of the Belzer Rebbe sitting calmly in the back. As was his custom when confronted with a difficult problem, the Rebbe began concentrating deeply yet quietly with the utmost assiduity.

Out of the darkness, an old man suddenly appeared. "Why are you stopped here? What are you waiting for?" Wordlessly, the driver pointed at the silent engine. The old man leaned over the hood, pulled a tool or two and some bolts from his leather belt and twiddled with the motor. Within minutes, the engine miraculously sprang back to life! Captain Shtaier whipped out some money and offered to pay their unknown savior but the old man shrugged him off. Dumbly, they watched him wandering off into the darkness and he was rapidly lost from view.[1]

They finally arrived in Przemysl at 4 a.m., and Captain Shtaier decided he needed a break at the Hungarian army base there. They parked the car at the central market and he hurried off with his driver. "Don't worry, we won't be long ...," he assured his passengers. But as the captain began to relax over a large meal, he quickly forgot the precarious plight of his Jewish charges waiting outside in the street. As he later admitted, he began to see the presence of the "*Csoda-Rabi*" (as he described the Belzer *tzaddik*) as a surefire security — and the unnatural phenomena accompanying their journey had persuaded him that he had Divine assistance!

When two and then three hours slowly passed without the return of either Captain Shtaier or his driver, the intense anxiety inside the car mounted. What could possibly have happened to them? Had they been arrested? Even if those two managed to extricate themselves from whatever temporary difficulties they had been caught up in, what might *chalilah* happen to the Belzer passengers in the meantime? If anything, their predicament was even worse than

---

1. Many years later, when the Belzer Rav related this eerie episode to the Sadigurer Rebbe, the Sadigurer Rebbe remarked that the wearing of a leather belt was characteristic of Eliyahu HaNavi! However, the Belzer Rav did not reply directly and merely smiled broadly and knowingly.

The central market in Przemysl where they waited for three hours

during the breakdown on the main road. Soon it would be daybreak and how would they fend off the inevitable interrogation without Captain Shtaier to shield them? There was a limit how long they could stay in the car. To where on earth had their escorts vanished?

Finally, after three hours, Captain Shtaier reappeared as large as life. "What happened? Where have you been? Were you arrested?" they asked. When Shtaier reassured them that nothing had gone wrong and he had merely been enjoying the Hungarian army's hospitality, their reaction was predictably angry. "How could you abandon us like that for three hours in the center of Przemysl? This is one of the headquarters of the *Wehrmacht*, with the Gestapo guarding the San River here! We could have been picked up at any moment ..."

In reply, Shtaier tried to mollify them by explaining that he had been held up for substantial time because neither he nor the driver could find the car; indeed, they thought at first it had been moved! Only when they began actively searching for it did they accidentally touch it and recognize its existence — so well was it concealed by the strange surrounding mist. "If we couldn't see it when we were looking for it and knew where it was, you can rest assured the

Germans wouldn't have seen you either!" While Captain Shtaier undoubtedly exaggerated the length of time they had spent searching for his car, he was unquestionably sincere in describing the protective haze that obscured the vehicle.

Shtaier had not returned empty-handed: He brought fruit and water for his passengers. Ominously, he had also procured several guns and hand grenades from Hungarian army stores. This naturally heightened the already strained tension in the car, though nobody said a word. However, the Rebbe refused to eat anything throughout the hair-raising journey. Instead, he covered both eyes with his hands — manifestly meditating with deep concentration — and his faithful *shammas* R' David Shapira had not the heart to disturb him.

East of Przemysl, on the River San, lay the old border marking the 1939 partition between German-occupied Poland in the northwest and Russian-occupied Poland in the southeast. Although both zones had later been annexed by Germany after its surprise attack in June 1941, the border was still heavily guarded by the Gestapo. Captain Shtaier directed them southeast toward Sambor, Drohovitch and Stryj before making a sharp turn southwest and doubling back across the Carpathian Mountains toward Turka and the new Hungarian border at Uzoc'kyj (Uzhok, after annexing Czechoslovakia's eastern areas). As they drove through one of Poland's large forests, Shtaier armed himself with one of the rifles, perhaps in anticipation of a partisan attack. Everyone froze in fear but fortunately nothing happened. Indeed, though countless German soldiers and police vehicles passed them on the road, none attempted to check them. They crossed various German controls and made several stops without mishap.

Probably by design, they arrived at the Hungarian border at an early hour — at 6 a.m. Thursday morning (fortuitously, Pesach Sheni) — when the guards were probably less alert. Captain Shtaier was equipped with false documentation purportedly signed by top Hungarian ministry officials certifying the Belzer entourage was really "three high ranking Russian generals captured on the Eastern front with major intelligence information of fortifications and strategy." This testimonial urged all authorities to cooperate in facilitating their journey. Furthermore, Shtaier had taken the precaution — via his counterintelligence contacts — of having the War Ministry issue a special request for all border controls to allow free passage to "the important Russian general and his companions."

Since the border area around Uzoc'kyj was heavily used by Hungarian army units, Shtaier did not envision any problems. Nonetheless, as they drew up at the barrier, Shtaier spoke directly to the Belzer Rav: *"Mir brochen eine grosse hilfe, machen sie gefeligest gebeht* — We need great assistance, please pray!" Surprisingly, they were to face more dangers on this part of the journey than they ever did in crossing occupied Poland. Although the border guards saluted Captain Shtaier smartly and showed him due respect, they still insisted on seeing his papers. When he flourished his impressive documentation, two Hungarian gendarmes in their distinctive feather-plumed hats came out to inspect "the generals" and were instantly suspicious. They addressed some questions directly at the passengers, in fluent Hungarian, but nobody answered. "Everybody step out of the car and show his papers!" they ordered briskly.

Immediately, Shtaier realized the game was almost up. He had made several fundamental errors: Despite dressing his party in uniforms, he had raised the suspicions of the gendarmerie in a sensitive army area. None of his top "generals" could speak Hungarian, Russian or any other Slav language; nor did they much look like military men. It looked as if his cover story would be completely blown. Not only was there every likelihood that his charges would be deported straight back across the border into the hands of the Gestapo with all that would mean for them, he would also not receive the large reward for which he had risked his life. Worse, he was now himself in deep trouble for forging documents and smuggling wanted fugitives.

Quick as a flash he grabbed a few bottles of choice wine stashed away for just such an emergency and raced off in the direction of the command post. The driver likewise disassociated himself from the scene by getting out and busying himself with the engine as if he were repairing some small fault. But inside the car there was pandemonium. Shtaier had vanished they knew not where, the driver was no help and the two gendarmes were getting more agitated and threatening by the minute. Although the Belzer Rebbe could not properly understand what the border guards were saying, he could see by their increasingly wild gestures that they wanted the three men to step out of the car — and on the double!

When the gendarmes saw how their orders were being ignored they became furious. Both drew their ceremonial swords and began swearing and cursing at the hapless passengers, urging them to get out without any more delay. Obviously, the Belzer entourage could not remain where they were if they wanted to avoid any violence. Reluctantly they began moving from their back seat. Suddenly the Rebbe intervened. "Don't get out! Stay here! Don't move!" Thus the impasse continued: the gendarmes threatening and gesticulating outside at the passengers esconced within, obstinately ignoring their orders. Only the ice-cold nerve of the "top Russian general" prevented the gendarmes from entering the car and physically ejecting them by force.

Meanwhile, a young messenger arrived from the command post with a cup of hot coffee for the driver. The driver managed to send a note back with this youth warning Shtaier of the danger they were in. Captain Shtaier had been using the interval to soften up the commandant by breaking open a couple of bottles for a convivial drinking bout while discussing politics and army gossip. When he received the terse note, he realized the time had run out. "See here," he drawled, displaying his papers. "I'm on a top secret intelligence gathering mission and these important men have vital information. They've agreed to talk as long as we handle them right. But your guards are being a little awkward. Usually that's right and that's their job — but not in this case ...

"Now it's not fitting that a top officer like myself should have to explain all this to low ranking border guards," continued Shtaier, pointing at his stripes and medals, "That's why I'm confiding the secret only with you — and I know I can trust you!"

The commandant, suitably flattered, agreed to walk out with Captain Shtaier and see what all the fuss was about. When he beheld the enraged gendarmes, wildly waving their swords about, he ordered them to immediately sheath their weapons and leave the passengers alone. They reluctantly obeyed and saluted while the commandant cast a cursory glance over Shtaier's papers. "Pray continue your journey," he announced grandly, lifting the barrier.

As they sped away, Captain Shtaier knew that this might not be the end of the matter. Most likely, the gendarmes were confiding their well-founded suspicions at this very minute. If the commandant realized how the cover story did not quite add up he would probably telephone the nearest control or police-post down the road to have them pulled in for questioning. Nor would they be too difficult to trace since all car numbers were logged at the border crossing.

Fortunately, he had prepared himself for just such an eventuality. As soon as it was safe, he ordered the driver to pull off the road into an adjacent potato field. Shtaier jumped out of the car and pulled a pair of false number plates from some hiding place. Quickly, he and the driver replaced the plates and buried the old ones deep in the ground. To further throw off any pursuit by the authorities, they turned off onto secondary roads to cross the border at one local checkpoint — the mountain pass they were driving through zigzags along the Slovak border — and re-enter Hungary at another checkpoint. Each time they approached these border controls, Shtaier again implored the Rebbe: *"Herr Rabbiner, nachmahl hilfen!"*

Even without pursuit, they found traveling in Hungary far more fraught with danger than their journey across Poland had been. At least the Poles and Germans retained some respect for the Hungarian pennant fluttering from their army staff car and let it pass unchallenged. But in the area beyond their border, bristling with army convoys and crawling with military police, the Hungarians wanted to know exactly what this vehicle with its strange passengers was doing here. Hardly had they successfully explained themselves to one group of suspicious soldiers than they were soon required to repeat the exercise to the next troop position along the road.

To their misfortune, it was a time of heightened tension between Hungary and Germany. Officially, these countries had been allies since November 1940 and Hungary joined in the June 1941 invasion of Russia. But Hungarian losses on that front coupled with their traditional enmity with Romania had spurred Regent Miklos Horthy to withdraw as many troops as possible and replace his pro-German prime minister with Miklos Kallay by March 1942. Kallay's increasingly neutral stance and softer approach to Jews — both native and refugee — had goaded the furious German Fuehrer to summon Horthy to Saltzburg for a severe dressing down during April 1943. As Kallay continued his policies, Hungarian forces prepared themselves for skirmishes with their "close allies" and were on a sharp lookout for fifth-columnists. So May 1943 was not the ideal time for Shtaier to smuggle in dubious looking fugitives.

Usually they got through by guile and bluff, as when they were stopped by a large Hungarian army convoy led by a general on a horse. "Who are you? What's going on?" he snapped suspiciously. In desperation, Captain Shtaier saluted the Hungarian general and whispered something and the general waved them on. Occasionally, they only escaped peril by apparently miraculous intervention. One army group blocked their way and were refusing to let them continue until they were satisfied with their credentials. Shtaier was at his wit's ends when an elderly Hungarian officer rode up on his horse. After perusing the documents, he signaled them through. "I've no idea who on earth that general was!" Captain Shtaier admitted in bewilderment.

Further on, a highly distinguished military commander halted their car and threatened dire penalties, until three generals suddenly appeared on horseback and ordered their release. Although Captain Shtaier subsequently made great efforts to discover the identity of those three mysterious generals, he was unable to do so.[2]

Most Polish refugees escaping across the Hungarian border were generally not safe until they reached Budapest and legalized their presence with the police's external division, the KEOKH. (If they were officially Jewish, they were then incarcerated under reasonable conditions; if they claimed "Aryan" status, they would stay at open camps outside the capital and report to the police once a month.)

---

2. When the Belzer Rav repeated this story at his 9th Shevat Thanksgiving *Seudah*, during 1957 — the last year of his life — one of his close chassidim replied, "The Bilgoraj Rav once said he was personally sure who the 'generals' were: his saintly father, Rebbe Yissachar Ber; his saintly grandfather, Rebbe Yeshie'le; and his fiery great-grandfather Rebbe Shalom!" At the time, the Belzer Rav remained noncommittal, merely smiling enigmatically; on a previous occasion, however, he had told the Sadigurer Rebbe he regarded this particular episode as "... *a nes, a pela-dik'er nes!*"

But until they registered in Budapest, they could be arrested at any time or place and deported back to the tender mercies of the Gestapo. Even those harboring "illegal" refugees were liable to be expelled to Poland with them. So the Belzer entourage was anxious to press on to Budapest without delay.

The first major Hungarian town they came to was Ungvar (Uzgorod), approximately a quarter of their way to Budapest. Because of the numerous holdups, checkpoints and evasive driving, it had taken them more than a day to travel the 160-odd kilometers from the Polish border. They were still in what was considered a border area — it had been annexed from Czechslovakia in mid-March 1939 — and their situation remained highly precarious. Yet when they finally reached the *kehillah* of Ungvar, Captain Shtaier refused to go any further!

"I'm sorry," he said wiping his brow. "But it's too hazardous for me to continue. If I had known what was involved in this smuggling trip, I wouldn't have done it for all the money in the world! Never again will I do anything like this! I'm sure the border police have been hunting for me ever since we bluffed our way through Uzoc'kyj. By now they must have circulated our description throughout the whole area so it's best if we split up. Besides, Ungvar has many religious Jews so you'll be quite comfortable here."

They tried to reason with him, pointing out how risky Ungvar was for refugees, how his contract stipulated he must deliver them safely to Budapest — but to no avail. Shtaier was adamant not to prolong this perilous enterprise; he refused even the Belzer Rebbe's specific request. Eventually, they agreed on a compromise. Since it was only a few hours to Shabbos, they would stay in Ungvar over the weekend and decide their next steps afterwards. First they had to find somewhere suitable to stay.

Before the War, many chassidim had traveled to Belz from Ungvar — a prominent, respectable *kehillah* — but their addresses were obviously not at hand. Shtaier parked on the main street while R' David Shapira went into the nearest Jewish shop to ask for the closest available chassid. The shopkeeper came out into the street and pointed out a bearded Jew walking toward them. *"Reb Yid,"* the *gabbai* asked apprehensively, "are you perhaps a *Belzer* chassid?" The elderly man looked him up and down in surprise since R' David was now disguised in a most modern suit with a short jacket and a flashy tie.

"My name is Zundel Berger," the man replied at last, "and I happen to be a *Belzer* chassid. What's the problem?" Indeed, R' Zundel was a respected member of the Belzer fraternity. R' David Shapira took a deep breath, walked up close and whispered in his ear, "The holy Rav, Reb Ahare'le, with his younger brother, Reb Mottele, have escaped here! They need somewhere to stay."

R' Zundel shook with both relief and fear — relief that the Belzer Rav was alive and fear for his present safety. For months, disquieting rumors had swept the Ungvar community, hinting that the very worst fate had befallen their Rebbe. Yet this relief was tinged with anxiety since it was strictly forbidden during wartime to take in any strangers — especially Polish refugees — under threat of the severest penalties. During this tense period, Ungvar was not a secure refuge for fugitives from either the Gestapo or Hungary's security police. However, there was no way he could leave his holy Rebbe out in the street so, as a loyal Belzer, he bravely elected to host the Belzer Rav and his brother over Shabbos.

He squeezed into the front of the car and directed them to his house. But as they entered, he took his first good look at the passengers and was deeply shocked. Both the "Rebbe" and his "brother" were now clothed in modern suits and ties and neither had beards or long *payos*. Obviously, these were shameless frauds; this could not possibly be his holy Belzer Rav! They hardly resembled the real thing. (Judging from rare photographs surviving his escape, the Belzer Rav without his distinctive beard was totally unrecognizable.)

In a rage, he screamed at them, "You Polish bandits! *Farbrechers*! So you want to save your miserable skins — but is nothing sacred? Did you have to abuse the holy name of the Belzer *tzaddik*? If not for the presence of this Hungarian officer, I'd throw both you liars out by the scruff of your necks!"

While R' David Shapira vainly tried to pacify R' Zundel Berger, the Belzer Rav made no direct attempt to confirm his identity. Instead, with his failing strength after almost sixty hours of fasting — the Rebbe picked up a *Tehillim* lying on the hall table and began reciting Psalm 111 with his customary fervor to thank Hashem for their miraculous escape. R' Zundel's son had personally visited Belz shortly before the War and when he heard the Rebbe's voice he cried out in astonishment, *"Ribbono Shel Olam! But that's the Rav! He and no other!"*

Deeply mortified, R' Zundel Berger made an abject apology but the Rebbe brushed the misunderstanding aside. Meanwhile, Captain Shtaier went down to the post office to place a long distance call to Budapest to inform the Rescue Committee that he had arrived in Ungvar with "both brothers." The Committee was overjoyed that the audacious plan had worked and frantically began organizing alternative schemes to smuggle the Rebbe to Budapest without delay. For the moment, they urged extreme discretion. The less who knew of the Rebbe's presence in Ungvar, the better. For their part, they would tell no one in Budapest the good news.

However, it was virtually impossible to keep it a secret in Ungvar. The overwhelming relief people felt upon learning that those awful rumors about the Rebbe were unfounded was palpable. The Rebbe seriously contemplated moving to a secret address and conducting a private *tisch* for only a select few but concluded it would be of little use. The excitement was too great. That Friday night, many chassidim tried to crowd into Mr. Berger's home to witness the *tefillos* and *tisch* and, as one later put it, "You could feel the *simchah* with your hands!"

Fortunately, their Shabbos passed peacefully and by Motza'ei Shabbos, the Belzer Rav felt sufficiently relaxed to relate some of the miracles that had accompanied their flight. Just then, Captain Shtaier returned for his new instructions and overheard some of the Rebbe's stories. "I'm amazed, Rabbi, that you have left out the greatest wonder of all: how the car was covered with a supernatural cloud!" he interjected. "All the way from Bochnia to the Hungarian border, nobody could see us. That was how I could allow myself to park in the center of Przemysl, confident no one would notice the car or its passengers!"

That Motza'ei Shabbos, urgent discussions were held to plan their next move. By then the Budapest Committee had succeeded in hiring an official ambulance from the Red Cross. In theory that ought to have been the perfect vehicle with which to conclude their escape. To their surprise, the Belzer Rav felt otherwise. Instead he stipulated that Captain Shtaier should complete the journey in his car! In any event, he insisted that Shtaier must accompany them all the way to Budapest. Apparently he perceived this officer of Hungarian counterintelligence as Heaven's emissary in his rescue. Most reluctantly, Captain Shtaier bowed to the *Wunder Rabbiner's* wishes.

Sunday morning, Shtaier pulled up outside the Berger household. As the Belzer party boarded his car, they noticed Captain Shtaier conferring with a mysterious gentleman — by his clothes and bearing, apparently a prominent member of Hungary's ruling hierachy. However, neither he nor Captain Shtaier deigned to enlighten them as to his identity and they were relieved when he made no move to hinder them.

Contrary to their hopes, the journey from Ungvar to Budapest was most difficult. By unfortunate coincidence that particular Sunday was also the day when Hungary's ruler, Regent Miklos Horthy, decided to visit the border area — annexed from Czechoslovakia — and inspect the defenses. Ever since they had drifted apart, Hungary was well aware that Germany was apt to unleash a sudden military attack on erstwhile allies or innocent neutrals as ruthlessly as if they were fighting long-standing enemies. As a precautionary measure, Hungary had established a network of clandestine bases and strongpoints along the Slovak and Polish borders. With tension rising, Horthy resolved to survey these bases and the likely routes of a German invasion. Without warning, the whole area between the border and fifty miles from Budapest was abruptly placed on a military footing, with all civilian traffic arbitrarily suspended while Horthy's retinue crisscrossed the region. No other vehicles were officially allowed to proceed without special permits. Since Captain Shtaier was not armed with these permits, their position was delicate in the extreme.

To make matters worse, they began experiencing minor breakdowns of their own. The first was nothing insurmountable — just a puncture — but it drew unwelcome attention to themselves. As their driver got out to change the tire, Shtaier took a blank sheet of stationery out of his briefcase and quickly wrote something down. Shortly afterwards, a military patrol pulled over to ask them what they were doing there and check their special permits. Captain Shtaier flourished his sheet of paper while he explained he was escorting these important prisoners to a certain prison. Amazingly, the military police accepted his strange explanation and drove off.

"For the past few hours we've been traveling on military roads without a permit," muttered Shtaier under his breath. "This was just about the biggest miracle so far but I don't know how we're to get past the final checkpoint ..."

A few miles down the road, they had another puncture; obviously, their lengthy flight across Poland and Hungary had taken its toll. While the driver was repairing the tire, which took longer than merely changing the wheel, Shtaier scribbled some more on his sheet of paper. Once again a passing military patrol slowed down suspiciously but Captain Shtaier pointed at his precious piece of paper and they drove on without making any further inquiries!

Eventually they arrived at the final checkpoint. Cars were waiting in line at the barrier; each was painstakingly checked as to its credentials. How were they to get through? Shtaier's cover story — his three "prisoners" had to be interrogated in Budapest urgently, that very day — was barely adequate and would not stand too close an examination, as they had already learned earlier. Worse still was their lack of even the basic documentation; not one car in line was being allowed past this checkpoint without a special permit.

As they reached the control, Captain Shtaier had an inspiration. He pulled out his sheet of paper and instructed the driver to keep on driving slowly toward the barrier without stopping. Captain Shtaier calmly waved the paper out of the car window while he smiled confidently at the sentries, all the time inexorably approaching the barricade. Astonishingly, the sentries blithely assumed the scribbled notepaper must contain the all-important permit and they hastened to tug on the rope, lifting the barrier. Out of the whole line of cars, they were alone in not being stopped for a thorough examination!

From then on it was a clear run to Budapest and they covered those last fifty miles in good time, finally arriving during twilight. That Sunday had been a long, grueling day. In more peaceful times, however, it was generally considered a day of joy and celebration — the 18th of Iyar, more familiarly known as Lag B'Omer, the 33rd day of the *Omer*. Now, as in days of old, they too had experienced some unusual *nissim* of their own and escaped the Bochnia ghetto barely three months before its final liquidation.

CHAPTER 18

THE
HUNGARIAN
EXILE

C OMPARED TO NEIGHBORING POLAND, HUNGARY
was an oasis of tranquility amidst German barbarism, yet
its Jews had already suffered many travails of their own.
In the previous century, Hungary was one of the first
states to vote delegates into parliament on a blatant anti-Semitic
platform. During 1919, pogroms raged in the provinces when the
abortive Communist government collapsed and Admiral Niklos
Horthy de Nagybanya marched to power. As the violence slowly
subsided, his government restricted Jewish admission to universities and eliminated most Jews from public service. The situation
stabilized somewhat under the government of Count Stephen de
Bethlen (1921-31), but Hungary's persecution of its Jews intensified
during the 1930's, following the example of Nazi Germany.

After Germany's annexation of Austria in May 1938, Hungary
further ratcheted up the repression with laws limiting Jewish employment, barring Jews from prominent positions in the media
and refusing trade licenses. Their landed property was rendered
liable to expropriation; citizenship and voting rights were restricted;
and entry to the professions severely limited. Other substantial

Munkatabor, forced labor

Jewish populations fell under Hungarian sway when Hungary allied itself with the German Axis to dismember Czechoslovakia in 1938 and early 1939, acquire parts of Romania in 1940, and occupy areas of Yugoslavia during 1941. Subsequently, Hungarian occupying forces massacred several thousand Yugoslavian Jews while deporting 17,000 former Czechoslovak and "stateless" Jews (i.e., those who lacked documentary proof of citizenship) to the Ukraine, where Nazi death squads murdered 11,000 and Hungary utilized the rest as slave laborers.

Native Hungarian Jews fared only relatively better during wartime. All Jews of military age were conscripted under army control — *munkatabor* — where they were compelled to undertake demeaning and humiliating labor in the icy wastes of the Ukraine. The army subjected religious Jews to extra persecution while creating kashrus and Shabbos observance difficulties in general. (Prewar Orthodox Judaism flourished mainly in the smaller towns, but much of the Jewish population in larger cities, and particularly Budapest where a substantial proportion lived, was assimilated to some degree.) Although Kallay's government refused to introduce the yellow star, and stopped any further deportations — rejecting Germany's "resettlement of the Jews as a final solution" until he received a satisfactory explanation as to where exactly they were being resettled — nonetheless he upheld the *munkatabor* forced-labor conscription and extended the employment restrictions and expropriations.

Jewish refugees in Hungary fared worse. To obtain asylum and freedom from deportation, most Jewish refugees had to masquerade as Polish "Aryans" and live a secret existence like latter-day Marranos. Hungarian security agents prowled favorite refugee haunts to apprehend non-Aryans while police regularly raided railway depots and bus depots for "illegal" aliens. Those caught were extradited back to Poland, their country of origin, straight into the hands of the Gestapo. Following extensive lobbying by Jewish welfare organizations, Jewish refugees beyond the border areas were more likely to be imprisoned than deported, and those who declared they were non-Jewish were duly registered as Aryans without too much fuss, though they had to register with the police once a month.

Obviously, legalizing the Belzer Rebbe's status with the authorities would not be easy; concealing his whereabouts, next to impossible. But first he had to be treated following years of deprivation. After a few hours' stay at the house of Mr. Shmuel Ber Barnet, the Belz Committee persuaded Dr. Duni, of Budapest Hospital In-Patients Department, to hospitalize both brothers for checkups. Graciously, he agreed to facilitate this without any charge or bribe. To conceal their identity, they were admitted to separate private wards and the Belzer Rav was registered as "Samuel Brown" (a common Jewish Hungarian name), aged 90! Such had been the effect of his almost continual mortification in sympathy with the overwhelming calamity; the Rebbe looked more like 90 than his true age of 63.

Unfortunately, every public ward of the hospital contained Jewish refugees who had recently escaped from Poland — mostly through Rav Weissmandl's smuggling network — and if they caught a glimpse of the Belzer Rav someone might recognize him. So, using various excuses, Dr. Duni moved all the Polish patients into a separate block. To further ensure the Rebbe's isolation and security, the Committee requested that nobody should dare visit the Rebbe or his brother in the hospital, an order strictly obeyed by Budapest's chassidim. Even R' Moshe Dovid Hollander, whose heroic efforts had paved the way for the Rebbe's escape, resisted the overwhelming temptation. Sadly, Hollander was conscripted into *munkatabor*, the army's forced labor battalions, on the very day of the Rebbe's discharge from the hospital, and so never met him.

Despite his travails and tribulations, the Rebbe never wavered from his meticulous attention to halachah. One of his chassidim, R' Aaron Maggid, asked a hospital maintenance worker to repair the door lock and when he had completed this small job, the Belzer Rav thanked the worker warmly, rewarding him with a large tip. That night, R' David Shapira, who was staying in the adjacent room, was shocked to hear his Rebbe groaning loudly. Fearing he had suffered some relapse, the *shammas* hurried in to see what was ailing him. Immediately, the Rav turned to him. "David! Please call Reb Aaron Maggid." As soon as Mr. Maggid arrived the Belzer Rebbe questioned, "Perhaps that worker was not paid yet? It is an *issur* to delay payment!"

R' Aaron was taken aback. "But the worker was a non-Jew to whom *lo solin* does not apply."

"Even so, *Chazal* taught us to behave strictly to promote peaceful relations," persisted the Rebbe.

"But the Rav gave him a respectable amount of beer money!"

The Belzer Rav waved that aside. "That was nothing, I just intended that as an extra — nothing more!"

"That worker is employed by the hospital. He gets a weekly wage and this is part of his job."

"Nevertheless," insisted the Belzer Rav, "it still smacks of a delayed payment." They had no option but to pay the worker within the hour so that the Rav could relax.

After six days in the hospital, it was decided to move the Rebbe to a different location and they requested a junior doctor to sign a release certificate. Since the Rebbe was reluctant to be examined by a non-Jewish doctor he agreed to remove only his vest. The doctor took one look at his emaciated chest and murmured, "I've met this patient before!" His memory took him back to a tour of duty in Lemberg (Lvov) before the War; then he had not been allowed to physically examine this famished gentleman and had to use a towel as a buffer. He did not recognize the Rebbe's face but he certainly recollected that unique physique. "This is no ordinary refugee — he is an important Polish Rabbiner!" he exclaimed angrily. "You can't fool me!" The Hungarian Committee, who had had no idea of this previous encounter, was caught and had no option but to promise the doctor a large reward — and a possible blessing from the great Rabbi — for holding his silence.

On Friday, 23 Iyar, 1943, the Belzer Rav moved into the large suburban house of R' Moshe Winegarten, the local *shochet* in Neu-Pest (or Ujpest, to the north of Budapest proper). The Committee hoped

Neu-Pest

a town suburb outside Budapest would be a safer location than an address in central Budapest, where acculturated Jews were unprepared for an inevitable influx of their Orthodox brethren adorned with beards, *payos* and chassidic attire. Contrary to their best efforts, the secret of the Belzer Rav's whereabouts soon leaked out and this led to friction with the local police force. In general, the Belzer Rav was unusually introspective and introverted during his first few weeks in Hungary. Once, he even came out of his room and begged the waiting crowds to leave him alone. "What do you all want from me? How can I possibly help? I am only flesh and blood!" However, within a few minutes he reappeared to beg their pardon.

For the first time since their flight from Przemyslany seventeen months earlier, the two brothers were separated when the Bilgoraj Rav remained secluded at the hospital for several more weeks, due to technical reasons. To safeguard his personal security he was allowed only a few close visitors, all of whom were amazed at his singular dedication to *avodas Hashem*. Although the fate of his family in the Ukraine was still shrouded in mystery and uncertainty, Rav Mottele spent every spare minute learning, day and night, in his hospital room. After five years of fear and deprivation, he was now free to review tens of pages of Talmud a day, drawn mostly from his phenomenal memory due to a wartime lack of *sefarim* at the hospital or in Budapest generally.

The Belzer Rav's bid for relative isolation in Neu-Pest was totally shattered that Shavuos (Wednesday and Thursday, the 9th and 10th of June, 1943), when almost 1,000 Belzer stalwarts located throughout Hungary turned up. Chassidim from Szombathely presented him with a *kolpik* (a narrow *shtreimel* traditionally worn by Polish Rebbes) but he refused to dress differently than the general Hungarian chassidic attire, though he secretly wore under his *bekeshe* the short "*galus* clothes" of his escape as a constant reminder of the travails of Polish Jewry. The Rebbe was pleased to welcome so many chassidim and led the prayers and festive meals as if they were back in Belz in days of old, yet his joy was tempered by fears of how the local police would react (bearing in mind the ominous precedent of Shavuos 1940 in Sokal) or whether the undesirable publicity would reach the ears of the Gestapo. His anxiety was not misplaced.

The first day's Shavuos *tisch* had always been extremely popular back in Belz, when the Belzer Rav personally sang three verses from Shabbos morning *zemiros* (*Yom Shabbason*) beginning with "*Uvo'u kulam bivris yachad; na'aseh venishmah, amru k'echad* — They all enrolled in the Covenant; 'We shall obey and harken,' they proclaimed as one." In a play on words, this *tisch* was colloquially known as the "*Uva'u kulam tisch*" or "Everybody arriving *tisch*," and thousands of visitors used to throng the streets and alleys of Belz. Those chassidim who recalled the memorable Shacharis, *Akdamos*, *Anochi* or Mussaf when Belz was in its heyday were close to tears. Emotions ran particularly high that afternoon at the *Uva'u kulam tisch* when the Rebbe sang "... *ha'am asher na'ah* — the nation that wanders, straying like sheep, may Hashem remember them favorably according to His *bris* and promise, so no harm befalls them, just as promised after Noach's flood." The Rebbe fervently repeated these sentiments three times and his intent was obvious: that the missing millions exiled or on the run should not *chalilah* be obliterated as at the *Mabul*.

The Rebbe giving sherayim at a tisch

After hundreds of chassidim descended on Neu-Pest, antagonistic officers began arresting them and demanding to see their release papers from the forced-labor battalions conscription.[1] Finally they swooped down on Mr. Winegarten's house, demanding to interview the *Csoda-Rabi* or "Wonder Rabbi" himself. His official position was delicate in the extreme: He had predictably rejected the option of masquerading as a gentile with a fictitious Aryan identity (despite being on the official Gestapo wanted list) and had not yet legalized his status with the Hungarian authorities.

The police commander entered the Belzer Rav's room with a number of policemen and demanded to see his citizenship papers. When these were not forthcoming, he ordered the Rav to accompany them to headquarters. Unfortunately, there were no influential chassidim present to smooth over troubled waters and no amount of special pleading could persuade the heartless commander to relent, at least temporarily. The police screamed at the Rebbe and threatened all sorts of dire consequences until he reluctantly agreed to go with them. He

---

1. Because of difficulties with kashrus and general mitzvah observance, many religious Jews evaded *munkatabor*.

dressed in warm clothing and walked slowly to the front door. Here he paused, placed his hand on the *mezuzah* and began fervently reciting several *pesukim*, as was his custom. Just then, the commander had an abrupt change of heart. "The Rabbiner may return to his room!" he announced. All the policemen left the premises on the assurance that his application for citizenship would soon be processed.

Because of this harassment, the Rebbe changed houses several times without prior notification and tried to restrict his *tisch* and *tefillos* — conducted in the traditional Belz ritual without deviation — to a select few, but to little avail. At the public *seudos* he spoke in Torah at length and repeatedly referred to the horrendous situation in Poland. (Although numerous stencil copies of his words were circulated among the Hungarian chassidim, apparently none survived the War.)

Since his arrival in Hungary, the Belzer Rav took a close interest in the welfare of refugees, questioning all who came into his presence about how they had escaped and whether there was any chance of rescuing others. Although he exerted his considerable influence to alert Hungarian activists to the vital liberation effort, most Hungarian Jews tended to discount all Polish atrocity stories as exaggeration and hyperbole. Later, the Belzer Rav issued his famous *p'sak* that to rescue their brethren from Nazi tyranny, one may exceed the statutory one-fifth maximum for general charity and spend everything one owns.

As the German war machine began to appear vulnerable, so grew the self-confidence of Hungarian Jewry, but in deference to the Rebbe, they did bestir themselves a little. In June 1943, Anglo-American troops invaded southern Italy, precipitating Mussolini's temporary overthrow while Russia's counterattack in the east smashed German forces and recaptured much lost ground. Yet the momentum of the Nazi murder and massacre machine never faltered. So the Belzer Rav requested that the Rescue Committee fund another rescue trip by Shtaier to Przemyslany, where his family was still trapped, but the brave captain adamantly refused to repeat these dangerous missions, though he regularly dropped in to reminisce with the *Csoda Rabi*.

After a forceful personal request by the Rebbe, Shtaier finally acquiesced for a huge sum, but his apprehensions were not unfounded.

He found that the Przemyslany ghetto existed only in a limited form — with most Jews already deported — and he was unable to enter the area or make contact with the remaining inmates. Furthermore, his prowling around the perimeter aroused the suspicion of the Gestapo who arrested him as a possible "Jew helper." Only his excellent credentials authenticated by the Hungarian army extricated him from a fate similar to those he hoped to save. He was released after a day's questioning and immediately returned to Budapest empty-handed.

Soon afterwards the worst tidings emerged from Poland: the ghetto had been totally liquidated and all Przemyslany's Jews deported to an unknown destination. Even so, those close to the Belzer Rav refused to believe the bitter news; surely some of the Rebbe's family had managed to find refuge with leading non-Jews who previously could always be persuaded to perform favors for money. While the names and addresses of the town mayor and other prominent non-Jews were being assembled and negotiations with Shtaier progressing (now that the necessity to penetrate the ghetto was no longer relevant), an escapee from Poland arrived in Budapest at the beginning of August with an urgent letter for the Rebbe.

This desperate letter was written by Yehoshua Hammer, a *bachur* who was hiding in a forest outside Lemberg together with Shlomah and Pinchas Frankel — elder sons of the Belzer Rav's son-in-law, Rav Shmuel Frankel. Their money had now run out and the Polish peasant who had been sheltering them for a hefty bribe had given them two week's notice to come up with the cash or he would throw them to the wolves! Distressingly, the letter had already taken a week to reach Budapest and only one week still remained to rescue the Rebbe's grandchildren. The letter was couched in the most bitter language and his chassidim could scarcely imagine the Rav's pain as he visualized their dire plight.

Captain Shtaier was furnished with a large sum of money for all eventualities and directed to Lemberg and Przemyslany with all speed. Once again his mission was unsuccessful and he returned within a few days. Apparently, that peasant had not bothered to wait the agreed fortnight; after one week he had driven

The Rebbe (right) at the inauguration of his brother-in-law, Rav Yochanan Twersky (left), in Rubichow

them from his house and the boys were soon caught and murdered by the Germans. Shtaier also brought letters from leading Przemyslany non-Jews detailing the awful annihilation of the Rebbe's family and close followers — none had survived.

Rebbe Moshe'le, the Belzer Rav's eldest son, had already been brutally murdered back in 1941 during the Przemyslany pogrom of 9 Tammuz (July 5th); now his wife and five children were slain together with his mother, the Belzer Rebbetzin. The Rebbe's other sons, R' Yisrael and R' Yehudah Zundel, were also slaughtered with their wives and children, as were his daughters and sons-in law: R' Yeshayah Zusia of Ostilla, R' Shmuel Frankel (both with seven children), R' Yisrael of Kaminka, R' Moshe Eliyakim Beriah of Hibniv (both with two children). Additionally, his brothers-in law, R' Yochanan and Rav Pinchas of Ostilla, were murdered with their wives and families in Nazi *aktions*. (Earlier, his brother, Rav Yehoshua, was murdered in Yaroslav and his brother-in-law, Rav Yochanan Twersky, was killed in a forest outside Rubichow, where he was Rav.) Strikingly similar to his unusual reaction at the brutal murder of his beloved son Rebbe Moshe'le in the Przemyslany pogrom, once again the Belzer Rav personally declined to observe mourning or utter even a mention for individuals, focusing rather on the wider calamity.

Meanwhile in Eretz Yisrael, they remained uncertain of the Rebbe's intentions: Did he still want to travel onwards to Palestine or did he consider Hungary a safe enough haven until this war was over? As soon as the Belzer Rav reached Budapest on Lag B'Omer, R' Shemayah Binder in Switzerland cabled Mr. Ortner, but that cable first arrived on June 10, 1943 (Motza'ei Shavuos):

> TO BERISH ORTNER 111 NACHALAT BINYAMIN TEL AVIV
> RABBI IN GOOD HEALTH AT OZER FRIED GIVE ROKACH'S
> TO ANGLO-PALESTINE BANK FOR JOSEPH KARAKOW
> FOR USA CABLE WHEN DONE BINDER ZURICH

The reference to "Ozer Fried" was meant to hint at Budapest
while "Rokach's" referred to money previously deposited with
Mr. Ernest Gelley of Nahariah on behalf of the Belzer Rav. Not
surprisingly, this rather explicit cable about deposits destined for
the Anglo-Palestine Bank would soon arouse the suspicions of
the British authorities. Simultaneously, a separate cable arrived
from England:

> TO BERISH ORTNER 111 NACHALAT BINYAMIN TEL
> AVIV WE RECEIVED LETTER FROM YOUR SON MOSHE
> SHEMAYAH TELEGRAPHED RABBI'S HEALTH GOOD BY
> OZER FRIED SHEMAYAH WORRIED AT NO NEWS FROM
> ERNEST ELIMELECH RUMPLER LONDON

Mr. Ortner replied immediately:

> TO ELIMELECH RUMPLER LONDON THANKS FOR
> TELEGRAM PLEASED THAT RABBI'S WELL ALL WAITING
> IMPATIENTLY HIS ARRIVAL HERE CERTIFICATES
> WAITING IN ISTANBUL PERSUADE SHEMAYAH TO
> ARRANGE RABBI'S TRIP HERE ORTNER

The next day Mr. Ortner also cabled Switzerland:

> TO SHEMAYAH BINDER ZURICH HAPPY AT RABBI'S GOOD
> HEALTH ALL WAITING IMPATIENTLY HIS ARRIVAL HERE
> CERTIFICATES READY CONTACT BARLAS ISTANBUL
> AND ARRANGE RABBI'S TRAVEL HERE BERISH ORTNER

Meanwhile, the British authorities weighed in, and on the same
day as Mr. Ortner replied to Zurich, he received the following official missive:

11 June 1943
B Ortner
111 Nachalat Binyamin Street, Tel Aviv
Our Reference 1/3788/43
Dear Mr. Ortner
Please forward to me full information regarding the contents of the two telegrams of 23/5/43 and also of 6/6/43 which you received from Mr. S. Binder of Zurich.
Please send your reply via either your bank or Barclays Bank.
I remain,
PP
On behalf of Inspectorate of Foreign Currency dealings.

When Mr. Ortner responded on the 16th of June via Barclays Bank, Jerusalem, he was careful to feign all innocence.

Dear Sirs,
Further to your letter of 11/6/43 (Ref:1/3788/43) I am pleased to reply as follows:
The telegram from Mr. S. Binder of 23/5/43 was delivered to me on 10/6/43. However, I have not received any telegram from Mr. Binder dated 6/6/43.
From the telegram of 23/5/43 I discovered the good fortune of Rabbi Rokach. This news was vitally important to me. The name Ozer Fried is not known to me. So too the name Joseph Karakow is unfamiliar, in whose benefit Rokach's belongings should be deposited in the Anglo-Palestine Bank. This name is also unknown to Anglo-Palestine Bank. Therefore I do not understand the whole telegram.
Besides which, I am not in possession of any money or belongings of Rabbi Rokach. As is well known, Rabbi Rokach is a great spiritual leader with admirers and followers around the world. Yet everybody knows that Rabbi Rokach has never been rich or owned property. As one of his followers, I am endeavoring to obtain on his behalf an entry visa into Palestine.
With great respect,
Yours sincerely,
Berish Ortner

That day, he finally received the missing cable of June 6th:

TO BERISH ORTNER NACHALAT BINYAMIN 111 TEL
AVIV PLEASE CABLE IF RECEIVED CABLE OF 23RD STOP
ALSO IF AFFAIRS OF GRANDFATHER AARON ARE IN
ORDER HE IS IN GOOD HEALTH AT STERN'S SHEMAYAH
BINDER ZURICH

"Stern's" was a reference to R' Chaim Mordechai Stern, owner of the famous kosher hotel and restaurant in Budapest. Meanwhile Reb Berish continued his campaign to bring the Rebbe to Eretz Yisrael and wrote to London on 17 Sivan 5703 (June 20th):

> To my honored friend the chassid Reb Chaim Nota Katz Ner Yair.
> London
> I was very happy to hear the news of the holy tzaddik shlita. We are all anxiously awaiting his arrival here. Due to the efforts of the Chief Rabbi R' Yitzchak Isaac Halevi Herzog shlita the Jewish Sochnut sent certificates to Istanbul for the Rebbe and his brother. All of us are waiting, that is both chassidim and non-chassidim, for their arrival here. Especially the great Torah learners, who ask me every day, when will we merit to see him? Surely it will be a great asset for Klal Yisrael if his holiness comes to our holy land. Persuade our friend R' Shemayah shlita that he should help hasten his coming ...
> Hashem Yisbarach should help that we should soon witness the blotting out of Amalek, yemach shemo vezichro!
> Your true friend in heart and soul,
> Dov-Berish Ortner

Likewise he wrote to Switzerland on Sunday 19 Sivan (June 22nd):

> To my honored friend, wealthy and famous chassid, Morenu Harav Shemayah Binder Ner Yair and to all the chassidim.
> Honored chassidim!
> It is impossible to describe to you the phenomenal joy throughout Eretz Yisrael and particularly in Jerusalem on finally hearing the news that his holiness Maran the Rebbe shlita is finally alive and well. Everybody — rabbanim, elder Belzer chassidim, other groups of chassidim, religious and non-religious — ask every day the well-being of the Rebbe shlita. And when they now hear, after such a long time, of

his good fortune they are all extremely happy and all wait with bated breath to see him here in the holy land.

When I first heard the good news on Erev Shavuos, I traveled up to Jerusalem for Yom Tov. We davened Mussaf at the Kosel Maaravi and prayed for the well-being of the Rebbe and his brother R' Mottele shlita, that we should merit to see them here soon, Amen!

The Chief Rabbi Herzog shlita too was overjoyed at the news and his wife commented, "Those who sow in tears shall reap with joy!" (Probably a reference to Mr. Ortner's breaking down in tears when first approaching Rabbi Herzog.) I firmly believe that when the Holy Ark — the holy Rebbe — travels to our land then Moshe will proclaim: Kumah Hashem vayafutzu oyevecha — Arise Hashem and smite Your enemies! Amen, speedily in our days.

I once heard from my uncle R' Mechele Zalkewer, may Hashem avenge his blood, who heard from the previous Rebbe, zechuso yagen aleinu, that he very much wanted to be in Eretz Yisrael. If we did not merit that, may we at least deserve to see the Rebbe shlita here in the holy land. Apparently that is the Will of Hashem.

I ask in the name of all Belzer chassidim and in the name of gedolei Yerushalayim that you help hasten their arrival here. If any help is still needed, Chief Rabbi Herzog and the Sochnut are still willing to assist to the best of their ability at any time.

Please pass these words from the depths of my heart to the holy Rebbe shlita and forward his reply.

Dov-Berish Ortner

Indeed, Mr. Ortner was not exaggerating the widespread interest in the Rebbe's fate. On Erev Shavuos, a press report had appeared in the *Davar*:

SAFETY FOR BELZ REBBE AND RABBI ROTH OF CZERNOWITZ

Yesterday, Rabbi Fishman received telegraphic intelligence from Istanbul that the Belz Rebbe and his brother are safe. So is Rabbi Roth of Czernowitz.

Until now there has been no news here of their whereabouts or safety and there was much concern for their health. The Belz Rebbe and his brother are in Budapest; Rabbi Roth is in Bucharest.

Although it was rather irresponsible of the left-wing newspaper to publish the present whereabouts of the Belzer Rebbe — which doubtless alerted German agents — it does reveal the depth of interest among all circles of Israel's population in the Rebbe's situation. Meanwhile Mr. Ortner made copies of his latest letter to Zurich and dispatched them to Rabbi Avrohom Babad, the Shotzer Rav (Rabbi Shalom Moskowitz), R' Elimelech Rumpler and other Belzer chassidim in London. This brought an enthusiastic response. The first cable was delivered on the 8th of Tammuz (July 11th):

TO BERISH ORTNER TEL AVIV RECEIVED LETTER RAV BROTHER AND YOSSELE YARZIBER ALL WELL TELEGRAPHING SHEMAYAH ABOUT PALESTINE TRIP AND AWAITING REPLY CHAIM NOTA KATZ LONDON

Just over a week later another — more forthright — cable arrived from London, on the 15th of Tammuz (July 18th):

TO BERISH ORTNER NACHALAT BINYAMIN 111 TEL AVIV REBBE AND BROTHER DESIRE PALESTINE RETRANSIT CONTACT GOLDIN HOTEL CONTINENTAL ISTANBUL THROUGH RABBI HERZOG TRY CERTIFICATE ALSO JOSEPH GOLD ABRAHAM BABAD LONDON

Both R' Chaim Nota Katz and Rabbi Babad (later Rav of Sunderland, in northern England; his impeccable English garbled by cable-ese) wrongly assumed that the Rebbe's loyal *gabbai*, the wise and perceptive Reb Yosel Gold of Yarotschev, must surely have accompanied the Rebbe through all his travels and travails — and by rights should escort him to Eretz Yisrael. In fact, he had remained behind in Przemyslany on the Belzer Rav's express instructions, to attend to the needs of the Rebbe's extended family trapped in the ghetto. Obviously they had not contacted Switzerland, where R' Moshe Gross had been in direct communication with Reb Yosel and leading members of the Belzer family via the Red Cross.

More interestingly, Rav Babad's confident assertion that both "the Rebbe and his brother desire Palestine" (sic) does not seem to have been based on direct information from the Belzer entourage! Neither the Belzer Rav nor the Bilgoraj Rav gave the slightest hint in public or in private that they had any intention of leaving Hungary in the near future. Certainly at that juncture, such an idea was furthest from the mind of both chassidim and other Hungarian Jews. Despite the persecutions and sporadic outbursts of virulent anti-Semitism, Hungarian Jewry in 1943 felt relatively safe and were confident that they would survive the War intact. All talk at that juncture was merely of finding a suitable locale for the Rebbe, perhaps in the provinces at a distance from Budapest. But even if the information in Rav Babad's cable might have been somewhat premature, the telegram itself was timely in the extreme. By spurring Mr. Ortner into early action, the efforts to secure the all important certificates succeeded — and just in the nick of time.

CHAPTER 19

ON THE MOVE
AGAIN

EVER SINCE THE POLICE RAID DURING SHAVUOS,
the Belzer Rav was anxious to find an alternative address.
Periodically, the Neu-Pest police would harass groups of
chassidim — particularly on Shabbos, when there was a
larger attendance — and arrest them on various pretexts, usually
for evading military forced labor. Naturally, this blatant display of
official racism by the authorities coupled with the resulting distress
to his followers was a constant source of dismay to the Rebbe.

At first he moved into the Budapest residence of Mr. Barnet at 56
Dohany utca. But that house was small, cramped and overheated,
which was a great strain on the Rebbe who was hypersensitive to
extremes of heat and cold. He soon relocated to Mr. Bernstein's
home on Dob utca, Budapest, which was larger and more airy.
Unfortunately, it was still far too small to accommodate visiting
chassidim, and Rosh Hashanah was rapidly approaching — countless chassidim would want to join the Rebbe.

The Belzer Rav summoned his leading followers and told them
that more suitable premises might be found in one of the smaller *kehillos* outside of Budapest. Besides, Budapest was accustomed to more

acculturated Jews and a large influx of chassidim would possibly spark off the Neu-Pest kind of police friction, but on a greater scale. Couriers were immediately dispatched to Pupa (or Papa, where the Rav, Rabbi Yosef Grunwald, was an ardent Belz supporter), Szombathely, Racsfehert (Ujfeherto, north of Debrecen) and Munkacs (where the Belzer family had sheltered during the previous World War). All these *kehillos* expressed an interest and while the Belzer Rav seemed to be inclining toward Racsfehert, his ever loyal chassidim R' Moshe Dovid Hollander and R' Avraham Direnfeld began constructing a spacious abode fit for the Rebbe in Pupa.

When the news leaked out of the Belzer Rebbe's imminent departure from Budapest, the local *kehilloh* was most upset, and frantic efforts were made to find suitable premises and to legalize the Rebbe's status. They succeeded in both, beyond the chassidim's fondest expectations. The communal building they offered the Rebbe at 32 Nagyatadi Szabo in the center of the Jewish district was large — four stories high — and spacious. During peacetime it had functioned as the communal school (with a small yeshivah on the upper floor) and although the main area had been subdivided into classrooms with temporary walls, once these were removed there would be ample room for *tefillos* and a *tisch*. Moreover, one of the tenants in the building, Mr. Reiner, agreed to forego his two well-appointed rooms in favor of the Rebbe, for a reasonable sum.

Although friction with the Budapest authorities could not yet be ruled out, the Belzer Rav carefully considered the proposal personally suggested by the Budapest *kehillah* president, and ultimately agreed to it. The Rebbe appointed R' Moshe Dovid Hollander to be in charge of the Rosh Hashanah preparations. Much groundwork had to be laid: removing the movable walls and school furniture, constructing a large enough table for the communal *tisch*, and obtaining the requisite benches (known as *"poilishe benk"*).

The Belzer Rav advised R' Moshe Dovid to have these benches manufactured wider than usual so that they could be used for sleeping as well as sitting. He foresaw that many of the chassidim would probably lack accommodation over the High Holy Days and would need somewhere to rest their weary bones. Indeed, those unusual benches would prove to be extremely useful for this purpose. Even while the building work was still going on, the Belzer Rav moved from Mr. Bernstein's house to Mr. Reiner's vacated flat, as it was far more suitable.

Besides the crowds of chassidim expected to arrive from the Hungarian provinces, hundreds of Budapest's Orthodox Jews would probably want to stop by — not to mention countless curious onlookers. Unfortunately, even after the school hall was cleared of furniture and removable walls, it would still be too small. So a ticket system was introduced to grant admission to loyal Belz chassidim for Rosh Hashanah and Yom Kippur, while official guards at the door insured it did not become overcrowded.

Meanwhile, the *kehillah* recognized that there was no way they could conceal the Rebbe's presence in Budapest or keep it secret. Instead, they persuaded Kallay's government that it would suit their international image if they ordered Budapest's police and immigration officials to leave this eminent Rabbinical leader strictly alone. Thus the Rebbe was permitted to live openly as a Jewish refugee, in stark contrast to most Polish fugitives — and with the Belzer Rav's occupation of the communal school, the four-story building attained almost diplomatic or extra-territorial status. Although they were fully aware that hundreds of illegal and unregistered Polish refugees had found sanctuary there, no detectives entered the premises or conducted searches.

Rarely had Budapest seen a spectacle as it did during the weekend of September 30 to October 2, 1943 (that year, Rosh Hashanah fell on Thursday/Friday). Bearded strangers — adorned with long sidelocks, spiky fur headgear and flowing prayer shawls draped carelessly over their shoulders, who were dressed mainly in black with shiny silk coats, thick knitted belts knotted around their midriffs, trousers tucked into black stockings — marched purposefully to and fro while youths and young children with twirling sidelocks and peculiar peaked black velvet caps trotted at their side. Non-Jews and non-Orthodox were equally nonplussed at the exotic sight and the news spread rapidly and widely of some *"Csoda Rabi"* who had recently arrived in Budapest. Obviously, this attention was most unwelcome when

Hungary harbored many anti-Semites and scores of enemy agents, and was still officially allied with Germany, but there seemed little likelihood of concealing the fact.

On Rosh Hashanah morning, the Belzer Rav dispatched his *gabbai* to borrow an *Ari Siddur* from a neighbor, Rav Avraham Shlomo Katz (Rabbi of Riskewe and later of Kiryat Yoel, Bnei Brak). "But I don't have the *Arizal's Siddur*," Rav Katz replied in surprise. Just then his community *shammas* arrived with a New Year's gift from their shul — an *Ari Siddur* written on parchment! Immediately, Rav Katz called the *gabbai* back and handed him the *siddur*.

The *tefillos* and *tisch* were maintained in the Belz tradition with no deviation. As was his custom, the Rebbe personally led the prayers at Mussaf, but since none of the regular *baalei tefillah* were available for Shacharis, the Bilgoraj Rav prepared himself on Erev Rosh Hashanah to lead the *davening;* the Rebbe instructed him on various points of *nusach.* Back in Belz, *baalei tefillah* specifically chosen for scholarship and piety rarely mixed with the chassidim throughout Elul, studying instead in their lodgings while clothed in white trousers and socks like Rebbes, eating the food supplied directly from the Rebbe's kitchen, and only emerging for daily *mussar* sessions with the Belzer Rav; the month of Elul constituted for them "one lengthy Rosh Hashanah."

The prayers began unusually early, on the express instructions of the Belzer Rav. Officially, the reason given was the wartime curfew; to his closest devotees, however, he revealed that he had a confidential motivation he would not disclose. Some of the younger chassidim had previously been among the famous *yoshvim* and they now swung into action as they would have done in Belz, before the War, personally preparing and cooking the festival *seudos* for the numerous guests over Yom Tov. Most of the expenses were defrayed by the Rebbe while each "*orach*" paid whatever he could afford. Naturally, the atmosphere in wartime Budapest bore only a faint reflection of the authentic aura of Belz in its heyday, but the Hungarian chassidim were well satisfied.

After *Havdalah*, the Belzer Rav summoned Reb Moshe Aaron Krunstein for a meeting that would cause much incredulity and speculation. As soon as Mr. Krunstein entered the room, the Rebbe informed him that he had secretly decided to leave for

Eretz Yisrael! "Can you contact the Swiss *askanim* by telephone? Under British rule, we will need certificates to enter Palestine." Reb Moshe Aaron was dumbfounded. Although the Budapest school premises might be only temporary, surely they could find somewhere else without taking such a drastic step. Until then all the talk had been about finding an alternative locale somewhere in the provinces. But traveling to Palestine during wartime? Was the Rav really serious? What were his reasons? And what did that mean for the future, here in Hungary?

A few days later, Rabbi Avraham Binyamin Sofer, Rav of Pressburg, arrived in Budapest on his way to Eretz Yisrael and took his leave from the Belzer Rav. The Rebbe ordered even his closest chassidim to leave his room while he confided in the Pressburg Rav; only his loyal *shammas*, Reb Shmuel Porgas, was permitted to remain. "We are also intending to go to Eretz Yisrael," announced the Rebbe. *"Zeits mochel Pressburger Rav,* if you could inspire the Belzer chassidim there to push things along? We would also be grateful if you would speak to Reb Dov Berish Ortner in Tel Aviv on our behalf."

As word of this request leaked out, speculation mounted. Perhaps the Rebbe was really serious after all! Yet what was wrong here in Hungary? Nothing too bad would happen to the Jews here — or would it? *Chas v'chalilah* had there been any Heavenly decree against the Hungarian Jews this Rosh Hashanah? Moreover, how would the Rebbe get hold of an entry visa? Although a transport of a hundred or so "Zionists" left Budapest every few months en-route to the Middle East on the famous Orient Express, hardly anybody believed that the Rebbe had a good chance of obtaining Palestine certificates.

Ever since Britain's infamous White Paper policy began under Arab pressure, Jewish immigration was severely restricted, few certificates were available and these were in the hands of the Zionist parties who saw most religious Jews as "anti-Zionist." Obviously, the party faithful would strongly object to the spiritual leader of the Belz chassidim — renowned for their zealous rejection of all modern movements, including secular Zionism — receiving one of their precious certificates or entering "their" homeland. Nevertheless, his

Chief Rabbi Herzog, flanked by Rav Mishkowski and Rav Botchko on his right, and Moshe Shapira and his son Yaakov Herzog on his left, chairing a Hatzalah meeting in Switzerland

loyal followers contacted their fellow chassidim in Switzerland and London with their Rebbe's request.

Actually, Mr. Berish Ortner had already been busy trying to obtain the vital certificates for the past two and a half months — ever since Rav Babad's cable of 15 Tammuz had surprisingly claimed that "the Rebbe and his brother desire Palestine." On receipt of this telegram, based on a misunderstanding or wishful thinking, Mr. Ortner had swung into action. That very day he left for Jerusalem and met with Chief Rabbi Herzog. Since the certificates previously sent to Istanbul had lapsed, he demanded that new ones be immediately issued. Now that the Rebbe was residing in Hungary and not directly under "enemy occupation," it ought to be easier to be accepted by the British authorities. Sadly, Rabbi Herzog informed him that the whole current quota of certificates had been used up — only a select few remained, reserved for "veteran Zionists." Yet Mr. Ortner persisted, insisting that the Belzer Rav was "a true veteran Zionist!"

"Does he not pray three times a day *Vesechezenah einenu beshuvchah leTzion*? That makes him an ideal Zionist! Is he not also a veteran in

Torah? He richly deserves such a certificate — without question!"
(Actually, this alleged restriction to "veteran Zionists" was misleading
since this category had been extended as "Veteran Zionists, Rabbis,
etc." — equally including leading Jewish personalities who were not
necessarily Zionist — as revealed by an internal *Sochnut* Memo of
Sept. '43, and their earlier applications to Britain's Commissioner for
Migration and Statistics who dealt with Palestine entry permits.)

In reply, Rav Herzog picked up the telephone and dialed
Mr. Moshe Shapira of the *Sochnut's* Aliya Department. After a
brisk conversation, Rav Herzog instructed R' Berish to go to Mr.
Shapira's office. When he arrived, Mr. Shapira asked him to formally submit his request in writing, detailing the Rebbe's precise
address; afterwards he would do everything within his power to
obtain new certificates for them. Accordingly, Mr. Ortner drafted,
typed out and handed over the following letter on the fast day
of 17 Tammuz:

> *The Jewish Agency for Eretz Israel*
> *Jerusalem, Eretz Israel*
> *17 Tammuz 5703, 20 July '43*
> *Re: The Belzer Rebbe & Escort*
> *1) The famous Belzer Rebbe, Aaron Singer, shlita, aged 67. 2)*
> *Rabbi Morderchai Pecsenik, Rav of Bilgoraj and brother of Belzer*
> *Rebbe, shlita, age 47. 3) Joseph Gold, aged 65, personal beadle of the*
> *Rebbe.*
>
> *They are presently residing at Mordechai Stern, hotel owner, of 7*
> *Rumbach utca, Budapest. According to a telegram that I have just*
> *received from his devotees in London, the Rebbe asks for assistance in*
> *their coming here. A copy of the telegram is hereby enclosed.*
>
> *As one of the Rebbe's closest followers, I hereby request the Jewish*
> *Agency for Eretz Israel in the name of the Belzer Rebbe, shlita, that*
> *you endeavor to assist the three above persons to come here.*
>
> *In the name of the Torah leaders in Eretz Israel, in the name of*
> *thousands of his admirers here in our land, I request you hasten their*
> *arrival here as soon as possible.*
>
> *With great respect,*
> *Yours sincerely,*
> *Dov Berish Ortner*

The next day Reb Berish had cabled his reply to London:

TO RABBI ABRAHAM BABAD LONDON WAS WITH
YOUR TELEGRAM IN JERUSALEM SOCHNUT STRAIGHT
AWAY SENT INSTRUCTIONS TO BARLAS ISTANBUL
TO ISSUE THREE CERTIFICATES FOR REBBE BROTHER
ALSO JOSEPH GOLD AND ARRANGE TRANSIT TELL
SHEMAYAH ALSO ASK BARLAS SAME BERISH ORTNER

Once again, he had clarified his quest by letter on the next day, 19
Tammuz (Thursday, July 22nd):

> *To the honored chassid etc. Moreinu Harav Avraham Babad, shlita,
> and all our fellow chassidim,*
>
> *I received your telegram and gave copies to Chief Rabbi Herzog, sh-
> lita, and the Sochnut. They told me they will send a telegram straight
> away to Mr. Barlas (the agent of the Sochnut's Aliya Department in
> Istanbul) and to Mr. Goldin (he deputizes for Barlas when he's away)
> — that they should use every avenue available regarding transit.
> They want our Rebbe to come here and they will help as much as is
> legally possible; also they will send certificates for the Rebbe's brother
> and Reb Yosel Gold — May Hashem Yisbarach help them. On your
> part, you should pressure the Chief Rabbi shlita and Mr. Barlas in
> this great enterprise.*
>
> *Please reply with information on your activities. Certainly, if I
> have any early information, I will pass it on to you.*
>
> *Best wishes from all of us to all of you.*
>
> *Your friend who seeks your best with heart and soul.*
>
> *Dov Berish Ortner*

For his part, Mr. Ortner, back on his trusty typewriter, maintained
the pressure on the *Sochnut* and the Chief Rabbi:

> *Mr. Moshe Shapira*
> *Aliya Department*
> *Jewish Agency for Eretz Israel*
> *POB 92 Jerusalem*
> *Thursday 4 Menachem-Av 5703, August 5, 1943*
> *<u>Re: Rescue of Belzer Rebbe shlita (Aaron Singer)</u>*
> *Dear Mr. Shapira,*

On July 20, 1943, I submitted the request to the Jewish Agency for Eretz Israel on behalf of the Belzer Rebbe, shlita, for assistance in coming here.

Today I received a letter from his devotees in London dated 20 August, which states inter alia:

"As you know, thank G-d his holiness Maran the Rebbe, shlita, his brother R' Mottele, shlita, and the shammas R' Yosel Gold are thankfully together all well. May G-d continue it thus in the future! The Rebbe very much wants to come to you in Eretz Yisrael. We are very pleased that the Chief Rabbi, Rav Yitzchak Isaac Halevi Herzog, shlita, has exerted himself on behalf of Maran, our Rebbe, shlita."

Behind the Rebbe's expressed request stand thousands of Klal Yisrael worldwide and particularly in Eretz Israel who await with longing for their imminent arrival here. Especially after the Amalekim yemach shemom murdered his brothers-in-law, the famous Rabbis Twersky, and also his sons and sons-in-law, zechusom yagen aleinu, with all their families, may Hashem Yisbarach avenge their blood.

I am confident that the heads of the Aliya Department in conjunction with the Rabbis who have the opportunity to help in this instance will do everything within — and beyond — their capabilities. To comply with the overwhelming wishes of the general public, surely they will assist in every way and with the greatest speed such a famous leader. After Hashem Yisbarach has helped him until now escape the hands of the tyrants yemach shemom, they must soon bring the Rebbe shlita to our holy land with Hashem's help.

I await your cherished reply so that I can inform his devotees in Switzerland, London and America who watch and wait for your rapid and vital assistance.

With great respect and true appreciation, and on behalf of the Belzer Rebbe.

Yours sincerely,
Dov Berish Ortner

This appeal duly brought the desired result and just over a week later the *Sochnut* dispatched a positive reply:

The Jewish Agency for Eretz Israel
Jerusalem POB 92
Mr. Dov B. Ortner

111 Nachalat Binyamin, Tel Aviv
August 16, 1943 (15th Av 5703)
Our Ref: 1607 /Z
Dear Mr. Ortner,
<u>*Regarding Rabbi Aaron Singer (Belzer Rebbe) & escort*</u>
In receipt of your letter of August 5, 1943 regarding emigration
of the above. We have approached the British Government for their
approval of the certificates of the Belzer Rebbe, Joseph Gold and
Mordechai Pecsenik. We are hopeful that the Government will fulfill
our request.
Respectfully yours,
M. Shapira
Aliya Department

Just when it appeared that their goal was within reach, a last minute hitch arose. R' Berish had been laboring under the mistaken impression that he was acting on behalf of all Belzer chassidim and — more importantly — the Belzer Rav. Apparently he was unaware that the London chassidim were instructing him on their own initiative and had not yet consulted their counterparts in either Switzerland or Hungary. That was why he (and they) had wrongly assumed Reb Yosel Gold of Yarotschev was safe in Budapest with the Rebbe; actually he had remained in the Przemyslany ghetto, which was then in its death throes with most of its inmates already murdered or deported; Reb Yosel *Hy"d* personally had vanished during the Sivan *aktion*. So the details of the Rebbe and his escorts' names and particulars were inaccurate. That understanding was somewhat shattered on 28 Av (August 29th) when he was again cabled from London:

TO BERISH ORTNER 111 NACHALAT BINYAMIN TEL AVIV NAME OF OUR RABBI IS ARON TWERSKY BORN 1872 BROTHER'S NAME IS MARKUS PECSENIK BORN 1890 FRIENDS NAMES ARE DANIEL SHAFRINSKY BORN 1894 AND SALOMON WEINSTOCK BORN 1905 PLEASE ASK AGENCY GIVE THEM CERTIFICATES PLEASE REPLY BABAD

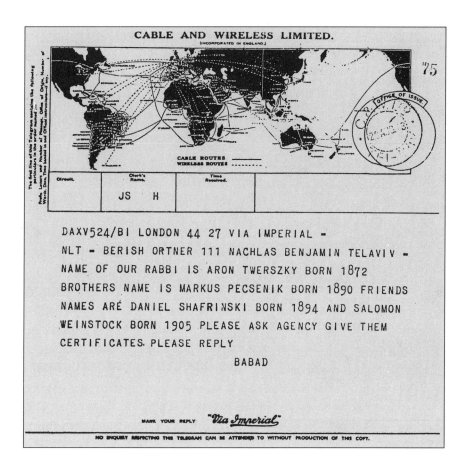

CABLE AND WIRELESS LIMITED.
(INCORPORATED IN ENGLAND.)

CABLE ROUTES
WIRELESS ROUTES

Circuit.	Clerk's Name.	Time Received.
JS H		

DAXV524/BI LONDON 44 27 VIA IMPERIAL -
NLT - BERISH ORTNER 111 NACHLAS BENJAMIN TELAVIV -
NAME OF OUR RABBI IS ARON TWERSZKY BORN 1872
BROTHERS NAME IS MARKUS PECSENIK BORN 1890 FRIENDS
NAMES ARE DANIEL SHAFRINSKI BORN 1894 AND SALOMON
WEINSTOCK BORN 1905 PLEASE ASK AGENCY GIVE THEM
CERTIFICATES. PLEASE REPLY
                        BABAD

MARK YOUR REPLY "Via Imperial"

NO ENQUIRY RESPECTING THIS TELEGRAM CAN BE ATTENDED TO WITHOUT PRODUCTION OF THIS COPY.

Obviously, Rabbi Babad had finally been contacted by the Swiss activists who had recommended those two substitute names. R' Shlomo Weinstock was the brother-in-law of R' Moshe Gross and as *shochet* in Bardejov, Slovakia, had been drawn into the network of rescue conspirators, hatching two rescue attempts — the second had almost succeeded in spiriting the Rebbe from Bochnia to Slovakia by train and cart. The Belzer Rav had recently adopted the surname Twersky, the name of his maternal family: Rebbetzin Basha Ruchamah was a granddaughter of Rebbe Aharon Twersky of Chernobyl. Likewise, his half-brother Rebbe Mottele had earlier taken his own maternal family name. Now Mr. Ortner was put in the embarrassing position of asking the *Sochnut* to allow last minute alterations to their bureaucratic procedures without delaying them any further. Putting the bravest face on it, he retired to his typewriter and began his correspondence anew with the *Sochnut*, the Chief Rabbi and even Judge Frumkin:

> *The Jewish Agency for Eretz Israel*
> *Aliya Department*
> *Jerusalem PO 92*
> *29th Menachem-Av 5703*
> *August 30, 1943*
> *Your ref: 1607/Z*
> *Regarding the Belzer Rebbe & Escort*
> *Dear Sir,*
>
> *Last month, on 20th July, I submitted a request to the Jewish Agency regarding the above — based on telegrams received from the Rebbe's devoted followers in London. These stated that the Belzer Rebbe asks for emigration certificates to our holy land, requesting help and assistance to this goal.*
>
> *Today I received a telegram from London dated 27th July again requesting certificates for the Rebbe and his escort. However, it states that the correct name of the Rebbe is "Aron Twersky." A copy of this telegram is hereby enclosed. The change of surname was undoubtedly necessary for understandable reasons.*
>
> *The eyes of the world are watching how the Jewish Agency for Eretz Israel will help save the Belzer Rebbe in time. Therefore I hereby request and beseech the Jewish Agency to immediately authorize the certificates of the Rebbe and escort; and correct the file of the Rebbe to his correct name "Aron Twersky" as stipulated in the latest telegram. If necessary, to also ensure that the Government quickly fulfill the request and authorize their rapid emigration here.*
>
> *With great respect and genuine regard, and on behalf of the Belzer Rebbe,*
> *Yours sincerely,*
> *Dov Berish Ortner*

❦

> *Erev Rosh Chodesh Elul 5703*
>
> *To his honor, Admoreinu VeRabbeinu Harav Hagaon Pe'er HaTorah etc. Hashem's messenger to save Jewish souls, Moreinu Harav Yitzchak Isaac Halevy Herzog, shlita,*

Chief Rabbi to Eretz Yisrael.

Regarding the Belzer Rebbe & Escort

Most honored Rabbi!

In this matter, I have just received telegrams from London (copies enclosed) that the Belzer Rebbe requests immediate dispatch of certificates to hasten their arrival here. They are presently in Budapest (Hungary).

I have already submitted a request by hand on July 20, 1943 to the Sochnut Jerusalem. The whole world is watching how the Chief Rabbi and the Jewish Agency handle this when it is within their hands to save the Rebbe and his brother. Only they have survived from the large, famous family murdered al kiddush Hashem, Hashem yinkom damam!

I am sure that his honor shlita will contact the Jewish Agency and do everything within his power for the rapid rescue of the Belzer Rebbe shlita and his brother so that I can soon assure the Rebbe's followers in America, London and Switzerland that the certificates have been authorized with Hashem's Grace and your help.

With fearful respect and genuine regard,

Dov Berish Ortner

❧

Erev Rosh Chodesh Elul 5703

To the wise, knowledgeable, noble and ethical Judge, Mr. Gad Frumkin shlita,

Regarding the Belzer Rebbe & Escort

Who am I to approach the learned Judge? Yet I base myself on the previous request by the leaders of the generation.

Peace and Blessings!

With regard to the request of the Lubavitcher Rebbe to your honor during 1941 to help rescue his relative the Tzaddik of Belz, shlita, I believe the time has now come to honor the tzaddik's request. "He who begins a mitzvah is enjoined to complete it" — particularly the mitzvah of saving a renowned tzaddik. Especially after the wicked Amalekim yemach shemam vezichram murdered his sons and brothers-in-law, the famous tzaddikim Twersky with all their families, Hashem yinkom damam speedily ...

> *I turn to your honor and I am sure that the honorable judge will now carry out the wishes of the Lubavitcher Rebbe, shlita, and after contacting the Jewish Agency will assist as far as possible.*
>
> *If by any chance your honor should need any more details I am always at your bidding.*
>
> *With due respect and genuine regard, and on behalf of the Belzer Rebbe,*
> *Dov Berish Ortner*

He also involved his Jerusalem comrades in the campaign:

> *To my friends.*
>
> *After receiving your letter I immediately spoke to Sternfeld who spoke to the publishers. But he said nothing's to be done at the moment while the strike's still on; afterwards they can talk business. Now I hear they've done all they could. Perhaps two of you can go to Rav Eliezerov (of Chevron) and tell him what now needs doing. Then he can accompany you to Frumkin — now they're in Hungary, it's quite legal to come here, not like before. Maybe he will influence Mr. Dubkin or Ben-Zvi. Perhaps then you'll get a straighter answer through him — but I think this must be kept top secret.*
>
> *I'm sure Shapira's doing everything he can and there's absolutely no need to press Rav Herzog further. Perhaps two of you can go to Rav Fishman, since he sent the telegram from Barlas. Don't tell him anything you learned from me so that you might hear instead what's in their files — a word to the wise is sufficient.*
>
> *Your friend,*
> *Berish Ortner*

Naturally, this latest development with the correct names confused and perturbed the bureaucrats at the *Sochnut* offices, who replied a week later:

> *The Jewish Agency for Eretz Israel*
> *Jerusalem*
> *Mr. Dov Ortner*
> *111 Nachalat Binyamin*
> *Tel Aviv*
> *September 7, 1943*
> *7th Elul 5703*

Regarding Belzer Rebbe & escort
Our ref: 1607 / Z
Dear Mr. Ortner,
Further to your letter of August 30 (29 Av) regarding the above. Originally, you approached us on behalf of Singer, Aaron (Belz Rebbe), Pecsenik, Mordechai and Gold, Joseph. As we informed you on August 16, we forwarded the above names to the Government Immigration Department.

To continue this process we must first know if the only change affects the surname of Rabbi Aron Twersky instead of Aaron Singer? Or do changes also affect the others, for instance, Pecsenik, Mordechai is described in your telegram as Pecsenik, Markus? Are there any alterations to Mr. Gold? Could you likewise let us know more details of the two others mentioned in that telegram: Shafrinsky, Daniel and Weinstock, Salomon.

We would like to deal with this matter so could you please furnish all the missing details by return?

Yours sincerely,
PP
Secretariat, Aliya Department

The Jewish Agency for Eretz Israel
Aliya Department
Jerusalem
10th Elul 5703
(September 10, 1943)
Regarding the Belzer Rebbe & Escort
Your ref: 1607/Z Aliya Dept.
Dear Sirs,
Thank you for your letter dated 7 Elul (September 7, 1943) re: the above and I hasten to reply.

1) From my request of 29 Av (August 30, 1943) with enclosed telegram, the only change was in the surname of the Rebbe shlita substituting "Aron Twersky" for "Aaron Singer," for reasons readily understood.

2) His brother's name, the Rabbi of Bilgoraj, shlita, from "Morderchai Pecsenik" to "Markus" in the latest telegram is no change at all.

Obviously, "Mordechai" is his Jewish forename while "Markus" is surely how he is currently registered in his Hungarian passport.

3) Regarding "Joseph Gold" there certainly has been no change. From my previous knowledge of him, he is a constant companion of the Rebbe shlita in all his travels. Also, he was always the regular prayer leader at the Rebbe's High Holy Days services.

4) Regarding the other names mentioned in the latest telegram, "Daniel Shafrinsky" and "Salomon Weinstock," I know of no more details than those contained in that telegram. However, I assume these are shammasim accompanying the above, to replace the two shammasim who were murdered by the tyrants yemach shemam — Hashem yinkom damam. According to a letter I received from a devotee in Geneva, Switzerland on November 25, 1942, the Jewish Agency at the time agreed to supply them with certificates.

Once again I request on behalf of the Belzer Rebbe shlita and in the name of thousands of his followers worldwide to endeavor to hasten their safe arrival here. May Hashem bless your efforts with success.

With great respect and genuine regard,

Dov Berish Ortner

❧

The Jewish Agency for Eretz Israel Jerusalem

Mr. Dov B. Ortner

Tel Aviv

September 23, 1943

23 Elul 5703

Our ref: Aliya Dept. 1607/Z

Dear Mr. Ortner,

Further to your letter of 10th this month, regarding the Belz Rebbe & escorts. We wish to inform you that we have included the names Twersky, Aron (instead of Singer, Aaron as previously, Belz Rebbe); Pecsenik, Markus; Gold, Joseph; Shafrinsky, Daniel; and Weinstock, Salomon in the list of Hungarian Rabbis and political leaders that we submitted to the Government on September 15, 1943.

Respectfully yours,

W. Gold

Secretary, Aliya Department

Now that the *Sochnut* had finally authorized the request for five certificates, all that remained to be seen was whether the British Administration would acquiesce to that request. Ironically, the last minute alteration of the Belzer Rav's surname from Singer — earlier registered as a refugee from occupied Europe and therefore suspect to British officials — to Twersky (allegedly a prominent Hungarian personality, previously unknown to the British) was more likely to speed up the process. Nevertheless, R' Berish kept up the pressure to tie up all the loose ends and on 27 Elul (September 27) cabled London:

> TO RAV BABAD LONDON SOCHNUT AGREED CERTIFICATES FOR RABBI ARON TWERSKY MARKUS PECSENIK JOSEPH GOLD DANIEL SHAFRINSKY SALOMON WEINSTOCK REGARDING TRANSIT SHEMAYAH SHOULD CONTACT BARLAS ISTANBUL ORTNER

So by Motza'ei Rosh Hashanah, when the Belzer Rav first voiced his desire to emigrate to Eretz Yisrael, his dedicated chassidim had already anticipated his wishes by a few months and had almost accomplished the difficult task. Meanwhile, the two brothers tried to persuade Hungarian Jewry to take the desperate plight of Polish Jews much more seriously. Privately, many Hungarians thought that all the many war atrocity stories were vastly exaggerated and the "Polish *farbrechers*" were just too lazy to work for their German masters! As the Bilgoraj Rav later lamented, "They simply didn't believe any of our accounts of Nazi outrages in Poland. We told them from our own personal firsthand knowledge and tried to depict the impending Nazi menace. But they wouldn't listen to a thing and instead put all their trust in the royal administration of Hungary, who opposed direct Nazi rule by their nominal allies and refused to betray Hungary's Jews." Their confidence in the durability of the liberal-royal government remained so steadfast that some honestly judged it safer to stay in Hungary than move to Palestine, a previous target of the German military until their defeat at El Alamein in October 1942.

On Motza'ei Yom Kippur, chassidim from Munkacs were urgently summoned to the Rebbe's room. At the head of the table sat the two brothers, and the Bilgoraj Rav spoke forcefully and at length. "All

Hungarian Jews have a sacred duty to rescue their brethren trying to escape the Nazi *Gei-Hinnom* — and especially the Jews of Munkacs! You live right near the border and many refugees are attempting to cross and hide. Even if it costs a lot of money you can ill afford, you still have to help! Here my brother, the Rav, has *paskened* that in this emergency of *pikuach nefesh* the normal conditions of not spending more than one-fifth of one's possessions do NOT apply!"

Few realized how the deceptively calm situation in Hungary was about to be shattered. Had they appreciated, as did the Belzer Rav, how they were in reality sitting on a smoking volcano which would erupt within eight months, they might have behaved differently. Certainly, the Belzer Rav sensed that his personal situation was far more precarious than it appeared, though the Rebbe's calm exterior betrayed nothing of impending problems.

CHAPTER 20

ON THE
WANTED LIST

A S THE REBBE HAD SUSPECTED, THE GESTAPO HAD
not taken his escape from Bochnia lightly, particularly
when this was followed by a stream of fugitives fleeing the ghetto to Slovakia. Initially, top Nazi officials
swiftly arrived from Krakow to make preliminary inquiries but
shortly afterwards most of the ghetto's Jewish administrators fled,
and the Gestapo set up a Committee of Inquiry to look into security
at Bochnia. After studying reports from their border controls, their
suspicions centered on the enigmatic captain of Hungarian counterintelligence who was personally known to several top-ranking
police officers.[1] In due course, a full report was sent back to Berlin.

In early August the blow finally fell when a thick envelope
landed on the desk of Budapest Police Foreign Persons' Division,
the KEOKH. It contained a stiff official complaint from the Gestapo
regarding Captain Shtaier as "a smuggler of Jews and suspicious
elements." At least Shtaier had the intelligence services to protect him, but the letter also contained an official request for the

---

1. Fortunately, they did not share their information with the Gestapo in Ukraine, who
had temporarily arrested Captain Shtaier in Przemyslany.

immediate extradition of the Belzer Wonder Rabbi, now residing in Budapest and hiding behind the name of "Samuel Braun, a refugee teacher." The Gestapo had included a photograph of the Rebbe but by a fortuitous oversight, it was actually a photo of the previous Rav, Rebbe Yissachar Dov!

Fortunately, the head of the division, Alexander Von Simonpla, was out of Budapest and one of his junior underlings handed the stern letter to the Police Commander, Dr. Ferdinand (Nandor) Batizfalvy. Batizfalvy was a genuine friend of Jews who had saved scores of refugees and he had no wish to comply with the Nazis' demands. Instead he misfiled the letter and "neglected" to report its existence either to his superiors or even to Alexander Von Simonpla on his return. He confidently assumed that the German bureaucrats would not pursue the matter and reassured leading Jewish activists that the Grand Rabbi was quite safe.

The next German demand arrived in mid-September — during *Aseres Yemei Teshuvah* — and by then Berlin had escalated their charges. Now they pressed for the extradition of the Bilgoraj Rav too, claiming both brothers had organized the wave of "illegal" escapes from Bochnia and had helped over 2,000 Jews flee to Hungary. Also, they demanded an internal Hungarian inquiry to apprehend and arrest any of their officers implicated in smuggling criminals and other undesirable elements. Since the Gestapo was obviously not going to drop the matter and was backed up by the powerful German ambassador to Hungary, it was impossible for Commander Batizfalvy to hush it up any longer. Furthermore, this time Berlin had taken the precaution of simultanously sending corresponding demands to the Hungarian Foreign Ministry.

Reluctantly, he handed over both letters to Alexander Von Simonpla. To his surprise and relief, Von Simonpla agreed to drag out the affair as long as possible to give the two rabbis a chance to escape. To both officials, it seemed best if the fugitives moved to another country, preferably beyond the long reach of the Gestapo. Despite his close contacts with the Jewish community, Commander Batizfalvy confided in none of them.

The first any of them knew of the looming catastrophe was on Sunday, October 10, the day after Yom Kippur, when an official police notice arrived at the Rebbe's address, asking him to present himself at the Budapest Police Foreign Persons' Division that Wednesday, October 13, which just happened to be Erev Succos! This laconic notice threw his chassidim into turmoil and panic. Officially, all aliens had to register with the police who issued them identity cards with their photo, after which they had to appear once a month. Officials of the KEOKH were notorious for their unsympathetic handling of Jewish refugees from Poland. At best they landed up in the alien's local prison on Rumbach-Sandor utca or at the *Unterenrungas Lager* for illegal immigrants; at worst they might be handed right back to the Gestapo! Until now the Belzer Rav had dealt with them at arm's length via various intermediaries; this demand for his personal attendance at their headquarters was most ominous.

Two of his closest chassidim, R' Yosef Salgo and R' Chaim Mordechai Stern, rushed to Mr. M. Kraus — a Budapest community leader who enjoyed close connections with top officials. Indeed it was he who had first introduced the Belz Rescue Committee to Captain Shtaier and had broached the idea of using him to smuggle the Rebbe to Hungary. Visibly upset and panic stricken, Salgo and Stern burst into Mr. Kraus' private office uninvited and began sputtering incoherently. Mr. Kraus stared at them in horror and shock. What terrible calamity had happened? When he finally managed to piece together their information — that the Belzer Rebbe had been urgently summoned to the KEOKH for questioning — he relaxed. "Is that all? So what's all the panic about? It's just a formality! If you're so concerned I will personally look into the affair, meet with the authorities and sort it out."

In reply, the two of them embraced him warmly, flung their hands around his neck and kissed him "like little children"! Mr. Kraus was immensely touched how grown, respected men should get so emotional at the fate of their Rabbi. He immediately called on Alexander Von Simonpla, head of the Division. Privately, Von Simonpla was surprised that Commander Ferdinand Batizfalvy had not already tipped off his excellent contacts within the Jewish community about these German demands. However, he merely turned to his secretary and asked for the relevant file. After carefully perusing its contents for a few minutes in silence, he gazed across the desk at Mr. Kraus and shook his head slowly. "This is a serious business! This is not the everyday affair of some obscure Polish refugee or other!" he explained somberly. "It's unusual and grave; it's government to government business! The German Embassy is also now involved and wants this Rabbi Samuel Braun escorted back to the Gestapo for questioning — we have to handle this very carefully."

From his long experience in dealing with top Hungarian officials, Mr. Kraus knew how they appreciated and reacted positively to being told the straight truth — rather than being deceived with duplicity or equivocation. So he confirmed that the refugee teacher Samuel Braun was none other than the Grand Rabbi of Belz but there was absolutely no accuracy in any of the other allegations, nor was there a smuggling ring run by Hungarian officers. He told Von Simonpla something of the history of the Belz dynasty and its reputation around the world, pointing out how Hungary would earn international kudos by giving the Rebbe sanctuary; besides, he was already planning to leave for Palestine and would surely be out of the country within weeks. A little judicious procrastination in complying with the German demands was needed, and the awkward situation would resolve itself to everybody's satisfaction.

Von Simonpla nodded sympathetically and summoned the police commander Dr. Batizfalvy. "Take this file under your control," he ordered. "We must deny that this suspect is the Wonder Rabbi of Belz. His place is in Palestine and certainly not in Germany!" Then he turned back to Mr. Kraus and spoke confidentially. "The flood of disciples coming to the Grand Rabbi ought to stop; it arouses the suspicions and ire of government or German agents. Better still if he stayed at a private house and kept his whereabouts secret."

Over the years, Mr. Kraus had been in almost daily contact with Dr. Batizfalvy, smoothing out communal and citizenship problems. He knew him as a fervent anti-Nazi who disliked protocol or red-tape and would easily waive unnecessary formalities. So he asked him to dispense with the need for the Rebbe to appear at police headquarters in person, but the police commander firmly rejected the suggestion. "As to drafting a suitable reply for the Germans, that we can do between ourselves," Dr. Batizfalvy declared, "but signing the official form confirming he is Samuel Braun that the

Grand Rabbi has to do himself! Besides," he added, softening a little, "I would like the opportunity to meet this great Rabbi myself. Let him come in a taxi, straight to my office. I won't keep him more than 5 minutes!"

It was difficult to reject this stipulation, raised in such a kind manner, especially when Dr. Nandor Batizfalvy was a truly noble gentile. But they did manage to delay the procedure. Instead of Erev Succos as scheduled, the Rebbe's attendance at police headquarters was postponed till shortly after Yom Tov. Throughout the wait, though those around him were very nervous — R' Yosef Salgo, in particular, repeatedly confided to Rebbe Mottele how at heart he dreaded this business would end badly — the Belzer Rav remained calm and collected. Certainly, none of the chassidim noticed the slightest change to his regular routine nor to any of Belz's traditions or customs.

Mindful of Alexander Von Simonpla's advice, modifications were made to the Belzer Rav's arrangements before Succos. Although the Rebbe did not immediately change his residence or location of *tefillos,* the Shabbos *tisch* was held privately at home and they sought to limit those coming to watch or participate. Instead of the hundreds who were usually present, everybody was now asked to stay away. Henceforth, two guards were stationed outside the Rebbe's residence to bar onlookers; only a few of those who had not been there for some time would be allowed in. In addition, all those under suspicion from the government (usually for evading army forced labor and popularly described as *"tamir venelom"* for their assuming false identities, dates and places of birth) were discouraged from congregating at the communal school building.

Naturally, these new restrictions caused much resentment, and scuffles occasionally broke out on the large balcony outside the Rebbe's apartment, but there was no other alternative beyond canceling the *tisch* entirely — and that the Belzer Rav would not hear of. As an added safeguard, the Belzer Rav's Hungarian documentation was secretly changed to "Twersky." Fortunately, Succos passed peacefully without further crisis or alarm. Yet despite all the precautions, larger crowds than usual thronged around the Rebbe, causing added problems whenever errands forced the *gabbaim* to push their way through.

From childhood, the Belzer Rav had inherited from his mother a meticulousness regarding ritually washing his hands, often and repeatedly, before any holy undertaking — and his apartment had no running water. Instead, buckets of water had to be fetched from a standpipe downstairs in the courtyard. One extremely late afternoon as time still available for Minchah prayers was rapidly running out, R' Shmuel Porgas was shouldering his way back through the crowded apartment with the Rebbe's bucket of water when an impetuous chassid plunged his hands into the bucket to wash his own hands! The *gabbai* was in a quandary: to bring fresh water might take too long, especially with the jostling crowds outside and inside the apartment, and the Belzer Rav was in a hurry. But as he approached, the Rebbe quickly turned to him and said, "*Zeits azoi gut*, pour the bucket out, wash it down and bring other water!" Later, after Minchah, he remarked, "You wanted to fool me?"

Besides many loyal chassidim who arrived from the provinces and could not be dissuaded from attending the *tefillos* or *tisch*, there was the added complication of *arba minim*. During wartime, Hungary was cut off from its usual supply and had to find these uncommon fruit and flora from its own resources. Young Belz chassidim from Pupa and Szombathely already began their search during Elul and somehow managed to locate *lulavim* and *hadassim*, but where to find *esrogim*? They were nowhere to be found throughout Hungary.

Finally, on Erev Succos, three *esrogim* arrived by mail from Switzerland. None of these were particularly fine specimens but they were at least kosher, and the *shammasim* decided to keep one for the Belzer Rav and send the other two to Budapest's Central Synagogue for the use of the wider community. But the Rebbe would not hear of it — that's too selfish, what about those in the provinces? Don't they deserve to perform this mitzvah too? Instead, the other two *esrogim* should be quickly dispatched to the nearest large *kehillos* outside Budapest. As for all the Jews in Budapest — they can take their turn with the Belzer Rav's *esrog*!

Despite the unwelcome attention this would inevitably attract from the authorities, thousands of Budapest's Jews lined up to recite the blessings over that sole *esrog*. Naturally, by the time they had finished handling the *esrog* it was bruised and discolored. Indeed, when the Rebbe unwrapped it on Friday, the second day of Yom Tov, the *esrog* was almost entirely black. Yet the Belzer Rav made his *berachah* over it with his customary fervor and then gazed at it lovingly. "*An esrog hadar ... an esrog hadar ...,*" he murmured in satisfaction.

That year, the third day of Succos was also Shabbos, which caused a small problem: during Chol HaMoed, Belz customarily sang at the *Melaveh Malkah* only four *zemiros* to distinctive tunes traditionally attributed to the Rebbe, Reb Elimelech of Lizhensk (Lezajsk). While the melodies for "*Eliyahu HaNavi*," "*Ish Chassid*" and "*Ribbono Shel Olam*" were well known, since these tunes were sung on other occasions, few knew the rarely used melody for "*Al Tirah Avdi Yaakov*" — and the Belzer Rav was unwilling to forego the slightest custom, even under wartime constraints. He summoned R' Yishai Hecht (originally a Belz resident) and proceeded to repeat the tune a few times until R' Yishai could confidently sing it together with the Rebbe. "At the *tisch*, I'm going to call on you to sing *Al Tirah Avdi Yaakov!*"

Shemini Atzeres and Simchas Torah were on Thursday and Friday, and they had only three *Sifrei Torah* at the Belzer *minyan* — a far cry from that unforgettable final Shemini Atzeres in Belz four years earlier, just before their *galus* began. Despite the evident emotional link with their recent past, great effort was exercised to endow the festival with much of its lively cheer and traditional gaiety. Two of the *Sifrei Torah* were borne by the Belzer Rav and Bilgoraj Rav respectively, and the third was circulated among the many guests. Once again the erstwhile *yoshvim* swung into action to feed and house the countless provincial chassidim and numerous refugees.

Shabbos Bereishis that followed immediately after Yom Tov was unseasonably cold, and Sunday October 24 was colder still, which presented a problem. This was the day scheduled for the Belzer Rav's visit to the police. Because he had hardly been outside since his arrival in Budapest, he had not acquired an overcoat or warm outer clothing; habitually the Rebbe was highly sensitive to cold and could not venture outside on such an extremely wintry day without

To the police headquarters

adequate protection. Quickly, the famous *gaon*, Rabbi Yisrael Weltz, proffered his personal rabbinical, fur-lined *peltz*, which was gratefully accepted. (Due to the last minute confusion, few noticed that the coat was really designed for a much taller man and dragged along the ground.)

The appointment had been arranged for 12:15 p.m. and the Rebbe endeavored to complete his strenuous regime of study, prayers and meditation earlier than usual. By 12 p.m. he was ready and the car journey took only a few minutes; accompanying him in the car were the Bilgoraj Rav, Mr. Yosef Salgo and Mr. M. Kraus. Although his companions were nervously convinced this was not a simple matter, the Belzer Rav seemed unperturbed. When Mr. Kraus assured him it was merely a formality and his domicile in Budapest had already been cleared with the authorities, the Rebbe pressed his hand warmly and declared, "I'm relying on you; continue doing your best!"

When they arrived, the police commander was already waiting outside. After welcoming them in, Dr. Ferdinand Batizfalvy asked a few simple questions which Mr. Kraus answered on the Rebbe's behalf before handing the official papers to the Rebbe for his signature. Suddenly Dr. Batizfalvy requested that he and the Rabbi consult a few moments privately in another office. Since the Rebbe understood no Hungarian at all, he turned to his companions for an explanation. In principle, the Belzer Rav had no objections, but he asked if one of his companions might accompany them as an interpreter. The police commander refused. "Surely the Rabbi understands German — no?" The Rebbe agreed that he could understand simple phrases in rudimentary German and Dr. Batizfalvy escorted him to another room. They were closeted together for nearly half an hour but what they discussed there was never revealed.

The Belzer Rav kept it a close secret and Dr. Ferdinand Batizfalvy rebutted all entreaties to divulge the details. Apparently Dr. Batizfalvy had stressed how the Hungarian government was not responsible for the ill-treatment of its Jews and Jewish refugees — they only acted badly because of German pressure and force of circumstances — and he was hoping that the Belzer Rav would convey this favorable gloss to the Allies on finally leaving Hungary. Evidently, they must have also talked about the Rebbe's plans to escape to Palestine and the Gestapo pursuit; certainly scarcely a day passed afterwards without the Rebbe inquiring how the process of obtaining certificates and transit visas was progressing. As he left police headquarters, the Belzer Rav thanked Dr. Batizfalvy for the courteous way the matter had been sorted out and the police commander got up and walked him to the front entrance. It was patently obvious that Dr. Ferdinand Batizfalvy was greatly impressed by this Wonder Rabbi.

CHAPTER 21

FINAL MONTHS IN HUNGARY

TWO WEEKS AFTER SUCCOS THEY RECEIVED more bad news from Poland. In early November, two Hungarian Jews entered the Belzer Rav's private rooms to report on the tragic death of his youngest brother, Rabbi Shalom, Rav of Apta (Opatow), at the age of 42. Rabbi Shalom had left Apta at the beginning of the war and had been staying temporarily in Drohovitch before moving to Stryj, not too distant from the Hungarian border. In the winter of 1943, he had made arrangements with two Polish smugglers to help him escape across that border but they abandoned him to his fate and he had to hide in the forest near the border. From there he had sent urgent letters via Polish peasants begging assistance from the Munkacs community (who had just been strongly exhorted by the Bilgoraj Rav after Yom Kippur to take a more proactive role in *hatzalah*).

By the time the community had finally dispatched two Jewish smugglers to ferry him across the border, he had already expired from the intense cold. When the smugglers had entered the forest they discovered his dead body lying among the trees and, recognizing who this was, gave him a decent Jewish burial. On their return

Rebbe Shalom of Apta

to Hungary, they had come to report directly to the Rebbe with their firsthand knowledge. At first he accepted the news with equanimity (just as he had all previous private sorrows) and after the smugglers left he did not refer to the painful subject for the next month.

Shortly before Chanukah, however, he had an abrupt change of mind. One night after Maariv, he summoned R' Chaim Shloma Friedman (who earlier helped smuggle the Rebbe from Przemyslany to Wisnicz and had recently escaped from the Bochnia ghetto during its final liquidation in Elul 1943) and asked him to interview the smugglers again. "*Zeits moichel,* find out exactly what happened with my brother Reb Shalom. Did they definitely recognize him? Did they bury him themselves? Do they remember where they buried him? Find out every small detail please. We need a *gevias edus* — a complete witness report."

When R' Chaim Shloma returned with the details, the Belzer Rav sent him to ask Rabbi Yonason Steif, Rav of Budapest, three *shailos*: Does the Rebbe have to keep *aveilus* on a "*shemuah rechokah,*" or distant tidings? For how long should he maintain this *aveilus*? Does he have to tear *kri'ah*? (Customarily, the Belzer Rav was rigorous on asking a *shailah* even where the halachah was simple and apparently obvious; as was his custom, he repeated these questions three times for greater emphasis.) While he waited patiently for R' Chaim Shloma's return with the *p'sak*, no one was allowed into the Rebbe's presence or received a *berachah*.

Rav Steif ruled that he has to sit *shivah* for half an hour and should tear *kri'ah*. Surrounded by a *minyan* of chassidim, *gabbaim* and *shammasim*, the Belzer Rav immediately slipped off his chair onto a nearby suitcase and sat in total silence for over 30 minutes. After seating himself in his chair for several moments, he stood up and eulogized his brother with a few short, pithy sentiments. "He was a *tzaddik* and a *yerei Hashem* and a chassid! A great dispenser of charity — he distributed abundant sums of money!" This behavior was most unusual for the Belzer Rav, who generally did not mark the death of any of his family during wartime — not even his beloved son, Rebbe Moshe'le, murdered in his vicinity during the first Przemyslany pogrom; obviously, he must have had some heavenly intent.

Rav Shalom Rokach, his youngest brother, was indeed exemplary in charity and saintliness. As a child he had remained unbelievably humble and recoiled from any élitism over his contemporaries. If ever he saw one of his classmates with torn clothes, he immediately exchanged them with his own. Although his personal lifestyle was frugal and ascetic, and his *hasmadah* a byword, he was kindness itself: his home was open day and night to all waifs and strays, who received food and donations in abundance. Quiet, friendly and patient, he was never known to have raised his voice in anger. Despite being a Rebbe in his own right, he remained a devoted chassid of Belz to the end.

Following the short *hesped*, the Rebbe took the opportunity to commemorate several prominent Belzer chassidim who had disappeared during the War, including R' Yaakov Berish of Rawa-Ruska (famous as *Baal Shacharis* on Rosh Hashanah, a notable *talmid chacham* with a total belief and dedication to the Belzer Rebbes, uncle of R' Berish Ortner), R' Mechel'e of Zolkove (one of the foremost *yoshvim*, amazingly unpretentious despite delivering five or six varied *shiurim* daily to hundreds of *bachurim* in Belz, likewise an uncle of R' Berish Ortner) and R' Yeshayah Prager (one of the Rav's closest chassidim, who forsook his rich background to devote himself entirely to Torah and *yiras Shamayim*), also of Rawa-Ruska. Only after he had paid significant tributes to their memories did the Belzer Rav revert to his regular schedule, bestowing *berachos* and advice.

It was obvious that he regarded his punishing schedule as vital. When a temporary *gabbai* with a misplaced compassion disobeyed the Rebbe's specific instructions and neglected to wake him after his painfully short sleep, reasoning that the exhausted Rebbe desperately needed more rest, Reb Aharon awoke with a start a few minutes later — visibly agitated. "By not waking me exactly on time," he reprimanded him angrily, "you endangered me and the whole world!"

Despite the enormous respect lavished on them in Budapest, the Bilgoraj Rav had always sensed that Hungary could not be considered as anything more than a temporary way station en route to somewhere safer.[1] Also, as the Bilgoraj Rav later recalled, ever since the Rebbe left Belz on Shemini Atzeres 1939 he had never stopped yearning and planning to live in the Holy Land despite the evident hardships. Indeed, before the War, he even had a separate timepiece in Belz adjusted to mirror the times of sunrise and sunset in Eretz Yisrael!

Following that fateful encounter with the KEOKH Division dealing with enemy aliens and refugees, they urgently had to find asylum elsewhere. Although various suggestions arose, including Switzerland, America and even remaining in Hungary (usually by those not privy to the highly secret extradition directives), the Rebbe would not hear of anywhere besides Eretz Yisrael. Nearly every day, the Bilgoraj Rav booked an international telephone call to R' Moshe Gross in Switzerland (in the era before direct dialing, this was a lengthy and complicated procedure, further complicated by precarious wartime communications). Nor did the flow of letters and cables between Palestine, England and Switzerland falter; as usual it was R' Berish Ortner who was most prolific with a stream of letters issuing from his typewriter:

> *The Jewish Agency for Eretz Israel*
> *Aliya Department*
> *Jerusalem P O B 92*
> *26 Tishri 5704*
> *October 25, 1943*
> *Your ref: 1607/Z*
> *Regarding the Belzer Rebbe & Escort*
> *Dear Sir,*

---

1. Even before the outbreak of war, when chassidim had assumed Germany would never dare attack Poland after Britain and France had guaranteed its independence, the Rebbe had confided to a close chassid, "Oh, what will the Jews do now? Where can they run to? In the last war they fled to Hungary and found shelter. But now all the borders are closed and who knows what will happen there ..."

Further to your letter of 25 Elul last, in which you kindly informed me that you included the names of the Belzer Rebbe and escort among the list of Hungarian rabbis and activists submitted to the government on September 15, 1943.

May I take this opportunity to ascertain the results of that important endeavor and what are the immigration prospects of this famous Rebbe? I have been repeatedly asked this by letter and telegram and I would like to notify his followers worldwide who await your positive reply with bated breath.

Thanking you in anticipation, with much respect.
Dov Berish Ortner

Baruch Hashem 29 Tishrei 5704 (October 28, 1943)

To Harav Hagaon etc. Moreinu Harav Avraham Babad, London.

After receiving your telegram of August 27, 1943, I tried to obtain the requested certificates from the Sochnut. On September 27, 1943 I telegraphed you that certificates for the Rav, shlita, Markus Pecsenik and three companions were authorized by the Sochnut and forwarded to the government for their final approval, and I asked that Shemayah should see to Barlas in Istanbul about the journey to Eretz Yisrael. I hope you got my telegram.

Now a refugee has arrived from Budapest and informed me that the Rav asked that everything be done to assist him in coming to Eretz Yisrael. But bringing such a journey to fruition is one of the hardest things and costs a lot of money. I am taking every possible step at the various institutions.

With great respect,
Dov Berish Ortner

Mr. Moshe Shapira
The Jewish Agency for Eretz Israel
Aliya Department
Jerusalem P O B 92
1 Marcheshvan 5704
October 30, 1943
Your ref: 1607/Z: Regarding the Belzer Rebbe & Escort

Who am I to approach Your Honor, but I base my request on that of the Gadol Hador.

Dear Mr. Shapira,

Shalom & Brachah!

When I received that telegram on July 17, 1943 from London from the Belzer Rebbe's shlita followers (that the Rebbe and his brother want to come to Eretz Yisrael and asked me to contact Mr. Goldin in Istanbul through Chief Rabbi Herzog, shlita) I was not at all surprised. I had heard it from the Rebbe's own lips ten years earlier on my immigrating to Eretz Yisrael. When I took my leave, the Rebbe told me of his hopes with Hashem's help to come to Eretz Yisrael.

On July 20, I gave you a copy of the telegram, with a request for the Rebbe and escort, and you assured me that as soon as the way was open, the Belzer Rebbe would be among the first to arrive here.

After his famous brothers-in-law from the Chernobyl dynasty were murdered with their families and after his holy sons were burnt alive in shul — by the sadists yemach shemam — together with their families and hundreds of others al kiddush Hashem — Hashem yinkom damam, the Jewish world in America, Switzerland and England began the rescue of the famous Rebbe of Belz and his brother; and Hashem Yisbarach helped them: Your Honor kept his important promise and arranged certificates for them.

It is a fact that different people have lately arrived from Hungary. Recently among them was Mr. Kasztner[2] from Hungary who came with a special message from the Belzer Rebbe: regards to his sister Mrs. Perlow and myself, plus a personal request to endeavor and assist their arrival here as soon as possible. He heard this directly from the Rebbe shlita, the day after Yom Kippur.

Since Mr. Barlas is leaving around now for Istanbul, I beg Your Honor in every way I can, and on behalf of the Belzer Rebbe, and also in the name of his large community of admirers worldwide and in the Holy Land, that Mr. Barlas immediately on his arrival in Istanbul obtain telegraphic approval from London of their authorization and

---

2. Obviously, this refugee and messenger was not the controversial Hungarian Zionist leader Dr. Israel Rudolf Kasztner who negotiated directly with the Nazis — negotiations that led to the release of two train transports from Bergen-Belsen but the deportation of the remaining Hungarian Jews — since he only arrived in Israel after the War.

the necessary transit visas to utilize this opportunity to bring them here. If others have managed it, I am sure Your Honor can likewise obtain them with Hashem Yisbarach's help.

Your Honor is assured the gratitude and blessings of the Belzer Rebbe. I remain,

Dov Berish Ortner

Two days after mailing this letter, R' Berish met Mr. Barlas personally at the *Sochnut* offices in Tel Aviv and handed over the following request plus two photographs of the Belzer Rebbe.

Mr. Chaim Barlas
The Jewish Agency for Eretz Israel
Jerusalem
3 Marcheshvan 5704
November 1, 1943
Your ref: 1607/Z
Regarding the Belzer Rebbe & Escort
Dear Mr. Barlas,

The Jewish Agency allotted certificates on behalf of Belzer Rebbe Aron Twersky, his brother Rebbe Markus Pecsenik & three companions and forwarded them to the government in London. The Belzer Rebbe and his escort are presently in Budapest (c/o Mr. Stern, Rumbach utca 7). A few days ago Mr. Kasztner arrived among the group from Hungary as a special messenger carrying a personal request from the Belzer Rebbe shlita to make every effort to assist his arrival here as soon as possible.

In the name of the Belzer Rebbe shlita I ask Your Honor, after receiving relevant information from the Jewish Agency, to endeavor to reach Istanbul to obtain telegraphic approval from London to speed their travel.

I pray that Agency officials who have worked so hard on this project shall complete their goal with success.

Respectfully yours,
Dov Berish Ortner

The next day (11/2/43), on Mr. Barlas' advice, the following cable was dispatched to the Red Cross, Geneva:

Baruch Hashem 6th Cheshvan 5704 (November 4, 1943)

To His Honor, Mr. Barlas, at the Jewish Agency, Jerusalem.

(Your ref: 1607/Z Regarding the Belzer Rebbe & Escort)

Further to our conversation at the Jewish Agency offices, Tel Aviv re: the emigration of the Belzer Rav and his companions from Hungary to Eretz Yisrael via the Jewish Agency. I am pleased to enclose the following information:

On September 15, 1943, the Jewish Agency for Eretz Israel Administration sent the list of certification including (1) Belzer Rebbe (2) his brother, Rebbe of Bilgoraj (3) their companions, as follows:

(1) Rabbi Aron Twersky born 1875; (2) Rabbi Markus Pecsenik born 1890; (3) Joseph Gold born 1890; (4) Daniel Shafrinsky born 1894; (5) Salomon Weinstock born 1905; (they are presently at Mr. Mordechai Stern, Rumbach utca 7, Budapest).

My request is (a) to inform them telegraphically that you have their certificates; (b) cable London for their authorization of these certificates; (c) to endeavor to bring them here as soon as possible; (d) inform me by telegram of their arrival in Istanbul and also here, so preparations can be made for lodgings, etc.

You can be well assured of the gratitude and blessings of the Rebbe and also the profound appreciation of thousands of his admirers worldwide.

Yours most respectfully,

Dov Berish Ortner

Mr. Ortner also drafted a telegram for Mr. Barlas to send to Gross in Geneva — immediately after he arrives in Istanbul — via the Red Cross informing the Rebbe of receipt of certificates. Mr. Gross was to reply directly to Barlas in Istanbul. However, even before Mr. Barlas left Palestine, the *Sochnut* had some good news for R' Berish:

The Jewish Agency for Eretz Israel
Jerusalem
Mr. Dov B. Ortner
111 Nachalat Binyamin
Tel Aviv
November 5, 1943
7 Marcheshvan 5704
Our ref: Aliya Dept. 1607/Z
Regarding: Belz Rebbe & Escort
Dear Mr. Ortner,
Further to your letter of October 30, re: the above, I am pleased to inform you that Mr. Barlas is shortly returning to Istanbul and will there do all in his power to help these gentlemen.
As you probably know, the Belzer Rebbe and his escort were included in the list of veteran Hungarian Zionists submitted on September 15, 1943 and have now been accepted by the government.
Respectfully yours,
Moshe Shapira
Aliya Department.

In the same post, the *Sochnut* sent five separate memos signed by A. Silberberg, of the Jewish Agency Secretariat, formally confirming that Rabbi Aron Twersky, Hungary 1607/Z was approved as No. (Z/270) M438/43. Markus Pecsenik, Hungary P/9042 was approved as No. (Z/188) M/438/43. Joseph Gold, Hungary 3760/G was approved as No. (Z/301) M/438/43. Salomon Weinstock, Hungary V/2794 was approved as No. (Z/290) M/438/43. Daniel Shafrinsky, Hungary SH/4047 was approved as No. (Z/220) M/438/43.

Thus less than a month after the Belzer Rav had publicized his wish to flee to Eretz Yisrael, and just over two weeks since he had met with the KEOKH, his dedicated chassid succeeded in procuring the vital certificates (only sixteen weeks — even from Rav Babad's early cable). Maintaining the lengthy, and often repetitive, correspondence was painstaking and boring but it had yielded the desired result. No mean feat, but much remained to be done both financially and organizationally — it was still touch and go whether they escaped before the Gestapo's patience ran out. There was a limit to how long the Hungarian strategy of denial and procrastination could last, especially when pro-Nazi magazines publicized the sensational scoop, replete with photos, of several leading *gedolim* hiding out in Hungary illegally under Aryan papers. Included among them was the Belzer Rav.

Although the specific charge that these rabbanim were using non-Jewish passports was false, the unwelcome coverage attracted dangerous publicity. Worse, German spymasters

Anti-Semitic Hungarians allege prominent Rabbis hide behind Christian identities

had mounted their own investigations and soon a stream of background information arrived on Commander Batizfalvy's desk to back up Gestapo's demands. The Germans could now quote the exact date "Samuel Braun" left the hospital, or the public venue of his Shabbos and Yom Tov *tisch* ... It could only be a matter of time before Hungarian officials would reluctantly have to submit to a formal German extradition warrant. Once again, R' Berish was the central address for outgoing and incoming mail and on November 7th he dispatched the following cable:

TO GROSS GENEVA INFORMED REBBE VIA RED CROSS ORTNER

> *The Jewish Agency for Eretz Israel*
> *Mr. Dov Berish Ortner*
> *111 Nachalat Binyamin, Tel Aviv*
> *November 10, 1943*
> *12th Marcheshvan 5704*
> *Dear Mr. Ortner,*
> *Further to your letter of November 4 re: Belz Rebbe and companions. I have taken note of all the details.*

It goes without saying that I will do everything feasible for the emigration of the Rebbe and family as quickly as possible. In this way we hope to be successful.

Respectfully yours,
Chaim Barlas

R' Berish was anxious to utilize Mr. Barlas' good offices to ensure the Rebbe's travel arrangements also went smoothly. As the man in charge on the spot in Turkey — the final destination of the Orient Express — he could mobilize *Sochnut* finance, influence and personnel where necessary to sort out any unforseen problems. Notwithstanding Mr. Barlas' explicit promise, R' Berish sought to increase the pressure by involving the Belzer fraternity of London and Switzerland, on 22nd November:

Baruch Hashem, 24 Cheshvan 5704

To my relative and friend, the renowned chassid Reb Chaim Nota Katz, London.

As I telegraphed you, under the influence of Chief Rabbi R' Yitzchak Isaac Herzog shlita, the Sochnut has given certificates for the Rebbe and companions by my efforts. With Hashem's help, these certificates are now in my possession; they were recognized as veteran Hungarian Zionists on September 15 and approved by the Government.

Chaim Barlas, the Sochnut representative in Istanbul, was just now in Eretz Yisrael and promised me to do everything in his power to bring them here as soon as possible. However, I ask that you also telegraph Mr. Barlas in Istanbul with the request that he hasten their arrival here.

In recent days, various refugees from Hungary have arrived and brought me regards from Maran shlita who asked that we make a great effort that he comes quickly to Eretz Yisrael. (I have done everything in my power that I am capable of to hasten their difficult journey. When they come now, they will need large sums. I hope that you too will do everything and assist in every way and with Hashem Yisbarach's help we will succeed.)

With every respect and regards,
Dov Berish Ortner

An identical letter was simultaneously sent to the chassidim in Switzerland. He also wrote again to the *Sochnut*.

The Jewish Agency for Eretz Israel
(Vaad Hatzalah)
Jerusalem
1 Kislev 5704
November 28, 1943
<u>*Your ref: 1607/Z*</u>
Regarding the Belzer Rebbe & Escort
Dear Sirs,
Further to your request, I enclose 4 photographs of the Belzer Rebbe shlita.

I must ask you for the moment to keep these for internal use only. For obvious reasons, these should not be used for any publicity in the newspapers until the Rebbe shlita reaches the safety of Istanbul.
Dov Berish Ortner

The Jewish Agency for Eretz Israel
Jerusalem
Mr. Dov Berish Ortner
111 Nachalat Binyamin
Tel Aviv
December 7, 1943
10th Kislev 5704
<u>*Our ref: Aliya Dept. 1607/Z*</u>
Regarding: The Belzer Rebbe & Escort
Dear Mr. Ortner,
Further to your letter of 19th last addressed to Mr. Chaim Barlas. Mr. Barlas has meanwhile returned to Turkey.

In this regard may we inform you that Mr. Barlas personally noted down before he left to deal with this matter — emigration of Belz Rebbe — urgently and with exceptional measures as soon as he reaches Turkey.
Respectfully yours,
P.P.
Secretary, Aliya Department

The next day, Mr. Ortner cabled Istanbul:

Meanwhile, Belz chassidim in America managed to send the urgently needed funds to Switzerland via a circuitous route. To avoid wartime currency restrictions, some $6,000 was entrusted to Dr. Isaac Lewin of World Agudah[3] for onward dispatch through New York's Polish Consulate to the Polish Consul in Berne, Alexander Lados — one of the *chassidei umas ha'olam* — where it was converted to 25,734 Swiss Francs. Lados' right hand man, Dr. Julius Kuhl (later of Miami Beach) was not only Jewish but also a former Belzer chassid! As the "Assistant for Jewish Affairs" he had already used his good offices to help countless Jewish refugees with hundreds of new passports and visas, and he had no hesitation in also issuing two new Polish passports for the Rebbe and Bilgoraj Rav that were passed on to R' Ch. Y. Eiss for Mr. S. Binder. For added security, Dr. Kuhl mailed spare passports directly to Budapest via the diplomatic pouch of the Papal Nuncio, Monsignor Philippe Bernardini, another of the virtuous Swiss-based diplomats who cooperated fully with the Sternbuchs and other *hatzalah* activists.[4]

With all major hurdles surmounted and ancillary problems overcome, Mr. Ortner might have hoped it would be smooth sailing from now on, but obstacles still presented themselves. Obtaining separate transit visas from Romania, Bulgaria, Turkey, Syria and Lebanon took some time. Even when these finally arrived, the famous Orient Express train service from Paris to Istanbul was abruptly suspended for technical reasons. Naturally, these frustrating delays made chassidim around the world quite nervous, and Mr. Ortner had to bear the brunt of their criticism. A larger problem lay in the mounting opposition in Hungary to the Rebbe's departure — an opposition that almost scuttled the Rebbe's travel plans entirely.

---

3. Later, their non-governmental representative at the U.N.

4. Sending money from America via the Polish Consulate in Berne was the same conduit that was used to clandestinely fund the Mirrer Yeshivah in Shanghai; both the Polish Consulate and the Papal Nuncio also permitted the use of their diplomatic couriers, confidential ciphers and Morse codes to convey secret messages to those trapped in occupied territory or to rescue organizations in America.

CHAPTER 22

DON'T LEAVE US!

A S NEWS SPREAD OF THE BELZER REBBE'S IMPENDING departure, many Hungarian Jews were horrified. Instinctively they had felt more secure since his arrival, protected somehow from the fluctuating fortunes of this awful war. Hungary's foreign strategy and its internal policy toward Jews had ebbed and flowed with the tide of military supremacy; German setbacks in Russia, North Africa, Italy and Greece led to Hungary's distancing itself from the Axis powers. Although Hungarian Jews had been spared the savage bloodletting unleashed on their brethren in all the countries surrounding them, intense German pressure — led by the self-styled Fuehrer who repeatedly summoned the Hungarian Cabinet to Klessheim Castle near Salzburg for brutal dressings-down — was periodically exerted on their Hungarian allies to inflict far harsher penalties on its Jews. Nonetheless many Jewish communal leaders, fortified by their close contacts with prominent members of government and the aristocracy, were supremely confident their communities would survive intact until war's end. Following Italy's temporary overthrow of Benito Mussolini — Hungary and Italy had traditionally been allies — Miklos Kallay, who had replaced the pro-German Laszlo Bardossy, was emboldened to even broadcast a peace speech in August 1943.

During Elul 5703 (September 1943), however, Germany invaded her closest Axis ally and launched a deadly persecution of Italian Jewry. Could they safely discount a similar fate for Hungary? Surrounded by hatred and evil, caught between hope and fear, the average Hungarian Jew could never be entirely sure what the uncertain future entailed, and so they clung to saintly, fatherly figures like the Belzer Rav with an emotion hard to quantify. If he was planning to leave, what did that mean for Hungary — or for them?

During the solemn prayers of Rosh Hashanah, they had undoubtedly pondered the fearful words, *"V'al hamedinos bo yei'amar...* Regarding each country it is decided on this day: Who is destined for the sword and who for peace? Who for hunger and who for abundance? And its mortals are remembered on this day — for life or for death! Who is not remembered on this day ...?" If, immediately after Rosh Hashanah, the Rebbe had decided to remove himself from Hungary as urgently as possible, what might that *chalilah* portend for their fate? What if those shock-horror nightmares from Poland were not fevered exaggerations? Naturally, communal leaders fretted over whether the Belzer Rav's hasty departure might spark widespread unease or even panic.

Hundreds and then thousands of Hungarian Jews flocked to the Rebbe's residence, eager for encouragement, wise counsel, or a "good word" before he left them. Unlike his reticent behavior on arrival in Hungary — and disregarding Alexander Von Simonpla's precautionary advice — the Belzer Rav instructed his *gabbaim* not to restrict the growing flow of visitors. *"A rachmanus auf die Yidden ... Ribbono Shel Olam, a rachmanus auf zei ..."* he was repeatedly heard to murmur; his closest chassidim could only speculate what their Rebbe had in mind.

A delegation of Belz chassidim urged him to remain in Budapest. "This is Hungary; you are safe here," they argued. The tide had turned for Russia; their superior forces were at the Hungarian border, and it seemed scarcely credible that the Nazis — falling back under military onslaught on all sides — would waste any effort or scant resources on attacking more Jews. "You're wrong, the war is not yet over," replied the Belzer Rav. "The Germans are always ready to pounce!"

Certainly, he appeared very troubled in spirit. When he had first arrived from Poland he had looked dreadful, as if the entire weight of the unbearable *galus* were pressing down on his thin shoulders. During his several months in Hungary his mood had lightened slightly but now his face again displayed deep pain and foreboding. Indeed, his whole appearance perceptibly underscored the many years of fasting and deprivation which had intensified under enemy occupation. Many communal leaders — including *tzaddikim* and well-meaning but guileless do-gooders — sought to dissuade the Belzer Rav from going through with his plans on grounds of health or security — and only a select few knew of the Gestapo extradition demands.[1]

"*Chas veshalom*, that long journey will be too much for the Rebbe's depleted *kochos!*" they asserted, and did not hesitate to enter the Rav's private rooms to argue their belief personally.

"Why abandon a safe haven for somewhere surrounded by enemies and danger?" protested others, equally vociferously. More unscrupulous activists tried to alarm the Belzer Rav with manufactured scare stories. Yet the Belzer Rav's determination remained unshaken. As he confided to his loyal *gabbai*, R' David Shapira, "Believe me, I don't want to travel away from here but it's *a gezeirah fun Himmel!*"

None of these tactics, however, had as much impact as the plaintive plea of countless individual petitioners who begged the Rebbe not to abandon them. "The presence of the *tzaddik* will surely protect all of us from all evil! We have tried to provide everything needed — what does the Rebbe lack here?" they wept. For the first time the Belzer Rav plainly hesitated. Although he clearly sensed how his destiny lay in Eretz Yisrael, he was emotionally torn by his deep commitment and overwhelming empathy to fellow Jews.

When the Rebbe made no reply, the Bilgoraj Rav leaped to his defense. From the first he had felt the situation in Hungary to be precarious; it was too beholden to Germany, too close to the

---

1. Incidentally, communal leaders exerted similar pressure on their own rabbanim wishing to flee and any who ignored their directives were rejected after the War.

massacres and enslavement; it might be only a matter of time before they too succumbed to the intense Nazi pressure. Should the Belzer Rav renounce this chance to depart Eastern Europe — whose days he believed to be numbered — they might be trapped forever. "Leave the Rebbe alone!" he bellowed furiously. "If you want to commit collective suicide, that's your affair! But why prevent our great *Manhig* from escaping their bloody clutches? Can't you see how we're sitting on a rumbling volcano? Hungarian independence is nothing more than an illusion; the Nazis are only just behind the scenes and they'll do whatever they like whenever they like. They could be in here at any minute! They've never shown any respect for neutrality or allies; they've no time for sentiment or protocol. We know firsthand just what they're capable of, the senseless murders or crazy games of persecutions you just cannot possibly imagine ... You just don't understand the dangers. Anyhow, who are all of you to presume to lecture my holy brother on what he should or shouldn't do?"

As the crowd reluctantly drifted away, insulted and angry, the Bilgoraj Rav continued forcibly, "Besides, the Belzer Rav is not leaving for his own sake, he has to go for the sake of Belz's future! I beg him to have mercy on us all and ignore them!" Fortunately, the sheer force of the Bilgoraj Rav's vehemence won the day and the Rebbe was forever grateful. As he later wrote and remarked repeatedly: "My brother, the Bilgoraj Rav, fought a great battle and won in the *zechus* of our holy father *z"tl*. It was due to him that I merited to get to Eretz Yisrael — *megalgelin zechus al yedei zakkai* — credit is brought about by those already credit worthy!"

Before they left Hungary, the Belzer Rav strangely seemed to involve himself in mundane matters, namely in seeking alternative premises. True, Alexander Von Simonpla, head of the KEOKH, had advised Budapest's communal leaders that the Rebbe ought to move to a less well-known address, away from crowds and unwelcome publicity. Yet this was plainly not the Rebbe's purpose since he continued to welcome all chassidim and petitioners unreservedly. The strange business suddenly began one morning. Without any warning, he asked his *gabbai*, R' Shmuel Porgas, to quickly find another apartment in a different part of town; he wanted to move now!

The attendants looked at the Rav in surprise; it was so convenient and comfortable where they were. Although he claimed his present premises were "too big," they knew the Rebbe rarely gave his true reasons — particularly when he had esoteric motives. Moreover, it was the day before Rosh Chodesh and ev-

Street sign for Budapest ghetto

eryone knew that Belz had a tradition not to change homes on Erev Rosh Chodesh just as they normally enter new premises only on a Friday. As if reading their thoughts, the Rebbe remarked, "*Yoh, yoh. Ich veis as haint iz erev Rosh Chodesh ober vos ken'ich tuen? Ich miz!* — Yes, I know it's Erev Rosh Chodesh; but what can I do? I must move!" The apartment they found was at quite a distance, yet the Belzer Rav insisted on packing up and relocating that very day. But not for long — scarcely a month passed before the strange scene repeated itself. This time his complaint was that it was "too small" and the Rebbe asked them to look in a different district. Once again the *gabbaim* hurried to fulfill his urgent request. A few weeks later they were on the move again. Before the Belzer Rav finally left Budapest, he had stayed at three temporary lodgings around the Jewish area.

Nobody could fathom what it was all about. Why the urgency? Why those particular streets? Why keep moving? It was only after the Germans set up a puppet administration in March 1944 while concentrating all Hungarian Jews into six zones for deportation that it became a little clearer. Most Budapest Jews were herded into a ghetto run by the notorious Arrow Cross. Although many died from starvation and ill-treatment, the majority — nearly 100,000 —managed to survive until liberation by the Russians. By uncanny "coincidence" the buildings at the four corners of the Budapest ghetto housed the last four apartments of the Belzer Rav! (The ghetto was bordered by Dohany, Karoly, Kiraly — and Nagyatadi Szabo where previously the Rebbe customarily had his *tisch* in the community building.) Doubtless, the Rebbe's *zechus* had cushioned future inmates of the ghetto — long before anyone would have believed they would ever dare establish a ghetto in Budapest!

Characteristically, the Belzer Rav remained eternally grateful to anyone who assisted him in acquiring lodgings. The man who arranged his apartment in the community building came for a blessing just before the Rebbe departed Budapest, and was presented with protective coins for himself and family — all twelve children.[2]

But this was still in the future and for the present there remained a number of loose ends to tie up before they could leave Hungary. Understandably, the delay made chassidim abroad fairly nervous and Mr. Ortner had to bear the brunt of their frustration and even criticism, as we can see from his letter of 20 Cheshvan (November 18, 1943) to Jerusalem.

> *Thursday, Chayei Sarah 5704,*
> *To my dear friend R' Hillel Vind ner yair.*
> *I just wrote to my friend R' Elimelech this week and I have no more news. I can only wait for the moment I hear the news that the Rebbe has finally arrived in Istanbul! What people are saying I cannot tell — There is a time to be silent; a time to talk, it says in Mishlei — and there are those who talk incessantly but might as well as remain silent for all the information they provide. We can only trust in Hashem.*
>
> *I deliberately gave the photographs to Barlas earlier, and I told him (from the Alesko Rebbe in the name of the Sar Shalom, the Rebbe's great-grandfather) that if one needs salvation or similar one should conjure up the tzaddik's image and Hashem will surely help. Now that I required him to work for our Rebbe, I wanted him to have his picture in front of him! At the time, I was most glad to see how my words impressed him. Now I am delighted to hear that Barlas has shown the photographs to his Rav. He also sent me a letter in his own hand promising to do everything within his power and hopes to succeed this way. What will I not do for the sake of our Rebbe?*
>
> *As for those chassidim who are broigez with me; I think they still need to learn something! Baruch Hashem I learned Chassidus from my uncles R' Mechele Zolkover and R' Yaakov Berish and similar*

---

2. All of them survived the War intact and immigrated to Bnei Brak; whenever he attended the *tisch,* the Rebbe greeted him warmly as, *"Meine baal habayis"*!

great people, and with Hashem's help I remember what they taught me. May Hashem Yisbarach aid me to do only what's necessary. Incidentally when the Rebbe comes here with Hashem's help, he will be without a beard — just as he came to Hungary.

R' Yosef Feldman's sons didn't have much to tell me but I spoke to the wife of one of them. She's a daughter of Weinberg, a Belzer chassid, and she tells me that Yaakov is serving the Rebbe (instead of R' Nachman Hirsch Singer, deported from Krakow). The Rebbe tells him several times a day to say some kapitelech of Tehillim for our Polish brothers. On Motza'ei Shabbos during the kvittel-reading he told Yaakov to tell her that he is soon coming to Eretz Yisrael with Hashem's help.

R' David Shapira was a wealthy man but when he saw he was bereft of wife and children, he gave most of his riches to save the Rebbe. He wants to come here with the Rebbe. She claims the Rebbe's always happy and doesn't accept many kvittlech. There's always a big crowd just as in Belz.

I close with best wishes. But I am surprised why you didn't write me when Barlas left. Even though I'm sure he informed R' Y. Goldman I still hope he's traveled there as he promised.

Wishing the best for you all and hoping for a yeshuah as soon as possible.

B. Ortner

Mr. Chaim Barlas' rabbi (to whom he showed the photos) was the famous Rav Velvel Soloveitchik of Brisk, Mr. Barlas' hometown, who had escaped to Israel from Warsaw via Vilna in the early years of the War. Despite his reputation as a formidable *misnaged*, he greatly respected the Belzer Rebbe — "I'm not surprised he exists without food or sleep; he's a *Himmel-mentsch* who derives his sustenance from Heaven!" — and he ordered Barlas to make every effort to obtain certificates for him. Mr. Goldman was the trusted secretary of Chief Rabbi Yitzchak Isaac Herzog. Hardly had Mr. Ortner sent this letter off when he received a letter from the leading Jerusalem chassidim, replete with alternative suggestions.

To our dear friend, Rav Berish Ortner.

Last Shabbos was the Yahrzeit of Maran (Rav Yissachar Dov on Chayei Sarah, 22 Cheshvan, November 20) and we observed it with dignity and enthusiasm. Today I received a letter of 26 Tishrei from my father and he writes that the Rebbe very much wants to come to Eretz Yisrael.

He also sent him an esrog which grows in his area of Switzerland as there were no Italian esrogim available this year in Switzerland. Nonetheless, the Rebbe was very happy with it.

Surely you sent a telegram last Friday to London with all I told you on the telephone: that is, that the chassidim there should approach Chief Rabbi Hertz to inform him that the telegram from Chief Rabbi Herzog is about the Rebbe, his brother and escort. They should see to it that he contacts the government ministry there to hurry them up as urgently as possible.

To my mind, it's worthwhile sending a telegram to R' Babad who is close to Rabbi Hertz and he should speak to R' Chaim Nota who is respected by Dayan Abramsky, the Head of R' Hertz's Beis Din.

Also have to send a telegram to R' Shemayah Binder that they should contact the English Consulate in Berne who is kept informed by London. They should influence him that he should inform us what's going on with the certificates immediately, by telegram not post.

This is very important and should not be trivial in your eyes. Or to rely only on Barlas, as if without him nobody can help.

I also want to tell you that I saw by ... a telegram from Griffel. Therefore we think it's worthwhile sending Griffel a telegram with a paid reply asking him what's new about the Rebbe and if he has any information himself. Ask him what else we can do. Also we should ask him to handle it as he promised. Since you have all the addresses you can arrange all this.

As you know he is now in Turkey and that's when Griffel's help is also urgent. We have seen how much he has already done for people. Those who have arrived in the last few weeks were being handled by him. Last Friday too another transport arrived ... Please keep us informed on everything you are doing, whether we meet Barlas in Tel Aviv or receive a letter, we must never forget that every minute counts.

With friendly wishes,
Elimelech Ashkenazi

R' Elimelech Ashkenazi was a prominent leader of the Belzer community in Jerusalem and had been intimately involved in the early rescue effort, before Mr. Ortner dedicated himself and his typewriter wholly to the cause. His father, R' Alexander Chaim Ashkenazi of Lugano, was among those to mail *esrogim* to Budapest on erev Yom Tov. Dr. Yaakov Griffel, the legendary rescue activist, was nominally on Istanbul's Vaad Hatzalah on behalf of Agudas Israel but acted rather as a freelance with his wages paid by the Feldman

Dr. Yaakov Griffel

family. Many religious families owe their lives to his wheedling vital certificates for them. He and Chaim Barlas did not see to eye but he spent day and night on the rescue effort, often dragging his cot into the *Sochnut* offices to intercept the overnight cables.[3] Obviously, Mr. Ortner preferred to place his reliance on Mr. Barlas, who was higher up the *Sochnut* hierarchy and had made him specific promises. Then on the 18th of Kislev (December 8, 1943), he received the following cable from London:

> ORTNER NACHALAT BINYAMIN TEL AVIV INQUIRE WHAT DIFFICULTIES CONFRONT RABBIS TRANSIT AND WHAT WE CAN DO HERE AGENCY SAY EVERYTHING CONFIRMED HERE CABLE REPLY BABAD

Once again R' Berish girded his loins and sat himself at his faithful typewriter to prompt the *Sochnut* into greater urgency. The following correspondence ensued:

---

3. Despite the friction between them, Barlas recognized Griffel's value in representing religious refugees; and on the final *Sochnut* list, the Belz entourage are penciled in as under Griffel's responsibility. When Hungarian leaders later criticized his prioritizing the Belzer Rebbe and other Orthodox Jews in that transport, leaving genuine Zionists stranded in Hungary after the Orient Express ceased operating via Bulgaria, Barlas replied — according to *Sochnut* archives — that he was committed to rescuing all Jews impartially, but Griffel's documentation for religious applicants was so efficient and impeccable, they were invariably processed first when time or other technicalities were pressing. After the War, Griffel took a crucial role with the Sternbuchs in assisting refugees in crossing borders, re-establishing communities and institutions, and extricating orphaned children from their Christian "guardians."

The Jewish Agency for Eretz Israel
Mr. Moshe Shapira
Aliya Department
Jerusalem P O B 92
18 Kislev 5704
December 15, 1943
Your ref: 1607/Z
Regarding the Belzer Rebbe & Escort
Dear Mr. Shapira,

Today I received this telegram from London where they ask the reason for the delay in the Belzer Rebbe's arrival. A copy of the telegram is herein enclosed.

I must entreat Your Honor to ask Mr. Barlas by telegram if transit has already been arranged. Also to instruct him to hasten via every avenue the arrival of the Rebbe and his companions to Eretz Yisrael so as not to miss the chance of getting here chas veshalom.

I await your immediate reply. Thanking you in anticipation.
With great respect,
Dov Berish Ortner

⊱⊰

Mr. Dov Berish Ortner
111 Nachalat Binyamin
Tel Aviv
December 19, 1943
22 Kislev 5704
Our ref: Aliya Dept. 1607/Z
Regarding: Belz Rebbe (Aron Twersky) & Escort
Dear Mr. Ortner,

Further to your letter of 15th this month, I would like to inform you that today we telegraphed our representative in Istanbul and asked him to do everything possible regarding the above. Also to inform us of what action has been taken.

With great respect,
M. Shapira
Secretariat, Aliya Department
The Jewish Agency for Eretz Israel
Jerusalem

Earlier, Mr. Ortner had asked to be cabled the estimated date of the Belzer Rav's arrival but though the reply was sent out a fortnight later, it took almost a month to arrive, on 10 Teves (January 6, 1944).

BERISH ORTNER NACHALAT BINYAMIN 111 TEL AVIV YOUR TELEGRAM OF 8/12 RECEIVED WILL INFORM JEWISH AGENCY AFTER RABBI TWERSKY ARRIVES JOSEPH GOLDIN ISTANBUL

The Jewish Agency for Eretz Israel
Mr. Moshe Shapira
Aliya Department
Jerusalem P O B 92
11th Teves 5704
7th Jan. '44
Your ref: 1607/Z
Regarding the Belzer Rebbe & Escort
Dear Mr. Shapira,
  Today I received a telegram from Istanbul with this message: "I will inform the Jewish Agency after Rabbi Twersky arrives. Joseph Goldin."
  Since I intend to journey to Beirut (Lebanon) to meet His Honor, the Belzer Rebbe, shlita, I would very much like to ask you a great favor. Could you please give instructions that I be urgently telephoned (Tel Aviv 2081) as soon as the Jewish Agency hears from Mr. Barlas of the Rebbe's arrival in Istanbul? I will gladly recompense any costs.
  Thanking you in anticipation. Best wishes,
  Berish Ortner

If R' Berish thought that was the end of the matter, he was quite mistaken. His success in influencing top ranking *Sochnut* officials or obtaining virtually unattainable certificates had been duly noted and *hatzalah* activists (including Rabbi Dr. Tuviah Lewenstein, Agudist and Rescue hero of Zurich) were anxious to utilize his excellent contacts as well as the name of the Belzer Rav. On 15 Teves (January 11, 1944) began a new series of cables.

> BERISH ORTNER TEL AVIV THE REBBE URGENTLY
> REQUESTS SEVEN MORE CERTIFICATES AND
> TELEGRAPHED YOU DETAILS PLEASE HELP AND
> TELEGRAPH WHAT CAN BE DONE ELIMELECH RUMPLER
> LONDON

On the same day, the Telegraphic Agency Censor, 132 Allenby Street, Tel Aviv, sent him a message notifying him that, "Any replies to telegram No. 7/Z of January 11, 1944 from Gross can only be sent via the International Red Cross if the recipient is in enemy territory." Later that day, two cables were delivered.

> BERISH ORTNER TEL AVIV 111 NACHALAT BINYAMIN
> YOUR LETTER TO BINDER RECEIVED HAVE SENT
> YOU NAMES FOR SEVEN CERTIFICATES FOR REBBE'S
> ESCORT WHICH RABBI LEWENSTEIN TELEGRAPHED
> RABBI HERZOG JOSEPH SALGO MOSES GRUNWALD
> ALEXANDER SALGO JACOB HERZOG EUGENE HERZOG
> RAPHAEL COHEN SHALOM PORGAS ALL WITH
> FAMILIES WE ARE SENDING GRIFFEL EXACT DETAILS
> ARRANGE IMMEDIATELY AND TELEGRAPH REBBE
> AND BROTHER LEAVING SOON GROSS GENEVA

> BERISH ORTNER 111 NACHALAT BINYAMIN TEL AVIV
> PLEASE CONFIRM 800 PALESTINIAN LIRA FOR REBBE
> VIA CHIEF RABBI HERZOG MORE FUNDS FOLLOWING
> RETTER LONDON

Marcus Retter was the honorary secretary of Dr. Schonfeld, the legendary English rescue activist but although R' Berish was willing to use his good offices, he was primarily anxious there should be no more delays and replied as such to both London (on 16 Teves) and Geneva (on 18 Teves) via the Red Cross. Although he personally handed a detailed letter three days later directly to Mr. Moshe Shapira at the *Sochnut*, he maintained a certain distance so as not to jeopardize the main objective:

ELIMELECH RUMPLER LONDON TRIED TO OBTAIN SEVEN CERTIFICATES GROSS SHOULD TELEGRAPH ME DETAILS PLEASE DEMAND REBBE AND BROTHER TRAVEL WITHOUT DELAY WILL BE AT RAV HERZOG BERISH ORTNER

GROSS GENEVA WE DEMAND IMMEDIATE TRAVEL REBBE AND BROTHER TAKING STEPS FOR SEVEN CERTIFICATES REQUESTED TELEGRAPH DETAILS BERISH ORTNER

The Jewish Agency for Eretz Israel
Aliya Department
Jerusalem P O B 92
21 Teves 5704
January 17, 1944
Your ref: 1607/Z
Regarding the Belzer Rebbe
Dear Sir,
I received a telegram from Switzerland informing me that Rabbi Dr. Lewenstein of Switzerland sent a telegram to Chief Rabbi Herzog shlita asking him to authorize seven certificates for: (1) Moses Grunwald (2) Joseph Salgo (3) Alexander Salgo (4) Jacob Herzog (5) Eugene Herzog (6) Raphael Cohen (7) Shalom Porgas from Budapest with their families.
Similarly, I received a telegram from London that the Belzer Rebbe shlita also requests that the immigration of these seven should be granted.
I enclose herein copies of the two telegrams and I ask the honorable Jewish Agency to certify their request.
Awaiting your reply,
With due respect,
Dov Berish Ortner

As he had previously intimated, Mr. Ortner was anxious to meet the Belzer Rav in person on his arrival in the Middle East and escort him into Eretz Yisrael. Yet that too was no easy matter. Lebanon, captured by the Free French (with British help) in 1941 and nominally an independent state, was still within the French empire. While the sympathies of most Frenchmen (though not their Arab subjects) lay with the British, France itself had not yet been liberated from German occupation. So the diplomatic status remained complicated, and obtaining an entry visa to the French colonies from British-governed Palestine was difficult. Furthermore, Mr. Ortner could not even provide a definite date for his entry into — or departure from — Lebanon since it depended on the Rebbe's travel arrangements which were not yet finalized.

Once again the Chief Rabbi, Rav Yitzchak Isaac Herzog, proved invaluable in cutting through international red tape. Eventually, the Lud police authorities and the French Consulate issued month-long exit permits and entry visas "for dates unspecified, depending on his receiving telegrams from Istanbul confirming Rabbi Twersky's travel to Palestine!" and cabled the same to Beirut. After that all Mr. Ortner could do was wait — patiently or impatiently — for news from Turkey or Hungary.

CHAPTER 23

TEARFUL DEPARTURE

BEFORE THEY LEFT HUNGARY, THEY HAD TO ATTEND to several urgent matters. One obstacle was the imprisonment of several activists for their involvement in smuggling Jews from Nazi occupation into Hungary. "I cannot leave here until they're released!" declared the Rebbe. "Some of them even had a hand in my escape — how can we abandon them to an awful fate?" But when Belz devotees tried to make contact, they found the authorities had treated this case with the utmost severity; instead of sympathizing with those rescuing their brethren from horrendous oppression, they condemned them out of hand for corruption, conspiracy, deception and forgery. Not only had the state security officials piled the charges up against them, now it was learned that these activists had been transferred to a notorious jail — from where, it was whispered, no prisoner ever left alive! Yet the Belzer Rav remained just as determined not to depart Hungary until they were free. The Bilgoraj Rav and other close chassidim were at their wit's end.

Finally the Belzer Rav advised them to seek the support of well-placed Hungarian Jews like Meir Heinrich. Mr. Heinrich had grown up in the townlet of Stoelweisenbourg where his father was rabbi and, after his arrival in Budapest, maintained excellent links with the Hungarian aristocracy and the ruling elite. One day, he was surprised to find an Orthodox Jew knocking anxiously on his door, saying: "The Belzer Rebbe would like to see you!"

Like most Hungarian Jews in the capital, Mr. Heinrich was neither a Belzer chassid nor indeed a chassid of any "Wonder Rabbi," but he had at least heard of the Rebbe of Belz and unhesitatingly accompanied the troubled gentleman back to the Rebbe's apartment. He was met by the Bilgoraj Rav who described the acute danger facing the Rebbe, who flatly refused to escape as long as those activists were not released. Mr. Heinrich understood their predicament and showed them every sympathy but insisted there was no way he could possibly help — whom did he know with any pull in that notorious prison? Just then another door opened and the Belzer Rav stepped into the reception room. Rebbe Mottele stood up to introduce him: "This is Reb Meir Heinrich who came to talk about those Jews in prison."

"*Azoi*? You are Meir Heinrich? I would like to appoint you my personal representative; on my behalf you should free those unfortunate Jews, victims of injustice. May you go with *mazel* and *hatzlachah*!" Long after the Rebbe returned to his room, his purposeful words hung in the air while the hitherto sophisticated and cosmopolitan Mr. Heinrich just sat there wondering how this Wonder Rabbi had placed him right at the center of this awkward situation, just as he was about to deftly extricate himself. In what way could he be his envoy? Just what did the Wonder Rabbbi mean? Abruptly he stood up and, after stammering some hasty farewell, stumbled out in a daze.

He had to clear his head. Only 1,000 meters southwest of the Jewish Quarter the mighty River Danube (Duna in Hungarian) snakes through Budapest and divides Pest from Buda, and Mr. Heinrich pensively gravitated to the large Belgrad *rakpart* (rampart) along the eastern bank. Lost in thought, he absent-mindedly crossed one of the five bridges that led to Buda — and collided with a well-built gentleman about his own age. He looked up with a start and his heart sank; with rising anti-Semitism, now was not the time to bump into top ranking generals, decorated with rows of medals. He was about to stammer some abject apology when the general grabbed him in a bear-hug. "Heinrich! Is it really you? My old pal!

Where on earth did you spring from? Don't stare at me like you've never seen me before — we grew up in Stoelweisenbourg and cut classes at school together!"

Thankfully he released his grip and Heinrich could finally catch his breath. "Am I glad to have bumped into you, ha-ha!" continued the general, unabashed. "I'm throwing an exquisite party tonight — I've been released from the Eastern Front and have been appointed governor of this monumental prison downriver! Say you're coming to my party as one of my best old friends; we'll have a good laugh, remembering old times!" After the general gave him the address and marched off across the bridge, Mr. Heinrich stood looking at his retreating back in amazement. What a coincidence, to meet up with an old acquaintance who had just taken control of the very prison holding those unfortunate Jews. This was one party he could not afford to miss.

Despite war rationing, the best wine and slivowitz flowed like water. For all his sophistication, when it came to drinking Meir Heinrich was no match for the general or his military comrades and though he kept to liqueurs, soon felt the affect. Fortunately, the general took it in good spirit and told his butler to find Mr. Heinrich a bed. He woke up the next morning in a strange bed with an awful hangover, but the general greeted him cheerfully enough and they were soon blissfully reminiscing about their school years and juvenile pranks.

Finally Meir seized the opportunity and began his pitch. "I can't believe that meeting after so many years was any coincidence! For the sake of our childhood friendship, I need a really big favor: In the prison under your charge are some Jews — they're innocent of serious charges and we must get them out, no questions asked!" At first the general would not hear of it; it was more than his job was worth. But after much begging and reasoning, the two of them hatched an ingenious plan together. Aided by some hefty bribes, these prisoners were surreptitiously exchanged with several inmates from a local lunatic asylum![1]

---

1. Mr. Heinrich visited the Belzer Rav the day before he left Budapest; the Rebbe thanked him profusely while Rebbe Mottele penned a special letter of gratitude. Meir Heinrich survived the Nazi invasion and eventually migrated to New York where he lived to a ripe old age; he cherished the thank you letter till the end, keeping it with him in a special wallet.

There remained another major priority before the Rebbe left — to somehow alert Hungarian Jewry to the real dimensions of the Nazi menace around them, both for their own future safety and on behalf of the countless fugitives. So the Belzer and the Bilgoraj Rebbes stepped up their efforts to awaken Hungarian Jewry to the vast valley of death and torment on their immediate borders and to encourage them to take a more active role in *hatzalah*. The Bilgoraj Rav personally raised substantial funds for those trapped in Poland — or hiding in Hungary without authorization, often masquerading as Aryans.

In early January 1944 (*Parashas Shemos*, 5704), the Belzer Rav urgently summoned wealthy Budapest Jews to the home of the renowned activist R' Chaim Roth, who headed Budapest's *chevrah kaddisha* and hosted almost every visiting Rav or Rebbe. The Rebbe opened the evening meeting with words of Torah; he then spoke about the urgency of extricating their oppressed brethren from Nazi-occupied lands and repeated his ruling that the normal limits on what may be spent on charity do not apply in this extreme case of *pidyon shevuyim* and *pikuach nefesh*; nor does the Talmudic restriction against ransoming captives above their nominal value apply to Nazi victims.

"From the Romans to the Middle Ages," the Rebbe said, "slaves were treated with some minimal respect; captives then had some value and most would survive, albeit amid acute hunger and deprivation. But not now, under the accursed Germans! All their victims confront atrocious danger at any moment. So *Klal Yisrael* is faced with a sweeping, overarching calamity.

"If necessary, we must give away all our possessions to save families and individuals — just as we would to save ourselves! Even then, we would still not be entirely fulfilling our obligations. We must also enlist our minds, our money, and our energy to save what can be saved from complete destruction — with *mesiras nefesh*! Hurry to their cause and raise a large army in defense of our people. In this *zechus* may you be spared from every affliction and evil decree," the Rebbe concluded.

For fear that any of those present did not fully comprehend the Rebbe's words or the gravity of the situation, the Bilgoraj Rav elaborated on his brother's speech in graphic detail, recounting the ongoing barbarity and mass murder. "Many Jews pay to be concealed in non-Jewish homes, but when their money runs out, they are callously thrown out into the street where they are soon picked up by Nazis. Others are still hiding out in the Polish forests, braving constant hunger and icy cold, always fearing raids from the Germans and their collaborators. With a fresh injection of money these Jews can be saved and smuggled into Hungary."

Three men were chosen from among those present at the meeting to form an ad-hoc committee. After they seated themselves in an adjacent room with the Rebbe, each participant was summoned separately to avow his individual donation in complete confidentiality. The large sum raised that evening was delivered, then and there, into the hands of experienced rescue activists working on behalf of Polish Jewry.

A week after this meeting the two brothers were guests of honor at a poignant affair. Now that the leaders of the Hungarian community clearly saw that the Belzer Rav was determined to leave despite their protests, they decided to host a farewell evening for them very shortly before their scheduled departure. The occasion was a *siyum* to commemorate the completion of *Masechta Succah* by the small Tiferes Bachurim Yeshivah under Rav Yonason Steif's guidance. The Tiferes Bachurim Yeshivah was situated on the top floor of the Budapest communal building (above the school) and catered to local boys unable to attend larger yeshivos outside Budapest. So the community combined both *seudos* and arranged an impressive gathering in the large hall downstairs, where the Rebbe had previously conducted his *tisch*.

Thousands attended and the top table was graced by leading rabbanim and prominent personalities. It made an unforgettable impression — particularly the Bilgoraj Rav's lengthy and thought-provoking *derashah* — and Hungarian Jews were still talking about it long afterwards. The wide-ranging speech covered an inordinate amount of ground, from a Torah discourse on *Masechta Succah* and the *Sedra*, halachah and Midrash, to trenchant comments on the world situation.

Describing the current catastrophe as the birth pangs of the Messiah — *Chevlei Mashiach* — Rebbe Mottele dismissed those "weak in *emunah*" who asked why it had not been predicted. Or why Torah leaders had not prepared plans for the emergency and saved whole communities? "Just as we cannot accept the manifest signs and wonders of false prophets to lose faith in the Word of Hashem, so must we surmount this difficult test too, with our *bitachon* intact. Criticizing *tzaddikim* was a typical tactic of the antireligious through the ages; besides, no one knows what the End of Days entails."

Hungarian Jewry deserved high praise for its strong Orthodoxy with meticulous adherence to mitzvos and Torah, behind the bulwarks founded in previous generations. Yet as an outsider, he could discern various weaknesses creeping in. "*Hischazku! Hischazku!*" he declared. "Strengthen your resolve and observance of tradition in the manner taught by the great Hungarian *gedolim* of yesteryear. Also, these precious *bachurim* should continue their learning program even on their return home, and continue to wear the traditional Jewish garments without following alien fashions."

Rebbe Mottele continued, "It is a tradition to take one's leave by quoting halachah, a difficult task in these trying times. Yet the question on everyone's lips is how to behave in our terrible circumstances? Every day brings further decrees, blow upon crippling blow rain down on our bleeding body. What should we do now? For the individual? For the community? What is possible? Perhaps we should join the political parties? All wait to hear the unequivocal halachah from the *gedolim*. Well, last week, we held a meeting at the home of Reb Chaim Roth and we clearly heard my holy brother Rebbe Aharon of Belz declare in fiery language why we must spend everything we've got to save the survivors.

"The previous halachic restrictions do not apply now that 'civilization' has reared its ugly head. Even in the dark ages, captives could survive with difficulty and it did not take more than their nominal value to ransom them. But since this evil civilization based on violence and threats thrives without conscience or humanity, our lives have been eclipsed by suffering and slavery. All the ground rules of justice and mercy to civilians and strangers have been swept

A pamphlet of the Bilgoraj Rav's final derashah before leaving Budapest

Chapter 23: Tearful Departure / 379

away. In the name of this false civilization, millions have been obliterated amid hatred and venom.

"Our pain is beyond endurance," cried Rebbe Mottele. "If we were only sold for slavery we might have held our silence, but we are treated as sheep to be slaughtered, beaten and humiliated in the grasp of every sadist and merciless mercenary. These wicked Amalekites plan to wipe out every Jew, male or female, old or young, so there is no greater mitzvah than to save Jewish lives with all the money available in the world — particularly as those under threat include thousands of *talmidei chachamim*, rabbanim and rebbes. We have seen it all with our own eyes! Thousands of Jews murdered with unbelievable savagery; the blood of brothers, sisters, fathers and children, *tzaddikim* and chassidim, runs together in a stream. We personally witnessed them grabbing tender young children and burning them with gas and fire! *Keil Nekamos* should avenge their spilled blood before our eyes."

At this point, the entire assembly burst out weeping as Rebbe Mottele continued. "Over this our hearts grieve, our eyes lament over the slain of our people, millions of pure souls — from babes and infants to elderly and venerable — butchered *al Kiddush Hashem*. There hardly exists a piece of Polish earth not drenched in Jewish blood. Many thousands more succumbed to famine; the irreplaceable loss is beyond restitution. Has such a catastrophe ever occurred before? To any other nation? Why? To what purpose? For how long? My heart burns within me on contemplating the cataclysmic tragedy. Pathetically, there survives not even one from a city, or two from a family! Just a pitiful few remnants hiding in the forests or mountains. Their world has been eclipsed, their primitive existence is scarcely life, amid fear and confusion, hunger and thirst."

The Bilgoraj Rav took a breath. "Certainly we must strain every muscle to save their lives and redeem them from hunger, rescue them from the sword in that kingdom of *Gei-Hinnom*. Beyond donating all our resources, it is our holy duty to assist the minority who survived the dangerous journey here. They are starving for bread but nobody feeds them; desperate for clothing yet no one clothes them; searching for accommodation but everyone turns them away — instead of welcoming them with warmth and encouraging them with sympathy. If necessary, you should go knocking on doors to awaken the rich and powerful to the refugees' plight; they are hungry and naked, friendless and forlorn.

"Where are my brothers to strive for those who have been through fire and water in Hashem's Honor?" He shouted. "Come! Do! Join! How? With heart and soul! Who? Everyone who steps forward! For whom? For every fugitive without question or preparation — and don't ask unfounded questions while the urgency prevails! Save souls, rescue families, work for their welfare without exception or distraction. Every second counts — how many have already perished from delay? Revive parched spirits in an arid wasteland. Awake from your slumber and abandon the mundane pursuit of riches; what value money when blood is being splattered at every crossroad! Do your duty flawlessly, support above your means — even if it means collecting — to assist these unfortunates."

The Bilgoraj Rebbe scanned the crowd and said, "So far Hungary has been spared the worst; however, as with the *eglah arufah* of old, the dead lie at your borders. But for the grace of Hashem, a similar fate threatens the Jews here! As the country closest to the murder it owes a debt of gratitude to Hashem and similarly ought to offer a sacrifice. In sheer appreciation you ought to donate overwhelmingly to the cause. With Hashem's help you have been safe until now; with Hashem's help you should be safe in the future. When my holy brother *shlita* laid down the *p'sak* that we have a duty to donate more than a fifth, to donate everything — he added that this is not some chassidus, nor to merely assuage pangs of conscience by going beyond the strict *din*. Instead this is the plain, unvarnished halachah! I repeat and reemphasize this *p'sak*: Remember it always and observe it in practice!"

Mindful of the Hungarian leaders' overriding desire to prevent panic, the Bilgoraj Rav encouraged the troubled audience, saying that they might yet escape the Nazi threat, and told them that the Rebbe's insistence on leaving was primarily based on personal reasons. "Many are scared for the future fearing the *tzaddik* seeks to escape because he sees dangers looming for Hungary — who will protect or save us? What will be our end? Therefore I must tell you what anyone close to my great brother already knows: he is not fleeing in terror. Back in Belz before the War, he had often expressed his wish to live in Eretz Yisrael. Despite the inevitable difficulties and *yissurim* that living there entails, the unquenchable love for the Holy Land still burns bright in his heart. He is drawn by its spiritual significance and not for any material benefit — otherwise, why not America or anywhere else overseas? Only in Eretz Yisrael can halachah be most clearly expounded, the *tzaddik's* prayers answered, and his wishes achieved."

Finally, the Bilgoraj Rav thanked the Hungarian community — and Budapest in particular — for their bountiful welcome, generous support and warm hospitality. He was grateful that despite their personal misgivings and objections, they were not blocking the Rebbe's departure. He ended with the fervent wish, "May you be blessed with children, life, sustenance and every success. Hashem — 'Who is above all comfort' — should swiftly perform something no mere mortal can possibly do: comfort us for the terrible losses; heal our gaping wounds; transform our mourning to happiness, from darkness to light, from distress to relief, from slavery to freedom. Rapidly, rapidly, in our own days may we witness every predicted salvation and condolence — *Zeits gezunt!"*

His force majeure of a speech delivered with a fiery passion was a sensation at the time and left an indelible impression on Hungarian Jewry long after the two brothers had departed. Their departure had been secretly scheduled for Monday, 21 Teves 5704 (January 17, 1944), and huge crowds flooded into Budapest to see the Belzer Rav and wish them *L'chaim U'l'shalom* before it was too late. "Perhaps," many thought fearfully to themselves, "we might *chas veshalom* never see the Holy Rebbe again!" Since Shabbos *Parashas Shemos* was to be the Rebbe's last weekend in Hungary, hundreds of chassidim streamed in from the provinces. Nearly every Belzer chassid in Hungary was there, plus a substantial section of Hungarian Orthodoxy.

The Rebbe could not exclude them from the *tefillos* or conduct a small, private *tisch* in his own apartment — as had been customary since the Gestapo lodged their extradition demand — yet that was vital if he was to maintain a low profile and keep his departure secret. Before reaching the relative safety of neutral Turkey, the trains of the Orient Express journeyed across territory either occupied by or friendly to Germany, and they had to pass through several checkpoints. Once Gestapo agents discovered the Rebbe's destination and date of embarkation, they would not have the slightest hesitation or difficulty in pouncing on the Belz entourage and dragging them back to Poland! Yet how could they disappoint all these loyal Belz supporters?

Bravely, they decided to conduct public *tefillos* and *tisch* at a larger venue for the last time. Instead of using the existing premises, they took over the communal Hannah Hall, then catering as a wartime soup kitchen, with a capacity exceeding 500 at any one time. No one who was there on that memorable Shabbos would ever forget the extraordinary experience or atmosphere. The Rebbe betrayed not the slightest tremor of fear at the ever present possibility of a last-minute denouncement to the Germans, even though the more visible his presence in Hungary, the more precarious his position in the eyes of government and official circles.

Worse, the date and method of his departure had unfortunately yet perhaps inevitably become one of the worst kept secrets among his chassidim in Budapest. Despite every effort, the sensitive news had spread. Every day, the Jewish Agency's Emigration Department in Vadasz Street, Budapest, was inundated with hundreds of phone calls from different chassidim with various queries: "Does one have to book tickets on the Orient Express the day before? Or can I buy tickets on the day?" "Will we be allowed to accompany the Belzer Rebbe all the way up to the Romanian border?" "Are the police likely to conduct one of their periodic swoops at the railroad depot searching for illegal aliens on the day the Rebbe's due to leave?" and many other similar inquiries. Obviously, it was an open secret and the chassidim intended to give him a grand send-off. But that could be catastrophic — and not just because the secret was out.

Previous Jewish transports to Palestine escorted to the train by large groups of relatives and well-wishers had already raised the hackles of anti-Semites and Nazis. The Orient Express from Paris usually arrived at 2:30 p.m. and 15 minutes later the Vienna express, generally carrying top-ranking German officers and officials, would draw in alongside at the adjacent platform. Whenever they disembarked and saw the platform crowded with Jews, they would sing the bloodthirsty *Horst Wessel Lied* and raucously chant anti-Semitic slogans to mar the celebrations. Those Nazis would surely notice if this crowd was much larger than normal, and they would soon realize that a popular and prominent Jewish personality was exiting Budapest. It would be fairly simple for them to discover the identity of the "Wonder Rabbi" and then the Rebbe would be in dire peril.

Even if he succeeded in leaving on the train, they could easily pick him up at the last checkpoint — Svilengrad, on the Turkish border. This was under German military control, which had troops stationed in the vicinity, and was the last but strictest border crossing of the whole journey. They would not think twice about removing passengers "for questioning," killing them on the spot or dispatching them on one of their death trains from Salonika or Athens, *chalilah*.

In a vain effort to minimize the danger, the Budapest communal leader, Mr. M. Kraus, met again with his old police contact, Commander Dr. Ferdinand (Nandor) Batizfalvy, to draw up contingency plans. They felt they had no choice but to restrict access by chassidim and the wider public to the barest minimum, and the Rebbe appeared to reluctantly agree to their arrangements. To further baffle pursuit and keep the masses at a safe distance, it was decided that the Belzer Rav should bid his public farewells a day early and relocate from his apartment to a secret address.

However, by Sunday, several thousand more well-wishers from the provinces arrived — in addition to those who were already there for Shabbos or lived in Budapest — and clamored to see the Rebbe. The large courtyard of his apartment was overflowing with visitors and the street outside was crammed with men, women and children. It had been intended that everyone should file past the Rebbe for a *berachah*, but this was impossible to manage with such a crowd; the door to his apartment had to be bolted tightly shut since early morning. Exceptions were made only for prominent personalities who were allowed to enter and present a *kvittel*, and even they had to breach one of Belz's hallowed *hakpodas* and climb in through the window!

If it was impossible to open the front door, how was the Belzer Rav himself to leave? They had no choice but to summon help from the police to clear a way through. By 2:30 p.m. the Rebbe was ready to move to his secret address. This was preceded by an announcement: "The Rebbe requests that no person go to the address where he is now going. Since there is such a large *olam*, the Rebbe will *bazegen zich* and bless everyone in general." As the Belzer Rav stepped onto the veranda outside his apartment, the huge waiting crowd fell silent — even those who had perched for hours on walls and flat roofs — and strained to hear the Rebbe's words. As was his custom when blessing a public gathering, he spread his hands as he proclaimed, "*Zeit mir gezunt, bliebst alle gezunt!* You should all be helped with all types of *yeshuas*! And have everything that's good!" After a tremendous *Amen* swept and reverberated across the square, the sounds of muted weeping could be clearly heard; not a few sensed that the Rebbe's *berachah* signified that ominous threats lurked just over their horizon.

Despite strenuous efforts by the chassidim and the police it was only with great difficulty that the Rebbe managed to pass through the crowd and descend the stairs. But once he reached the street, the way to his waiting car was clear because the police had earlier forced everybody back and kept them at a safe distance while blocking the road to traffic. Once in the car, they made the short journey to the "secret address," none other than the residence of his loyal chassid, R' Yosef Salgo.

In compliance with the Rebbe's instructions, few people dared disturb his retreat, but a *seudas pereidah* (farewell meal) had been prepared for select communal leaders. The Belzer Rav was in an uncommonly good mood despite the looming dangers. He summoned his *shammas* R' David Shapira and asked him to invite his most intimate chassidim to this *seudah* since it would be nothing less than a private *tisch*. Worried that this might tire the Rebbe on the eve of a most exhausting journey, R' David tried to bring the *seudah* forward to the early evening but the Belzer Rav would not hear of it.

Indeed, this *tisch* lasted for approximately six hours, almost till daybreak, and the Rebbe enjoyed no sleep that night. Instead, he sought to strengthen his followers in *emunah* and *bitachon*, speaking of the perpetual battle with Amalek who seeks to corrupt *Klal Yisrael*, body and soul. He described how "we must fortify the defenses against the eternal enemy and prepare to sacrifice our lives *al Kiddush Hashem!*" Slowly, he distributed the customary *sherayim* to all present in a calm and collected manner, as if he were safe in Belz and not about to embark on a fateful journey.

At this late stage, the Bilgoraj Rav composed a flowery and effusive letter in the name of the Rebbe and countersigned by leading Polish émigrés (including the Bobover Rebbe). Addressed to the legendary communal leaders, Mr. Philip Freudiger and Mr. Y. A. Stern, it thanked them profusely on behalf of the pitifully few Polish refugees for their superhuman efforts to alleviate the refugees' plight. "Surmounting all obstacles, ignoring every danger, to sustain with warmth and self-sacrifice those weak of strength and bereft of help. To this day they stand ready to protect their unfortunate brethren with all their strength and powers ..."

As morning dawned, the Rebbe prepared to *daven,* but he first summoned a close chassid, R' Chaim Shloma Friedman. Obviously, almost all those immigrating to Palestine on *Sochnut* documents had Jewish identities and would naturally possess cultural and ethnic paraphernalia, but the Jewish Agency Emigration Department in Budapest thought otherwise. Because of previous brushes with Gestapo customs controls, they warned all immigrants traveling on the Orient Express that to avoid close Nazi scrutiny, they must leave behind all religious objects and conceal any distinctive Jewish appearance by not wearing typical Orthodox clothing and removing their *peyos* and beards — advice particularly relevant in the Belzer Rav's precarious position. For this last task R' Chaim Shloma would be ideal, since he was now clean-shaven, and had adopted an Aryan identity after fleeing to Hungary. Although busy packing up the Rebbe's belongings, he came straight away but had to wait from 9 a.m. until after 1 p.m. while the Belzer Rav completed his lengthy prayers and devotions. Only then was he summoned to the inner chamber.

Besides the *gabbaim* a few bystanders were also present, but time was pressing — the Orient Express was due to depart at

2:30 p.m. — so R' Chaim Shloma apprehensively stepped forward. Obviously, cutting off his revered Rebbe's beard was no easy task, but this was not the first time it was done. Sadly, the Belzer Rav had already had his beard shaven before: on fleeing Bochnia eight months previously and on the earlier flight from Premyzslany during Chanukah 5702. And on the most recent occasion in Bochnia, R' Chaim Shloma had likewise been chosen to carry out the deed. Then he had been extremely nervous and the Belzer Rav, who had accepted the violation of his deeply-held principles with calm resignation, had encouraged him in his task. Not so on this occasion.

As soon as the electric shaver touched his holy beard, the Rebbe roared angrily. *"Vos veht zein mein tachlis; vos veht zein mein sof? Oy Vei! Oy Vei! Ich hob mech nisht gerechent az ich vill mich nach broichen absheren die bord! Ich hob gemeint az doh iz shoin dos letzter galus und ich vell nisht darfen gehen veiter in galus arein. Oy! Oy Vei!* ... What's to be the end? Woe to me! I didn't expect I'd need cut my beard again. I thought this was to be my last exile! Woe to me!" These and similar sentiments were repeated over and over again in a furious monologue while everybody in the room fearfully retreated up against the far wall; those in the outer chamber were similarly shaken by the uncustomary shouting. Even after his beard and long sidelocks were removed, the Rebbe seethed with anguish, especially when he again had to exchange his traditional attire for modern clothing — or, as he branded them, *"Deutsche klieder!"*

As this traumatic episode drew to a close, the Belzer Rav ordered that all his hair-shavings be collected together and buried in a safe place. Strangely, he stipulated that none of those present — not even his loyal *gabbaim!* — may shake hands and wish him, *"L'chaim U'l'shalom"* except for R' Chaim Shloma, though he presented his *gabbaim* with coins as *"letz-gelt"* and also gave R' Chaim Shloma a two-pengo piece as a *"shemirah."* As he handed a coin to his *shammas* R' Shmuel Porgas, he implicitly warned him of the ominous future: *"Der rashah* is not human — he's a *meshugene hunt!* He has betrayed us to all seventy nations in the this world and to their seventy celestial masters in the world above! From him one must flee, but if one flees then *Der Eibeshter* helps!"[2]

As soon as the Rebbe was suitably dressed in his "*galus-clothes*," two high-ranking plain-clothes detectives entered the room. They had been designated by KEOKH police headquarters to escort him safely out of the country, at least to the Romanian border. Although his chassidim and well-wishers had respected his instructions not to invade his secret sanctuary, by now a substantial crowd had gathered outside Mr. Salgo's house and a path had to be forced through to the waiting taxi. Several private cars and hired taxis were parked nearby with the intention of accompanying the Rebbe to the railroad depot, but as his taxi sped away it was enveloped by a strange unworldly mist similar to that which had covered them on their flight across Poland! Whether the Belzer Rav — or Heaven — believed this journey was just as dangerous no mere mortal of our generation can possibly know, but it certainly made any pursuit doubly difficult. However, most chassidim already knew the taxi's destination but they came up against a more concrete obstacle in the burly form of Budapest's constabulary.

Since 1 p.m. Monday, January 17, 1944, all access to Keleti Palyaudvar (the Eastern Railroad Depot) had been strictly barred by one hundred police officers! It all began when the helpful communal leader, Mr. M. Kraus, had voiced his misgivings to the police commander, Dr. Ferdinand Batizfalvy: Surely a large, excitable crowd on the Orient Express platform must inevitably attract the unwelcome attention of top-ranking German officers and officials disembarking from the Vienna express alongside. There might be mob violence or worse — and what might happen to the Belzer Rav then? Or later, when he

---

2. Indeed, Mr. Porgas spent the coming months on the run and even succceeded in helping countless others without being caught, ascribing his miraculous escapes to the Rebbe's protective coin. Amazingly, on the day of Budapest's liberation by the Russian army this coin inexplicably vanished and was never seen again. When he eventually reported his numerous escapes to the Belzer Rav and mentioned this strange episode, the Rebbe smiled knowingly and repeated to his Israeli *gabbai*, R' Shalom Fogel, "Did you hear that, Shalom? What Shmuel says? The *matbe'a* suddenly vanished ..."

Budapest's Keleti Palyaudvar (Eastern Railroad Depot)

had to pass through their various controls? Yet how could the *kehillah* prevent a huge multitude from gathering or hope to control them?

In response, Commander Batizfalvy stationed his men at the main train station to guard every entrance and also at local railroad depots along commuter routes to prevent anyone from bypassing the police cordon by train. They had strict orders to bar anyone without tickets or a valid passport and visas from leaving the country; nor would any tickets be sold today for travel on the Orient Express. This way, only the approximately fifty Palestine immigrants and genuine Orient Express passengers should get through. Most of those planning to accompany the Rebbe on the train out of Hungary would have to abandon the idea.

Anyone with a chassidic or Orthodox appearance had a particularly hard time of it. At the nearby Kelenfeld Bahnhof, police even dragged chassidim (including Mr. Chaim Shloma Friedman) off commuter trains and held them at police stations until the Orient Express was well on its way. In addition, Messrs. Salgo and Stern had been unofficially requested to pass around the word among their fraternity that on no account would the police allow any well-wishers — chassidim or otherwise —

In better times, the Rebbe blesses multitudes of chassidim from the window of a train

anywhere near the train, to avoid German repercussions. However, this message had precisely the opposite effect.

At first it appeared as if the police operation was totally successful. At 2:30 p.m., when the Orient Express was due, the long train platforms were unusually empty of bystanders. Since hardly a chassid had ventured to enter the imposing rail terminus, Dr. Batizfalvy fretted that all his precautions had been overdone and a thorough waste of resources. Surely one hundred of his most trusted police officers had more important things to do with their time. Ten minutes slowly passed; the Vienna express was expected shortly, yet there was still no sign of the Orient Express. Finally a telephone message was relayed to the stationmaster: for technical reasons there would be a lengthy delay. The Vienna express quietly came and went, disgorging and collecting passengers; all had long since dispersed and Keleti Palyaudvar had returned to hushed silence when its unaccustomed repose was abruptly shattered by the raucous arrival of the Orient Express.

What an extraordinary sight! Generally, that prestigious international train carried no more than 800-odd passengers in secluded comfort. On this occasion it was overflowing with over 2,000 people — mostly chas-

Ticket for the Orient Express

sidim! They were all over the carriages, hanging out of the windows, clinging to the steps, sitting on the roof; there was not an inch of space for another soul! To avoid all police restrictions, they had secretly traveled westward across Hungary to near the Austrian border and boarded the Orient Express at earlier stops, where bewildered railroad staff were overwhelmed by the unexpected onslaught.

Within seconds the rail terminus was suddenly bustling with boisterous chassidim all eager to give their beloved Rebbe a worthy send-off. Few of them realized how every smattering of noise and excitement increased the mortal danger threatening their revered leader. Yet what could be done? Both Mr. Kraus and Dr. Batizfalvy exchanged rueful glances and lifted their hands in shocked despair. They had tried their utmost with the best of motives but the chassidim had outwitted them. They could do no more; Heaven alone could deliver the Belzer Rav from the naïve foolhardiness of his well-meaning followers.

With some difficulty and the assistance of Dr. Batizfalvy, the Rebbe mounted the steep carriage steps and took his place. As soon as he and the Bilgoraj Rav were seated, Mr. M. Kraus took his leave and withdrew to the platform where Dr. Batizfalvy was waiting for him, for once looking at a loss and emotional. "Do you think I can also get a blessing from the *Csoda-Rabi* (Wonder Rabbi)?" he asked plaintively. Mr. Kraus passed the request back to the Rebbe, who beckoned the police commander into his carriage.

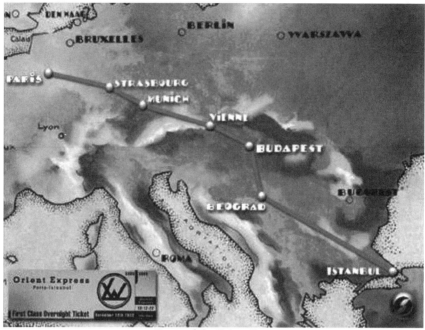

Route of the Orient Express

Dr. Batizfalvy bent forward respectfully and kissed the Belzer Rav's hand while he blessed him, "... May you merit to survive the coming days in peace ... You should successfully save as many Jews as possible ..."[3]

Finally the whistle blew, the conductor signaled to the locomotive driver and the Orient Express puffed slowly out of Budapest. The Rebbe's countenance clearly betrayed his profound sadness at parting from so many of his loyal chassidim. Hundreds of his followers wept openly. "We cried on remembering earlier meetings or partings from our Rebbe during his various travels before the War," some later recalled. "Then we came in many thousands; how

---

3. Within two months, the police commander was to play a crucial role in protecting Hungarian Jews in Swiss *schutzhauser* (safe houses) or rescuing them from the death marches during the Arrow Cross terror, and many owe him their lives. In reward for his selfless bravery, Switzerland granted him honorary citizenship and he eventually escaped via Zurich to South America. That he miraculously avoided being arrested at the Russian invasion (as was Raoul Wallenberg) he gratefully ascribed to the *Csoda-Rabi's* blessing.

different this sad occasion is from our glorious past! We also cried because with the *tzaddik* leaving us, who knew what the future might bring! Was this the lull before the storm? And then we cried for joy. At least he was escaping blood-soaked Europe! In his weakened condition, we feared he would not be able to take any new shocks ..."

It was the afternoon of Monday, 21 Teves 5704, during the week of *Parashas Va'eira*, eight months since they had escaped to Hungary — and the Belzer Rav had never been so alone. Despite all the cables and correspondence, no *gabbaim* were traveling with him and even his loyal brother, Rebbe Mottele, was not close at hand. Budapest's Jewish Agency Emigration Department had advised the fifty or so emigrants to split up and travel in separate carriages to avoid too close attention from German officials. Only the two non-Jewish detectives stood on guard outside his carriage. Yet how could the Belzer Rav fend for himself on this lengthy, strenuous journey after years of fasting and self-mortification? For now, a few of his closest chassidim still accompanied him, up until the Romanian border. But that was only the first and shortest leg of the trip. What solution had they for the major part of the voyage?

In peacetime, the journey on a direct route from Budapest to Turkey should have taken only between five and six days to reach Eretz Yisrael. Usually first-class passengers on the famous international luxury line crossed borders without changing trains, but during wartime they often had to disembark and make do with various wagons supplied by the respective countries. Moreover, the route was no longer direct, connections were often uncoordinated and trains frequently were canceled even when they were not a target of enemy action. The problems began already in Hungary. The official route led southeast straight through the eastern flank of Yugoslavia, but Yugoslavia was a hotbed of partisan activity. Although ostensibly under a harsh German occupation, several Italian and *Wehrmacht* divisions were unable to defeat the Serbian guerrillas and by 1944 the Axis forces were in retreat. Railroad tracks were a favorite target of the partisans and the Germans had no choice but to divert the Orient Express through Romania and Bulgaria.

So instead of heading southeast out of Budapest, the train first headed east to Bekescsaba (the *kehillah* of "Csubba" near Gyula on the present Hungarian border), then southeastward toward Arad (which was then on the border, after Hungary occupied chunks of Romania in August 1940) before taking the secondary railtrack that meandered in a southeast direction through the mountains to Bucharest. All this twisting and turning took most of the day, so they reached Arad — their first stop — only early on Tuesday morning. Here the two top-ranking detectives were scheduled to disembark, as were the few chassidim accompanying the Belzer Rebbe.

One of these, Mr. Avigdor Salgo, the young married son of R' Yosef, was entrusted by the Rebbe with a message for Dr. Batizfalvy. Confiding some details of that secret session with the police commander, the Rebbe revealed how the Hungarian police had agreed to delay searching for him until he left the country. As soon as Dr. Batizfalvy received a personal message that the Belzer Rav was safely across the Hungarian border, the police could honestly inform the Bochnia Gestapo that their wanted man was nowhere to be found. But what if the Gestapo flashed a "Wanted Notice" to all checkpoints along the Rebbe's route? For how long would his identity and destination remain secret?

CHAPTER 24

BETWEEN THE BOMBS

VIOLENT ANTI-SEMITISM AND DISCRIMINATION flourished in Romania even before the War, yet over three-quarters of a million Jews continued to reside there, and vibrant Judaism flourished in Crishana-Maramuresh, Bucovina and Bessarabia. After World War I, Romania flouted its international obligations to treat all its citizens, including Jews, equally, and in 1938, many were stripped of citizenship. Like Hungary and Poland, Romania had German-influenced "border rectifications" — initially surrendering north Bucovina and Bessarabia to Russia, north Transylvania to Hungary and south Dobruja to Bulgaria. At the outbreak of war, fresh laws were passed expelling Jews from all government service, business corporations or gainful employment; transferring Jewish property to Romanian owners; and subjecting Jews to forced-labor conscription.

Widespread pogroms organized by the army began with the 1941 invasion of Russia; later, thousands were shipped off in cattle-cars without food or water to die of suffocation or shooting; hundreds of thousands were murdered in Bessarabia; army units joined the extermination squads in southern Russia and shocked even the brutal Germans; finally, 200,000 Jews were deported to Transnistria where less than one-quarter survived in appalling conditions. Early in the War, a commissar had been appointed to oversee ghettos and deportation; then in 1942, plans were agreed upon with the SS to deport Romania's remaining Jews "to Lublin." But the government retracted and instead floated the idea of ransoming all its Jews to Palestine. No mass exodus resulted from these protracted negotiations, but shortly before the Rebbe's arrival, some survivors of Transnistria were allowed home. Until the Germans' retreat from Romania eight months later, the fate of its Jews remained exceedingly precarious.

Nonetheless, as the Orient Express drew into Arad they had a surprise. On the platform waited a large welcoming crowd, with many quite emotional. Apparently the route and timing of the Rebbe's secret escape had leaked outside Hungary. Although Romania was linked to the Axis powers and had initiated some horrific pogroms and barbaric deportations, it seemed obvious that the Jews still enjoyed some security. The large, excited crowd was led by the Timisoara *rosh hakahal*, Mr. Abraham Shonbraun.[1] The Belzer Rav blessed them all armly and with feeling.

As the train pulled away, the religious passengers — who had been dispersed among the carriages when they left Budapest — now gathered around the Rebbe to ask for his blessing. He was pleased to see that he was not as alone as he had thought; however, everyone else had also left their religious objects behind, in keeping with their instructions. He noticed a young *bachur* among the passengers, Moshe Silber from Budapest, and motioned him aside. Quietly the Rebbe asked him: Would he mind assisting him, now that he had no *gabbai* or *shammas*? The boy gladly accepted the great responsibility and fulfilled the task of attending to the frail and weakened Rebbe throughout the journey with alacrity. When Moshe revealed that he had hidden a pair of *tzitzis* in one of his suitcases, the Rebbe laughed approvingly and said he would use them each time he *davened*. Yet

1. Timisoara or "Timosvar" itself, 30 miles south of Arad, was on the main rail track to Bucharest from northeast Yugoslavia, but that route took it too close to the dangerous border for comfort.

he warned the young boy not to wear them but return them to their hiding place.

Meanwhile Mr. Shonbraun entered the Rebbe's carriage, announced his intention to accompany them to Bucharest and asked if he might attend to the Rebbe's needs. At first the Belzer Rav refused since the Timisoara *rosh hakahal* was a wealthy and respected figure who might find it demeaning to minister to the Rebbe's personal requirements, but he relented after Mr. Shonbraun persevered. When Mr. Shonbraun heard that no one had any religious items, he presented the Rebbe with his expensive pair of *tefillin*. Eagerly and quickly, the Rebbe donned the *tefillin* before handing them over to the Bilgoraj Rav and Moshe Silber. The Rebbe recognized, though, that it would be too dangerous to take these *tefillin* with him; they still had to go through several German checkpoints.

Another half an hour brought them to Birzava where a further lively reception awaited them on the platform. Obviously, the Rebbe and his plans were well-known to Romanian Jews. From then on it was a straight but lengthy run to Bucharest, the capital of Romania. Here they would all have to disembark and stay overnight since there was no direct connection to Turkey. Once again an excited crowd — including prominent Belz chassidim — waited to greet him; but they also had some unpleasant news to impart.

Back in Budapest, police had suddenly swooped down on every Orthodox Jew out of doors with a beard, *peyos* and long jacket — taking them in for questioning and detaining them overnight. This was unprecedented. Anti-Jewish measures had been periodically enacted in the past but they had never discriminated between different types of Jews. Surprise, confusion and then panic spread as several hundred religious Jews were picked up throughout the day, since many had a great deal to hide. Most had been evading the harsh forced-labor conscription and had been hiding out in Budapest where it was considered relatively safer. Now they had to prove their identity, produce documents and explain their presence in Budapest.

Ominously, this police activity began with a raid on the Belzer Rav's recent lodgings, where they conducted a thorough search and arrested a few of the Rebbe's close devotees. The resulting tumult soon appeared in the national newspapers, which were apparently fully briefed by official sources yet could offer no explanation for the mysterious investigation. Only those aware of Germany's extradition proceedings against the Belzer Rav could perhaps guess that this was nothing more than an elaborate charade by Dr. Batizfalvy to persuade the Gestapo that his officers were actively "searching" for the elusive *Wunder Rabbiner*.

Community leaders were about to approach the police to ascertain what was going on and see if they could possibly extricate anyone from custody, when most detainees were released as suddenly as they had been arrested. Batizfalvy's tactic must have been convincing and by the next day, Hungarian authorities were able to formally inform German officials that the Rabbi had apparently fled the country. Obviously, this information exacerbated the danger for the Belzer Rav, who was still traveling through German-controlled territory.

Consequently, Dr. Batizfalvy cabled the *Centrala Evereilor din Romania* (National Center for Romanian Jews) in Bucharest warning the Rebbe to hurry to neutral Turkey before the Gestapo caught up with him. This telegram was passed on to a second cousin of the Belzer Rav, Rabbi Elazar Twersky, who was the wartime *shochet* in Bucharest and was known as the Pultishaner Rebbe. Following intensive consultations with leading Belzer chassidim, they decided to advise the Rebbe, upon his arrival in the Romanian capital, not to stay in Bucharest for a few days as planned but to continue his journey with all speed.

When the Orient Express finally drew into Gara de Nord — Bucharest's main railroad depot — late on Tuesday, a large crowd was patiently waiting to greet the Belzer Rav. Here most passengers disembarked, including the Belzer and Bilgoraj Rebbes, since there was no direct connection with the Orient Express to Turkey. Indeed, during wartime there was no guaranteed timetable or train schedule through Bulgaria, their next destination. When his chassidim confided the disquieting news and telegram from Budapest, the Rebbe remained calm and displayed no fear. But he deferred to their conclusion not to delay his departure. Up until that moment, he had planned to stay in Bucharest for several days — at least until after

Shabbos (*Parashas Va'eira*). Under international law, the Gestapo had no jurisdiction to arrest him outside Poland, Hungary or Germany, but few Germans cared for such legal niceties and had already dragged Polish Jewish travelers off this train in the past.

The Jewish Agency had reserved rooms at central Bucharest's most prestigious hotels for all the Palestine immigrants, but the Rebbe requested that he be allowed to arrange his own accommodation. The two brothers were desperate for some rest and they quickly made their way to the Pultishaner Rebbe. Within minutes, their secret was out. Many Bucharest Jews joined the Rebbe for Minchah before filing past to wish *"Shalom."* After Maariv, communal leaders came on a courtesy visit and the Belzer Rav entertained them with an impromptu *tisch* despite his intense tiredness. The talk turned to the German atrocities in Poland and the Bilgoraj Rav recounted a few episodes of the horrifying brutality he knew from firsthand experience or had heard directly from witnesses. However, the Rebbe took no part in this conversation, apparently absorbed in a meditative reverie. Later the talk switched to the past glory of Belz. As everyone relived their personal memories, someone muttered sadly *"... Ahh,* those were the days ... the glorious *malchus* of Belz ... that time is gone and we'll never see its like again ..."

Suddenly, the Rebbe sprang up, his reverie interrupted, his tiredness and frailty forgotten, his age and weakness ignored, his sorrowing face aflame beyond recognition — *"Chas veshalom!* We are assured from my grandfather's household (the Sar Shalom) that Belz will remain a niche where they will serve *Hashem Yisbarach* until the coming of Mashiach!"[2]

The Rebbe had little rest that night. Hundreds of petitioners clamored to see him with their personal problems. The Belzer Rav patiently and calmly listened to all their concerns and took a particular interest in the fate of Polish refugees. He and the Bilgoraj Rav were able to retire only in the early hours of the morning, yet they had to leave Bucharest at daybreak if they wanted to get across the

---

2. In later years, the Pultishaner Rebbe often recalled this unforgettable experience: "That episode I will never forget; the roar of the Belzer Rav '... until the coming of Mashiach,' will remain with me forever!"

Bulgarian border and connect with the express train to Turkey. In Romania they had been welcomed with every courtesy and respect; sadly, Bulgaria was to be a totally different scenario.

In contrast with Romania, Bulgaria's Jews had suffered relatively little persecution in the years leading up to the War. Even under SS pressure, their wartime treatment cannot be compared to that of their coreligionists in neighboring countries linked to the German Axis powers — though they only narrowly escaped deportation to the death camps. At first Bulgaria remained neutral but its political sympathies were broadly pro-German, and Bulgaria later initiated its own anti-Jewish legislation. (Since these were somewhat milder than the Nuremberg race laws, this sadly led the already assimilated Jews into a rising trend of intermarriage and baptisms.)

In March 1941, the situation deteriorated when Germany pressed for transit facilities and bases to facilitate their invasion of Greece. In return, Bulgaria annexed western Thrace from Greece with its 6,000 Jews, and Macedonia from Yugoslavia with its 8,000 Jews (earlier they had taken the Dobruja district in southeast Romania). As German influence grew, Jews were increasingly subjected to curfews and special taxes and their radios and phones were confiscated. The cabinet reached a secret deal in the summer of 1942 to abandon all Bulgarian Jews already living in German-occupied areas, while scheming to expel all Jews from Bulgaria and confiscate their possessions. The Yellow Star was introduced; Sofia's Jews were forced to live in a designated area of the capital; all unemployed Jews were evicted from urban cities, and Jewish property was confiscated. Finally, top SS officials arrived to negotiate their deportation "to the East" and their evil plans were set in motion during March 1943.

When the secret leaked out, the Bulgarian government backed down but the deportation of over 11,000 Jews from Thrace and Macedonia to Treblinka death camps went ahead while Sofia's Jews were expelled to the provinces. However, by the time the Belzer Rav was passing through their territory, German setbacks in Russia and Italy had encouraged the Bulgarians to take a more lenient line and they eventually began negotiating the transfer of all their Jews via Turkey to Palestine. Like the Romanian negotiations, nothing much came from months of bargaining.

The bridge from Giurgiu to Ruse across the River Danube

The border between Romania and Bulgaria is defined by the River Danube (Dunarea to the Romanians and Dunav to the Bulgarians) flowing toward the Black Sea; and the main rail track to Sofia, the Bulgarian capital, crosses the river at Ruse. Nowadays, one can buy an international train ticket from *Bucuresti Gara de Nord* (Bucharest Northern Station) on the 481-*Rapide* direct to Sofia and undergo a standard customs and passport check en route during the ten-hour journey. Not so during wartime, with tense relations between Romania and Bulgaria — both ostensible allies in the German Axis — over disputed border territory. So, some seventy kilometers south of Bucharest, the train halted on the Romanian side of the Danube at the border town of Giurgiu (Dzurdzu to the Bulgarians), where passengers disembarked and crossed the bridge on foot to the Bulgarian border town of Ruse (Ruschuk) where the Sofia *Accelerat* (express) was waiting.

Border controls of Romania and Bulgaria respectively were situated at each end of this bridge. Romanian customs inspectors have long had a bad reputation for rudeness and corruption, and they were then known to be particularly severe in their search for smuggled currency and valuables, a search that could take an hour or two. The Rebbe's train reached Giurgiu at noon midday, so they would have just enough time to catch the Bulgarian express, due to depart at 2:30 p.m. from Ruse. Unfortunately, the bridge itself was closed for repairs and there were long queues for small river ferries that took only a few passengers at a time. Even so, the customs officials refused all pleas to hurry their procedure; if anything, they were more pedantic and aggressive than usual.

The Belzer Rav also had to wait his turn in the freezing cold, which was most difficult for him. Worse was to come. When he finally reached the customs shed, the inspector dealing with him was a rude, uncouth fellow and quite possibly anti-Semitic. He roughly shoved the Rebbe aside and thrust his hands into the Rebbe's coat pockets. Moshe Silber was horrified. It was bad enough that the Rebbe was not exempt from a customs check because of his age and frailty, but how could one treat such a revered leader of thousands like a common criminal? Angrily, Moshe Silber stepped forward and slapped the custom officer's hand. Instantly he knew he had made a terrible mistake. But it was too late; it could not be undone.

Within seconds, the shed was in uproar. The Romanians were furious. Never in their experience had anyone dared raise a hand to a top official. The frustrated train passengers were equally angry — with the custom officers for their overbearing attitude and delaying tactics. As mutual insults and recriminations gave way to blows, Moshe Silber realized that if he did not sort out this mishap quickly, he would be jailed and the Rebbe would be dispatched back to Hungary — and the Gestapo! He pulled away from the fracas and raced up to the senior commander. Fortunately, he spoke a fluent Romanian.

"I'm sorry. It's all my fault! Please forgive me. But your officer did not realize with whom he was dealing. This gentleman is very important to the Jews — one of the most important in the world! That's why I was suddenly overcome and reacted the way I did when he was being searched. But I'm sorry — I know I still shouldn't have done it. Please forgive me ..."

The commander listened in silence. Finally, he put away his notebook. "Okay. I might be prepared not to make out a full report. But

first I must know who this important gentleman is!" Moshe Silber paled. The Rebbe was safe only as long as he traveled incognito as "Aron Twersky." How could he trust this official with the secret? Only under great pressure did he grudgingly reveal that this was a leading, prominent Rabbi. Moshe Silber handed the commander a substantial "present" for agreeing to forgive him. "You're very lucky," remarked the commander as he pocketed the money. "By rights, I could jail you all for a long time!"

By then it was very late and the commander positioned the Rebbe, Moshe Silber and the Bilgoraj Rav at the front of the queue for the ferry. Although they were among the first to cross the Danube, they still had to clear the Bulgarian passport checks in Ruse. These were not as awkward as the Romanian customs, but these officials too saw no reason to hurry. So what if this group missed the connection to Turkey? There was another Sofia express due in two or three days' time! None of their frantic pleas helped; the callous officials painstakingly went about their task, regardless.

When they finally reached the rail platform, they were just in time to see their train puffing out of the station! What should they do now? How could the Belzer Rav — old, weak and highly sensitive to cold — wait for two or three days during January at this drafty rail depot, open to the wind, rain and snow? Besides, it could be dangerous now that his identity was known to some. Should they return to Bucharest and go through the whole ordeal again in two days' time? What about Batizfalvy's warning telegram? Besides, the Rebbe's true identity was hardly a secret there in Romania.

Desperately, Moshe Silber began searching for suitable rooms for hire in Ruse. As he walked around the rail depot, he discovered quite by accident that there was actually another train going to Sofia and it was due in that night. However it was not an *Accelerat* express service — anything but. It was a slow *Personal* commuter train, stopping at every tiny junction along the line. Also, it used a secondary track on a roundabout route so that it would take days to reach Sofia whereas the express managed it in a matter of hours. Yet what choice did they have? For all the inconvenience they would inevitably face, it was far safer than lingering in Ruse for up to three days.

Traveling on that commuter train was more fraught with danger than they had anticipated. The commuter train, with second-class seating only, was already crowded with peasants and locals who elbowed everyone aside in their scramble to get the best seats. As they were about to board, Moshe Silber suddenly realized they had mislaid one of the Belzer Rav's suitcases; it must have happened during all that confusion when rushing to catch the *Sofia Accelerat*. Unfortunately, this was the suitcase that contained all the kosher food, plus other valuables. The Rebbe told him to forget it, it was not important enough. Besides, if Moshe went off to look for it, he would be leaving the Rebbe alone and vulnerable amidst those rough peasants — "Please don't forsake me here by myself!"

While Moshe appreciated the Belzer Rav's concern, he chose to ignore it because of this new emergency: How could the Rav manage for the next week without food? So what choice did he have? Leaving the Rebbe standing at the foot of the steep carriage steps, he raced off to search for the missing case. Despite an exhaustive hunt throughout the station and train, it was nowhere to be found. Perhaps, one of the railroad porters or customs officials had stolen it. Fortunately, the Bilgoraj Rav still had a small amount of food which they could share.

When Silber got back to his carriage, he had a terrible shock. The Rebbe had suffered a bad fall! Appallingly, he was still lying, groaning quietly, on the platform where he had fallen; no one had come to his assistance. Apparently, a large crowd of boarding passengers had come up behind him and the crush had forced him up the steep steps. In his weakened state, after years of fasting, sleeplessness and deprivation, he was unable to mount the stairs without assistance — and certainly not when jostled by a crowd of crass peasants. (At the best of times in Belz, the Rebbe had walked slowly and with difficulty; even standing was an effort. Only on Shabbos did he eat and drink in abundance, stand upright, walk sprightly and appear healthy — almost a different person.) At the second step he had slipped and fallen back onto the platform.

Inwardly berating himself for abandoning the Belzer Rav because of his frantic search for food, Moshe Silber gently lifted him up the stairs and assisted him to a safe seat. The Rebbe had suffered bad bruising and severe shock; he had almost fainted from the pain. Indeed, Moshe Silber considered it a miracle that the Rebbe was able to continue the difficult journey. Despite his pain and injuries, the Belzer Rav did not complain, merely remarked poignantly, "Didn't I ask you not to leave me? To just forget the suitcase? I told you I'll willingly forego those supplies ..."

Indeed, the Rebbe would not eat a thing throughout the long journey — just as he had not during their shorter flight across Poland — until they were through the last German checkpoint. Nor would he have a drink besides a few sips of warm water, though they still had some kosher milk from Budapest. Whenever he was offered food or liquid, he would always refuse by asking, "Have we still got any more of their checks to go through?" The dangerous possibility that the Gestapo would catch up with them was never far from his thoughts.

Their commuter train was not a direct line to Sofia and after a day's travel, they had to disembark and wait a few hours for the connecting train. Fortunately, the railroad staff recognized the Belzer Rav as a distinguished personality and set aside a private room for them to wait in. Until then the Rebbe had not relaxed or

Sofia Tsentralna Gara

rested for a moment, as he had refrained from eating and had been constantly murmuring prayers or learning.

Paradoxically, all this time they were essentially traveling in the wrong direction — Sofia was in the far west of Bulgaria whereas Istanbul, their final destination, was to the southeast. Although the distance between Sofia and Bucharest is less than half that between Budapest and Bucharest, their journey time was to take twice as long. Part of the delay was intense air activity. Allied warplanes had finally achieved some measure of supremacy in the skies; besides engaging in numerous airdrops for the guerrilla bands in neighboring Yugoslavia, they had embarked on a bombing campaign of strategic targets in the Balkans, singling out Bulgarian rail traffic for special attention.

As the train got closer to Sofia, the rail staff became increasingly panicky. Wild rumors of British or U.S. planes attacking all moving trains were rife among passengers and crew; nor could station staff and signalmen offer any accurate information or reassurance. Periodically, their train would halt in the middle of nowhere with no explanation. Often they could hear heavy thumps in the distance, which sounded suspiciously like bombing. Though the train they were on was never attacked or shot at, they could all smell the distinct whiff of danger and fear.

When they finally reached Sofia Tsentralna Gara (Sofia Central Station) on Thursday night, they had an awful shock. It had suffered a major air raid the previous day with enormous "collateral damage." Half the large rail depot was destroyed and some trains had taken direct hits — including the *Sofia Accelerat* they had missed at the border! Apparently, it had just pulled in when the heavy raid began. Its passengers, including some Hungarian Jews, were among the many killed and wounded, and those who escaped did so by a miracle.

The Rebbe's entourage realized thankfully that their intense frustrations at the border were a blessing in disguise. Had the awkward custom officials not delayed them, they would certainly have been on that ill-fated train. Truly, *Hashem directs the footsteps of man (Tehillim 37:23)* and *protects the feet of His chassidim ...* (*I Shmuel* 2:9). Naturally, they were eager to leave the danger area as soon as possible and their connection to Turkey was already waiting. But the confusion and chaos in the half-ruined station — littered with debris, and the dead and dying — was indescribable. Nevertheless, they managed to board on time and the train immediately left on the last leg of the Orient Express' lengthy journey to Istanbul.

Now their route swung sharply back to the east, heading toward the border crossing into Turkey. As they climbed through the foothills, the heavy bombing was constant, heightening the fear and tension, yet amazingly they escaped any direct hit.

More worryingly, the Rebbe had become extremely weak from his unremitting fasting. It was not just painful to watch; the Bilgoraj Rav and Moshe Silber were becoming increasingly concerned it might *chalilah* cause lasting damage. Yet the Belzer Rav refused all their entreaties and maintained his self-imposed regime. Finally, on Friday midday, they reached Stara Zagora and their fourth or fifth border check — by then the exhausted passengers had lost count! They were only approximately 80 kilometers distant from the Turkish border, but this area was seen as part of German-administered Greece (Bulgaria had annexed northern districts of Greece during the War).

Once again they had to disembark and change trains. Because of the war situation, only open-topped Greek railway wagons were available, more suited for ferrying freight or livestock, quite a far cry from the opulent luxury of the world famous Orient Express! The weather was

*Reb Moshe Silber
at his wedding;
to his right
is the Bilgoraj Rav*

typical for that time of year — January 21 — and as their train picked
up speed, the cold was palpable. At the best of times, the Belzer Rav
was highly susceptible to extremes of temperature, and now, after five
days of fasting, he began shivering uncontrollably.

Frantically, Moshe Silber hunted around for something to protect
the Rebbe from the freezing cold. The Belzer Rav was wearing only
unfamiliar modern clothing with no warm outerwear; certainly no
Rabbinical *peltz*! Several fellow Jewish passengers kindly agreed to
relinquish their woolen seat covers and Moshe solicitously wrapped
these around the Rebbe, together with any scarves and towels he
managed to collect. However, the weakened Rav objected for fear
these might perhaps contain linen threads (and constitute *shaatnez*).
So concerned was Moshe Silber with the Rebbe's physical condition
that he felt this was surely a case of *pikuach nefesh* and he ignored
the Rebbe's vehement objections. Even so, the Belzer Rav continued
to suffer severe cold and was only slightly relieved.

Despite his distress, he persevered in his refusal to eat or drink.
"Have we still got any more checks to go through? How much longer do we have to go?" In fact, the next border crossing was the last
— and the worst. According to seasoned travelers in the know, the
Germans stringently controlled the final checkpoint at Svilengrad at

the crossing into neutral Turkey. They were backed up by troops from a nearby *Wehrmacht* base and apparently took a close interest in any Jewish passengers. The Rebbe was deeply perturbed. He had always felt that if the Gestapo were going to drag him off the train at any point, contrary to international regulations, it would be here where they were directly involved. So he asked Moshe Silber to cut his beard (or rather stubble) again for extra security. Unfortunately, they did not have a battery shaver or clippers, and a razor was obviously out of the question. Eventually, Moshe obtained some old fashioned hair removing cream that was unpleasant to use and reeked of singed hair.

When they finally reached Svilengrad in the late afternoon, they discovered those reports of a rigorous and stringent check were not exaggerated. Their train was shunted onto a rail siding and the inspection began. All baggage was exhaustively searched; all documents and papers were meticulously scrutinized. Moshe Silber and the Bilgoraj Rav were very much afraid the harsh officials would utilize the opportunity to belabor this aged and frail Jew, even if they did not discover his true identity.

Ultimately, the inspectors arrived at the compartment containing only two passengers: the Belzer Rav and Moshe Silber. The Rebbe appeared to be in some meditative trance, huddled in his corner and continually mumbling quietly to himself. Since he was totally ignoring the inspection, Moshe Silber jumped up to deal with the inspectors. One was a plainclothes Greek policeman, the other obviously a German whom Moshe Silber judged to be a high ranking Gestapo officer. Standing at the door of their compartment, the German official glanced down a typed list of passengers registered by the Jewish Agency and asked for their names.

"I'm Moses Silber and this is Aron Twersky," replied the boy meekly.

"What belongings do you and he have? And what are you carrying in those suitcases."

"Nothing much," answered Moshe, emptying his pockets. "Our small suitcases only have some food and a few clothes. I'll get them down if you want."

Instead of replying, the German stared at the strange old man slumped in the corner, swathed in scarves, obviously old and

4, ZALMAN SHAZAR AVE.
POSTAL ADDRESS: P.O.B. 92
JERUSALEM 91920
PHONE 526155
FAX 527029

הארכיון הציוני המרכזי
CENTRAL ZIONIST ARCHIVES

מען למכתבים: ת"ד 92
ירושלים 91920
טלפון 526155
פקס 527029

(III Unhgary)   - 4 -

No.- Name and Surname.-   Address.-
157.-LICHTENFELD Ignac..........Budapest
158.-LINK Zsigmond and fam......Palestine Office,Budapest
159.-LINKENBERG Armin............c/o Orthodox Community,Budapest
160.-LILLING Johanna............Meszaros u.50 Kassa
161.-LIPKOVISZ Fritz and wife....Palestine Office,Budapest
162.-LOBLE Lorand,Dr.and Fam....Rozsa ut.62,Budapest
163.-LOEWY Jozsef and fam.......c/o Paneth Jenö,Budapest
164.-LOEWBEER Emanuel and fam...Palestine Office,Budapest
165.-LOEWINGER Andor and fam.....c/o Pro Palestina,Kiraly ut.93.Budapes
166.-LOEVINGER Morio and fam...Léva
167.-LORAND Zoltan,Dr.and fam...Szabadka,or c/o Pro-Palestina,Kiraly
                                ut.93,Budapest VI
168.-LUKACS-LEITNER Zoltan......Nagyvarad
169.-LUSTIG Andor and wife......Kolozsvar
170.-LUSTIG Nandor Dr.,and wife..Ujvidek
171.-MAVSKOPF Desider...........c/o Felderbaum Vilmos,Vagselye
172.-MAY Chana Dr.and daughter...Somogy megye,tabori orvos,Karad or c/o
                                Kun Jozsefne,Pozsony u.51.,1,Budapest
173.-MEDGYES Karoly and fam......Kossuth Lajos ter 4.Budapest V
174.-MOLDAVAN Ignac and fam......Beregszass
175.-MOLNAR Vilmos,Dr...........Nagyvarad
176.-MOSKOVICS Salamon and fam...Munkacs
177.-MUELLER Samuel Benjamin.....Heves Megye,Paszto
         Chief Rabbi
178.-MUELLER Maximilian..........c/o Mrs.Ilona Brody,28,Kadar Ucca
                                Budapest
179.-MAGY Ferenc,Dr.and fam......Ujvidek
180.-NATHAN Kalman and fam.......Szolnokmegye
181.-NATHAN Sandor,Dr.and fam....Palestine Office Budapest
182.-NEUBURG Oedön and fam.......Wesselenyi 21,Budapest
183.-NEUMANN Arpad and fam......Palestine Office,Budapest
184.-NEUMANN Elek and fam........Nagy-Peleske/Szatmar Megye
185.-NORMAND Miriam(Anni)........Nagy-Sandor u.21,Nagyvarad
186.-PAUNC Frigyes and fam.......Ujvidek
187.-PARTOS Imre and fam........Izabella u.70,Budapest VI
188.-PECSENIK Markus,Rabbi.......c/o Mordehai Stern,Hotel Rombach
                                utca,Budapest VII
189.-PERL Aron and wife..........Debrecen
190.-PETERI Lipot................Almassy ter,Budapest
191.-PFEIFFER Izsak,Dr.Rabbi.....Monor
192.-POLANITZER Izidor and wife..Muranyi 51,Budapest
193.-POLACEK Zsigmond and fam....Sombor
194.-POZNER Sandor..............Nagyvarad
195.-PRAGER Hirsch,Rabbi.........SzatUarnemeti
196.-QUITTNER Leopold............c/o Daroczi Vilmosne,Jozsef krt.25,
                                Budapest
197.-RABBINOWITZ Baruch,Chief
            Rabbi...........Budapest
198.-REICH Jozsef and fam........Palestine Office,Budapest
199.-REICH Filip.................c/o Dr.Reich Sandor,Szent Domonkos,
                                ut.7,Budapest XIV.
200.-REINITZ Jozsef and fam......Ungvar
201.-REISNER Markus..............c/o Samuel Frey,Szombathely,Www
                                xxxxxxhgut
202.-RINGLER Hermann and fam.....Marmarossiget
203.-ROSENBAUM Gizella..........Istvanter 3,Toma vm.Paks Szent
204.-ROSENFELD Endre and fam.....Marosvasarhely
205.-ROSENFELD Vilmos and fam....Pozsonyi ut.38,Budapest V
206.-ROSNER Samu,Dr.and fam......Tiszaujlak

The passenger list (from Turkey border control;)
The Bilgorai Rav is no. 188 and the Belzer Rav is no. 270

sick. Then he abruptly shook his head and signaled the boy not to open their baggage. *"Es is nicht nehtig. Ich walte nicht diesen alten man balestingen!"* He repeated this sentiment ("It's not important. I don't want to disturb this old man!") several times to the Greek official before exiting the compartment. This was almost unheard of — not to inspect the baggage, but instead to refrain from asking awkward questions and show compassion and humanity to an elderly Jew. Perhaps the Rebbe's charisma had an effect even on heartless Germans.

As the compartment door shut behind them, Moshe Silber sank back into his seat heaving a deep sigh of relief. "What's happened, Moshe? What is the matter?" the Rebbe asked him. Evidently he had indeed been in a deep pensive reverie and had really not been aware of his surroundings. When Moshe Silber told him they had passed the dreaded inspection with flying colors, *b'ezras Hashem*, the Rebbe's whole demeanor changed. His face lit up, he shook off his exhaustion and frailty and was suddenly invigorated. Once the inspectors had completed their task, the wagons were shunted back onto the main line and coupled to a Turkish locomotive that was already waiting with other passenger cars. Turkish soldiers boarded the train to guard them for the last 200 kilometers.

Just as they moved off, the winter sun began to set. *Shabbos Va'eira* was rapidly approaching — their first Shabbos in true freedom for four and one quarter years. Because of the accumulated delays, they were still many miles short of Istanbul and it was far too dangerous to disembark close to the border. All the religious passengers (some revealing for the first time their Jewish identity) joined the Belzer Rav in his compartment for *Tefillas Shabbos*. As customary in the chassidic (*Nusach Sefard*) tradition, Minchah began with the recital of "*Hodu* ..." (*Tehillim* 107, which celebrates the release from prison, those healed from sickness, and those who made it safely through deserts or across the seas). For this unique occasion, the Rebbe ordered a change: The second verse that aptly declared, "Proclaim it, those redeemed by Hashem, liberated from their oppressor's hand ...," they were told to repeat three times — which was the Rebbe's habitual manner of emphasizing an important point. He too reiterated that verse with unusual vigor and feeling.

The Belzer Rav was like a man reborn, his countenance lit with an inner joy, and *Kabbalas Shabbos* proceeded amid great animation and excitement. The *chazzan* leading the prayers sang *Lechah Dodi* to extremely lively and joyful tunes. Subsequently, the Rebbe listened to *Kiddush* recited by one of the passengers on loaves of dried bread brought from Budapest. Finally he was prepared to break his long fast — on an apple and some homemade jam — but only after he kissed Moshe Silber's smuggled *tzitzis* warmly! Even from this tiny meal he ate only a little and distributed the rest as *sherayim*. Then he conducted a mini-*tisch*, singing *zemiros* and reciting Torah. Before reciting Torah he would customarily announce, "*Shtipps zech nisht* — Please don't push!" and he made this ritual declaration during this journey even when only the Bilgoraj Rav, Moshe Silber and few other fellow passengers were present! Perhaps, there was an esoteric, other-worldly purpose to this simple announcement.

CHAPTER 25

THROWN INTO PRISON

T HROUGHOUT THE MIDDLE AGES, TURKEY HAD been a haven for Jews escaping persecution in Spain, Italy, Germany and Poland, and so it was again during the Second World War. Yet there was a time when the Turkish Government wavered and contemplated throwing its lot in with the Axis powers, as it had during the First World War. Under intense German diplomatic pressure in late 1942, Turkey had considered waiving its neutrality and granting German forces transit and bases — effectively negating the glorious victory at El Alamein and once more placing Palestine, not to mention Turkey's own Jews, in mortal danger. Fortunately, they thought better of it after meeting with Winston Churchill. Many *hatzalah* activities were centered, or at least had representatives, in Turkey; relations with their Jewish citizens were a happy contrast to those in neighboring Greece.

On Shabbos morning, the Orient Express terminated at Sirkeci, Istanbul's European train station on the Golden Horn (the lower western side of the Bosporus Straits straddled by Turkey's former ancient capital, Constantinople). Yet the foreign passengers were not allowed to disembark until they underwent a final security

Sirkeci's rail depot

check. As they sat in their seats waiting, the Bilgoraj Rav noticed a substantial crowd had walked to the station to welcome them to freedom. But when this was pointed out to the Rebbe, he groaned deeply — perhaps remembering the many thousands of excited chassidim who used to greet him on his pre-War travels in Galicia, Poland and Hungary — and cried out sadly, "And what of the *bachurim* and *yungerleit*? Where are they all now ...?"

Many in the waiting crowd were genuine admirers; others were curious onlookers hoping to catch a glimpse of a famous escapee from Nazi persecution. All were shocked at his appearance. Old and bowed, with dimmed eyes; his face lined with pain and suffering; his features imprinted with the entire history of *galus*. Mr. Chaim Barlas, the *Sochnut* representative, also met him on the platform and when he noticed tears in the Belzer Rav's eyes, he remarked that the Rebbe ought to feel relief and joy at his escape. The Rav replied, "That's a miracle and a tragedy combined since so pitifully few have been rescued."

Among the welcoming throng was the renowned religious activist, Mr. Segal, who had come to deal with any unforeseen problems. Apparently, the Rebbe had already heard of him and shook his hand warmly while granting *Shalom* before asking if there was anywhere private where he could rest. In reply, Mr. Segal conducted him to the grand hotel room booked by the *Sochnut*. Mr. Segal had stocked it before Shabbos with milk, fish and challos whose kashrus was beyond doubt. After a short recess, the Rebbe walked with an entourage to a nearby shul to *daven* Minchah before conducting a festive *shalosh seudos* and *tisch*, with all the traditional tunes and rituals, that lasted until the late hours — just as in Belz of old. Following *Havdalah*, the Belzer Rav summoned the local *shochet* and asked the Bilgoraj Rav to check if his *chalof* (*shechitah* knife) was sharp yet smooth and free from imperfections. However, the Rebbe personally did not eat from his *shechitah*, since he never ate meat on weekdays.

After a couple of days in Istanbul, according to the *Sochnut* schedule they should have left for Eretz Yisrael on Monday, 28 Teves (January 24, 1944). However, the Rebbe was much weakened by his prolonged fast, his nasty fall and the abiding fear of the Gestapo. Eventually a doctor came to examine him and pronounced him unfit to travel. Instead he advised at least a week of total rest and relaxation. The Jewish Agency's Istanbul office, under direct instructions from Jerusalem, was most accommodating and understanding. It provided quiet and secluded accommodation (at Hotel Continental, where *Sochnut* officials themselves stayed, overlooking Tepebasi park in the Beyoglu district) for the Belzer and Bilgoraj Rebbes, exchanged their train tickets for a week later and notified the British and other transit authorities of the change in plan. In all they would be in Turkey for ten days.

Yet they were to enjoy little rest. Because of the excitement within the Turkish *kehillah*, people burdened with personal and general problems came knocking at all hours. Interestingly, although most of Istanbul's rabbanim visited, greater regard and more profound respect were displayed by the Sephardi *chachamim* than by the Ashkenazim. And not only Jews came by. High ranking diplomats and officials were also interested in the Rebbe's views and opinions. The British Consul had a number of queries about living conditions in Nazi-occupied territories, and asked other political questions as well. The U.S. ambassador sent his representative, who likewise had several inquiries about living conditions in occupied Europe and asked for all possible details. Then came the consul of the Free

French (representing the French Government in exile led by General De Gaulle) as well as the consul of the Polish government in exile with similar queries — the latter consul wanted to know if after the War, the Rebbe would return to Belz.

During the Belzer Rav's short stay in Istanbul, he summoned one man who had already been there for six months and knew his way about. "Do you know where the old Jewish cemetery is? Where is the burial place of the famous *mekubal*, Rav Naftali Katz, who wrote the *Semichas Chachamim* and passed away here on 24 Elul 5479. *Zeits moichel*, could you please visit his grave with a message? He once declared that 'the path that he couldn't take to Eretz Yisrael would eventually be taken by his descendant, twelve generations later!' Please inform him that eleventh-generation descendants are now doing it!"

The various *hatzalah* committees and charities also wanted a detailed report of the travail of European Jewry and priorities of rescue. Because of his immense tiredness and frailty, the Belzer Rav delegated his brother the Bilgoraj Rav to deal with all these visiting diplomats. The Bilgoraj Rav replied patiently and at length — meetings often went on for hours — and he forcefully pressed that everyone do his utmost to save the surviving remnant before it was too late. However, the Rebbe himself personally penned a sincere letter of gratitude to Dr. Julius Kuhl at Bern's Polish Consulate and urged him to assist other refugees. Even years later, Dr. Kuhl could barely conceal his admiration for the Rebbe, who immediately after his fearful flight across occupied Europe just one step ahead of the Nazis, coupled with the searing loss of his close family and many multitudes of chassidim, could find the energy and time to thank even those who played but a small part in his rescue.

The Bilgoraj Rav also gave a telling interview to the influential *Ha'aretz* newspaper, datelined Sunday, January 28 (3 Shevat):

> LET US DIE WITH THE PHILISTINES!
> *From our own correspondent, Chaim Baltsan, Istanbul.*
> *Rabbi Aaron Rokach, the Rebbe of Belz, and his brother Rabbi Mordechai Rokach, the Rebbe of Bilgoraj, have arrived here in Istanbul. They miraculously escaped from Poland after indescribable*

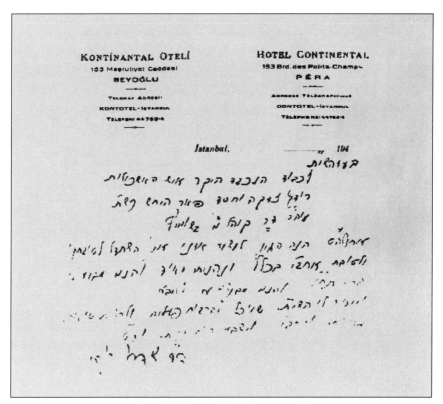

The Rebbe's letter of thanks to Dr. Kuhl

horrors. But their wives, children and all their families were murdered there ...

The Bilgoraj Rebbe told me, "From Polish Jewry, nothing is left! Besides 100,000 souls who are dying slowly in the slave labor camps, there are perhaps another 50,000 in hiding. The ghetto inhabitants of Warsaw and Bialystock chose to 'die with the Philistines.' Perhaps Polish Jewry in general, both old and young, might have been prepared to act likewise at the beginning of the oppression. But the Nazis hid their repugnant plans of mass murder until the last moment."

Meanwhile, many in Eretz Yisrael were under the mistaken impression that the Rebbe was on the way there as scheduled and expected to see him on Thursday, 2 Shevat. Even his loyal chassid Mr. Berish Ortner was confused. At first, when Mr. Gross in Geneva cabled that the Rebbe had departed Budapest, he had sought

«תמות נפשנו עם פלשתים...»

הרבי מבילגוראי שבא ביחד עם הרבי מבלז לאיסטנבול מספר על השמדת
יהודי פולין. — בני משפחת הרבי מבלז נרצחו על ידי הנאצים

מאת סופרו המיוחד של "הארץ". באסטנבול, חיים בלצן

חרבי מבלז

הרבי מבלז חה
בדרך לארץ

צעדי הממשלו

על הגבול הטורקי

The Ha'aretz report (note the official photograph)

to ensure there would be no last-minute hitches on his entry to Palestine:

> Mr. Moshe Shapira
> The Jewish Agency for Eretz Israel
> Aliya Department
> Jerusalem P O B 92
> 24 Teves 5704
> January 20, 1944
> <u>Your ref: 1607/Z:</u> Regarding the Belzer Rebbe
> Dear Mr. Shapira,
> With great joy and heartfelt gratitude, I take pleasure in informing Your Honor that I received a telegram today from Geneva that the Rebbe and his brother shlita left this Monday en route here.
> When I was in Jerusalem, I asked the Chief Rabbi, HaGaon Rav Yitzchak Isaac Herzog, shlita, to ensure the Rebbe does not experience difficulties at the border etc. The Chief Rabbi instructed me to ask Your Honor on his behalf — who will certainly do everything

418 / RESCUING THE REBBE OF BELZ

necessary in this regard. I am sure Your Honor will fulfill the Chief
Rabbi's request.

With respect and admiration,
Yours sincerely,
Dov Berish Ortner
P. S. Enclosed copy of the above telegram.

Also, Mr. Ortner contacted Palestine newspaper editors to ensure
that press coverage of the Belzer Rav's arrival would be fair and
favorable.

Motza'ei Shabbos, 27 Teves 5704
January 23, 1944
FOR THE ATTENTION OF ALL NEWSPAPER EDITORS
Dear Sirs,
According to telegrams from Switzerland & London, the Rebbe the
Tzaddik of Belz, and his Brother shlita will arrive here this coming
Friday, 3 Shevat, from Turkey and will stay in Haifa over Shabbos.

Since many of his admirers within the Yishuv have been await-
ing their arrival with extreme impatience and would like to travel to
Haifa to welcome them, I would ask you to make room for this report
in your paper.

Respectfully yours,
Dov Berish Ortner

◈⟋⟍◈

Mr. Joseph Hoftman
President, Journalists' Federation
Tel Aviv
Motza'ei Shabbos, 27th Teves 5704
January 23, 1944
Regarding the Belzer Rebbe shlita
Dear Mr. Hoftman,
Due to the arrival of the Belzer Rebbe and entourage, I would
like to ask you, as President of the Journalists' Federation, a favor
in the name of thousands of his supporters here and worldwide. As
you are aware, Jews now arriving from Hungary via Romania and
Bulgaria have had to travel without beards to avoid danger en route
and it is extremely likely that the Belzer Rebbe too will arrive beard-
less. Obviously the journalists will want to photograph him at the

The Rebbe's official photograph

border or inside the country. But that will be inadvisable because (a) it will not be respectful either to him or to our nation in Eretz Yisrael and around the world and (b) this might endanger many, many Jews forced to flee under false identities and non-Jewish appearance. Therefore I have prepared photos of the Rebbe with his previous image and I would ask Your Honor to explain to all the newspapers that anyone wishing to print a photo should only use the enclosed copies. Also, they should word their reports in such a way that they do not endanger other Jews who need to be rescued from the Nazis' clutches, Heaven forbid.

Respectfully yours and thanking you in anticipation,
Dov Berish Ortner

Two days later, he received the following cable:

B ORTNER TEL AVIV REBBE AND BROTHER LEFT ISTANBUL TODAY PLEASE MEET THEM REPLY TO 189 MULLWAY LETCHWORTH HERTS CHAIM NOTA KATZ

Although he raised substantial sums for Belz's needs, R' Chaim Nota Katz's new address in Letchworth (a modern rural town where many of London's religious Jews had evacuated to escape the flying bombs) was actually nothing more than a garage — sparsely furnished with just two beds and two chairs — and shared with another prominent Belzer chassid, R' Nachman Dachs! In this telegram, R' Chaim Nota based himself on the *Sochnut* schedule, but the Rebbe's departure had been delayed for another week. Yet this was enough to confuse R' Berish, who rushed off to Beirut on a false errand (fortunately, the *Sochnut* managed to extend his visa). A return cable was dispatched that day:

> ELIMELECH RUMPLER LONDON FATHER LEFT TODAY
> FOR SYRIA TO WELCOME REBBE REBBE LEAVING
> ISTANBUL TODAY FRIDAY I WILL TELEGRAPH HIS
> ARRIVAL MOSHE ORTNER

Two days later, Thursday, R' Chaim Nota sent another cable:

> TELEGRAPH WHEN RABBI ROKACH ARRIVED PLUS
> EXACT ADDRESS TO CHAIM NOTA KATZ LONDON
> KATZ

Finally, on Sunday, 5 Shevat, the Ortner family replied by letter:

> *Baruch Hashem, Sunday Beshalach es Ami, 5704*
>
> *To the famous chassid etc. Reb Elimelech Rumpler and all the chassidim.*
>
> *After receiving Reb Chaim Nota Katz's telegram that the Rebbe shlita had left Istanbul for the Holy Land, my father traveled Tuesday for Beirut (Syria) to welcome the Rebbe and his brother shlita. The visas for Syria had been prepared some time ago. On Friday, a few hundred people traveled to Haifa — the first town where they were expected to spend Shabbos. Only that day did we hear from other train passengers who arrived from Istanbul that the Rebbe will leave only on Monday Parashas Beshalach as they needed a rest after the long and difficult journey.*
>
> *So we all returned from Haifa as we had come, hoping that this Friday the Rebbe and brother — accompanied by my father — will finally arrive at Haifa. At Haifa everything was already prepared for their welcome. The reaction to the Rebbe's arrival in the Yishuv and Jewish newspapers was powerful and glowing hot. The important, serious newspapers carried background articles with his old photograph. Throughout the week, every day had some information in the papers of his coming. Everyone's waiting with bated breath for his arrival. Even Radio Jerusalem on Motza'ei Shabbos carried the news of his delay for another week.*
>
> *I would ask you to give over the contents of this letter to R' Chaim Nota since I simply don't have the time to write to him individually. I sent you a telegram today and will send all future telegrams to*

Haydarpasa ferry and rail depot

you. Also, I would ask you to pass this on to our friend R' Shemayah Binder and R' Moshe Gross with all the above details. Incidentally, we have not heard from R' Moshe Gross the dates for the seven certificates despite the telegram we sent. Without exact dates it is impossible to complete that task successfully. To my knowledge, Rav Herzog has meanwhile received your sefer.

We are already very happy for the day the Rebbe and brother shlita arrive here in peace and we'll tell you his address as soon as he decides.

Best regards to Your Honor, R' Chaim Nota and all the chassidim.
Your friend,
Moshe (ben Dov-Berish) Ortner

Finally, their impatient wait was over; on Tuesday, 7 Shevat (February 1, 1944), the Belz entourage finally left on the last leg of the journey to Eretz Yisrael.[1] Since Istanbul straddles the Bosphorus Straits between the Black Sea and the seas of Marmara and the Mediterranean, they had to sail with the Karakoy ferry for nearly an

---

1. Not Monday, as assumed by the other immigrants, since the Belzer Rav personally preferred traveling on Tuesdays, which is twice described as "good" in *Bereshis* 1:12.

hour to Kadikoy Pier near Haydarpasa train station on the south-eastern end of the straits, where trains to Russia and Asia begin. The rail track to Syria (Suriye to the Turks) was laid in the days of the Ottoman Empire and meanders in a southeastern direction up steep hills and down sheer valleys across Anatolia and through the Taurus Mountains. The Belzer entourage was accompanied by many well-wishers and at every major stop that boasted a *kehillah*, excited crowds of Sephardim gathered to cheer the *tzaddik* on his way to the Holy Land. It took them all day to cross Turkey, and they reached the Syrian border in the early hours of Wednesday morning.

Less than 50 kilometers across the border was the first major rail junction, at the ancient *kehillah* of Halab (Aram Zovah, now known as Allepo). Here all foreign visitors — or "aliens" — from Nazi-held territory had to disembark for a vigorous search and debriefing by the British secret service (after the British army, together with the Free French, had occupied this part of the French empire and offi-cially granted Syria independence). As if they were dangerous spies, each passenger was taken separately into an examination room where high-ranking officers pored through each piece of luggage before emptying the passengers' pockets. Then the "aliens" were subjected to a barrage of trick questions about their experiences and opinions of the Third Reich. In addition, everyone had his height measured and photographs taken. The whole process took several hours, particularly the cross-questioning.

However, the Belzer Rav was not very cooperative with the secret-service personnel. As a general rule, the Rebbe had always weighed every word carefully before he replied to any query, but here this genteel behavior only aroused the officer's suspicions. The more aggressive the questioning, the less cooperative the Rebbe be-came. When he was answering only in monosyllables, the frustrated inspector abruptly concluded he had heard enough.

Peremptorily, he ordered that "Rabbi Twersky" and his brother "Rabbi Pecsenik" be arrested together with several other passen-gers, pending further investigation! He was adamant he would not release Rabbi Twersky until "he told us all he knew!" Unfortunately, there was no one around to explain to this officious bureaucrat who the refined personality with whom he was dealing actually was.

Nor could anyone persuade him to stop treating the Rebbe as if he were a common criminal.

Everybody accompanying the Belzer Rav was horrified. It was bad enough that an international spiritual leader of countless thousands should be subjected to the same onerous formalities as everyone else — but to arrest him and take him away for questioning! As far as police officers of British Special Branch (the counter-espionage division) were concerned, this Rabbi could go right back where he came from unless he "opened up," and there was nobody in Halab with the requisite influence or political clout to countermand them. So near to Eretz Yisrael and yet so far ...

Once again Heaven had "prepared the cure before the illness" — and yet again the Angel of Mercy was Chief Rabbi Herzog. Because of the confusion over the date of the Rebbe's departure, Mr. Berish Ortner had been stranded in Beirut since the beginning of Shevat. If he returned to Palestine he could not come back to Beirut without applying for another visa; nor could he journey on to Halab in northern Syria without fresh papers. (Although Beirut, Lebanon and Syria generally were newly liberated territories of the French empire, the area bordering Turkey was under stricter military administration.) On 7 Shevat R' Berish was gratified to see a familiar face: Rav Herzog was leading an entourage of prominent *hatzalah* activists on a top-secret mission to Turkey and London, hoping to rescue war-afflicted children. The Chief Rabbi had specially arranged his itinerary so that he would meet the Belzer Rav en route and smooth away any impediment, should that be necessary. Since Rav Herzog had played a leading role in obtaining the certificates and extricating the Rebbe, Mr. Ortner saw it as a favorable omen that he would be the first to welcome him to Eretz Yisrael. Rav Herzog promised to tell the Rebbe that Mr. Ortner was waiting for him in Beirut.

By Divine Providence, Rav Herzog caught up with the Belzer Rebbe in Halab, just when and where the Chief Rabbi's unique leverage was most needed. As his train pulled into Halab station that Wednesday morning, he asked the local Jews, "Has any great rabbi or *tzaddik* arrived here today?"

"Yes — the *Inglesi* have taken him down to the police station!"

Apparently, Rav Herzog did not appreciate the full seriousness of the situation and decided to wait on the platform while sending his son Yaakov Herzog to ascertain what was going on. Yaakov was thoroughly shocked by what he found. The Belzer Rav was held in a damp basement of the Syrian police house, together with another fifteen Jewish fugitives from Nazi slaughter, and was being cross-examined by three British officers. As before, the Rebbe was answering slowly and hesitantly, weighing each word carefully. After Yaakov introduced himself and requested the Rebbe's release, the chief examiner replied brusquely, "He's not going anywhere until he answers our questions fully and properly!"

Yaakov Herzog asked the Belzer Rav directly, "Why is Your Honor not telling them anything?" But the Rebbe merely replied dismissively, *"Ich redd nisht mit de goyim!"*

At this impasse, Yaakov returned to report back to his father. The Chief Rabbi left the rail station and urgently demanded to see the Syrian authorities and the British general in command of the entire police unit. He insisted on the Rebbe's release forthwith, dwelling on his genteel personality, his exalted standing among international Jewry, his obvious physical weakness — and hinting at the likely repercussions if he was detained unnecessarily or a moment too long. The general was inclined to agree despite the protests of his team of investigators. As a compromise, he released the Belzer Rav immediately while holding the Bilgoraj Rav for detailed questioning on behalf of both of them. He claimed he could not free the Bilgoraj Rav from all investigation without specific permission from Supreme Army Headquarters!

When Yaakov Herzog saw how the weakened Rebbe was unable to walk from years of fasting and self-mortification — he literally had difficulty moving his feet or standing — he gently lifted him up and carried him out of the police house to a safer venue. Rather than take the Rebbe to wait for his brother at the rail station, where he was liable to elicit unwelcome attention from irksome Syrian officials, he was booked into a nondescript Arab hotel where he would be safer. Unfortunately, neither Rav Herzog nor any of his entourage would be able to wait with him since their urgent rescue mission was operating on a very tight schedule. Instead, Yaakov Herzog and Dr. Yaakov Griffel, the legendary *hatzalah* pioneer, rushed to the Jewish

*Rabbi Herzog and entourage
at the Aleppo hotel*

Quarter and woke up Mr. Yona Cohen, an Israeli Sephardi journalist who was then in Halab working on youth education on behalf of *Aliya Bet* ("illegal" Zionist immigration). It was not yet 8 a.m. on a cold winter's morning and Mr. Cohen stared blearily at his two agitated visitors. "What's the emergency? What's happened?"

Not one to mince words, Dr. Griffel came straight to the point. "You're about the only *Frenk* in town who knows what a Rebbe of chassidim is! A few hours ago, the Belzer Rebbe and his brother came across the Turkish border and the Syrians arrested them both on behalf of the British! They say it's just a formality, but can you imagine what an insult this is to the Jewish *Yishuv*? Here they've just escaped from the Nazi murderers in Poland and the British arrest them for being enemy citizens! By a miracle, Chief Rabbi Herzog was passing through here with us and Mordechai Elias.[2] They've already got the Rebbe released but there will be a long wait until his brother Rebbe Mordechai gets out — and meanwhile we must carry on our journey. So can you stay with the Belzer Rebbe until they leave Halab?"

Hurriedly, Mr. Cohen pulled himself together and accompanied them to the Arab hotel. It was small and dingy, and the Belzer Rav's room was tiny and narrow. To Mr. Cohen's journalist's eye, the Rebbe looked short, frail and malnourished; his face, now shorn of his beard, was lined with all the suffering and pain of Polish Jewry. Just then the Chief Rabbi swept in with more members of his entourage and Mr. Rachamim Nechmad, Halab *kehillah* president. Their meeting was short but deeply emotional. The Rebbe well knew of Rav Herzog's selfless efforts on his behalf and on behalf of *hatzalah*

---

2. The famous lawyer and legal adviser to the *Vaad Leumi* who defended Jewish religious practice at the Wailing Wall (*Kosel HaMaaravi*) during the infamous "*Mishpat HaKosel*" Inquiry.

generally. Trying to stand up in honor of his benefactor, he gripped the arms of his chair and painfully began pushing himself upright. Rav Herzog rushed forward to spare him the trouble. They met as the Belzer Rav was half erect and for a long moment they embraced each other warmly. Then the Rebbe suddenly burst into bitter sobs.

More than any words could possibly do, those heartfelt tears summed up the awesome tragedy of Polish Jewry. Nobody in that small room was unaffected; everybody wiped tears from his eyes. Privately, the Chief Rabbi was staggered at the Rebbe's appearance as he later reminisced:

"I remembered the Belzer Rav well from several encounters at Marienbad Spa (Marrianske Lazne) in Czechoslovakia before the War. It was an ideal place to personally meet the pre-War spiritual leaders of European Jewry and I became closely acquainted with the Rebbe. So I was shaken to the core to see him in his distress. I can never forget the impression he made on me then in Halab; it remains embedded deep within my heart. I couldn't even recognize his face, shorn of his beard and *payos*. Bent, broken, sad and suffering, with unfamiliar — indeed alien — clothes, eyes shedding tears, cutting a figure that cried out for Heavenly Mercy. It is too difficult to describe our traumatic embrace; at that moment the full significance of his miraculous escape really sunk in. I sensed that the Belzer Rav too felt similarly.

"Nonetheless I stifled my searing emotions, muffled my anguish and sought instead to comfort and encourage the Rebbe. I told him of my enormous joy at his astounding deliverance, and of the great rejoicing throughout the whole Jewish *Yishuv*. I stretched out my hand to take *Shalom* but he indicated he first wanted to wash his hands. Glad for the opportunity to be *meshamesh* the saintly *gaon* and *tzaddik*, I hurriedly brought in a pitcher of water and a bowl before we shook hands ..."

Recovering somewhat, the Rebbe asked the Chief Rabbi when his brother, Rebbe Mottele, would be released. Both Rav Herzog and Dr. Griffel hastened to reassure him that everything possible was being done to extricate him. Meanwhile, two unexpected visitors stepped into the Rebbe's room. The first, a tall Arab, was the Syrian police chief who whispered to Mr. Yona Cohen, "Is this the important *Yahud* who came here today?" The second visitor was a special photographer invited to record the meeting between the Belzer Rav and the Chief Rabbi. But the Rebbe refused, saying he had never allowed this before. Finally, in deference to Rav Herzog for whom he felt an immense debt of gratitude, he succumbed to their repeated persuasion and had his photo taken with Rav Herzog, his son Yaakov, Dr. Griffel, Mr. Nechmad — and the Syrian police chief! This photo still exists and, without his distinctive beard, the Rebbe is totally unrecognizable.[3]

By then it was almost 9 a.m. and time for the Chief Rabbi's connecting train to Turkey. Apologizing profusely that he was unable to accompany the Rebbe back to Eretz Yisrael or even wait with him in Halab, he hastily took leave on behalf of his entourage. Just before they left the hotel, Mr. Elias suggested that perhaps the Rebbe might consider changing his suit. It was not looking its best after a couple of weeks' travel. But the Belzer Rav refused. "As long as I'm still in *galus*, there's no point in changing my *galus*-clothes! Only when I get to Eretz Yisrael can I think of wearing different clothes." Before they departed Halab, they again pressed the Syrian authorities to quickly release the Rebbe's brother, "Rabbi Markus Pecsenik," and they promised to do so.

Despite these solemn assurances, the Bilgoraj Rav was not freed until evening. Throughout that Wednesday, Mr. Cohen kept the Rebbe company and saw to his scant needs. When inquiring about Mr. Yona Cohen's name, the Rebbe asked if he understood Yiddish. "*Lo!*" admitted Mr. Cohen, explaining that he was a Sephardi from Eretz Yisrael. The Rebbe lifted his eyes with joy (generally, he rarely looked up) and, in a heavily accented Ashkenazi Hebrew, remarked thoughtfully, "Really? A Sephardi from Eretz Yisrael? You are the

---

3. Instead of being embarrassed by this episode, the Belzer Rav valued the opportunity to display flexibility when required. His saintly father, Rebbe Yissachar Dov, had likewise been reluctant to pose for photographs, and when regulations requiring passport photos were introduced, chassidim persuaded Lemberg officials to make an allowance on his behalf. When they reported back he thanked them but remarked it must be permitted where necessary — "What do you want? That everybody else should be in *Gei-Hinnom* and I alone shall be the *tzaddik* in *Gan Eden*?" The Belzer Rav later related both episodes publicly when reprimanding a young chassid whose stringent leanings prevented him from joining festive meals or *seudos mitzvah*.

first Sephardi I have met!" After a slight pause, he asked "Of whom are there more in Eretz Yisrael — Ashkenazim or Sephardim?"

Following this short conversation, the Rebbe retreated into silence and then began mumbling quietly to himself — for several hours. Mr. Cohen was naturally unaware of the Belzer Rav's custom to review countless pages of *gemara*, commentaries and Kabbalah — by heart if necessary — before embarking on *davening*, and he at first thought mistakenly that he must be engaged in some lengthy prayer. Only at 3 p.m. did he realize that the Rebbe was about to begin Shacharis! Before *tefillah*, the Belzer Rav searched around for some water with which to wash his hands. Mr. Cohen sprang up to assist him but the Rebbe refused. "You said before you were a Kohen! So you mustn't serve me!"

By now, Mr. Cohen was ill at ease. It was mid-afternoon and the saintly and malnourished *tzaddik* had not had a morsel to eat all day. Mr. Cohen rang up the household of Mr. Rachamim Nechmad, the *kehillah* president, to ask for some kosher food. Shortly afterwards they brought round a meal fit for a king! Yet the Rebbe refused it all. Only after much persuasion did he reluctantly pick out a home-baked *kichel* and drink a single glass of tea. While drinking his tea, he resumed his conversation about Eretz Yisrael and its growing Jewish population. "Are there many yeshivos there? Are they opening up new ones? Where is it best to live — Yerushalayim or Tel Aviv? Or anywhere else? There must be religious Jews in other towns too, no?"

Mr. Cohen was disappointed that they did not discuss the dire situation in Europe. Rumors of unspeakable atrocities in Poland, the Rebbe's homeland, had swept Eretz Yisrael, yet the Rebbe avoided the subject altogether and did not even refer to his own miraculous salvation. What about the few survivors? Or was it all too painful? Summoning up his courage, Mr. Cohen remarked in a trembling voice, "Rebbe! It is an *eis tzarah l'Yaakov*! What will happen?" The Belzer Rav clutched Mr. Cohen's fingers. "Hashem's *yeshuah* comes in a blink of an eyelid. *B'ezras Hashem* there will eventually be a salvation for *Klal Yisrael*. But we need *emunah*; a strong *emunah* in Hashem ...," he murmured in a muted tone, almost as if he were speaking to himself.

After a few more salutary questions about life in Eretz Yisrael, the Belzer Rav returned to his regime of reviewing Torah by heart. Meanwhile, Mr. Cohen suddenly remembered the chassidic custom of obtaining blessings from religious leaders. Searching through his pockets, he found a Syrian banknote. Folding it up, he placed it on the table and requested, "*Rebbe, barcheini!*" The Rebbe asked him about his activities in Halab and Eretz Yisrael before clutching his fingers and feeling them. Then he uttered a short prayer and blessing. A local young Jewish boy walked in; he had received a *Sochnut* certificate and was about to immigrate to Palestine. Mr. Cohen tried to persuade him to request a blessing too. When he finally realized the significance of a *berachah* from the famous *tzaddik*, he got quite excited — he put down a monetary *pidyon* and likewise received a blessing. These were the only Sephardim in Halab to obtain *berachos*.

Wednesday evening, the Bilgoraj Rav had finally satisfied the pedantic British officials and answered all their questions at length. He joined the Rebbe at the small hotel and likewise bestowed a blessing on Mr. Yona Cohen. *Sochnut* officials also came to report on their arrangements for the continuation of their journey. The Rebbe was anxious to proceed with all speed. "We are already so near to Eretz Yisrael, I don't want to spend another Shabbos outside the Holy Land unnecessarily."

They took the first train out to Tripoli on the Lebanese coast and a hired taxi at the terminus immediately took them farther down the coast to Beirut, the Lebanese capital, where there was a small *kehillah*. All this way, they were accompanied by two *Peltours* travel representatives who sorted out the details on behalf of the *Sochnut*. The closer they got to Eretz Yisrael, the more their journey was delayed as the Rebbe continually wished to ritually wash his hands — as he did before any holy enterprise — and they detoured into Arab villages to buy a huge pitcher of water. At Beirut, a waiting crowd of approximately two hundred local Sephardim plus some twenty Israeli businessmen stood eagerly at the northern outskirts, led by the indefatigable R' Berish Ortner. At 10 a.m. Thursday morning, a car could be seen on the distant horizon approaching along the coastal road. To their great joy and relief, this was indeed the taxi bringing the Rebbe and the Bilgoraj Rav.

As soon as the Rebbe saw Mr. Ortner, he turned to the Bilgoraj Rav who had never seen R' Berish before and cried out, "*Dah host di, Berish*! (Here you have Berish)!"[4] R' Berish was overwhelmed with unadulterated joy; he later wrote that his feelings at that moment were indescribable. With hot tears running unashamedly down his face, R' Berish recited with fervent emotion three separate *berachos*: *Mechayei Meisim*, the standard *Shehecheyanu* and *She'chalak Mei'chochmaso Li'rei'av* (on an outstanding Torah scholar). On each blessing the Rebbe answered "*Amen!*"

As they stepped from the taxi, Mr. Ortner mentioned that he was their "Yehudah!" (Yehudah had been sent by Yaakov Avinu to prepare Goshen in Egypt.) "On Lag B'Omer 5693 the Rebbe had sent me to Eretz Yisrael, and with Hashem's help I opened the way for the Rebbe!" The Belzer Rav accepted *Shalom* from a few people and then asked if there was a warmer place where he could receive everyone. They got back into one of the *Sochnut* taxis and drove to Hotel Sapir, the only Ashkenazi hotel in Beirut with an acceptable standard of kashrus.

In a large reception room where the Rebbe was more comfortable, many came to greet him, including Rav Bachbut, Beirut's Chief Rabbi, with several rabbanim and dignitaries of the Sephardi *kehillah* — including a 100-year-old *chacham* who arrived on a stretcher! The Ashkenazi Rabbi, Rav Benzion Lechtman, also came with some *kehillah* members. Mr. Wallenstein, *Ha'aretz's* correspondent, was also present, as was the hotel proprietor, Mr. Sapir's son, who was a Jewish soldier on leave from serving in Eretz Yisrael. The Rebbe blessed the latter with success and speedy salvation for all of Israel, wherever they are.

In Beirut, the Ashkenazim had only a small shul whereas the dominant Sephardi community had a large, beautiful synagogue — Beit Knesset Magen Abraham — donated by the wealthy Sassoon family. Someone mentioned to the Belzer Rav that a shul nearby had a tradition that Eliyahu HaNavi had been revealed there. Despite his exhaustion, the Rebbe immediately expressed a wish to see this

---

4. Subsequently, Mr. Ortner was the only person the Rebbe customarily addressed familiarly by his first name without any title.

Beirut; the Shul is left of center

shul. However, he was advised this would be physically difficult for him since access required walking up many steps. The Bilgoraj Rav visited the site instead.

Meanwhile, Mr. Ortner unwrapped a large *lekach*-cake that he had brought from home. The Rebbe took a piece and distributed *sherayim* to the large assembly. Afterwards, the Belzer Rav asked R' Berish if he had *tallis* and *tefillin* with him. Mr. Ortner replied proudly that he still had his *tefillin* which R' Zelig Sofer from Hibniv (Uhnow) had written. "Excellent!" remarked the Rebbe, and they went to a nearby side room where he could *daven* undisturbed. But R' Berish had left his fur-lined winter coat draped over a chair, and the Rebbe said, "Berish! Take your *peltz'el* with you!" Mr. Ortner tried to explain to the Belzer Rav that there were no thieves about, *chas v'chalilah*! "No matter," insisted the Rebbe, "You have to guard your property so that none should be tempted to even think of stealing! That's what it says in the *yotzros*-prayers for Shavuos."

When the Belzer Rav had donned *tallis* and *tefillin*, R' Berish asked to hear the Rebbe's *berachos* since he had not merited to hear them for years. The Rebbe readily articulated the *berachos* loudly and clearly, just as on Yom Kippur in Belz (when the Rebbe *davened* very loudly). Everybody present was very emotional. After prayers, the Rebbe had a tiny breakfast with a little coffee, and by 3 p.m. they were on their way again.

As before, they traveled in *Sochnut* taxis (with *Peltours* representatives escorting them until the border) and their joy on the final lap to Eretz Yisrael was great indeed. After two hours of motoring down the coastal road, they reached the old border near Nekoura at 5 p.m. Thursday, February 3, 1944 (9 Shevat 5704 — a date forever celebrated by Belz chassidim). Although it was wartime and the border was closely guarded by French soldiers who usually checked baggage and papers meticulously, they showed the Rebbe due respect. On the information that this was an important and revered personality, they saluted smartly and allowed the entourage to pass through with only a cursory examination.

Once across the border, their taxi halted and the Rebbe tore *kri'ah* on reaching the Holy Land. Before they started off again, R' Berish requested permission to present the first *kvittel* in Eretz Yisrael.

"Have you already written it? Very good then, give the *kvittel* to me and the *pidyon* to the Bilgoraj Rav!" Shortly afterwards they reached Nahariah, where they stopped for Minchah. But the Belzer Rav revealed that it was too difficult for him to disembark and remained in the taxi.

During the last 28 kilometers to Haifa via Akko, several delegations came out to meet them, including the Vaad Leumi and the Haifa community; two carloads of Belzer chassidim brought silk *bekeshes* and fur *spodiks* for both the Belzer and Bilgoraj Rebbes. However, the Rebbe refused and declared his intention of wearing his modern suit — "*galus*-clothes" — for another week (except for Shabbos). "*Ich vill noch gehn a'bissel mit die klieder. Zollen die Yidden zehn vi azoi mir haben ausgezehn bei dem rasha!*"[5]

At 6 in the evening they finally reached Haifa and drove to their host, R' Chanina Kahane, a veteran Belz chassid who owned a large ground-floor apartment at 52 Halutz Street, Hadar Hacarmel, and put it at the Rebbe's disposal (the Bilgoraj Rav stayed upstairs). The entrance was decorated with a temporary portal embellished with flowers and a large "*Baruch Haba.*" A huge crowd was waiting, policed by the local constabulary, and they greeted the Belzer Rav with immense feeling and tremendous rapture. (Privately, many Belz chassidim were distraught and embarrassed at seeing their beloved Rav clean-shaven and dressed in modern clothes — looking nothing like his true self. Often it was the Rebbe who initiated the conversation and never failed to recognize each chassid individually, even those he had seen only once before.) The two Chief Rabbis of Haifa, R' Markus and R' Kaniel, paid their respects, as did representatives of various religious organizations, parties and institutions. While blessing the rabbinical deputation, the Belzer Rav instructed them to relay his *berachos* to the whole Jewish *Yishuv*. "May we merit that *Hashem Yisbarach* helps us to experience true salvation and the complete Redemption very soon!"

---

5. Even after that week had passed, the Rebbe continued wearing the *galus*-clothes under his Rebbe-garments for a lengthy period.

CHAPTER 26

ERETZ YISRAEL'S WELCOME

LTHOUGH THE JEWISH *YISHUV* WAS STILL relatively small, its reaction to the Belzer Rav was extraordinary. Thousands upon thousands came to greet him in Haifa, Tel Aviv and Jerusalem. Sephardim who had never heard of the Belzer Rav before were enamored of his saintly personality, kissing the air, walls, floor — anywhere the holy *tzaddik* had passed! Many thousands more followed his movements when religious and non-religious newspapers alike published his itinerary or commented on his deeds and opinions. Naturally, publications like *Haderech* and *Kol Yisrael* (both funded by Agudas Israel) published enthusiastic editorials, but even secular flagships such as *Ha'aretz* or *Haboker* carried favorable reportage. According to *Haboker*, the Rebbe took a great interest in the *Yishuv* as soon as he arrived, and spent a good part of his first Thursday night in Haifa cross-questioning his hosts about the young colony's budding enterprises — even fish breeding! — and was gratified by what he heard. Meanwhile, Rebbe Mottele described their harrowing journeys across German-occupied territory, their perilous border crossings and their rapturous welcome in Hungary and Turkey. He also spoke of non-Jews who secretly assisted persecuted Jews.

Among the Haifa crowds, the Belzer Rav noticed a former fund-raiser of Kollel Galicia, and a slight smile played about his lips — the gentleman had been an inordinate nuisance both to his employers and the Rebbe himself, and was not much appreciated by the chassidim now. "Do you know who this man is? Anybody from Poland wanting to immigrate to Eretz Yisrael before the War experienced great difficulties and had to wait a long time for a certificate. But the minute he merely uttered a desire to leave Poland, everybody, from the President of Kollel Galicia down, hastened to obtain his certificate and even paid his travel expenses!"

Similarly, he made a great fuss over another unconventional visitor the next day: the son of R' Yisrael Hibniver (of Hibniv or Uhnow, in the Rawa-Ruska district) who was a great Torah scholar and had taught all the Rebbe's sons. The Rebbe welcomed the son effusively and jokingly exclaimed, "Before we arrived I confided to my brother my anxieties on coming to a strange place, until I suddenly remembered you and remarked, 'Reb Yisrael's Feivele is here and will surely look after us!' " When he noticed how bystanders looked askance at his unusual warmth, since "Feivele" was a modern, clean-shaven Jew and hardly the typical Belzer chassid, the Rebbe continued: "You wonder at Feivele's welcome? A pity you didn't know his father! Under the *Deutscher*, one Purim in Bochnia when the situation became impossible and all Jews lived in constant fear, my R' Yisrael got up to crack jokes and sing *grammen* (witty rhymes) till people felt easier. To do that one needs heavenly inspiration — that was my R' Yisrael! He could have been a Rebbe of chassidim in his own right!"

Their first Shabbos in Eretz Yisrael — fortuitously, also *Shabbos Shirah* (*Parashas Beshalach*) — was celebrated in tradition and style. Friday morning, speculation was rife in Haifa: Where would the Rebbe *daven*? All the synagogues had individually proffered their invitations. Eventually he decided to attend central Beis Hamedrash Hagodol in Hadar Hacarmel. Chassidim, admirers and curious onlookers lined the route from Rechov Hachalutz to the shul. Because the local police had difficulty controlling the crowds, they roped off all these streets to traffic and kept all sightseers behind the rope. Only thus was it safe for the Rebbe and entourage to walk down the center of the road. At 7 p.m. the Rebbe finally arrived to a congregation of well over 1,000. *Kabbalas Shabbos* was completed by 9 p.m. but the Rebbe then went to the nearby Hotel Stern to rest. Only at midnight did he return home to conduct his *tisch,* which lasted until 2 a.m. Despite the late hour, this exhilarating *tisch,* replete with *zemiros* and tradition, was so overcrowded it was considered dangerous. Yet few were prepared to yield their places or forego the unique opportunity.

Shabbos morning, the police again roped off the streets to allow the Belzer Rav access to and from shul in safety. To the congregation's delight, the Rebbe chanted the *Shirah* as was his custom, despite his weakness and exhaustion. Everybody was relieved when this Shabbos ended peacefully with no mishap, despite the severe overcrowding. Paradoxically, while the sheer *simchah* of the general public in Haifa was unchecked, the relief and joy of Belz chassidim at their Rebbe's freedom was tempered by their deep shock at his appearance, shorn of beard and *peyos,* bereft of family, bowed down by the communal calamity. To those old-timers who remembered the authentic *Shabbos Shirah* back in Belz, this Shabbos and *tisch,* wonderful though they were, were hardly comparable. As with the consecration of the Second Temple in the days of Ezra, the youngsters, who knew no better, rejoiced, while the oldsters lamented. True, the Belzer Rav personally changed not one iota from the hallowed traditions and ritual of old. But what of the majority of their brethren still trapped — or worse — in Poland and occupied Europe?

Although the Rebbe never revealed any inner sadness, the "*Torah*" he delivered on this occasion was poignant as it was apt. "Why does the *Shirah* begin with words in the future tense: *Az yashir* — Then will Moshe and the *Bnei Yisrael* sing? To teach us the lesson of *Techias Hameisim*! Yet why associate the unadulterated joy of *Krias Yam Suf* with Resurrection of the Dead? Why remind us just then of the sad fate of death? But the *Bnei Yisrael's* happiness was not complete; only *chamushim* — one fifth — had merited to escape Egypt. Sadly, four-fifths of the *Bnei Yisrael* had recently perished during the plague of darkness. So their joy at their liberation and the destruction of their enemies was tempered by their grief at the fate of their brethren. Only a firm belief in *Techias Hameisim*, knowing that their brothers and sisters would eventually join them in the fullness of days, enabled them to sing the *Shirah* with the required *simchah!"*

Newspapers in general were most impressed by the excitement and devotion displayed by chassidim. Throughout Friday, they reported, guests flooded into Haifa from across Eretz Yisrael. All hotels were packed full; private apartments had to be converted into makeshift dormitories to cope with the extra demand. The Belzer Rebbe's apartment was under constant siege and only a strong police presence at the entrance kept the clamoring crowd outside from surging in.

Ha'aretz was struck by the episode of the *shochet*. Since Haifa was not renowned for its high standards of kashrus, Jerusalem's chassidim had brought a special *shochet* with them for Shabbos. Although the Belzer Rav's supreme scruples in halachah formed an integral part of his personality since youth, he refused to avail himself of the *shochet's* services. "I have a tradition from my saintly father (Rav Yissachar Ber *zt"l*) that where an established *shechitah* already exists, one must use their *shochtim* to avoid division and conflict."

Yet the chassidim persisted, "Now that we've already brought him all this way, discarding him is tantamount to shaming him in public!" The Belzer Rav was adamant. "Nor may we disgrace the community either, by importing an outside *shochet!"* he retorted. To placate the chassidim, he added, "Once my saintly father *zt"l* visited a small village in Hungary and his followers wanted to summon a skilled *shochet* from a nearby town. But my father *zt"l* rejected the plan and declared that he preferred to eat from the local man instead of an outside expert — anything rather than humiliate an entire *kehillah!"* Finally, one of Haifa's *shochtim* was called and the Belzer Rav checked his *chalof* (knife), as usual, before entrusting him to slaughter their chickens. *Ha'aretz* also reported a charming anecdote from a Jerusalem correspondent who had earlier met the Rebbe in Marienbad Spa in 1934:

On hearing that Rebbe Ahare'le was also at the spa, I went to his quarters that evening to join them for Minchah and Maariv. Despite the simplicity (Belz does not drag out the prayers) it still held a special quality. Several of us newcomers, including rich businessmen from Karlsruhe, lined up to wish Shalom Aleichem and he asked us individually where we were from. When I mentioned I was from Jerusalem, he left the rich businessmen and replied delightedly, "Oh, so you are a Yerushalmi!" — merely because I originated from Jerusalem, and although he did not know my identity. I don't think I ever met another Jew who displayed such happiness because I was a Jerusalem Jew! He seemed more attached to Jerusalem than to Belz or anywhere else. Perhaps he subconsciously sensed a kindred soul overcome with subliminal longings for the holy city.

Later while strolling through the forest, I met the Rebbe with his whole entourage walking toward me. From the distance, the Rebbe called out, "Yerushalmi!" and as I approached, he welcomed me with visible elation. This piqued the interest of members of his entourage and I had to disclose some of my family details. One chassid, obviously well informed of Jerusalem's affairs, turned and declared, "Rebbe, don't believe him! He's not an ordinary lay person; he's heavily involved in major matters there!" We discussed several topics and the Rebbe continued to enjoy my company and show me every sign of welcome ...

The Belzer Rav and his brother rested for a full week in Haifa, until the following Thursday. Petitioners continued to throng to the Rebbe's residence, as did various dignitaries and politicians, including British officials. All were implored to do their utmost for Jews under Nazi tyranny. Later the two brothers were to take this pressing cause to the wider public.

Wednesday afternoon and evening were also the occasion for a festive *seudah*, the traditional *peiros tisch* in honor of 15 Shevat, the New Year for Trees. This was the first time the Rebbe could celebrate it in the Holy Land with Eretz Yisrael's fruit. Since his arrival, he was meticulous to have all seven fruits — even at great cost — with which the Torah praises the proverbial land of milk and honey, and it was just as important to have many types of fruit as large quantities. This *tisch* went on till the early hours since it was also a *seudas pereidah*, a farewell meal to Haifa before they left the next day.

As the Rebbe departed Haifa at 10 a.m. Thursday morning, there was a large crowd waiting outside R' Chanina Kahane's apartment in Halutz Street to wish them farewell — estimated by chassidim to be in the thousands — and the entourage drove away in three cars. All along the way, Jewish settlements excitedly cheered them on, their children lining the road and occasionally waving flags. From among the excited crowd outside Petach Tikva, the Belzer Rav immediately recognized Mr. Ezra Gross, who had served him in Munkacs twenty-two years earlier when Ezra was still a boy. "For many years I've been hoping to meet you again! Do you recollect if all the *sefarim* I borrowed there were safely returned when we left?" Mr. Gross hastened to reassure him: "I remember it well — I was quite young then and some of those volumes were pretty heavy! But every last *sefer* was returned to its rightful owner." The Rebbe beamed at him. "*Yasher koach*, Ezra, for alleviating my conscience! I've worried about them for so many years!" Despite two world wars and unimaginable torment, these were the "minor details" that troubled the Rebbe.

The entourage agreed to R' Berish Ortner's suggestion to break the long journey at Tel Aviv, and here the welcome was extraordinary. In anticipation of their arrival, the Agudah youth movement had organized all *chadarim* and schoolchildren, with flags in their hands, to wait at the city entrance. Thousands more waited outside 79 Rothschild Avenue, Mr. Ortner's private residence, and the surrounding streets were black with onlookers. Chassidim clung to trees, roofs, balconies — anywhere to obtain a good view of their beloved leader. As the cars drew up around 1 p.m., the crowd surged forward, completely engulfing the Rebbe's car. The police officers and uniformed civil defense personnel in attendance to maintain order had major difficulty forcing a way through the crush to the apartment. Once inside, the Belzer Rav completed Shacharis and partook of a tiny breakfast before meeting the chassidic Rebbes of Tel Aviv, various rabbinical leaders and religious and political delegations, but there was no way he could receive every individual outside. Instead, accompanied by his brother, he ventured onto the

Posters announcing the arrival of the Rebbe

balcony and blessed the entire crowd by reciting the *Shehecheyanu berachah* — complete with the requisite *Shem* — and adding (according to *Ha'aretz*) "*Und die gantze Yiddishe stot!*" This blessing was answered by a deafening "*Amen!*"

Representatives of the municipal administration invited the Belzer Rav to establish himself in Tel Aviv, and he promised to consider the proposal. (In those early years, before Bnei Brak had earned its place on the map, many religious Jews and institutions were situated in Tel Aviv, the first totally Jewish town, while Jerusalem had a large Arab presence and security was fragile.) When the excitement had subsided somewhat and the Rebbe had rested, they continued the journey to Jerusalem.

All the previous welcomes were as nothing compared to that mounted in Yerushalayim — nobody could recall a greater *simchah* experienced by religious Jewry. Kollel Galicia (representing the Belz district in Poland) took a leading role in organizing the ecstatic reception: all yeshivos and schools closed for the occasion and the

Yishuv Hayashan played an active part in the celebrations. That afternoon, Meah Shearim resembled a ghost town, its shops shuttered as most of its inhabitants had gone to greet the Rebbe. From midday, women and children dressed in their Yom Tov finery streamed toward the Old Age Home at the entrance to the city (where the official reception was to take place) and filled the square outside. A special detachment of local police had already taken up positions and it was only by a strenuous effort that they kept roads to Tel Aviv open for traffic.

Approximately 1,000 people walked all the way to Motza, the first scheduled stop before entering Yerushalayim. The Belz entourage finally arrived there at 4:30 p.m., and several hundred chassidim cried out excitedly, "*Baruch Haba!*" "*Yechi Harebi!*" or "*Yechi Hatzaddik!*" The Belzer Rav managed to bless a few of the large crowd and also met delegations of rabbanim — Eidah Charedis, Agudah and Mizrachi. As the entourage moved off to Jerusalem, these chassidim chased after them with all their strength. Any empty trucks that happened to be passing were quickly flagged down, chassidim clambering aboard within seconds, and they soon entered Yerushalayim, singing and cheering.

At the Jerusalem entrance, a huge crowd waited — estimated at 20,000, an enormous amount for that period. The Rebbe had been expected at 4 p.m. and when they saw the entourage in the distance and heard the chassidim singing on the trucks that followed, the massive roar, "*Yechi Harebi!*" broke out and thousands surged forward, totally overwhelming the police presence. They raced up to the Rebbe's car and covered it completely, many clinging onto the roof and sides! With great difficulty, it succeeded in slowly maneuvering toward the gateway of the Old Age Home but it could proceed no further.

Many of the chassidim had brought wine and *mashkeh* to celebrate and now they toasted each other with, "*L'chaim! L'chaim!*" while Jerusalemites — particularly residents of Meah Shearim — broke into impromptu renditions of their famous dances. As growing rings of dancers encircled his car, the Rebbe was finally extricated from the vehicle. Dressed in the traditional fur-lined *peltz* and *shtreimel*, accompanied by his loyal brother and assisted by the struggling policemen, the Rebbe slowly made his way through the crush to the shul that formed part of the complex.

Waiting inside to greet him were leading chassidim; religious, political and institutional representatives; delegates of the Rabbanut and Polish Consulate; R' Moshe Blau and Dr. Weshitz on behalf of the municipality; and tens of influential or lucky chassidim. One of the policemen attempting to keep order also presented a personal petition on his sick grandmother's behalf; on hearing the name, the Rebbe — whose phenomenal memory remained unscarred by his experiences — remarked "I remember your *bubba* from years ago, when she sent a *kvittel* to Belz!" Members of the *Yishuv Hayashan* presented the Rebbe with a white silk *bekeshe* traditionally worn by Jerusalem chassidim during the *Yamim Noraim*. However, the Belzer Rav pointed out that this was not the custom in Belz, where even the Rebbe on Yom Kippur wore a simple linen *kittel* over his regular black *bekeshe*, but promised to wear it during his baking of matzos on Erev Pesach.[1]

The less fortunate crowd outside clamoring to catch a glimpse climbed nearby trees or onto the roof — some even tried to enter via the roof! In the feverish scramble, windows and doors were broken and other material damage inflicted. The entourage remained ensconced in the shul during the mounting turbulence. After some two hours, they attempted to proceed to their temporary accommodations in Sanhedria but the previous chaotic scene repeated itself until they were finally seated in their car. For a time it almost looked as if they would not make it!

Chassidim ran after the Rebbe's car all the way to Sanhedria, and on his arrival at R' Mendel Frankel's apartment, another fresh and substantial crowd was standing outside in eager anticipation. When the entourage pulled in they were again greeted with delight and exhilaration. Here, the Rebbe managed to receive *Shalom* from the

---

1. One Shabbos, the Rebbe approached a prominent Jerusalem chassid, Rav Yosef Lieberman, fondled his white *bekeshe* admiringly and confided, "I heard from my father how my grandfather once remarked that *baruch Hashem* his father — the Sar Shalom — never wore white on Shabbos, otherwise he too would have been forced to. Once I heard that statement, I could not change our custom. But you certainly can wear these clothes!"

smaller and more orderly crowd and blessed them personally with an imminent *yeshuah*. That Thursday night he was also able to receive rabbanim from Ashkenazi, Sephardi, Yemeni, Iraqi and other communities; prominent leaders of the Old City and new Jerusalem were likewise able to attend. Later, among the stream of visitors who came to welcome the Belzer Rebbe to Yerushalayim was Mr. Moshe Shapira, of the Jewish Agency's Aliya Department. The Rebbe asked him to convey his deep-felt gratitude to the *Sochnut* and its officials for all their exertions on his behalf and also for arranging his journey onward from Istanbul to Eretz Yisrael. The Rebbe related some of his torment in Poland and described the awful situation there.

In Jerusalem too, he reiterated his enormous respect for the entire *Yishuv* and reacted strongly to any disparagement of non-religious areas. When the Rav of Meah Shearim introduced himself and added smugly, "I proclaim true Eretz Yisrael lies within Meah Shearim — all the rest is just Palestine!" the Rebbe retorted, "*Azoi zogst die*? Now let me tell you *my* conversation with the Bilgoraj Rav on reaching Eretz Yisrael: My brother remarked that Eretz Yisrael was *baruch Hashem* 100 percent better than we had imagined, to which I replied that it's better by 200 percent! After all, Haifa is a town ... (here the Rebbe stopped short of articulating any nasty comments on Haifa's reputation) ... yet we had a Shabbos there we couldn't have imagined years ago back in Belz!"

While in Jerusalem, the Rebbe was offered some fruit after a meat meal. He reached out, took the fruit but then immediately put it back. When his *gabbai* inquired why, the Belzer Rav suggested he ask their *baal habayis* if the platter was not perhaps *milchig*. After some thought his host finally remembered that several years earlier the plate had been used for a dairy meal on *one* occasion!

Interestingly, when Rav Isser Zalman Meltzer came to visit him, the Rebbe confided that "*Baruch Hashem* during that whole time under the *Deutsche* I didn't waive even one *minhag Yisrael*!" In a lengthy conversation they discussed sunrise, sunset and nightfall and how these affected the *zemanim* for Shacharis, Minchah and Maariv. "Here in Eretz Yisrael, darkness follows sunset quickly and suddenly, unlike in Poland where it's drawn out," the Rebbe declared and as a consequence, Belz in principle no longer *davened* Minchah shortly before Maariv as they had in *der heim*. Rav Meltzer was most impressed by the Rebbe's breadth of knowledge combined with depth of feeling, and on leaving his room exclaimed admiringly, "I knew he was great in Kabbalah but I never realized how great he is in revealed Torah!" Later, when Rav Meltzer was discussing with a fellow Lithuanian Rosh Yeshivah the Rebbe's unavoidable delays in praying Shacharis, he described the Belzer Rav as the personification of the *Targum* to *Koheles* 8:5: "The times of prayer,

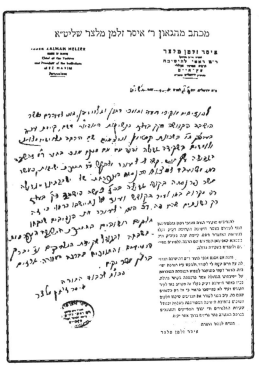

A letter from Rav Isser Zalman Meltzer in support of the Yeshivah of Belz

truth and halachah are recognized in the hearts of the wise"!

That Shabbos, *Parashas Yisro*, the Rebbe's first Shabbos in Yerushalayim, was celebrated in style. Not only chassidim were present, a large percentage of the religious *Yishuv* came out of respect and curiosity. The *tisch* and *tefillos* were conducted at the Zion Orphanage (directed by Mr. Blumenthal) in the Bucharian district, where the Rebbe stayed temporarily. Because of the heightened interest, Agudah's Jerusalem branch arranged for a police detachment to be stationed outside the orphanage throughout Shabbos. *Kiddush* was recited only shortly before midnight and the packed *tisch* lasted until 2 a.m. Shacharis started late and there was great excitement since the Rebbe was expected to lead the Mussaf prayers himself — in honor of his grandfather, Rebbe Yeshie'le, whose *yahrzeit*, 23 Shevat, would fall during the following week. However, Mussaf was likewise delayed and only ended in the late afternoon. After the "midday" *tisch* and Minchah, the *shalosh seudos* went on till late in the evening as is customary in Belz, which seemed to live beyond the confines of time. Nor did the Rebbe's regular hour-long breaks known as "*hafsakos*" disturb their equanimity.

Many prominent rabbanim, Jerusalemites and chassidim who were unable to attend the *tisch* during Shabbos visited the Zion Orphanage after they had made *Havdalah* — although Shabbos was still being celebrated in all its glory by the Belz assembly. As customary, after the Rebbe recited Torah, lighted candles were brought to the *tisch* before the fish, known traditionally in Belz as "*lechtige-fish*," was served to the Rebbe. As usual, he would turn the large platter this way and that, selecting a small morsel and distributing the rest as *sherayim*, signaling to the *gabbai* to whom to give portions. Following *bentching* and Maariv, the Rebbe personally recited *Havdalah* and signaled to the chassidim to sing "*Hamavdil*" and "*Eliyahu HaNavi*." By now it was already the early hours of Sunday morning.

Immediately after *Havdalah*, the Rebbe instructed his *gabbai*, "Call Berish to my room!" When Mr. Ortner arrived, he found both the Belzer Rav and Bilgoraj Rav awaiting him. After the Rebbe personally looked round to check that there were no curious chassidim eavesdropping on their conversation, he began, "Tell me, Berish — when are you returning to Tel Aviv?"

"*Im yirtze Hashem*, tomorrow morning, Sunday," replied Mr. Ortner, a little puzzled.

"And at what time will you be going?"

"I can travel even at 6 a.m.," offered Mr. Ortner (it was already past 4 a.m.!).

"Excellent," said the Rebbe, rising from his seat. "Leave then at 6 a.m. I want you to rent a residence for me in Tel Aviv — because I intend to live there!"

R' Berish just stared and gaped. He was totally dumbfounded; this was akin to a thunderclap on a clear day. Everybody had naturally expected the Belzer Rav to settle in Yerushalayim, especially after such a glorious Shabbos. Recovering a little, Mr. Ortner began apologetically, "I had thought, just as everyone else thought, that the Rebbe will certainly wish to live in the Holy City of Jerusalem ..." But the Belzer Rav replied firmly, "The holiness of Yerushalayim is so great that I can't live here! Besides, I have hidden reasons why I cannot settle here! But I can't reveal these to anybody."

After some thought, R' Berish suggested that rather than Tel Aviv, perhaps the Rebbe might move to the more religious townships of Bnei Brak or Petach Tikva.

"I want to live *davka* in Tel Aviv! I'll give just one reason: I've heard that whenever there are Arab riots *chas veshalom*, they close off Tel Aviv to all Arabs — unlike anywhere else. That shows it's a totally Jewish town and that's where I want to live! Please don't ask me for reasons because I cannot divulge them under any circumstances! Therefore, please hurry. Go early tomorrow to look for an apartment. If only I had somewhere there tomorrow, then I would already go now, immediately! But keep this whole affair completely secret until I give you permission to disclose it."[2]

Mr. Ortner saw there was no point in prolonging the discussion, and as a loyal chassid he was prepared to fulfill the Rebbe's every wish. Yet he asked if he could involve his young son, Moshe, in this since it would be difficult for one person alone to search for property in Tel Aviv. Only after the Rebbe was assured that Mr. Ortner's son would definitely keep the secret did he agree. Then Mr. Ortner suggested that it might be worth considering buying a property rather than renting it since that would dispense with any possible problems with landlords. (Indeed, after the huge tumult engendered by the Belzer Rav's short visit, there would be few landlords in Tel Aviv who would be entirely relaxed at having such a famous neighbor or tenant.) The Belzer Rav agreed to that proposal and blessed R' Berish that Hashem should grant him success in finding the right property.

Immediately upon his return to Tel Aviv, Mr. Ortner began an extensive search for a suitable address. Within two to three days, he had several in view: Two bungalows on Rothschild Avenue and Firberg Road respectively, a two-story house at 63 Ahad Ha'am Street, and a five-room house with a large three-dunam garden in

---

2. Interestingly, the Rebbe had earlier discussed living in Tel Aviv with Mr. Yona Cohen in Halab; and on his short visit to Tel Aviv the Rebbe had promised to consider their proposal to establish himself there. According to R' Shmuel Porgas, his *gabbai* in Budapest, the Belzer Rav had already expressed his wish to settle in Tel Aviv while still in Hungary.

Petach Tikva. Rather than report back in person and arouse unnecessary speculation among Belz chassidim, Mr. Ortner sent his son instead.

On Thursday 23 Shevat, Moshe Ortner arrived in Jerusalem where the Belzer Rav was conducting a *tisch* in honor of his grandfather Rebbe Yeshie'le's *yahrzeit*. As soon as the Rebbe saw Moshe Ortner, he told him he would call him to his room right after the *tisch*. Once again the Bilgoraj Rav was present when the Rebbe inquired about what he had to offer.

"Well, there are several possibilities including a two-story house in Tel Aviv for £10,000 and also a most suitable, comfortable building in Petach Tikva with five rooms and large grounds for only £3,000," replied Moshe. "£10,000 is very large amount and we only have £800 that the English chassidim sent to Chief Rabbi Herzog. Perhaps the Rebbe will consider buying the house in Petach Tikva that is only £3,000?"

In reply, the Belzer Rav rose from his seat and gripped Moshe's lapel. "Now listen carefully to what I'm telling you! Petach Tikva is a Jewish town — *a scheiner Yiddishe shtott* — I've passed by there and seen it. But I have concealed reasons why I can live only in Tel Aviv."

"Yet — if we don't have the money?"

"Don't worry — there will be money *im yirtze Hashem*. Now the Bilgoraj Rav will come to Tel Aviv this Sunday to have a look at this house. If he approves of it, buy it straightaway! And I would like to be in Tel Aviv for next Shabbos already! But until then it must remain a secret; absolutely nobody should know."

That Sunday, Rebbe Mottele duly visited the house and was highly impressed. "It could almost have been specially built for my brother *shlita*!" he enthused. They all returned forthwith to Jerusalem where he and R' Berish described the layout of the house. When R' Berish mentioned that the large room to the north (later fondly known as the *"graiser-stieb"*) might be suitable for a *tisch*, the Rebbe turned smilingly to the Bilgoraj Rav and remarked, "You see? I told you Berish understands everything! Even to find a suitable place for a *tisch*!" The Belzer Rav was particularly pleased that the property owners selling the house were descendants of the Yerushalayim Rav, Rabbi Yosef Chaim Sonnenfeld. Under the instructions of the Rebbe, a limited company was set up — "Beis Belz Ltd." — with himself, the Bilgoraj Rav and Mr. Ortner as shareholders; the contract stipulated vacant possession by Rosh Chodesh Nissan (March 25, 1944; i.e. just over a month's time) at a price of £10,000. Now they had the onerous task of raising the money. They also had to contend with the active opposition by bands of Jerusalemites who tried to persuade the Belzer Rav that Tel Aviv was not a religious city like Jerusalem: "The Rebbe should know that some people there drive their cars on Shabbos!" — but he refused to believe them.

Mr. Ortner summoned Belz chassidim and other interested parties to urgent meetings at his house. Although none of the Belz chassidim then in Eretz Yisrael were wealthy (including Mr. Ortner, who had often abandoned his business affairs for his Rebbe's cause), nonetheless they somehow managed to raise quite an amount. Together with short-term loans taken out by Mr. Ortner this came to nearly £6,000, which still left a shortfall of £4,000. Under the Rebbe's instructions, the Bilgoraj Rav contacted chassidim in free Europe and America for their assistance.

Until these letters arrived, none had an inkling of the Belzer Rav's surprising plans. Now they learned that "... for totally secret reasons which cannot be revealed, his holy decision is that it is impossible for him to reside in Yerushalayim ... certain groups in Yerushalayim mounted protests and persuasion to change his mind ... eventually he revealed he had many hidden reasons for his decision not to remain in Yerushalayim ... he urgently wants to move to Tel Aviv before Pesach ... because of the shortage of money he is in great anxiety that perhaps his plans will not be successful ... everyone assumes that as a respected personality above party politics he could raise the spiritual profile of Tel Aviv ... his followers abroad can play an essential role in this ..." The Rebbe's insistence on taking up residence in Tel Aviv by Pesach at the very latest led the Bilgoraj Rav to speculate he was concerned for the possible view of the *Chasam Sofer* (*Yoreh Deah* 236) that the *korban pesach* may be sacrificed in Yerushalayim even nowadays and therefore wanted to avoid that dilemma by maintaining sufficient halachic distance to exempt himself from this obligation.

The first time the Belzer Rav visited the *Kosel HaMaaravi* was a tense occasion and his preparations were extraordinary. The Rebbe seemed gripped by an inner fire, and, after immersing himself in a *mikveh*, gave strict and repeated instructions that nobody may touch him throughout the way to the *Kosel*. He retold several stories from his saintly forebears relating to the holy sites and repeated how his father Rebbe Yissachar Dov (who had, of course, never visited Eretz Yisrael) once remarked, "I am totally familiar with the *Kosel HaMaaravi*, with all its details and *pitchifces*! Inside the *Kosel* there is a doorway which cannot be seen, and with that too I am familiar!" Surprisingly, after his fervent *tefillos*, Reb Aharon instructed one of his followers to roundly curse Hitler at the *Kosel* — contrary to his routine stringency never to mention him by name so as not to "give power to the *Sitra Achra*!"

That Purim the Belzer Rav prayed at the *beis hamedrash* of Kollel Warsaw. As customary, he read the *Megillah,* and several Kabbalists among the congregation recognized that the special emphasis he always gave to certain words and phrases was in accordance with the *kavannos* of the famed *mekubal*, Rav Shalom Sharabi. Their suspicions were confirmed during his repeat *laining* the next morning. Although the Rebbe was well-versed in esoteric knowledge and mystic practice, he tried to conceal his wisdom in this field much as he did his enormous breadth in revealed Torah.

Despite the large crowds, the Rebbe tried to remain sensitive to every individual. Once he was being assisted up the steep stairs to Batei Warsaw and the crush was enormous. Yet a young son of one of the neighbors boldly stepped forward, held out his hand and announced in a piping voice, "*Shalom Aleichem!*" The child was quickly elbowed aside by the *gabbaim* but when his voice reached the Belzer Rav, he looked round, took a few steps back, clutched the child's hand with a fatherly smile and returned the greeting. Similarly, if a *gabbai* ever ordered a child out during the *tisch*, the Rebbe would have him gently called back with the order repeated as a request.

After a nine-and-a-half week sojourn in Yerushalayim, following successful fundraising by his chassidim, the Belzer Rav finally moved to Tel Aviv on 11 Nissan (April 4, 1944), on a Tuesday shortly before Pesach. (Belz customarily move into new premises on Erev Shabbos, but that year Friday was also Erev Pesach. Tuesday was usually the day the Rebbe preferred for embarking on journeys and enterprises.) The next day, *Ha'aretz* gave this news item due prominence:

> BELZ REBBE ARRIVES IN TEL AVIV TO SETTLE
> *With great warmth Belz chassidim yesterday greeted the Rebbe, Rabbi Aharon Rokach, who left Jerusalem to establish himself in Tel Aviv. At midday, groups of chassidim waited at the main Jerusalem-Tel Aviv highway near Mikveh Yisrael. As he arrived with his brother and Jerusalem chassidim, they joined the entourage into the Hebrew Town.*
>
> *The house, 63 Ahad Ha'am Street, had been specially bought by his chassidim in Eretz Yisrael, America and England. The entrance was decorated with a large baruchim habaim. On arrival in Tel Aviv, the Rebbe first waited a short time at Mr. Ortner's residence, 79 Rothschild Avenue, before moving into his own home.*
>
> *Before leaving Jerusalem, the Rebbe took his leave from Chief Rabbi Herzog who had come to pay a courtesy call. This was a return visit after the Rebbe had earlier called on Chief Rabbi Herzog at his private residence.*
>
> *All the rooms in the Rebbe's new home in Tel Aviv were busy until late last night with chassidim, well-wishers and on-lookers ...*

In keeping with the hopes expressed in the Bilgoraj Rav's letter, the Rebbe did elevate Tel Aviv's religious landscape over the next decade — particularly in the vicinity around 63 Ahad Ha'am Street. He was to slow the precipitate flight of the religious from Tel Aviv and help perpetuate the original Orthodox character of the town. He strongly advised chassidim to persevere with the struggle for Tel Aviv's soul rather than abandon it for the more conducive religious atmosphere and education in other townships. "What happened in *der heim*? Did chassidim not stand at their shop entrance or otherwise come into contact with all their neighbors?" In one instance when a young boy had the traditional *chalakah* (first haircut), he had him paraded up Allenby Street — freshly shorn with long *peyos* — as a worthy example to emulate.

While visiting war refugee children, the Rebbe gently asked, "Where are your peyos like his?"

Even when living in Tel Aviv, the Belzer Rav refused to believe it was an irreligious city. When a bus engine could be heard in the distance, he insisted the driver "must have forgotten it's Shabbos ..." His subsequent attitude to the more secular residents was extraordinary — reminiscent of the saintly Berditchever Rebbe — incredibly finding the best gloss on their behavior. They ate pork "in anticipation of Messianic times!"; they smoked on the Sabbath because they were "unaware of Shabbos restrictions"; they did not don *tefillin* because they could not guarantee the required physical sanctity; people stole because "all the world belongs to Hashem!" He once remarked that one has a duty to explain the actions of a difficult Jew just as one endeavors to *"farenfer a schvere Rambam!"*

When R' Berish railed against *"Yiddishe goyim"* during elections, the Rebbe peremptorily interrupted him. "It's forbidden to speak thus about Jews!" He ordered R' Berish to wash and dry his hands three times on the Rebbe's towel before repeating ten times, *"Yehudim! Yehudim!"* to remove the detrimental effect. Likewise, when a petitioner from Los Angeles asked for a blessing to relocate to a better area since his current Jewish neighborhood was *"niderik* and *gemeine,"* he was first made to repeat three times, "There are no low or depraved Jews in Los

Angeles," since no such concept as a depraved Jew exists! "Weak Jews" rather than "irreligious Jews."

Dr. Much, the Rebbe's personal eye doctor, who visited him every week, was non-religious, but when he notified them he could not call over Pesach, the Belzer Rav remarked admiringly, "He's probably meticulous not to eat outside his home on Pesach and afraid we might offer him something!" During the year, they once served the doctor some wine. Since the Rebbe did not share in the drink, the chassidim explained that he rarely drank except on Seder-night when he imbibed plenty. The doctor replied, "Of course, I personally make my own raisin wine and borscht before Pesach — and fast on Yom Kippur." The Belzer Rav was greatly impressed and remarked afterwards, "When Mashiach comes he will have the task of returning those Jews who were unable to withstand all the tests of time for various reasons. When he meets a Jew who makes Pesach wine and borscht himself and also fasts on Yom Kippur — he will derive enormous *simchah*!"

Sixty-three Ahad Ha'am Street, the Rebbe's house, contained a flourishing garden with flowering plants and trees, and on noticing it, the Rebbe asked his loyal chassid R' Yisrael Klapholtz to do the gardening! After buying the correct tools and water hoses he was to tend the beautiful garden nearly every other day. Even more surprising, the Rebbe kept up a keen and detailed interest in the garden, occasionally descending to ground level to inspect its progress. The whole affair was an enigma to Mr. Klapholtz and the many visitors to Belz: Such a saintly man, absorbed all day in Heavenly matters, should spare time and sentiment for such a worldly and apparently mundane hobby?

When the Belzer Rav noticed R' Yisrael's deep puzzlement, he reminisced that his *Zeide* Rebbe Yehoshua had likewise had a garden planted around his house, but one chassid took a deep dislike to the idea and ruined everything the gardener had planted. Although Rebbe Yeshie'le had pleaded in protest to this chassid and had hinted that he had a higher, esoteric purpose, the man rudely replied, "I don't want my Rebbe to have a garden!" Indeed, he repeatedly destroyed whatever the gardener planted, "while my *Zeide* never said another word to the man ..."

Mr. Klapholtz was almost as puzzled as before but faithfully tended the Rebbe's garden from Pesach until shortly before Rosh Hashanah. Before the new year was about to begin, the Belzer Rav told R' Yisrael, "Do you see? Until now you have looked after the garden well and did all I asked. But now the year of *Shemittah* has arrived! Take all your tools and hoses and put them carefully away in a locked room — till after *Shemittah!*" Only then did they realize the Rebbe's intent.

On their arrival in Eretz Yisrael, the Belzer Rebbe and the Bilgoraj Rav also sought to revive education as taught according to age-old methods. Famously, Belz had always retained a sincere regard for traditional *chinuch: cheder* children were encouraged with charming ceremonies during Chanukah and Simchas Torah. On the last day of Chanukah, the children would form a procession, carrying the latest acquisitions of *sefarim,* and file past the Rebbe's window to be blessed with success in learning. During the Simchas Torah morning *tisch,* the younger boys would be marshaled as a band of "holy sheep" led by a slightly older "shepherd," dressed appropriately. After a chorus of "bleats" and a short question and answer chant, they were specially treated to the Rebbe's *sherayim* shared out by the "shepherd." In common with many chassidim, their boys did not have their hair cut before the age of three, nor wear a *cappel* and *tallis katan,* or recite *berachos.* On their third birthday they were taken, wrapped in a *tallis,* to the *cheder,* to their *aleph-beis melamed* for the sweet ceremony of studying the holy letters — specifically *taf, shin, yud.* Only at the age of five did they begin learning *Chumash,* and the *Chumash seudah* was mandatory. After beginning with *Vayikra,* their study of *Chumash* followed the weekly *Sedra* cycle. Many of these old traditions have experienced a remarkable revival over recent decades, but in 1944 it was an uphill task.

On 24 Iyar, the Bilgoraj Rav issued the following letters in support of *Yaldei Yisrael* (established in the wake of the *Yaldei Teheran* scandal):

> *I have been instructed by my brother, the holy Rav shlita, to encourage the generous among us to support Yaldei Yisrael. To quote his words, he has already been able to value and esteem the great enter-*

prise, educating children according to the traditions we have inherited from our holy forefathers, zechusam yagen aleinu, and integrate them correctly. Therefore he requests that you strengthen and support this institution of Yaldei Yisrael so the honorable activists can widen their activities with renewed strength while our brethren here and abroad donate generously to the cause.

And my holy brother shlita blesses all those involved in establishing or supporting this great mitzvah that we merit to see the advancement of Keren Yisrael and the holy Torah, and that we merit the complete Geulah very soon.

Signing under instruction of my holy brother, the Tzaddik of Belz Mordechai Rokach

❧

The rousing proclamations published by my holy brother, the Tzaddik shlita, and other gedolim and tzaddikim of our generation on behalf of Yaldei Yisrael do not need our endorsement, particularly as their words constitute a whole Torah of their own. Children's education is not merely a private duty of individual fathers but also the responsibility of the general public. For the benefit of the child without parents, Yehoshua ben Gamla organized a system of teachers available in every area and town (Bava Basra 21) and it is recorded in Rambam and Shulchan Aruch, Hilchos Melamdim, as halachah.

Not only must a teaching system be available but it should also be linked with a holy and conducive atmosphere to direct their young hearts toward yiras Shamayim and Torah. Chazal tell us that they first began that program in Yerushalayim, where children could witness great holiness and the Kohanim performing the sacrifices, thus encouraging them to piety and Torah study (Tosefos ibid.). Although the strict parameters of the original institution may no longer be valid, the spirit of that takanah remains totally relevant. Even outside Yerushalayim, their surrounding atmosphere should be pure and sanctified, steering their hearts toward Torah and spirituality. Certainly we have a sacred duty in this terrible situation where pitifully few survive from thousands of saintly children, brutally murdered al Kiddush Hashem or thrown from the roofs in front of our eyes!

Believe me, at the worst times, trapped under terrible conditions in the depth of galus, when the ghettos were subjected to awful "deportations," *our religious brethren risked their lives on behalf of general chinuch. And especially on behalf of those children who had been torn from the bosom of their family by the hands of the reshaim. How can we excuse ourselves if we do not offer support to the innocent young lambs amid peace and prosperity?*

Yet I remain hopeful that Am Yisrael will respond to the needs of Yaldei Yisrael and to the call of Gedolei Yisrael, giving with open hands and in generous spirit. Thus will the directors and volunteers of this holy institution be able to widen the confines of kedushah and enroll those children, orphaned from their parents, under the wings of the Shechinah. In this merit may we witness the salvation and comfort of all Israel.

Writing for the sake of our strengthened religion,
Mordechai Rokach (Rav of Bilgoraj)

The Bilgoraj Rav repeated these sentiments near the end of Sivan when he spoke at the foundation-stone laying of Sinai Talmud Torah, Tel Aviv. Speaking "on behalf of his brother and all the Rebbes" (as reported in the religious weekly *Hayesod*, Friday 2 Tammuz) he delivered a fiery *derashah*:

It is no coincidence that only days after the international fast day the foundation stone for this Talmud Torah is being laid. Years ago the Torah warned us that when we are beset by "many troubles ... because Hashem is no longer among us ..." Every fast day spurs one to teshuvah and to review past behavior because we believe nothing happens by accident; we have no option but to confess our sins. And the only tried and tested remedy against "many troubles" and hard times is strengthening Torah. As that Torah chapter concludes, "And now write for yourselves this song ..." If you involve yourselves in Torah and good deeds, in educating the children to Torah, we can be spared the tribulations of Ikvesa D'Meshicha (the End of Days).

Secular education is supported by the wider public and even by some among us. But recent visitors from outside who have come to settle here can better discern how the children here are apt to absorb the holy light of Torah. Every child has a natural, independent inclination to Torah because his roots stem from holiness — zera kodesh.

"Educate each child according to his nature," every Jewish child has a natural affinity to Torah.

How often we ought to protest against the scandal of those few living embers from the Nazi conflagration who were given over to an educational system alien to their spirit and foreign to their sainted fathers' tradition!

"When King Solomon married Pharaoh's daughter, a stake was driven into the sea on which was eventually built the large city of Rome." Secular education helps build Rome, not Jerusalem! Now after the fall of Rome we have gathered to lay a stone for a veritable Mishkan of Torah, thus planting a Torah stake in the sea of Tel Aviv.

The reference to those "living embers" obviously referred to the sad saga of *Yaldei Teheran*, where orphaned survivors of religious parents who escaped via Teheran in '42 were allocated almost entirely to exclusively non-religious schools by the Jewish Agency.[3] The world fast day mentioned in his opening remarks was actually declared by the Belzer Rav on behalf of those trapped in the Nazis' fiendish grasp.

---

3. Out of the 733 escapees, only 30 children were permitted to enlist in religious institutions and another 40 absconded later. Of these fortunate few, many were brought by their counselors to the Belzer Rav for encouragement in Torah study and piety, often returning of their own volition for Shabbos and Yom Tov.

CHAPTER 27

OUR BROTHERS IN DISTRESS AND CAPTIVITY

D ESPITE THEIR FORTUNATE ESCAPE, THE TWO brothers never forgot their less fortunate brethren still trapped in the Nazi noose. Indeed, they were among the first to bring a realistic appraisal of the sheer enormity and intensity of the torment to the wider Israeli public. Right from their arrival in Haifa, the Bilgoraj Rav was disturbed at the overwhelming composure bordering on indifference displayed by the *Yishuv* to their coreligionists' fate. After four years of Nazi oppression, he lamented, with its murder machine working at full blast — still only a handful take the dire situation seriously! So he embarked on a series of speeches and interviews (mainly in the Agudah and other religious publications) to shock the public into action, dwelling alternately on the physical and spiritual heroism displayed in the face of oppression, the natural need for revenge, and the urgent necessity for funds and assistance.

An early opportunity arose when he and the Belzer Rav were invited to visit the Tiferes Yisrael Yeshivah in Haifa by the Rosh Yeshivah, Rabbi D. M. Robman. The Belzer Rav declined because of continuing frailty but the Bilgoraj Rav came to deliver a forthright address, reported in *Hayesod* weekly, 24 Shevat.

> *"I am deeply impressed by my visit here," said the Bilgoraj Rav. "Even from the distance one can hear the roar of Torah study from the precious bachurim learning with diligence and fervor. Before I arrived in Eretz Yisrael, I was told that Haifa is a non-religious city. To the delight of myself and my brother, the Belzer Rebbe, I can confirm now that we have been greatly disillusioned — for the best! If socialist Haifa, the workers' city, can boast a yeshivah with more than eighty talmidim in comfortable conditions and a luxurious dormitory block, then one may not slander Haifa for being irreligious!*
>
> *"May I take this occasion to convey scenes from your chaverim in Poland. The oppressor yemach shemo decreed that all pupils who abandon their studies and join the slave labor would be saved from death ... Yet our holy talmidim" he cried out, his voice breaking with emotion, his eyes filling with tears, "sacrificed their lives, sanctified Hashem's Name and would not discontinue limud haTorah!"*

The evening before they left Haifa, he had a widely reported opportunity to voice his distress to an adult audience — at what should have been a routine public ceremony. The occasion that Wednesday evening was the foundation-stone laying for a new marble *aron hakodesh* at the old, central *beis hamedrash* in Haifa. After short speeches by Mr. Teitelbaum (on behalf of the executive) and Chief Rabbi Baruch Markus, Rebbe Mottele dwelt at length and in detail on the war atrocities, reducing the large congregation to tears. His spellbinding address lasted well over an hour and the second part was devoted entirely to the war situation.

> *"... I have discovered that the public in the Holy Land does not fully believe the terrible horror that has befallen our nation in exile. Sadly, the bitter truth is many, many times worse than anything you have heard! All that is known in the free world is but a drop in the ocean of massacres battering European Jewry. To all those doubters, I can bear witness from my own personal experience that all current descriptions are as nothing compared with the awful truth. On leaving Hungary, I saw with my own eyes wagonloads of Italian Jews being transported to their death in Poland. Elderly, women, young children,*

pushing their shrunken hands through the bars, begging for "Water!
Water!" But the Gestapo troops did not allow anyone to approach the
death train and assist the captives. I saw prisoners crazed from thirst
attacking each other and biting their flesh!

People talk glibly about the murder of thousands of children. But
no words can possibly describe how Nazis kill children. They even
force the mothers to witness the "ceremony" of their childrens' mas-
sacre! There have been cases where the parents have been forced from
their beds to be present at the execution! Just to multiply the pain
and torture ...

This aron hakodesh here will have steps as did the Menorah in
the Mikdash, yet no steps were allowed for the Mizbe'ach since that
symbolized humility and teshuvah. But the Deutsche are incapable
of genuine teshuvah! They allegedly repented after the last war, yet
now they have reverted to type — behaving as the German barbarians
did thousands of years ago when they were the greatest murderers at
large. Their 20th-century descendants adorn themselves in the cloak
of culture and civilization merely to dominate the world and destroy
it. Anyone who thinks they will eventually repent is mistaken; they
are the accursed sons of Satan and their offspring cannot possibly
atone for their devastation. Many ask how we, merciful sons of merci-
ful ancestors, are capable of avenging ourselves on this archenemy,
but we have to pray that Heaven implants in our souls passion for
vengeance and retaliation. Until the horrendous fate of our holy, pure
brothers is avenged, we will never find peace to the end of days!

According to the Mizrachi party's *Hatzofe*, the Bilgoraj Rav bellowed *"Keil nekamos Hashem, Keil nekamos hofia* — these murders
must be avenged! None of the *Deutsche* are innocent of this heinous
crime. Send help!" The Rav screamed, "Save every soul that can still
be saved!" One socialist newspaper, *Davar*, reported on 17 Shevat
that the Bilgoraj Rav asked emotionally:

How dare the Jews of Eretz Yisrael doubt the veracity of atrocity ac-
counts? How dare they remain indifferent? Rather they should give
away their last pennies to save those few souls still left!

We have a duty to rescue every Jewish child still alive as we would
a Sefer Torah! The 600,000 letters in each Sefer Torah symbolize the

members of Klal Yisrael. Hashem declares (according to Chazal), "My candle is in your hands and your candle is in My Hands! If you look after My candle, I will guard yours!" Just as we protect the Sifrei Torah by constructing an aron hakodesh, so too are we duty bound to save the "Torah letters floating in the atmosphere" — the remaining survivors. Then Hashem will guard our candle, the ner Hashem, nishmas Adam! May we merit together with the she'eiris hapleitah to witness the coming of Mashiach here, in the Holy Land!

This oration made an enormous impression on ordinary laymen and newspaper correspondents alike. Finally, several of the Bilgoraj Rav's newspaper interviews were published, mostly on Thursday, 23 Shevat (February 17, 1944), when they were already in Jerusalem. One Agudah publication, *Haderech*, carried his private interview with Yaakov Katz that had lasted until 2 a.m., with the Bilgoraj Rav recounting some blood-curdling episodes and painting scenes of spiritual heroism.

When one workplace in Krakow was closed down, six hundred girls lost their employment. Since the Germans had no further need for them, they decided to get rid of them all and mustered Jewish slave-laborers to dig mass graves. When the girls heard of their fate, they broke into a dance! And that is how they went to their death! Happy that they were destined for a better world, with their virtue intact and their reputations unblemished!

In one Galician town, the Gestapo approached the Jews and offered to escort them group by group across the border. It was agreed that after the first paying group was safely across the border and had sent reassuring letters, they would proceed with the other groups. But the first group was taken outside the town and forced under threats to write a letter "confirming they had reached their destination" before being murdered with their wives and children. With this trick, hundreds more were taken to their death, fooled into thinking their predecessors had been saved. Hashem yinkom damam.

One of the first kehillos to be massacred was Brzezany in Galicia. On Yom Kippur, six hundred of its prominent members were dragged out to be murdered with the utmost cruelty. Kosow suffered the same fate as did Stanislawow, Kolomia and other towns. Some towns were rendered

R' Chaim Yisrael Eiss

Judenrein, including Tarnow, where some were murdered and the rest "resettled" or ausiedlung, as they deceptively call it. Just one example of their brutal sadism: one top German officer did a "kindness" for a Jewish decorator who plastered and painted his private quarters with dedication and earned his total satisfaction. As a reward for his work, he shot him while remarking, "You at least are worth a German bullet!"

The decree came from above to destroy, liquidate and murder to an exact schedule. One day the havoc is visited on one town, the next day it is somewhere else's turn.

The same publication carried another wide-ranging discussion with R' Fishel Gelernter and Mr. S. Z. Mozes (who described Rebbe Mottele as "... precious, pleasant, good natured ...; besides his Torah brilliance and saintliness, he is extremely perceptive in world affairs. Despite his relief and joy at reaching safety, his lined face reveals the past trauma ...").

He[1] first registered his gratitude for their miraculous liberation and although hester panim — a Divine veil cloaking everything in overwhelming darkness and confusion — reigned generally, every individual experienced miracles and exceptional wonders beyond natural circumstance. The Bilgoraj Rav singled out the late R' Chaim Yisrael Eiss of Zurich (whom he remembered from his earlier visits to Belz) as a shining example of hatzalah activity.

Everybody in Poland strengthened themselves till their last breath in belief, trust and supreme bravery. "Take, for instance, charity. When Western Galicia still had enough to eat, they dispatched food parcels to Eastern Galicia. When they heard of one area where they were starving, another area would step in and support them."

Even while the Bilgoraj Rav was hiding from the Gestapo, he endangered himself to discover the situation of various kehillas and personalities nearby and faraway — including rebbes and famous rabbis — and send some assistance.

_____

1. The Bilgoraj Rav.

The Bilgoraj Rav was the personal contact between many kehillos, and also collected details and materials on the varying situation in Galicia and their assistance campaigns. Spiritual life endured at all times and in the worst of situations — clandestine shtiebels were full and Torah study persisted. Education in the religious networks never stopped. Chadarim existed where hundreds of children learnt although these were threatened by danger from all sides. It needed mesiras nefesh, literally, to sustain Torah chinuch in every town and village.

When he was in Przemyslany, several chassidim secretly gathered in his house, spending their time just how they would have before the War, without any modification. Whenever they drank a l'chaim they would toast each other, "To be safe and spared any mishap." That was the sole wish and prayer on everyone's mind. Yet one young man asked that he be blessed that, "His children grow up to be pious with good deeds!" The Rav was astonished. During such precarious circumstances where everybody else sought safety, he sought the blessing of good children? Ultimately the Rav assured him that in the merit of educating his children for Torah and Chassidus he would surely deserve protection!

No words can describe what happened or everything one saw — it was beyond belief! Human imagination is too limited to articulate the events raining down on individuals or communities. The sadism was harrowing and ghastly. Jews were forced out in the depths of winter, in the worst cold imaginable to work outside with only paper clothing to cover them. The suffering was so unbearable that they begged to be shot instead.

The Polish tragedy went through three stages: When war broke out with Russia, the situation of Eastern Galicia (that had been bearable until then) deteriorated. When America joined the War, the persecution entered another stage. The cruelty reached a new pitch when Russian troops scored their first successes. The persecution itself went through two stages. At first Jews were exiled from place to place to dispossess them and make them easier prey to loot. Then began the period of deportations to death. Initially, no one knew what these deportations or "resettlement" meant since the Nazis used tricks and *various ruses. Only afterwards did they hear from Congress Poland the fate of the deportees, and they warned the Galician kehillos of what to expect.*

The Bilgoraj Rav had been at the center of assistance campaigns and on hearing these first reports, he was so affected that his health collapsed and he became dangerously ill. His saintly brother, the Belzer Rav, had to treat him personally. As far as he could recall, the main headquarters of destruction then were Belzec and Malkinia. The persecution intensified throughout the Reich and occupied territories till the end of 1942.

As to mounting a revolt? This was discussed in all circles and when realization dawned that there was nothing to lose, the religious Jews and chassidim also joined the battle. It was a natural reaction — Haba l'horgoch, hashkeim v'horgo! But Polish Jews' bravery was conspicuous in the religious arena, risking their lives for Torah and mitzvos which led to amazing feats of Kiddush Hashem. In many areas, Jews hid in concealed "bunkers." Escapees picked up by the Gestapo were often assured by the reshaim that they would be unharmed if they only disclosed the whereabouts of their bunkers. Otherwise, they would be shot on the spot! Yet all of them, even young children, would not surrender their comrades, declaring they would rather die than betray other Jews to slaughter! That is their sole revenge: The Nazis had not managed to break Jewish unity. Among other episodes, the Bilgoraj Rav remembered one young man in Bochnia who was about to be executed in the Jewish cemetery. But before his murder, he proclaimed in front of them that he saw his revenge: they had not managed to extract details of Jewish bunkers — and he saw his reward by at least receiving a Jewish burial!

In the Krakow labor camps, Jews would get up early to pray secretly. The Nazis found out and captured thirty-six Jews in tefillin. All were murdered. There were thousands of other examples of self-sacrifice and Kiddush Hashem ...

"All reports publicized so far on the number of Jews surviving in Poland cannot be totally accurate since solid facts are hard to come by and difficult to verify. All that we can safely surmise is that a relatively small remnant are in hiding and a larger group is still alive in slave labor camps. There are various avenues of rescue," the

Bilgoraj Rav concluded, "but we have to rouse public opinion here in Eretz Yisrael and abroad to the plight of the survivors." Personally, he hopes to utilize all his strength for the hatzalah effort.

The reference to that brave man in Bochnia probably refers to Hershel Zimmer and his son from Krakow who officially baked bread for Bochnia's slave workers and secretly smuggled bread to "illegal" Jews in hiding. They withstood excruciating torture and died "happy at being executed for delivering Jews from hunger!"[2]

On the same Thursday, the *Kol Yisrael* carried his interview with R' Moshe Porush (Glikman) which took place against a background of back-to-back meetings and visits. Drawing a heartbreaking sigh the Bilgoraj Rav began:

> *"The situation is far, far worse than you here or our brothers in America imagine. It's time the Jewish public and world nations learnt the true situation under Nazi occupation and roused themselves to hatzalah. I have the impression that you assume it is merely a rerun of the old story: Just as there were pogroms in certain towns or countries, so it is now in Poland. On the contrary, the present situation is completely different. The war against the Jews manifests itself there by their total obliteration chas veshalom. Everything was preplanned beforehand, operating from conviction and to a fixed strategy! It looks almost as if the Germans are more interested in eliminating the Jews than in winning the war against the Allies!*
>
> *"From the first, the Germans ensured that Jews had no weapons to stage a possible revolt; they were always in charge of the situation, initiating attacks and taking care no Germans were harmed. They planted spies in the camps and ghettos. Once anyone had hidden a weapon, he was straight on line for execution.*
>
> *"It is frightening to hear how Krakow and its surrounding kehillos were destroyed. It started with a decree forcing all Jews to vacate Krakow but allowing them the choice of where to go. Many went to nearby Bochnia, but during 1942, Bochnia was converted to a ghetto. During Sivan all remaining Krakow Jews were deported and*

---

2. R' Hershel was a Bobover *talmid* and had earlier used his position as Judenrat secretary to smuggle out official stationery, typewriter and ink to forge lifesaving documents and permits.

the same fate befell the other towns during Av. On 12 Elul, the Jews of Bochnia were deported and the ghetto was converted to a closed camp. That deportation was horrifying. In one day 90 percent — 7,200 — were deported in cattle trucks while over 1,000 were tortured and machine-gunned to death. Besides the unbelievable cruelty, the Nazis played games with their victims. For instance, the Rav was officially freed but when he walked innocently home he found the killers waiting for him at the entrance — shooting him and his wife on the spot."

The Bilgoraj Rav detailed their fateful encounter with Bochnia's Camp Commandant at the Rebbe's residence on Parashas Shekalim where Muller was favorably impressed. After that, when Muller discovered a Sefer Torah, he did not tear it to shreds as previously but dispatched it to the Rebbe. Also, he freed other rabbis from the slave labor and allowed them to live in the Rebbe's vicinity.

Contact between Polish towns and neutral countries was maintained until the end of 5702. According to reports, Warsaw's situation was very good until then; Jews profited and established factories and other enterprises. But between the end of that year and the beginning of the next, the situation changed and they decreed that no Jew may send mail. Once a maid was shot on the spot for dropping a Jew's letter into a mailbox!

The Bilgoraj Rav described the unbelievable generosity to charity. Everyone, rich and poor alike, supported the general fund to assist the penniless. People gave much more than they could afford. They all concluded that if they had enough for a month or two, then they should donate to the poor. And they gave generously. When there was an appeal for Pesach matzos, thousands gathered within minutes, each with their donation! "We cannot quantify the communal enthusiasm for charity. They were content with the minimum and everybody 'felt a blessing in the food.' "

Exceptional was the sheer bravery of Jews, especially the youngsters. At first the German decree stated that all who registered for work would not be deported. Even so, many, particularly Gur and Belz chassidim, ignored all these assurances and refused to work on Shabbos — despite the argument that this could endanger their lives, literally sakanas nefashos. Instead they arranged shiurim and learnt with enormous diligence. Also, they traveled from area to area spread-

ing Torah, surmounting all obstacles. Anyone who knows the reality of Nazi rule in those days can imagine what mesiras nefesh was entailed in traveling from one place to another to establish shiurim. Yet they were extraordinarily successful! Everyone recognized this supreme bravery as uniquely Jewish. Ultimately, the orders came from Berlin to deport them all — including those who permitted themselves to work on Shabbos in the belief that it would save their lives ...

Inevitably, all these interviews and speeches had a cumulative effect on the public mood. The time had now come to spur the community into action and they decided to call for a "World Fast and Day of Prayer" on the traditional *Yom Kippur Katan* (Thursday, 28 Adar) before Rosh Chodesh Nissan. The Belzer Rav called on the revered Gerrer Rebbe, Rav Avraham Mordche Alter, who was frail and mostly housebound since his escape from Warsaw in the early years of the War. The Rebbe of Gur immediately agreed to issue a joint declaration:

> *Holy City of Jerusalem, May it speedily be rebuilt!*
> ### TO OUR HONORED BROTHERS
> ### IN THE HOLY LAND AND ABROAD
> *After witnessing how the Nation of Israel is trapped in distress rachmanah litzlan, we have found it most important to declare a Fast Day for Klal Yisrael's tefillos on Thursday, 28 Adar, this year! Men and ladies from eighteen years old upwards should fast on this day. The elderly and weak should redeem their fast with charity.*
>
> *On the day of the taanis, they should gather in the shuls and batei medrash to recite Tehillim and prayers. Also to repent with complete teshuvah while accepting the yoke of Torah and mitzvah observance in their entirety.*
>
> *In this merit may Hashem behold the travail of His people and have mercy on the remnant. May we merit the geulah sheleimah very soon, in our days.*
>
> *Awaiting salvation and the rapid elevation of Keren Yisrael.*
> *(signed)*
> *Avraham Mordechai Alter, of Gur*
> *Aharon Rokach, of Belz*
> *Mordechai Rokach, Rav of Bilgoraj*

This proclamation was countersigned by the leading Rabbis and Torah scholars. Mr. Ortner also obtained the signatures of the various chassidic Rebbes in Tel Aviv including Husyaten, Chortkov, Sadigura-Przemysl, Boyan and Zlatapoli. Sadly, the international Fast Day was held against the grave background of heartbreaking news from abroad — the full-blooded invasion of Hungary, almost the last sanctuary of religious Jews in Europe!

Its fragile independence was abruptly shattered, its puppet administration swept aside and an estimated 800,000 Jews suddenly fell within the direct grasp of the bloodthirsty Nazis. Paradoxically, it was German military reverses in Italy, Russia and Romania which led to the German occupation of its official ally. Irritated by Hungary's peace feelers to the West, Regent Horthy and his cabinet were summoned to Klessheim Castle near Salzburg on March 17, 1944 for a personal dressing-down by the self-styled Fuehrer. While they were thus isolated, German tanks rolled over the border and by the time the cabinet returned two days later (Sunday, 24 Adar) the occupation was complete. Fortunately, the Belzer Rav had escaped their rapacious clutches by just two months.

A new puppet administration was established but now the real rulers were the SS under Edmund Veesenmayer — and Berlin's deportation experts had simultaneously arrived with the tanks. Once again, extermination of the Jews took precedence over Germany's desperate struggle to avoid defeat and invasion. Harsh anti-Jewish legislation was swiftly enacted on 5 Nissan and all Jews concentrated into six zones. Since they were clearly losing the battle against Russia in the east and facing an impending Anglo-American invasion in the west, the German murder machine was in a tremendous hurry to destroy as many Jews as possible. Everything they had learned in the last ten years about terror, ruthlessness, guile, organization and the exploitation of accomplices was rapidly put into motion. Naturally, Eretz Yisrael was shocked by the latest news.

On Tuesday 26 Adar, the Belzer Rav led a large congregation in chanting *Tehillim* at the *Kosel HaMaaravi*. They began with Psalm 90 (the allocation for the "Fifth Day") and recited loudly, accompanied by tears and emotion. When they reached Psalm 102, the Rebbe broke down and cried uncontrollably like a young baby. On his return to his temporary residence, he brokenheartedly led the prayers for Maariv.

That Thursday, the international Fast Day duly took place on 23 March, and thousands crowded into Meah Shearim Yeshivah. Many *Gedolei Yisrael* were present and although the Gerrer Rebbe had expressed his wish to attend, his failing physical strength did not allow him. Instead he sent his sons to read a personal letter. After Minchah, the Belzer Rav mounted the *bimah* and in a tearful voice stated, "I am not worthy enough to rebuke other Jews! But anybody may repeat words of *mussar* and *hisorerus* ... The Noam Elimelech writes that every generation has its special mitzvos that should be performed to perfection. Our generation's special duty is to correct and repair failings in religious education, family purity and Sabbath observance!" Since the Rebbe was in a heightened emotional state — his face constantly changed color from glowing passion to a lifeless pale white, his short sentences were punctuated with deep-felt sighs and chanted in the *mussar nigun* customarily used on Yom Kippur eve — his half-hour *derashah* roused the congregation to repentance and demanded a personal *cheshbon hanefesh* from everyone.

Then the Bilgoraj Rav delivered a fiery speech for approximately 90 minutes, describing the stark reality of Poland's predicament and their short sojourn in Hungary, elaborating on its holy, pure yeshivos and *Talmud Torahs*. Once again everybody present burst into loud weeping. He urged them not to delay; something could still be saved but everybody here was still too lethargic. The subsequent chapters of *Tehillim* were recited with deep feeling. At first, the congregation was led by the Rebbe and, after his departure, by the Bilgoraj Rav.

To coincide with the fast a passionate proclamation was issued on the same day, on behalf of the "Yishuv for Hatzalah" fund:

> *Acheinu Bnei Yisrael in Eretz Yisrael!*
> *The despairing cry of the remnants of our people reaches us from the depths of the land of tyranny — Help! The surviving remnant are in terrible straits but there are still some that can be saved and there are still ways of saving them with Hashem's help.*
> *The month of Nissan has been proclaimed a month of charity for*

כרוז האדמו"רים

ומען מפעל "הישוב להצלה"

בזה"ת, כ"ח אדר תש"ד, ירושלים עיה"ק.

אחינו בני ישראל אשר בארץ הקודש!

קול שוועת יתר הפליטה של בת עמנו מגיע אלינו מארצות
תוריה: חצילו! שארית פליטת ישראל נתונה בצרה איומה ויש
עד מי להציל וישנם עוד דרכים להצלה, בשעה"ת.
חודש ניסן תובעין כאחוזה צדקה להצלה. חוב קדוש על כן
עלינו. שבכל זיח גיצלנו, להשתתף כולנו במסעל זה למען הצלת
ישראל. יתן כל אחד כפי כוחו ויותר מכוחי.

ובימים י"א — י"ב — י"ג — ניסן חבע"ל ישתתף כל אחד
במסעל הכללי "הישוב להצלה", כסי אשר ירשות עליו ועל כל
מסורת ביתו, ובזכות זה ח' חפתורח החמציל יפרת ויצל וירחם על
שארית עמו ישראל.

אברהם מרדכי   ישראל במוה"ר   אהרן רוקח
אלטר (מנור)   מרדכי פיי בש (מהושיאסין)   סבבז

נחום מרדכי במוה"ר ישראל מרדכי רוקח
(ממשורסקוב)
(באאמז"ד זצ"ל)   ישראל במוה"ר יצחק זצ"ל
סבעלזא אבד"ק   (מבוען)
ביללגורייא)
יעקב במוה"ר
יצחק מבאחוט
אברהם יעקב
במוה"ר יש ראל (מסאד'נודה)
מרדכי שלום יוסף במוה"ר
אהרן (מסאדינורה-פשמישל)
צבי ארי' בהרה"צ מרדכי
יוסף זצ"ל, (סולאמזשול).

The appeal for hatzalah

rescue. Therefore there rests a holy duty upon us, who have been spared by Hashem's assistance, to join this great enterprise for Hatzalas Yisrael. Everyone should contribute as much as he can and more.

The 11th, 12th and 13th of Nissan have been set aside for this general fund, "Yishuv for Hatzalah," for all to respond, according to how he and his family have been assessed. In this merit, may Hashem the Redeemer and Rescuer have mercy on the remnants of His people.

Among those who signed this appeal were the Rebbes of Gur, Belz, Husyaten, Chortkov, Bilgoraj, Boyan, Bohush, Sadigura-Przemysl and Zlatapoli. Heartbreakingly, the horrendous events in Hungary did not stand still and less than three weeks after the invasion — even before Pesach — the deportations to the Polish death camps began, rising to a daily transport of 12,000 Jews. (Over the next few months, to the 17th of Tammuz, nearly 450,000 Jews from the different zones were to disappear on the death trains.) On Monday, 22 Iyar (May 15, 1944), the Belzer Rav summoned a Rabbinical conclave in Tel Aviv which lasted all day. The rabbis were shocked and horrified when the Bilgoraj Rav related graphic details of the Holocaust. A delegation was promptly dispatched to Jerusalem comprising — besides the Bilgoraj Rav — the Viznitz Rebbe, Sadigura Rebbe, Sadigura-Przemysl Rebbe and Munkacs Rebbe.

After a preliminary meeting at the Gerrer Rebbe's residence (his frailty prevented his personal attendance but he sent a message that he joined their efforts with all his heart) they met with Chief Rabbi Yitzchak Isaac Herzog and Chief Rabbi Uziel, R' Yitzchak Meir Lewin, Mr. Moshe Shapira, Mr. Binyamin Mintz, Rav Yaakov Henoch Sancowitz, Rav Shmuel Aaron Webber (all of Vaad Hatzalah), Dr. S. Lemberger and R' Yosef Feldman (both from Hungary, the latter funded the legendary Dr. Griffel). They discussed ways of arousing public involvement in last-ditch rescue efforts and decided on various courses of action. Urgent cables were also sent to the U.S. government's Aid Committee and other institutions and personalities.

Two days later, even the secular newspapers reacted to the call of the rabbis. Take, for instance, *Ha'aretz* of Wednesday, May 17:

*A specific campaign to awaken the Yishuv and the nation world-
wide ... against the background of the Holocaust suddenly unleashed on
the Jews of Hungary and Romania trapped in the Valley of Death. Also
to arouse general public opinion across the world ... to save the surviving remnants in Europe whose despairing cry reaches us daily ...*

Actually, although in a precarious state, Romanian Jewry was
fortunately spared in 1944 once the retreating Germans had not the
means to continue rounding up Jews.

The Agudist *Kol Yisrael* was more strident, calling for a complete
change in priorities — privately and publicly — and openly basing
themselves on the Bilgoraj Rav's testimony:

*These are not exaggerations or conjecture, nor artificial pessimistic
supposition! Reality, concrete facts are the sadistic horrors heard
over the last few years — these reflect the unvarnished truth! It is
a fact that the torturers abuse our blood-brothers in whichever way
they think fit. It is a fact that Acheinu Bnei Yisrael in exile are being
murdered with every cruelty and vengeance. Occasionally in the past
we heard faint echoes of atrocities; every so often we received information from distant nations or resistance fighters about horrendous
bloodbaths inflicted on our brethren. Although we heard, we could not
believe they were abandoned to slaughter or that the killers were so
active. From the distance we could not fathom the true depth of suffering befallen the Jewish tribes in exile. Our ears were not attuned to
the chorus of shrieks erupting from our brothers dying by fire, water,
famine and thirst.*

*At best we accepted only half or less of the horror stories. We
thought they were suffering persecution but not wholesale murder;
we believed their situation was awful but not that children and babies were expiring from hunger and dehydration. Who could have
imagined mothers being forced from bed to witness the murder of
their offspring! But what we refused to believe until now has now
been confirmed by an eyewitness who observed the breadth and depth
of the calamitous churban and felt the pain and anguish of a nation,
downtrodden and despoiled. All of us have heard the shocking report
of this witness, his words have been broadcast by all publications;*

religious and non-religious alike have heeded up the testimony of this recent emigrant.

Together with a concern to save our brothers from the Valley of Death, we must also empathize with their travail and destruction for without brotherly sympathy there can be no brotherly assistance. And without the overriding aim of saving our brothers, rescue attempts will hardly get off the ground. We have been taught that when sufferings arise we must immediately improve our behavior in accordance with Torah and mitzvos; as this torment advances we must examine our conscience and correct our ways for the better.

On the Rebbe's insistence all rabbanim, institutions and groups — even non-religious — were recruited to the rescue cause and when a delegation of Mizrachi rabbanim protested at working with the irreligious, the Rebbe uncharacteristically shouted at them, "At a time like this when Jewish blood is being spilled like water and it's genuine *pikuach nefesh,* you want to play politics with their lives?" (Although he dispatched the Bilgoraj Rav to collaborate with them he privately remarked, "One has to know how far one can go with Mizrachi.") Despite the rising anxiety and flood of urgent cables, some bureaucrats yet managed to resist the tidal wave of public opinion. Neither the British authorities stationed in the Middle East nor Jewish Agency leaders would countenance an attempt of Hungarian Jews to negotiate a halt to the deportations for $2,000,000 and 50 trucks. Their emissary, Mr. Joel Brand, arrived on the Syrian border on 8 Sivan (May 30th) but he was arrested and held incommunicado while the death trains continued running. Another international fast day was proclaimed for Monday, 14 Sivan (June 5), signed by all the leading rabbanim in addition to the above Rebbes:

The sword of the oppressor is being wielded above the heads of the last remnant in occupied Europe — Hungarian Jewry. A terrible danger hovers over the remaining members of Hashem's people. Frightening reports reach us daily.

Jewish blood is being spilled like water. Millions of our brothers are being killed and destroyed — amid unbelievable cruelty and unnatural deaths al Kiddush Hashem throughout Europe captured by the oppressor. The holy sanctuaries, relics of our heritage, have been destroyed and ruined.

Therefore we call on all our brethren in the Holy Land to a day of fasting, repentance and prayer on Monday, 14 Sivan, 5704. On that day, all our brethren should gather in the synagogues to pour out their hearts in tefillah and supplication, begging for Heavenly mercy on His remnant being slaughtered like sheep!

Everyone above eighteen years old should fast on that day, men and ladies, besides the old and infirm who may redeem their fast with charity. After Minchah the standard Vayechal ... should be lained and Tehillim recited, then they should all sit on the floor for a short period in mourning over the enormous Churban wrought by Hashem in His anger. For our great sins, nearly all of us have to mourn our relatives in Europe!

The masses of Klal Yisrael must beg for mercy, repent fully and strongly call to Hashem that He save the remnants of His people. Hashem, the Guardian of Israel, should watch from Heaven the torment of His people, avenge the blood of His servants and punish their enemies, declare an end to our sufferings and redeem us to a complete Geulah, speedily in our days!

During July, as reports of the brutal deportations were publicized around the world (mainly by the indefatigable George Mantello at the Salvadorian Consulate in Geneva), high level representations finally persuaded the Regent Horthy to halt the death trains. At the end of August 1944, the pro-German puppet administration was ultimately toppled and the "deportation experts" removed. Relief, however, was short lived. As Russian forces crossed the Hungarian border during October — amid renewed Hungarian peace overtures — the Germans organized a counter-coup, kidnaping Horthy's son and forcing him to appoint the fascist Arrow Cross under Ferenc Szalasi. Two days later, October 18 (1 Cheshvan), the "deportation experts" were back in full force.

A veritable reign of terror was inflicted on Budapest until some 160,000 Jews were incarcerated in a cramped ghetto to be tormented by the Arrow Cross. Since transport was scarce, the Polish death camps overrun by the Russians, and the death trains officially suspended by Berlin, thousands of starving Hungarian Jews were forced to tramp hundreds of kilometers in unbearable "death marches" through winter rain and snow to the Austrian border. The death toll, estimated at over 30 percent, horrified even Szalasi, but all Hungary's efforts to halt these forced marches were ignored. By the time the Russians eventually took Budapest during February 1945 (Shevat-Adar) after a merciless siege, some 70

Desperate Budapest Jews besiege the Swiss Embassy for lifesaving papers

percent of Hungarian Jewry had joined their murdered brethren.

Sadly, all attempts to rescue remnants of the large Belzer dynasty proved equally futile. Although reports received while the Rebbe and his brother were still in Hungary implied that most of their family had been slaughtered, subsequent intelligence seemed to indicate that a few members were still alive. Scarcely a fortnight after escaping to Eretz Yisrael, on Wednesday 22 Shevat (February 16, 1944), the Bilgoraj Rav wrote a warm letter to the London chassidim, addressed in particular to R' Chaim Nota Katz and R' Elimelech Rumpler.

> *Baruch Hashem Who saved us from the lions' mouth and granted us life to merit ascending to the Holy Land. May Hashem Yisbarach grant the same to the surviving remnant.*
>
> *Words are insufficient to praise Hashem for the nissim and wonders performed for us. Several times we were in terrible danger and Hashem saved us from Satan's sword! Now my holy brother shlita has asked me to write the following:*
>
> *He blesses you that the zechus of your mitzvah, your efforts on our behalf and rescue, should stand you in good stead to be protected from all dangers or problems, allowing you to nurture your children to Torah and piety amidst satisfaction and prosperity. We also want to tell you that we have received welcome information that my sister-*

in-law, the Rebbetzin Malkah tichye, and our brother-in-law, the tzaddik Rav Pinchas of Ostilla and his wife — our sister — are all still alive baruch Hashem but in terrible conditions, HaMakom yerachem! We have received word that they ask for assistance and rescue.

... and my holy brother the Rebbe shlita blesses you that you succeed in all your endeavors for the best; we should hear good news from the surviving remnant; the perceived value of Klal Yisrael should rapidly rise and the Geulah should arrive soon.

In the name of my holy brother: Blessing you that his tzaddik's blessing should take root in Heaven and blossom here on earth.

Rebbe Pinye'le of Ostilla

Mordechai, son of the Holy Rebbe of Belz

Unfortunately, this latest information was not correct. The Rebbe's wife (and cousin) Rebbetzin Malka, famous for her practical charity, had been killed in Przemyslany during 1943, *Hashem yinkom damah*, while Rav Pinchas Twersky and his wife, Rebbetzin Chanah Rachel, had survived only a little longer. "Rebbe Pinye'le," as he was popularly known, had been a rising star in the chassidic and Torah firmament. His first twenty years of marriage were spent in Belz where he became extremely close to his father-in-law, Rebbe Yissachar Ber, adopting Belzer customs and traditions, though a Chernobyl descendant and son of the Rachmistrivka Rebbe. Saintly since his childhood, generous to a fault, his unassuming modesty masked a phenomenal depth and breadth in Torah scholarship. His rebbetzin matched him in remarkable generosity. His tenure as Rav of Ostilla, Volhynia for some nine years (1923-1932) marked him as a Rebbe and leader. Later he relocated to the Galician city of Przemysl where his fame spread.

At the invasion, he was on the Nazis' wanted list as a recognized leader so he dressed in simple clothes and went into hiding in Sambor. In the winter of 1941 he even participated in a collection for the starving refugees in Siberia without matzos or wine for Pesach;

for Succos he managed to obtain a rare *esrog* from Sanok shortly before Yom Tov. In the first *aktion*, on Tuesday, August 4, 1942, his daughter-in-law bravely stepped outside her safe bunker with her crying toddler rather than endanger the other inhabitants. That *aktion's* death train passed through Rawa-Ruska a day later and they were murdered at Belzec the next day, 23 Av. At the next *aktion*, on Shabbos, October 17, 1942, the family bunker was discovered and all (besides the youngest son) were dragged to the death trains. But after nightfall, they managed to rescue Rav Pinchas and his rebbetzin, who were heartbroken at the mass slaughter of their close family and entourage — five sons and almost twenty grandchildren — among them their oldest son, Rav Yeshayah Meshulam Zusia, a son-in-law of the Belzer Rav, with seven children.

During Chanukah (December 1942), all the survivors were forced into a tiny, insalubrious ghetto surrounded by barbed wire where Rav Pinchas fell deathly ill with typhus. Doctors despaired of his recovery and he personally looked forward to a "luxury death" — peacefully, at home in bed! Yet he recovered by Purim in time for the *Megillah* reading. Shabbos, April 10th saw another cruel *aktion* where the Rav and Rebbetzin were imprisoned together with another 900 Jews. Despite the best efforts by the local Judenrat head, he managed only to save Rav Pinchas alone. All the rest, including his wife Rebbetzin Chanah Rachel (the Belzer Rav's sister), were machine-gunned into a large pit at the cemetery on Wednesday, 9 Nissan.

At the next *aktion* on Shabbos, May 22, 1943, both Rav Pinchas and his youngest son Yitzchak were caught and dispatched to Belzec death camp where they were murdered, probably on Monday, 19 Iyar, 34th day of the *Omer*. He and his descendants were renowned for their Torah scholarship, piety and charity. Only one member of his large family escaped, his daughter Rebbetzin Triena, wife of the Skverer Rebbe, who immigrated to America after the War and reestablished their dynasty.

Indeed, most of the Belzer Rebbe's closest descendants had been ruthlessly wiped out. Besides his stepmother (i.e. the Bilgoraj Rav's mother) Rebbetzin Chayah Devoire'le, the Belzer Rav lost three precious sisters and two brothers plus their children and grandchildren.

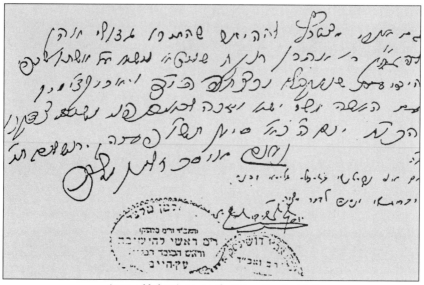

*As an added stringency, the Belzer Rav insisted
on a Hetter Meah Rabbanim before remarrying*

Among his murdered brothers and brothers-in-law were — besides
the Ostilla Rav — luminaries such as the rabbanim of Rawa-Ruska,
Hrubieszow, Apta (Opatow, for whom the Rebbe briefly sat *shivah*
in Budapest) and the Rebbe of Yaroslavl. From his immediate offspring, the Rebbe had four daughters and five sons. Two sons had
died as children (several apparently healthy newborns had also
died shortly after birth) and his second daughter, Rebbetzin Mirel,
died tragically at a young age in 1938. The only member of the family not to display any emotion at this tragedy was her father Rebbe
Aharon; later her husband and two children were murdered.

At an early stage of the oppression, the Rebbe's oldest son Rebbe
Moshe'le was burnt alive in the Przemyslany shul and though the
Belzer Rav was present in Przemyslany and escaped capture then
only by a miracle, he hardly reacted beyond remarking, *"A chessed
fun Der Bashefer* — now I too have paid my dues and presented my
korban!" Later Rav Moshe's wife and five children were murdered.

The Rebbe's oldest daughter, Rebbetzin Rivka Miriam Frankel,
was murdered with seven children. The Rebbe's other daughters,
Rebbetzin Adel Twersky (daughter-in-law of Rav Pinchas of Ostilla)
and Rebbetzin Sarah Brachah Rosenfeld with two sons, were killed,

The Rebbe (second from left) and the Bilgoraj Rav (second from right) gracing the wedding of their relative, Rebbe Itzikel Rokach (third from left), father of the present Machnovke Rebbe

too. Two other sons, Rav Yisrael with his two sons and Rav Yehudah Zundel with two daughters, were likewise slain. The Bilgoraj Rav's oldest daughter, Alte Bas Zion, died in 1931 at the age of 3, while his second daughter, Rivka Miriam was murdered together with his wife, Rebbetzin Sheva (Rabinowitz) in Kobrin, Russia.

As Rashi famously comments in *Parashas Beha'aloscha*: ... to teach us the distinction of Aharon, *shelo shinah* — that he never changed throughout years of holy *avodah*. This scale of tragedy could have broken a lesser man but there was no noticeable change in the behavior or devotions of the Belzer Rav. Following a certain calamity he once made an astute observation: There is no greater pain than losing a loved one, though an orphan's grief is markedly less than that of a parent on being bereaved of a child. A father who loses his offspring can feel as if his entire world has been abruptly destroyed in his lifetime and often cannot come to terms with his tragic ordeal. Yet when other children are dependent on his care, he will normally suppress his personal pain to put on the bravest face, especially in front of the children.

Here the Belzer Rav's entire world — children, grandchildren, siblings, stepmother, chassidim, contemporaries, et al. — had literally been destroyed in his lifetime; yet he voiced no complaints nor allowed anyone else to do so! During his short respite in Budapest, as news spread of the probable destruction of his family, a famous Hungarian Rav and a leading Belzer chassid sought to comfort him and began with the customary phrase, "The Rebbe should know of no more pain ..." But the Rebbe sharply interjected, "Does Your Honor suspect of me that perhaps I ever experienced pain? *Chalilah*! Not a bit of it! Never in my life did I suffer any distress![3] Please, I insist, repeat now three times that you retract these words!" (As later recalled by the Ponevezher Rav, Rabbi Shlomo Yosef Kahaneman.)

This was a remarkable personification of the words of the *Tanna D'Vei Eliyahu Rabbah* (Ch. 27) "... from here they stated: The Talmud scholar of the generation endures the sins of the generation, keeping the pain so intimate that none can recognize it beyond *HaKadosh Baruch Hu* alone!" The Belzer Rav did not mark even those *yahrzeits* whose dates were indisputably authenticated — such as that of his beloved son Rav Moshe'le who was cruelly murdered in his proximity — perhaps sublimating his private bereavement within the overwhelming communal catastrophe.[4] Yet he likewise opposed instituting a new national day of mourning as inappropriate. Notwithstanding his personal ordeal, he had all the time and every sympathy for other people's problems — whether substantial or trivial.

In general, once rescue efforts ceased, he rarely discussed the war years for fear that even the faintest trace of complaint against heavenly

---

3. The Rebbe had a remarkably stoic acceptance of physical ailments. Since his first year of marriage, he suffered chronic stomach and intestinal pain which only lessened slightly on his arrival in Eretz Yisrael; even there these remained so excruciating that he once revealed, "Believe me, the *yissurim* I experience I would wish only on a *goy* who persecutes and oppresses Jews!" Likewise his eye disease. Yet he constantly concealed his pain. Although a fish bone lodged in his throat caused unbearable torment during one Shabbos *tisch*, he maintained his smiling, bright countenance so that nobody realized, and he merely hurried the remainder of the *seudah*. But as soon as the *tisch* ended and everybody left, a Tel Aviv doctor was urgently summoned and allowed to switch on a lamp "since it's *pikuach nefesh*!" The doctor was frankly amazed that the Rebbe had been able to withstand terrible pain for so long just to spare his chassidim any distress; to his growing wonder, the Rebbe first asked him where he came from and who his father was before yielding to treatment!

4. Interestingly, when donating the customary *machatzis hashekel* on *Taanis Esther*, he would first give twice on behalf of himself and his current Rebbetzin, then quietly on behalf of his martyred rebbetzin, and then repeat the donation countless times — apparently on behalf of his murdered children and grandchildren.

justice might inadvertently cross one's mind. (Soon after the Belzer Rav's arrival in Eretz Yisrael, Rabbi Shimon Aharon Polansky — the phenomenal *gaon* famous as the "Tepliker Rav" — tried to question him about the ongoing Holocaust, but the Rebbe replied that one must not discuss subjects which may invite sinful thoughts. Whenever he later spoke of the Rebbe, the Tepliker Rav would weep quietly while remarking, "What *madreigos* in *yiras cheit* that *tzaddik* has achieved!") Nonetheless, despite the passage of years, he never forgot the anguish and suffering of those fateful years. On occasion, he would wear the modern "*galus*-clothes" he had escaped in beneath his rabbinical attire. The private wooden chair on which he now sat (in Belz, their personal chair traditionally accompanied them on all visits) was a plain and simple piece of furniture without upholstery, and he rigidly refrained from reclining in spite of his advancing age and weakness.[5] Nor would he accept expensive gifts "until there is peace in the world ..."

His view on the Second World War was distinctive as was his attitude to the State of Israel. Unlike other *gedolei Yisrael*, he saw the extraordinary persecution not as *Chevlei Mashiach* — the earth-shattering events presaging the birth pangs of the Messianic Age — but described them cryptically as a "*Gezeirah fun Himmel*, a Heavenly Decree." When Rav Isser Zalman Meltzer voiced the hope that those unbearable torments were a portent of Mashiach's imminent arrival, the Rebbe replied, "The *tefillos* of the great Rebbe, Reb Elimelech of Lizhensk, have already repealed *Chevlei Mashiach;* instead these were Heavenly Decrees we must accept with love!" Interestingly, it is said that throughout Sunday, 21 Adar II (March 31) 1940 — Rebbe Elimelech's *yahrzeit* during the first year of the invasion — the Belzer Rav had stood at the window anxiously waiting for Mashiach to arrive, only to be bitterly disappointed by nightfall. Since the Noam Elimelech had accepted upon himself the birthpangs of the Messiah, Rebbe Ahare'le had fully expected Mashiach on that auspicious day! Perhaps that was also why he had sent two emissaries to the Noam Elimelech's *kever* on his *yahrtzeit* in 1939, shortly before the invasion.

---

5. His simple chair and *shtender* are now preserved behind glass in the grand Jerusalem shul.

The Bilgoraj Rav in Paris in the summer of 1949 on behalf of the Rebbe

He viewed the independent *medinah* as neither ushering in the longed for Redemption nor revealing the profane hand of Satan. Instead he described its establishment as a "*chessed*, now Jews will have somewhere with unrestricted access to which to escape!" and encouraged his chassidim to settle there.

On his escape, the Belzer Rebbe had become remarkably close with his younger brother, the Bilgoraj Rav, from whom he refused to part. When Rebbe Mordechai married Rebbetzin Miriam Glick during Nissan 1947,[6] the Rebbe insisted he find an apartment close by, remarking, "*Chalilah* he should leave me — he is my right hand! It's impossible I should exist without him for even a minute!" Indeed he represented the Rebbe at most events or conferences and the Rebbe consulted him before every major decision. This was in addition to the Bilgoraj Rav's ceaseless efforts for war survivors: obtaining welfare, housing and employment, or arranging *shiduchim* and weddings on their behalf. On 8 Shevat 1948, the Bilgoraj Rav was *zocheh* to his first and only son — the future Rebbe Yissachar Dov — and on 15 Shevat the Belzer Rav was delighted to be *sandek* at his nephew's *bris*. At the

---

6. Both brothers remarried after the War, but the Belzer Rav's subsequent marriage was not blessed with offspring.

pidyon haben the two Kohanim active in their rescue, R' Chaim Nota Katz of London and R' Moshe Gross of Geneva, officiated.

Barely a year later, the Rebbe dispatched the Bilgoraj Rav on a mission to strengthen and encourage survivors and emerging Belz congregations in Europe — promising his brother his own spiritual powers of blessing! Throughout the summer of 1949, the Bilgoraj Rav faithfully carried a personal message from the Rebbe:

The Bilgoraj Rav's final resting place in Teveriah

"That *rasha* meant to wipe out all Jews, every one of us! Every Jew who survived the War, whether in captivity or freedom, it was only because he was accompanied by angels on each side!" At the end of the summer their father, Rebbe Yissachar Dov, appeared to him in a dream and instructed him to return home immediately! He arrived back in Eretz Yisrael before Yom Kippur 5710 and fell ill during Chol HaMoed Succos. The Rebbe visited him for the last time on 24 Marcheshvan and Rebbe Mordechai underwent major surgery the next day (November 17, 1949) but did not survive. He was only 47 years old and had been at the peak of his powers.

Thousands joined the cortege as it slowly made its way to the Teveriah *beis hachaim*, weeping bitterly. Such a talented, multifaceted soul! A renowned orator; a facile writer; a quick, razor-sharp mind; yet so kind, easygoing and humble. What a loss to *Klal Yisrael*! What a loss to his young son! What a loss to his saintly brother!

The only person to betray little emotion was, once again, the Belzer Rebbe. Just as the Rebbe had accompanied his brother to the *chuppah* — and officiated at the *bris* and *pidyon haben*[7] — so did he accompany him to the grave. Hashem gives, Hashem takes, that is the will of Hashem to be accepted unquestioningly.

---

7. He now took the tender orphan under his personal care as if he were his own son until his own *petirah* seven short years later.

CHAPTER 28

THE FINAL YEARS

A
S THE BILGORAJ RAV HAD REPEATEDLY DECLARED, the Belzer Rebbe had not sought to escape his Nazi pursuers merely to save his own life or for personal comfort, rather he did so on behalf of the wider public. Indeed, the Rebbe had seen his survival as a crucial part of Belz's destiny, and was ever mindful of the Sar Shalom's ringing declaration: "Belz will remain a niche where they will serve *Hashem Yisbarach* until the coming of the Mashiach!"[1] On the Belzer Rebbe's safe arrival in Eretz Yisrael, he confided to his close chassidim his desire to prepare a fresh generation "with whom we need not be ashamed to go out and welcome Mashiach!" He had always seen *chinuch* as crucial, and when transcribing his *berachah* to donors of the *maamados* appeal he would personally add," ... and blessing that you merit to

---

1. When the Boyaner Rebbe of America later visited, he asked if it was true that the first Rebbe of Belz had predicted that providing an authentic Torah education in the generation before Mashiach would prove as hard a test as the *Akeidah*. Rav Ahare'le replied, "That I never heard! But I personally heard my grandfather's assurance that he had paved the way in Belz for every Jew seeking *yiras Shamayim* and *ahavas HaBorei* until the Mashiach!"

raise your children to Hashem's Torah and veneration." He particularly bemoaned the irreplaceable loss of Belz's unique band of holy *yoshvim* — "Their memory is too painful; among them were those personally capable of being Rebbes and accepting *kvittlech*!" So it was no coincidence that he instructed his brother, the Bilgoraj Rav, to found the first traditional *cheder*, Machzikei Hadas, in Yafo near Tel Aviv, during 1948.

The Rebbe's plans and ambitions were in direct contrast to the evil machinations of Satan's cohorts. In 1943, when the extermination program was at full blast, the lurid Nazi propaganda sheet *Der Sturmer* published a special number with pre-War photographs of

Im ehemaligen Marienbad
Sie kommen an und wollen sich nicht fotografieren lassen

The infamous Nazi propaganda sheet "Der Sturmer"

leading Polish and Galician "Talmudists." Under a famous photo of the Belzer Rav out taking the air at a health spa, surrounded by admiring chassidim, the notorious Streicher had triumphantly added an ominous caption: "Such pictures, the world will no longer see!" It was only due to the superhuman efforts of the Rebbe and other prominent survivors that *Der Sturmer's* dire — yet entirely probable — prediction did not come true (which was mainly why the Belzer Rav had been so high on the Gestapo's Wanted List; their unremitting hunt for his whereabouts had dogged his every step from Poland to Israel).

And not only *Der Sturmer.* In the face of the excited welcome that overwhelmed the young *Yishuv* on the Belzer Rav's arrival in Eretz Yisrael, one old-time *maskil* wrote bitterly in a secular periodical: "We had sought freedom, unfettered with the *kapota*, discarded when we threw out the painful *galut* inheritance! We had no idea that the primitive Judaism of Galicia would again raise its head among us. We marched to the vision of Herzl and Nordau and thought we had left the last of these cults and rites behind in Poland. Yet now he seeks to replant it on this soil. Our land has to be healthy — and only healthy. Whoever tries to reintroduce the cult of Rebbes is planting the seeds of *galut* in Eretz Yisrael ..." Contrary to the worst machinations of the Nazis or the disdain of anti-religious intellectuals, Belz's future today seems assured by a string of respected *mosdos* and teeming *shtiebels* around the world, headed by a charismatic leader.

Nowadays most chassidic groups boast their own yeshivos and *chadarim* as a matter of course, but in the aftermath of the devastating European *Churban*, it was fairly unusual — and a radical step for Belz in particular. When other chassidic groups established yeshivos in pre-War Poland, Belz had looked on with a mixture of ambivalence and scorn. As usual it was extremely loath to depart from time-honored tradition, and Belz had always marched to the memorable maxim of the Chasam Sofer: "*Chadash assur min HaTorah!*" If a system of *shtiebels* and *yoshvim* had produced an enviable crop of phenomenal *talmidei chachamim*, why institute change? So it was not an easy decision for the Belzer Rav to make. The origins of the idea can be traced back to Monday, 16 Teves 1945.

The Talmud Torah's registration with the mandate authorities

— תלמוד תורה
מחזיקי הדת דחסידי בעלזא
תל־אביב, רח' עין יעקב 15

ב"ה

הננו שמחים להודיע לצבור החרדים, הרוצים לחנך את בניהם על טהרת הקודש
בדרך אבותינו הק' נ"ע והשואפים לראות בהם דור ישרים "בורד, שבע"ה עלתה בידינו
לרכוש עבור התלמוד תורה בית גדול ומשוכלל וחצר רחבת ידים עם גן ואויר צח

והננו מודיעים בזה שהלימודים בזמן הבע"ל מתחילים בעו"ה בר"ח מרחשון.
מתקבלים תלמידים לכל הכתות.
וכ"כ מקבלים תלמידים לישיבה קטנה בגיל שתים עשרה שנה אלו שלמדו
כבר גפ"ת.
וכן מתקבלים ילדים קטנים מגיל שלוש ומעלה אשר עומדים תחת השגחה מיוחדת
של משגיח מומחה ר"ש
התלמידים מקבלים גם ארוחת צהרים במסעדה של הת"ת.
לאלו הגרים רחוק מתקיים שרות טקסי בכל חלקי העיר.
התלמידים מתחנכים בחינוך מקורי לתורה ויראת שמם ובדרך ארץ ע"י מלמדים
מומחים ות"ח וירא" השם העושים מלאכתם באמונה ואשר הרוא' פרי טיב בעמלם
שהעמידו עשרות תלמידים לישיבות לשם ולתפארת.

התלמיד תורה שלנו אושר רשמית כבר'ים מיכר.

הורים הרוצים לרשום את בניהם יפנו למשרד הו "ת, רח' עין יעקב 5
עד כ"ח תשרי.

Poster announcing the opening of the Belzer Talmud Torah in Tel Aviv

R' Berish Ortner had come to visit the Rebbe and was asked if he could perhaps remember from his youth any episode or comment by Rebbe Yehoshua, the Rebbe's beloved grandfather. Mr. Ortner recalled that when Rebbe Yeshie'le had visited the shul at his home-town Hibniv (Uhnow), the Rav had remarked, "My father *zt"l*, the Sar Shalom, foretold how twelve famous synagogues would be situated near the future *Beis HaMikdash* to serve as sanctuaries for Mashiach — and my shul in Belz will be one of them! And I add that this shul in Hibniv will be another one of them!" While the Rebbe was digesting this, Mr. Ortner respectfully added, "Now we can see that these shuls have been destroyed like the *Beis HaMikdash*; when that is speedily rebuilt so will those have to be. Since Your Honor is in the Holy Land, I think it is perhaps an opportunity to fulfill the wishes of holy leaders *zt"l* that Torah is learned here, within a framework similar to what we had back in Belz. Therefore it is important to establish a *Talmud Torah* in Tel Aviv and a yeshivah in Jerusalem where they can continue studying according to our fathers' tradition until the coming of the Mashiach!"

The idea was as ambitious as it was radical. Belz in Eretz Yisrael was then in its infancy. Their *shtiebel* in Jerusalem was fairly small, initially used solely for Shabbos, and only established a few years previously — shortly before the War. The Rebbe asked how this could be arranged. "Easy! I'll draw up the rules of the charity and get them certified by the government. Once that's out of the way, one can open up! But first these rules will have to be shown to a religious lawyer to check for errors and I'll show them to the Rebbe for his approval," said R' Berish.

The Belzer Rav agreed to the plan but added, "You speak sense yet I wish this all be kept strictly secret. I know that you can keep a confidence, but what about any others brought in to help?" Reb Berish hastened to reassure him. "If I relay the Rebbe's instructions that they may not reveal a thing until they have permission, they will surely obey."

With the Rebbe's heartfelt blessing, Mr. Ortner hurried to com-plete the formalities. Although the Rebbe was pleased with the charity's rules, he objected to the title "Yeshivas Belz." Instead, Mr. Ortner suggested a title commemorating the Rebbe's murdered

ב"ה

מודעה רבה לאורייתא!

שמחים אנו להודיע לכל מוקירי התורה
בארה"הקודש כי פתחנו את

ישיבת בעלזא

בנשיאותו של כ"ק מרן אדמו"ר שליט"א מבעלזא

בירושלים עיה"ק בשכונת קטמון

ומתקבלים תלמידים מצוינים
ומופלגים בתורה שיקבלו חינוך והדרכה
בג"פת וחידושי תורה וכו'

ע"י ר"מ הישיבה הרב הגאון המפורסם

מוה"ר יהושע דייטש שליט"א

מלפנים אבדק"ק בראהוו

בעת רב ימ"ץ שכונת כית-ישראל וקסמון בירושלים תי"ו

התלמידים יקבלו אש"ל בבית התבשיל וכפנימי' של הישיבה.

ההרשמה בכל יום בשעה 7–9 בערב
בשכונת קטמון רחוב המלכים 25

תשרי תש"י

ההנהלה

A poster announcing the opening of the Belzer Yeshivah in Yerushalayim

Various letters from the Rebbe requesting that the chassidim support the yeshivah

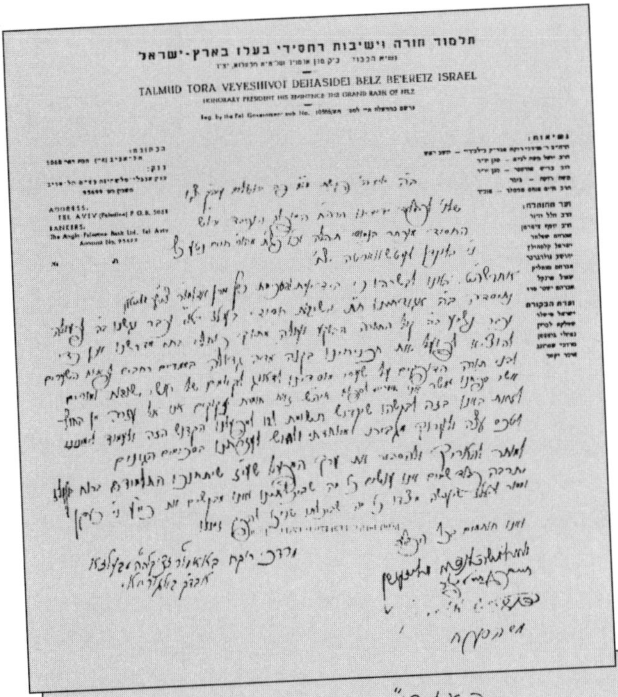

תלמוד תורה וישיבות דחסידי בעלז בארץ-ישראל

TALMUD TORA VEYESHIVOT DEHASIDEI BELZ BE'ERETZ ISRAEL

HONORARY PRESIDENT HIS EMINENCE THE GRAND RABBI OF BELZ

ADDRESS: TEL AVIV (Palestine) P.O.B.

A letter from the Bilgoraj Rav soliciting funds for the yeshivah

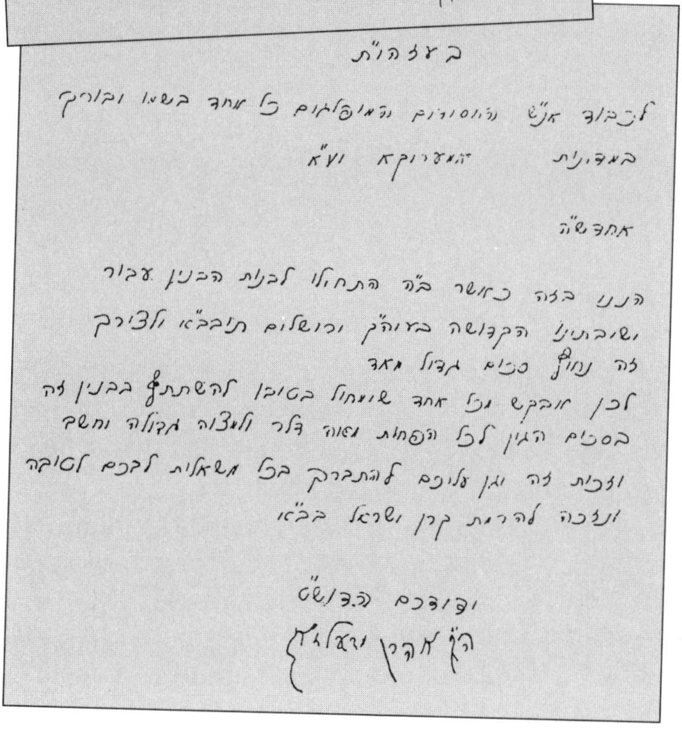

בעזהו"ת

לכבוד אנ"ש הנדיבים והמופלגים כל אחד בשמו יבורך

במדינות האמריקא ויע"א

אחדש"ה

הנני בזה כאשר ב"ה התחילו לבנות הבנין עבור
ישיבותינו הקדושה בעיה"ק ירושלים תובב"א ולצורך
זה נחוץ סכום גדול מאד
לכן מבקש מכל אחד שיחול בטובו להשתתף בבנין זה
בסכום הגון לכל הפחות מאה דלר ולמצוה גדולה יחשב
וזכות זה יגן עליהם להתברך בכל משאלות לבבם לטובה
ונזכה להרמת קרן ישראל בב"א

ידידכם הדו"ש
הק' אהרן מבעלזא

A letter from the Rebbe in support of the yeshivah

children, but that was likewise unacceptable; they eventually settled on "Yeshivos D'Chassidei Belz." A committee of thirteen was chosen (to reflect the Thirteen Attributes of Mercy) with the Belzer Rav as president, the Bilgoraj Rav as chairman, and Mr. Ortner with R' Yoel Moshe Landau, Rav of Lizhensk, as joint vice-chairmen. (Characteristically, Mr. Ortner was to treat his honorary position with the utmost seriousness, attending all meetings, galvanizing individuals, composing and typing letters at his faithful typewriter, until his health failed.) Even after they received official approval, the Rebbe wanted the plan kept secret until after Pesach at least.

For various technical reasons, neither the *Talmud Torah* nor the yeshivah opened its doors for the next few years. (But the earlier registration with the Mandate authorities proved prescient in sidestepping the newly installed Israeli government's attempts to block "new religious schools" from opening.) Meanwhile, the security situation in Palestine deteriorated with rising Arab-Jewish tension, the imminent relinquishing of the British Mandate and the likely Declaration of Independence. Surviving Belzer chassidim in Europe, many of whom had settled in Antwerp on the Rebbe's advice and had founded a traditional *cheder* as early as 1946, were concerned for their frail leader's safety. With the help of Dr. Yaakov Griffel in Paris, a temporary Belgian entry visa was obtained, and his loyal chassid, R' Chaim Shloma Friedman (who had survived the remainder of the war in Hungary by a series of miracles) was dispatched to escort the Belzer Rav to Antwerp. Traveling on a rickety old plane run by Pan-African Airlines — the only service still operating to the danger zone — Mr. Friedman landed at Haifa (Lud was still under British control) and finally arrived in a blacked-out Tel Aviv late at night.

The Rebbe listened carefully to the proposal and promised to consider it overnight. However, he remained firm in his decision not to forsake the vulnerable *Yishuv* — "I dwell among the people; now when *Yiddishe bachurim* have to stand guard at the borders, how can I leave Eretz Yisrael?" Instead he would press ahead with the plan to establish Belzer *mosdos* with the help of world Jewry.

The Rebbe's refusal to leave Eretz Yisrael seemed incomprehensible to his American chassidim when viewed against the threats of neighboring Arab states to invade and crush any Jewish state at birth. The chassidim offered him sanctuary in America until the danger was over, and argued that journeying there would be doubly useful as he could use his personal presence in America to raise large funds for his *mosdos*. Since they were certain that he would finally bow to their rescue plan, they confidently went ahead in arranging all the necessary papers, but the Belzer Rav refused to leave — even after air raids began and he found it difficult to descend into shelters in his weakened state.

However, the drive to reestablish Belz and its institutions continued unabated. Although Mr. Friedman had a new family and had joined the Antwerp diamond trade, he relocated yet again to Israel to help in this sacred task. The Jerusalem yeshivah finally opened in the Katamon district in early 5710 — a year after the Tel Aviv *Talmud Torah* — with just ten *bachurim*, but both soon grew apace under the Rebbe's gentle encouragement. The Rebbe publicized a rare letter explaining the need to establish Yeshivos D'Chassidei Belz "to train the hearts of the youth who have been wandering several years in *galus, lo aleinu,* in the ways of their saintly fathers and to see to all their needs ..." Circulars also invited exceptional *bachurim* from the general public to apply for adequate food and accommodation in addition to a thorough Torah education (no mean offer during Israel's post-independence recession and rationing). The Rebbe took an exceptional interest in both *mosdos*, setting the curriculum, choosing the subjects and insisting on sufficient stipends to allow his pupils to study in comfort and peace of mind. At regular intervals, they were invited to his room for guidance in *yiras Shamayim* and Chassidus and were usually advised to study the *Kedushas Levi, Maasei Rokeach* and similar works. Pure Torah study of *Shas* and *Poskim*, however, always took precedence.

The opening *shiur* was delivered by the Rebbe himself at his private residence and ended with a word-play on the Aramaic acronym of the six *Sidrei Mishnayos* — *"Zeman Nekat"* — which teaches us to "grasp time": eat and sleep when you need to, otherwise grasp all available time for the Holy Torah! Even when the Belzer Rav spent his summers in Katamon near the yeshivah,[2] the students were forbidden to attend his Maariv prayers — usually conducted at a late hour — for fear of *bitul Torah*. Indeed, they were allowed to visit the Rebbe only at fixed intervals for the same reason. Often the Rebbe would dispatch his *gabbai* to the *beis hamedrash* to spur them on to greater enthusiasm in learning. The Belzer Rav felt personally responsible for the financial upkeep of those early *yoshvim*, according them precedence even over his own family's needs — after all, hadn't they sacrificed all materialistic pursuits for the sake of spiritual growth? Although shortages and economic difficulties frequently plagued the early years of the Israeli state, the *yoshvim* were spared every inconvenience and worry. (Similarly, he continued the Belzer Rebbes' traditional practice of secretly supporting scores of respectable families in Jerusalem and elsewhere — plus dispatching regular stipends to the gentle poor via his *gabbaim* — even when the Belz establishment was not yet firmly established in Eretz Yisrael.)

Just as in pre-War Poland, where he had campaigned for traditional *chinuch* in every minute detail, so too did he do in Israel. He frequently blamed inclement weather or unseasonal colds on the fact that the children studied a fixed curriculum of *Chumash* instead of following the weekly cycle of *Sedras*. All pupils, especially of the more traditional *chadarim*, were welcomed to his *tisch* with cake and cookies. "*Chinuch*," declared the Belzer Rav, "has to be performed in its entirety — just as pure oil was needed for the Chanukah miracle, although impure oil could, strictly speaking, have sufficed." For the selfsame reason he instructed a bar mitzvah boy who *bentched* with a *zimun* for the first time to personally finish the whole cup of wine rather than drink only most of it as he usually had.

To the end the Belzer Rav plowed an individual furrow, unswayed by outside opinions or pressures. His views on communal issues and Agudas Yisrael are a case in point. Traditionally, Belz had resolutely maintained a zealous stance against *Haskalah*, Zionism and

---

2. The Rebbe's summer furlough in Jerusalem from Tammuz to Succos became an annual event with a large pilgrimage of chassidim and well-wishers accompanying his car to and from the Katamon district. Over the years the convoy grew so large that it occasionally raised the suspicions of Jordanian army and U.N. armistice lookouts on the cease-fire line, who feared it might be Israeli army maneuvers!

socialism; and when Agudas Yisrael was founded, Belz remained steadfastly on the outside. Yet they were no strangers to communal activism. Already in 1878 — long before the establishment of Agudah — Rebbe Yehoshua pioneered the government-sanctioned *Machzikei Hadas* movement with its own weekly newspaper to counteract the growing trend toward Reform in Galicia; and both Rebbe Yissachar Ber and Rebbe Aharon who succeeded him continued this organizational activity. Nonetheless, Belz in Poland refused all entreaties to join Agudas Yisrael and was popularly seen as hostile.

On hearing rumors of Rebbe Yissachar Ber's antagonism to the new religious party, Rebbe Avraham Mordche Alter of Gur had planned to journey to Munkacs (where the Belzer leadership had fled during First World War) until Mr. Dovid Schreiber, the Belzer Rebbe's confidant in Vienna, revealed the basis for Belz's reluctance: Rebbe Yissachar Ber was not opposed to the Agudah in principle, otherwise he would have campaigned against it publicly and vigorously, as was his wont. Rather, he preferred to remain outside to retain his total objectivity and allow him to criticize it without qualm where necessary. Later an Agudah delegation led by Rav Meir Shapiro and R' Yitzchak Meir Lewin visited Holeszyce (where the Rebbe stayed temporarily until Belz recovered from war damage) in 1923; they were warmly received by Rebbe Yissachar Ber, who even accompanied them to the *beis hamedrash* to publicize his blessings for their success. Then the delegates met with Rebbe Aharon, already renowned for his saintliness, who assured them, "Don't take any notice of rumors or carping! I tell you that your movement is an *Agudah L'sheim Shamayim!*" (*Letters of the Gerrer Rebbe*, 60 and *Memoirs of R' Yitzchak Meir Lewin*).

Now, on arrival in Eretz Yisrael over twenty years later, Rebbe Aharon assured the Agudah delegation, "I see the Agudah in Eretz Yisrael as similar to *Machzikei Hadas* that my *Zeide* founded back there ..." At that early period in the new state's history, Agudas Israel and branches of Poalei Agudah and Pagi were the only groups self-confident, motivated and organized enough to oppose the powerful political *apparatchiks* who held most levers of power, be it immigration, employment, housing, rationing, welfare or schooling. For the battered remnant of war survivors — penniless, hungry, bewildered, desperate — the Agudah, which established an alternative educational network, was often their only religious lifeline (as it was later for the Sephardi *aliyah*). Although never associated with any political party and rarely taking a public stance on religio-political issues, the Belzer Rav proved a constant source of advice and encouragement to Israel's Agudah behind the scenes, and allowed his chassidim to take part.

He saw little point in boycotting elections or refusing state aid for religious schools and concurred with the common consensus that independent religious institutions such as *Chinuch Atzmai* could receive government sponsorship, rebutting the view of opposing *gedolim* from outside Eretz Yisrael — "After all, the government is only returning a small percentage of the taxes they collect from Orthodox Jews and they do not have to abstain from their own money." When a delegation of *kannaim* came to see him he reprimanded them, "How many *Talmud Torahs* have you built? How many yeshivos have you opened? Is it a *chochmah* to discourage those spreading Torah?" Similarly, he upbraided a delegation of nationalist rabbis because their institutions strayed from the traditional mold.

Since the government provided 60 percent of the religious schools' budget, supplementary funds had to be raised in America. Opinion among U.S. rabbanim and Rebbes remained divided as to whether *Chinuch Atzmai* should be permitted to receive government funding, so they decided to dispatch an emissary to ascertain the authoritative views of the Belzer Rav. Rebbe Yehudah Aryeh Perlow of Novominsk duly traveled to Eretz Yisrael to meet the Belzer Rebbe, who confirmed his earlier statements, adding, "Although my own yeshivah will not take from them for private reasons, everybody else ought to take ... you can also publicize: Whoever adds to the school funding will be recompensed from Heaven!"

At the first elections to the Knesset during Teves 1949, he willingly appended his signature to public calls urging voters to support the Religious Bloc. In fact, he went further and rewrote the entire proclamation, obviously seeing this as a holy task, since he spent much time weighing each word and washing his hands intently after finally writing down each crucial word — remarking, "Other Rebbes may sign my *nusach* if they wish, otherwise this should be issued separately!" Addressed to the "Honored *Yereim*," it pointed out how crucial it was to battle for observance of Torah and religion in the *medinah*, and to pass laws based on *Daas Torah*, and ended by blessing everyone with "everything good" and that they should further merit witnessing the Torah's elevation and the complete Redemption.

When his draft was shown to the other Rebbes, the Rebbe of Sadigur commented approvingly, "We can see how this has been written with *kedushah* and *taharah*!" and suggested to the Rebbe of Gur: "Although we have already signed the previous proclamation, perhaps we ought to suspend those and append them to this instead?" — which is exactly what happened. And when a chassid asked wonderingly, "Is it really a mitzvah to vote in the Knesset elections?" the Belzer Rav nodded. "A mitzvah like matzah?" persisted this chassid. The Rebbe shook his head sadly. "A mitzvah like *maror*!" he murmured.

Despite his best efforts to shore up the Orthodox community in Tel Aviv, he was appalled at the cynical proposal to dilute the all-religious township of Bnei Brak by annulling its autonomy and merging it with Tel Aviv. He met privately with his distant relative Mr. Israel Rokach (previously Tel Aviv mayor, then minister of the interior), and successfully demanded that the whole idea be shelved. Likewise, he recognized Rav Avraham Yeshayah Karelitz (the *Chazon Ish*) as the supreme halachic authority there — "*Der Torah Yid fun die Torah shtetle!*" When young Bnei Brak chassidim trekked to his Tel Aviv *tisch*, he suggested that instead of relying on leniencies they should accept the Chazon Ish's ruling that this distance is beyond *techum Shabbos*, since the area was still undeveloped.

Notwithstanding ideological reservations about the secular state, he encouraged the influx of religious personalities and infrastructure. When the Rebbe of Przeworsk, Rav Yitzchak Gewirtzman, arrived in Paris via Siberia, he sent a *kvittel* asking whether he should settle in America or Eretz Yisrael. The Belzer Rav decisively replied, "*A shailah* whether he should come to Eretz Yisrael or *le-havdil* America? Certainly a *Yid* like him should come to Eretz Yisrael and reside in one of the holy cities of either Tzefas, Yerushalayim or Chevron. Since we don't possess Chevron at the moment, his choice lies between Yerushalayim and Tzefas — and there is more *yiras Shamayim* in a single corner of Eretz Yisrael than in the entire America!" (For personal reasons, however, "Reb Itzikel" eventually moved to Antwerp.)

The fact that the Belzer Rav was now recognized as an indisputable leader of the generation did not prevent him from accepting criticism. Quite the reverse; his abiding humility ensured that he rated himself as insignificant! Late Monday night, May 11, 1953, he was visited by Rebbe Avraham Yehoshua Heschel of Kupcyznice (who had escaped from Vienna to New York), accompanied by Rebbe Avraham Friedman of Sadigura-Tel Aviv. In an hour-long, free-ranging conversation they discussed *shidduchim*, Mashiach, neighborhoods, travel, Yerushalayim, Mount Carmel and Eliyahu HaNavi, before the Kupcyznice Rebbe gently chided him about what he had for breakfast. But on discovering it had consisted of nothing more than a glass of coffee and a cube of sugar, he was horrified. Renowned for his kindness and good heart, the Kupcyznice Rebbe could not accept that the Belzer Rav ate so little — yet the Rebbe insisted he just could not eat any more, he had stomach problems! "But your father used to eat properly," the Kupcyznice Rebbe pressed him.

The Belzer Rav waved that aside, "*Ah, 'meila*, my father was a *malach*, an angel — I cannot compare with him! I could even have a *hetter* to eat before *davening* but I just can't because of my stomach ..."

Until now their conversation had been very good-natured but now it took a serious turn as the Kupcyznice Rebbe announced solemnly, "Belzer Rav! I would like to give you some words of *mussar*!"

At that, the Belzer Rebbe was filled with awe and trembling. Thrusting his hands into his *gartel*, he stood waiting expectantly for his guest's words of rebuke: "I would like to admonish the Belzer Rav for afflicting his body so much! I would suggest he be more generous in his intake of food, for the sake of strengthening his weakened body — and the world needs him so badly!" Then the two honored guests found out that the Belzer Rav had eaten nothing since his meager breakfast almost twelve hours earlier and wanted to leave immediately so the Rebbe could have an evening meal, but the Belzer Rav would not hear of it. At the end of their hour-long

An American poster announcing the cornerstone-laying of the new yeshivah building

conversation he accompanied them to the front door and waited while they descended the stairs. Only after he completed the Maariv prayers did he consent to partake of his minimal evening repast.

When the Kupcyznice Rebbe returned to Eretz Yisrael (four years later) and once again came to visit, the Belzer Rav greeted him at the threshold of his room with, "Kupcyznice Rebbe! We are commanded to obey the words of the sages. Since your last visit, whenever I'm finished eating, I add an extra spoonful in honor of *mitzvah lishmo'a divrei chachamim!*"

Although the Belzer Rav rarely attended meetings or public affairs, he made a noted exception for the sustained battle against female conscription to the army or national service, which he perceived as a decree against the very future of *Klal Yisrael*.[3] Besides taking an active interest in the entire campaign, he joined the presidium at a massive Jerusalem demonstration on Wednesday, 10 Av 1953 — timed to coincide with the Knesset debate — and even addressed the crowd: "The decree mandating 'National Service' or army conscription for ladies and girls is an *issur min haTorah* that includes several transgressions. We must pray that the government

---

3. Since Hapoel-HaMizrachi and Mizrachi representatives backed the irreligious government's campaign, he ordered all chassidim to sever their membership with the party, even if that meant forfeiting their health insurance. The implied *chillul Hashem* of an ostensibly religious party currying favor by disparaging *gedolei Yisrael* and pious Jews angered him to the degree that he expressed rare criticism and voiced sentiments so strident that he insisted these not be repeated outside his circle.

withdraw this *geizerah* and Hashem should help that the complete *geulah* should rapidly take place in our days, Amen."

His attention never strayed far from the concept of Mashiach. Whenever discussion ranged over the religious, political or military situation he would remark on the imminent Redemption. "Mashiach is ready to come at any moment, may Hashem help that he reveals himself soon." Sometimes he would plead plaintively that Hashem should inspire everyone to *teshuvah*, so Mashiach will arrive immediately. On other occasions he would quote his father: "Mashiach can come during peace or war — Hashem should help it should take place during peacetime. Whatever the generation — Mashiach will find *an eitzah* for his generation!"

Meanwhile the Belzer Rav encouraged the continued growth of his *mosdos*. Since the Jerusalem yeshivah had outgrown its rented premises it was decided to construct a multi-purpose campus. Contracts were signed on 12 Adar 1953 for a large plot of land on the edge of the Machneh Yehudah district, behind the old Shaarei Zedek Hospital — and opposite the designated Knesset site. Predictably, this surprising address aroused opposition and at first the district zoning commission tried to prevent the erection of a *charedi* stronghold in proximity to state institutions. Orthodox circles also questioned the advisability of being situated beyond the "safety" of religious areas. Surely the distance would dissuade many from attending the yeshivah! And what chance was there of encouraging a chassidic community to flourish in its shadow?

Yet the Rebbe remained adamant that this was where he wanted the new Belzer World Center to be. Perhaps the motivation behind this was similar to his earlier decision to settle in Tel Aviv rather than in a religious township, and in time the secular neighbors became accustomed to the growing presence of earnest chassidic young men dressed in their traditional garb. On Tuesday, 2 Elul 1954, thousands gathered for the festive occasion celebrating the ceremonial laying of the foundation stone. When the Belzer Rav was handed the brick, he asked for some mortar "so it should stand firm!" and as he laid it in the prepared hole, he declared, "I am laying this stone so that Jewish youth can study Torah and *yiras Shamayim* here; I also stipulate that they should be permitted to eat, drink, and sleep therein;

ישיבה דחסידי בעלזא

ועד הבנין

בנשיאות כ״ק מרן אדמו״ר שליט״א

ת״ד נגס   בעה״ק ירושלים תובב״א   שלכלם 55584

ב״ה

מודעה רבא לאורייתא!

הננו שמחים להודיע לכל אוהבי ומוקירי התורה ולומדי׳

שא״ה ביום שלישי פ׳ שופטים ב׳ אלול תשי״ד

בשעה 5 אחה״צ נתקיים

הנחת אבן הפנה

ע״י

כ״ק מרן אדמו״ר שליט״א

לבנין הישיבה דחסידי בעלזא בירושלים

על המגרש שנרכש למטרה זו בקצה רחוב אגריפס

ובסביבת מחנה יהודה - מאחורי בית־החולים ולך|

הקהל החרדי מוזמן להשתתף בשמחת מצוה זו

ועד הבנין

A flyer inviting everyone to attend the cornerstone-laying

The desolate field where the Yeshivah of Belz would be built
(note: The sign in the picture reads: This is the spot where the Yeshivah of Belz will be built)

and for any other purpose (this was obviously to avoid the halachic restrictions of a *beis haknesses*) ... May the building be completed soon and may we merit to greet Mashiach speedily in our days."

Two years later, during October 1956 at the time of the Sinai Campaign (Israel's first major war since its War of Independence), his behavior was extraordinary, clashing with many time-honored customs. It was widely rumored that he had been consulted by David Ben-Gurion, and as soon as the call-up began and anxious soldiers queued up for the Rebbe's *berachah*, he began lengthy *tefillos*. After the outbreak of hostilities, upon arriving for *Kabbalas Shabbos* on *Parashas Chayei Sarah*, he paused at the *mezuzah* of his room for a significant period while praying silently yet fervently. Then he approached the Shabbos lights as customary but stood there — for three solid hours! — while *davening* without respite. Few words were audible besides a repeated, "*Shabbos Kodesh zol meigen zein!*" Actual Friday night *davening* began only at midnight and on its completion he retired to his room where he continued his prolonged prayers — until 20 minutes before daybreak! Only then did he ask somebody to make *Kiddush* on his behalf, and he declined to conduct his usual *tisch*.

The Rebbe at the cornerstone-laying ceremony
(The present Rebbe as a young boy is circled in white; he is standing behind R' Berish

These lengthy *tefillos* continued throughout the week. On one occasion the Belzer Rav stood praying in his room for six solid hours without a break though he was habitually so weak he could barely walk or stand without assistance. On 25 Cheshvan 1956, the Bilgoraj Rav's *yahrzeit*, he sent emissaries to his *kever* in Teveriah with a personal message for his departed brother: "Please meet our holy *zeides* and beg that they arouse Divine Mercy before the *Kisei HaKavod* on behalf of the inhabitants of Eretz Yisrael who require enormous compassion."

The next Friday night, *Kabbalas Shabbos* was again substantially delayed due to the Rebbe's devotions, but the third week, *Shabbos Vayetzei*, was even more remarkable, though Israel's role in the war was essentially over. At 11 a.m. Shabbos morning, the door of his room was opened as usual so the Belzer Rav could hear *Krias HaTorah*. However, when *leining* reached the significant words, "*VeYaakov halach ledarko ...*" ("Jacob went on his way ...," in the middle of *maftir*), he instructed them to pause while he again began praying.

Eventually, when considerable time passed, his chassidim continued the *leining* and completed Mussaf while the Rebbe remained

Lekach and bronfin at the Chanukas HaBayis

engrossed in fervent prayer — throughout that Shabbos and even after nightfall! In fact, he continued these long after midnight, until 3:55 a.m., constituting an unbroken *tefillah* of over sixteen hours! Throughout these exceptional entreaties, he appeared consumed by an inner fire that cast a fear and trembling upon those around him. Obviously he was but tenuously attached to this world, and when he inadvertently touched one hand with the other, he cried out in anguish, *"Oy!* Who touched me?" until they reassured him it was none other than himself. With hindsight, only ten months later, that timing of 3:55 a.m. Sunday morning was to prove ominously significant.

These unusual *tefillos* continued over the coming months and there were days when he remained closeted in his room, unavailable to accept *kvittlech*. Generally the Belzer Rav felt *kvittel*-reading to be so vital that he left instructions they could disturb even his minimal couple of hours set aside for rest whenever there was a medical or life-threatening emergency. But in the aftermath of the Sinai Campaign it was sometimes impossible to interrupt his prayer vigils even for the most dangerously ill. During that fateful period there were also days when he went entirely without even those paltry amounts of food and drink he normally allowed himself — despite the pleadings of his *gabbaim* and chassidim. Inexorably, this intensified regime of self-mortification and concentrated prayer increased the toll on the Rebbe's weakened physique; and he had already endured seventy-seven years of self-discipline and denial.

On 8 Kislev he hosted his annual *yahrzeit seudah* for his saintly grandfather, Rebbe Aharon of Chernobyl. During the customary *l'chaim*, he declared, "Rebbe Aharon of Chernobyl *zechuso yagen aleinu* was the leader of Eretz Yisrael and we plead with him that since *Klal Yisrael* needs *nissim* — both natural and unnatural, both here and abroad — so we ask him to go and inspire *rachamim* before the *Kisei HaKavod*." During this period he made the surprising statement that above and beyond the accursed Nazis' raging enmity against Jews, which he had personally witnessed, the *bnei Yishmael* harbored yet greater hatred!

Despite — or perhaps because of — his intense concern for the physical safety of Israel's population, he retained a close interest in the progress of Belz's institutions; belying his advanced years and frailty, he encouraged their development with all the vigor and initiative of a young man. New York's Belz chassidim had established congregations and *chadarim* in both Crown Heights and Borough Park during 1951; Montreal chassidim followed their example a year later. During 1954 Montreal chassidim went further and inaugurated their first religious girls' school, Bnos Yerushalayim; Antwerp did likewise in 1955. For technical reasons, construction of the Jerusalem yeshivah had lagged behind schedule and the Belzer Rav summoned R' Moshe Ortner, whom he had appointed to lead the building program. "Could you please hurry the builders? When I come to Jerusalem this summer as usual, I would like to reside in the new building! Can it be finished this summer?" The Rebbe's rooms were designed to be part of the complex and under his encouragement the work was conducted at a faster pace. By Tammuz, the dormitory block, dining hall and the Rebbe's apartment were duly completed before his arrival.

This was not the only Belzer project to be completed in haste that year. The growing influx of chassidim in Bnei Brak had made their temporary premises increasingly cramped. But that left them with an awkward dilemma. Their first *shtiebel* had been established three years earlier at the private shul of R' Yechiel Benedict, but it had always been far too small to house their *cheder*. When the idea was floated of erecting a combined *Talmud Torah* and enlarged *shtiebel* on an empty plot, some feared the Rebbe — with his heightened sensitivity for people's feelings — would be reluctant to vex Mr. Benedict, whose generosity had sustained them until then. Moreover, there was a well-known *kepeidah* (principle) from the Sar Shalom, founder of the Belz dynasty, not to establish a separate *shtiebel* where it might cause dissension. When a hesitant delegation of Bnei Brak chassidim met the Rebbe late at night, Thursday 12 Tammuz, in Tel Aviv to discuss their plans, they met with a double surprise: Not only did the Belzer Rav bestow his agreement but he warmly encouraged them to complete the formalities urgently. "For my part I would like you to sign the contract with the present owners tonight!"

"Tonight?" asked his astonished chassidim. "But it's already midnight!"

"So do it immediately tomorrow, Erev Shabbos before noon, and may Hashem be with you!" Indeed, the business was completed the next day, before the Rebbe left for his annual summer furlough, but it was several weeks before the chassidim realized the cause of the great hurry.

When the Belzer Rav arrived in Jerusalem on Sunday, 15 Tammuz, the first half of the completed yeshivah campus was consecrated in the presence of a massive crowd from all over Eretz Yisrael. Few of the bystanders — or those who missed the joyful ceremony — realized then just how historic this occasion was to be in the annals of Belz. Some three weeks after arriving in Yerushalayim, the Rebbe was troubled by a disturbing dream. "I saw a *gemeineh chalom, zehr a gemeineh chalom*, should I make anything out of it?" he asked his *shammas*. As the *shammas* tried to calm him, he continued "… in my dream I saw my father *zt"l* wearing his Shabbos clothes and *shtreimel*. I can't remember whether it was Yom Kippur or not but Erev Yom Kippur it certainly was … And my father *zt"l* recited some Torah and I didn't understand it but I did not want to ask him to repeat it." To the Rebbe's consternation, this troubling dream was repeated a fortnight later, on Thursday, 18 Av (August 15).

None of the large congregation who gathered that *Shabbos Parashas Eikev* noticed any changes in the Rebbe's countenance or schedule; only the closest discerned just the slightest haste. At the Friday night *tisch*, he repeated his father's commentary on *Koheles* 9:10, about how those who leave behind children or *talmidim* advancing along the path of Torah are considered still living beyond the grave; their offspring's continuation of their *derech* assists their own spiritual development in Heaven. That is why we say in *Krias Shema*: "*Lema'an yirbu yemeichem v'yemei beneichem ... k'yemei hashamayim al ha'aretz.*" The parents' otherwise static spiritual existence in *shamayim* will be similar to their existence *al ha'aretz* when their lives are bound up with that of their living children or students. He ended by commenting that if the new generation goes in the path trodden by their holy fathers then they will be considered still alive since their influence continues; that way they merit "long life," life with *yiras Shamayim*, a continuation to a lifetime of *kedushah* in the way of *Hashem Yisbarach*. Significantly, these words were to remain his final legacy about how the youth should follow in Hashem's ways.

As he finished delivering this Torah, his facial expression abruptly changed. Those closest realized there had been some deterioration in his health but few recognized how grave the situation really was. Despite his setback, the Rebbe continued to study and pray throughout the night, barring all visitors and foregoing any rest. At 9 o'clock Shabbos morning, overcome by weakness, he fell into a fitful sleep. He was awakened only with difficulty, but when his *gabbaim* suggested they summon a doctor, the Rebbe refused. An hour later they realized the situation had deteriorated further and only with difficulty and much effort was he able to reply to their questions. A local doctor was called, then the legendary Dr. Falk Schlesinger, who diagnosed that it was extremely serious — apparently the Belzer Rav had suffered a brain hemorrhage while delivering his *tisch-Torah*. When Professor Halperin arrived in the afternoon, it was decided to move the Rebbe to the nearby Shaarei

Zedek Hospital. At 6 p.m. his *talmidim* carefully carried him on his bed to the hospital.

The bitter news spread like wildfire. Synagogues and *shtiebels* commenced mass *Tehillim* recitals amid tears and wailing. As fear and trepidation permeated Jerusalem, thousands spontaneously gathered outside the hospital hoping for better news (it was only with difficulty that police managed to clear Yaffo Road for the public transport beginning the Motza'ei Shabbos schedule from the nearby Central Bus Station). Also, at the close of Shabbos cables were sent to all chassidic centers and prominent Rebbes, pleading for *tefillos* and blessings while prayers in Jerusalem did not cease for an instant. After midnight a delegation set out for Meron to pray at the Tomb of Rabban Shimon bar Yochai. Hospital staff, too, worked unceasingly in a desperate effort to save the Belzer Rebbe's life. However, the Gates of Heaven were closed to their desperate entreaties and, surrounded by crowds of tearful chassidim who had rushed to his ward to cry out *"Shema Yisrael!"* the pure soul of the Belzer Rav passed over to the world of everlasting life. The time was early Sunday morning, 21 Av 5717 at 3:55 a.m. — exactly the time

The huge crowd at the levayah

Thousands of people make their way to the cemetery

that the Rebbe had some ten months earlier completed his lengthy prayer vigil during the Sinai Campaign!

All were stunned by this rapid turn of events. Despite the Rebbe's extraordinary exertion in prayer over the last few months, despite his increased frailty, despite his advancing age, no one had suspected that the end was so near or would come so quickly. Indeed, it was barely thirteen and a half years since he had reached Eretz Yisrael and safety. For all the groundwork of a robust infrastructure, Belz in Eretz Yisrael was still in its infancy. They felt totally bereft since the majority of the holy family had already been murdered by the Germans, and though his nephew Yissachar Dov was actively being groomed for the succession, he was still only 9½ years old at the time. The blow had fallen like a bolt of darkness at midday. Nor were Belzer chassidim alone in their shock. All chassidim recognized the saintly leader as one of the supreme *manhigim* of the age — particularly since the *petirah* of Rebbe Avraham Mordche of Gur some ten years earlier — and one of the select few who retained and transmitted the wisdom of earlier generations.

Among wider circles too, the unique holiness and humility, the special ability to bestow blessings coupled with a deep concern

The present Rebbe at the grave site at the end of the shivah

and regard for all of *Klal Yisrael,* had made a profound impression. During his final years he had become familiar to ever more people in Eretz Yisrael, religious and non-religious alike. Medical specialists would send him their most desperate cases; respectable businessmen arrived with complicated financial predicaments; the common people brought their uncommon problems. All had met the other-worldly, famished saint on his simple wooden chair in his modestly furnished room, dispensing blessings and advice in a barely audible whisper. Many had even witnessed open miracles; all had sensed they were in the presence of the transcendental, a relic from another era, another world. Now he was gone.

In numbed silence, his sorrowing *talmidim* carried him on his bed back to the half-completed yeshivah. The crowd of well-wishers that had been growing throughout the night burst into heartrending tears and wailing — old and young alike — as the hallowed remains were placed on the ground and surrounded by countless candles. All adjacent rooms and halls were quickly filled by weeping mourners reciting *Tehillim,* their numbers steadily augmented by arrivals from out of town after the unexpected news was broadcast over state radio. Since the Rebbe had left no instructions as to his

The matzeivah of the Rebbe in Yerushalayim

preferred burial place, precedence was initially given to the ancient chassidic plot in Teveriah where the Bilgoraj Rav had been laid to rest seven years earlier, on the Rebbe's directions. However, the leading chassid and renowned *posek*, Rav Dov Berish Wiedenfeld, ruled that the *levayah* and burial should rather take place in Yerushalayim, and they settled on the new *Rabbanim* section on Har HaMenuchos, Givat Shaul, where a clear space of four *amos* could be left all around the tomb.

After the traditional *taharah* in the yeshivah's newly consecrated *mikveh*, the funeral began in the early afternoon. Rabbi Yehoshua Deutsch, Rav of Katamon, on behalf of the Rebbe's chassidim and many admirers, delivered a short eulogy in the *beis hamedrash* and pleaded that the Belzer Rebbe defend *Klal Yisrael's* interests from his elevated position in Heaven just as he had on earth. By then thousands from Jerusalem and throughout Israel flocked unceasingly to the Machaneh Yehudah district, including many who knew of the Rebbe only by reputation and had never seen him personally. Even chassidim from abroad managed to arrive in time, ferried in by chartered airliners. All the neighboring alleyways, streets, courtyards and fields rapidly filled with men, women and children — many with their outer clothes ripped in mourning. Yeshivah students together with police finally forced a path through the crowd, and at 3 p.m. the cortege set off down Agrippas and Yaffo Roads toward Givat Shaul.

Along the route all work ceased and shops closed out of respect. Traffic was halted and diverted to side roads; even the main entrance to Jerusalem was closed and vehicles funneled via Ein Kerem-Eshtaol. The huge *levayah* proceeded slowly, heads bowed in grief; from different directions could be heard uncontrolled sobbing. The *mittah* was carried all the way by his chassidim who had previously immersed in a *mikveh* and ripped their clothing. Despite the fierce sun, the massive crowd walked the entire route; several fainted and were given first-aid by Israeli ambulance crews who accompanied the cortege. After 2¼ hours they finally reached Har HaMenuchos and the vast area turned black with mourners. Many pressed forward to the grave which rapidly filled with *kvittlech*. After Jerusalem's traditional *hakafos*, the *aron* was laid to final rest amid the recital of Thirteen *Middos* and bitter weeping. It was some time before chassidim could tear themselves away from their Rebbe's last resting place.

In those early years, Jerusalem had never experienced a *levayah* quite like it. In addition to the enormous number of ordinary people — unofficial estimates ranged from 40,000 to 50,000 — from all walks of life and strata of society, the funeral was graced by all the leading Rebbes, roshei yeshivah, rabbanim, community activists, chassidim and pious individuals. The loss was perhaps best summed up by his close confidant of yesteryear, Rabbi Shalom Moskowitz, Rav of Shotz in Romania and later of London, England: "... The holy and pure Rebbe whom the whole world testified was the undisputed *tzaddik hador* in our generation ... guarded most wonderful and frightening *madreigos* ... like the *Tanna* Rebbe HaKadosh, he hardly benefited from this material world throughout his life — not eating, drinking, nor sleeping — instead his entire life was an unending saga of *dveikus* ... How many times did we see open *ruach hakodesh*? ... The fiery angels in Heaven must have trembled when they saw such a holy body ... It is many years since such a holy body has ever been on earth ... This world has suffered a tremendous loss, an irreplaceable loss ..."

Since that fateful day until the present, his burial site on Har HaMenuchos near Givat Shaul has been an annual pilgrimage destination and place of prayer, especially on his *yahrzeit*, 21 Menachem-Av. As the Rosh Yeshivah, Rav Shalom Brander, so aptly put it: "The masses of *Klal Yisrael* throng to pour out their hearts at the site where the heart of Israel lies buried!" Likewise, the previous Rebbe of Skver remarked in his later years, "There will never be anyone else who so loved another Jew! You can recognize that at his tomb!"

For the next decade, Belz found it difficult to recover from the mortal wound, yet his legacy of *mosdos* founded with his blessing continued to thrive. On the thirtieth day after his *petirah*, 21 Elul, a massive crowd gathered near Yerushalayim Street in Bnei Brak for the foundation-stone laying for the Belz *Beis HaMedrash* and *Talmud Torah*. The stone was laid by the Rebbe's cousin and brother-in-law, Rabbi Shalom Rokach, Rav of Sokal. Although an

Posters announcing the groundbreaking
for the Beis Medrash in Bnei Brak

Posters announcing the inauguration
of the Beis Medrash in Bnei Brak

Posters announcing the laying of the
cornerstone and the chanukas habayis
of the new Belzer Shul in Yerushalayim

Students of the Belzer Talmud Torah in its early years

immense mood of sadness pervaded the ceremony, some comfort was derived that at least the light of Belz continued to shine brightly. After an intense campaign of fundraising and feverish construction, an impressive three-story building — architecturally reminiscent of the roof moldings of the historical shul destroyed in Belz — comprising a spacious *shtiebel, kollel,* plus eight classes and kitchen facilities for the Machzikei Hadas Talmud Torah was completed by the first *yahrzeit*! Later the City Council renamed the street "Ha'Admur MiBelz" and new Belz *mosdos* continued to flourish in the surrounding vicinity.

In Tel Aviv too, the Machzikei Hadas Talmud Torah, the first to be founded by the Belzer Rav in Eretz Yisrael, had retained the Rebbe's unlimited attention and interest even after similar *chadarim* were established in Bnei Brak and Jerusalem. Accordingly, his chassidim continued to nurture its growth while moving one section into the Rebbe's house and establishing a *yeshivah ketanah* and *kollel.* The *graiser-stieb* where the Rebbe's *tisch* was conducted once again resounded with the sound of Torah and *kedushah.*

Meanwhile in Jerusalem, immediately after the Belzer Rav's *petirah,* his chassidim launched an emotional funding campaign on behalf of the half-completed yeshivah and issued a rousing proclamation signed by Rav Dov Berish Wiedenfeld of Tchebin (Trzebinia), Rav Akiva Sofer of Pressburg and Rav Dovid Shperber of Brashav (Brasov or Brasso in Transylvania, midway between Klausenburg and Bucharest). Eventually, a five-story, seventy-room campus was consecrated with due flair and style, and the occasion was graced by leading rabbanim. Over the next decade, the yeshivah was led by the renowned *talmid chacham,* Rav Shalom Brander, and proudly carried the flag for Belz and the Rebbe's legacy.

Since 1966 these *mosdos* have been under the able leadership of the Belzer Rav's successor, his charismatic nephew, Rebbe Yissachar Dov, who has nurtured the enormous growth and success of Belz and its numerous institutions until the present day.

The Belz Bais Hamedrash erected by the present Rebbe, dominates the northern Jerusalem skyline

CHAPTER 29

ELIEZER NASAN LANDAU

REB LEIZER PLAYED A PROMINENT ROLE IN THE BELZER Rav's survival — not only facilitating his daring escape to Hungary but ensuring that he subsisted safely for sixteen months under the direct scrutiny of the feared Gestapo, in the Krakow ghettos destined for extermination. Mr. Landau was not the only one to have close connections with Nazi henchmen; sadly, during wartime many sought to curry favor by doing the nefarious bidding of the Nazis even at the expense of their fellow Jews. Reb Eliezer was unusual in using his considerable influence not for betrayal but entirely to save lives, countless lives. Thousands upon thousands owed their very existence to him and his family's bravery, guile, charm, quick intelligence and bluff — as do the dynasties of Belz and Bobov. Indeed, the Rebbes of Belz and Bobov openly admitted as much, as did the legendary hero of rescue: Rav Michoel Ber Weissmandl.

Reb Eliezer's contact with the unpredictable Germans began innocently enough. The family then lived in Krakow, a large and famous *kehillah* and the former capital of Polish kings, but now it was

Reb Leizer Landau before the German invasion

the seat of power for Hans Frank, officially the governor general of occupied Poland, who fancifully described himself as "the German King of Poland." It was also the center of the SS and Gestapo who wielded the real — and brutal — power across Poland and its death camps. Mr. Landau's livelihood derived mainly from money changing, which was strictly illegal under the German regime; it was forbidden for Jews to own more than a paltry amount of any currency. Word of his financial activities eventually reached the Gestapo, which dispatched a search squad to Landau's house.

When they arrived, Mr. Landau was not at home but they rummaged through the house, looking for foreign currency, but without success. Yet they did turn up a small stock of food items including coffee beans, various cans of preserves and other foodstuffs unavailable in wartime Poland — even to the Germans. Gruber, the Gestapo officer in charge, queried suspiciously, "What's this?" and Mrs. Sarah Landau hastily replied, "Nothing much, this is our food. If you want, we can supply you with some of the same as well." Gruber then asked, "How much?" and Mrs. Landau assured him, "*Klien gelt!*" Gruber digested this in silence for a long minute before he finally announced that he wanted to see Mr. Landau at Gestapo headquarters as soon as possible.

Generally, most Jews did not return alive or unscathed from a visit to the Gestapo, and R' Eliezer ventured there the next day only after prolonged prayers and tears. Following his own instincts, he tentatively offered Gruber coffee and tinned Portuguese sardines at a minimal price. Fortunately, Gruber agreed to accept assorted foodstuffs that were otherwise unobtainable. But Gruber was not satisfied with this and kept summoning Mr. Landau on various pretexts — and each time he demanded more. After some time Gruber introduced him to *Obersturmfuhrer* Wilhelm Kunde, apparently because they worked closely together and Gruber was afraid of him. Kunde was even greedier than Gruber but the connection proved very valuable.

Although Gruber was sent to the eastern front and never heard from again, great salvation was obtained from Kunde; from this tiny beginning thousands were eventually saved, including the Belzer Rav. For every release of arrested Jews, Kunde would receive not just expensive food items but valuable jewelry and gems. Eventually, Kunde introduced Mr. Landau to his colleague Heinrich, who was likewise amenable to releasing captives at a price. With time, both rose through the ranks until they headed the Jewish Section of the Gestapo, effectively ruling over hundreds of thousands of Jews. This allowed Mr. Landau to free many prisoners incarcerated in the Gestapo dungeons at the Muntupli Fortress. Yet each rescue attempt was fraught with risk and he would often tell his family, "Hashem alone knows if I'll even return!"

One example of many was later graphically described by Camille Hammer.[1] "Several days after the final *aktion* in Krakow in 1942 that decimated the ghetto, the German police conducted a manhunt for all Jews who hid outside the ghetto. These were Jews whose papers lacked the round stamp of the German authorities, the stamp that granted life, at least temporarily ... The police arrested many like me who had a permit to reside in Krakow, but on that day they demanded to see that special stamp too. To our bad luck we did not have the vital stamp since we didn't really need it — we lived outside the ghetto. Nonetheless, the *reshaim* arrested all of us with about fifty other Jews who had work and residency permits in Krakow; all were destined for Auschwitz and the only one to save us was Leizer Landau, masquerading under the name of Schmidt.

"The police truck arrived, loaded us all on and drove to a large building. They showed us to the cellar and we had to walk the gauntlet between lines of young gendarmes who hit us with rubber truncheons and kicked us mercilessly. Finally we reached another corridor lit with a dim bulb; at the end of this corridor was the cellar and our temporary prison. It already contained about thirty captives — eighty altogether — only some of whom I knew, but we were all miserable and fearful of our untimely end ... The only person who could possibly help us was Schmidt (Landau) and since I knew that he was scheduled to be in Krakow that day, my only hope was that he would somehow hear of our plight. I even whispered to my neighbor that there's still a chance, Reb Leizer's in Krakow! I was sure that if he discovered our emergency, he would risk his life

---

1. Later of Tel Aviv and a factory owner in Kfar Saba, manufacturing air mattresses.

— as he already had time after time, to save even individuals. Every single Jew was as precious in his eyes as fifty or a hundred.

"It happened exactly as I'd trusted. Somebody phoned him about our imprisonment and he immediately employed his connections and pressed for our release. An officer entered our cellar and summoned the first captives to fill in forms in a top-floor office. I was among the fifth or sixth group to be called and my details were recorded in the presence of several gendarmes. And then I saw Schmidt! He had entered the lions' den! I cannot describe my emotions then, I was close to tears. He stationed himself on the stairs leading from the cellar to the office. Like a heavenly angel, Reb Leizer came by himself and told us he would not rest until he freed us all. I ran down the stairs to share the knowledge with the other captives in the cellar. At the welcome news the men and women burst into tears and fell about me.

"As we afterwards discovered, Schmidt had discussed the whole rescue with Kunde and his men who promised to sort it out. Yet Schmidt remained nervous lest the presence of the gendarme chief might ruin their plan. Torn with internal misgivings, he decided to check it out for himself — at certain risk to his own life since the headquarters of the gendarmerie allowed no stranger access. When he entered the cellar from the back, we instinctively sensed his appearance, quelling our disquiet and trauma. But when the gendarme chief noticed him, he screamed, 'The colossal nerve of a Jew! Stand in line with the others!'

"Schmidt had undertaken enormous personal risk to ascertain whether Kunde's men had kept their word and really had come over to rescue us — now he too was suddenly arrested and his papers confiscated. He came up to me and confided, 'I think we're all lost.' But it didn't take long before he was suddenly called out ... Then followed feverish negotiations between the gendarmes and the Gestapo but although we heard the words we could not comprehend much of what they were talking about. We awaited an uncertain future, full of dread. Suddenly we were informed that we were all leaving, we're all freed!

"When we returned to Bochnia, two or three of us who knew Reb Leizer personally went round to his house; we realized our liberty must have cost him a hefty bribe. We told him straight, 'Leizer! We know your activities cost a pretty penny and we'd like to pay you for it.' But he smiled his charming smile, kissed us and produced a bottle of wine or spirits and declared, 'That you're alive is the greatest payment for me!' as we drank a *l'chaim*."

Although Mr. Landau accepted no money on that occasion, usually he had no choice since his only bargaining tools were diamonds and expensive presents. With his indispensable contacts, he could have sold his influence dearly and made a sizable fortune — as others did — but he was more concerned to save and assist the oppressed populace.

He also had more time and sympathy for the ordinary *amcha* — the powerless masses — than for the influential elite. Often when he appeared in public, Reb Leizer was trailed by desperate men and women beset by all the problems that a callous German officialdom could devise. Yet Reb Feivush Stempel, the Bobover Rebbe's *mechutan*, once urgently approached Mr. Landau for a favor in the ghetto and became agitated when Mr. Landau remained too busy listening to all the "ordinary" people. Reb Feivush was not used to being ignored. Before the War he had been extremely well connected financially, politically and dynastically — the family owned a chain of hotels; he was a founder of the Polish Agudah and represented them in *Sejm*; he was a *kehillah* leader in Krakow; and his son married the Bobover Rebbe's daughter. Reb Feivush did not hesitate to openly remonstrate with Mr. Landau but Reb Leizer merely replied, "My dear Reb Feivush, when else will these poor people have a chance to speak to me? Your problems, however, I can sort out at any time!" — and turned back to the simple *amcha* with his warm smile and patience!

Opportunities to buy off Nazi decrees by judicious presents were known to outsiders too, and the German industrialist Oskar Schindler (of "Schindler's List") reportedly confided to the infamous Dr. Kastner in Hungary that "Heads of the Krakow Gestapo are bribeable." When the Germans captured Lemberg in 1940 and arrested the Bobover Rebbe with other Jewish leaders, Mr. Landau tried to have him brought to Krakow for "questioning," but his efforts proved as fruitless as several other similar schemes throughout

Poland to save Rebbe Benzion Halberstam. Yet this method did at least succeed in rescuing other Jews arrested outside Krakow. Later Reb Leizer was instrumental in saving Rebbe Shlomo Halberstam, who resurrected Bobov Chassidus after the War; Reb Leizer's sister, Mrs. Yocheved Sheindel Korngut, rescued the Bobover Rebbe's young son — later his successor — Naftul'che, captured during a doomed escape bid to Slovakia and, due to her heroism, the only prisoner there to elude the firing squad.

Salvation came not only from bribing influential Nazis. Another stratagem crucial in avoiding deportation was "bunkers" — concealed rooms or holes in the ground where fugitives could hide temporarily in squalor and privation until the "selection" was over. But for that to succeed one had to be forewarned when extermination squads were likely to strike. More importantly, they had to be convinced the fate of the deportees was so much worse than their precarious ghetto existence that it was worth risking life and limb to disobey German orders and evade their search teams or bloodhounds. During one notorious incident, the deputy head of the Jewish police wrested his own daughter, son-in-law and two grandchildren from their bunker and delivered them against their will into the clutches of the killers — who promptly dispatched them to the death camps. Immediately afterwards, even as the *aktion* was continuing, he was overcome with remorse and rushed round to the Landaus weeping and wailing, "Did I do the right thing or no? Is it really only a labor camp they're going to? Tell me, please!" When he was met with silence, he became utterly hysterical, lying down on the floor with terrifying shrieks, demanding to know if he had acted correctly. Surprisingly, even when the terrible truth did leak out as to what "an unknown destination" or "*nach austen*" really meant, few dared believe it or break the conspiracy of silence. Mr. Landau was not one of them.

During one of his conversations with Kunde, the high-ranking officer had disclosed where all those long cattle boxcars from Krakow were destined: the death camp at Belzec. Reb Leizer did not hesitate to immediately confide this to his wife who was as actively involved in *hatzalah* as he was. By that time the Landaus had moved to Bochnia and when Dr. Shenfeld, a member of Bochnia's underground, heard a "selection" was shortly due, he approached Mr. Landau for assistance in obtaining a German stamp certifying him as a vital worker. Sadly, these stamps were in extremely short supply and Landau was unable to help him. "What shall I do?" Dr. Shenfeld asked in desperation.

"Do whatever you possibly can! Hide in any bunker — you should know they're not taking people to work camps but to annihilation camps!" Reb Eliezer confided. After hearing that from such a reliable source, Dr. Shenfeld no longer trusted those who claimed it was safer to assemble for selection under German orders. Instead he secreted himself away and survived the war. To this day Dr. Shenfeld cannot forget Landau's self-sacrifice in helping so many, nor his bravery in disclosing the secret despite the danger.

Similarly, since Krakow rather than Warsaw was the nerve center of Nazi activity, Reb Leizer would tip off other communities when deportations or raids by extermination squads were imminent. For instance, Rivka Pinkesevitch[2] and her brother among many others survived in the Tarnow ghetto for another year after being forewarned of an impending deportation.

In a remarkable act of bravery, Reb Leizer would even venture aboard the death trains in a desperate venture to save "vital workers." As part of the fiendish Nazi plot, these cattle-cars would take an inordinate amount of time to reach their destination, often being sidelined into sidings or secondary railroad tracks for many hours so their human freight, crammed tight without food or water and precious little air, would be more dead than alive when they finally reached the extermination facilities and could put up no resistance. Even when these trains were accessible to the public, armed guards zealously prevented Jew and non-Jew from approaching or responding to the desperate cries for water. Yet Mr. Landau dared to step where others feared to tread.

On occasion he boarded the dreaded death trains personally to dispense food and water. Once a long-distance train halted near Bochnia and he even obtained official permission to supply them with sustenance — the shrieks and cries of those tormented victims

2. Née Horowitz, the Bais Yaakov heroine immortalized in *To Vanquish the Dragon*.

were terrifying in the extreme. Rarer still, he sometimes managed to remove some of the doomed passengers, and during 1943, while stumbling inside a darkened, unlit cattle-car, he came across the diminutive figure of Rebbe Shime'le Zolkover, the holy *mekubal* and Rosh Yeshivah of *Chachmei Lublin*, and offered to save him. Yet Rebbe Shime'le adamantly refused to follow him out — declaring, "My place is with my people!"— although it was glaringly obvious what their fate would be. (Previously, when Rebbe Shime'le had been seized in *tallis* and *tefillin*, he had been recognized by a Jewish policeman who tried to free him — but received the same response.)

In one frightening episode, as Mr. Landau was still inside a death train, the doors were suddenly bolted shut again and the train began jerkily moving off! Miraculously, Kunde found out in the nick of time, ordered the train to a halt and released him! A relative asked him where he found the nerve and courage to dare take such risks. "Whenever I enter the lions' den," Reb Leizer replied gravely, "I try to imagine it's my own son Kalman who is trapped — if he were in such a predicament, would I hesitate then?"

But even when his son was at risk, he still engaged in *hatzalah*. Kalman came home one Shabbos and noticed a parked car with a community dignitary, Mr. Benjamin Landau, sitting inside. "Reb Binyamin!" he called out. "What are you doing here?" At this, the Nazi driver sprang angrily out of the car, grabbed Kalman viciously by the throat and began smashing his head against the car door.

As it later transpired, Reb Binyamin had been arrested on suspicion. The arresting officer previously had been promised an expensive ring and was now in town, and knowing the Landaus were home over Shabbos, he had come to pick it up before going on holiday — leaving his driver in charge of his human prey. Fortunately, Kalman's cries alerted Reb Leizer to Reb Binyamin's plight, but his efforts proved fruitless on this occasion and he was released only after several weeks' persuasion. Yet the fracas with Kalman and then Reb Leizer's resultant intervention possibly spared him from being shot at the outset.

Perhaps Mr. Landau derived some of his courage from his saintly and learned father-in-law, Reb Leizer (Elazar) Tiefenbrun, who

Reb Leizer Tiefenbrun

displayed total disregard for the Nazis. Although he descended from the rich and respected family of Reb Abish'l Kaner, by the onset of World War II he took little interest in daily affairs. He spent all his time studying or praying, and even while asleep would customarily murmur words of Torah to himself; he painstakingly recorded his Torah thoughts with ink he had prepared himself. During the week Reb Tiefenbrun would retire to bed fully clothed — even with shoes and black beaver hat! — with his walking stick in hand, in full expectation that Mashiach would arrive at any minute.

A bloodthirsty and widely feared Nazi by the name of Bogusch burst into the Landau home one night on the pretext that a light had been showing from one of the back windows despite the strict blackout. "You've been signaling to the enemy!" he bellowed as he began a violent search. In a back room he came across Reb Tiefenbrun (who stayed with his influential son-in-law) and pulled up short at the sight of the chassidic Talmudist replete with beard and long sidecurls, by that time a rarity under German occupation. Reb Leizer was innocently eating a modest flour mixture after fasting all day, but at the unexpected sight Bogusch began cursing and blaspheming. "Let's see where your G-d is now!" he screamed.

On hearing the blasphemy, Reb Tiefenbrun calmly returned to his simple supper — which provoked Bogusch to fever pitch. Advancing on his victim, he deliberately removed his revolver from his holster and placed it against the old man's head. It was obvious to everyone in the room that the homicidal Nazi who had already murdered countless Jews in cold blood was about to pull the trigger. Anybody else in that situation would have been paralyzed with fear, yet Reb Leizer Tiefenbrun fearlessly swallowed his supper as if there were no gun grinding against his forehead, as if Bogusch and all his cohorts had never existed; he never even uttered the final *Vidui*! The tension was finally broken when another daughter, Mrs. Shasha Lev, interjected, *"Mein herr!* Can't you yourself see that this man is not normal?" Bogusch stared at her before replying, "Yes. Yes. He's obviously not normal. It's a shame to waste a German bullet on him!" before withdrawing his gun and leaving the room.

That was not his only brush with death. On another occasion, Reb Tiefenbrun was discovered and dragged away by two German officers. A young grandson, Luzer Lev, ran after them and tried to wrest the old man from their tight grasp. When his feeble struggles proved ineffectual, he tried to bite one of the officer's hands. Obviously, no German would stand for this and the Nazi angrily pulled out his gun. Surprisingly, the other German intervened, "Stop! Stop! He's a *brave yunge*! Let the old man go!"

Reb Tiefenbrun once took it into his head that he must immerse himself in the Krakow *mikveh,* and no amount of pleading by the family could shake his resolve. The ritual baths had long been closed on German orders; it was extremely perilous for a bearded Jew to appear on the streets in the traditional attire and he had no permit to travel between Bochnia and Krakow. No matter, he remained determined to go. How he managed to get there, evade the patrols or find admittance, the family never knew, but he returned safely, mission accomplished. Mr. Landau, his son-in-law, consulted him regularly and benefited from his encouragement.

Two other personalities who motivated him greatly and were always there for advice and freely devoted their prayers and blessings to him were, of course, his Rebbe, Rav Yeshayeh Halberstam of Czchow (Chechov) — the youngest son of the Divrei Chaim who founded the Sanzer dynasty; the Landaus were from a Sanzer family — and the Belzer Rav. Due to highly placed connections, Mr. Landau was heavily involved in smuggling the Belzer Rebbe into Bochnia, aiding his escape to Krakow, providing him with lifesaving certification as a vital worker, protecting him from both the Gestapo and the ghetto commandant, facilitating his flight to Hungary, preventing his last-minute arrest, and coping with the aftermath by assuaging the Judenrat and the commandant.

Indirectly, he also helped defray the needs of the Belzer family, among other prominent personages. Emile Weitz, who had been successfully spirited into the relatively safe haven of Bochnia by Mr. Landau, was a wealthy businessman from Warsaw — it was claimed he lent the Joint at the onset of war the astronomical amount of $100,000 (tantamount to millions nowadays). On Mr. Landau's recommendation, he agreed to maintain Rabbinical families, and since Mr. Landau's 13-year-old son Kalman — now a respected Rosh Yeshivah in Tchebin, Jerusalem — found favor in Weitz's eyes, he entrusted him with large sums for poverty-stricken ghetto inmates. The young Kalman would distribute stipends to Rebbe Shaye'le, the Belzer brothers and the Vielipoli Rebbe every Thursday. Mr. Landau had set up a group of such wealthy businessmen to support him since he required enormous sums for his *hatzalah* work — and later, to keep the ghetto functioning.

Although he had always sought to maintain as low a profile as possible, he was forced to step into the breach when the ghetto almost collapsed at the end of August 1942; yet even afterwards he held no official position vis-a-vis the Germans. That crisis began with the brutal *Einsatzgruppen* raid on Bochnia that left only 1,500 survivors out of 8,000, saw the all-powerful ghetto boss Salo Greiber tortured and murdered, and put to rest the hope that enterprises and slave workers vital to the war effort might be spared from the Nazis' murderous blood lust. Worse, on the day following the three-day *aktion*, the workshops and machinery were set on fire, as was the massive Nazi warehouse of raw materials — exposing the Bochnia ghetto as critically vulnerable. Clearly *Wehrmacht* influence could not match that of Gestapo and SS, and it was crucial someone enjoying the confidence of those with dominant power swiftly reorganize the ghetto workshops.

Mr. Landau was the obvious choice. He had a line to top officials at German headquarters in Krakow, and he had the charm and guile to wheedle concessions and avoid interference; he had proven time and again he had the best interests of his fellow Jews at heart and he had the ability and bravery to save them. After great perseverance and substantial bribes he succeeded in resurrecting the Bochnia ghetto as a closed slave-labor camp (*zwangs-lager*) under the control of the Gestapo — its only chance of survival. SS Officer Kunde in Krakow and Bochnia Gestapo Chief Schoemburg, both callous murderers, took a direct interest while the day-to-day running was in the hands of the authoritarian *Lagerfurhrer* Muller. Mr. Landau regularly supplied Schoemburg with quality processed meat (for which he was so grateful, he would affectionately escort Reb Leizer's young son Kalman to the door after deliveries) and he rapidly had Muller eating out of his pocket after a faked phone call allowed Muller to "overhear" an animated conversation with an unidentified top Nazi receiving expensive gifts and foodstuffs.

Although the persecution of Jews in Poland had reached its final stage and most ghettos and camps around them were methodically being liquidated in short order, Bochnia even expanded its enterprises under the protection of the Gestapo. Workshops producing brushes, socks, sweaters, leather goods, toys, handcrafts, tailoring and more labored in three shifts, 1,500 workers to a shift. As far as Nazi officers were concerned, that craft of tailoring was the prime reason for Bochnia's survival. The ghetto had several expert tailors fashioning well-cut uniforms for Gestapo commanders and the other killers; their expertise earned the outspoken praise of the Germans, who claimed the native Poles just couldn't compete.

The Jews, however, were motivated solely to cheat extinction. Many slave workers were aged 60 or over but after they shaved off their beards and procured false papers, Landau registered them as between ten and twenty years younger. Likewise, children were registered as teenagers; they in particular strained themselves to keep the factory wheels turning. They needed to: Mr. Landau "employed" rabbanim and other *klei kodesh*, totally unsuited to work, who sat in the workshops publicly reciting *Tehillim*, studying the *Sedra*, holy books and *Zohar*! His factories were equipped with an alarm system and at the approach of outsiders, the bell would ring, the *sefarim* would be hastily hidden and the machines would hum at top speed for the German war effort.

Surprisingly, although it was his bribes and drive that kept the workshops and ghetto going, Reb Leizer remained in the background. For instance, R' Berel Frankel, from the noted family of factory owners in the industrial town of Bilitz-Bielsko, formally employed the 350 expert tailors after scrounging eighty-five sewing machines from every possible source, and was the ostensible employer of the Belzer Rav. As he later recalled, "Bochnia ghetto was seen as a safe haven, sucking in Jews from all the demolished ghettos and camps; following every *aktion* in the Krakow district, fugitive Jews would flee in our direction to smuggle themselves in. Amazingly, the Gestapo was well aware of this influx but wasn't particularly bothered: Raising no obstacles and expressing no interest where these new arrivals had fled or originated from, they simply ordered us to accept anyone capable of work. But the Gestapo's lax attitude frightened us, it lent weight to their explicit bragging: 'What difference if we get the Jews today or tomorrow? None of them can escape our clutches in any event!' So we realized the respite in Bochnia could not last, our ghetto too would be liquidated eventually."

Indeed, following the vicious *aktion* of Elul/August 1942, another — equally brutal — was scheduled for Kislev/November, just three months later. Fortunately, the Landaus' elaborate banquet of fancy foods washed down with intoxicating drink followed by persistent pleading — primarily by Mrs. Sarah Landau — managed to persuade Kunde to ignore his orders and call the *aktion* off after "only" 1,000 victims were liquidated;[3] and this non-compliance was ingeniously concealed by suitably bribing Kunde to falsely register a death train from Western Europe as coming from Bochnia. Immediately after they extracted the desired promise, Mr. Landau dispatched his son Kalman to check on the well-being of the Frankel family. Naturally, the boy was horribly afraid to leave the sanctuary of their home outside the ghetto, protected by the fiction of foreign citizenship, and venture into the inferno where a blood-curdling *aktion* was still possibly in progress. All they had was the word of a drunken SS officer that it was finally over! Their house overlooked

---

3. As detailed in Chapter 13.

the road to the local Jewish cemetery and Kalman had clearly seen two wagons loaded with the latest victims, their blood dripping onto the roadside!

Yet his father insisted and the boy dutifully went. On the way he met truckloads of gendarmerie returning from the slaughter but they did not molest him (apparently, Reb Leizer's bravery and charmed existence extended to his family). The ghetto was as silent as the grave since no Jews yet knew the danger had passed, and the Frankel family quite naturally refused to open the door or reply to his repeated hammering. Only after he yelled out his name did Mrs. Frankel finally open the door a crack and confirm they were unscathed. They and their extended family survived the war — which they ascribed to the Landaus — and one daughter later married Rabbi Rafael Soloveitchik, son of the Brisker Rav.

Mr. Landau's bravery and concern for his fellow Jews was rigorously tested when an underground group of "Matisovskim" was captured in Krakow. This heroic movement is a story in itself [4] and owes its inspiration to a young *baal teshuvah* by the name of Matisyahu (Matis) Gellman of Vienna. He in turn was inspired during the 1930's when he heard a speech of the charismatic Torah leader Rav Meir Shapiro of Lublin. Overcome with a new resolve, he returned to the land of his fathers — Poland — and their religion, wholeheartedly. He eventually gravitated to Gur, whose young chassidim were organized into several groups popularly known by the name of their youthful leader or "commandant." One of the most fiery and "sharpest" groups was the "Matisovskim," led by Matis Gellman, which really came into its own during the German occupation. The members fearlessly refused to be cowed, defied all German regulations and curfews, never removed their distinctive long *peyos* or beards, would not register with the German authorities or undertake any work for them. Collectively, they would gather in underground *shtiebels* and yeshivos to study together in attics or cellars, sharing their meager meals and keeping *Yiddishkeit* alive with a chassidic fervor.

---

4. Indeed, their exploits have been immortalized in *Eileh Shelo Nichne'u* by R' Moshe Prager.

The main base of their activity was Krakow, but they had large off-shoots in Warsaw — where they survived until the Uprising — and other major Polish communities. Matis Gellman, who miraculously smuggled himself from one center to another to provide encouragement (and arrange *shidduchim*!), vanished in the early years of the war and the group derived some Torah guidance from Rav Moshe Betzalel, brother of the Gerrer Rebbe. The "Matisovskim" also earned enormous respect from contemporary *gedolim*, including the Belzer Rav, who met them during his three-month stay in the Krakow ghetto and who made himself available to them whenever they called. He encouraged them to devote themselves entirely to Torah, despite the dangers — their reward in the Next World would be immeasurable. When he eventually met up with the old Gerrer Rebbe in Jerusalem, he remarked on their amazing *mesiras nefesh* and praised them highly. Likewise, when Moshe Schonfeld, a young Matisovsky, escaped to Bochnia and introduced himself to the Bilgoraj Rav, the Rav immediately asked him, "Are you a member of the Gerrer *chevrah*? Really, one ought to stand up for you!"

Inevitably, as the Krakow ghetto was relentlessly dismantled, a bunker of these brave souls was discovered, as were several relatives of the Gerrer Rebbe. Since Bochnia was in daily contact with Krakow via the *Bau-Dienst* slave laborers, the awful news rapidly reached them with an urgent message: There is only one possible way to release these captives still being held in the ghetto local prison, and that was through Kunde — and the only effective way to approach Kunde was via Reb Eliezer Landau. Knowing the Belzer Rebbe's high regard for the group, Moshe Schonfeld hastened to acquaint him with the dire situation.

Immediately, the Rebbe summoned Mr. Landau to his room and began lauding these young Gerrer chassidim to the Heavens. Even Moshe Schonfeld was surprised by the way the Belzer Rav extolled their virtues. As he later recalled, Eliezer Landau did not hesitate for a second and obeyed the Rebbe's slightest wish without question. Grabbing some jewelry and gold as "presents" or bribes, he bravely set out for Krakow though he knew full well this was a most dangerous mission — many Nazis in Krakow sought his and the ghetto's downfall. It was no secret that a clandestine power struggle raged between the Gestapo, recipients of Mr. Landau's largesse, and an important group within the SS led by Armon Goeth, the bloodthirsty commandant of the notorious Plaszow Camp, who schemed to destroy Bochnia and its workshops. Yet once the Belzer Rebbe asked him, Reb Leizer would not refuse.

Any rising hope of saving the Gerrer group was very quickly dashed. Instead, that night the Bochnia ghetto heard the shocking news — despite his influential contacts the great *shtadlan* himself had been arrested! He had first rushed to Kunde and asked him, "What will be the fate of those arrested in the bunker?" When the Nazi replied shortly, "They'll all be shot!" Mr. Landau threw his up hands in simulated shock and prepared to bargain and bribe. "What a waste," he argued. "These are strong, young men who could make excellent workers when we in Bochnia have a desperate shortage of workers — and are prepared to pay well for them. We need them urgently — let them join the war effort for Germany!"

Large bribes and arguments eventually wore Kunde down until he finally growled, "*Gut*! You can take them ..." But before Mr. Landau could relax with relief, he delivered another hammer blow: "Just remember — I'm officially only in charge within Krakow. How you transfer them to Bochnia is your concern!" Nonetheless, knowing that every second counted, Reb Leizer raced to the prison and, armed with Kunde's instructions, hastily released several captives and moved them to other premises in Krakow while he searched for a safe method to transport them to Bochnia as "urgently needed experts." But one of the Nazi guards at the prison informed Goeth that some of his prisoners had been released. Goeth came running and immediately ordered Landau's arrest!

"Ho! ho! ho!" he guffawed cruelly. "What have I caught here? No less than the Jewish king of Bochnia ghetto!" Landau shook with fear; all his worst nightmares were realized. Quickly, Goeth had him brought into the Plaszow Camp where he had full control. After personally administering a brutal beating, he ordered him to prepare the gallows for his own hanging. How can one describe what was going through Reb Eliezer Landau's mind at the time? Conflicting thoughts raced in rapid succession.

At first, he believed all was lost, he had overestimated his own power, he had relied too much on his influence with the Gestapo, which favored the continued existence of the Bochnia ghetto. Now he was in the hands of the dreaded SS, which sought the destruction of all Jews, useful or not. Then he pulled himself together. Was he not a *shaliach mitzvah* on a holy errand to save Jewish prisoners? Had he not come here on the express command of the holy Belzer Rav? Surely in that *zechus* he should escape harm. His heart told him that the *tzaddik* of Belz would not forsake him.

With the warped civility of a Nazi killer, Goeth asked him if he had any last requests. Reb Leizer appealed for *tachrichim* and a *siddur* to recite the final *Vidui* and, after searching around, the Nazis produced a long, white silk shirt and white socks. Strangely enough, this odd attire was to help save his life.

When the terrible news of Landau's capture got back to the Bochnia ghetto, there was profound panic. The very existence of the ghetto — and their survival — depended on him. Everybody was terrified at what might happen to the man who risked his life to save fellow Jews, and then worried about their own future. Without Reb Leizer to protect them, the SS would soon carry out their long-held wish to destroy their labor camp and exterminate its workers. Mrs. Sarah Landau, a formidable *hatzalah* activist in her own right, approached both Shoemburg and Kunde to save her husband.

Meanwhile, everyone in the ghetto fervently began reciting *Tehillim*. His Rebbe, the elderly Rav Yeshayeh of Czchow, wept openly as he prayed for Eliezer Nasan Landau's life, while the Belzer Rav — who had sent Landau out on this dangerous mission — took it worst of all. He locked himself in his room, refused to allow anyone in, nor permitted any other disturbances while he strained himself mightily in prayer to save his faithful *shaliach*. At the very last minute, as Landau was about to be hung at the gallows in the center of Plaszow Camp, Goeth changed his mind slightly — seeing him dressed in those weird white clothes tickled his fancy.

Rather than just kill him then and there, he ought to make a public spectacle of murdering a powerful leader of the Jews. He would force all his Jewish prisoners to attend, plus perhaps a few cronies. So what if Landau has to wait a little longer? Let him sweat!

Fortunately, the delay allowed a few Gestapo officers to arrive and though they had not the slightest reluctance to kill Jews, they did want to save Landau, who had been very useful to them with bribes and "presents." A furious row broke out between them and Goeth as they asserted the continued merit of the Bochnia ghetto while the SS pressed for its destruction together with its Jewish leader.

All the while, Landau stood at the gallows, helplessly watching as he held the rope noose in his hands, waiting for the order to hang himself. He saw himself as already having one foot in the next world, yet he followed the debate with close interest. He knew his Gestapo contacts would not relent so easily. Not only did they value the Bochnia ghetto as a rich source of bribes, it was a useful counterweight to German industrialists under rival SS protection. Since they had arrived in the nick of time, before the noose tightened around his neck, they would not capitulate to Goeth without a struggle.

For a lengthy hour, the heated argument raged back and forth. Suddenly the bloodthirsty Goeth approached Reb Eliezer angrily, drew his revolver and bellowed furiously, "It's a shame to waste a German bullet on an accursed Jew like you! Here, take this ...," and he rained a murderous blow with his gun on Landau's head. Reb Leizer Landau fell to the ground with blood pouring down his face. Only then did Goeth relent. But the other Gestapo officers snarled at Landau and ordered him to get up and leave straightaway. "Get out of here and keep your nose out of business that doesn't concern you!" Happy to be alive, Landau limped away with an open wound in his head while Goeth directed his pent-up anger at his other victims from the Gerrer bunker, and they nobly sacrificed their lives *al kiddush Hashem*.

Late that night, when Reb Leizer returned to Bochnia heavily bandaged — he bore the scars and trauma to the end of his life — everyone was greatly relieved. Although he had been unable to save the young chassidim, at least he miraculously escaped their fate, and the ghetto was safe for the moment, though their situation remained precarious. The Belzer Rebbe was particularly pleased to see him. Part of his reward came on the last day of Pesach (April 26, 1943), shortly before the Rebbe's escape.

Only a *minyan* of ten Jews — including their host — was allowed to join the last Pesach meal with the Belzer Rav. The Rebbe sat at the head of the table with the Bilgoraj Rav on his right, and four on each side. Nearest on the right was Mr. Landau, and when the customary *kneidlach* made from crushed and boiled matzah flour were served up (traditionally Belzer chassidim ate soaked matzah products only on the last day of Pesach) Reb Eliezer Landau suddenly blurted out, "Let the Rebbe give us *kneidlach* and let these redeem us from the other *kneidlach!*" obviously referring to Nazi bullets and bombs.

The Rebbe immediately pushed the dish away and sat for a few long minutes lost in heavenly contemplation until he sensed an opportune time had arrived. With his face aflame, he hurriedly began sharing out the *kneidlach* while exhorting, "*Giech! Giech! Giech!* — Quickly! Quickly!" Indeed, all ten present survived the war intact! Although the escape of the Landau family was not in the same class as that of the Belzer Rebbe, they experienced several miracles of their own.

By 1943, everybody in the Bochnia ghetto knew its days were numbered and frantically sought ways to elude Nazi clutches — and Reb Leizer's need was more imperative than most. His close shave in trying to rescue the "Matisovskim" was not his only brush with Goeth. At the final liquidation of the Krakow ghetto, many Jews eluded capture by hiding in bunkers and, despite their best efforts, the Nazi search teams did not succeed in uncovering all of them. With a massive bribe, Mr. Landau managed to extricate about seventy fugitives from a large bunker and bring them to Bochnia. Unfortunately, this amazing coup soon became common knowledge and leaked back to Goeth who, predictably enough, was furious at being cheated of more victims and swore revenge.

Goeth instructed his deputy to even the score. One night he arrived in Bochnia without warning and ordered the Ghetto *Ordnungdienst* (police force) to round up the seventy escapees. Meanwhile he took a top Jewish policeman, Naftali Rapps, a religious bachelor who risked his life for countless favors and mitzvos, to accompany him to the Landau home — and assist in his arrest! He barged in and summarily commanded Mr. Landau to get dressed and come with him. While he spoke to Mr. Landau, Mrs. Landau seized the opportunity to spring from her bed, jump out of the window and run for assistance. Meanwhile Reb Leizer quickly dressed and then asked the SS officer if he could use the bathroom for a second. To everyone's amazement, he agreed, and Mr. Landau hastily escaped into the street! After a few minutes the Nazi became suspicious and shouted to him to hurry up and come out immediately. When he received no response, he pushed the door open and found the bathroom empty.

Angry at being outwitted, he ordered the two oldest Landau children, Kalman and his 9-year-old sister Channah, to get dressed and follow him. Kalman apparently dressed too slowly for the impatient German's liking and because he was unable to do it any faster, Goeth's deputy began to beat him with his club. At this the boy began shaking so uncontrollably that he was totally unable to dress himself and had to be helped. Finally the two children were taken into the German's car and they began to drive down the road — to the local Jewish cemetery! By now Kalman was convinced that they were both about to be promptly shot and he sobbingly confided to his sister in Polish, "We're soon going to be killed!"

"Don't worry," replied his little sister calmly, with the example of her father in mind. "I've got a nice ring on this finger, I'll give him that!" Meanwhile, Naftali Rapps quietly advised the SS officer that he was heading in the wrong direction; he turned the car round and brought them back to the police backyard. The police station was lit up like day and groups of men were lined up against the wall. The two children were likewise ordered up against that wall and Kalman discovered that these men were part of the seventy escapees who had already been rounded up. "It looks like we're soon going to be shot!" they whispered fearfully.

Meanwhile, Mrs. Sarah Landau was still running in the direction of Shoemburg, unaware that her husband had already escaped and her eldest children had been arrested. As she ran through the dark streets long after the curfew, a Polish detective saw her and aimed his gun at her. Quick-wittedly, she screamed out that she was escaping armed robbers who had attacked their house and asked if he wouldn't mind escorting her to the local Gestapo chief. Kalman and his sister were still up against the wall when Shoemburg strode in shouting, *"Was is das? Was is los?* What is this, what's going on?" He summoned Goeth's deputy to his office and upbraided him for entering his jurisdiction on police business without consulting him. After some argument Shoemburg ordered him to leave. Since the Gestapo was ranked higher than the SS, the deputy had to obey and the Jews were all freed. Kalman and his sister were meant to sleep the rest of the night in the police chief's room, but he was trembling so uncontrollably they held him tight in a vain attempt to stop the shaking. When Kunde heard the story, he warned Mr. Landau to do everything possible to "leave the area and hide. Otherwise there's no escaping Goeth, he'll certainly vent his anger."

Flee? How could he forsake his father-in-law or the ghetto? His father-in-law, Reb Leizer Tiefenbrun, was old and frail. Even if he finally agreed to reluctantly remove his beard and *payos*, he was hardly fit to trek through the foothills of Slovakia or smuggle himself across borders. And how would the ghetto manage without Landau? He was vital to protecting its many inmates, including Rebbe Shaye'le and the Belzer Rav. He had solemnly promised the *Judenrat* he would not leave until after he had mollified the Gestapo if the Belzer Rav fled. Yet Heaven paved the way for his escape and "prepared the medicine before the illness."

It all began some time earlier and with another classic case of *hatzalah*. Gestapo Chief Shoemburg's favorite tactic was to travel the railcars passing through Bochnia, looking for Jewish-looking passengers masquerading under false papers. When he found suspicious passengers, he would lead them straight to the Jewish cemetery and shoot them dead — even if he was unsure whether they were native Poles! Since his home overlooked the road to the cemetery, Mr. Landau saved Jewish lives by providing many presents. One day the family noticed that Shoemburg was leading a girl to the cemetery and called Mr. Landau. He was not far away and managed to reach the cemetery just as the girl was standing at the open grave. Shoemburg smiled satanically and remarked, "This is not one of yours! She's not a Jew — she's Polish."

Reb Leizer stared at the girl who was shaking like a leaf and felt sure she was Jewish. He turned to the Gestapo chief and flattered him. *"Mein Herr!* Nobody can compare with your expertise in recognizing faces! You took her off the train because you thought she looked Jewish — and I'm sure you're right. She is a Jew!" But at this point the poor girl screamed, "I'm not a Jew!" However, the flattery had helped and after Mr. Landau took him aside to beg and plead, Shoemburg relented — but only if she admits in front of him that she's really Jewish and was vainly trying to fool him.

Reb Leizer walked up to her and declared emotionally in Yiddish, "My name's Eliezer Landau and I can see you're Jewish. I've received a promise that if you'll admit your Jewishness, he'll release you." Yet because of her fear, she was adamant that she was not Jewish. The longer he stood and begged, the more obstinate she became. Shoemburg lost patience and, waving his loaded revolver, shouted at Mr. Landau, "You must leave here immediately!" But Mr. Landau refused to withdraw and begged for another minute. He turned to the girl — and burst into tears! "Why are you doing this to yourself?" he asked her.

Now she too broke down and fell in front of him, weeping and wailing, "I'm Jewish! I'm a Bais Yaakov teacher and the only survivor from my *shtetle*!" Then she pulled herself together, stood up and admitted to Shoemburg that she was indeed a Jew and begged his pardon. The killer released her — for which he was duly rewarded by Landau. Although by this stage of the war Jews had been slaughtered in the millions and their blood ran like water, Reb Leizer was still concerned enough for a single, unknown soul to risk his life; he took *hatzalah* so seriously that he could be reduced to tears. Surely it was more than coincidence that this episode led to the rescue of the Landau family.

The girl was brought back to the Landau home where Mrs. Landau fed and revived her. Until Reb Leizer procured work permits, she stayed with them for several days. They had done this for other refugees in the past and had even hidden those on the run — including Rumek Anisefeld from the Krakow resistance — in a secure bunker below the house. The Bais Yaakov teacher was eventually appointed secretary at one of the workshops but after a short spell suddenly vanished into thin air. The Landaus checked with the workers, even called in the Jewish police, but could find no trace of her.

Months later, as the Belz entourage considered escaping with the Hungarian counterintelligence agent, a non-Jewish woman arrived at the Landaus' house, sat down on the floor and took off her shoe! From here she retrieved a secret note with instructions on how to cross the Slovak border on foot with the help of Slovakian smugglers who were very familiar with the routes. To their great surprise, the Landaus discovered that this messenger had been sent by none other than the missing girl! It turned out that she was the fiancée of Mr. Ben-Zion Kalb of Kezmarok in Slovakia, located within 30 kilometers of the Polish border and a favorite jump-off point for smugglers. Ever since the Germans occupied Poland, he had been trying to extricate his fiancée, and after three years he had succeeded with Rebbe Michoel Ber Weissmandl's help. When Shoemburg had dragged her off the train, she had been trying to get closer to the border. She had kept her escape plans secret even after Mr. Landau had rescued her — until she finally crossed to safety. Now she had sent this messenger to repay the Landaus for saving her life.

The Belzer Rav decided to flee directly to Hungary rather than travel the physically difficult route through Slovakia,[5] and after the immediate repercussions of his escape died away — again largely as a result of judicious bribes — Mr. Landau decided to explore this Slovak option for himself. By this time Reb Leizer Tiefenbrun had passed away and merited a Jewish burial, so they would no longer have the burden of carrying him across the difficult terrain of two borders. Rather than rely on the note or word of Slovakian smugglers, they decided to send two reliable young men: Rumek Anisefeld (who had earlier hidden in the Landau bunker) and Moshe Schonfeld, the youthful "Matisovsky." They traveled to Zakopane, a skiing and hiking center and now a national park, on the Slovak border.

Two days later, there was a knock on Landau's door and Kalman ran to open it — and saw an unforgettable sight: Anisefeld, the tall, strong, brave resistance fighter, stood white, shaken and in tears. "It's *kaput*! Finished! The experiment failed completely!" After he was a little more coherent, he reported that they had spent a night

---

5. As detailed in Chapter 15.

climbing over the high Carpathian Mountains and successfully crossed the Slovak border, but they were discovered by Slovakian border guards who shot at them. Schonfeld was killed but Anisefeld jumped down a steep cliff and ran for his life. Not knowing how to continue, he returned to the Landaus. He was to survive the War and eventually become an Israeli ambassador on the African continent under the assumed name of Nir Gad.

Actually, Moshe Schonfeld too had survived — and without a scratch! Famous for his sharp intelligence and quick thinking, he had immediately thrown himself to the ground and played dead when he heard shots. The patrol came up to him and looked him over but as he didn't move a muscle, they left without molesting him. As soon as it was safe he successfully continued his escape. He also made it to Eretz Yisrael, where he married a daughter of the Agudah leader, Reb Itche Meir Lewin, and was honored as *baal tefillah* for the *Yamim Noraim* at the court of the Gerrer Rebbe. But the Landaus were not to know all this just then and they were in despair. How were they to evade Goeth's evil grasp? They could feel the ground burning beneath their feet.

After consulting with local *tzaddikim*, Reb Leizer decided he had no choice: He had to try the Slovak option despite the initial failure. In a bold step, he also decided to inform Kunde before he fled! One could not know which way Kunde might react but he might need his help if they were caught — of which there was every likelihood: Since his family's faces were recognizably Jewish and they were traveling to Zakopane by railroad, there was the obvious danger they may get arrested, and then his connections with Kunde might again prove useful. To his surprise and relief, Kunde was glad to hear the news. "See here, you know all I've done for you. It's because I've realized for some time that we're losing the war! You, who have done so much for your fellow Jews, should remember me! And after this war's over you shall bear witness how I helped whenever I could!"[6]

---

6. In any event, this barefaced duplicity did not help him and SS Officer Wilhelm Kunde of Kiel was duly sentenced to death at Nuremberg.

Mr. Landau was quick to exploit Kunde's secret fears and entreated him to protect the Jews of Bochnia and not dispatch them to the death camps. Kunde promised to do his best to prevent its liquidation unless he received explicit instructions from Berlin. Mr. Landau pressed further: "I'm leaving behind my large family, many relatives. Could I introduce my elder sister who, with your assistance, can help my family and other Jews?" After Kunde agreed, he met Mrs. Yocheved Sheindel Korngut (wife of Reb Yankev Shea), who was also active in *hatzalah* and had earlier saved Naftult'che, who later became Bobover Rebbe.

Kunde kept his promises and allowed Mrs. Korngut leverage similar to that of her brother. Her regime lasted only a couple of months, but during that interim many Jews absconded to Slovakia while new routes and stratagems were discovered. Hundreds of families fled before it was too late and even after she joined them and migrated to Eretz Yisrael,[7] Kunde did not dismantle the ghetto, allowing the majority of its inmates to make good their escape.[8] There seems no logical explanation for its lasting longer than most Polish ghettos other than Kunde's solemn promise to Mr. Landau. Inevitably, of course, its final end arrived during August 1943 amid blood and fury.

By then the Landau family was relatively safe and sound. The night before their escape, Reb Leizer took his leave from his Rebbe, Reb Shaye'le of Czchow, *Hashem yinkom damo*, amidst tears and high emotion. The elderly Rebbe lit two candles and accompanied Mr. Landau outside while holding the burning candles in his hands. Earlier, the Rebbe had given Kalman a small piece of material, cut from the sleeve of a garment of his holy father — the Divrei Chaim. The next morning, a month after the Belzer Rav's departure, they left on the train to Zakopane. Heaven smiled upon them and the rail journey passed without incident, as did their crossing the Carpathian Mountains on foot that night. All the way, they repeat-

---

7. She eventually married the Torah giant, the Ozrower Rebbe, author of the *Aish Dos*.

8. The official bulletin of the *Sochnut's Vaadat Hatzalah* notes that "from May 1943 until March 1944, an estimated 3,500 ghetto inmates successfully escaped — a substantial proportion being from Bochnia."

edly recited, "Levi Yitzchak ben Sarah Sasha" (the Berditchever Rebbe's personal name) as a *segulah* and evaded both the Gestapo and the cruel Slovak guards.

They made for Pressburg and Rebbe Michoel Ber Weissmandl — who had organized the smugglers' network on which the Slovak escape route depended — since Reb Leizer was anxious to discuss *hatzalah* with this legendary hero. Like Mr. Landau, Rebbe Michoel Ber was prepared to bargain and plead with the German devils themselves. His book *Min HaMeitzar* searingly describes how a combination of bribes, guile and bluff succeeded in halting the Slovak death trains from October 1942 until the Slovak uprising in 1944. He wrote, paraphrasing a Hebrew alliteration, "I discovered the power of money and tears," to great effect. Although they had never met each other personally before, the two men fell on each other like soul brothers, embracing and crying bitter tears.

Then they closeted themselves in a private room for several hours to examine rescue options for the remnants of Polish Jewry. As Rabbi Weissmandl records in his book (p. 170) "… We are presently saving several families from there. A few days ago the great activist Reb Eliezer Landau from Bochnia passed through with our help. As is well known, by his good connections with some of the *reshaim*, he saved thousands upon thousands from death to life with *mesiras nefesh*. And these connections were solely money (not collaboration) … He came here to awaken the Jewish community to take mercy on their brothers and save thousands of precious souls with money …"

The family stayed in Pressburg for several days and Kalman slept in the same room as Rebbe Michoel Ber and witnessed his activities at first hand. But Rebbe Michoel Ber and Reb Leizer did have one difference of opinion — over a foster child in Reb Leizer's care. The story began earlier, back in Bochnia, where the Landaus had lived just outside the ghetto, overlooking the road running alongside the ghetto fence. Mr. Landau was once walking home when he noticed a young boy on the other side of this fence shadowing his movements. Why was this child following him from inside the ghetto? He strode over to the wooden enclosure and called through, "What do you want?"

"*Pan* Landau, save me!" replied the boy in agitation. "My name's Zalman Langweig-Lipschitz, son of the *dayan* Reb Chaim. And I'm the only one left!" Reb Leizer did not hesitate for a second. He retraced his steps, entered the ghetto and removed the boy on some excuse — and took him home with him. If he had room for eight children of his own, surely he would have room for another. The orphan remained at home with them and when they escaped to Slovakia, Reb Leizer — quite naturally! — took him along. In Pressburg, Rebbe Michoel Ber was very impressed by the young boy. "Leave him here with me and I'll look after him! His place is in yeshivah, not wandering across Europe pretending to be a non-Jew. Let me enroll him in my own yeshivah, in Nitra." (Nitra was one of the few yeshivos still functioning in Eastern Europe, despite the Nazis.)

Instead of relief at being released of his burden, Mr. Landau would not hear of it. The boy was in his care, he felt responsible; besides, he did not feel Slovakia was safe. It had always been anti-Semitic and violent, quick to pass anti-Jewish laws; three-quarters of Slovak's Jews had already been deported, and it was run by a Jew-hating Catholic priest under Nazi guidance and with a pro-Nazi government. But Rebbe Michoel Ber was charismatic too and wore him down with persuasive arguments. Eventually Mr. Landau relented after Rav Weissmandl promised that if ever the situation in Slovakia deteriorated, he would send him to Hungary, where they were headed. (Zalman did indeed begin learning in Nitra with great diligence and *hasmadah*; sadly he was killed together with the other *talmidim* when the yeshivah was liquidated.)

The Landaus were in a hurry to leave Slovakia for the relatively safer sanctuary of Hungary, and Rebbe Michoel Ber arranged for smugglers to lead them across the border and onto a train for Budapest, from where they were less likely to be sent back to Poland. After a whole night of trekking on foot, they crossed the border safely near Gyor but the next part of the plan went seriously wrong. The railroad depot at Gyor was crawling with border police searching for suspicious foreigners, and when the smuggler hired to buy their tickets saw the heightened security he fled in panic — and abandoned them high and dry at an orchard on the outskirts of town.

Gyor Bridge (the shul is visible in the background)

Despite the danger, Mr. Landau did not lose his cool and calmly stepped up to the window to order tickets to Budapest. But the rail staff could only understand Hungarian, while none of the Landaus spoke or understood Hungarian. Desperately he tried German (he spoke a fluent *Hoch-Deutsch*, of course), but got nowhere. Rather than draw attention to himself, he retired to a quiet bench where they conferred quietly about what to do next. Obviously they couldn't stay there and wait to get arrested.

Even if they somehow obtained tickets, how would they get on the right train when they couldn't read Hungarian either? How would they know which train to board? By Hungarian standards Gyor was a large and picturesque county town — and a major depot with several tracks running through. Besides trains to Budapest, they could just as easily board a train to Papa (Pupa), Veszprem or even back to Slovakia and Austria by accident! They were in a total quandary. Any second now the border police would notice them; whenever they caught suspicious characters near the border they normally handed them straight over to the Germans, their military allies.

Suddenly the Landaus noticed an eccentric figure entering the depot. He wore a white cap perched uneasily on his abundant, shoulder-length hair and he sported a full beard. Obviously, he

Gyor rail junction

was a typical Bohemian, possibly an artist or musician. When this outlandish character noticed them sitting forlornly on the bench, he sidled up to them — and began whispering to them in Germanic Yiddish! All were scared to exchange more than a few words in case they might be overheard and betrayed to the authorities. *"Bleib da, ich vellen kaufen billeten* — Wait here while I buy you tickets."

But their main surprise came when they were safely aboard the Budapest Express. Once no other passengers were present in their compartment, the Bohemian turned to them and asked, "Are you by any chance called Eliezer Landau?" Normally, Reb Leizer was never at a loss for words, but now his jaw dropped open, the color drained from his face and he stared at the stranger in complete shock, his mind spinning. How on earth did the man know that? Never in this lifetime had they met before! "How do you know my name?"

"My name is Amram Gestetner and the way you see me now is not my normal get-up; I'm not really a Bohemian but a religious Jew! When I realized how difficult it would be to pass myself off as an ordinary Hungarian in these dangerous times without shaving off my beard — which I was reluctant to do — I hit upon the idea of growing this long, wild hair. I live now in Budapest but my parents actually come from Gyor and are buried here. Today is my father's *yahrzeit* but I didn't intend to come back here because it's dangerous for Jews to be so close to the border. But last night the Belzer Rebbe — who arrived in Neu-pest a month ago — appeared to me in a strange dream, almost like the Baal Shem Tov! He reminded me that tomorrow is my father's *yahrzeit* and instructed me to visit his grave. He further told me that I'll see Eliezer Landau with his family at the railway station in great danger — and to please help him since he had done so much to help the Rebbe!

"When I woke up," continued Mr. Gestetner as Mr. Landau listened open-mouthed, "I wasn't sure what to do. Should I take any notice of this bizarre dream? I haven't been back these past seven years. Yet how could I ignore it — after all, it was indeed my father's *yahrzeit*! In the end I decided to brave the danger of coming here and praying at my late father's grave. I hardly entered the railway depot on the way back from the cemetery when I saw you and your family. That's when I realized the dream must be true!"

True to his visionary instructions, Mr. Gestetner brought them safely to Budapest and then hosted them in his house for several weeks.[9]

The Landaus stayed in Budapest for over six months while they waited to slip across the Romanian border and hopefully travel to Eretz Yisrael. Shortly before they sneaked into Romania, the Belzer

---

9. Reb Amram, from a renowned Hungarian family, had long been a Belzer chassid, and when the Rebbe arrived in Budapest, presented him with a silver tray via his son, Rav Nasan, now a leading district Rav in Bnei Brak. In 1930, the Belzer Rav had neatly solved a difficult dilemma for him: Hungarian Orthodoxy countrywide was run by the Central Orthodox Office in Budapest, which proposed various revisions to their original regulations formulated at the time of *Austritt* in 1869 relating to the status of communal *shochtim*. Vehemently opposed to any changes, Reb Amram insisted these revisions be put to the vote throughout the pre-World War I borders of Hungary — including large swaths of Romania, Czechoslovakia, Yugoslavia and Austria, where chassidic leaders and their large communities were sure to reject the changes. But the Central Office successfully persuaded government ministers to confine the vote to present-day Hungary where modern and *Oberlander* rabbis were in favor, since allowing "foreigners to meddle in Hungarian Jewish affairs would be unpatriotic!" In desperation, Reb Amram traveled to Belz to consult with his Rebbe. Belying his unworldly demeanor, the Belzer Rav replied, "*Adarabah!* Just the opposite! It's unpatriotic to refuse the old areas a say! It shows that Hungary has abandoned any hope for the return of its ancestral lands!" This intuitive argument struck a chord with the politicians and swayed the legislators. Sadly, Reb Amram did not survive the War, *Hashem yinkom damo.*

Rav left for Palestine on the Orient Express, and Mr. Landau, accompanied by his son Kalman, went to see him a few hours before the departure. Though officially non-Jews, they managed to push through the immense and emotional crowd surrounding the apartment and somehow or other enter the Rebbe's room.

The Rebbe invited Reb Leizer to sit at his table while Kalman stood at his side while they spoke for a few minutes. "Since I'm leaving now, I'll give you a letter!" the Belzer Rav announced. Just then, their tete-a-tete was interrupted by the arrival of some prominent rabbanim, coming to take their leave. But not long afterwards Reb Leizer was invited back and the Rebbe handed over a glowing testimonial, written— unusually — entirely in his own hand! It was an extremely warm letter, describing how Mr. Landau had saved thousands of Jews. Indeed, despite their own precarious position — officially non-Jewish refugees — he even pursued rescue efforts from Hungary, to smuggle the pitiful remnants out of Poland by any means. Sadly, he came under suspicion and when their temporary premises were searched by Hungarian security officials, he became terrified lest the Rebbe's letter "incriminate" him as a Jew and activist, and cause him to be deported back to Poland. With a heavy heart, he tore the Rebbe's precious testimonial to shreds and destroyed the "evidence."

This letter, however, was not the sum total of the Belzer Rav's gratitude. As soon as he reached Jerusalem, during February 1944, while staying with R' Zalman Ashkenazi, he summoned the vice-president of the Hatzalah Committee for Polish Jews, Dr. Isaac Kister, then an active lawyer who helped refugees in an honorary capacity, later the district judge for Tel Aviv. Dr. Kister was shocked by the Rebbe's appearance — "his whole demeanor reflects the harrowing destruction of Polish Jewry!" — and after the customary greeting, revealed that he came from a small village outside Przemysl. In his youth, as Dr. Kister privately recalled, he had often heard almost legendary stories told of Rebbe Yissachar Ber's first-born. To Dr. Kister's surprise, the Rebbe remembered his family too — his father as a community leader in Musczic visited Belz fifteen years earlier — despite the countless visitors plus soul-destroying suffering that had transpired since then.

"Now, since I've heard you have influence and connections, I have a very important request: You must persevere in getting a Palestine entry certificate for Mr. Eliezer Landau who is stuck in Hungary!" Dr. Kister was struck by how the Rebbe could not praise this Landau highly enough and, in an effort to persuade him, quoted many instances of his rescue work under impossible conditions. Dr. Kister also got the impression that the Belzer Rav deliberately repeated Landau's name so often in order to drive the message home. "His official name is Lazer Landau, according to his passport, and I insist you do everything possible to rescue this precious man and bring him here!" When Dr. Kister tried to explain how vexatious this request was when Hungary was full of countless refugees desperate for certificates, the Rebbe summoned Mr. Isaiah Horowitz, president of the Hatzalah Committee for Polish Jews, and repeated his emphatic demand on behalf of Mr. Landau.

Meanwhile, the Landaus made it to Romania and Mr. Landau registered his interest in immigrating to Eretz Yisrael with Zionist organizations. By July 1944, they had an escape plan: Youth Aliya hired three decrepit but large fishing boats that between them could cram over 1,000 passengers on board for the sea voyage. Since these were not motor driven, it could take several days to sail down the coast, past Bulgaria to Turkey and safety. The rescue committee organizing the ships and selecting the passengers was run partly by religious volunteers who were scrupulous to act fairly and impartially, disregarding favors or influence, in the belief that this would ensure the passengers some Divine protection. Unfortunately, others with less scruples did accept bribes — with disastrous consequences.

The three ships, *Marina*, *Mefkura* and *Bulbul*, docked at the large Black Sea port of Constanta (some 240 kilometers due west of the capital, Bucharest) on Thursday, August 3, 1944, and began taking on passengers. The smallest and best ship, the *Marina*, loaded first, but could take only 300. Many fought to board the *Mefkura*, but it managed only another 350 desperate refugees and fleeing Romanians. The third and most decrepit boat, the *Bulbul*, took the last 410, including the Landaus — though its safe capacity was only 100. Though the three ships weighed anchor together, *Marina* raced far ahead and was only a distant speck by nightfall; the *Mefkura* too made steady progress while *Bulbul* lagged several miles behind. By the next day, *Chamishah-Asar b'Av*, they were passing German-occupied Bulgaria but they were not molested — at first.

After nightfall that Friday night, the dark sea ahead of them suddenly burst into flames and many passengers became hysterical, screaming and shrieking. Their fears were not unfounded. Without warning, three German gunboats had sunk the *Mefkura* at midnight, ruthlessly and viciously, in a three-stage attack. First they torpedoed the defenseless fishing vessel, then they machine-gunned the passengers on deck and released killer dogs to slay anyone in the water, and finally set fire to the wreckage and watched it burn all night.[10] However, eight did survive the nightmare: three members of the crew and five Jewish passengers.

The repercussions on the *Bulbul* were also serious. Their captain, a middle-aged, mercenary fisherman, resolved not to be massacred together with his Jewish cargo and, threatening the passengers with a rusty revolver, forced them below deck while he intended to abandon ship and take off with the single dinghy. But he was overpowered by three young passengers and tied up while the sailors apprehensively dropped anchor, awaiting developments. During the next hours, the passengers prayed frantically as they watched the flames slowly subside into a shapeless glow and the long night slowly turn to day. The Landaus were particularly perturbed; they had close family aboard the *Mefkura*.

At daybreak, *Shabbos Nachamu*, they could finally try to ascertain what was going on: Through telescopes they watched with bated breath as the German boats calmly returned to Bulgaria — and thankfully ignored the *Bulbul*. Fearfully, they sailed toward the vicinity of last night's flames and came across an awful sight: shattered timbers, tattered sails, battered suitcases, sodden clothing, waterlogged bodies, all the miserable debris of a shipwreck — until alert passengers saw some of the pitifully few survivors and pulled

---

10. Later it transpired that two Polish-British spies had bribed their way on board with vital intelligence; German agents had discovered this and were determined that nobody from the *Mefkura* should remain alive to tell any tales.

them aboard. One pregnant lady even managed to swim to safety with a 2-year-old child clinging to her back, and gave birth to a healthy child two days later!

Suddenly Reb Leizer Landau gave a scream and pointed frantically. "Over there! Over there! That girl! It's my niece! It's Chaya Sarah Korngut!" They all watched as the 17-year-old desperately swam toward their ship. When she was finally close enough, a sailor tossed a life-preserver nearby. Determinedly, she plunged after it, slipped beneath the waves — and was never seen again!

As if that trauma were not enough, the *Bulbul* ran into more trouble shortly before Motza'ei Shabbos, this time off the shores of Turkey, when it ran aground on a large rock. Now they were truly stuck, in the middle of nowhere. Since the hull was pierced below the water line, they dared not try floating away, while the Turkish coast on the horizon appeared desolate with little sign of life. They remained stranded there for several days, cut off from civilization or assistance, while their food stocks slowly petered out. Finally the Turkish army reluctantly came to the rescue, ferrying them to shore in small boats capable of carrying only seven to eight passengers at a time.

But at least they were alive and relatively safe. After witnessing the destruction of the *Mefkura*, nobody felt like complaining, not even when they had to tramp through the hilly coastal landscape toward Istanbul. At least the younger children were seated on mules since they could not manage the steep hills; there were no paved roads in this desolate landscape and no other transport was available. Weary and dejected, the refugees trekked for nearly ten days from one poor hamlet to the next, escorted by soldiers on horseback. Goaded by the army, the villagers would bring out bread, fruits and vegetables, including potatoes, at night; then the refugees would lie down to rest on the dry, hard, sun-baked earth.

One night as they slept, Mrs. Shasha Lev, Mr. Landau's sister-in-law, suddenly exclaimed confidently: "We will reach Eretz Yisrael!" Apparently, her saintly father, Reb Leizer Tiefenbrun, with whom she had been so close, had just appeared to her in a dream to instruct that when the family arrives in the Holy Land and meets his brother-in-law, Reb Naftali Hager, in Jerusalem, they should repay an old debt!

Finally they reached a paved road and were trucked into Istanbul. They were met by *Sochnut* officials and the legendary Dr. Yaakov Griffel before being ushered into a local Jewish school, hastily converted in a dormitory. After resting for a few days, they followed the same route traveled by the Belzer Rav seven months earlier — the Karakoy ferry across the Bosphorus to the railroad depot; then a train to Syria, climbing the steep hills and sheer valleys across Anatolia and through the Taurus Mountains to Aleppo (Haleb); then on through Lebanon to the Palestine border. Soon after reaching Eretz Yisrael during Elul, Mr. Landau journeyed to Jerusalem in the full expectation of meeting Reb Naftali Hager and repaying his father-in-law's debt — as instructed in that mysterious dream! They met the elderly Reb Naftali on Erev Rosh Hashanah in Batei Ungar, Meah Shearim, and he kindly invited the whole family to his home over Yom Tov.

Following Rosh Hashanah, when Mr. Landau asked him if there was any money owed by Reb Leizer Tiefenbrun, Reb Naftali immediately denied being owed anything. Only when told of the strange dream during the trek through Turkey did he reconsider; after much thought he admitted that perhaps, as an added stringency, there possibly might be something outstanding from a temporary partnership they had once had. Since the Landaus had just arrived and needed money both for an apartment and for establishing a small business, Reb Leizer arranged to repay the forgotten debt in monthly installments. Indeed, he faithfully paid up month by month — and immediately after the final payment, Reb Naftali Hager passed away!

After that Rosh Hashanah the Landaus decided to settle in Tel Aviv, and the Belzer Rav invited them to his two-story house at 63 Ahad Ha'am St. — recently bought with so much self-sacrifice. "Take this place until you find lodgings to rent," he offered. "You can stay here with your family!" Meanwhile the Rebbe remained in Tzefas till after Succos.[11]

---

11. While in Tzefas his *gabbai*, Reb Hillel Vind, asked him if he would like to visit *kivrei tzaddikim* as customary, but the Belzer Rav replied, "They say Rabbi Leibele Eiger wore his *shtreimel* from Rosh Chodesh Elul till after Succos! While we don't wear our *shtreimel* during the week, at least we won't visit cemeteries during these holy days."

נ ע י צ ה   ן ו י כ ר א ה   י ז כ ר מ ה

האַרכיון הציוני המרכזי
CENTRAL ZIONIST ARCHIVES

Name and surname	age	relations resp. acquaintances

1Landau Leser born. Brzesko 17.12.1898   Simon Kornitzer, Tel-Aviv
  -'-   Sala   -'- Perlstein Dembica 13.5.-/Shederot Rotshild 41
  -'-   Kalman -'- Brzesko 1.2. 1931 /1902
  -'-   Maria -'-   -'-   10. 6. 1930
  -'-   Anna   -'-   -'-   5. 6. 1932
  -'-   Herik -'-   -'-   10. 5. 1934
  -'-   Leonora-'-   -'-   5.4. 1936
  -'-   Leon   -'-   -'-   5. 7. 1940
(durch Freudiger, Budapest Csakt ut. 9)

2) Loew Josef born. Frystak 10. 5. 1897   Simon Kornitzer, Tel-Aviv
  -'- Sosia -'- Perlstein in Dembica 4.5.1900 Shederot Rotshild 41

3) Loew Lazar born. Brzesko 4.6. 1920   Simon Konitzer, Tel-Aviv
  -'- Naftali -'-   -'-   18.8. 1930   Shederot Rotshild 41
  -'- Zelda   -'-   -'-   3.3. 1931
  -'- Sala   -'-   -'-   10.9. 1934
  -'- Kalman -'-   -'-   20.10.1934
  -'- Salamon -'-   -'-   4.4. 1933
(durch Freudiger, Budapest Czaky ut. 9)

4) Glück Mauric born .   7.10.1898   Dr. J. Pollak, Tel-Aviv
  -'- Eriestina -'- Szatmarnemeti 24.4.1929   Geula 32
  -'- Josef born.   -'-   -'-   2.8.1930
  -'- Victor -'-   -'-   -'- 27.10.1934
  -'- Fani(wife) Schwartz Franciska at Nagynuiszsaty 30.8.1905
  -'- Leo   born. Bratislava 16.10.1910
  -'- Borbala   -'- Spitzer -'-   11. 5.1915
  -'-(Gyoer)Robert-'- Bratislava 3. 5.1941
  -'- Erwin   born. Budapest   8.3. 1943
  -'- Bela   -'- Bratislava 16. I.1912
  -'- Johanna   -'- Löew Beer Vienna10.8.1920
(per Spitzer Budapest, Icabella 66)

5)
Silber Armin born. Istvanhuta   8.11.1908   Silber, Tel-Aviv
  -'- Rachel   -'- Landau Ungvar 10.10.1920   Shederot Ben Jehuda 13
Budapest, Kiraly ut. 14

6) Gellis Margit born.   1912   Simon Kornitzer, Tel-
  -'- Michafel -'-   1915   Aviv, Shederot Rot-
  -'- Alfred   -'-   1918   shild 41
  -'- Eugen   -'-   1921

Soporon, Becsiut 5

7) Wolf Baruhh Mendel born. Oswiecim 30.6.1885   Dr. Schwarzbard, Tel-
  -'- Scheindla   -'- Krakau 7.12.1885   Aviv , Shederot Rot-
  -'- Lieba   -'-   28.6.1918   shild 41,House Heller
  -'- Josef   -'-   28.4.1919
  -'- Sari   -'-   3. 3.1922
  -'- Nathan Aaron -'-   16.6.1927

c/o Silber, Budapest, Kiraly ut. 14

8) Landau Sara(Mr. Henoch's widow) born Krakau 1872   Dr. Schwarzbard,
  -'- Perla   -'-   '-' 1905   Tel-Aviv, Shederot
  -'- children 1927,1932,1936,1940(1940)   Rotshild 41,House
c/o Ebert Efraim, Budapest, Dohany ut. 28   Heller

Dr. Griffel's list; the Landau family is first on the list

The Belzer Rav was renowned for showing gratitude for the slightest favor, so the fond regard the Rebbe harbored for Mr. Landau was made obvious on several occasions. In 1949 Reb Leizer came to the Belzer *tisch* on Rosh Hashanah and the Rebbe asked him if he had washed his hands for challah yet. As he went off to wash, the Rebbe confided in his *shammas*, Reb Yitzchak Landau (a relative), "That man has saved thousands of Jews, including myself!" Likewise, when he once joined the Belzer *minyan* in Jerusalem, the Rebbe honored him with *maftir* while repeating the identical sentiments to the Naroller Rav.

Just as the Belzer Rav had helped him obtain entry into Israel, so did he protect him against British officialdom. When Reb Leizer was unfairly accused of "collaboration" with the Nazis, the Rebbe sent his brother, the Bilgoraj Rav, to testify warmly on his behalf. Those who had lost money on failed rescue attempts or whose relatives were not among the liberated became so overwrought and aggrieved, they were prepared to inform against honest saviors like Mr. Landau. A typical example occurred during the Landaus' first year in Tel Aviv, when they prayed in the same synagogue as Mr. Akiva T., who had been a good friend before the War. At the beginning of the War, Akiva had escaped to Russia, leaving his wife and children behind in the Bochnia ghetto.

As the first few survivors dribbled into Israel, speaking of Mr. Landau's rescue successes while Akiva's wife and children had vanished with the countless millions, he immediately blamed Mr. Landau for their deaths. Without giving him a chance to explain himself, he angrily stopped speaking to him and instead instigated no end of problems. Some time later, however, Akiva's wife and children actually turned up in Tel Aviv — having no idea that *he* was alive! When they met, she revealed to him that she and her children had been saved several times by Mr. Landau, and it was only due to him that they were still alive. Mortified, Reb Akiva rushed to the Landaus and broke down in tears, begging Reb Leizer's forgiveness for all the pain he had caused him.

These few inevitable critics were far outweighed by grateful survivors who unashamedly attributed their existence to Reb Leizer Landau. Wherever his children have traveled — around

Eretz Yisrael, Europe, and especially America — often, as they are introduced by name, they are regularly accosted by total strangers thanking them for their father's exploits. But since neither they nor their parents ever kept a record of these people, there is no "Landau's List" comparable to Oskar Schindler's, though Reb Leizer's ventures were incomparably more daring and the consequences if caught were perilous beyond measure.

Prominent personalities — besides the Belzer Rav, Bilgoraj Rav and Rebbe Michoel Ber Weissmandl — likewise articulated their admiration. When the Rav of Mattersdorf, Rabbi Simchah Bunem Ehrenfeld, visited Eretz Yisrael in 1959, his father-in-law, Rebbe Shmuel Zeltenreich (Czackower Rav) wrote him. "... if you could also call upon someone to whom we owe a great debt from the days of anger and destruction — and tell him you have my instructions to visit him and inquire of his welfare — it's Moreinu Eliezer Landau. Tell him I wrote you that it's worth visiting him and making acquaintance with the man who achieved great and wonderful things with *mesiras nefesh* on behalf of our Jewish brethren. He literally saved many souls from unnatural deaths at the hands of the Nazis *yemach shemam*. Happy is his lot in this world and the next! At that time I was there, in the Land of *Gei-Hinnom*, and I constantly remember his blessed acts for the good ..."

Again, when the late Bobover Rebbe — who painstakingly rebuilt that Chassidus and dynasty after the War — had a large reception in Bat Yam on visiting Eretz Yisrael in his later years, among those who came to greet him was Reb Zvi Landau. When he was introduced to the Rebbe as "Reb Leizer Landau's son," the Bobover Rav sprang excitedly to his feet. "*Aiye*! Your father saved me! Your father saved me! The whole realm of Bobov that you see — is only in the merit of your father!" In the shade of such glowing accolades, any criticism fades into insignificance.

The memories of his War years never left Mr. Landau, particularly his fateful confrontation with Goeth, when the noose already lay around his neck. Just as the scars of his head wound remained with him to the day he died, so did the realization of how close he had come to losing his life; every minute from then on was *geshenkte yahren* (years that were a gift). In memory of his salvation he would donate vast sums of money every Purim to the needy and *tzedakah gabbaim* of all circles — as a successful and generous Tel Aviv businessman, his was a popular address throughout the year — and in the last year of his life he was eagerly anticipating the annual ritual. Sadly it was not to be. Purim night 1989, as he was awaiting the first callers, he took ill and never recovered; he passed away a month later on the first night of Pesach, at the age of 82.

The *levayah* that first day of Chol HaMoed of an "ordinary *baal habayis*" was extraordinary. It began in Yerushalayim where the present Belzer Rav publicly addressed the *niftar*: "When you reach Heaven, tell them you saved his holiness Rebbe Aharon of Belz, the Rav of Bilgoraj, many other good Jews and hundreds of Jewish souls. You can go in peace and rest in peace until the final awakening."

When the cortege reached Tel Aviv it was joined by hundreds of religious Jews, including communal leaders and Rebbes, before it continued on to the Shomrei Shabbos cemetery in Zichron Meir, Bnei Brak. Here again, additional hundreds swelled the funeral, including many War survivors, and it was an emotionally dramatic moment when one of his rescuees, Rabbi Dovid Frankel, declared that in his family alone there are hundreds of offspring who all owe their lives to Reb Leizer! Fittingly, since Reb Leizer remained a staunch and crucial supporter of *Kollel Aish Dos* till the end, he was finally laid to rest near his brother-in-law, the Ozrower Rebbe, author of *Be'er Moshe* and *Aish Dos*.